PRAISE FOR
THE BOOK OF BASKETBALL

"Simmons' crazed genius and uncommon attention to the NBA stand out. . . . This is the ultimate book for the connoisseur of sports minutiae, an exhaustively curated NBA guide."   —*Slate*

"Research has given Simmons an unusually keen eye for the game, which he uses to try to resolve some of basketball's thorniest debates. . . . He can flat out write."   —*The New York Times Book Review*

"Ambitious, definitive . . . The opinionated Simmons will be entertaining to all NBA junkies."   —*The Post and Courier* (Charleston, SC)

"Damn enjoyable . . . Simmons is a smart aleck, but he's also doggedly thorough with his facts and writes with authority."   —*BookPage*

"Captures the visceral joy of a true fan . . . Simmons pulls it off with a mesmerizing mix of statistics, wild pop-culture riffs, and tons of humor."   —*ScrippsNews*

"A must-read for any NBA fan."   —*The Denver Post*

"Guaranteed to make you laugh out loud."   —*USA Today*

"Hilarious."   —*The Oregonian*

"Engaging . . . a great read for sports fans."   —*SmartMoney*

"[An] incredible epic . . . masterfully written and thought-provoking."
                                                          —*Cleveland*

"One of the best things I've read about sports . . . detailed with love and a passion for the game."   —*The Florida Times-Union*

"Packed with knowledgeable and historical insights and full of statistics and hilarious footnotes (two words I thought I'd never see together), this book will entertain an NBA fan for weeks."
                          —Myles Knapp, *The Sacramento Bee*

Now I Can Die in Peace:
How the Sports Guy Found Salvation Thanks
to the World Champion (Twice!) Red Sox

THE BOOK OF
BASKETBALL

THE BOOK OF
BASKETBALL

THE NBA ACCORDING TO THE SPORTS GUY

BILL SIMMONS

BALLANTINE BOOKS TRADE PAPERBACKS | NEW YORK

ESPN
BOOKS

Published in the United States by ESPN Books, an imprint of ESPN, Inc.,
New York, and Ballantine Books, an imprint of The Random House
Publishing Group, a division of Random House, Inc., New York.

BALLANTINE and colophon are registered trademarks of
Random House, Inc. The ESPN Books name and logo
are registered trademarks of ESPN, Inc.

Grateful acknowledgment is made to HarperCollins Publishers for
permission to reprint an excerpt from *The Franchise* by Cameron Stauth.
Copyright © 1990 by Cameron Stauth. Reprinted by permission
of HarperCollins Publishers.

Library of Congress Cataloging-in-Publication Data
Simmons, Bill.
The book of basketball : the NBA according to the sports guy / Bill Simmons.
          p.   cm.
Includes index.
ISBN 978-0-345-52010-4
eBook ISBN 978-0-345-51311-3
1. Basketball.   2. National Basketball Association.   I. Title.
GV885.1.S46 2009
796.323.'640973—dc22   2009036006

Printed in the United States of America

www.ballantinebooks.com
www.espnbooks.com

2 4 6 8 9 7 5 3 1

Book design by Jo Anne Metsch

For my father and for my son.
I hope I can be half as good of a dad.

INTRODUCTION

You might be standing in a bookstore right now. You might be leaning against a sofa in someone's house. You might be sitting on the john. You might be taking a bath. You might be shopping at one of those dollar stores, sitting on a beach, riding in a car, reading a free e-book preview. You might be sitting in a library or a Starbucks and wondering if the guy two chairs away is surfing porn on his iPad. You might be planning on clubbing someone to death with this thing—and really, you probably could—and wanted to read the first few pages before you did the deed. Regardless, you are thinking one of the following four things.

1. "This monstrosity was a no. 1 bestseller? A 700-page book about *basketball*? How the hell is that possible?"
2. "I forgot Bill Simmons used to write! Now he's hosting that terrible ESPN show with Dan LeBatard, *No, You're Wrong!* What a sellout."
3. "This is the book that billionaire owner loved, so he hired Simmons as GM and it was a total disaster! I think they're still suing each other. I always wanted to read this thing."
4. "Wait, I already bought the hardcover . . . now he wants me to buy the paperback? Greedy bastard."

I hear you on no. 4. I do. If I couldn't make the paperback better than the hardcover, it wasn't worth releasing. That's why I tightened it (cutting thirty pages of fat), fixed every factual error (all of them harmless, but still), then filled the extra space with new material and seventy new footnotes.[1] I added two new "What Ifs?" I updated the Hall of Fame Pyramid, changing a few rankings (biggest winner: Dwyane Wade) and rewriting the Kobe, LeBron, Wade and Howard sections. Same number of pages, better book. And our new virtual guide (www.bookofbasketball.com) allows you to follow up on any magazine articles, games, plays, YouTube clips or anecdotes mentioned in the paperback with one exception: Greg Oden's dong.

Until the bitter end, I resisted my publisher's demands for a finished edit. They wanted it after the 2010 Finals; I wanted to wait until LeBron made his decision. Every instinct I had told me, "Something weird is going to happen." Something did. That's the thing about the book of basketball—it never stops rewriting itself. After LeBron picked Miami, I realized this book will never be finished. For my own sanity, I needed to stop working on it. Five years was enough. There will never be another version. I promise. You have my word.[2]

Bill Simmons
September 1, 2010

1. When I told Gladwell that I had spent eight weeks on my paperback, he laughed and said, "Are you kidding? *Nobody* does extra work for a paperback!" Yeah, but still.
2. Well, until 2015. Or unless some crazy NBA-related shit happens and I have to rewrite it again. Or unless I go broke. Actually, forget I promised anything.

FOREWORD

Malcolm Gladwell

1.

Not long ago, Bill Simmons decided to lobby for the job of general manager of the Minnesota Timberwolves. If you are a regular reader of Bill's, you will know this, because he would make references to his campaign from time to time in his column. But if you are a regular reader of Bill's column, you also know enough to be a little unsure about what to make of his putative candidacy. Bill, after all, has a very active sense of humor. He likes messing with people, the way he used to mess with Isiah Thomas, back when Thomas was suffering from a rare psychiatric disorder that made him confuse Eddy Curry with Bill Russell. Even after I learned that the Minnesota front office had received something like twelve thousand emails from fans arguing for the Sports Guy, my position was that this was a very elaborate joke. Look, I know Bill. He lives in Los Angeles. When he landed there from Boston, he got down on his hands and knees and kissed the tarmac. He's not leaving the sunshine for the Minnesota winter. Plus, Bill is a journalist, right? He's a fan. He only knows what you know from watching games on TV. But then I read this quite remarkable book that you have in your hands, and I realized how utterly wrong I was. Simmons *knows* basketball. He's serious. And the T-wolves should be, too.

2.

What is Bill Simmons like? This is not an irrelevant question, because it explains a lot about why *The Book of Basketball* is the way it is. The short answer is that Bill is exactly like you or me. He's a fan—an obsessive fan, in the best sense of the word. I have a friend whose son grew up with the Yankees in their heyday and just assumed that every fall would bring another World Series ring. But then Rivera blew that save, and the kid was devastated. He cried. He didn't talk for days. The world as he knew it had collapsed. Now that's a *fan,* and that's what Simmons is.

The difference, of course, is that ordinary fans like you or me have limits to our obsession. We have jobs. We have girlfriends and wives. Whenever I ask my friend Bruce to come to my house to watch football, he always says he has to ask his girlfriend if he has any "cap room." I suspect all adults have some version of that constraint. Bill does not. Why? Because watching sports is his *job*. Pause for a moment and wrap your mind around the genius of his position. "Honey, I have to work late tonight" means that the Lakers game went into triple overtime. "I can't tonight. Work is stressing me out" means that the Patriots lost on a last-minute field goal. This is a man with five flat-screen TVs in his office. It is hard to know which part of that fact is more awe-inspiring: that he can watch five games simultaneously or that he gets to call the room where he can watch five games simultaneously his "office."

The other part about being a fan is that a fan is always an outsider. Most sportswriters are not, by this definition, fans. They capitalize on their access to athletes. They spoke to Kobe last night, and Kobe says his finger is going to be fine. They spent three days fly-fishing with Brett Favre in March, and Brett says he's definitely coming back for another season. There is nothing wrong, in and of itself, with that kind of approach to sports. But it has its limits. The insider, inevitably, starts to play favorites. He shades his criticisms, just a little, because if he doesn't, well, what if Kobe won't take his calls anymore? This book is not the work of an insider. It's the work of someone with five TVs in his "office" who has a reasoned opinion on Game 5 of the 1986 Eastern Conference semifinals because he watched Game 5 of the 1986 Eastern Conference semifinals in 1986, and then—just to make sure his memory wasn't playing tricks on him—got the tape and rewatched it three times on some random Tuesday morning last spring. You and I cannot do that because we have no cap room. That's why we have Simmons.

3.

You will have noticed, by now, that *The Book of Basketball* is very large. I can safely say that it is the longest book that I have read since I was in college. Please do not be put off by this fact. If this were a novel, you would be under some obligation to read it all at once or otherwise you'd lose track of the plot. (Wait. Was Celeste married to Ambrose, or were they the ones who had the affair at the Holiday Inn?) But it isn't a novel. It is, rather, a series of loosely connected arguments and riffs and lists and stories that you can pick up and put down at any time. This is the basketball version of the old *Baseball Abstracts* that Bill James used to put out in the 1980s. It's long because it *needs* to be long—because the goal of this book is to help us understand the connection between things like, say, Elgin Baylor and Michael Jordan, and to do that you have to understand exactly who Baylor was. And because Bill didn't want to just rank the top ten players of all time, or the top twenty-five, since those are the ones that we know about. He wanted to rank the top ninety-six, and then also mention the ones who almost made the cut, and he wanted to make the case for every one of his positions—with wit and evidence and reason. And as you read it you'll realize not only that you now understand basketball in a way that you never have before but also that there's never been a book about basketball quite like this. So take your time. Set aside a few weeks. You won't lose track of the characters. You *know* the characters. What you may not know is just how good Bernard King was, or why Pippen belongs on the all-time team. (By the way, make sure to read the footnotes. God knows why, but Simmons is the master of the footnote.)

One last point. This book is *supposed* to start arguments. I'm still flabbergasted at how high he ranks Allen Iverson, for example, or why Kevin Johnson barely cracks the pyramid. I seem to remember that in his day K.J. was unstoppable. But then again, I'm relying on my memory. Simmons went back and looked at the tape some random Tuesday afternoon when the rest of us were at work. Lucky bastard.

CONTENTS

THE BOOK OF
BASKETBALL

A FOUR-DOLLAR TICKET

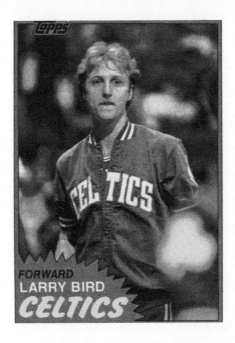

DURING THE SUMMER of 1973, with Watergate unfolding and Willie Mays redefining the phrase "stick a fork in him," my father was wavering between a new motorcyle and a single season ticket for the Celtics. The IRS had just given him a significant income tax refund of either $200 (the figure Dad remembers) or $600 (the figure my mother remembers). They both agree on one thing: Mom threatened to leave him if he bought the motorcycle.

We were renting a modest apartment in Marlborough, Massachusetts, just twenty-five minutes from Boston, with my father putting himself through Suffolk Law School, teaching at an all-girls boarding school, and bartending at night. Although the tax refund would have paid some bills, for the first time my father wanted something for himself. His life sucked. He wanted the motorcycle. When Mom shot that idea down, he called the Celtics and learned that, for four dollars per game, he could purchase a ticket right behind the visitors' bench. Nowadays, you can't purchase four boxing pay-per-views or a new iPod for less than $150. Back then, that money secured a seat five rows behind the visitors' bench at the Boston Garden, close enough to see the growing bald splotch on Kareem's head.[1]

My father pulled the trigger and broke the news to my mother that night. The conversation probably went something like this:

DAD: Good news, honey. I bought a season ticket for the Celtics. I'll be spending thirty-five nights a year inside the Garden by myself,[2] not including playoff games, so you'll have to stay home with Billy alone on those nights because we don't have enough money to get a babysitter. Also, I used up nearly the entire income tax refund. But I couldn't resist— I think they can win the title this year!

MOM (*after a long silence*): Are you serious?

DAD: Um . . . I guess I could take Billy to some of the games. He could sit on my lap. What do you think?

MOM: I think we got married too young.

If she *did* say that, she was right; my parents separated five years later. In retrospect, maybe the motorcycle would have sped things up. But that's how close I came to missing out on a childhood spent inside the Garden.[3] If Mom had agreed to the motorcycle, maybe Dad would have wiped out and become the next Gary Busey. Maybe we would have missed five championship seasons. Maybe I wouldn't have cared about basketball as much. Maybe you wouldn't be kicking yourself for spending money on this book right now. Life is strange.

We bought into Celtic Pride at the perfect time: they were coming off 68 wins and an unlucky break late in the '73 playoffs, when John Havlicek separated his shooting shoulder running through a screen and Boston fell

1. That's the first of about 300 unprovoked shots at Kareem in this book. Just warning you now. Kareem was a ninny.
2. The C's played six home games in Hartford each year in a misguided effort to expand their New England fan base. The experiment ended in the late '80s when they realized three things: the players hated traveling for 47 games a year, they could make more money playing at home, and most important, it was fucking Hartford.
3. We'll be referring to the Boston Garden as "the Garden" and Madison Square Garden as "MSG" for this book. Why? Because it's my book.

to an inferior Knicks team. Despite the lost championship and a wildly popular Bruins squad that shared the Garden, the Celts had gained local momentum because of Havlicek and reigning MVP Dave Cowens, a fiery redhead who clicked with fans in a way Bill Russell never did. After struggling to fill the building during Russell's astonishing run (eleven titles in thirteen years from 1957 to 1969), the Celtics were suddenly flourishing in a notoriously racist city. Was it happening because their best two players were white? Was it happening because of the burgeoning number of baby boomers like my father, the ones who fell in love with hoops because of the unselfishness of Auerbach's Celtics and Holzman's Knicks, who grew up watching Chamberlain and Russell battle like two gigantic dinosaurs on Sundays, who were enthralled by UCLA's win streak and Maravich's wizardry at LSU? Or was Cowens simply more likable and fan-friendly than the enigmatic Russell?

The answer? All of the above.[4] Maybe the city would have accepted an African American sports hero in the fifties and sixties—eventually it accepted many of them—but never someone as complex and stubborn as Russell. The man was moody and sullen to reporters, distant and unfriendly to fans, shockingly outspoken about racial issues, defiant about his color and plight. Russell cared only about being a superior teammate and a proud black man, never considering himself an entertainer or an ambassador of the game. If anything, he shunned both of those roles: he wanted to play basketball, to win, to be respected as a player and person . . . and to be left alone. Even when Auerbach named him the first black professional coach in 1966, Russell didn't care about the significance of the promotion, just that there was no better person for the job. Only years later would fans appreciate a courageous sports figure who advanced the cause of African Americans more than any athlete other than Muhammad Ali. Only years later would we fully empathize with the anguish and confusion of such a transcendent player, someone who was cheered as a basketball star and discriminated against as a human being. Only years later would Russell's wary, hardened demeanor fully make sense.

4. Boston's deep-seated racial issues bubbled to the surface one year later, thanks to a divisive decision to proactively integrate Boston's public schools and all the ugliness that followed. Although, looking back, it was probably a red flag that Reggie Smith and Jim Rice were the only black guys on the Red Sox for like 40 years and everybody was fine with this.

Unlike Russell, Cowens didn't have any baggage. There was nothing to figure out, no enigma to be solved. The big redhead dove for every loose ball, sprinted down the court on fast breaks, crashed the offensive boards and milked every possible inch of his talents. He hollered at officials with a booming voice that bellowed to the top rows of the Garden. He punctuated rebounds by grunting loudly and kicking his feet in different directions, which would have been fine except this was the Tight Shorts Era, so everyone constantly worried about his nuts careening out of his shorts like two superballs. When he stomped to midcourt to jump center with the towering Abdul-Jabbar, his nemesis and the league's best player at the time, Cowens always looked like a welterweight preparing to trade punches with a heavyweight. There was something fundamentally unfair about the matchup, like our real center had called in sick. Then the game started and we remembered that it wasn't a mismatch. Cowens lured Kareem away from the basket by draining 18-footers, robbing Milwaukee of its best shot blocker and rebounder. Defensively, Cowens made up for an eight-inch height difference by wearing Kareem down and making him work for every field goal attempt. Over and over again, we'd watch the same bumpy dance between them: Jabbar slinking toward his preferred spot on the low post, a wild-eyed Cowens slamming his chest against Kareem's back and dramatically refusing to yield another inch, finally digging in like a *Battle of the Network Stars* competitor in the last stages of a tug-of-war. Maybe they didn't make sense as rivals on paper, but they brought out the best in each other like Frazier and Ali—Cowens relishing the chance to battle the game's dominant center, Kareem unable to coast because Cowens simply wouldn't allow it—and the '74 Finals ended up being their Thrilla in Manila. The Celtics prevailed in seven games, with the big redhead notching 28 points and 14 rebounds in the clincher. So much for the mismatch.[5]

The ultimate Cowens moment happened when Mike Newlin flopped

5. Both guys had a defining moment in Game 6: Kareem drained a clutch sky hook to save Milwaukee's season in double OT, and Cowens stripped Oscar Robertson and skidded 20 feet along the floor going for the ball. No clip defined a player more than that one, with the possible exception of the 340 times (and counting) that Vince Carter went down in a heap like he'd been shot. By the way, if you think Kareem is going to take a beating in this book, wait until we get to Vince.

for a charge call against him. You didn't do these things to Cowens; nobody valued the sanctity of the game more than he did.[6] He berated the referee under the basket, didn't like the guy's response, screamed some more, then whirled around and spotted Newlin dribbling upcourt. Sufficiently enraged, he charged Newlin from behind at a 45-degree angle, lowered his shoulder like a football safety and sent poor Newlin sprawling into the press table at midcourt. Watching it live (and I happened to be there), it was a relatively terrifying experience, like being ten feet away in Pamplona as a pissed-off bull targets an unsuspecting pedestrian. And that wasn't even the best part. While pieces of Newlin were still rolling around the parquet floor like a shattered piggy bank, Cowens turned to the same referee and screamed, "Now that's a fucking foul!" So yeah, Cowens was white and Russell was black. But Cowens would have been worth four bucks a game if he were purple. Same for Havlicek. Because of them, my father stumbled into a Celtics season ticket and never looked back.

Our first season coincided with the Celtics winning their first title of the post-Russell era and the suddenly promising Simmons era. My memories don't kick in until the following year, when we moved to Chestnut Hill (fifteen minutes from the Garden) and Dad started bringing me more regularly. The people in our section knew me as a miniature sports encyclopedia, the floppy-haired kid who chewed his nails and whose life revolved around the Boston teams. Before games, the Garden's ushers allowed me to stand behind our basket on the edge of the court, where I'd chase down air balls and toss them back to my heroes. I can still remember standing there, chewing my nails and praying for an air ball or deflected jump shot to come bouncing toward me, just so I could grab it and toss the ball back to a Celtic. When I say this was thrilling for a little

---

6. After the '76 season, Cowens took a leave of absence and found a job at a local raceway, where he had an office and everything. Then he came back at the 32-game mark like nothing ever happened. Later, it came out during the '77 playoffs that Cowens had spent a night driving a cab around Boston and collecting fares. The funny thing is, you're reading this right now convinced that I'm joking. Nope. We need to redo Cowens' career in the Internet era—imagine message board threads with titles like "Dave Cowens picked me up in a cab last night!"

kid . . . I mean, you have no idea. This was like going to Disneyland forty times a year and cutting the line for every ride. I eventually built up enough courage to wander over to Boston's bench[7] and make small talk with the amused coaches, Tommy Heinsohn and John Killilea, leading to a moment before a Buffalo playoff game when a *Herald American* photographer snapped a picture of me peering up at an injured John Havlicek (wearing a baby blue leisure suit and leaning on crutches), then splashed the photo across the front page of its sports section the following day. By the time I turned six, you can guess what happened: I considered myself a member of the Boston Celtics. That spawned my racial identity crisis in the first grade (fully described in my Red Sox book) when I gave myself the Muslim name "Jabaal Abdul-Simmons." I didn't know any better. I wanted to play for the Celtics and most NBA players were black. Besides, I had more in common with them—my favorite sport was black, my favorite player (Charlie Scott) was black, my favorite comedians (Flip Wilson, Jimmie Walker, and Redd Foxx) were black, most of my favorite TV shows (*Sanford and Son, The Jeffersons, Good Times, The Mod Squad*) starred blacks, and I even made my mother take me to Roxbury in 1975 to see Keith Wilkes' one and only movie, *Cornbread, Earl and Me*.[8] It pissed me off that I was white. So I made my first-grade teacher call me "Jabaal," wrote "Jabaal" on my homework and tests, colored my own face in drawings and that was that.

Meanwhile, the '76 Celts were hanging on for one last championship run. Silas and Havlicek had seen better days. A washed-up Don Nelson— that's right, the same guy who later coached Milwaukee and Dallas—was playing with a protruding potbelly that made him look like the beleaguered dad in about ten different seventies sitcoms. Every key player (including Cowens and Jo Jo White, the best guys on the team) had already peaked statistically, only we didn't have young legs off the bench because

---

7. Yes, once upon a time, a little kid could wander onto the court before games, stand next to the home team's bench and talk to the coaches and players. Sigh.

8. Wilkes played Cornbread, a high school star gunned down in the movie. When the murder scene left me bawling, my mom was relieved because she had been worried we might not make it out of the theater alive. She claims that everyone was pissed we were there. I was too young to remember what happened; the only part I don't believe is Mom's claim that I played dice in the men's room afterward.

Auerbach had uncharacteristically butchered a few draft picks. Golden State looked like the prohibitive favorite until the defending champs self-destructed in Game 7 of the Western Finals under bizarre circumstances: in the first few minutes, Phoenix's Ricky Sobers jumped Warriors star Rick Barry and landed a few punches before teammates pulled him off.[9] At halftime, Barry (a notorious prick) watched the tape and realized his own teammates hadn't leaped in to save him. Fuming, he spitefully refused to shoot for most of the second half—no lie, he *refused* to shoot—playing hot potato anytime someone passed him the ball. And that's how a 42–40 Suns team advanced to the Finals, upsetting the defending champs on their home floor as their best player played an elaborate game of "eff you" with his teammates.

So that was one break for the Celtics. The other one happened organically: this was the final year before the ABA/NBA merger, the league's weakest season for talent since the Mikan era. For most of the decade, the ABA had been overpaying talented prospects from high school and college, including Julius Erving, Maurice Lucas, Moses Malone, David Thompson and George Gervin, all breathtaking athletes who would have pushed the rigid NBA in a more stimulating direction. Each league offered what the other was lacking: a regimented, physical style highlighted by the selflessness of its players (the NBA) versus a freewheeling, unpredictable style that celebrated individual expression (the ABA). When the leagues finally merged, three years of disjointed basketball followed—team-first guys awkwardly blending their talents with me-first guys—until everyone worked out the kinks,[10] the league added a three-point line,

9. Great subplot: Barry wore a wig that season (these were the days when you could do such a thing without getting mocked on the Internet) and after the fight, Barry seemed more concerned with readjusting his wig than with wondering why Sobers jumped him. If you ever get hold of the Warriors media guide, check out how Barry's hair recedes each season until the '76 team picture, when he suddenly has a full head of hair, and then he's back to being bald in the '77 team picture again. Now he has plugs. Don't ask why I love this stuff.

10. Two new wrinkles/problems that we'll cover in detail later: First, some players stopped giving a crap because they had guaranteed big-money contracts. Second, cocaine became fashionable for a few years before everyone realized, "Hey, wait, this drug is addictive and destructive and expensive. There's really no upside here!" We never knew there was a problem until a Nuggets game in 1979 when David Thompson tried to snort the foul line.

Bird and Magic arrived and the game landed in a better place. The '76 Celtics were too old and slow to make it after the merger, but we didn't realize that yet. We also didn't realize that white guys like Nelson had a better chance of eating the shot clock, digesting it, and crapping it out than guarding the likes of Erving and Thompson. The game was changing, only nobody could see it yet.

After Boston and Phoenix split the first four games of the Finals, Game 5 started at nine o'clock to accommodate the wishes of CBS, a network that didn't totally care about the league and had no problem tape-delaying playoff games or moving them to wacky times. Know what happens when you start that late for a crowd of loony Boston fans during a time when anyone could afford a ticket to the NBA Finals? You end up with the rowdiest, craziest, drunkest Boston crowd of all time. With four full hours to get plastered before the game and another three during the game itself, not only will the collective blood alcohol level of the crowd never be topped, neither will the game. I'd tell you more, but I snoozed through the fourth quarter, Phoenix's remarkable comeback and the first two overtimes, sprawled across my father and the gracious people on either side of him.[11] With seven seconds remaining in double OT, I awakened with the Celts trailing by one and everyone standing for the final play. (In fact, that's why I woke up, because everyone in our section was standing.) Almost on cue, I watched Havlicek haul in the inbounds pass, careen toward the basket (dribbling with his left hand on a bad wheel, no less), then somehow brick home a running banker off the wrong foot just before time expired, leading to the scariest moment of my young life: thousands of delirious fans charging the court, with many of them leapfrogging people in my section to get there. It was like a prison riot, only a benevolent one. And I was half asleep when it happened.

You know the rest: the officials ruled that one second remained, referee Richie Powers got attacked by a drunken fan, the Suns called an illegal time-out to get the ball at midcourt, Jo Jo drained the technical free throw, Gar Heard made the improbable turnaround to force a third OT (I remember thinking it was a 50-footer at the time), then the Celtics narrowly

---

11. My father still makes fun of me about this. In my defense, I was six. In his defense, it was the most famous NBA game ever played.

escaped because of the late-game heroics of Jo Jo and an unassuming bench player named Glenn McDonald. Even though I slept through some of the best parts, Jabaal Abdul-Simmons became the coolest kid in school the following day—not just because I attended the most famous basketball game ever played, but because my parents allowed me to stay awake until one-thirty to see it.[12]

We clinched the franchise's thirteenth championship in Phoenix two days later. Within two years we devolved into one of the league's most hapless teams, which wasn't necessarily a bad thing for the Simmons family: not only could Dad (barely) afford a second ticket by then, but thanks to a fleeing base of paying customers, they upgraded our seat location to midcourt, right alongside the Nancy Parish Memorial Tunnel (I'll explain later), where players, coaches, and referees entered and exited the arena.[13] My seat happened to be two rows in front of Dad's seat—we couldn't get two together unless we moved away from the tunnel, which we didn't want to do—but I could hop under the railing, stand in the tunnel and chat with him during time-outs. Even better, a bizarre collection of injured players, old-timers and media personalities gathered in the tunnel and watched a quarter or two, leading to one of my favorite childhood memories: a washed-up Marvin "Bad News" Barnes standing eighteen inches away from me, milking some bogus injury, wearing a full-length mink coat and leaning against my railing. Every few minutes, after a good Celtics play, he'd nod at me with one of those "What it *is*, Tiny White Dude!" smiles on his face. And since I wasn't over my racial identity issues yet, I spent the entire time marveling at his coat and hoping he'd legally adopt me. Didn't happen. Although we did have this exchange:

ME (*finally mustering up the courage after three quarters*): Mr. Barnes, when are you coming back?

---

12. When we came home, Dad and I were so wired that we made food and watched TV. A *Charlie's Angels* rerun was on—the show that had just taken off a few weeks before—and I remember thinking, "So this is what happens when you're up late? You can watch TV shows with half-naked female detectives running around?" A future night owl was born that night, my friends.

13. Not only did I spend my formative years sticking my right hand out hoping for famous high fives, but you can see me on TV during half of the great games of the Bird era. I spend more time on ESPN Classic than the Sklar brothers.

BAD NEWS (*gregarious*): Wrgrghjsdhshs nmdmakalkm nbbd jsjajajp ldksaksjhj, lil' man![14]

The News only played thirty-eight games for us, but that exchange personified everything. Celtic Pride had been tossed out the window in less than twenty-four months. Nelson and Hondo retired. Silas and Jo Jo were dumped under bitter circumstances. A miserable Cowens lost some of the fire that made him special. Heinsohn was canned so that he could realize his potential as the biggest homer in the history of sports announcing.[15] Worst of all, Auerbach nearly jumped to the Knicks after owner John Y. Brown recklessly traded three first-rounders for Bob McAdoo without telling Red first. In the old days, head cases like Barnes and McAdoo never would have *sniffed* the Celtics. We had become just another struggling team in a struggling league, a desperate franchise making desperate moves and searching for an identity. Then, just as quickly, everything changed. Auerbach won the power struggle with John Y.,[16] drafted Larry Bird as a junior eligible in 1978 and had the foresight to wait a year for Bird to graduate from Indiana State.[17] Even as the franchise was going to hell, we had a potential savior on the horizon. Following an acrimonious contract dispute, Bird signed for a then-record five-year $3.25 million deal, strolled into camp and transformed a 29-win laughingstock into a 60-win juggernaut within a few weeks. As far as reclamation projects go, it happened even more quickly than Swayze cleaning up the Double Deuce (and we didn't even have to hire Sam Elliott). We mattered again. Larry Legend

14. This was one of my two favorite moments of 1978, along with the time my buddy Reese and I realized that if one of us was holding the feet of the other, we could steal all the change from the bottom of the fountain at the Chestnut Hill Mall and buy hockey cards with the money. Good times!

15. I had a reader joke once, "Tommy is as objective during Celtics games as Fred Goldman when the topic is O.J."

16. John Y. owned the Braves and "traded" them for the Celtics in a complicated deal that involved seven players, two picks (one turned out to be Danny Ainge) and cash. Boston's previous owner, Irv Levin, moved the Braves to San Diego and renamed them the Clippers. So if John Y. had forced out Red, he would have been directly responsible for Clippers East and Clippers West. We also probably would have traded Bird's rights to New York for Toby Knight and Joe C. Meriweather.

17. We had 12 months to sign Bird before he reentered the draft, so everyone in New England jumped on the ISU bandwagon as Bird carried the undefeated Sycamores to the '79 NCAA Finals. They were more popular in New England than BC and Holy Cross that year.

would capture three championships and three MVP awards, help save the NBA and become the most popular Boston athlete ever. During that same time, I hit puberty, graduated from high school and college and started living in Boston on my own. By the time Bird's career ended in 1992, my life was just beginning.

Now . . .

Consider the odds. From the time I could walk, my love for playing and following sports dwarfed everything else. I developed a special connection with basketball because my father bought a single season ticket only after my mother vetoed his motorcycle career. After catching two titles in our first three years, a calamitous chain of events crippled the franchise and frightened off so many fans that my dad and I leapfrogged into the best possible seats in the best basketball arena in the world, and as if that weren't enough, our seats got upgraded right before one of the five greatest players ever joined the team. This wasn't just a lucky chain of events; this was like winning the lottery three different times, or better yet, like Justin Timberlake bagging Britney Spears, Jessica Biel, Scarlett Johansson and Cameron Diaz in their primes, only if he had added Lindsay Lohan, Angelina Jolie and Katie Holmes[18] for good measure. I spent my formative years studying the game of basketball with Professor Bird and relishing every subtle nuance that went with it. There was something contagious about watching someone constantly look for the extra pass; by osmosis, his teammates became just as unselfish, even potential black holes like McHale and Parish. It was like watching a group of relatively humorless guys spend time with an inordinately funny guy; invariably the inordinately funny guy raises everyone else's comedy IQ.[19] When you watched Bird long enough, you started to see the angles he was seeing; instead of reacting to what had just happened, you reacted to the play as it was happening. *There's McHale cutting to the basket, I see him, get him the ball, there it is . . . Layup!* Bird gave us a collective sixth sense, a more sophisticated way of appreciating the sport. It was a gift. That's what it was.

18. I threw Katie in here for old times' sake. It's not her fault that Tom Cruise turned her into a mannequin.

19. When I worked on Jimmy Kimmel's show, we called this the Adam Carolla Corollary. Carolla always found a humorous angle on anything; eventually, everyone else became funnier just trying to keep up with him.

And that's why you're reading this book. I grew up watching basketball played the right way. Guys looking for the open man. Guys making the extra pass. Guys giving their best and coming through in big moments. By the time Bird retired, I had earned my Ph.D. in hoops. When your favorite team lands a transcendent player in your formative years—Magic on the Lakers, MJ on the Bulls, Elway on the Broncos, Gretzky on the Oilers, or whomever—it really *is* like winning the lottery. Even twenty years later, I can rattle off classic Bird moments like I'm rattling off moments from my own life. Like the time he sprang for 60 as Atlanta's scrubs exchanged high fives on their bench,[20] or the time he dropped 42 on Dr. J in less than three quarters, frustrating Doc to the point that they started strangling each other at midcourt.[21] I have a hundred of them. Bird's greatest moments also became some of mine. Funny how sports work that way. I find myself missing those buzzworthy Bird moments more and more, the ones where everyone in the Garden collectively realized at the same time, "Uh-oh, something magical could happen here." Suddenly there would be a steady murmur in the arena that resembled the electricity right before a rock concert or a championship fight.[22] As soon as you felt the buzz, you knew something special was in the works. You probably think I'm a raving lunatic, but I'm telling you, anyone who attended those games knows exactly what I'm trying to describe. You could feel it in the air: *Larry's taking over.*

For nearly all of his first two seasons ('80 and '81), there was a barely perceptible distance between Bird and Boston fans, a wall erected from his end that we couldn't break through. Painfully shy with the press, noticeably unsettled by prolonged ovations, Bird carried himself like a savant of sorts, someone blessed with prodigious gifts for basketball and little else. This was a man who didn't mind that one of his nicknames was "the Hick from French Lick." We assumed that he was dumb, that he couldn't ex-

---

20. I did not make this up. There were four times in the second half of that game (March 12, 1985) when the Hawks subs either jumped up in delight with their arms raised, fell on top of each other in disbelief or slapped palms.

21. This was the most shocking and improbable sports fight that ever happened. Happened 20 feet in front of me. I will never forget it. Like seeing Santa throw down with the Easter Bunny.

22. I thought about throwing in "the last two minutes right before a girl-on-girl show starts at a bachelor party" here and decided against it.

press himself, that he didn't really care about the fans, that he just wanted to be left alone. This changed near the end of Game 7 of the Eastern Finals, the final act of a remarkable comeback trilogy against Philly. Unequivocally and unquestionably, it's the greatest playoff series ever played: two 60-win teams and heated rivals, loaded rosters on both sides,[23] two of the greatest forwards ever in starring roles, four games decided on the final play, the Celtics winning three straight elimination games by a total of four points. Everything peaked in Game 7, a fiercely contested battle in which the referees tucked away their whistles and allowed things to morph into an improbable cross between basketball and rugby. You know the old saying "There's no love lost between these two teams"? That was Game 7. If you drove to the basket for a layup or dunk, you were getting decked like a wide receiver going over the middle. If you snuck behind a big guy to potentially swipe his rebound, you were taking an elbow in the chops. If you recklessly dribbled into traffic hoping for a bailout call, better luck next time. This was a man's game. You'd never see something like it today. Ever.

Meanwhile, the fans weren't even fans anymore, more like Romans cheering for gladiators in the Colosseum. Leading by one in the final minute, Philly's Dawkins plowed toward the basket, got leveled by Parish and McHale, and whipped an ugly shot off the backboard as he crashed to the floor. Bird hauled down the rebound in traffic, dribbled out of an abyss of bodies (including three strewn on the floor, almost like the final scene of *Rollerball*) and pushed the ball down the court, ultimately stopping on a dime and banking a 15-footer that pretty much collapsed the roof. Philly called time as Larry pranced down the floor—arms still raised, soaking in the cheers—before finally unleashing an exaggerated, sweeping fist pump. Bird never acknowledged the crowd; this was the first hint of emotion from him. He finally threw us a bone. We went absolutely ballistic and roared through the entire time-out, drowning out the organ

23. Bird and Erving (four MVPs), Robert Parish (NBA top fifty), Kevin McHale (ditto), Tiny Archibald (ditto), Maurice Cheeks (one of the top point guards that decade), Andrew Toney (most underrated player of that decade), Bobby Jones (best sixth man of his generation), Cedric Maxwell ('81 Finals MVP), Darryl Dawkins, Caldwell Jones, M. L. Carr, Gerald Henderson, Rick Robey . . . now that's a playoff series! The lesson, as always: expansion ruins everything.

music and cheering ourselves hoarse when the horn signaled the players to return to the floor.[24] When the Celtics prevailed on a botched alley-oop and everyone charged the floor, Bird remained there for a few seconds at midcourt, jumping up and down like a schoolgirl, holding his head in disbelief as fans swarmed him. Of all the great victories from the Bird era, that's the only nontitle time where Boston fans loitered outside the Garden for hours afterward, honking horns, exchanging high fives and hugs, chanting "Phil-lee sucks!" and turning Causeway into Bourbon Street. We wanted Bird to be the next Russell, the next Orr, the next Havlicek. For the first time, it looked like he might get there.

Nothing that followed was a surprise: Bird's first championship in '81; his first MVP award in '84; his memorable butt-kicking of Bernard and the Knicks in Game 7 of the Eastern Semifinals; and then a grueling victory over the despicable Lakers in the '84 Finals that featured the definitive Larry performance, Game 5, when it was 96 degrees outside and 296 degrees inside a Garden that didn't have air-conditioning. Fans were passing out in the stands. Well-dressed housewives were wiping sweaty makeup off their brows.[25] Fat Irish guys had armpit stains swelling on their green Celtics T-shirts. Even the dehydrated Lakers team couldn't wait to get back to California; Kareem and Worthy were sucking from oxygen masks during time-outs. Of course, Bird loved the ruthless conditions, ending up with 34 points and 17 rebounds as his overheated minions rooted him on. As Bird was finishing them off in the fourth, the Lakers called time and M. L. Carr started fanning Bird with a towel . . . and Larry just shoved him away, insulted. Like M.L. was ruining the moment for him. Imagine breaking down in Death Valley on a 110-degree day, only if you were trapped inside your car with seventeen other people. That's how hot the Garden was that night, only we didn't care. All we knew was that Bird was God, the Lakers were wilting like pussies and we were part of the whole thing. We were sweating, too.

24. One of the many great subplots of the pre-Jumbotron era: the Garden fans rewarding the team with a standing ovation through the entire time-out. That was our ultimate stamp of approval. Like a "you did that for us, we'll do this for you" thing. Now we're too busy watching the kiss cam or gawking at cheerleader nipples.
25. My seat was next to one of those classy Wellesley/Weston housewives who wore great jewelry and looked like she got groomed four times a week. Even *she* was sweating. I don't think her sweat glands had ever been triggered before.

Those were the games when Bird and the Garden worked like Lennon and McCartney together. Can you imagine him playing in the TD Banknorth Garden and looking mildly appalled during a time-out as dance music blared and overcaffeinated flunkies fired T-shirts into the crowd with cannons? Me neither. When the Bird era crested in 1986, it was the ultimate marriage of the right crowd and the right team: a 67-win machine that finished 50–1 at home (including playoffs). Remember the scene in *Hoosiers* right after Jimmy Chitwood made the "I play, Coach stays" speech and joined the team, when they had that inspiring "this team's coming together" montage? That's what every home game felt like. The season ended with Bird walking off the floor in Game 6 of the Finals, fresh off demolishing the Rockets with a triple double, his jersey drenched with sweat and the crowd screaming in delight. It was perfect. Everything about that season was perfect. And to think my dad could have bought that stupid motorcycle.

Only one question remained: how many more memorable years did Bird have in him? During his apex in '86 and '87, he increased his trash-talking (nobody was better)[26] and started fooling around during games (including one time in Portland when he decided to shoot everything left-handed), like he was bored and kept upping the stakes to challenge himself. There was the famous story of the first three-point shootout, when he walked into the locker room and told everyone they were playing for second. Or the time he told Seattle's Xavier McDaniel exactly where he was shooting a game-winning shot, then lived up to the promise by nailing a jumper right in X-Man's mug. You could fill an entire documentary with those anecdotes; that's what NBA Entertainment eventually did by producing *Larry Bird: A Basketball Legend.*[27] As the game-winners and stories kept piling up, number 33 moved onto Boston's Mount Rushmore with Orr, Williams and Russell. We thought he could do anything. We thought he was a superhero. When they announced the starting lineups

26. My personal favorite: Bird once told Indiana's Chuck Person before a game that he had a Christmas present for him. During the game, he made a three in front of the Pacers bench, turned to Person and said, "Merry fucking Christmas."
27. On IMDb.com, this is also listed as *The Passion of the Christ.*

before games, Bird came last and his introduction was always drowned out by an unwritten rule that all Celtics fans screamed at the top of their lungs as soon as we heard the words, "And at the other forward, from Indiana Sta . . ." We didn't cheer him as much as we revered him.

When Lenny Bias overdosed two days after the 1986 draft, Bird lost the young teammate who would have extended his career, assumed some of the scoring load and reduced his minutes. The man's body betrayed him in his waning years, worn down by too many charges taken, too many hard fouls, and too many reckless dives for loose balls. Hobbled by faulty heels and a ravaged back, stymied by a wave of athletic black forwards that were slowly making the Kelly Tripuckas and Kiki Vandeweghes obsolete[28]—guys Bird always feasted on in the past, by the way—poor Bird could barely drag his crippled body up and down the court. He was doing it all on memory and adrenaline. During his final two seasons ('91 and '92), he'd miss three or four weeks of the schedule, spend nights in the hospital *in traction* to rest his back, then return with a cumbersome back brace like nothing happened.[29] Invariably, he'd add another game to his ESPN Classic resume. Like the famous Game 5 against Indiana in '91, when he banged his head against the floor, returned Willis Reed–style, then carried the Celts past the Pacers. Or the 49-point outburst against the Blazers on national TV, when the crowd chanted, "Lar-ree! Lar-ree!" *before* he obliged with a game-tying three in regulation. This was like watching Bird karaoke. Everything crested during a home playoff game against the '91 Pistons, when a struggling Bird couldn't get anything going, then an actual bird flew out of the rafters and halted play by parking itself defiantly at midcourt. The crowd recognized the irony and immediately starting chanting, "Lar-ree! Lar-ree! Lar-ree!" For the only time in the entire series, our crippled hero came alive. He started hitting jumpers, a bunch of them, and the Celtics pulled

28. It's too bad that Bird's prime just missed Scottie Pippen, the greatest defensive forward ever and a fantastic foil for Bird. By the time Pippen matured, Bird was on his way out. Our loss.

29. Bird's back brace made him look fat and misshapen, kinda like Ralph Macchio in *Karate Kid 3*. He couldn't move by the second round and still dominated a do-or-die Game 6 against the '92 Cavs with his perimeter passing (16 points and 14 assists). Then the Cavs realized before Game 7, "Wait, he can't dribble; all we have to do is hound him when he has the ball and attack him defensively!" They won by 18 and shot 59%. Sad ending for the Legend.

away for a crucial victory. As we joyously filed out of the Garden, my father asked me, "Did that really just happen?"

It did. I think.

When Bird finally retired in '92, it happened for the right reasons: his body couldn't handle an NBA schedule anymore. Unlike Magic, he never came back or lowered himself to an Old-Timers Game.[30] Unlike Jordan, he never would have toiled away on a mediocre team past his prime. He walked away and stayed away. The Celtics never recovered. Actually, that's an understatement. Bias had gotten the ball rolling, but when Bird retired, the Celtics passed away and became something else. Then Reggie Lewis dropped dead, and McHale retired, and the Garden got knocked down, and M. L. Carr screwed things up, and we lost the Duncan lottery, and Rick Pitino screwed things up, and Chris Wallace screwed things up, and Danny Ainge screwed things up, and somewhere during that torturous stretch the Celtics stopped being the Celtics. Three different times after Bird hung up his Converse Weapons, my father nearly gave up his suddenly expensive seats and couldn't do it. After the 2007 Celtics shamefully tanked their way to 61 losses and still couldn't land Kevin Durant or Greg Oden, the team sent him a 2007–8 bill for midcourt seats priced at $175 per ticket. Yup, the same price for a single season ticket in 1974 couldn't cover half of one game in 2008. Nobody would have blamed Pops for cutting ties after such a miserable season; there was one week where he nearly pulled the trigger. In the end, he couldn't walk away. Had he given up those tickets and watched the Celtics turn things around from afar, he never would have forgiven himself. So Dad renewed and hoped for the fifteenth straight spring that one lucky break would launch us back to prominence, whether it was a trade, a draft pick or Brian Scalabrine developing superhuman powers after being exposed to a nuclear reactor. He hoped for another game like the famous Bird-Dominique duel,[31] when Larry had come through enough times that you could literally feel it com-

---

30. Or even worse, in Magic's case, a Legend/Celebrity 3-on-3 or 3-Ball on All-Star Weekend.

31. Game 7 of the '88 Eastern Semis: 'Nique drops 47 but Bird explodes for 20 in the final quarter, including one sequence where they swapped five baskets in a row, saving the game and earning a gushing "You are watching what greatness is all about" line from Brent Musberger.

ing before it happened. After that masterpiece of a sporting event—really, it was a life experience—we were too wired to head right home, so we found an ice cream shop called Bailey's in Wellesley and ordered a couple of hot fudge sundaes. I don't think we said anything for twenty solid minutes. We just kept eating ice cream and shaking our heads. What could you say? How could you put something like that into words? We were speechless. We were drained. We were lucky.

You can't walk away from the potential of more Bailey's moments, even if the NBA stacks heavy odds against such bliss happening. Once the league expanded to thirty teams, luck became a greater factor than ever before. You need luck in the lottery, luck with young players, luck with trades, luck with everything. Phoenix landed Amar'e Stoudemire only because eight other teams passed on him. Portland landed Greg Oden when they had 5.3 percent odds of getting the first pick. Dallas landed Dirk Nowitzki because Milwaukee thought it would be a good idea to trade his rights for Robert Traylor. New Orleans landed Chris Paul only because three teams stupidly passed on him. Shit, even Auerbach landed Bird because of luck. Five teams could have drafted him before Boston and all five passed. That's the NBA. You need to be smart and lucky. When Lewis passed away seven summers after Bias' tragic death, the Celtics stopped being lucky and definitely stopped being smart. That didn't stop my father from steadfastly renewing those tickets every summer with his fingers crossed, hoping things would somehow revert to the way they were.

As strange as this sounds, it's more painful to live the high life as a basketball fan and lose it than to never live that high life at all. Imagine a basketball team as an airplane—if you never flew first class, you wouldn't know what you were missing every time you crammed yourself into coach. But what if you spent a few years traveling first class, reclining your seat all the way, relishing the leg room, sipping complimentary high-end drinks, eating steak and warm chocolate chip cookies, sitting near celebrities and trophy wives and feeling like a prince? Head back to coach after that and you're thinking, "Wow, this sucks!" Well, that's what an income tax refund bought my father in 1973: two remarkable decades of basketball, a boatload of happy memories, forty or fifty potentially splendid nights a year, and just when you thought it couldn't get any better, a chance to follow the entire career of one of the greatest players ever . . . and after everything slowed down and the Celtics downgraded from first to coach, the hope against hope that it was a temporary setback and we might get upgraded again. Even if it meant paying first-class prices for coach seats every year, my father didn't care. He was ready to get invited to the front of the plane again. He would always be ready.

The decision was made: Every spring, he would keep paying that bill. No matter what.

For anyone who didn't see Bird in his prime—or Magic, or Jordan, or the '70 Knicks, or the '01 Lakers, or any other magical player or team that resonated with fans—it's difficult to comprehend the meaning of those previous three paragraphs unless you lived through them. Bird's impact eroded over time, something that inevitably happens to every great athlete once he or she retires.[32] Stories and anecdotes endure, as do YouTube clips and ESPN Classic cameos, but collectively, it's never enough. In the spring of 2007, I stumbled across NBA TV's replay of Havlicek's farewell game, which was showing on a Sunday morning when the only people watching were probably me and the Havliceks. Two things stood out about that game. First, the opening tip-off was delayed for eight and a half minutes because Celtics fans wouldn't stop cheering after Hondo was introduced. Let's see that happen in 2009 with . . . anyone.[33] And second, according to CBS' ancient-looking halftime graphics, Havlicek's statistical resume on April 9, 1978, looked like this:

Most games played (1,269)
Most playoff games played (172)

32. Bird's prophetic quote in 1986: "All I know is that people tend to forget how great the older great players were. It'll happen that way with me, too."
33. Eight minutes 30 seconds. That's longer than "Stairway to Heaven"; Hulk Hogan pinning the Iron Sheik for the WWF title at MSG; the total amount of time it took the Pats to finish their final drive of Super Bowl XXXVI (including stoppages); all of the sex scenes from *Basic Instinct* combined; Stevie Wonder's longest Grammy acceptance speech; the amount of time that passed before we stopped believing that Ricky Martin was straight; Act One of the first *Chevy Chase Show*; the climactic fight scene from *Rocky*; the amount of time that David Beckham made soccer relevant in America again; and any of Jeff Ross' roasts on YouTube.

Only player to score 1,000 points in sixteen straight seasons
Third in career scoring (26,895 points)
Second in career minutes played (46,407)

Seeing those numbers three decades later, my gast was flabbered. Yeah, I remembered Hondo carrying us to the '76 championship, and I remembered that he was one of the best players of his time, a physical freak of nature, someone who routinely played 42 to 44 minutes a night without tiring. Throughout his final season, I recall opposing teams showering him with gifts at every stop.[34] But third in scoring, second in minutes and first in games played? John Havlicek? I did some digging and found that Hondo made thirteen straight All-Star teams, four All-NBA first teams and seven All-NBA second teams; he played for eight title teams and won the 1974 Finals MVP; and he earned one of 11 spots on the NBA's thirty-fifth-anniversary team in 1980. To this day, he ranks tenth in points, eighth in minutes and seventh in playoff points. By any measurement, he remains one of the twenty best players ever. But if you asked a hundred die-hard NBA fans under thirty to name their top twenty, how many would name Havlicek? Three? Five? Shit, how many of them could even spell "Havlicek"?

Which begs the question: does greatness have a shelf life?

A few weeks after that Havlicek telecast, young LeBron James dropped 48 points on Detroit to singlehandedly save the Cavs-Pistons series (as well as the '07 playoffs, which were on life support). Clearly, something monumental had happened: not only did Marv Albert bless the performance as one of the greatest in playoff history, but it felt like a tipping point for LeBron's career, the night he tapped into his considerable gifts and lifted himself to another level. When talking heads, columnists, bloggers and fans raced to put the night into perspective, for once the hyperbole seemed justified. More than a few people played the "MJ was great, but he never had a game like that" card, as if Jordan's remarkable career had to be demeaned for everyone to fully respect what LeBron had ac-

---

34. The farewell tour for retiring stars was a goofy tradition in the '70s and '80s that peaked with Julius Erving in '86 and stopped after Kareem retired in '89. There was a ton of emotion both times—with Doc because we were going to miss him, and with Kareem because we were so happy to see him go.

complished. In my ESPN.com column the following day, I wrote that Jordan never physically overpowered an opponent the way LeBron ramshackled the Pistons, comparing it to Bo Jackson wreaking havoc in his prime.

By the weekend, after everyone had calmed down about the "48 Special," I found myself recalling some of Jordan's killer moments—how he coldly destroyed Drexler in the '92 Finals, how he prevailed against the rugby tactics of Riley's Knicks, how he stole Game 7 against the '98 Pacers by repeatedly getting to the line, how he ended his Chicago career with the incredible layup-steal-jumper sequence in Utah—and regretting that, like nearly everyone·else, I had fallen into the "let's degrade the old guy to coronate the new guy" trap. I had always sworn never to do that. One of my favorite books is *Wait Till Next Year,* in which a sports columnist (Mike Lupica) and a screenwriter (William Goldman) trade chapters about a particularly crazy year in New York sports. Writing from the fan's perspective, Goldman submitted an impassioned defense of Wilt Chamberlain's legacy called "To the Death," one of my favorite pieces and a major influence on this book. According to Goldman, great athletes fade from memory not because they're surpassed by better ones, but because we forget about them or our memories are tainted by things that have nothing to do with their career (like Bill Russell being a lousy announcer or O.J. being a lousy ex-husband). Here's the killer excerpt: "The greatest struggle an athlete undergoes is the battle for our memories. It's gradual. It begins before you're aware that it's begun, and it ends with a terrible fall from grace. It really is a battle to the death."

This piece was published in 1988, back when Bird and Magic were at the height of their superpowers and Jordan was nearing the same breakthrough that LeBron eventually enjoyed in Detroit. Already saddened that we would be poking holes in them someday, Goldman predicted, "Bird and Magic's time is coming. It's easy being fans of theirs now. Just wait. Give it a decade." Then he wrote an entire mock paragraph of fans picking apart their games in the year 2000, complaining that Magic couldn't guard anyone and Bird was too slow. He ended with this mock quote: "Sure [Bird] was good, and so was Magic—but they couldn't play today." Maybe it hasn't happened yet because of the uniqueness of their games, the symmetry of their careers, and the whole "Bird and Magic saved the NBA" myth (we'll get there). But with Jordan? It's already happening. As recently as 1998, we collectively agreed Jordan was the greatest player we would ever see. That didn't stop us from quickly trying to replace him with Grant Hill (didn't take), Kobe Bryant (didn't take), LeBron James (taking), and Kobe again (sporadically taking). Everyone's willingness to dump Jordan for LeBron in 2007 was genuinely perplexing. Yeah, the "48 Special" was a magnificent sporting event, but it paled in comparison with a twenty-year-old Magic jumping center in Philly in place of an injured Kareem, playing five positions, slapping up a 42–15–7 and willing the Lakers to the 1980 title. If that happened today, pieces of Skip Bayless' head would be scattered across Bristol.[35]

So what makes us continually pump up the present at the expense of the past? Goldman believed that every era is "so arrogant [and] so dismissive," and again he was right, although that arrogance/dismissiveness isn't entirely intentional. We'd like to believe that our current stars are better than the guys we once watched. Why? Because the single best thing about sports is the unknown. It's more fun to think about what *could* happen than what already happened. We know we won't see another Bird or Magic; we already stopped looking. They were too unique. But Jordan . . . that one is conceivable. We might see another hypercompetitive, unfathomably gifted shooting guard reach his potential in our lifetime. We might. So it's not that we want LeBron to be just as good as MJ; we need him to be *better* than MJ. We already did the MJ thing. Who wants to rent the same movie twice? We want LeBron to take us to a place we haven't been. It's the same reason we convinced ourselves that Shaq was better than Wilt and Nash was better than Cousy. We didn't know these things for sure. We just wanted them to be true.

There's a simpler reason why we're incapable of appreciating the past. As the Havlicek broadcast proved to me, it's easy to forget anything if you stop thinking about it long enough, even something as fundamentally ingrained in your brain as "My favorite basketball team employed one of the

---

35. Note to anyone reading in 2075: Bayless was a TV personality who took extreme positions until he was fired in the summer of 2010 after LeBron dumped Cleveland to sign with the Heat and a frothing-at-the-mouth Bayless, in his rush to excoriate LeBron for stabbing Cavaliers fans in the back, briefly morphed into a fire-breathing, eight-foot dragon and killed all 17 people in the studio. You can find the clip on YouTube—just search for "Bayless + dragon."

best twenty players ever when I was a little kid and I watched him throughout my childhood." Once upon a time, the Boston Garden fans cheered Hondo for 510 seconds. And I was *there*. I was in the building. I cheered for every one of those 510 seconds and it was the only happy memory of that entire crummy season. But that's the funny thing about noise: eventually it stops.

So that's what this book is about: capturing that noise, sorting through all the bullshit and figuring out which players and teams and stories should live on. It's also about the NBA, how we got here and where we're going. It's way too ambitious and I probably should have stuck to an outline, but screw it—by the end of the book, it will all make sense. I swear. Just know that I'm getting older and the depreciation of sports memories bothers me more than I ever thought it would . . . especially in basketball, a sport that cannot be grasped through statistics alone. I wanted to write down my memories, thoughts and opinions before I forget them. Or before I get killed by a T-shirt cannon during a Clippers game. Whatever comes first.

Take Bird, for instance. In the big scheme of things, number 33 was an extremely tall and well-coordinated guy who did his job exceptionally well. That's it. You can't call him a superhero because he wasn't saving lives or making the world a better place. At the same time, he possessed heroic qualities because everyone in New England bought into his invincibility. He came through too many times for us. After a while, we started expecting him to come through, and when he *still* came through, that's when we were hooked for good. I know this was the case because I lived through his prime—whether I have developed enough credibility in your eyes as a basketball thinker is up to you[36]—but I'm telling you, that's how Boston fans felt in the spring of 1987. Unfortunately, you can't glance through Bird's career statistics in the *Official NBA Register* and find the statistic for "most times the fans expected their best player to come through and he actually did." So here's a story about his most memorable game-winning shot, a shot that didn't actually go in.

36. This is a completely unbiased book except for the ongoing digs at Kareem and Vince. Even someone like Kobe, who could be called a conniving, contrived, unlikable, philandering, socially awkward fraud of a human being in the wrong hands, will be handled with the utmost respect. I promise you.

After winning three MVP awards, the Legend was rattling off the greatest run of his career in the spring of '87, single-handedly dragging an aging roster through three punishing rounds despite a broken foot for McHale (gamely kept playing) and injuries to Bill Walton and Scott Wedman (both out), as well as sprained ankles for Parish and Ainge (playing hurt). Um, those were only five of the best seven guys on the team. When we were finished in the waning seconds of Game 5 of the Eastern Finals, Bird saved the season with his famous steal from Isiah, which remains the loudest I ever heard the Garden in my life, the only time I remember the upper balcony actually *swaying* because everyone was jumping up and down in sheer delight. That's the great thing about sports: when you hope for something improbable to happen, 4,999 times out of 5,000 it never happens, but then there's the 5,000th time, and for God's sake, it happens. That was the Bird steal. Two games later, he finished Detroit with a variety of backbreaking shots down the stretch, including a ludicrous 15-foot lefty banker that had to be seen to be believed.[37] At this point, we were convinced that Bird couldn't be stopped. He just kept raising his game to another level; how high could he go? Down by one in the final 30 seconds of a must-win Game 4, the Celtics tried to run a play for Bird, but James Worthy smothered him and held his jersey to keep him close.[38] Somehow the ball rotated around and back to Bird's side. Worthy stupidly left him to jump out on Danny Ainge, leaving the Legend open in the corner for a split second.

(Insert sound of fifteen thousand people gasping out loud.)

DJ swung the ball to Bird, who planted his feet and launched a three right in front of the Lakers' bench.

(Insert sound of fifteen thousand people pleading, "Threeeeeeeeeeee . . .")

Swish.

---

37. I missed this one because my high school prom was scheduled the night before in Connecticut. My uncle Bob sat in my seat and ended up getting shown numerous times on CBS. Also, I didn't hook up on prom night or even come close. Number of times I've regretted not getting up early that Sunday morning and making the 150-minute drive: 280,975.

38. Where were the refs? You got me. I watched this game recently and screamed at the refs after one of their 20 awful calls down the stretch, prompting my confused wife (listening from the kitchen) to ask, "Don't you already know what happens in this game?" Yeah, but still.

(Insert sound of fifteen thousand people screaming, "Hrrrrrrrrrrr-aaaaaaaaaaaahhhhhhhhhhh!")

If they stopped the game right there and announced that Bird would walk across the Charles River, not only would I have been the first kid there, I would have brought my camera. We stood and cheered and screamed and stomped our feet through the entire time-out, never thinking we would blow the game after what we had just witnessed. The Lakers ran their patented "let's get the ball to Kareem and the refs will bail him out" play and got him to the free throw line. He made the first and missed the second, leading to an egregious no-call from Earl Strom where Mychal Thompson slammed into McHale and Parish and caused them to knock the rebound out of bounds. Lakers ball. That opened the door for Magic's spine-crushing baby sky hook that McHale would have blocked if he wasn't playing on a *freaking broken foot*. (Sorry, I'm still bitter.) Now there were just two ticks left on the clock and the Lakers were jumping around and blowing each other . . . but we still had Thirty-three. Everyone in the building knew Larry was getting the ball. Everyone in the building knew we were still alive.

So what happens? The Lakers stick two guys on Bird. Somehow, he breaks free at midcourt (seriously, how the hell does this happen?), slides down the sideline, grabs the inbounds pass, controls his momentum long enough to set his feet for a split second right in front of Riley, steadies his upper body for a nanosecond, and launches a wide-open three in front of the Lakers bench. At that precise moment, standing in front of my seat at midcourt with pee probably dripping down my leg, I would have bet *anything* that the shot was ripping through the net. I would have bet my baseball card collection. I would have bet my Intellivision. I would have bet my virginity.[39] I would have bet my life. Even the Lakers probably thought it was going in. Watch the tape and you will notice Lakers backup Wes Matthews crouched on the floor and screaming behind Bird in sheer, unadulterated terror like he's about to watch someone get murdered in a horror movie. You will hear the fans emit some sort of strange, one-of-a-kind shrieking noise, a gasping sound loosely translated as, "Holy shit, we

---

39. Again, no luck on prom night.

are about to witness the greatest basketball shot ever!" Hell, you can freeze the tape on the frame before the ball strikes the rim. It looks like it's going in. It should have gone in.

It didn't go in.

When Bird released the shot, his body was moving directly between me and the basket; you could have drawn a straight line over the arc of the ball and extended it over Bird's head right to me. Two decades later, I can still see that moon shot soaring through the air on a direct line—it was dead-on—knowing immediately that it had a chance, then feeling like Mike Tyson had floored me with a body punch when the ball caught the back of the rim. Bird missed it by a fraction, maybe the length of a finger-nail. It couldn't have been closer. You cannot come closer to making a basketball shot without actually making the shot.[40]

Here's what I remember most. Not the sound in the Garden (a gasp of anticipation giving way to a prolonged groan, followed by the most deafening silence imaginable),[41] or the jubilant Lakers skipping off the court like they were splitting a winning Powerball ticket twelve ways (they knew how fortunate they were), or even the shocked faces of the people around me (everyone standing in place, mouths agape, staring at the basket in disbelief). Nope. It was Larry. As the shot bounced away, he froze for a split second and stared at the basket in disbelief even as the Lakers celebrated behind him. Just like us, he couldn't believe it.

The ball was supposed to go in.

The split second passed and Bird joined the cluttered group of players and coaches leaving the floor. When he walked through the tunnel by me and my father, he seemed just as confused as anyone.[42] The rest of us remained in our seats, shell-shocked, trying to regroup for the walk outside, unable to come to grips with the fact that the Celtics had lost. If you saw

---

40. In one of the kajillion NBA documentaries made this decade, Worthy admits that he still has nightmares about that shot going in. And he *won* the series.

41. I would put this shot against any moment in NBA history where a crowd makes two of the loudest noises possible that are completely opposite in the span of two seconds: *hrrraaaaaaaaaaaaa-ohhhhhhhhhhhhhhh.* There was never a louder *hrrrraaaaaaaaaaaaaaaaa-ohhhhhhhhhhhhhh* moment.

42. You can see me at the end of this one, right before James Brown interviews Magic—I'm wearing a blue polo shirt and kinda look like Kirk Cameron during the second season of *Growing Pains.* Also, I look like a doctor just told me that I have VD.

Saving Private Ryan in the theater, do you remember how every paying customer was paralyzed and couldn't budge as the final credits started to roll? That's what the Garden was like. People couldn't move. People were stuck to their seats like flypaper. We went through the seven stages of grief in two minutes, including my father, who was slumped in his seat like he had just been assassinated. He wasn't showing any inkling of getting up. Even when I said to him, "Hey, Pops, let's get out of here," he didn't budge.

A few more seconds passed. Finally, my father looked at me.

"That was supposed to go in," he groaned. "How did that *not* go in?"

More than twenty-two years have passed since that night . . . and I still don't have an answer for him. For everything else, I have answers.

I think.

ONE

THE SECRET

I LEARNED THE secret of basketball while lounging at a topless pool in Las Vegas. As I learned the secret, someone's bare breasts were staring at me from just eight feet away. The person explaining the secret was a Hall of Famer who once vowed to beat me up and changed his mind only because Gus Johnson vouched for me.

(Do I tell this story? Yes. I tell this story.)

Come back with me to July 2007. My buddy Hopper was pushing me to accompany him for an impromptu Vegas trip, knowing that I wouldn't turn him down because of my Donaghy-level gambling problem. I needed permission from my pregnant wife, who was perpetually ornery from (a) carrying our second child during the hot weather months in California and (b) being knocked up because I pulled the goalie on her back in February.[1] But here's why I'm an evil genius: with the NBA Summer League happening at the same time, I somehow convinced her that *ESPN The Magazine* wanted a column about Friday's quadruple-header featuring my favorite team (the Celtics), my favorite rookie (Kevin Durant), and the two Los Angeles teams (Clippers and Lakers). "I'll be in and out in thirty-six hours," I told her.

She signed off and directed her anger at the magazine for making me work on a weekend. (I told you, I'm shrewd.) I quickly called my editor and had the following exchange.

ME: I don't have a column idea this week. I'm panicking.

NEIL (*my editor*): Crap. I don't know what to tell you; it's a dead month.

(A few seconds of silence ensues.)

ME: Hey, wait . . . isn't the NBA Summer League in Vegas right now?

NEIL: Yeah, I think it is. What would you write about, though?

ME: Lemme see what the schedule is for Friday. *[I spend the next 20 seconds pretending to log onto NBA.com and look this up.]* Oh my God— Clippers at 3, Celtics at 5, Lakers at 6, Durant and the Sonics at 7! You have to let me go! I can get 1,250 words out of that! *[Neil doesn't respond.]* Come on—Vegas? The Celtics and Durant? This column will write itself!

NEIL (*after a long sigh*): Okay, fine, fine.

Did I care that he sounded like I had just convinced him to donate me a kidney? Of course not! I flew down on Friday, devoured those four games and joined Hopper for drunken blackjack until the wee hours.[2] The following morning, we woke up in time for a Vegas Breakfast (16-ounce

---

1. The term "pulling the goalie" means "eschewing birth control and letting the chips fall where they may." Usually couples discuss pulling the goalie before it happens . . . unless it's Bridget Moynahan. In my case, I made the executive decision to speed up plans for kid number two. This did not go over well. I think I'm the first person who ever had a positive home pregnancy test whipped at them at 95 mph.
2. This is a bald-faced lie—we both got crushed at $50 tables at the Wynn and were in bed by 1:00 a.m. I didn't want to ruin the story.

coffee, bagel, large water), then headed down to the Wynn's lavish outdoor blackjack setup, which includes:

1. Eight blackjack tables surrounding one of those square outdoor bars like the one where Brian Flanagan worked after he fled to Jamaica in *Cocktail*. Once you've gambled outdoors, your life is never quite the same. It's like riding in a convertible for the first time.
2. Overhead mist machines blowing cool spray so nobody overheats, a crucial wrinkle during the scorching Vegas summer, when it's frequently over 110 degrees outside and 170 degrees in every guy's crotch.
3. A beautiful European pool tucked right behind the tables. Just so you know, "European" is a fancy way of saying, "It's okay to go topless there."[3]

If there's a better male bonding experience, I can't think of one. For our yearly guys' trip one month earlier, we arrived right before the outdoor area opened (11:00 a.m.) and played through dinner. For the first three hours, none of the sunbathers was willing to pull a Jackie Robinson and break the topless barrier, so we decided the Wynn should hire six strippers to go topless every day at noon (just to break the ice) and have their DJ play techno songs with titles like "Take Your Tops Off," "Come On, Nobody's Looking," "We're All Friends Here," "Unleash the Hounds" and "What Do You Have to Lose? You're Already Divorced." By midafternoon, as soon as everyone had a few drinks in them, the ladies started flinging their tops off like Frisbees. Okay, not really. But two dozen women made the plunge over the next few hours, including one heavyset woman who nearly caused a riot by wading into the pool with her 75DDDDDDDDDDDs. It was like being there when the Baby Ruth bar landed in the Bushwood pool; people were scurrying for their lives in every direction.[4]

So between seedy guys making runs at topless girls in the pool, horny

---

3. It's never a bad thing when "European" is involved—that word always seems to involve nudity or debauchery. Even in porn (which is centered around those two things, anyway), you throw the word "European" in the title and the movie suddenly seems ten times more appealing. Um, not that I buy porn or anything.

4. The thing about European-style pools is that most of the uninhibited women who go topless are usually people you'd never want to see topless . . . like this lady, who looked like one of the Wild Samoans from the WWWF, only with 75DDDDDDDDDDDs. Those breasts are burned in my brain forever. And not by my choice.

blackjack dealers getting constantly distracted, aforementioned moments like the Baby Ruth/multi-D episode, the tropical feel of outdoors and the Mardi Gras/beads element of a Euro pool, ten weeks of entertainment and comedy were jam-packed into eight hours. Things peaked around 6:00 p.m. when an attractive blonde wearing a bikini joined our table, complained to the dealer, "I haven't had a blackjack in three days," then told us confidently, "If I get a blackjack, I'm going topless." The pit boss declared that she couldn't go topless, so they negotiated for a little bit, ultimately deciding that she could flash everyone instead. Yes, this conversation actually happened. Suddenly we were embroiled in the most exciting blackjack shoe of all time. Every time she got an ace or a 10 as her first card, the tension was more unbearable than the last five minutes of the final *Sopranos* episode. When she finally nailed her blackjack, our side of the blackjack section erupted like Fenway after the Roberts steal.[5] She followed through with her vow, departed a few minutes later, and left us spending the rest of the night wondering how I could write about that entire sequence for *ESPN The Magazine* without coming off like a pig. Well, you know what? These are the things that happen in Vegas. I'm not condoning them, defending them or judging them. Just understand that we don't keep going because some bimbo might flash everyone at her blackjack table; we keep going for the twenty minutes afterward, when we're rehashing the story and making every possible joke.[6]

Needless to say, wild horses couldn't have dragged Hopper and me from the outdoor blackjack section during Summer League. We treaded water for a few hours when I ran into an old acquaintance who handled PR from the Knicks, as well as Gus Johnson, the much-adored March Madness and Knicks announcer who loves me mainly because I love him. Gus and I successfully executed a bear hug and a five-step handshake, and just as I was ready to make Gus announce a few of my blackjack hands ("Here's the double-down card . . . *Ohhhhhhhh! it's a ten!*"), he implored me to come over and meet his buddy Isiah Thomas.

Gulp.

5. This was such a great moment that I had to go with back-to-back Hall of Fame pop culture and sports analogies. I mean, those were two of the biggies. I'm talking about the analogies.
6. And also because some bimbo might flash everyone at our blackjack table.

Of any sports figure that I could have possibly met at any time in my life, getting introduced to Isiah that summer would have been my number one draft pick for the Holy Shit, Is This Gonna Be Awkward draft. Isiah doubled as the beleaguered GM of the Knicks and a frequent column target, someone who once threatened "trouble" if we ever crossed paths.[7] This particular moment seemed to qualify. After the PR guy and I explained to Gus why a Simmons-Isiah introduction would be a stupefyingly horrific idea, Gus confidently countered, "Hold on, I got this, I got this, I'll fix this." And he wandered off as our terrified PR buddy said, "I'm getting out of here—good luck!"[8]

I played a few hands of rattled blackjack while wondering how to defend myself if Isiah came charging at me with a piña colada. After all, I *killed* this guy in my column over the years. I killed him for some of the cheap shots he took as a player, for freezing out MJ in the '85 All-Star Game, for leading the classless walkout at the tail end of the Bulls-Pistons sweep in '91. I killed him for pushing Bird under the bus by backing up Rodman's foolish "he'd be just another good player if he weren't white" comments after the '87 playoffs, then pretending like he was kidding afterward. (He wasn't.) I killed him for bombing as a TV announcer, for sucking as Toronto's GM, for running the CBA into the ground, and most of all, for his incomprehensibly ineffective performance running the Knicks. As I kept lobbing (totally justified) grenades at him, Isiah went on Stephen A. Smith's radio show and threatened "trouble" if we ever met on the street. Like this was all my fault. Somewhere along the line, Isiah probably decided that I had a personal grudge against him, which simply wasn't true—I had written many times that he was the best pure point guard I'd ever seen, as well as the most underappreciated star of his era. I even defended his draft record and praised him for standing up for his

7. This encounter took place about six weeks before the kooky trial for Anucha Browne Sanders' sexual harassment lawsuit against Isiah and Madison Square Garden became a national story, effectively murdering Isiah's tenure with the Knicks and leading to a sad episode in October '08 when Isiah apparently overdosed on prescription meds. It's never been clear if the overdose was intentional or not. Can you tell my editors told me, "Write this footnote carefully"?

8. You know things were bad with me and Isiah when the Knicks PR guy decided, "Instead of sticking around to help thwart a PR holocaust, I'm going to flee the premises like O.J. and A.C. taking off for Mexico." I don't blame him.

players right before the ugly Nuggets-Knicks brawl that featured Carmelo
Anthony's infamous bitch-slap/backpedal. It's not like I was obsessed with
ripping the guy. He just happened to be an easy target, a floundering NBA
GM who didn't understand the luxury tax, cap space, or how to plan
ahead. For what I did for a living, Isiah jokes were easier than making fun
of Flavor Flav at a celebrity roast. The degree of difficulty was a 0.0.

With that said, I would have rather been playing blackjack and drinking vodka lemonades than figuring out how to cajole a pissed-off NBA
legend. When a somber Gus finally waved me over, I was relieved to get it
over with. (By the way, there should be no scenario that includes the
words "Gus Johnson" and "somber." I feel like I failed America regardless
of how this turned out.) Gus threw an arm around me and said something like, "Look, I straightened everything out, he's willing to talk to you,
just understand, he's a sensitive guy, he takes this shit personally."[9] Understood. I followed him to a section of chairs near the topless pool, where
Isiah was sipping a water and wearing a white Panama hat to shield himself from the blazing sun. As we approached, Gus slapped me on the back
and gestured to a female friend who quickly fled the premises, like we
were Mafia heads sitting down in the back of an Italian restaurant and
Gus was shedding every waiter and busboy. *Get out of here. You don't want
to be here for this.* Meanwhile, Isiah rose from the chair with a big smile on
his face—he'd make a helluva politician—saying simply, "Hi, I'm Isiah."[10]

We shook hands and sat down. I explained the purpose of my column,
how I write from the fan's perspective and play up certain gimmicks—
I like the Boston teams and dislike anyone who battles them, I pretend to
be smarter than every GM, I think Christmas should be changed to Larry
Bird's birthday—which made Isiah a natural foil for me. He understood
that. He thought we were both entertainers, for lack of a better word. We
were both there to make basketball more fun to follow. He didn't appreciate two things I had written: that he destroyed the CBA (which he
claimed wasn't true) and how I lumped him with other inept GMs in a

9. After seeing him in action, I'm totally convinced that Gus Johnson can resolve
any feud, controversy, or territorial matter within 25 minutes: Bloods-Crips, Richards-
Locklear, Shiites-Sunnis, TO-McNabb, the Gaza Strip, Vick-PETA, you name it. He's like
a cross between Obama, Jay-Z and Cyrus from *The Warriors.*
10. Totally underrated part of the story: "Hi, I'm Isiah." As if there potentially could have
been some confusion.

widely read parody column called "The Atrocious GM Summit."[11] That led to us discussing each move and why he made them. He admitted two mistakes—the Jalen Rose trade (his fault) and the Steve Francis trade (not his fault because Larry Brown insisted on it, or so he claimed)—and defended everything else. Strangely, inconceivably, each explanation made sense. For instance, he explained the recent Randolph trade by telling me (I'm paraphrasing), "Everyone's trying to get smaller and faster. I want to go the other way. I want to get *bigger*. I want to *pound* people down low." I found myself nodding like Steve Lawrence and Eydie Gormé in *SNL*'s "Sinatra Group" sketch. *Great idea, Chairman! I love it! You're a genius!* Only later, after we parted ways and I thought about it more, did it dawn on me how doomed his strategy was—not the "getting bigger" part as much as the "getting bigger with two head-case fat asses who can't defend anyone or protect the rim and are prohibitively expensive" part. You get bigger with McHale and Parish or Sampson and Olajuwon. You don't get bigger with Eddy Curry and Zach Randolph.[12]

But that's not why I'm telling you this story. After settling on an uneasy truce about his job performance, we started remembering those unforgettable Celtics-Pistons clashes from the eighties: how their mutual hatred was palpable, how that competitiveness has slowly eroded from the league because of rule changes, money, AAU camps and everything else. Today's rivals hug each other after games and pull the "I love you, boy!" routine. They act like former summer camp chums who became successful CEOs, then ran into each other at Nobu for the first time in years. *Great to see you! I'll talk to you soon—let's have lunch!* When Isiah's Pistons played Bird's Celtics, the words "great to see you" were not on the agenda. They wanted to destroy each other. There was

11. I gathered all the inept 2006 GMs for a fake conference panel where they gave tips on how to completely suck at their job. Isiah ended up stealing the fake show.

12. His funniest-in-retrospect explanation was for the hideous Jerome James signing. As Isiah spun it, he signed James to be his center, then had a chance to land Curry a few weeks later and went for it. A bummed-out James felt betrayed and never dedicated himself, but hey, Isiah had a chance to get a young low-post stud like Curry and it was worth the risk. I swear, this made sense as he was saying it. He swayed me enough that I never had the urge to sarcastically quip, "Hey, anytime you can lock up Eddy Curry and Jerome James for $90 million and lose two lottery picks, you have to do it."

an edge to those battles that the current ones don't have. I missed that edge and so did Isiah. We both felt passionate about it, passionate enough that—gasp—we were legitimately enjoying the conversation.[13]

I was getting comfortable with him. Comfortable enough that I had to ask about The Secret.

And here's where I won Isiah over—not just that I asked about The Secret, but that I remembered it in the first place. Detroit won the 1989 title after collapsing in consecutive springs against the '87 Celtics and '88 Lakers, two of the toughest exits in playoff history because of the nature of those defeats: a pair of "why did that have to happen?" moments in the Boston series (Bird's famous steal in Game 5, then Vinnie Johnson and Adrian Dantley banging heads in Game 7), followed by another in the '88 Finals (Isiah's ankle sprain in Game 6). The '89 Pistons regrouped for 62 wins and swept the Lakers for their first championship, vindicating a controversial in-season trade that shipped Dantley and a draft pick to Dallas for Mark Aguirre. That season lives on in Cameron Stauth's superb book *The Franchise,* which details how GM Jack McCloskey built those particular Pistons teams. The crucial section happens during the '89 Finals, with Isiah holding court with reporters and improbably offering up "the secret" of winning basketball. Here's an edited-for-space version of what he tells them on pages 310 and 311. The part that matters most is in boldface.

It's not about physical skills. Goes far beyond that. When I first came here, McCloskey took a lot of heat for drafting a small guy. But he knew that the only way our team would rise to the top would be by mental skills, not size or talent. He knew the only way we could acquire those skills was by watching the Celtics and Lakers, because those were the teams winning year in and year out. I also looked at Seattle, who won one year, and Houston, who got to the Finals one year. They both self-destructed the next year. So how come? I read Pat Riley's book *Show Time*

13. Proving yet again that I can get along with *anyone* on the planet as long as they like basketball. You could dress me in red, drop me into a Crips neighborhood, tell me that I have 12 minutes to start a high-caliber NBA conversation before somebody puts a cap in my ass . . . and I would live.

and he talks about "the disease of more."[14] A team wins it one year and the next year every player wants more minutes, more money, more shots. And it kills them. Our team has been up at the Championship level four years now. We could have easily self-destructed. So I read what Riley was saying, and I learned. I didn't want what happened to Seattle and Houston to happen to us. **But it's hard not to be selfish. The art of winning is complicated by statistics, which for us becomes money. Well, you gotta fight that, find a way around it. And I think we have.** If we win this, we'll be the first team in history to win it without a single player averaging 20 points. First team. Ever. We got 12 guys who are totally committed to winning. Every night we found a different person to win it for us. Talked to Larry Bird about this once. Couple years back, at the All-Star Game. We were sitting signing basketballs and I'm talking to him about Red Auerbach and the Boston franchise and just picking his brain. I don't know if he knew I was picking his brain, but I think he knew. Because I asked one question and he just looked at me. Smiled. Didn't answer.

Whoa.

A few pages later, with the Pistons on the cusp of sweeping the Lakers, Isiah rants about Detroit's perceived lack of respect from the outside world:

Look at our team statistically. We're one of the worst teams in the league. So now you have to find a new formula to judge basketball. There were a lot of times I had my doubts about this approach, because all of you kept telling me it could never be done this way. Statistically, it made me look horrible. But I kept looking at the won-loss record and how we kept improving and I kept saying to myself, Isiah, you're doin' the right thing, so be stubborn, and one day people will find a different way to judge a player. They won't just pick up the newspaper and say, oh, this guy was 9 for 12 with 8 rebounds so he was the best player in the game. **Lots of times, on our team, you can't tell who the best player in the game was.**

14. The "Disease of More" ranks right up there with *The Tipping Point* and the Ewing Theory as one of the three greatest theories of the last 35 years. No sports theory gets vindicated more on a yearly basis. The complete list of "Disease of More" NBA champs: '67 Sixers, '71 Bucks, '75 Warriors, '77 Blazers, '79 Sonics, '80 Lakers, '92 Bulls, '00 Lakers, '04 Pistons. And let's throw in the following NBA Finalists: '67 Warriors, '81 Rockets, '86 Rockets, '93 Suns, '95 Magic, '96 Sonics, '99 Knicks, '03 Nets.

'Cause everybody did something good. That's what makes us so good. The other team has to worry about stopping eight or nine people instead of two or three. It's the only way to win. The only way to win. That's the way the game was invented. But there's more to that. You also got to create an environment that won't accept losing.

Forget for a second that, in two paragraphs of quotes, Isiah just described everything you would ever need to know about winning an NBA championship. I always wanted to know what The Secret was. If you noticed, *he never fucking said it.* Even more frustrating, nobody ever asked him again.[15] And I had been wondering about it since I was in college. Now we were sitting by a topless pool in Vegas and he seemed to be enjoying my company, so screw it. When was this scenario ever happening again? I set up the question and asked him.

Isiah smiled. I could tell he was impressed. He took a dramatic pause. You could say he even milked the moment.

"The secret of basketball," he told me, "is that it's *not* about basketball."

The secret of basketball is that it's not about basketball.

That makes no sense, right? How can that possibly make sense?

For the next few minutes, Isiah explained it to me. After coming soooooooooo close for two straight postseasons, the chemistry for the '89 team was off for reasons that had nothing to do with talent. Chuck Daly needed to give Dennis Rodman more playing time, only the Teacher (Dantley's nickname, in an ironic twist) wasn't willing to accommodate him. And that was a problem. Rodman could play any style and defend every type of player; he gave the Pistons unique flexibility, much like Havlicek's ability to play guard or forward drove Russell's last few Celtics teams. There was also a precedent in place from when John Salley and Joe Dumars came into their own in previous seasons; Isiah and Vinnie Johnson gave up minutes for Dumars, and Rick Mahorn gave up minutes for Salley. But when Rodman started stealing crunch-time minutes from Dantley, the Teacher started sulking and even complained to a local writer.

15. Although this wasn't surprising. The lack of ingenuity with questions from sports reporters has never been anything less than appalling. None of these dolts followed up on The Secret, but I bet they asked questions like "Isiah, how excited would you be to win a title?" in 40 different forms. Then they went back to the press room and fought over the last four bags of Cheetos.

You couldn't call it a betrayal, but Dantley had undermined an altruistic dynamic—constructed carefully over the past four seasons, almost like a stack of Jenga blocks—that hinged on players forfeiting numbers for the overall good of the team. The Pistons couldn't risk having Dantley knock that Jenga stack down. They quickly swapped him for the enigmatic Aguirre, an unconventional low-post scorer who caused similar mismatch problems but wouldn't start trouble because Isiah (a childhood chum from Chicago) would never allow it. Maybe Dantley was a better player than Aguirre, but Aguirre was a better fit for the 1989 Pistons. If they didn't make that deal, they wouldn't have won the championship. It was a people trade, not a basketball trade.[16]

And that's what Isiah learned while following those Lakers and Celtics teams around: *it wasn't about basketball.*

Those teams were loaded with talented players, yes, but that's not the only reason they won. They won because they liked each other, knew their roles, ignored statistics and valued winning over everything else. They won because their best players sacrificed to make everyone else happy. They won as long as everyone remained on the same page. By that same token, they lost if any of those three factors weren't in place. The '75 Warriors self-combusted a year later because of Barry's grating personality and two young stars (Wilkes and Gus Williams) needing better numbers to boost their free agent stock. The '77 Blazers fell apart because of Bill Walton's feet, but also because Lionel Hollins and Maurice Lucas brooded about being underpaid. The '79 Sonics fell apart when their talented backcourt (Dennis Johnson and Gus Williams) became embroiled in a petty battle over salaries and crunch-time shots. The '81 Lakers were bounced because Magic Johnson's teammates believed he was getting too much attention, most notably fellow point guard Norm Nixon, who resented having to share the basketball. The '83 Celtics got swept by Milwaukee for a peculiar reason: they had *too many* good players and everyone wanted to play. The '86 Lakers lost to Houston because Kareem

---

16. In the '88 Playoffs, Dantley played 33.9 MPG and Rodman 20.6 MPG. When the Pistons cruised to the '89 title, Aguirre averaged 27.1 MPG and Rodman 24.1 MPG. Dantley/Rodman averaged a combined 26.5 PPG and 11.6 RPG in '88, followed by 18.4 PPG plus 14.4 RPG from Aguirre/Rodman the following spring. So they sacrificed eight points per game for better defense, rebounding and chemistry. And it worked.

wasn't an alpha dog anymore, only Magic wasn't confident enough to supplant him yet. The '87 Rockets imploded because of drug suspensions and contract bitterness. Year after year, at least one contender fell short for reasons that had little or nothing to do with basketball. And year after year, the championship team prevailed because it got along and everyone committed themselves to their roles. That's what Detroit needed to do, and that's why Dantley had to go.[17]

"So that's the secret," Isiah said. "It's not about basketball."

The secret of basketball is that it's not about basketball.

These are the things you learn in Vegas.

When I was talking to Isiah that day, his affection for those Pistons teams stood out almost as vividly as the pair of exposed nipples eight feet away. This didn't surprise me. I remembered his appearance on *NBA's Greatest Games*,[18] when he watched Game 6 of the '88 Finals with ESPN's Dan Patrick. The Lakers couldn't handle point guards who created shots off the dribble, as we witnessed during Sleepy Floyd's legendary twenty-nine points in one quarter one year earlier.[19] If someone like Sleepy gave them fits, you can only imagine how they struggled against Isiah Lord Thomas III when he needed one more victory for his first title. Smelling blood in the third quarter at the Forum, he dropped fourteen straight points with a ridiculous array of shots, doing his best impression of Robby Benson at the end of *One on One*... right until he stepped on Michael Cooper's foot and crumbled to a heap. Poor Isiah kept trying to stand, only his leg wouldn't support him and he kept falling to the ground. At the time, it was like watching those uncomfortable few seconds after a racehorse suffers a leg injury, when it can't stop moving but can't support itself, either.

17. The Teacher was blindsided by the trade. When he finally played Detroit later that season, he sought out Isiah before the opening tip, leaned into him and said *something* that rattled Isiah. It was the NBA's version of "I know it was you, Fredo." He would never win an NBA ring. But Teacher, you have to understand—it wasn't about basketball!

18. This show ran on ESPN2 in the mid-'90s: Patrick watching classic games with one of its participants. I think I was the only one who watched it.

19. Their other weakness: Kareem stopped rebounding somewhere during the '84 season. Plus, he was starting to look like a bona fide alien with goggles, a shaved head and that gangly body. All Lakers games in '88 and '89 should have kicked off with Kareem climbing out of a UFO. But that's irrelevant here.

Anyone who ever played basketball knows how an ankle sprain feels at the moment of impact: like Leatherface churning his chain saw against the bottom of your leg. You don't come back from a badly sprained ankle. Hell, you can't even walk off the court most times. Isiah didn't stand for ninety seconds before getting helped to his bench. You could practically see Detroit's title hopes vanishing into thin air.

Except Isiah wouldn't let the injury derail him. He chewed on his bottom lip like a wad of tobacco and transferred the pain. When the Lakers extended their lead to eight, Isiah hobbled back into the game, fueled on adrenaline, desperately trying to save Detroit's title before his ankle swelled. He made a one-legged floater. He made an off-balance banker over Cooper, drawing the foul and nearly careening into the first row of fans. He drained a long three. He filled the lane for a fast-break layup. With the final seconds of the quarter ticking away, he buried a turnaround 22-footer from the corner—an absolutely *outrageous* shot—giving him a Finals record 25 for the quarter and reclaiming the lead for Detroit. This was Pantheon-level stuff, win or lose. CBS headed to commercial and showed a slow-motion replay of that aforementioned layup: Isiah unable to stop his momentum on that ravaged ankle, crashing into the photographers under the basket, then gamely speed-hopping back downcourt as his teammates cheered from the bench. On the Goosebump Scale, it's about a 9.8. We always hear about Willis Reed's Game 7 cameo against the Lakers, or Gibson taking Eckersley deep in the '88 World Series. Somehow, Isiah's 25-point quarter gets lost in the shuffle because the Pistons ended up losing the game (and the series).[20] Seems a little unfair. Nobody was more of a warrior than Isiah Thomas. In retrospect, that was his biggest problem: maybe he cared a little *too much*. If that's possible. Actually, that's definitely possible. Because when ESPN finished rerunning that third quarter, they returned to the studio and Isiah Thomas was crying. He had never seen the tape before. He couldn't handle it.

20. That Game 6 defeat ranks among the most brutal ever. Even with Isiah barely able to move by game's end, Detroit led by three with 60 seconds to play. Time-out, L.A. Byron Scott hit a jumper in traffic (102–101, 52 secs left). Isiah ran the shot clock down and missed a one-legged fall-away (27 secs left, time-out L.A.). Kareem got bailed out by a dubious call (Laimbeer's "bump" on a sky hook), then drained two clutch FT's with 14 secs left. Then Dumars badly missed a runner coming out of the time-out. Ballgame. If healthy, Isiah swings that final minute of Game 6. I am positive. But that's basketball—you need to be good *and* lucky.

What followed was breathtaking. Just know that I watch all these shows. I watch every *SportsCentury,* every *Beyond the Glory,* every HBO documentary, everything. I eat this stuff up. And with the possible exception of the Cooz breaking down during Bill Russell's *SportsCentury,* no moment ever matched what transpires after Patrick asks a simple question about Game 6: "Why does it bother you?"

The words hang in the air. Isiah can't speak. He dabs his eyes, finally breaking into a self-conscious smile. The memories come flooding back, some good, some bad. He's overwhelmed. Finally, he describes how it feels to play for a championship team. To a tee. And he does it off the top of his head.

"I just . . . I . . . I never watched this," Isiah mumbles, dabbing his eyes with a handkerchief. "You just . . . you wouldn't understand."

Patrick doesn't say anything. Wisely.

Isiah takes a second to collect himself, then he keeps going: "That type of emotion, that type of feeling, when you're playing like that, and you know, you're really going for it . . . you're *going* for it. You put your heart, your soul, you put everything into it, and . . ."

He chokes up again. Takes another moment to compose himself.

"It's like, to look back on that, to know that all we went through as a team, and the people, and the friendships and everything . . . you just wouldn't understand."

He smiles again. It's a weird moment. In any other setting, he would come off as condescending. But he's right: somebody like Patrick, or me, or you . . . none of us could understand. Not totally, anyway.

Isiah keeps going. Now he *wants* Patrick to understand.

"You know, like you said, to see Dennis, the way Dennis was, to see Vinnie, to see Joe, to see Bill, to see Chuck, and to know what we all went through and what we were fighting for . . . I mean, we weren't the Lakers, we weren't the Celtics, we were just, we were *nobody.* We were the Detroit Pistons, trying to make our way through the league, trying to fight and earn some turf, you know, and make people realize that we were a good team. We just weren't the thing that they had made us."

Patrick steps in: "You weren't Show Time, you weren't the Celts, you were the team that nobody gave credit to."

"Yeah," Isiah says, nodding. Now he knows. He knows what to say. "And seeing that, and feeling that, and going through all that emotion, I mean, as a player, *that's* what you play for. *That's* the feeling you want to have. When twelve men come together like that, you know, it's . . . it's . . ."

He struggles for the right words. He can't find them. And then, finally: "You wouldn't understand."

He's right. We wouldn't understand. And as it turned out, even Isiah didn't totally understand. He took over the Knicks in 2003, failed to heed the lessons of those Pistons teams, and got replaced five years later.[21] Of all the unbelievable things that transpired during the "Thomas error"—no playoff wins, a sexual harassment suit, two lost lottery picks, four straight years with a payroll over $90 million, fans protesting inside and outside MSG in his final season—what couldn't be explained was Thomas' willingness to overlook precisely what worked for his Detroit teams. How could such a savvy player become such a futile executive? How could someone win twice because of chemistry and unselfishness, then disregard those same traits while rebuilding the Knicks? Once upon a time, Detroit couldn't find a prototypical back-to-the-basket big man to help Thomas offensively, so GM Jack McCloskey smartly surrounded him with unconventional low-post threats, effective role players and streak shooters. When McCloskey realized they still couldn't outscore the Celtics or Lakers, he shifted the other way and built the toughest, most athletic, most flexible roster possible. By the '87 Playoffs, the Pistons went nine deep and had an answer for everyone. On paper, it's the weakest of the superb teams in that 1983–93 stretch. But that's the thing about basketball: you don't play games on paper. Detroit captured two titles and came agonizingly close to winning two more.

Again, Isiah was there. He watched McCloskey build that unique team. He knew there was more to basketball than stats and money, that you

---

21. After getting waxed by Boston in the '85 Playoffs, McCloskey realized he had three keepers (Isiah, Vinnie and Laimbeer) and nobody else with the right mix of athleticism and toughness to hang with Boston. He selected Dumars with the 17th pick, traded Kelly Tripucka and Kent Benson for Dantley and turned Dan Roundfield into Mahorn (a physical forward who could protect Laimbeer). In the '86 draft, he picked Salley 11th and Rodman 32nd, hoping Detroit could wear down Bird with young legs off the bench. That same summer, he stole backup center James Edwards from Phoenix. It's the most creative 12-month stretch ever submitted by an NBA GM. McCloskey built a future champion around Isiah without making a single top-10 pick or trading anything of real consequence.

couldn't win and keep winning unless your players sacrificed numbers for the greater good. So why place his franchise's fate in the hands of Stephon Marbury, one of the most selfish stars in the league? Why give away two potential lottery picks for Curry (an immature player and a liability as a rebounder and shot blocker) and compound the mistake by overpaying him? Why keep adding big contracts like he was running a high-priced fantasy team? What made him believe that Randolph and Curry could play together, or Steve Francis and Marbury, or even Marbury and Jamal Crawford? Why ignore the salary cap ramifications of every move? It made no sense. He had become Bizarro McCloskey. Every time I watched Isiah sitting glumly on the Knicks bench for that final season with a steely "There's no way I'm qutting, I'm not walking away from that money, they're gonna have to fire me" mask on his face, I remembered him sitting at the Wynn's outdoor pool utterly convinced that a Curry-Randolph tandem would work. How could someone learn The Secret and still screw up?

I have been obsessed with that question ever since. Year after year, 90 percent of NBA decision makers ignore The Secret or talk themselves into it not mattering that much. Fans overlook The Secret completely, as evidenced by the fact that, you know, it's a secret. (That's why we live in a world where nine out of ten basketball fans probably think Shaquille O'Neal had a better career than Tim Duncan.) Nobody writes about The Secret because of a general lack of sophistication about basketball; even the latest "revolution" of basketball statistics centers more around evaluating players against one another over capturing their effect on a team. When, in February 2009, Michael Lewis wrote a *Moneyball*-like feature for the *New York Times Magazine* about Shane Battier's undeniable value, he listed a bunch of different anecdotes and subtle ploys, as well as decent statistical evidence that explained Battier's effect defensively and on the Rockets as a whole, but again, it was nothing tangible. (Although Lewis unknowingly came up with two corollaries to The Secret: one, that your teammates are people you shouldn't automatically trust because it's in each player's selfish interest to screw his teammates out of shots or rebounds; and two, that basketball is the sport where this is most true.) You couldn't quantify Battier's impact except with victories, opponent's field goal positions, plus-minus variables, statistics that hadn't been created yet[22] and his high ranking on the unofficial list of Role Players That Every Peer Would Want on Their Team. And that's what I love about basketball most. You don't need to watch a single baseball game to have an opinion on baseball; you could be stuck on a desert island like Chuck Noland,[23] have the 2010 *Baseball Prospectus* randomly wash up on the shore, devour every page of that thing and eventually have an accurate feel for which players matter. In basketball? Numbers help, but only to a certain degree. You still have to watch the games. Check out Amar'e Stoudemire, who scores 22 to 25 points a night for Phoenix, grabs two rebounds a quarter, screws up defensively over and over again, botches every defensive switch, doesn't make anyone else better, doesn't create shots for anyone else and doesn't feel any responsibility to carry his franchise even as Phoenix pays him as its franchise player. Did Amar'e get voted by fans into the West's starting lineup for the 2009 All-Star Game with the Nash era imploding and the Suns shopping him more vigorously than Spencer and Heidi shopped their fake wedding pictures?[24] Of course he did.

The fans don't get it. Actually, it goes deeper than that—I'm not sure who gets it. We measure players by numbers, only the playoffs roll around and teams that play together, kill themselves defensively, sacrifice personal success and ignore statistics invariably win the title. The 2008 Lakers were 3-to-1 favorites over Boston and lost the Finals; to this day, Lakers fans treat the defeat like it was some sort of aberration. We have trouble processing the "teamwork over talent" thing. San Antonio was the most successful post-Jordan franchise and nobody understands why. Duncan was

---

22. We created one on page 403 just for him: nitty-gritties. Someone like Battier transcends stats. I thought it was fascinating that, in the same week Lewis' complimentary piece was released, (a) John Hollinger's "player efficiency rating" on ESPN.com ranked Battier as the 53rd best small forward and 272nd overall out of 322 players, and (b) Houston was shopping Battier.

23. *Cast Away* is on my Mount Rushmore for Most Rewatchable Cable Movie of the 2000s along with *Anchorman, Almost Famous* and *The Departed.* They should make *Cast Away 2* as a thriller where Chuck Noland loses his mind and makes hookers wear volleyballs over their heads when he has sex with them, eventually starts killing them, then escapes police by living outdoors and using his survival skills from the first movie. Like a combination of *First Blood* and *Silence of the Lambs.* You would have paid to see this in the theater. Don't lie.

24. For everyone after 2025: Spencer and Heidi were a reality TV couple who disappeared shortly after this book was published when Satan decided, "Even *I* can't take it anymore," and dragged them into the bowels of hell.

the best post-Jordan superstar and nobody understands why. But here's the thing: We have the answers! We know why! Look at how McCloskey built those Pistons teams. Look at how Gregg Popovich and R. C. Buford handled the Duncan era. Look at how Red Auerbach handled the Russell era. Look at why so many fans (myself included) still remember the '70 Knicks[25] and '77 Blazers. Here's what we know for sure:

1. You build potential champions around one great player. He doesn't have to be a super-duper star or someone who can score at will, just someone who leads by example, kills himself on a daily basis, raises the competitive nature of his teammates, and lifts them to a better place. The list of Best Players on an NBA Champ Since Bird and Magic Joined the League looks like this: Kareem (younger version), Bird, Moses, Magic, Isiah, Jordan, Hakeem, Duncan, Shaq (younger version), Billups, Wade, Garnett, Kobe. It's a list that looks exactly how you'd think it should look with the exception of Billups.[26]

2. You surround that superstar with one or two elite sidekicks who understand their place in the team's hierarchy, don't obsess over stats, and fill in every blank they can. The list of Best Championship Sidekicks Since 1980: Magic, Parish/McHale, Kareem (older version), Worthy, Doc/Toney, DJ, Dumars, Pippen/Grant, Drexler, Pippen/Rodman, Robinson, Kobe (younger version), Parker/Ginobili, Shaq (older version), Pierce/Allen, Gasol. You would have wanted to play with everyone on that list . . . even Younger Kobe. Most of the time.

3. From that framework, you complete your nucleus with top-notch role players and/or character guys (too many to count, but think Robert Horry/Derek Fisher types) who know their place, don't make mistakes

25. My editor (known as Grumpy Old Editor from now on) adds, "I was watching an MSG special on Clyde and he mentioned being pissed about Willis winning the '70 Finals MVP because Frazier thought he deserved it, which was certainly true if you based it on the numbers. But then he said that as he thought about it he realized he would have never done what he did in Game 7 if Willis hadn't inspired him. The Secret, again."

26. Billups led the '04 Pistons during a discombobulated season when the rules swung too far in favor of elite defensive teams who made threes and limited possessions. Plus, the Shaq/Kobe era completely imploded that season, with half the team embroiled in "I'm not talking to that mothafucka anymore" fights . . . and yet they *still* could have won the title if Karl Malone hadn't gotten hurt.

and won't threaten that unselfish culture, as well as a coaching staff
dedicated to keeping those team-ahead-of-individual values in place.
4. You need to stay healthy in the playoffs and maybe catch one or two
   breaks.[27]

That's how you win an NBA championship. Duncan's Spurs push the
formula one step further, pursuing *only* high-character guys as role players and winning just once with a squeaky wheel (Stephen Jackson in 2003,
and he was jettisoned that summer). Popovich explained their philosophy
to *Sports Illustrated* in 2009: "We get guys who want to do their job and go
home and aren't impressed with the hoopla. One of the keys is to bring in
guys who have gotten over themselves. They either want to prove that they
can play in this league—or they want to prove nothing. They fill their role
and have a pecking order. We have three guys who are the best players, and
everyone else fits around them." In a related story, Duncan's teams have
won 70 percent of their games for his entire career. This can't be an accident. But how do you keep stats for "best chemistry" and "most unselfishness" or even "most tangible and consistent effect on a group of
teammates"? It's impossible. That's why we struggle to comprehend professional basketball. You can only play five players at a time. Those players
can only play a total of 240 minutes. How those players coexist, how they
make each other better, how they accept their portion of that 240-minute
pie, how they trust and believe in one another, how they create shots for
one another, how that talent/salary/alpha-dog hierarchy falls into
place . . . that's basketball. It's like falling in love. When it's working, you
know it. When it's failing, you know it. Bill Russell (in *Second Wind*) and
Bill Bradley (in *Life on the Run*) played for famously magnanimous teams
and described their inner workings better than anyone:

> Russell: "By design and by talent the Celtics were a team of specialists,
> and like a team of specialists in any field, our performance depended on
> individual excellence and how well we worked together. None of us had
> to strain to understand that we had to complement each other's special-

27. Every fan of the Suns from 2004 to 2007 just rammed this book against their heads.

ties; it was simply a fact, and we all tried to figure out ways to make our combination more effective . . . the Celtics played together because we knew it was the best way to win."

Bradley: "A team championship exposes the limits of self-reliance, selfishness and irresponsibility. One man alone can't make it happen; in fact, the contrary is true: a single man can prevent it from happening. The success of the group assures the success of the individual, but not the other way around. Yet this team is an inept model, for even as people marvel at its unselfishness and skill involved, they disagree on how it is achieved and who is the most instrumental. The human closeness of a basketball team cannot be reconstructed on a larger scale."[28]

Russell: "Star players have an enormous responsibility beyond their statistics—the responsibility to pick their team up and carry it. You have to do this to win championships—and to be ready to do it when you'd rather be a thousand other places. You have to say and do the things that make your opponents play worse and your teammates play better. I always thought that the most important measure of how good a game I'd played was how much better I'd made my teammates play."

Bradley: "I believe that basketball, when a certain level of unselfish team play is realized, can serve as a kind of metaphor for ultimate cooperation. It is a sport where success, as symbolized by the championship, requires that the dictates of the community prevail over selfish personal impulses. An exceptional player is simply one point on a five-pointed star. Statistics—such as points, rebounds, or assists per game—can never explain the remarkable interaction that takes place on a successful pro team."

In different ways, Russell and Bradley argued the same point: that players should be measured by their ability to connect with other play-

28. That same dynamic doubles for any military unit or dorm hall of college freshmen: the human closeness cannot be reconstructed on a larger scale.

ers (and not by statistics). Anyone can connect with their teammates for one season. Find that connection, cultivate it, win the title, maintain that connection, survive the inevitable land mines, fight off hungrier foes and keep coming back for more success . . . that's being a champion. As Russell explained, "It's much harder to keep a championship than to win one. After you've won once, some of the key figures are likely to grow dissatisfied with the role they play, so it's harder to keep the team focused on doing what it takes to win. Also, you've already done it, so you can't rely on the same drive that makes people climb mountains for the first time; winning isn't new anymore. Also, there's a temptation to believe that the last championship will somehow win the next one automatically. You have to keep going out there game after game. Besides, you're getting older, and less willing to put up with aggravation and pain . . . When you find someone who at age 30 or 35 has the motivation to overrule that increasing pain and aggravation, you have a champion."[29]

I didn't see the words "stats" or "numbers" in there. It's all about winning. You can tell which current teams may have discovered The Secret well before the playoffs. The Celtics finished the 2007–8 preseason as a noticeably tighter group; already rejuvenated by the Garnett/Allen trades, traveling together in Italy without cell phones had bonded them in an unconventionally effective way.[30] They hatched their own catchphrase, "Ubuntu," a Bantu-derived word that roughly means "togetherness." They hung out even after returning to the States; instead of three players heading out for a movie or postgame dinner, the number invariably shaded closer to nine or ten. Before every tip-off, Eddie House and James Posey stood near the scorer's table and greeted the starters one by

---

29. That section finished like this: "Rarely will you see an athlete who hasn't put on 10 or 15 pounds over a full career, but even rarer are the ones who don't put on the same amount of mental fat. That's the biggest killer of aging champions, because it works on your concentration and your mental toughness, which are the margin of victory; it prevents you from using your mind to compensate for your diminished physical skills." I like the concept of "mental fat." Does this mean a thirty-five-year-old Eddy Curry would have real fat *and* mental fat? What's that gonna look like?

30. Kudos to Doc Rivers for smartly banning all mobile devices on the trip. Although I think the players were still allowed to order porn in their hotel rooms.

one,[31] with Eddie performing elaborate handshakes and Posey wrapping them in bear hugs and whispering motivational thoughts. Bench guys pulled for starters like they were the whitest, dorkiest tenth-graders on a prep school team. When the starters came out for breathers, the roles reversed. And that's how the season went. The player most responsible for that collective unselfishness (Garnett) placed third in the MVP balloting because of subpar-for-him numbers; meanwhile, the Celtics jumped from the worst record in 2007 to the best record in 2008. Where's the statistic for that? (Shit, I forgot: it's called wins.) But that's what makes basketball so great. *You have to watch the games. You have to pay attention. You cannot get seduced by numbers and stats.* Even as I was frantically finishing the hardcover book, I couldn't help noticing LeBron's '09 Cavaliers developing Ubuntu-like chemistry and raving about it constantly—how much they loved each other, how (pick a player) hadn't enjoyed himself this much playing basketball before, and so on. Talking about it, they had that same look in their collective eye that a buddy gets when he's raving about killer sex with his new girlfriend: *This is amazing. I've never had anything like this before.* And I was thinking, "Where did I just read something like this?" Then I remembered. It was a quote from a December 1974 *Sports Illustrated* feature about the Warriors:

> There are a super group of guys on this team. Players who put the team ahead of self. I think basketball is the epitome of team sport anyhow, and we've got players now who complement one another for the sake of the team. Team success is what everyone here is after. I've never seen a guy down on himself after he had a bad performance, as long as we won. In the past he might have been more concerned about his poor shooting, and even if we had happened to win the game he wouldn't have been any happier.

31. Even if you could describe Posey's man hugs as corny, homoerotic or genuinely uncomfortable (especially if you were sitting in the first few rows), they symbolized the closeness of that team. After the Hornets imported Posey for $25 million that summer, I watched Posey dole out man hugs for Chris Paul and David West; for the first time, I can say that I watched other men hug and felt wistful about it. The NBA: where questioning your sexuality happens!

You know who said that? Rick Barry. That's right, the single biggest
prick of that era. Something clicked for him on that particular Warriors
team: he was feeling it, he felt comfortable discussing it . . . and yes, he
earned a Finals MVP trophy six months later. Any time a star player raves
about his team like Barry did, you know that team is headed for good
things. You just do. Of course, any team can channel a collective unselfishness for one season. How do you keep it going after winning a title
and the riches that go with it? Former Montreal goalie Ken Dryden explained that winning

> becomes a state of mind, an obligation, an expectation; in the end, an at-
> titude. *Excellence.* It's a rare chance to play with the best, to be the best.
> When you have it, you don't want to give it up. It's not easy and it's not al-
> ways fun . . . when you win as often as we do, you earn a right to lose. It's
> losing to remember what winning feels like. But it's a game of chicken. If
> you let it go, you might never get it back. You may find it's a high-paid,
> pressureless comfort to your liking. I can feel it happening this year. If we
> win, next year will be worse.[32]

Russell lived for that pressure, defining himself and everyone else by
how they responded to it:

> Even with all the talent, the mental sharpness, the fun, the confidence
> and your focus honed down to winning, there'll be a level of competition
> where all that evens out. Then the pressure builds, and for the champion
> it's a test of heart. . . . Heart in champions has to do with the depth of
> your motivation, and how well your mind and body react to pressure. It's
> concentration—that is, being able to do what you do under maximum
> pain and stress.[33]

32. This is from *The Game,* Dryden's excellent account of his final season with the Montreal Canadiens, a team that played in something called the National Hockey League.
33. I felt the same way as I was frantically trying to finish the hardcover with a deadline
hanging over my head. Do you think Russell used cigarettes, booze, coffee, Pilates and a
$2,000 Relax the Back chair to repeatedly come through under stress en route to 11 ti-
tles? Or was that just me? It took me so long to finish that I actually started smoking
again (just two or three per day when I was writing, for the nicotine rush) *and* quit
smoking again, and the two events seemed like they happened 10 years apart.

So really, repeating as champions (or winning a third time, or a fourth) hinges on how a team deals with constant panic (not wanting to lose what it has) and pressure (not only coming through again and again, but trusting it will come through). You can handle those phenomena only if you've got a certain framework in place, and as long as the superstar and his sidekicks remain committed to that framework. Wilt captured one title ('67) and was traded within fourteen months. He only cared about winning one title; defending it wasn't as interesting, so he gravitated toward another challenge (assists). Meanwhile, Russell still ritually puked before big games in his thirteenth season. He had enough rings to fill both hands and it didn't matter. He knew nothing else. Winning consumed him. Merely by being around Russell and feeding off his immense competitiveness, his teammates ended up caring just as much. You can't stumble into that collective feeling, but when it happens—and it doesn't happen often—you do anything to protect it. That's what makes great teams great.

And that's why we remember the Jordan-Pippen teams so fondly. What cemented their legacy wasn't the first five titles but the last one, when they were running on fumes and surviving solely on pride and Jordan's indomitable will. My favorite stretch happened in the Eastern Finals—Game 7, trailing by three, six minutes to play—when the exhausted Bulls wouldn't roll over for a really good Pacers team that seemed ready to knock them off. Remember Jordan beating seven-foot-four Rik Smits on a jump ball, or Pippen outhustling Reggie Miller for a crucial loose ball in the last few minutes? Remember how the Bulls crashed the offensive boards[34] that night and did whatever it took to prevail? Remember how Jordan struggled with dead legs and a flat jump shot, so he started driving to the basket again and again, willing himself to the foul line like a running back moving the chains? Remember Jordan and Pippen standing with their hands on their knees at midcourt in the final seconds, completely spent, unable to summon enough energy to celebrate? They would

---

34. Weird stats from that game: MJ/Pippen shot 15 for 43; Chicago missed 17 of 41 FTs; Rodman did nothing (22 minutes, 6 boards); and Indy shot 48% (Bulls: 38%). So how did the Bulls do it? They had 22 offensive rebounds and 26 second-chance points, and they controlled the ball like a hockey team down the stretch—from the 7:13 mark to the 0:31 mark (when they clinched the game), they held the ball for 270 of a possible 402 seconds. And that includes 20–25 seconds of dead time when the clock kept running after they made baskets. Incredible game to rewatch.

not allow the Bulls to lose that game. You don't learn about a great team or great players when they're winning; you learn about them when they're clawing to remain on top. By contrast, the Shaq/Kobe Lakers only won three titles when the number should have been closer to eight. Since it was mildly astonishing to watch them implode at the time, I can't imagine how it might look for fans of subsequent generations.

Wait, they had two of the top three players in basketball at the same time and only won three titles in a diluted league? How is that possible?

For the same reason that downgrading to Aguirre made the '89 Pistons better. For the same reason that everyone in the eighties would have committed a crime to play with Bird or Magic. For the same reason that players from Russell's era defend him so vehemently now. For the same reason that every player from the last dozen years would have rather played with Duncan than anyone else. It's not about statistics and talent as much as making teammates better and putting your team ahead of yourself.[35] When a team of talented players can do it, they become unstoppable for one season. When they want to keep doing it and they can sublimate their egos for the greater good, that's when they become fascinating in a historical context.

For the purposes of this book—loosely described as "evaluating why certain players and teams mattered more than others"[36]—I couldn't find that answer just through statistics. I needed to immerse myself in the his-

35. Weird parallel: The best wrestlers are held to this standard within their ranks. For instance, Ric Flair and Shawn Michaels are considered to be the best of their respective generations. Why? Because they sold the shit of their opponents. They could have a great match against anybody, even if it was someone with four moves like Hulk Hogan or Undertaker. Only three sports work this way: basketball, hockey and wrestling. That's right, I just called pro wrestling a sport. You have a problem with that? *Huh?*

36. This should be a riveting sell on the talk-show and talk-radio circuit. I think I'm going to lie and pretend that there's a chapter in here that definitively answers the questions "Did Jordan get suspended for gambling?" "Was the 1985 lottery fixed?" "Was Tim Donaghy acting alone?" "Did Kobe really do it?" and "Was Wilt Chamberlain's 20,000 figure an elaborate way of covering up the fact that he was gay?" When they ask for more info, I'll just say, "Look, you'll have to read the book." Then I'll kill the rest of the time talking about how Barry wore a wig during the 1976 Playoffs. There's no way in hell that Stephen Colbert won't be riveted by that.[P1]

P1. FYI: It's our first new footnote for the paperback (each will be marked with a "P"). I did Colbert's show on October 29, 2009; turned out he was more enthralled by my Kobe/Teen Wolf comparison (page 572).

tory of the game, read as much as I could and watch as much tape as I could. Five distinct types of players kept emerging: elite players who made themselves and everyone else better; elite players who were out for themselves; elite players who vacillated back and forth between those two mind-sets depending on how it suited their own interests;[37] role players whose importance doubled or tripled on the right team; and guys who ultimately didn't matter. We don't care about the last group. We definitely care about the middle three groups and we really, really, *really* care about the first group. I care about guys who ralphed before crucial games and cried on television shows because a simple replay brought back pain from years ago. I care that someone walked away from a guaranteed title (or more) because he selfishly wanted to win on *his* terms, and I care that someone gave away 20 percent of his minutes or numbers because that sacrifice made his team better. I care about glowing quotes from yellowed magazines and passionate testimonials from dying teammates. I care about the things I witnessed and how they resonated with me. And what I ultimately decided was this: when we measure teams and players against one another in a historical context, The Secret matters more than anything else.

One final anecdote explains everything. Right after Russell's Celtics won the last of their championships in 1969, a crew of friends, employees, owners and media members poured into Boston's locker room expecting the typical routine of champagne spraying and jubilant hugs. Russell asked every outsider to leave the locker room for a few minutes. The players wanted to savor the moment with each other, he explained, adding to nobody in particular, "We are each other's friends." The room cleared and they spent that precious piece of time celebrating with one another. Lord knows what was said or what that moment meant for them. As Isiah told Dan Patrick, we wouldn't understand. And we wouldn't. After they reopened the doors, Russell agreed to a quick interview with ABC's Jack Twyman, who started things out with the typically shitty nonquestion that we've come to expect in these situations: "Bill, this must have been a great win for you."

Russell happily started to answer: "Jack . . ."

37. Kobe alert! Kobe alert!

The rest of the words didn't come. He searched for a way to describe the feeling. He couldn't speak. He rubbed his right hand across his face. Still no words. He finally broke down for a few seconds—no crying, just a man overwhelmed by the moment. You know what he looked like? Ellis "Red" Boyd during the climactic cornfield scene in *The Shawshank Redemption*. Remember when Red finished Andy's emotional "hope is a good thing" letter, fought off the lump in his throat, stared ahead with glassy eyes and couldn't even process what just happened? The moment transcended him. You could say the same for Russell. The man had reached the highest level anyone can achieve in sports: the perfect blend of sweat and pain and champagne, a weathered appreciation of everything that happened, a unique connection with teammates that he'd treasure forever. Russell knew his '69 team was running on fumes, that they were overmatched, that they probably shouldn't have prevailed. But they did. And it happened for reasons that had absolutely nothing to do with basketball.[38]

Bill Russell would never play another professional basketball game. He had milked The Secret for everything it was worth, capturing eleven rings and retiring as the greatest winner in sports history. He clung to that secret until the bitter end. When his journey was complete, he rubbed his eyes, fought off tears and searched for words that never came. By saying nothing, he said everything.

Nearly three decades later, a crew from NBA Entertainment interviewed Wilt Chamberlain about his career. The subject of the 1969 Finals came up.

"No way we should we have lost to Boston," the Big Dipper muttered in disbelief. "Just no way. I mean . . . I *still* don't know how we lost to Boston."

He laughed self-consciously, finally adding, "It's a mystery to me."

Of course it was.

---

38. Just like Isiah, he tried to pass The Secret on after his playing days and failed in Seattle and Sacramento. It's never been explained why the same legends who embraced The Secret or at least understood it (Russell, MJ, Bird, Magic, Cousy, Baylor and McHale, to name seven) couldn't apply that same secret to teams they were running. It's like the opposite of VD—you can't pass it along.

TWO

RUSSELL, THEN WILT

CENTER   BOSTON CELTICS   6
BILL RUSSELL

THE GREATEST DEBATE in NBA history wasn't really a debate. I think this is strange. For instance, you might believe that the greatest television drama of all time was *The Sopranos*. I believe it's *The Wire*. If we knew each other and this came up after a few drinks one night, I would refuse to talk about anything else until you conceded one of three things:

1. "You're right, I am an idiot, the greatest television drama of all-time was *The Wire*."
2. "I don't know if you're right, but I promise to plow through all sixty-five episodes of *The Wire* as fast as possible and then we can continue this debate."
3. "You're bothering me. I need to get away from you."

Those would be the only three acceptable outcomes for me. Still, it's a subjective opinion—I might believe *The Wire* can't be approached, but ultimately I can't prove it and can only argue my side. That's it. But if we were arguing about the greatest debate in NBA history—Bill Russell or Wilt Chamberlain?—I can prove Russell was better. There's a definitive answer that involves common sense, firsthand accounts, relevant statistics and the valuable opinions of teammates, fellow players, coaches and educated writers who watched them battle for ten straight seasons.[1]

You know what it's like, actually? O. J. Simpson's murder trial. A few days after the Goldman/Brown killings, when the Juice made his aborted attempt to flee to Mexico, an overwhelming majority of Americans assumed he was guilty. His criminal trial started and we learned about a pattern of corruption and racism within the L.A. Police Department. We discovered that much of the blood evidence was mishandled. We watched the overwhelmed prosecution team unforgivably botch its case. But none of it mattered *because this guy had to be guilty.* After all, his blood dripped all over the crime scene, he didn't have an alibi during the time of the murders, he had a mysterious cut on his left middle finger that matched the drips of blood from someone who fled the crime scene, he had a history of threatening and beating his wife, there were no other suspects and it seemed proposterous that so many inept policemen and forensic scientists could collaboratively conspire to frame someone on such short notice.[2]

Smartly, if not reprehensibly, the defense team battered the race card home—that was their only chance to get a guilty person acquitted, even if it meant splintering the country and damaging the relationship between blacks and whites in the process—and lucked out because many of the dense jurors couldn't understood the damaging DNA evidence in the pre-*CSI* era. To everyone's disbelief, O. J. Simpson walked. Facing more competent attorneys and a lesser level of proof one year later, the Juice was pulped in a civil trial and ordered to pay the Goldman/Brown families $30 million

---

1. FYI, you can use this same set of factors to prove that nobody was more whipped than Lionel Richie on the day he wrote "Truly."

2. O.J. intersected with NBA lore in 1994, when we watched helicopter footage of his white Bronco driving through southern California (in a botched attempt to evade police) split-screened with a crucial Game 5 of the Rockets-Knicks Finals. Here's how bad that Finals was: even Knicks and Rockets fans were more interested in the car chase.

in punitive damages. Fifteen years later, even though we haven't convicted anyone for the murders of Nicole Simpson and Ron Goldman—shit, we haven't even found a potential suspect—more and more Americans believe Simpson was innocent or not conclusively guilty. Give it another fifteen years and even more will believe he was framed. By the year 2035, nobody under forty will remember the details, just that O.J. walked and that maybe, just maybe, that meant he was innocent. None of this changes the fact that O.J. either killed two people himself or was "involved" with the dirty deed in some other way. It's impossible to come up with any other reasonable conclusion. Unless you're insane.

Same goes for the Russell-Chamberlain debate. Wilt was more talented; Russ gave his teams a better chance to win. Wilt had a greater statistical impact; Russ had a greater impact on his teammates. Wilt peaked in the regular season; Russ peaked in the playoffs. Wilt shrank from the clutch; Russ thrived in the clutch. Wilt lost nearly every big game; Russ won nearly every big game. Wilt averaged 50 points for one season; Russell was voted Most Valuable Player by his peers that same season. Wilt was traded twice in his career; Russ never would have been traded in a million years. Wilt was obsessed with statistics; Russ was obsessed with winning. Wilt cared about what fans, writers, and critics thought; Russ only cared what his teammates thought. Wilt never won a title in high school or college and won only two as a pro; Russ won two in college and eleven in the NBA. Wilt ignored The Secret; Russell embraced it. I shouldn't have to waste an entire chapter on them for two indisputable reasons: Russell's teams always beat Chamberlain's teams, and Wilt was traded twice. Right there, it's over. And really, it was over when Russell retired in 1969 as the greatest basketball player ever.

But a few years passed, and then a few more, and then a few more. Chamberlain's numbers started to look more and more implausible. The "debate" heated up again. Now I have to waste a whole chapter debunking the six most common myths of the Chamberlain-Russell debate.

MYTH NO. 1:
RUSSELL HAD A BETTER SUPPORTING
CAST THAN WILT

There isn't a simpler team sport to understand than basketball: if two quality opponents play a seven-game series, the dominant player should prevail as long as the talent level on both sides is relatively equal. We have sixty years of hard-core evidence to back this up. Since the 1976 merger, only one Finals result still doesn't make sense on paper: when the '04 Pistons soundly defeated a more talented (but quietly imploding) Lakers team,[3] a wake-up call for a league that had been slowly gravitating toward lower-scoring games, fewer possessions, swarming, physical defenses and a much slower pace. As long as the talent level between two teams is *relatively equal,* the team with the best player should win. So the supporting-cast card works with Russell and Wilt only if we prove that the talent disparity was *not* relatively equal. Right off the bat, it's almost impossible because the NBA didn't expand to ten teams until 1967, giving everyone a good supporting cast (even the crummy teams). People seem to think Russell played with only Hall of Famers and poor Wilt was stuck carrying a bunch of beer-bellied bums; not only is that erroneous, but it would have been impossible given the numbers. Imagine the current NBA if you removed every foreign player, chopped the number of black players in half, then cut the number of teams from thirty to eight. Would every team end up with three All-Stars and four or five solid role players at worst? Of course. Welcome to the NBA from 1956 to 1966.

Here's how the seasons shook out after Russell entered the league:

1957. Russell joins Boston mid-December after playing in the Melbourne Olympics, then the Celts squeak by Philly (featuring Hall of

3. Rule changes in place by 2005: no hand checking (making it easier for quick guards to penetrate); 8 seconds to advance the ball over midcourt (not 10); resetting the shot clock to 14 seconds instead of 24 in certain situations; whistles for offensive isolation plays (no overloading players on one side); a relaxing of illegal zones; and an implicit understanding that moving high screens were now okay (as long as you didn't stick your knee or foot out on the pick).

Famers Paul Arizin and Neil Johnston) in the playoffs and meet St. Louis in the Finals. Boston has two stud guards in their prime (Bill Sharman and '57 MVP Bob Cousy) and three terrific rookies (Russell, Heinsohn, and Frank Ramsey), while St. Louis has Bob Pettit (two-time MVP), Macauley (Hall of Famer) and Slater Martin[4] (Hall of Famer, second-team All-NBA that season), as well as Charlie Share, Jack Coleman and Jack McMahon (three highly regarded role players). Since Boston won Game 7 in double OT,[5] it's safe to say these two teams were equally talented.

1958. The Hawks exact revenge thanks to up-and-comer Cliff Hagan (second-team All-NBA, Hall of Famer) and Russell's badly sprained ankle.[6] Again, even talent on both sides.

1959. Boston starts to pull away: three All-NBA first-teamers (Russell, Cousy, and Sharman), two promising guards (Sam and KC Jones), the best sixth man (Ramsey) and one of the best scoring forwards (Heinsohn). Even then, they needed seven games to get past Syracuse (led by NBA Top 50 members Dolph Schayes and Hal Greer) before easily sweeping Elgin and the Lakers. Through three years and two titles, Russell and the Celtics had the most talent exactly once.

1960. Boston handles Philly in six and needs seven to defeat a Hawks team with four Hall of Famers (including newcomer Lenny Wilkens). Mean-

---

4. One of my favorite NBA names: Slater Martin. Just reeks of the '50s, doesn't it? He played with Whitey Skoog, Dick Schnittker, Dick Garmaker, Vern Mikkelsen, Lew Hitch, George Mikan and Ed Kalafat on the '56 Lakers. Now those were some white guys! As far as I can tell, that's the only two-Dick team in NBA history.

5. My vote for the most underrated NBA game: double OT, Game 7. It ended with Boston scoring with 1 second left, followed by St. Louis player-coach Alex Hannum calling time-out to set up a play from underneath his own basket, where he'd whip a full-court football pass off the other backboard, then it would ricochet to Pettit at the foul line and he'd quickly shoot. What happened? Hannum threw the ball 90 feet, it bounced off the backboard right to Pettit and he missed the game-tying shot. This actually happened. Can't we put Gus Johnson in a time machine and have him announce this one?

6. The Hawks won their four games by six points total. I'm guessing a healthy Russell would have made a difference in two of those.

while, Wilt wins the MVP as a rookie playing with Arizin (ten straight All-Stars), Tom Gola (five straight All-Stars, Hall of Famer), Guy Rodgers[7] (four All-Stars) and Woody Sauldsberry ('58 Rookie of the Year, '59 All-Star). Boston had more firepower, but not by much. Wilt wasn't exactly stuck playing with Eric Snow, Drew Gooden, Sasha Pavlovic, Larry Hughes and Turdo Sandowich like 2007 LeBron.

1961. We're kicking off a two-year stretch for the most loaded NBA team ever: Boston easily handles Syracuse and St. Louis for title number four. Meanwhile, Philly gets swept by a weaker Nats team, leading to Wilt throwing his first coach under the bus after the season (a recurring theme).[8]

1962. Still loaded to the gills, Boston needs seven games to defeat Wilt's Warriors and an OT Game 7 in the Finals to defeat Baylor, Jerry West and the Lakers. I'm telling you, everyone had a good team back then.[9]

1963. The first sign of trouble: Sharman retires, Cousy and Ramsey are slipping and rookie Havlicek isn't Hondo yet. Boston needs seven games to hold off Cincy (led by Hall of Famers Oscar Robertson, Jack Twyman and Wayne Embry) and another six to beat the Lakers.[10] Meanwhile, Philly moves to San Fran, finishes 31–49 and misses the playoffs with Wilt, Rodgers, Tom Meschery (an All-Star), Al Attles (KC Jones' equal as a defensive stopper) and Willie Naulls (four-time All-Star). But hey, if they'd

---

7. Another great '50s sports name: Guy Rodgers. I actually tried to convince my wife to name our son Guy, but she couldn't get past making cutesy talk with a baby named Guy. I thought it would be cool because we could have said things like "Look at the little Guy" or "He's been a good Guy." Regardless, we need more Guys. Some other classic NBA names from the '50s that would work for dogs at the very least: Woody, Archie, Bo, McCoy, Harry, Clyde, Forest, Nat, Arnie and Elmer.

8. Coaches Wilt threw under the bus: Neil Johnston, Dolph Schayes, Alex Hannum, Frank McGuire, Butch van Breda Kolff.

9. Weird fact: Russell won MVP but didn't make first-team All-NBA.

10. One of Boston's greatest achievements of the Russell era: never losing to a team that featured West and Baylor in their prime. Everyone just casually overlooks this one.

won more games, maybe Wilt wouldn't have averaged 44.8 points that season.[11]

1964. Cousy retires and no Celtic makes first-team All-NBA, but that doesn't stop Boston from beating a stacked Cincy team (led by Oscar and rookie of the year Jerry Lucas) and easily handling Wilt's Warriors in the Finals (now with future Hall of Famer Nate Thurmond aboard). Boston won without a point guard or power forward this season—other than Russell, they didn't have a top-twenty rebounder or anyone average more than five assists—but we'll give them a check mark in the "most talent" department for the last time.[12]

1965. Ramsey retires and Heinsohn fades noticeably in his final season. Undaunted, the Celts finish with their best record of the Russell era (62–18) and smoke L.A. in the Finals thanks to their Big Three and a monster year from Satch Sanders. As for the Warriors, they self-destruct and lose seventeen in a row, eventually trading Wilt for 30 cents on the dollar to Philly.[13] For the first time, Wilt's team matches Boston's talent with shooting guard Hal Greer (ten straight All-Star games), Lucious Jackson (an All-Star power forward who finished eighth in rebounding that season), swingman Chet Walker (seven-time All-Star), point guard Larry Costello (six-time All-Star) and two quality role players (Dave Gambee and Johnny Kerr). That's why the Sixers-Celtics series comes down to the final play of Game 7 at the Garden, with Havlicek stealing the inbounds pass as Johnny Most screams, "Havlicek stole the ball! Havlicek stole the ball!"

11. In *The Last Loud Roar*, Bob Cousy writes that Cincy gave Boston everything they could handle; he headed into the '63 Finals expecting the Lakers would beat them. The X-factor was Tommy, who quit smoking a few weeks before the playoffs, dropped 14 pounds and destroyed Rudy LaRusso in the Finals. You have to love it when NBA Finals were decided by things like "somebody quit smoking."

12. Hidden fact from the Russell era: KC Jones was abominable offensively. Playing 30 to 32 minutes a game post-Cousy, KC averaged 7.8 points and 5.3 assists, shot 39 percent from the field, and didn't have to be guarded from 15 feet. How can a defensive specialist make the Hall of Fame by playing 9 years, starting for 4, and never making an All-Star team? Was he better than Al Attles? Was he even half as good as Dennis Johnson?

13. At one point they were 10–34. Would a healthy MJ have ever played for a 10–34 team? What about a healthy Bird or a healthy Magic?

1966. Heinsohn coughs up a fifteen-pound oyster and retires, KC Jones is fading fast and the Celts are forced to rely on aging veterans (Naulls and Mel Counts)[14] and castoffs from other teams (Don Nelson and Larry Siegfried) to help the Big Three in Auerbach's final season. For the first time with Russell, they don't finish with the league's best record as Philly edges them (55 wins to 54). As usual, it doesn't matter—Boston beats Philly in five and wins Game 7 of the Finals against L.A. by two points. Philly had more talent this season. On paper, anyway.

1967. KC retires, another veteran castoff comes aboard (future Hall of Famer Bailey Howell) and Russell struggles mightily to handle the first year of his player-coach duties.[15] From day one, it's Philly's year: given an extra boost by rookie Billy Cunningham and Wilt's sudden revelation that he doesn't need to score to help his team win (more on this in a second), the Sixers roll to their famous 68-win season, topple the Celtics in five and beat the Warriors in six for Wilt's first title. This was the perfect storm for Wilt—his strongest possible team against Boston's weakest possible team.

1968. Wilt leads the league in assists and Philly finishes eight games better than the Celtics. The aging Celts rally from a 3–1 deficit in the Eastern Finals to advance, then beat a really good Lakers team for Russell's tenth title. After the season, Philly trades Wilt to L.A. for 40 cents on the dollar.[16]

1969. With Russell and Jones running on fumes, everyone writes the Celtics off after they finish fourth in the East. In the first round, they beat

14. Underrated aspect of the Russell era: Five aging vets signed with Boston hoping for a free ring (Naulls, Carl Braun, Wayne Embry, Clyde Lovellette and Woody Sauldsberry). Nowadays, these guys would just sign with Phoenix or Miami because of the weather.

15. Russell's inadequacies as a player-coach emerged as a dominant theme: he'd forget to rest guys or bring them back in and basically sucked. The next year, Russell delegated to teammates and named Havlicek and Jones as his de facto assistants, turning it into a professional intramural team where players subbed themselves and suggested plays during time-outs. This worked for two straight titles. Naturally, no NBA team since 1979 has tried it.

16. Wilt was traded twice in his prime: once for Paul Neumann, Connie Dierking, Lee Shaffer and cash, once for Archie Clark, Darrall Imhoff, Jerry Chambers and cash. Wilt defenders stammer whenever this gets mentioned.

a favored Sixers team in five. In the second round, they beat a favored Knicks team in six—the same group that wins the 1970 title and gets blown for the next twenty-five years by the New York media as the Greatest Team Ever. In the Finals, as 9-to-5 underdogs to the Lakers, they rally back from a 2–0 deficit and win Game 7 in Los Angeles.

So here's the final tally: Over a ten-year span, Russell's teams clearly had more talent than Wilt's teams for four seasons ('61, '62, '63 and '64) and a slight edge in Wilt's first season (1960). In '65, Philly and Boston were a wash. From '66 through '69, Wilt played for stronger teams, making the final record 5–4–1, Russell. For six of those ten seasons, you could have described the talent disparity as "equal" or "relatively equal." After Russell retired that summer, the '70 Lakers lost the famous Willis Reed game in Game 7 of the Finals; the '71 Lakers suffered a season-ending injury to Jerry West and lost to the eventual champions, the Bucks; the '72 Lakers won 69 games and cruised to Wilt's second title; and the '73 Lakers lost a Finals rematch to the Knicks. Wilt retired after a ten-year stretch in which he played in the 1964 Finals and lost, then played for teams talented enough to win a championship *every single year for the next nine.* So much for Russell being blessed with a better supporting cast. If there's a legitimate gripe on Wilt's behalf, it's that Russell was lucky enough to have Auerbach coaching him for ten years. Then again, Red is on record saying he never could have coached a prima donna like Wilt. Also, if you're scoring at home: Russell played with four members of the NBA's Top 50 at 50 (Havlicek, Cousy, Sharman and Sam Jones); Wilt played with *six* members (Baylor, West, Greer, Cunningham, Arizin and Thurmond). And Russell's teammates from 1957 to 1969 were selected to twenty-six All-Star games, while Wilt's teammates from 1960 to 1973 were selected to twenty-four. Let's never mention the supporting-cast card again with Russell and Chamberlain. Thank you.

MYTH NO. 2:
RUSSELL WASN'T A VERY GOOD OFFENSIVE PLAYER

Here's where history treated Russell unfairly. We glorify the unselfish passing of the '70 Knicks, Wes Unseld's one-of-a-kind outlets and Walton's altruistic play on the '77 Blazers, yet Johnny Kerr was the league's first great passing center and Russell came next. Remember how Portland's offense revolved around Walton's passing in '77?[17] The Celtics ran every half-court play through Russell after Cousy retired because they lacked a true point guard. When you watch Russ on tape, his passing jumps out nearly as much as his defense—not just his knack for finding cutters for layups, but how easily he found streaking guards for easy fast breaks directly off blocks or rebounds. Here's what Havlicek wrote in his imaginatively titled 1977 autobiography, *Hondo,* about the first post-Russell season: "You couldn't begin to count the ways we missed [him]. People think about him in terms of defense and rebounding, but he had been the key to our offense. He made the best pass more than anyone I have ever played with. That mattered to people like Nelson, Howell, Siegfried, Sanders and myself. None of us were one on one players. . . . Russell made us better offensive players. His ability as a passer, pick-setter and general surmiser of offense has always been overlooked."

So why doesn't Russell get credit for his passing? *BECAUSE WALTON WAS WHITE AND RUSSELL WAS BLACK!* Just kidding; I was doing a Stephen A. Smith impersonation.[18] Actually, Russell doesn't get credit for the same reason that everyone thinks he played with eight Hall of Famers every year for thirteen seasons or that his teams were always more talented than Wilt's teams: because people don't know any better, and because it's easier to regurgitate something you heard than to look it up. Four things

---

17. Walton averaged 5.5 assists per game in the '77 Playoffs. Russell averaged five assists or more in seven different playoffs, including 6.3 a game in the '65 Playoffs (when it was much tougher to get credited for an assist). For his career, Russell averaged more playoff assists (4.7) than any center who ever played more than 30 playoff games.

18. For anyone reading this after 2030: Stephen A. Smith was an ESPN personality whose gimmick answered the question "What would it be like if somebody argued about sports with their CAPS LOCK on?"

stand out when watching Russell on tape: his passing (superb), his shot blocking (unparalleled), his speed getting down the court (breathtaking), and his unexpected talent for grabbing a rebound, taking off with it, and running the fast break like a point guard (has to be seen to be believed). Russell was like a left-handed, infinitely more cerebral Dennis Rodman, only if Rodman had Walton's passing talent, David Robinson's athletic ability and Michael Jordan's maniacal drive, and if Rodman could block shots like Josh Smith unleashed on the WNBA for an entire season.

(Would you have enjoyed playing with such a player? I thought so.)

MYTH NO. 3: STATISTICALLY, WILT CRUSHED RUSSELL

Wilt's first nine offensive seasons were unlike anything that's happened before or since. He averaged 37.6 points and 27.6 rebounds as a rookie, then 38.4 and 27.2; 50.4 and 25.7; 44.8 and 24.3; 36.9 and 22.3; 34.7 and 22.9; 33.5, 24.6 and 5.3 assists in '66; 24.1, 24.2 and 7.8 with a record 68.3% FG shooting in '67; and 24.3, 23.8 and a league-leading 8.6 assists in '68. For his career, he *averaged* 30.1 points, 22.9 rebounds and 4.4 assists in the regular season. On paper, it's staggering.[19] Russell's career offensive numbers can't compare except for rebounds—he averaged 15.1 points, 22.5 boards and 4.3 assists per game, peaking in 1960 (18.2 points, 24.0 rebounds) and 1964 (15.0 points, 24.7 rebounds and 4.7 assists). In their head-to-head matchups, Wilt handed it to Russ statistically, although Auerbach and the old Celtics swear that Russ played possum for three quarters, allowed Wilt to accumulate stats and then smothered him

---

19. Bob Cousy wasn't as staggered. Here's what he wrote in 1964's *The Last Loud Roar:* "Basketball is a team game. When it becomes a one-man operation, as it did after Chamberlain came to Philadelphia, it just doesn't work. You cannot expect nine other guys to submerge themselves and their abilities to one man. It particularly doesn't work when the man everybody else is feeding isn't helping the others whenever and wherever he can . . . the argument can be made that Chamberlain only suffers from a poor supporting cast. If you have a man who makes better than 50 percent of his shots, the argument goes, why shouldn't you concentrate on getting the ball to him whenever possible? Carrying that to its logical conclusion, I would have to ask why you should ever let any other player on the team shoot at all. No, statistics mean nothing in basketball." Amen, Cooz! I love when a Hall of Famer proves my point.

in the fourth; he'd also relax during blowouts and allow meaningless numbers that didn't matter (knowing that Wilt was obsessed with stats). Russell played 911 games in the last ten years of his career, with an astounding 142 of them coming against Wilt (15.6 percent). By all accounts, Russ pulled a perpetual rope-a-dope against Wilt along the lines of Ali in Zaire, when Ali allowed Foreman to punch himself out, then finished him off later in the fight. Russ saved most of his anti-Wilt tricks for big games and big moments.

Here are their head-to-head stats in 142 games (including playoffs):

Wilt: 28.7 points, 28.7 rebounds
Russ: 14.5 points, 23.7 rebounds

At this point, you're thinking, "Come on, Simmons, this is crazy. You have no case." Well, here are some more stats for you:

Wilt's record against Russell: 58–84
Russ's record against Wilt: 84–58

Hold on, we're just getting started. Check out their playoff numbers.

Wilt: 160 games, 22.5 points, 24.5 rebounds, 4.2 assists, 47% FT, 52% FG
Russ: 165 games, 16.2 points, 24.9 rebounds, 4.7 assists, 60% FT, 43% FG

Hmmmmmmm. Russell's numbers jumped and Wilt's numbers dipped dramatically when there was money on the line, even though Wilt was routinely his team's number one scoring option and Russ was number four or five. Sure, Wilt averaged three more baskets a game, but everything else was even and Russell happened to be a superior defensive player, teammate, basketball thinker and crunch-time guy. Which is how we end up with the following statistics:

Wilt's record for the Conference Finals and NBA Finals: 48–44
Russ's record for the Conference Finals and NBA Finals: 90–53

And these:

Wilt's record in Game 7's: 4–5
Russ's record in Game 7's: 10–0

And these:

Wilt's record in elimination games for his team: 10–11
Russ's record in elimination games for his team: 16–2

And these:

Wilt: 2 championships
Russ: 11 championships[20]

So yeah, by any statistical calculation, Wilt Chamberlain was the greatest regular season player in NBA history. I concede this fact. For the playoffs? Not so great.

And then there's this: since the Celtics didn't need his scoring, Russell spent his energies protecting the rim, helping out defensively, controlling the boards, getting good shots for teammates and filling the lanes on fast breaks. In the process, he became the most dominant defensive player ever—nobody comes close, actually—and it's statistically impossible to calculate his effect on that end.[21] Russell routinely swallowed up the extended area near the rim, handling all penetrators and displaying a remarkable knack for keeping blocks in play. Whereas Wilt famously swatted shots like volleyball spikes for dramatic effect, Russell deflected blocks to teammates for instant fast breaks; not only did those blocks result in four-point swings, but Auerbach's Celtics were *built* on those four-

20. And if you're looking for a degree of difficulty, Russell coached himself for the last two titles. Why doesn't that ever get factored in? Imagine MJ winning those final two titles in Utah as a player-coach.
21. In Terry Pluto's *Tall Tales,* Heinsohn claims that Russell's defense was worth 60 to 70 points per game. Take that one with a grain of salt because he's the same guy who compared Leon Powe to Moses Malone.

point swings. That's how they went on scoring spurts, that's what stands out every time you watch those teams, and that's why they kept winning and winning—they had the perfect center to launch fast breaks and the perfect supporting cast to execute them. Opponents eventually gave up challenging Russell and settled for outside shots, which doesn't sound like a big deal except this was a notoriously poor era for outside shooting.[22] So Russell affected every possession even without swatting shots, almost like a bouncer at a rowdy bar who kicks ass for a few weeks and eventually lowers the fight rate to zero just by showing up. If that weren't enough, Boston's scorers famously saved their energies on defense because they had Russell lurking behind them to cover every mistake, so offense-first guys like Cousy, Sharman, Heinsohn and Sam Jones found themselves in the dream situation of worrying about scoring and that's it.

Can you capture that impact statistically? Of course not. They didn't start keeping track of blocks until 1973, so there's no quantitative way to prove Russell's dominance on the defensive end; it's like trying to measure Chamberlain's offense dominance if nobody kept track of individual points, so we were forced to rely on stories from writers, teammates and opponents, like, "There was this one game in Hershey, Pennsylvania, when Wilt really had it going against the Knicks. I swear, he musta had 100 points!"[23] Wilt matched Russell's rebounding numbers and probably blocked more shots than any non-Russell center, but his defense couldn't compare for two reasons. First, he wasn't a natural jumper like Russell, someone who sprang up at a moment's notice and jumped multiple times on the same play. (Since Wilt was carrying more weight, he was forced to

22. This was before the three-point line, basketball camps and picture-perfect jump shots, when teams took a ton of shots and threw up a ton of bricks. Of the great guards who peaked in the '50s, Cousy was a 37.5% shooter; Sharman, 42.6%; Slater Martin, 36%; Bob Davies, 37%; Guy Rodgers, 38%; Richie Guerin, 42% and Dick McGuire, 39%. Only when Sam Jones, Jerry West and Hal Greer emerged did the prototypical two-guard take shape; long-range shooting specialists didn't start making a mark until the mid-'70s. So someone who protected the basket had an even greater effect back then.

23. It's exceedingly possible that Russell was good for 8 to 15 blocks per game in the playoffs. Just researching this chapter, there were three different playoff games in the '60s when an author or narrator casually mentioned in their summary that Russell had 12 blocks.

set his feet, bend his knees and then jump, almost like someone leaping over a moving car. Many opponents learned to time those jumps and float shots over his considerable reach.[24] You didn't have the luxury of timing anything with Russell.) Second, Wilt was continually obsessed with a bizarre streak—for whatever reason, he wanted to make it through his entire basketball career without fouling out, so he'd stop challenging shots with four or five fouls even if he was hurting his team in the process. I'm not making this up.

(Seriously, I'm not making this up.)

(Wait, you don't believe me? Here's what John Havlicek wrote in *Hondo:* "Wilt's greatest idiosyncrasy was not fouling out. He had never fouled out of a high school, college or professional game and that was the one record he was determined to protect. When he got that fourth foul, his game would change. I don't know how many potential victories he may have cheated his team out of by not really playing after he got into foul trouble.")[25]

Translation: Wilt cared about statistics more than winning. If they kept track of blocks in the sixties, the Dipper would have become obsessed with those numbers (especially as they compared to Russell), dumped the never-fouled-out streak and inadvertently turned into a dominant defensive player, almost by accident, possibly someone who won five or six titles instead of two. But there was no statistical rush from defense. So Wilt settled on raking up offensive numbers, spiking blocked shots like volleyballs and pursuing his inane streak of never fouling out. It wasn't until the '66–'67 season that Wilt realized his teams were better off if he concentrated on rebounding, passing and defense. Here's how he described that

---

24. Sam Jones made an art form of this, adding little insults with each shot like "Too late" or "Sorry, Wilt" every time he sank a jumper. One time Wilt flipped out and chased him around the Garden, so Sam grabbed a photographer's stool to fend him off. If this happened in 2010, I'm almost positive it would lead *Around the Horn.*

25. Hondo's take on Russ: "There was never a player who could control a game defensively like him. You could see the shooters just cringing every time they got within his range. Sometimes he would start out very strong, in order to discourage his man completely. Other times he would allow a man to score some early baskets, then later on, when the guy wanted to attempt the same move in a crucial situation, he would find that Russell would prevent him from doing it. . . . The end of the game was really Russell's time. In a close game, he was incredibly alive."

epiphany in his autobiography, *Wilt: Just Like Any Other 7-Foot Black Millionaire Who Lives Next Door* (now that's a title!):[26]

> I was 30 years old when the '66–'67 season began, and I was maturing as a man, and learning that it was essential to keep my teammates happy if I wanted my team to win.

[As far as epiphanies go, that ranks somewhere between Pete Rose admitting that he had a gambling problem and John Holmes glancing down at his fourteen-inch schlong and realizing he needed to try porn. Better late than never, I guess.]

> I not only began passing off more and scoring less, I also made a point of singling my teammates out for praise—publicly and privately.

[Wow! What a sacrifice! What a guy! So wait . . . if you're trying to win basketball games, it's a good idea to be unselfish and to act like a good teammate instead of hogging the ball and blaming everyone else when you lose? Are we sure? Do we have confirmation on this?]

> I realize now that this is the kind of thing that helped make O. J. Simpson's teams at USC and Bill Walton's teams at UCLA so successful. The same is true of Joe Namath and the Jets.

[Um . . . Wilt? The same was true for Bill Russell—you know, number 6 on the Celtics, the team that knocked you out of the playoffs every spring?]

> O.J. and Bill and Joe always praise their teammates. They remember the name of every key guy who throws a key block or makes a good assist or a good defensive play, and they tell the player—and the press—all about it. That can't help but make the player try even harder the next time, instead of maybe letting down, subconsciously, because he's tired of being ignored and hearing how great you are all the time.[27]

26. This is an entertaining book that includes stories about Wilt getting blown by stewardesses on airplanes and stuff. Here's one case where Wilt really didn't get enough credit for something. *Wilt* should have won a Pulitzer, or at least a National Book Award.

27. Later in life, Wilt executed this unselfish mind-set to perfection on the set of *Conan the Destroyer,* which went on to become the most unintentionally funny action movie of the '80s other than *Gymkata.* Even as an actor, Wilt was breaking records.

[I don't know, Wilt—this sounds too crazy. I thought basketball was an individual sport. They don't keep stats for praising your teammates. I think you're wrong.]

I was just learning this lesson in 1966, and it was reflected in my statistics.

["Granted, I threw away the first seven years of my career and everyone hated playing with me, but you have to hand it to me—I *did* learn the lesson."]

Instead of me averaging 40 points a game, we had a great scoring balance. Hal Greer averaged 22.1, Chet averaged 19.3, and Billy averaged 18.5. Luke Jackson and Wali Jones also averaged in double figures. That's the kind of balance Boston always had.

[The Celtics won the title every year for Wilt's first seven years in the league. Only in 1967 did it occur to him that his teams should start emulating what worked for the best teams? Yeesh. Nobody ever said Wilt was a brain surgeon.][28]

After he embraced "unselfishness" and won his first title, in classic Wilt fashion, he lost interest in winning and became obsessed with assists. Suddenly Wilt was passing up easy shots to set up teammates, checking the scorer's table multiple times per game, complaining if he felt like he hadn't been credited for a specific assist, lambasting teammates for blowing his passes and taking an inordinate amount of delight in leading the league in '68 (a record he bragged about more than any other).[29] As with

28. In *A Few Good Men,* this would be the trial scene when Cruise grabs the rule book from Kevin Bacon and asks Noah Wyle to find the part about going to the mess hall for dinner. In other words, I just scored major points with my case by digging up these Wilt quotes. Even better, I got to read the story about Wilt getting blown by the stewardess again.

29. From Bill Libby's enjoyable 1977 biography of Wilt (*Goliath*): "A couple of times he went to a teammate with a hot hand and told him he was going to give him the ball exclusively because the other guys were wasting his passes and he wouldn't win the assists title this way." What a team player, that Wilt. In that book, Libby mentions that, for all the hullabaloo about Wilt being such a ladies' man, "a surprising number of players and reporters say they've never seen Wilt with a woman." Come on, Wilt couldn't have been gay! He was a lifelong bachelor, he loved clothes and he loved cats! Where is this coming from?

anything else he did, Wilt failed to strike the right balance and settled into a bad habit of being *too* unselfish, taking only two shots in the second half of Game 7 against Boston while his teammates floundered around him. The heavily favored '68 Sixers blew a 3–1 lead and choked in Game 7 at home, but as Wilt pointed out in his book, "Hal hit only eight of 25 shots. Wali hit eight of 22. Matty hit two of ten, Chet hit eight of 22. Those four guys took most of our shots and hit less than a third of them. But I got the blame."

So much for the lessons of Walton, Namath and Simpson. What did we learn about Russell, Chamberlain, and statistics? Well, Wilt's teams re-volved around his offense and Russell's teams revolved around his de-fense. Wilt coexisted with his teammates; Russell made his teammates better. Wilt had to make a concerted effort to play unselfishly and act like a decent teammate; Russell's very existence was predicated on unselfish-ness and team play. In the end, Russell's teams won championships and Wilt's teams lost them.

Russell 11, Chamberlain 2. Those are the only two numbers that matter.[30]

MYTH NO. 4:
WILT WAS A GREAT GUY

Was Wilt a great guy to approach in the airport? Absolutely. Was he great to interview for a magazine or a talk show? You betcha. Did the people who knew him have great stories about him? No question. Was he gener-ous with his money? Of course. If you were a stewardess, was this some-one you would have wanted to blow under an airplane blanket? Apparently, yes. For such a good guy, it's bizarre that Wilt sucked so much as a teammate. He just didn't grasp the concept. For the first six years of his career, he hogged the ball, became infatuated with scoring records and demanded to be treated differently than his teammates. When things fi-nally fell apart on the '65 Warriors, legendary *L.A. Times* columnist Jim Murray wrote, "[Wilt] can do one thing well—score. He turns his own team into a congress of butlers whose principal function is to get him the

---

30. Although, again, *Conan the Destroyer* was a great freaking movie.

ball under a basket. Their skills atrophy, their desires wane. Crack players like Willie Naulls get on the Warriors and they start dropping notes out of the window or in bottles which they cast adrift. They contain one word: 'help.' "[31] Even when Wilt played more unselfishly and copied Russell's game, he couldn't maintain it for more than a year. He openly clashed with every coach except two—Frank McGuire (who let him shoot as much as he wanted, leading to the 100-point game) and Alex Hannum (and only because Hannum challenged him to a fight to get him to listen).[32] He blamed teammates and coaches after losses, feuded with teammates who could have helped him (most famously, Elgin during the '69 season) and demeaned opposing players to the press to make himself look better. He had a nasty habit of distracting his own team at the worst possible times—like the '66 Eastern Finals against Boston, when *Sports Illustrated* released a controversial Chamberlain feature before Game 5 in which he ripped coach Dolph Schayes and destroyed the morale of his team.[33]

Some believe that Wilt achieved too much too soon, that he never understood the concept of teamwork because he'd been the center of attention (literally) since he was in high school. In his Chamberlain-Russell book *The Rivalry*, John Taylor writes that Auerbach believed Warriors owner Eddie Gottlieb "spoiled Wilt something fierce. A lot of times, Wilt didn't even travel with his teammates. He was out of control. Auerbach doubted that he himself would have been able to coach Wilt. . . . Wilt spent that year with the Globetrotters, tasted the big money and stardom, and he began thinking that he was more important than his coach or teammates. Goty, afraid of losing the big draw, let him get away with it. Chamberlain had become convinced that people came to games in order to see him and that, therefore, the point of every game was to give him an opportunity to play the star. There was a certain box office logic to this thinking, but it made Chamberlain uncoachable, in Auerbach's view, and

31. That's the same Willie Naulls who landed on the Celts one year later and won two straight titles with Russell. Hmmmmmm.
32. Wilt played for 9 coaches in 14 years. I love that stat.
33. Even Wilt admitted this in his book, writing, "The stories created quite a furor, and I'm not sure the 76ers ever got back in stride during the playoffs." Although, in classic Wilt fashion, he blamed the magazine for not waiting to run the piece.

as long as he was uncoachable, any team he played on would never become a real winner."[34]

If you're wondering how Wilt was regarded around the league, here's the ultimate story: When San Fran shopped him in '65, the Lakers were intrigued enough that owner Bob Short asked his players to vote on whether or not he should purchase Chamberlain's contract. The results of the vote? Nine to two . . . *against.*

Nine to two against!

How could anyone still think this was the greatest basketball player ever? In the absolute prime of his career, a playoff contender that had lost consecutive Finals and didn't have an answer for Russell had the chance to acquire Wilt for nothing . . . *and the players voted against it!*[35] Would they have voted against a Russell trade? Seriously, would they have voted against a Russell trade in a million years?

(Note: if this were the O.J. trial, that last paragraph would be the equivalent of O.J. trying on the bloody glove.)

MYTH NO. 5:
A COUPLE PLAYS HERE AND THERE
AND WILT COULD HAVE WON JUST AS MANY
TITLES AS RUSSELL

Nearly every NBA champ had a pivotal playoff moment where they needed a big play and got it, but that doesn't stop Wilt's defenders from ignoring this reality and making excuses for every one of his near-misses: the '60 Eastern Finals (Wilt injured his right hand throwing a punch in Game 4); Game 7 of the '62 Eastern Finals (a controversial goaltending

---

34. One thing Wilt can't be blamed for: during a 1965 game in Boston, 76ers owner Ike Richman died of a heart attack while sitting at the press table next to the Philly's bench. If you had to pick a superstar whose owner might drop dead during a big game, you'd have to pick Wilt, right? Strangest part of the story: they carried Richman out and the game kept going. How heartless was that? Nowadays, I'd like to think we'd postpone a game even if one of the Maloofs dropped dead. Although nobody would be able to tell for about a quarter.

35. The best part of this story? I found out about it from Wilt's autobiography. He didn't even seem that bitter, explaining, "I guess guys like Elgin Baylor and Jerry West were afraid I'd come to L.A. and take some of their glory away." Yeah, Wilt, I'm sure that was it.

call proved the difference); Game 7 of the '65 Eastern Finals (Russell nearly wore goat horns[36] before Havlicek saved him); Game 1 of the '68 Eastern Finals (right after Martin Luther King Jr. was killed, when Sixers coach Alex Hannum never had his team vote on whether or not they should play, allegedly killing the morale of the team, even though they won Games 2, 3 and 4); Game 7 in '68 (when Wilt's supporting cast went cold); Game 7 of the '69 Finals (when Wilt "injured" his knee in crunch time); and Game 7 of the '70 Finals (when Willis Reed's reappearance ignited the MSG crowd and Walt Frazier destroyed West). That's all fine. Just know that Wilt's teams sucked in the clutch *because Wilt sucked in the clutch.* The fear of losing overwhelmed him in big games. Terrified of getting fouled because of his dreadful free throw shooting, he played hot potato or settled for his patented fall-away (the one that landed him fifteen feet from the basket and away from rebounds), and he didn't want to foul anyone if he had four or five fouls because, you know, it would have interfered with his laughable no-fouling-out streak. That made him nearly useless in close games, like a more tortured version of Shaq from 2002 to 2007, only if Shaq was afraid to foul anyone and had a persecution complex.[37]

Here's what NBA great Rick Barry wrote about Wilt in his autobiography, *Confessions of a Basketball Gypsy,* which has the worst cover in the history of sports books:[38]

> I'll say what most players feel, which is that Wilt *is* a loser. . . . He is terrible in big games. He knows he is going to lose and be blamed for the

36. With five seconds left, Wilt cut Boston's lead to one. Russell's ensuing inbounds pass hit one of the wires that held the basket up, a fluke play that doubled as an automatic turnover and nearly cost Boston the season. Wilt loved to bring this up afterward, pointing out again and again that Russell was as capable of choking as anyone. This is like Lindsay Lohan hearing that Dakota Fanning sipped champagne at a wedding one night, then screaming, "See, see, I'm not the only messed-up one!"

37. One of the hidden subplots of Game 7: Hondo said later that he jumped the inbounds pass for Hal Greer partly because he was waiting for it; he knew Wilt wasn't getting the ball because Wilt never wanted to get fouled in big moments (so there was no way they were running the play for him).

38. It's a photo of Barry standing in an airport and holding a bag and a basketball. He's not even really looking at the camera. He looks put out, like he's posing for a picture for an Asian tourist who didn't know who he was and just wanted a picture of a tall white guy. It's spectacular.

loss, so he dreads it, and you can see it in his eyes; and anyone who has ever played with him will agree with me, regardless of whether they would admit it publicly. When it comes down to the closing minutes of a tough game, an important game, he doesn't want the ball, he doesn't want any part of the pressure. It is at these times that greatness is determined, and Wilt doesn't have it. There is no way you can compare him to a pro like a Bill Russell or a Jerry West . . . these are clutch competitors.

Holy smokes! Some harsh words from a guy who wore a wig for an entire NBA season four years later. But let's examine those Game 7's in '68, '69 and '70 again. In the first one, Wilt took two shots after halftime and steadfastly kept passing to his ice-cold teammates, then blamed them afterward because they couldn't make a shot. In the second one, Wilt banged his knee and asked out of the game with five minutes to play, enraging van Breda Kolff (who refused to put him back in, even if it meant costing the Lakers the title) and Russell (who uncharacteristically slammed Wilt that summer, launching a feud that lasted nearly twenty-five years). In the third one, Willis limped out and drained those first two jumpers, only it never occurred to Chamberlain, "Wait, I have a one-legged guy guarding me, maybe I should destroy him offensively!"[39] He just didn't get it. Wilt never understood how to win; if anything, losing fit his personality better. Here's how Bill Bradley described Wilt in *Life on the Run:*

> Wilt played the game as if he had to prove his worth to someone who had never seen basketball. He pointed to his statistical achievements as specific measurements of his ability, and they were; but to someone who knows basketball they are, if not irrelevant, certainly nonessential. The point of the game is not how well the individual does but whether the team wins. That is the beautiful heart of the game, the blending of personalities, the mutual sacrifices for group success. . . . I have the impression that Wilt might have been more secure with losing. In defeat, after

39. When Reed limped off early in Game 5, Wilt somehow got shut down by a woefully undersized Dave DeBusschere and New York's pressure defense during their rousing 16-point comeback. Wilt finished with 22 points but took only three shots in the second half. Three shots? The fact that he threw up a 45–27 in Game 6 only made it worse.

carefully covering himself with allusions to *his* accomplishments, he could be magnanimous. . . . Wilt's emphasis on individual accomplishments failed to gain him public affection and made him the favorite to win the game. And, simultaneously, it assured him of losing.[40]

Here's another way to look at it: there are very few clutch stories about Wilt Chamberlain. His three finest moments were probably Game 7 against the '65 Celts, when Wilt was magnificent in defeat with 30 points and 32 rebounds; the clinching game of the '67 Boston-Philly series, when he ripped Boston apart with a ridiculous triple double (29 points, 36 rebounds, 13 assists); and the clinching Game 5 of the '72 Finals, when he destroyed an undersized Knicks team with a near-quadruple double (24–29–9 and 8 blocks). He's the same man who once explained to *Sport* magazine, "In a way, I like it better when we lose. It's over and I can look forward to the next game. If we win, it builds up the tension and I start worrying about the next game." Would Russell have ever said something like that? What do you think? Here were some of the famous clutch Russell games:[41]

Game 7, 1957 Finals. As a rookie, Russell notches a 19–32 and makes what everyone agrees was the most phenomenal play of his career—scoring a game-tying basket near the end of regulation that carried him into the stands, regrouping and somehow chasing down Jack Coleman from behind and blocking Coleman's game-clinching layup. This whole sequence ranks incredibly high on the I Wish We Always Had TV Coverage for Sports scale.

Game 7, 1960 Finals. Russell scores 22 points and grabs 35 rebounds in a blowout of the Hawks. Ho-hum.

Game 7, 1962 Eastern Finals. In the year Wilt averaged 50 a game, Russell holds him to 22 in Game 7 (and scores 19 himself).

40. Pages 157–60 of Bradley's book double as a psychological profile of Wilt's loserdom. No joke.
41. Thanks to Elliott Kalb's informative book *Who's Better, Who's Best in Basketball* for the stats you're about to read. If you're an NBA fan, buy this book. It's great. Even if I disagreed with almost all of it and he painfully overrated Shaq.

Game 7, 1962 Finals. Russell scores 30 points, makes 14 of 17 free throws and grabs an NBA Playoffs record 40 rebounds in an overtime win over the Lakers (the Frank Selvy game). Everyone agrees this was the definitive Russell game—near the end of regulation, every forward on Boston's roster fouled out (Heinsohn, Sanders and Loscutoff), so Russell had to protect the basket and handle the boards by himself. Unbelievable: *30 points and 44 rebounds?*

Game 7, 1965 Eastern Finals. Although Havlicek saved him from goat horns, Russell submitted a near triple double (15 points, 29 rebounds and 9 assists) that nearly would have been a quadruple double if they'd kept track of blocks back then.[42]

Game 7, 1966 Finals. Celts beat L.A. by 2; Russell notches 25 points, 32 rebounds and God knows how many blocks.

Game 7, 1968 Eastern Finals. Russell scores 12 but holds Wilt to 14 . . . and for good measure, he coached the winning team.

Looking back, Wilt had five chances to knock Russell out of the playoffs in '68 and '69 with a superior team—including two Game 7's at home—and only needed to submit *one* monster performance to pull it off. Each time, he couldn't do it. Each time, Russell's inferior team prevailed. Each time, Wilt whined about it afterward. If Jerry West was Mr. Clutch, then Wilt was Mr. Crutch.

MYTH NO. 6:
PLAYERS AND COACHES FROM THE ERA ARE SPLIT OVER WHO WAS A GREATER PLAYER

You have to believe me: I read every NBA book possible to prepare to write this one. No stone was left unturned—during the summers of '07 and '08,

---

42. Which raises a question: why the heck didn't they keep track of blocks back then? How hard would that have been? This is the first of 79 times I will complain about this.

I spent more time on www.abebooks.com than Abe did. While poring over these books, I searched for insight on the Russell-Chamberlain debate and kept a tally of every player, coach and media member willing to go on the record. (You can see a complete list of those books at the end of this one.) And I'm not sure what was more amazing—how many of them praised Russell or how many of them crushed Wilt (including people who played with him and coached him). Since we could fill this entire book with quotes from people praising Russell's unselfishness, competitiveness and clutchness, let's narrow it down to six Wilt-related quotes that explain everything:

Butch van Breda Kolff (in *Tall Tales*): "The difference between Russell and Wilt was this: Russell would ask, 'What do I need to do to make my teammates better?' Then he'd do it. Wilt honestly thought the best way for his team to win was for him to be in the best possible setting. He'd ask, 'What's the best situation for me?' "[43]

Jerry West (in *Goliath*): "I don't want to rap Wilt because I believe only Russell was better, and I really respect what Wilt did. But I have to say he wouldn't adjust to you, you had to adjust to him."

Jerry Lucas (in *Tall Tales*): "Wilt was too consumed with records: being the first to lead the league in assists, or to set a record for field goal percentage. He'd accomplish one goal, then go on to another. Russell only asked one question: 'What can I do to make us win?' "[44]

Jack Kiser (in *Goliath*): "Russell pulled the con job of the century on Chamberlain. He welcomed Wilt to the league. He played father-figure. He told him, man, you're going to better all my records, but you have

43. Butch benched Wilt for the last five minutes of Game 7 of the '69 Finals knowing that if the Lakers lost the game, he'd get fired. And he did. That's how strongly he disliked Wilt.
44. I couldn't fight off Grumpy Old Editor from chiming in any longer. His take on Lucas: "Lucas should talk—he never met a stat he didn't squeeze until it was dead."

things to learn and I'm going to teach you because I admire you.[45] He made friends with him. He got Wilt to the point where Wilt worried about making him look bad. . . . Wilt hated to lose, but he liked Bill so much that he didn't like losing to him. Wilt could destroy Russell when he was inspired. But he held back just enough to get beat. He tried to win over Russell, but he wasn't driven like he was against guys he disliked. I might point out Russell never said a bad word about Wilt until the night he retired and he hasn't stopped rapping him since."

Bill Russell (in *Second Wind*): "It did seem to me that [Wilt] was often ambivalent about what he wanted to get out of basketball. Anyone who changes the character and style of his play several times over a career is bound to be uncertain about which of the many potential accomplishments he wants to pursue. It's perfectly possible for a player not to make victory his first priority against all the others—money, records, personal fame, and an undivided claim to his achievements—and I often felt Wilt made some deliberate choices in his ambitions."

Wilt Chamberlain (in *Wilt*): "To Bill [Russell], every game—every championship game—was a challenge, a test to his manhood. He took the game so seriously that he threw up in the locker room before almost every game. But I tend to look at basketball as a game, not a life or death struggle. I don't need scoring titles or NBA championships to prove that I'm a man. There are too many other beautiful things in life—food, cars, girls, friends, the beach, freedom—to get that emotionally wrapped up in basketball.[46] I think Bill knew I felt that way, and I think he both envied and resented my attitude. On the one hand, I think he wished he could learn to take things easier, too; on the other hand, I think he may have felt that with my natural ability and willingness to work hard, my teams could have won an NBA championship every year if I was as totally com-

---

45. According to *SI*'s Frank Deford, Russell once told Wilt, "I'm probably the only person on the planet who knows how good you really are." I'm almost positive that Mario Lopez never said this to Mark-Paul Gosselaar.

46. That sentence easily could have been Vince Carter's high school yearbook quote.

mitted to victory as he was. . . . I wish I had won all those championships, but I really think I grew more as a man in defeat than Russell did in victory."

That might be true. But I'd rather have the bathroom puker on my team, the most beloved teammate of his era, the guy who didn't care about statistics, the guy who always seemed to end up on victorious teams in close games, the guy who finished his career as the greatest winner in sports, the guy who was singularly obsessed with making his teammates better and doing whatever it took to prevail. I'd rather have Bill Russell. And so would anyone else in their right mind.

The defense rests.

THREE

HOW THE HELL DID WE GET HERE?

WHILE TRYING TO absorb six-plus decades of NBA history, one question keeps popping up: *How do we put everything in perspective?* If Wilt averaged 50 points a game for an entire season, what does that really mean? Would he average 40 a game now? Thirty? Twenty? Could the '72 Lakers win 33 games total if they were playing in 2009? Were the '96 Bulls the greatest team of all time or just the most successful? I can't answer these questions without putting some sort of elaborate context in place. When I tell you that Oscar Robertson's season-long triple double wasn't as impressive as it seemed, you'd have to take my word unless you saw every relevant rule change, innovation, talent glut/dearth, statistical whim, big-picture mistake and trouble patch laid out from 1946 to 1984. Why stop there? Because that's when the NBA, for better and worse, became the league it is now. Stylistically, creatively, fundamentally and talent-wise, you could transport any good player or team from 1984 to 2010 and they would be fine (and in some cases better than fine).

Think of the NBA like America's comedy scene and everything will fall into place. Ever watch tape of Milton Berle, Bob Hope or Sid Caesar performing on their top-rated shows in the 1950s? Lots of mugging, lots of easy jokes, some cross-dressing, more mugging, tons of self-flagellation, even more mugging. It's bewildering that they were considered geniuses at the time. But they were. Nobody was bigger. (Kinda like George Mikan and Dolph Schayes, right?) When Lenny Bruce, Woody Allen, Bob Newhart and the Smothers Brothers pushed comedy in a different direction in the sixties—astute observations, hyperintelligent premises—they were considered geniuses of the highest order. (Kinda like Oscar, Elgin, Wilt and Russell, right?) But you know what? If you YouTubed any of those guys in their primes, you wouldn't laugh much. Only during the Ford presidency did comedy start to look like it does now: Richard Pryor's acerbic take on the African American experience, George Carlin's pointed riffs, *Saturday Night Live*'s ballsy redefinition of televised sketch comedy, Steve Martin's intentionally absurd stand-up act, even young observational comics like Jay Leno and David Letterman who had been influenced by Carlin and Bruce. (Kinda like Julius Erving, Bob McAdoo and Tiny Archibald redefining the limits of speed and athleticism with the NBA.) The 1977–1982 stretch saw iconic movies capture similar strides, like *Caddyshack, Animal House, Stripes* and *The Blues Brothers,* all funny movies fueled by drugs, recklessness and individualism. (Kinda like the NBA when it was being led by the likes of Pete Maravich, George Gervin, David Thompson and Micheal Ray Richardson.) Then the eighties rolled around and comedy settled into the era of over-the-top humor, sarcastic irony and "Did you ever notice . . . ?" jokes that, for better and worse, still make us laugh now. Letterman's groundbreaking NBC show. Howard Stern's equally groundbreaking radio show. Eddie Murphy's *SNL* impressions and stand-up acts. A little cable show called *Mystery Science Theater 3000.*[1] Stand-ups like Jerry Seinfeld and Sam Kinison. Consistently funny movies like *Trading Places, Beverly Hills Cop, Night Shift, Fletch* and *Ferris Bueller's Day Off.* All of that stuff holds up even today.

1. *MST 3000* and Letterman created the unintentional comedy genre: mocking things that weren't originally intended to be funny. Nearly 15 years later, I unveiled the Unintentional Comedy Scale on ESPN.com, with Dikembe Mutombo's voice earning a perfect 100 out of 100 and at least 20 different professional golfers earning a zero (because of the little-known rule that you must endure six electroshock treatments upon getting your PGA Tour card).

By the mid-eighties, the comedy world had figured it out and reached the place it needed to be. But it didn't just *happen*. The civil rights struggle, three assassinations (JFK, RFK and MLK) and a growing discontent about Vietnam altered the comedy scene in the sixties; people became more serious, less trusting, more prone to discuss serious issues and argue about them. That's how we ended up with Woody and Lenny. The seventies were marred by a polarizing war and the Watergate scandal, pushing disillusioned Americans into cynical, outspoken and carefree directions (drugs, free sex, etc.), a spirit that quickly manifested itself in comedy. The comedians of the late seventies and early eighties learned from everyone who had pushed the envelope—what worked, and more importantly, what didn't work—and developed a more somber, reflective, sophisticated attitude stemming from how the previous generation's pain shaped their perspective. A perspective that, for better and worse, hasn't really changed since. And now we're here. Were Bird and Magic better in '84 than LeBron and Wade are right now? It's a nice debate. Was Eddie Murphy funnier in '84 than Chris Rock is right now? It's a nice debate. But if you're asking me whether a *Get Smart* episode from 1967 is funnier than a *South Park* episode in 2009, no. It's not a debate.

So it's all about context. The ebbs and flows of the years (and with the NBA, the seasons) affect our memories and how we evaluate them. If we're figuring out the best players and teams of all time—don't worry, we're getting there—we need to examine every season from 1946 (year one) through 1984 (year thirty-nine) and the crucial developments that helped us get here. Consider it a brief and only intermittently biased history of how the NBA became the NBA.[2]

---

2. That was nearly the title for this book: *A Brief and Occasionally Biased History of the NBA.* The titles I loved most (but ultimately was talked out of): *Tuesdays with Horry*[P2] . . . *Love Child of the Basketball Jesus . . . Tell Me How My Book Tastes . . . Where a Pulitzer Happens . . . The Greatest NBA Book I've Ever Written . . . Majerle and Me . . . The Hoops Testament . . . Black Men Can Jump . . . The Second Best Basketball Book Ever . . . I Love This Game . . . I Should Have Been Black . . . The Basketball Bible . . . A White Man's Thoughts on a Black Man's Game . . . Secrets from a Topless Pool in Vegas . . . The Association . . . Weekend at Bernie Bickerstaff's.*

P2. *Tuesdays with Horry* was the best title; I didn't have the balls to go with it. When this book improbably hit number one on the *New York Times* best-seller list for nonfiction, who got bumped to number two? You guessed it . . . Mitch Albom. Damn it all.

1946–54: GROWING PAINS

Heading into the summer of '54, everyone thought the NBA was going down in flames. And they believed it for five reasons.

Reason no. 1. Without rules to prevent intentional fouling, stalling and roughhouse play, league scoring dropped to an appalling 79.5 points per game. Every game played out like a Heat-Knicks playoff slugfest in the mid-nineties, only with clumsy white players planting themselves near the basket, catching lob passes, getting clubbed in the back and shooting free throws over and over again. If you were protecting a lead, your point guard dribbled around and waited to get fouled. If you were intentionally fouling someone, you popped him to send a statement. Players fought like hockey thugs, fans frequently threw things on the court and nobody could figure out how to stop what was happening. You can't really overstate the fan-unfriendliness (I just created that word) of the stalling/fouling tactics. There was the time Fort Wayne famously beat the Lakers 19–18. There was the five-OT playoff game between Rochester and Indy in which the winner of each overtime tap held the ball for the rest of the period to attempt a winning shot, leading to a bizarre situation in which Rochester's home fans booed and booed and ultimately started leaving in droves even with the game still going. The '53 Playoffs averaged an unbelievable *eighty* free throws per game. The anti-electrifying '54 Finals featured scores of 79–68, 62–60, 81–67, 80–69, 84–73, 65–63 and 87–80. You get the idea.

Reason no. 2. The league suffered its first betting scandal when Fort Wayne rookie Jack Molinas was nabbed for wagering on his own team.[3] Even after Molinas had been banned and commissioner Maurice Podoloff prohibited gambling on any NBA games, the damage was done and the league took an inordinate amount of abuse on sports blogs and radio shows.[4]

---

3. It's hard to believe that Boston College didn't give Molinas an honorary doctorate.
4. They didn't have these things in 1954. Just wanted to make sure you were paying attention. Although it would have been fun to read blogs with mean-spirited names like "Bob Cousy's Lisp."

Reason no. 3. The '54 playoffs were screwed up by an ill-fated "What if we slapped together a six-game round robin with the top three teams in each conference?" proposal, which led to the Knicks getting knocked out in a nationally televised quagmire that lasted longer than any NFL game. According to Leonard Koppett, "The game encompassed all the repulsive features of the grab-and-hold philosophy. It lasted three hours, and the final seconds of a one-point game were abandoned by the network. The arguments with the referees were interminable and degrading. What had been happening, as a matter of course, in dozens of games for the last couple of years, was shown to a nationwide audience in unadulterated impurity."[5]

Reason no. 4. Since everyone traveled by train and bus back then, the league stretched only from Boston to Minnesota, with just three "major" television markets in place (Boston, Philly and New York) and seven smaller markets (Minneapolis, Syracuse, Baltimore, Rochester, Fort Wayne, Indianapolis and Milwaukee). Let's just say that the Minneapolis-Syracuse Finals in '54 didn't knock *I Love Lucy* out of the number one Nielsen spot.[6]

Reason no. 5. The lily-white league desperately needed some, um . . . how do we put this . . . um . . . I want to be politically correct . . . you know, especially after the whole Imus/Rutgers thing . . . so let's just say this as discreetly as possible . . . um . . . well . . . *the league needed more black guys!*

1954–55: THE LIFESAVER

When Syracuse owner Danny Biasone[7] created the 24-second shot clock, his brainstorm didn't do much except for speeding up possessions, elimi-

5. Koppett's book *24 Seconds to Shoot: The Birth and Improbable Rise of the NBA* proved to be an enormous help for this chapter. He's dead, but I'd like to thank him anyway.
6. Our top five shows in 1954: *I Love Lucy, Dragnet, Arthur Godfrey's Talent Scouts, You Bet Your Life* and *The Chevy Show* featuring Bob Hope. Isn't it weird that someone 55 years from now will look at the 2010 top five and say, "I wonder what the hell happened on *American Idol*?" just like I wondered, "I wonder what the hell happened on *Arthur Godfrey's Talent Scouts*?"
7. Four great Biasone facts: he was born in Italy and did the Ellis Island thing; he made his money owning a bowling alley; he wore long, double-breasted coats and Borsalino hats; and he smoked filtered cigarettes. I don't know what Borsalino hats are and that still sounds fantastic.

nating stalling, hiking league scoring by 13.6 points per team and basically saving the league. How did he arrive at 24? Biasone studied games he remembered enjoying and realized that, in each of those games, both teams took around 60 shots. Well, 60 + 60 = 120. So Biasone settled on 120 shots as the minimum combined total that would be acceptable from a "I'd rather kill myself than watch another NBA game like this" standpoint. And if you shoot every 24 seconds over the course of a 48-minute game, that comes out to . . . wait for it . . . 120 shots! Biasone came up with the idea in 1951 and spent three years selling the other owners on it, even staging an exhibition game for them in August 1954, using a shot clock, to prove the idea worked. That's how we ended up with a 24-second clock. Of course, the nitwits in Springfield didn't induct him until 2000, which would have been touching if poor Biasone hadn't been dead for eight years. Really, inventing the shot clock and saving professional basketball wasn't enough of an accomplishment to make the Basketball Hall of Fame for forty-one years? And you wonder why I'm blowing it up later in the book. Personally, I think we should create a $24 bill and put Biasone's picture on it.

The karma gods rewarded Biasone when Syracuse beat Fort Wayne in seven for the '55 title[8] (the second-lowest-rated sporting event of all time behind Fox's *Celebrity Boxing 2*). Coincidence? I say no. Scoring cracked 100 per game by the '58 season. One year later, Boston beat Minnesota by a record score of 173–139, with Cousy finishing with 31 points and a record 29 assists. And the NBA never looked back.

One other essential change: the fouling rules were revamped. A limit was placed on team fouls (six per quarter, followed by a two-shot penalty); an offensive foul counted as a team foul but not free throws unless the offending team was over the limit; and any backcourt foul counted as a team foul. The first change prevented teams from fouling throughout games without repercussions; the second change sped up games; and the third change made teams pay a price for fouling anywhere on the court. Sounds like three simple, logical, "why the hell didn't they always do that" tweaks, right? It took the league *eight years* to figure it out.

---

8. Also noteworthy: Earl Lloyd and Jim Tucker became the first black players to play for a championship team.

I'd compare the NBA's first eight years to the first eight years of porn (1972–80)—yeah, some good things happened and everyone who was there remembers those years fondly, but ultimately we moved in a much better, more logical, and more lucrative direction. The porn industry didn't take off until it transferred everything to videotape; the NBA didn't take off until it created a shot clock.[9]

1955–56: MIKAN II: ELECTRIC BOOGALOO

After his '56 Lakers floundered to a 5–15 start and attendance petered, Big George stepped down as general manager, made an ill-fated return[10] and couldn't handle the game's increased speed. As Koppett described it, the plodding Mikan "simply wasn't equipped for the 24-second game. The widened foul lane he could handle; the constant running he could not." And I'm supposed to rank Mikan as one of the top thirty players of all time? Bob Pettit filled Mikan's void by winning the league's first MVP trophy, leading the league in scoring and rebounding for a Hawks team that fled Milwaukee for St. Louis before the season—in retrospect, a bad career move given the success of *Happy Days* two decades later.[11]

1956–57: RUSSELL

Boston's Red Auerbach traded future Hall of Famers Ed Macauley and Cliff Hagan for Russell's rights before the 1956 draft. Why? Because he

---

9. Extending this analogy, Bob Cousy was Seka, Dolph Schayes was Marilyn Chambers, Joe Fulks was Harry Reems, Red Auerbach was Gerard Damiano and George Mikan was definitely John Holmes.

10. Keeping the Mikan-Holmes analogy going, this comeback went about as well as the last two years of Johnny Wadd's career, when he became a junkie and dabbled in gay porn to support his habit.

11. We definitely would have seen Richie Cunningham wearing Hawks T-shirts and jerseys, and possibly a retro cameo with Pettit and Clyde Lovellette wearing bad wigs and pretending they were 20 years younger, then Clyde insulting the black chef at Arnold's and Fonzie kicking his ass.

needed a "modern" center who could handle the boards, protect the rim, and kick-start fast breaks for his speedy guards. Red anticipating in 1956 exactly where the sport was heading—to a T—remains his single greatest accomplishment. Well, that and living into his mid-eighties even though he lived on Chinese food and went through cigars like breath mints. For the Celtics, Russell carried them to the '57 title. For the NBA, Russell imported previously foreign concepts like "jumping," "dunking," "shot blocking" and "blackness." The ultimate win-win.

1957–58: BASKETBALL CARDS

After Bowman's 1948 set bombed with fans, Topps waited a full decade before trotting out its first NBA set. Eighty players (including veterans like Cousy and Schayes) suddenly had their own "rookie card." Six decades later, it's practically impossible to find those cards in mint or near-mint condition for obvious reasons (the set sold poorly) and less obvious reasons (most of the cards were miscut, off-center, and either overprinted or underprinted).[12] Russell's short-printed rookie trails only Mikan's '48 Bowman rookie (worth $9K-plus in near-mint condition) in the Most Valuable Basketball Card Ever race. Another four years passed before Fleer made an ill-fated, one-year jump into the card business with a now-valuable, hard-to-find 1961–62 set that featured rookies for Wilt, West and Oscar (and might be the least exciting cards ever made). Three sets, three failures. No more basketball cards were produced until the 1969–70 season, when Topps released a "tall boy" set of ninety-nine cards that doubled as rookies for Kareem, Hondo, Willis, Pearl, Frazier and Cunningham.

Why is this important? Every relevant rookie card from 1946 to 1970 can be found in the '48 Bowman, '58 Topps, '62 Fleer and '70 Topps sets. If this book becomes the *Da Vinci Code* of NBA books, I'm using part of my financial windfall to buy these four sets in mint condition. The rest of

12. Pettit's quadruple-printed card remains the easiest to find. Go figure, they quadruple-printed Pettit (white) and single-printed Russell (black). I'm sure this was a coincidence. Russ' rookie fetches from $500 to $15,000 depending on its condition.

the money will be spent on a Manhattan Beach house on the water, a minority stake in the Clippers that includes courtside seats, a BMW M6 convertible, hookers, divorce lawyers, a Hollywood production company that takes a ton of meetings and lunches but never actually produces anything, and expensive Zegna shirts that show off my chest hair. Move over, Donald Sterling—there's a new sheriff in town.

1958–60: COLORIZATION

Not only did Lakers rookie Elgin Baylor follow Russell's lead by bringing hang time, explosiveness and midair creativity into the league, but Wilt Chamberlain was finishing a one-year Globetrotters stint[13] and planned on joining Philadelphia the following year. (The Warriors had drafted Wilt as a territorial pick in 1955 when he was a senior in high school. Don't ask.) Anticipating his arrival, the league created an offensive goaltending rule, nicknamed the Wilt Chamberlain Rule, that prohibited offensive players from tipping shots on the rim. The rule evolved over the years because, in the tape of Wilt's 73-point game in '62, he redirected a number of jump shots from teammates into the basket *before* they hit the rim, something that wouldn't be legal now. They had to have tweaked the rule in the mid-sixties. By the way, you know you've arrived in life when you get a rule named after you.[14]

The Dipper exceeded all expectations in his rookie season, averaging a record 37.6 points, capturing the Rookie of the Year, MVP, and MLBHC (Most Likely to Bang Hot Chicks) awards and even inspiring NBC to expand its telecasts to Saturday and Sunday afternoons.[15] On the other hand, Wilt became so frustrated by constant pounding from smaller op-

13. Once the NBA started stealing black stars away from the 'Trotters, it was only a matter of time before the 'Trotters morphed into something else—namely, a fan-friendly hoops team that did tricks, whupped the Generals, and had a sweet *Wide World of Sports* run. You know who loved them? Young Jabaal, that's who.

14. Other rules or phrases named after NBA players or personalities: the Ted Stepien Rule, the Magic Johnson Rule, the Trent Tucker Rule, the Jordan Rules, Hack-a-Shaq, the Larry Bird Exception, the Allan Houston Rule and the Ewing Theory.

15. You know what's really weird? The network's number one announcing team in 1959 was Marv Albert and Hubie Brown.

ponents that he briefly retired in the spring of 1960. With other stars like Cousy complaining about the interminable length of the season[16] (as well as constant traveling, low salaries, the physical toll from a brutal schedule and the league's refusal to protect them from doubleheaders and back-to-back-to-back games), the NBA suddenly faced its second crisis: a public breach with its stars. This wouldn't fully manifest itself for another four years. And then? It manifested itself. Like a bitch.

1960–61: THE SCORING BOOM

Not necessarily a good thing. Why? Nobody played defense, and every game looked like a disjointed All-Star contest or even worse a college pickup game where nobody runs back on D because they're sweating out the previous night's keg party. The '61 Celtics led the league in scoring (124.5 per game) and averaged 119.5 field goal attempts and 33.5 free throw attempts. To put those numbers in perspective, the 2008 Celtics averaged 76 field goal attempts and 26 free throw attempts per game. That's insane. Play suffered so badly that NBC dropped the NBA one year later despite a memorable '62 Finals.[17] The following season ('63), commissioner Maurice Podoloff slapped together a production team to "broadcast" the All-Star Game and the NBA Finals, then sold a syndication package to local affiliates around the country like it was *Cheaters* or *The Steve Wilkos Show.* Unbelievable.

Because of the inordinately high number of possessions, the statistics from 1958 to 1962 need to be taken with an entire shaker of salt and possibly a saltwater taffy factory.

Within five seasons, scoring increased by 18.6 points, field goal attempts increased by more than 4 per quarter, there were nearly 18 more rebounds available for each team and shooting percentages improved as teams played less and less defense.

---

16. Teams routinely played 25–30 preseason games as well as a 72-game regular season and any playoff games, and the guy who did the schedule back then was apparently suffering from a major head injury. Details to come.

17. The other factor: every new NBA star was black. Well, then! Down the road, NBC made up for this apparent burst of racism by greenlighting *The Cosby Show, The Fresh Prince of Bel-Air* and even the unwatchable *A Different World.*

YEAR	G	FGA	REB	FG%	PPG
1956–57	72	6,809	4,494	38.0	99.6
1957–58	72	7,333	5,160	38.3	106.7
1958–59	72	7,368	5,043	39.5	108.4
1959–60	75	8,151	5,513	41.0	115.4
1960–61	75	8,642	5,789	41.5	118.1

Then the '62 season rolled around and the following things happened:

1. Wilt averaged 50 points
2. Oscar averaged a triple double
3. Walt Bellamy averaged a 32–19
4. Russell averaged 23.6 boards and fell two behind Wilt for the rebound title

Hard to take those numbers at face value, right? And that's before factoring in offensive goaltending (legal at the time), the lack of athletic big men (significant) and poor conditioning (which meant nobody played defense). I watched a DVD of Wilt's 73-point game in New York and two things stood out: First, he looked like a McDonald's All-American center playing junior high kids; nobody had the size or strength to *consider* dealing with him. Second, because of the balls-to-the-wall speed of the games, the number of touches Wilt received per quarter was almost unfathomable. Wilt averaged nearly 40 field goal attempts and another 17 free throw attempts per game during his 50-point season. Exactly forty years later, Shaq and Kobe averaged a *combined* 52 points a game on nearly the same amount of combined field-goal/free-throw attempts.[18] Things leveled off once teams started taking defense a little more seriously, although it took a full decade to slow down and resemble what we're seeing now statistically (at least a little). Here's a snapshot every four years from 1962 on. Notice how possessions, rebound totals and point totals began to

18. When MJ scored 37.1 per game in the '87 season, he averaged just 27.8 shots and 11.8 free throws. All right, maybe we didn't need the word "just" in there.

YEAR	G	FGA	REB	FG%	PPG
1961–62	80	8,619	5,713	42.6	118.8
1965–66	80	8,195	5,458	43.3	115.5
1969–70	82 .	8,147	4,336	46.0	116.7
1973–74	82	7,697	3,955	45.9	105.7
1977–78	82	7,615	3,863	46.9	108.5 .
1981–82	82	7,236	3,565	49.1	108.6
1985–86	82	7,268	3,572	48.7	110.2
1989–90	82	7,146	3,538	47.6	107.0
1993–94	82	6,924	3,526	46.6	101.5
1997–98	82	6,536	3,407	45.0	95.6
2003–04	82	6,545	3,461	43.9	93.4[19]
2007–08	82	6,683	3,442	45.7	99.9

drop; how shooting percentages kept climbing; and beyond that, how the numbers jumped around from '62 to '74 to '86 to '94 to '04 to '08.[20]

Compare the numbers from '62 and '08 again. Still impressed by Oscar's triple double or Wilt slapping up a 50–25 for the season? Sure . . . but not as much.

1961–62: THE FIRST RIVAL

Abe Saperstein's American Basketball League died quickly, but not before planting the seed for two future NBA ideas: a wider foul lane (16 feet) and a three-point line. The ABL also gambled on "blackballed" NBA players, including Connie Hawkins, who averaged a 28–13 for Pittsburgh and won the league's only MVP award. In the one and only ABL Finals, the Cleveland Pipers defeated the Kansas City Steers, three games to two, with future Knicks star Dick Barnett leading the way. The ABL disbanded midway

19. That season sucked. We even had Al Michaels calling play-by-play for ABC that year with "I'm only here because they offered me a shitload of cash" vigor.

20. The numbers from '94 to '04 dropped because of overcoaching, superior defense, far fewer possessions, overexpansion, more physical play and a noticeable dearth of elite talent (thanks to bad drafts, the influx of high schoolers and youngsters getting paid too soon).

through its second season, with the league-leading Steers declared league "champs." Good rule of thumb: if you have a franchise named the Kansas City Steers in your professional sports league, you probably aren't making it. If you have a team called the Hawaii Chiefs, you almost definitely aren't making it. And if you name a team (in this case, the Pittsburgh Rens) after the abbreviation for "Renaissance," you *definitely* aren't making it.[21]

1962–63: THE VOID

When Bob Cousy retired after getting his sixth ring, the Association lost its most popular player and someone who ranked alongside Mickey Mantle and Johnny Unitas from a cultural standpoint. Cooz got treated to an ongoing farewell tour throughout the season, as well as the first-ever superemotional retirement ceremony that featured Cooz breaking down and some leather-lunged fan screaming, "We love ya, Cooz!" Who would step into the Cooz's void as the league's most beloved white guy? Did West have it in him? What about Lucas? Yup, the league was becoming blacker and blacker . . . and if you were a TV network thinking about buying its rights in a bigoted country, this was *not* a good thing.

(On the flip side, with Lenny Wilkens thriving on the Hawks and Oscar running the show in Cincy, the old "blacks aren't smart enough to run a football or basketball team" stereotype started to look stupid . . . although it never really disappeared and even resurfaced as a key plot line during season one of *Friday Night Lights* in 2007.)[22]

21. Also, the number of black NBA players increased to 25 out of a possible 96 (26 percent). Actual quote from Al Attles in *Tall Tales:* "I came into the league in 1960 and the word was that there could be up to four blacks per team." Nowadays, only New England prep schools think like this.

22. This was the astonishing two-parter in which an older assistant set off a racial powder keg by saying Smash Williams was better off as an RB than a QB. If *FNL* was MJ's career, Lyla Garrity's slam-page episode would be the 63-point game in Boston (the coming-out party), the two-parter with Smash would be the '91 Finals (when the show's considerable potential was realized), the story arc where Landry and Tyra killed her stalker was MJ's baseball career (far-fetched and a complete waste of time) and seasons three and four were like Jordan's last three title seasons (cementing its reputation as the greatest sports-related drama ever). Glad I got that off my chest.

1963–64: THE SIT-DOWN STRIKE

January 14, 1964, Boston, Massachusetts.

(We're going with a paragraph break and parentheses to build the dramatic tension. Sorry, I was feeling it.)

Frustrated by low wages, excessive traveling and the lack of a pension plan, the '64 All-Stars make one of the ballsiest and shrewdest decisions in the history of professional sports, telling commissioner Walter Kennedy two hours before the All-Star Game that they won't play without a pension agreement in place. With ABC televising the game and threatening Kennedy that a potential TV contract will disappear if the players leave them hanging in prime time, Kennedy agrees fifteen minutes before tip-off to facilitate a pension deal with the owners. Attica! Attica! Attica!

How this night never became an Emmy Award–winning documentary for HBO Sports remains one of the great mysteries in life. You had Boston battling a major blizzard that night. You had every relevant Celtic (current or retired) in the building, including the entire 1946–47 team, as well as a good chunk of the league's retired stars playing an Old-Timers Game before the main event. You had an All-Star contest featuring five of the greatest players ever (Wilt, Russell, West, Oscar and Baylor) in their primes, as well as a number of other relevant names (Lucas, Havlicek, Heinsohn, Lenny Wilkens, Sam Jones, Hal Greer) and the greatest coach ever (Auerbach) coaching the East. You had Larry Fleisher advising the players in the locker room, a powerful lawyer who brandished significant influence with the players down the road.[P3] You had the first instance in American sports history of professional stars risking their careers and paychecks for a greater good. And ultimately, you had what turned out to be the first pen-

---

P3. Fleisher's footnote got accidentally bumped from the hardcover. He's a lost hero (or villain, if you hate how ticket prices skyrocketed) in NBA history—the mastermind who mobilized the players' union, secured free agency and eventually paved the way for every terrible eight-figure contract. I'd rank him as the fifth-most-important nonplayer in NBA history, trailing only Danny Biasone, Red Auerbach, David Stern and Doug Christie's wife.

sion plan of the modern sports era, the first real victory for a players' union in sports history.[23] Other than that, it was a pretty boring night.

Halberstam unearthed two classic tidbits while reporting *Breaks of the Game*. First, the leaders of the "let's strike" movement were Heinsohn, Russell and Wilkens. The votes were split (Halberstam's estimation: 11–9 in favor) and a few influential stars wanted to play and negotiate later . . . including Wilt Chamberlain. Even during far-reaching labor disputes, Wilt did whatever was best for him. Classic. And second, just when it seemed like the dissenting players might convince everyone else to play, Lakers owner Bob Short sent a message down to the locker room ordering West and Baylor to get dressed and get their asses out on the court, sending the entire locker room into "Screw these guys, we're not playing!" mode. And they didn't. The seeds for free agency and big-money contracts were planted on this night. Again, you're telling me this wouldn't be a good HBO documentary? Where's Liev Schreiber? Somebody pour him a coffee and drive him to a recording studio!

In general, the NBA was veering in a healthier direction. Walter Kennedy replaced Podoloff as the league's second (and, everyone hoped, more competent) commish.[24] The Celtics became the first to routinely play five blacks at the same time as opponents emulated their aggressive style—chasing the ball defensively, keeping a center underneath to protect the rim, and using the other defenders to swarm and double-team. With the degree of difficulty rising on the offensive end, the athleticism of certain players started to flourish. You know *something* was happening since attendance rose to nearly 2.5 million and ABC forked over $4 million for a five-year rights deal despite a dearth of white stars.

The network handed its package to Roone Arledge, an innovative young executive who eventually helped revolutionize television with his work on *Monday Night Football, Wide World of Sports,* the Olympics, col-

---

23. Cousy started the Players Association in 1954, although its initial goals were to curb the endless barnstorming tours and get players paid for personal appearances. Not until the mid-'60s did they begin to make headway on medical plans, pension plans, the reserve clause and everything else. Our first two presidents of the Players Association? Holy Cross grads! Who says the Cross couldn't crack the Ivy?

24. And with that, we'd never have another white celebrity named Maurice.

lege football, and even *Nightline* (the first show of its kind).[25] According to Halberstam, "What ABC has to prove to a disbelieving national public, [Arledge] believed, was that this was not simply a bunch of tall awkward goons throwing a ball through a hoop, but a game of grace and power played at a fever of intensity. He was artist enough to understand and catch the artistry of the game. He used replays endlessly to show the ballet, and to catch the intensity of the matchups . . . he intended to exploit as best he could the traditional rivalries, for that was one of the best things the league had going for it, genuine rivalries in which the players themselves participated. Those rivalries, Boston-Philly, New York–Baltimore, needed no ballyhoo; the athletes themselves were self-evidently proud and they liked nothing better than to beat their opponents, particularly on national television. They were, in those days, obviously motivated more by pride than money, and the cameras readily caught their pride." For the first time, the NBA was in the right hands with a TV network.[26]

1964–65: THE BIG TRADE

When the struggling Warriors sent Wilt (and his gigantic contract) back to Philly for Connie Dierking, Lee Shaffer, $150,000, Baltic Avenue, two railroads and three immunities, the trade rejuvenated Philly and San Francisco as NBA cities—both would make the Finals within the next three years—and was covered like an actual news event. In fact, "Chamberlain traded!" may have been the NBA's first unorchestrated mainstream moment. Put it this way: Walter Cronkite wasn't mentioning the NBA on the *CBS Evening News* unless it was something like "Celtics legend Bob Cousy retired today." I've always called this the Mom Test. My mother was never a sports fan, so if she ever said something like, "Hey, how 'bout that Mike Tyson, can you believe he bit that guy's ear off?" then

---

25. I loved Arledge for coming up with *Superstars* and *Battle of the Network Stars,* two of my favorite shows as a kid. If not for him, I never would have seen Charlene Tilton's hard nipples in the softball dunk tank or the watershed Gabe Kaplan–Robert Conrad 100-yard dash (the "USA 4, USSR 3" of reality-TV moments).

26. You have to admire me for running a Halberstam excerpt when he's an infinitely better writer. I have no ego. I'm like Russell—I don't care about stats.

you knew it was a huge sports moment because the people who weren't sports fans were paying attention. Anyway, Wilt getting traded definitely passed the Mom Test. Also, I think Wilt slept with the Mom Test.

(One other biggie that year: with Tommy Heinsohn retiring after the season, Oscar Robertson replaced him as the head of the players union. I just love the fact that we live in a world where Tommy once led a labor movement. *Elgin, I gotta tell ya, I absolutely* love *your idea for a dental plan! Bing, bang, boom! That's a Tommy Point for you, Mr. B!*)

1965–66: RED'S LAST STAND

I always loved Red Auerbach for announcing his retirement *before* the '66 season started, hoping to motivate his players and drum up national interest in an "Okay, here's your last chance to beat me!" season. Like always, he succeeded: Boston defeated the Lakers for an eighth straight title in Red's much-hyped farewell,[27] given an extra jolt after Game 1 of the Finals when Auerbach announced that Russell would replace him as the first black coach in professional sports history.[28] Like everything Red did, the move worked on both fronts: Boston rallied to win the '66 title, and Russell turned out to be the perfect coach for Russell (although not right away).

Red's retirement marked the departure of old-school coaches who didn't need assistants, bitched out officials like they were meter maids, punched out opposing owners and hostile fans, never used clipboards to diagram plays and manned the sidelines holding only a rolled-up program. He controlled every single aspect of Boston's franchise, coaching the team by himself, signing free agents, trading and waiving players, making draft picks, scouting college players, driving the team bus on road trips, handling the team's business affairs and travel plans, performing il-

27. Leading by 10 with 40 seconds left, Red lit up his victory cigar right before a furious comeback—the Lakers scored 8 straight before the C's finally ran out the clock. Imagine the Auerbach era ending with the biggest choke in sports history *and* a jinxed final victory cigar.
28. Back then, they called Russell the first "Negro" coach. That phrasing eventually faded away, much to everyone's relief, especially Vinny Del Negro's.

legal abortions on his players' mistresses and everything else.[29] That's just the way the league worked from 1946 to 1966. Red was also something of a showman, putting on foot-stomping shows when things didn't go Boston's way, antagonizing referees and opponents, and lighting victory cigars before games had ended. Until Wilt usurped his title, Red served as the league's premier supervillain, the guy everyone loved to hate even as they were admitting he made the league more fun.

With players finally earning real money and achieving fame on a mainstream level, the player-coach dynamic was shifting—it was becoming more difficult to scream at players Lombardi-style or make them run wind sprints until they keeled over, that's for sure—and salary hikes made it harder to keep great teams together.[30] Auerbach lowballed his players by convincing them they'd make the money back in the playoffs; he knew that if they bought into that bullshit, then he'd never have to worry about motivating them. Once salaries started climbing past a certain point, you couldn't play the playoff-money card. Like always, Auerbach read the league's tea leaves perfectly and left at the perfect time. From the moment Biasone created the shot clock, Red determined where the sport was heading, embraced the influx of black players and capably handled the enigmatic Russell, a ferocious competitor, lazy practice player and overly sensitive soul who was affected by everything he couldn't control: the plight of African American athletes, his lack of acceptance in Boston, the lack of a labor agreement, Wilt's reported salary, even the civil rights movement and his place in it. Other than Muhammad Ali, Russell was the single most important athlete of the sixties and it's impossible to imagine him playing for anyone else, as evidenced by the fact that Red never gave us the chance. They were a perfect match, a little Jewish guy from Brooklyn and a tall black guy from Louisiana bringing out the best in each other, dominating the league for a solid decade and changing the way basketball

29. Just kidding. All Red did was arrange the illegal abortions. Okay, that was a joke, too. Should I just get out now? Yeah, I should get out now.

30. Wilt signed for $100,000 before the '66 season; Russell received $100,001 (yes, intentional). From a prestige/credibility standpoint, those contracts made the NBA seem just as stable as the NFL and Major League Baseball. *Look, our guys make big money, too!* You have to love the fact that we once lived in a world where rich athletes were considered a positive.

was played. Will a professional basketball coach ever matter that much again? No. No way.

1966–67: THE SECOND RIVAL

The American Basketball Association formed in February of 1967 and announced plans for its first season in October. The intentions of the league's founders were unclear: did they want to compete with the NBA or force a potentially lucrative merger? Within a few months, they named George Mikan commissioner, announced franchises for ten cities (New York,[31] Pittsburgh, Indy, Minny, Oakland, Anaheim, Dallas, New Orleans, Houston and Denver) and promised to (a) sign current NBA players and incoming rookies (happened); (b) get themselves a TV contract (didn't happen), (c) play with a multicolored ball and a three-point line (happened), and (d) encourage their players to grow gravity-defying afros, dunk as much as possible and try all kinds of drugs (happened).[32] Instead of accepting that a rival was inevitable, NBA owners panicked and moved up their expansion plans, adding five more teams (Chicago, San Diego, Seattle, Milwaukee and Phoenix) over the next three years and then three more (Portland, Cleveland and Buffalo) for the 1970–71 season. As an ABC executive joked in *Breaks,* when they put in a clause in the 1965 TV contract allowing ABC to cancel if any NBA team folded, they should have gone the other way and placed a limit on the number of expansion teams. After all, nothing ruins a sports league faster than overexpansion, diluted teams and the death of rivalries, right?[33] Throw in competition for players, a potential antitrust lawsuit and the new Players Association potentially challenging

31. This franchise moved to Long Island because it couldn't land enough game dates in NYC. And you wondered why Dr. J grew big hair.

32. I exaggerated. Speaking of afros, Oscar Gamble's 1976 baseball card has been in the glove compartment of every car I ever owned; it's a good-luck charm. One time I was pulled over for speeding and when I was searching for my license and registration, the Gamble card fell out. I noticed the cop trying not to smile, so I muttered something like, "That card cracks me up." The cop let me go with a warning. The moral of the story: everyone loves big-ass afros.

33. Gary Bettman ignored these lessons and tried a similar strategy with the NHL, nearly destroying it in the process. And he came from the NBA! I love professional sports.

the reserve clause, and suddenly things weren't looking so rosy for the National Basketball Association. Although nobody knew it yet.

1967–71: THE BROKEN MIRROR

That would be Spencer Haywood. He was bad luck. For everyone. Sure, you make your own bad luck to some degree, and in this case the NBA allowed salaries to escalate too rapidly during the latter part of the sixties. In 1966, Knicks rookie Cazzie Russell (the number one overall pick) signed a three-year, $250,000 contract, pushing the Association into the "okay, guys, you don't have to have a second job during the summers anymore" era. The following year, college star Elvin Hayes passed up ABA money (and the chance to play for Houston) for a $350,000 deal with the Rockets. Jimmy Walker (Jalen Rose's dad) parlayed the ABA's interest into a lucrative $250,000 package with Detroit, becoming the first of dozens of talented young NBA players who didn't reach their potential partly because somebody paid them too much too soon. Warriors star Rick Barry jumped leagues, signed with Oakland and became the first professional athlete to dispute the reserve clause in contracts (a clause that allowed teams to keep a player's rights for one year after his contract ended). The legal challenge went poorly and Barry spent the season as Oakland's TV announcer. As far as career moves go, this ranked right up there with David Caruso ditching *NYPD Blue* and Andy Richter leaving Conan O'Brien's show. On the bright side, *somebody* had to challenge the reserve clause, right?[34]

Here's the irony: even as money was poisoning professional basketball for the first time, the NBA couldn't have been in better shape as a whole. During the 1967–68 season, the Lakers opened up the league's first state-of-the-art arena (the 17,000-seat L.A. Forum), attendance topped 4.4 million, ratings rose from 6.0 (1965) to 8.9 in 1969, and ABC even televised a few prime-time playoff games (including Game 7 of the 1969 Finals dur-

---

34. Baseball player Curt Flood gets credit for standing up to The Man and paving the way for a new era of sports contracts, only Barry did the same two years earlier. So why doesn't he get credit? Because Rick Barry was a dick. I keep telling you!

ing May sweeps). But everyone was getting greedy: players, owners, agents, you name it. And you know how that plays out.

Enter the Broken Mirror. Haywood started his professional career when Lew Alcindor did, so we can blame his bad karma for swaying the NBA's number one pick that year: Phoenix would have been a better market for Big Lew, but Milwaukee won the coin toss and the Suns took Neal Walk second.[35] Haywood became the first nonsenior to play professionally, signing with the ABA's Denver Rockets as a "hardship" case and unwittingly giving the ABA an enormous advantage: now the ABA had first crack at nonseniors and high schoolers because the NBA stuck by its antiquated four-year draft eligibility rule. So you could blame Haywood for the eventual influx of underclassmen and teenagers who nearly submarined the NBA in the 1990s, as well as the NBA preventing more dangerous Haywood signings by arranging a merger in May 1971. The NBA accepted ten ABA teams (everyone but Virginia). In return, the ABA dropped its antitrust suit, each ABA team agreed to pay $1.25 million over ten years and ABA teams were deprived of TV money until 1973. The NBA Players Association quickly sued to block it, arguing that the merger created a monopoly and preserved the unconstitutional reserve clause. The ensuing legal dispute (nicknamed the Oscar Robertson suit) would drag on for another five miserable years. In retrospect, it's hard to fathom how the NBA could have handled twenty-eight teams in 1972, so the timing of that lawsuit looks like divine intervention. Regardless, I blame the Broken Mirror (Haywood) for putting it in motion.

After winning three ABA awards as a rookie (MVP, Rookie of the Year and All-Star MVP),[36] Haywood left tread marks fleeing for the 1970–71 Sonics after realizing his quote-unquote three-year, $450,000 Denver contract only paid him $50,000 per year, then another $15,000 annually for twenty years starting when he turned forty. He had been victimized by a brilliant ABA

---

35. I watched a Suns-Hawks '70 Xmas game and Walk was the hairiest NBA player ever: chest hair, neck hair, shoulder hair, you name it. So what were the odds of an extremely hairy white center named Neal Walk becoming an All-Star? I say 0.000000004 percent.
36. Haywood won All-Star MVP along with a 1970 Dodge Challenger and a $2,000 RCA television. Nice! That might be my favorite prize ever—not just for sports, but for any game show, raffle or anything else. Do you think Spence was driving the Challenger when he dropped the RCA off at an L.A. pawn shop 8 years later?

trick called the Dolgoff plan, in which they offered contracts with deceivingly high dollar figures but backloaded most of the deals. How did they pull off such chicanery? According to *Loose Balls*, by routinely bribing agents to talk their clients into those deals.[37] (The bigger problem arose when NBA stars used those artificially high numbers to negotiate legitimately high deals, leading to the salary explosion that transformed the NBA as we knew it. And not in a good way. Well, unless you enjoy watching wealthy, coked-out, passionless basketball. Then you were pumped.) Haywood signed with Seattle and successfully contested the NBA's hardship rule, leading to a slew of prospects filing early and claiming financial "hardship" even though nearly all of them were getting paid under the table in college.[38]

Haywood symbolized an increasingly erratic sport: wealthy and empowered just a little too soon, looking out for himself only, thriving during an era with too many teams and younger stars being given too much money and responsibility waaaaaaaaay too soon. That's how the seventies became the Too Many, Too Much, Too Soon era. The Broken Mirror became its defining figure, peaking too early, earning a ton of money and spending it just as fast, switching teams every few years (always after letting the previous one down), helping to destroy the post-Bradley Knicks, souring Sonics coach/GM Bill Russell on professional basketball, marrying a celebrity (the model Iman), developing a massive cocaine problem and even being involved in the single greatest known coke story in NBA history (we'll get there). It can't be a coincidence that Spencer Haywood retired after the 1982–83 season and the league immediately took off. It just can't.

1971–72: THE STREAK

Why hasn't anyone made a documentary about the '72 Lakers? You had the league's most beloved star and tragic figure, Jerry West, winning his

---

37. If you think agents are scumbags now, they were ten times more scumbaggy in the '60s and '70s. Makes you wonder if Scott Boras came from the past.

38. ABA owners created the phrase "hardship case" to make the Haywood signing seem more palatable to the outside world and give it a perceived legal framework. In other words, the phrase meant nothing. Awesome.

first title on a 69-win team. You had Elgin retiring two weeks into the season and becoming the first superstar to retire without winning a ring,[39] paving the way for Dan Marino, Charles Barkley, Karl Malone and every other star who took heat for falling short. You had Wilt playing the way we always wanted him to play. You had an increasing number of Hollywood celebs hitting home games at the "hip" L.A. Forum, a trend that Doris Day had pioneered in the early sixties. Best of all, you had L.A.'s 33-game winning streak, which happened in a diluted league but remains remarkable when you remember the previous record was 20 (the '71 Bucks).[40] I'll save my thoughts on the '72 Lakers for the "Keyzer Söze" chapter, but let's rank that streak against the unbreakable records in NBA history. Here's my top ten:

1. **Wilt's 50 per game.** Perfect storm of the right era, the right guy, the right rules and the right ball hog. We might not see 40 a game again, much less 50.

2. **Wilt's 55-rebound game.** Since nobody has come within 20 boards of this mark in the past two-plus decades, and since it's difficult for an entire team to snare 55 rebounds these days, I'm declaring this one safe. The guy who came within 20? (Wait for it . . . wait for it . . .) Charles Oakley in 1988.

3. **Russell's eleven rings.** Too many teams, too much movement, too tough to keep a great team together for more than a few years. I just can't imagine someone getting twelve. Even if someone had a Horry-like career as a role player and played contender roulette for fifteen years, landing in the right situation over and over again, could they get twelve? Nobody had better timing/luck than Horry and he *only*

---

39. Elgin's ring (they gave him one) was probably whipped against the wall of his Clippers office 17,000 times since 1972. He qualifies for the Ewing Theory because the Lakers ripped off a 33-game win streak right after he retired, but that's unfair because it took so much dignity for him to walk away from a guaranteed title. He left with his head held high. In other words, it was the complete opposite of how GP's career ended.

40. It took another 36 years before anyone even broke 20 again—when the '08 Rockets won 22 straight.

has seven. Could someone be 55 percent luckier than Big Shot? I don't see it.[P4]

4. **L.A.'s 33-game win streak.** Like Bob Beamon's long jump in Mexico, only if he jumped 39 feet instead of 29 feet. Here's how it happened: you had a veteran, experienced, talented nucleus that had been together for years dismantling a diluted league that, except for Milwaukee and Baltimore, had seen too much player movement because of expansion and the ABA. In a three-season span from 1969 to 1972, we witnessed four of the thirteen longest streaks ever: 33 games, 20 games, 18 games and 16 games (the '71 Bucks again). Coincidence? No way.

I have a goofy theory on the 33-gamer: Bill Sharman took over the Lakers that year and may have been the first "real" NBA coach ever. Back then, NBA game days consisted of players showing up an hour before the game, farting around, then getting advice from coaches like "Keep Willis off the boards" and "Don't let Monroe kill us" while everyone smoked Marlboro Reds. Sharman was a stickler for detail, conditioning and repetition—things today's generation takes for granted but everyone ignored in the fifties and sixties— forcing his players to stretch every day, pushing them to eat healthy and quit smoking, scheduling game-day shoot-arounds so players could get accustomed to rims and shooting backgrounds at different arenas, requiring them to watch game films and basically doing everything that modern coaches do. For a veteran team like the Lakers, those little things pushed them to another level. He also handled Chamberlain better than any other coach, becoming the first to convince Wilt to buy into Russell's rebounding/shot-blocking routine, even pulling a Jedi mind trick by soliciting Wilt's opinions and ideas all season so Wilt felt part of everything that was happening.[41]

P4. A career highlight: Bob Cousy sent me a surprisingly heartfelt note about how much he enjoyed *TBOB*. His one gripe: he thought Russell's eleven rings should have been number one here, writing, "The greatest accomplishment in American team sports pro history was the Celtics' dominance from 1957 to 1969. Eleven championships in thirteen years will never be topped." Good point.

41. No joke: I adopted Sharman's strategy as a parenting tactic with my daughter. Keep her off the pole! I gotta keep her off the pole!

The Dipper sacrificed a ton of shots but fully embraced the whole unselfishness/teamwork thing,[42] and over everything else, that's what made his team so great. So yeah, on paper, it doesn't make sense that the '72 Lakers were better than the '69 Lakers . . . but when you factor in a diluted league, Sharman's influence and Wilt's reinvention, it makes sense.

5. **George McGinnis' 422 turnovers.** Disclaimer: this happened in the ABA. McGinnis holds the first (422), second (401), and third (398) all-time turnover spots, making him the Chamberlain of turnovers.[43] The NBA didn't start keeping track of turnovers until the '78 season, robbing us of two landmark George years before he notched 312 in 1978 and a whopping 346 in 1979. Who made more turnovers over the years, George McGinnis or Rachael Ray? Will we ever see someone else average more than five turnovers a game without getting benched or killed by his own fans? If I'd had my column back in the mid-seventies, I would have been ragging on George constantly: between his ball-stopping habits, ugly one-handed jumper, moody attitude and disinterest in defense, George took more off the table than any "superstar" ever. You can't believe how much McGinnis secretly sucked until you watch his stink bomb in the '77 Finals. I know he peaked two or three years earlier (most famously with a 52-point, 37-rebound game in 1974) and had a miserable series, but still, you can't tell me someone that sloppy and simple to defend belonged on a championship team.[44] I can't imagine anyone breaking George's hallowed 422 or averaging a quadruple nickel like he did in '75 (29.9 points, 9.2 boards, 6.3 assists and 5.3 turnovers). Kevin Porter and Artis Gilmore set the current NBA record with 360 turnovers apiece in '78. Allen Iverson ap-

---

42. In '71, Wilt averaged a 20–18–4 and shot 54.5%. In '72, Wilt averaged a 15–19–4 and shot 64.9%. He attempted 1,226 FGs and 669 FTs in '71; that dropped to 764 FGs and 524 FTs in '72. So he *did* sacrifice.

43. Too bad they didn't keep track of TOs when Wilt played—that's another record he would have gone out of his way to break. Can't you hear Chick Hearn saying, "My God, what is the Big Dipper doing? He just intentionally sailed his tenth pass of the game into the stands!"

44. In fairness to George, he led the '73 Pacers in scoring when they won the title, then carried the '75 Pacers to the Finals and averaged a stunning 32–16–8 in 18 playoff games with a jaw-dropping 111 TOs. George also had 8 TOs in the '74 ABA All-Star Game. The guy couldn't toss his car keys to a valet without someone else catching them.

proached that mark with 344 in 2005; nobody else in the 2000s topped 320. George, your record is safe. Future generations will remember you as the one and only member of the Quadruple Nickel Club.

6. **Wilt's 100-point game.**[45] Kobe's 81-point game made this one seem slightly breakable. The right perimeter player at the right point in his career with the right touch of officiating could definitely challenge it with help from the three-point line. In his 81-point explosion, Kobe played 42 minutes and made 21 of 33 two-pointers, 7 of 13 threes and 18 of 20 free throws against a mess of a Toronto team. (The key for Kobe that night: Toronto's perimeter defenders were Jalen Rose, Mike James, Morris Peterson, Joey Graham and a washed-up Eric Williams. Those guys couldn't have stopped a David Thompson nosebleed.) So let's tweak those numbers slightly, have him hog the ball a little more and make him slightly more accurate. Had he played 46 minutes and made 24 of 37 two-pointers, 10 of 15 threes and 22 of 24 free throws, that's exactly 100 points. Look at the two sets of numbers again; is the second set *that* big a stretch from the first?

7. **Chicago's 72-win season.** The perfect storm of the right era (the league at its most diluted), right team (a pissed-off Bulls team hell-bent on reclaiming its throne) and right alpha dog (a possessed Jordan coming off his "baseball sabbatical" and a humiliating playoff defeat). I can't imagine anyone finishing a season with fewer than 10 losses. It's too improbable.

8. **Scott Skiles' 30-assist game.** Some perfect storm potential because the record happened against Paul Westhead's nonsensical '91 Nuggets team that attempted Loyola Marymount's run-and-gun style and failed so memorably. Whether it's broken or not, let's agree that we'll never see another balding white dude shell out 30 assists again.[46]

---

45. Wilt almost made this list a fourth time for shooting 72.7 percent from the field in '73. That one feels breakable to me—if the right aging, gigantic center came along who only shot dunks and layups, it could fall. Rigor Artis shot 67 percent in '81 and 65 percent in '82. Maybe 43-year-old Shaq will do it.

46. Pete Maravich holds the white-guy record for points (68); Jerry Lucas for rebounds (40); Mark Eaton for blocks (14); John Stockton for steals (9); and Dan Majerle/Rex Chapman for threes (9). Peja Stojakovic had 10 threes in a game but I don't count the Euros as true white guys. Just a personal thing with me.

9. **Rasheed Wallace's 41 technicals.** In just 77 games! In other words, Sheed averaged an astonishing 0.53 technicals per game for the 2000–01 season; it's like Teddy Ballgame's .406 but for semi-homicidal sports marks.[P5]

10. **Jose Calderon's 98.1 free throw percentage.** This just happened—Calderon made 151 of 154 free throws in '09 and shattered Calvin Murphy's seemingly insurmountable 95.8 from '81 (right before they changed the 3-to-make-2 rule). Murphy made 206 of 215 FTs and still holds the 200-plus record. Larry Bird holds the 300-plus (93%, 319 for 343) and 400-plus (91%, 414 for 455) records. And Dirk Nowitzki (91.5%, 536 for 586) holds the 500-plus record. Regardless, don't feel bad for Murphy because he still owns one of the great records in sports history: fourteen kids by nine different women, the unofficial siring record for athletes as far as I'm concerned. Put that thing away, Calvin! And you wondered why they called him the "Pocket Rocket."

1972–73: THE DOUBLE CROSS

During the final year of its latest four-year contract with ABC—the network that helped nurture professional basketball into a mainstream force—the NBA negotiated a deal with CBS mandating that the winning network *had* to show NBA games starting between 1:00 and 2:00 p.m. on Saturday afternoons. Since ABC couldn't dump crucial college football games in October and November, a bitter Roone Arledge dropped his right of first refusal and decided to destroy the NBA on CBS. Which he did. Easily. Arledge promoted the living hell out of his Saturday college football games and crushed the Association in the ratings, quickly turning it back into a Sundays-only TV entity. Then he expanded *Wide World of*

P5. Sheed was the only player ever ejected from the McDonald's All-American Game. It's true. Before the 2009–10 season, he landed in Boston and cruised through the regular season so indefensibly that I snapped in March and wrote a 3,600-word column declaring him my least favorite Celtic ever (and my dad's as well). Sheed partially redeemed his shit-bomb of a season by playing himself into decent shape as the playoffs went along. By mid-June, his 38DD man boobs had dropped to 34B's and he even played 35 minutes in Game 7 of the Finals without dropping dead. So that was a bonus. I'd like to thank him for being my 2010 Sobering Reminder that I'm an idiot for caring about professional sports.

Sports to Sundays, where it did an eye-opening 12.0 rating and thrashed the NBA every week like a redheaded stepchild. If that weren't enough, he rolled the dice with trash sports like *Superstars* and *World's Strongest Man;* and even those programs beat the NBA. Within a year, the NBA's ratings had dropped 25 percent (from 10.0 to 8.1) and when college hoops took off on NBC, suddenly the NBA was cranking out third-place finishes every Sunday. As Halberstam wrote in *Breaks of the Game,* "Along Madison Avenue it became known as Roone's Revenge."

Why would the owners screw over a network that saved its league? Apparently the newer owners were jealous of the NFL's lucrative contract with ABC, as well as the attention lavished on *Monday Night Football,* feeling they'd never be better than number three on ABC's depth chart behind pro football and college football. I'd throw in this theory: for thirty solid years, this was the dumbest league going. These guys couldn't figure out how to align divisions or eliminate jump balls at the beginning of every quarter, so *of course* they'd be dumb enough to sabotage their ABC alliance and start a feud with the most powerful TV executive alive. According to Halberstam, only one relevant NBA voice argued against the double cross: Auerbach, who appreciated ABC's efforts and asked the salient question, "You don't really think a man like Roone Arledge is going to take this lying down, do you?" Everyone ignored Red and pushed for the switcheroo to CBS, paving the way for everything that would happen over the next ten years: free-falling ratings, nontelevised Game 7's, tape-delayed Finals games and sweeping public apathy.[47]

1973–74: THE WAR THAT COULDN'T BE WON

When two sides battle, normally there's a winner and a loser. When the ABA and NBA battled, everyone lost. The ABA was hemorrhaging money and going through commissioners like they were Starbucks baristas,[48] while the NBA was suffering in five distinct ways. In order:

---

47. The lesson, as always: don't mess with the karma police.
48. There were six ABA commishes in all: Mikan, Jack Dolph, Bob Carlson, Mike Storen, Todd Munchak and Dave DeBusschere. Here's a good rule of thumb: if your fledgling league has 6 commissioners in 9 years, you probably aren't making it.

1. Bidding wars and swollen contracts damaged the new generation of
   NBA up-and-comers. Sidney Wicks, Haywood, Hayes, Walker, Sam
   Lacey and Austin Carr suffered right away; McAdoo, McGinnis (after
   crossing over in '75), Maravich and Archibald suffered eventually.
   When those players should have been enjoying their primes in the late-
   '70s, only Hayes was contributing to a contender. We also had sketchy
   players making significantly more money than their coaches, creating
   its own legion of problems that Heinsohn explained beautifully in his
   award-winning autobiography, *Give 'Em the Hook:*

   > Darryl Dawkins is the perfect example. The guy could have
   > been a monster, should have been a monster, but nobody
   > had the controls. Armed with a long-term contract, Darryl
   > had the security of dollars coming in. I've seen this happen
   > so many times. . . . It's not just the length of the contract that
   > hurts, it's the length of the guaranteed lifestyle. Unless you're
   > talking about athletes who are truly dedicated to the game,
   > the only time these guys bear down is when their security is
   > threatened. I used to talk about this with Cousy, who began
   > coaching the Kings in Cincinnati the same year I took the
   > job in Boston. One night he started telling me about Sam
   > Lacey, his rookie center—how he was pessimistic about
   > him because Sam wouldn't do this, Sam wouldn't do that,
   > and just didn't take very well to coaching. "Cooz," I said.
   > "I don't know what you expected. You guys just signed
   > Sam for some serious dough, didn't you? So obviously
   > he must assume management thinks quite highly of him.
   > And his wife certainly thinks he's great. His mother thinks
   > he's great. His agent thinks he's great. You're the only guy
   > telling him he's not great. So, Cooz, who do you think he's
   > going to listen to?" Cooz agreed, then he watched me polish
   > off seven glasses of Scotch and a pack of Marlboro Reds in
   > less than two hours before letting me drive home. I vaguely
   > remember driving into a stop sign and hitting a homeless
   > guy. The cops let me go because I was Tommy Heinsohn.

Those guys got a round of Tommy Points that night! Bing, bang, boom![49]

2. The ABA kept bowling over the NBA's top referees with Godfather offers, stealing four of the top six (John Vanak, Joe Gushue, Earl Strom and Norm Drucker), improving the quality of ABA games and leaving the NBA in a legitimate bind.[50] By the '76 season, as Hubie Brown told Terry Pluto, "The officiating at the end of the ABA was like the players—it was just an incredible amount of talent, just staggering. And nobody knew it. The officials were a bigger secret than the players." Only Hubie could lapse into hyperbole while discussing ABA officials.

3. NBA scoring dropped from 116.7 in 1970 to 102.6 in 1974. You could attribute some of the decline to better defense and better coaching; older guards like Frazier, Jo Jo, Bing, Goodrich and Norm Van Lier setting a deliberately slower pace; a famine of overall offensive talent; and waaaaaaaay too many guys named Don and Dick. The '70 teams averaged 116.7 points on 99.9 attempts and shot 46.0 percent from the field. The '75 teams averaged 102.6 points on 91.2 attempts and shot 45.7 percent from the field. Free throw attempts were roughly the same (24.5 per team in '70, 25.0 in '75), so every '75 game had about seventeen fewer total possessions than a '70 game. Why, you ask?

   (You really want me to say it?)

   (Fine, I'll say it.)

   Too many white guys! Okay? All right? I said it! The league needed more black guys! The ABA stole too many of them! It was a freaking problem! Okay?

---

49. I made those last five sentences up. Sorry, Tommy. By the way, he's the only NBA author to repeatedly use the word "baby" in his prose, as in "Kareem was great, but Cowens was better, baby!" Strangely, this would become a broadcasting crutch for the insufferable Tony Siragusa two decades later.

50. This was one of the ABA's underrated achievements, right up there with Villanova and Western Kentucky being forced to forfeit their 1971 records and NCAA tournament prize money because ABA commish Jack Dolph left his briefcase open at the '71 All-Star Game and reporters noticed signed contracts for Howard Porter and Jim McDaniels. I nominate this for Dumbest Commish Moment Ever. Not even Gary Bettman can top it.

To be fair, it wasn't "blacks" as much as "young athletes." Here's how the clash played out for relevant rookies from '71 through '75:

1971: Austin Carr, Sidney Wicks, Elmore Smith, Fred Brown, Curtis Rowe, Clifford Ray, Mike Newlin, Randy Smith (NBA); Julius Erving, Artis Gilmore, George McGinnis, Ralph Simpson, Tom Owens, Johnny Neumann, Jim McDaniels, John Roche (ABA)

1972: Bob McAdoo, Paul Westphal, Jim Price, Kevin Porter, Lloyd Neal (NBA);[51] George Gervin, James Silas, Jim Chones, Brian Taylor, Don Buse, Dave Twardzik (ABA)

1973: Doug Collins, Ernie DeGregorio, Mike Bantom, Kermit Washington, Kevin Kunnert (NBA); Larry Kenon, Swen Nater, John Williamson, Caldwell Jones (ABA)

1974: Bill Walton, Jamaal Wilkes, Tom Burleson, Scott Wedman, Tom Henderson, Campy Russell, Brian Winters, Truck Robinson, John Drew, Phil Smith, Mickey Johnson (NBA); Moses Malone, Marvin Barnes, Maurice Lucas, Billy Knight, Bobby Jones, Len Elmore (ABA)

1975: Gus Williams, Alvan Adams, Darryl Dawkins, Lionel Hollins, Junior Bridgeman, Bill Robinzine, Joe Bryant, Ricky Sobers, Kevin Grevey, Lloyd Free, Bobby Gross (NBA); David Thompson, Marvin Webster, M. L. Carr, Dan Roundfield, Mark Olberding (ABA)

Scoring those five years like rounds in a prizefight: 10–8, ABA; 10–9, ABA; 10–9, ABA; 10–9, NBA; 10–10, even. From a quality-of-play standpoint, the ABA grabbed nearly every athletic rebounder and exciting perimeter scorer, forcing the NBA to keep trotting out

51. Those were the only '72 draft picks who played 350-plus career games and averaged 10-plus points. The next seven picks after LaRue Martin (number one) and McAdoo (number two): Dwight Davis, Corky Calhoun, Freddie Boyd, Russ Lee, Bud Stallworth, Tom Riker, Bob Nash. I swear I didn't make these names up.

the likes of Dick Gibbs and Don Ford every night.[52] If HBO's Harold Lederman was judging, he'd probably say, "*OHHHHHH*-kay, Jim— I have to give this one to the ABA. Maybe the NBA landed more role players and fringe starters, but Jim, out of the twenty best incoming rookies from 1971 to 1975 (Erving, Gervin, Wicks, McAdoo, Kenon, Westphal, Moses, Nater, Barnes, Gilmore, McGinnis, Walton, Silas, Wilkes, Lucas, Thompson, Collins, Knight, Buse and Bobby Jones) the ABA landed *fourteen* of them, including five who could potentially put asses in seats. They landed the biggest punches, pushed the envelope with high schoolers and robbed the NBA of nearly every exciting athlete! I have the ABA winning, 49–46!"

Considering the NBA had eighteen teams at the time, that was a pretty significant shortage of incoming talent, no? That's why I have trouble taking the numbers from '72 to '76 seriously—particularly some of the gaudy scoring/rebounding numbers that don't jibe with the drop in scoring—because such a relatively small talent pool spread was stretched over twenty-eight teams and two leagues. Imagine if you removed all the European players from the 2009 NBA, forbade the Eastern and Western Conferences from playing each other, then directed 75 percent of the most talented rookies to one conference for five solid years. Wouldn't the stats be skewed? Wouldn't you take the respective conference championships a little less seriously?

4. Julius Erving blossomed as basketball's most exciting player and a legitimate box office draw, winning 1974 MVP and Playoffs MVP awards, getting an endorsement deal with Dr. Pepper and gracing the cover of *Sports Illustrated*'s March 15 issue: a picture of Julius dunking as his head broke up the comically unsophisticated headline "What's Up? Doc J." Even if fans couldn't see him on TV, the buzz surrounding

---

52. The number of semiathletic white small forwards from the mid-'70s is staggering: in '76 alone, we had Don Nelson, Ford, Gibbs, Bill Bradley, Dick Snyder, Tom and Dick Van Arsdale, Scott Wedman, Jack Marin, Keith Erickson and Larry Steele playing 20-plus minutes a game (and Kenny Reeves for the Bulls). Anytime you have a position that features two Dons and three Dicks and your league is supposed to be entertaining, that's probably not a good thing.

Doc had made him *cooler* than any NBA player. With the Lakers and Knicks fading and the NBA's younger stars failing to resonate with the public, for the first time the ABA finally had something the NBA needed, and a merger seemed more likely than ever. Alas, the Oscar Robertson suit was still holding it up. The NBA was like a separated rich guy who falls for a mistress from the wrong side of the tracks (the ABA), develops a relationship with her kid (Doc) and wants to marry her even though it's probably the wrong idea . . . only he has to wait another five years for the divorce to clear and keeps wondering if he's doing the right thing getting married again. I think that analogy made sense. I'm almost positive.

5. In the spring of '74, Utah drafted high schooler Moses Malone and stole him away from the University of Maryland with a four-year, $565,000 deal. That's right, the ban on high schoolers had been lifted for professional basketball. Poor Moses ended up making an unprecedented life adjustment, moving from Virginia to Utah at the tender age of nineteen and living on his own without the ability to put a decent sentence together. Like Josh Baskin in *Big*, only with more Mormons and more mumbling.[53] For the NBA, it was one more body blow: instead of Moses becoming a household name at Maryland and progressing at his own pace, the best center prospect since Kareem would be learning bad habits in a floundering league. Within a year, Utah went under and Moses was stuck playing with Marvin Barnes on the Spirits of St. Louis. Not exactly the ideal mentor.[54]

(Only one bright spot this season: San Diego lured Wilt to the ABA, but the NBA blocked the deal and Wilt was stuck coaching the Q's all season. Wilt took it seriously for about a month, then less seriously, and by the midway point of the season, he was no-showing games. S.D. finished last

---

53. Look, you can't discuss young Moses without mentioning that, as many claim, he initially expressed himself mostly through grunts. The iconic Moses story: during his second ABA season, Moses injured his foot and the trainer couldn't find anything wrong with it. Moses disagreed by simply saying, "Foot broken." And it was.

54. It's a good thing that Moses didn't end up on the '75 Spirits: they had Marvin Barnes at his crazy apex, New York schoolyard legend Fly Williams, legendary head case Joe Caldwell and a swingman named Goo Kennedy. That's right, Bad News, Fly and Goo on the same team! Too bad they never signed Splooge Simpson.

in league attendance with less than 1,900 per game. In Wilt's defense, they didn't keep coaching stats at the time so he couldn't come up with any individual goals.)

1974–75: RACIAL PROGRESS . . . OR NOT

The 1975 Finals made sports history: for the first time, a championship game featured two black coaches—Al Attles for Golden State, KC Jones for Washington—and if that weren't enough, they were wearing superhip seventies leisure suits! (Somebody needs to start a website called My Favorite 100 Al Attles Disco Suits. Every time they cut to him on the bench, it looks like he's waiting on line for Luis Guzman's club in *Boogie Nights*.) Jones took heat because CBS' inside-the-huddle cameras kept catching him crouching submissively during time-outs as assistant Bernie Bickerstaff furiously diagrammed plays and seemed to be the one coaching the team. So what if Bickerstaff happened to be black as well? This just proved that blacks shouldn't be coaching NBA teams. Or something. Poor KC got fired a year later and didn't get another crack at a head coaching job until 1983.[55]

You know what? We can do better for 1974–75. My favorite subplot was Oscar shattering the Great Player Turned Incomprehensibly Bad TV Analyst barrier. It's unclear why CBS believed Oscar would have clicked with TV audiences when he had a (deserved) reputation for being humorless and cantankerous. Maybe they just wanted a big name. But Oscar tanked so badly that they dumped him for former referee Mendy Rudolph. Mendy Rudolph? Now *that's* insulting. Here's what fascinates me after the fact: a whopping eight of the twenty-five all-time greatest players were legitimately horrendous on television, but that didn't stop the networks from repeatedly hiring the latest available legend under the whole "Hey, he's a huge name, he'll be fine!" theory before eventually weaning themselves off

---

55. I defy you to find a weirder coaching resume than the one belonging to KC Jones: Brandeis University (head coach, '67–'70); L.A. Lakers (assistant, '72); San Diego Conquistadors (head coach, '73); Bullets (head coach, '74–'76); Celtics (assistant, '79–'83; head coach, '84–'88); Sonics (head coach, '90–'91); New England Blizzard of the women's ABL ('97–'98). My head hurts.

the hare-brained idea (although we still see it with the NFL). Here's the official NBA Legends Turned Horrible TV Personalities chronology.

Elgin Baylor ('74). CBS teamed him with Brent Musburger and Hot Rod Hundley for its inaugural NBA season, only Elgin struggled so mightily that the network replaced him *during* the '74 playoffs. As soon as the Warriors were eliminated, they dumped him for Rick Barry for the Conference Finals.[56] Can we get Elgin's CBS work on YouTube? Can someone make that happen for me?

Oscar Robertson ('75). Stood out for a couple of reasons. First, he never looked at the camera. *Ever.* It was like the camera was the sun and he didn't want to get blinded. Second, he had absolutely nothing to say, so he made up for it by making a variety of unprofessional sounds as the game was happening: You know, like "Ohhhhhhhhhhh!" and "Yes!" Oscar always sounded like he was getting a lap dance in the CBS Champagne Room. The network couldn't get rid of him fast enough after the season, sparing us from seeing an inevitable "The Big O No!" headline if the Oscar era lasted too long.[57]

Rick Barry ('75–'81). Moonlighted as a playoffs color guy if the Warriors were done playing, coming off like the annoying guy at your Super Bowl party who played a year of college football and thinks that gives him the right to criticize and nitpick everything that's happening. When he retired and joined CBS full-time for the '80–'81 season, Barry's TV career fell apart following an incredible moment during Game 5 of the Finals, when CBS showed a picture of a few members of the '56 Olympic basketball team (including a young Russell with a big grin on his face), leading to this exchange:

GARY BENDER: Rick, who do you think that guy is over there?

56. That had to be doubly insulting for Elgin—not just getting booted, but booted and replaced by Rick Barry? That's like having your college girlfriend dump you for the biggest douche on the varsity crew team.
57. It's really a shame that the dude who runs the "Awful Announcing" blog wasn't around back then.

BARRY (*attempting his first joke ever*): I don't know, it looks like some fool over there with that, um, that big watermelon grin there on the left.[58]

(*CBS cuts from the picture to a dumbfounded Russell with the words "watermelon grin" still hanging in the air. He glances back and forth between Gary Bender and Barry with a "Did he just say what I think he just said?" look on his face. Three excruciating seconds pass.*)

BENDER (*still smiling, although he may have been shitting himself*): Who is that guy? (*Pause*) That's you, Bill. Don't you recognize that picture?

RUSSELL (*not smiling*): Nope.

Did it end there? Noooooooooo! Only fifteen seconds later, with Russell still steaming, Barry tried to loosen things up by handing the pictures to Russell on camera. As Barry kept asking over and over again, "You sure you don't want these?" a seething Russell turned his entire body away from Barry toward Bender, who tried to defuse things by telling Rick, "You might want to leave this one alone." And Barry *still* kept going until Russell finally said coldly, "No, I don't want 'em." Unequivocally the most awkward sports-TV moment that didn't include Joe Namath and Suzy Kolber. You couldn't even believe it as it was happening. Needless to say, Barry's contract was not renewed. And that's an understatement. (Of course, if this incident happened in today's overly PC era, Barry would quickly disappear from planet Earth like Michael Richards did.) Barry eventually found a second life on TBS, providing play-by-play for the '85 Eastern Finals with—you're not gonna believe this—Bill Russell! Who's the genius who came up with that idea? That was like Mike Tyson getting freed from jail and immediately hosting the 1996 Miss Black Teen USA pageant.

---

58. I showed this clip to the Sports Gal, who defended Barry by saying, "He didn't mean it that way. Look at the way he was smiling. It looks like a half watermelon. I really don't think he meant it the bad way. Maybe he didn't know what it meant. Did he get fired?" Um, yes. Yes, he did.

John Havlicek ('78). A late addition to the Musburger-Barry team for the '78 Finals,[59] Hondo said absolutely nothing and flatlined for seven games. Was this really a surprise? I loved Hondo, every Boston fan loved Hondo, but he's not exactly someone you'd want giving the best man's speech at a wedding.[60] I remember watching one of those Finals games on NBA TV at like three in the morning, seeing Hondo introduced in the beginning, getting excited, then thinking he had gotten sick or something because we didn't hear him speak for the next forty-five minutes. Nope. He was just sitting there. You can't even give him a grade other than "incomplete" or "possibly in a coma."

Bill Russell ('80–'83). Well received during his first run in the early seventies, Russell was unprepared/uninterested/un-(fill in any other adjective that suggests life) the second time around and couldn't carry the load himself after Barry was fired. Actually, he sounded like my dad every time he falls asleep during a Red Sox game, wakes up in the late innings and mumbles, "Wait, what happened to Beckett? Did we take him out?" That was Russell for three solid years. Although you can't blame him because he worked with Barry for one of them. Maybe he was heavily medicated.

Moses Malone ('86). Okay, we're cheating here—CBS used Moses as a pregame/halftime/postgame studio guy for Game 4 of the '86 Finals, an awesome game overshadowed by CBS' decision that it would be a good idea for Moses to speak extemporaneously on live TV. Teamed with Musburger and Julius Erving (no slouch himself in the Horrible TV Guy department), Doc came off like a cross between Eddie Murphy and Jesse Jackson compared to Moses. It's hard to figure out what CBS was thinking here. I mean, it's not like Moses was getting more articulate as the years passed—we were only three years removed from his "Fo fo fo" prediction and his nickname within the league was "Mumbles" Malone. The more I'm

59. These were the days when networks routinely had all-white broadcast teams without considering the racial implications. Now we've swung the other way—you're only allowed to have two white guys on a studio show and that is *it*! You hear me? Only two!

60. A great rule of thumb for the "Would he be good on TV?" question: could you see him giving a funny best man's speech? If not, then don't hire him. Proving my point: I'd want to attend any wedding where Charles Barkley gave the best man's speech. And so would you.

thinking about it, I wonder if someone at CBS lost a bet—as in "Okay, if you win, I'll pay for our golf trip to Scotland, but if I win, you *have* to use Moses Malone as a TV guy for a Finals game." Whatever the reason, this was the only NBA telecast ever that needed closed captioning.[61]

Magic Johnson ('92–'97). NBC signed Magic right after he retired and it seemed like a layup. Nobody was more personable or likable than Magic, right? Then the telecasts started. Magic giggled during plays without provocation, kept interrupting Marv Albert and Mike Fratello, and tied every play or storyline into something that had happened while he was playing for the Lakers. You also couldn't really understand him because, for whatever reason, it always sounded like he was eating a ham sandwich. Of course, I loved having Magic around because he was like a never-ending *SNL* skit. The Knicks would take the lead on a Ewing shot, then the Bulls and Jordan would answer with a basket, and suddenly Magic would start screaming, "Patrick was down on his end sayin', 'I'm gonna win this game' and Michael came back down and said, 'Uh-uh, big fella, you ain't winnin' on my court!' "[62] There was something undeniably entertaining about listening to Magic provide color for games, the same way it's entertaining when you see a pedestrian trip or a buddy puke all over himself at a bachelor party. When NBC mercifully moved Magic to the studio, it wasn't the same; he was just annoying and had nothing to say. What's strange is that Magic went away for a while, returned on TNT and developed into a decent sidekick for Kenny and Charles. I have no rational explanation for this. None.

Julius Erving ('97). Hands down, the worst studio analyst of all time. And that's a *strong* statement. Only two years before, Joe Montana appeared on NBC's NFL show and may have been dead for all we knew. I remember waiting for Jonathan Silverman and Andrew McCarthy to jump in right before every commercial and wheel Montana's corpse out of the TV

---

61. Every NBA DVD should have three audio choices: English, Spanish and Moses Malone. I'm not apologizing at any point in my life for these Moses jokes. The man couldn't speak English and didn't seem interested in learning how to try. What else can I tell you?
62. Magic absolutely loved the phrase "winnin' time." Every pivotal moment revolved around "winnin' time," as in "Michael knows right now it's winnin' time!"

frame. Still, it wasn't surprising that Montana stank—we didn't like him for his personality, just for banging hot blondes and winning Super Bowls. It's not like our expectations were high. But Doc was one of the few NBA stars to successfully strike that delicate balance between "articulate spokesman and ambassador" and "slick dude who lives for dunking on heads." It was incomprehensible that Doc would suck on TV. Seeing him stammer awkwardly on the air, say nonsensical things like "Great players make great plays" and perform the deer-in-the-headlights routine was a little disarming. Every time the camera homed in on him, you could actually feel the tension in the studio. It was tangible. Before one Houston-Utah playoff game, Doc made history by predicting, "I think the key for Houston will be when Hakeem gets the ball, how fast he decides to either shoot, dribble or pass." That's an actual quote. I remember my old roommate Geoff and I spending the next fifteen minutes trying to determine what other options Hakeem could possibly have had on a basketball court, ultimately deciding on these: (a) turn the ball over, (b) call time out, (c) pass out, (d) shit on himself, or (e) drop dead. It was an unforgettable moment, as evidenced by the fact that I can remember where we were watching the game when it happened. Poor Dr. J. Some people just aren't meant to be on television.[63]

Isiah Thomas ('98–'00). NBC made a big deal about this hiring because, you know, Isiah was a great player, which means he'll be a great TV guy, right? (Whoops, I forgot—there's no correlation whatsoever.) Well, he didn't have much to say—which didn't matter much because partner Bob Costas was rusty from a twenty-two-year play-by-play layoff and treated every game like it was a radio telecast[64]—and you could barely hear Isiah because his meek, high-pitched voice was drowned out by any semiexcited crowd. When Detroit canned Doug Collins midway through the season, NBC signed him for a three-man booth (Costas, Collins and Isiah), a

63. Yes, I include myself.
64. Here's what Bob sounded like that first year (say this urgently out loud): "Scottie dribbles to the left . . . Mullin is on him . . . Scottie passes to Jordan . . . Jordan makes a move to his left . . . dribbles twice . . . gives it up to Kukoc . . . here's Kukoc . . . Kukoc on the drive! . . . *It goes in!* . . . and the Bulls lead *eighteen to sixteen! . . . Kukoc has six points for the Bulls! . . . Now here's Jackson dribbling it up the floor for Indiana . . .*" And so on. I hate when play-by-play guys talk too much. We have a TV. We can see.

problem because Collins was roughly ten thousand times more competent than Isiah (even if he suffered from Rick Barry–itis). Now Isiah couldn't get a word in edgewise, and even if he did, we couldn't hear him. By the time the Finals rolled around, you could practically hear the voice of NBC's producer imploring Collins to keep including Isiah in the broadcast. YouTube[65] the '98 Finals some time and watch how many times Collins starts a sentence with something like, "And Isiah, you know better than anyone that you can't pick up your dribble" or "I don't think the Jazz can hold Chicago off with Jordan playing like this . . . " Pause while NBC's producer screams in Collins' ear. ". . . Right, Isiah?" Holy shit, was it awkward. That may have been the worst three-man booth ever. NBC moved Isiah to the studio for the next two years, where he had nothing to say and spent most of the time grinning crazily like Gene Hackman's right-hand man in *No Way Out* just before he shoots himself. But everything paid off during the postgame celebration for the 2000 Finals: Peter Vecsey capped a classic two-month, I-don't-give-a-shit-if-you-fire-me run where he took more cheap shots than Claude Lemieux by totally blindsiding poor Isiah, randomly telling him on live TV as they were recapping everything, "And I just found out that you're the next Pacers coach!" Poor Isiah didn't know what to do; he hadn't even looked as flustered after Bird stole the ball in the '87 playoffs. The best part was Vecsey standing there with a defiant smirk while Isiah stuttered and stammered in front of a national TV audience. Phenomenal stuff. It made the entire lousy Isiah-on-TV era worth it.[66] (Unfortunately, it wised up the network executives for good. Not only did we never see Vecsey on network TV again, we've never seen another NBA Legend Turned Horrible TV Personality—although there's always a chance ABC will be dumb enough to hire Shaq when he finally retires. I have my fingers crossed.)

65. That's right, I used "YouTube" as a verb there. Sorry, I was feeling it.
66. At the time, I wrote "It's too bad Vecsey can't be the sideline reporter for the Oscars, just so he could interview people like Matt Damon and say things like, 'I guess that's why you're telling friends that you want to dump Winona Ryder!' That stunned look of resignation/horror/disgust/embarrassment that Vecsey constantly evokes should have an impact beyond the sports world."

1975–76: THE DUNK CONTEST

Two unforgettable moments stood out during a chaotic season that featured Kareem's trade to Los Angeles; two commissioner hirings, two NBA high schooler signings; three ABA teams folding; a bitter legal fight between Philly and New York over George McGinnis; the threat of a merger hanging over everything; the world-renowned triple-OT game (Phoenix-Boston); and a now-legendary ABA Slam Dunk Contest that put David Thompson on the map, turned Doc into a demigod and laid the groundwork for the creation of NBA All-Star Weekend. If you could pick one image that defined each league from 1970 to 1976, you'd pick Cowens skidding across the floor in the '74 Finals and Doc dunking from the foul line in the Dunk Contest. One league played with passion and did all the little things, while the other league embraced the schoolyard elements of the game, but in either clip you'll see fans jumping out of their seats. Still, basketball purists discounted the ABA because nobody played defense and everyone went for their own stats, so the fact that the league's signature moment happened in a Dunk Contest wasn't helping matters.

Doc's foul-line dunk had to be the most exhilarating basketball moment that didn't happen in an actual game. For one thing, nobody had seen one of these contests before, so they didn't know what to expect; once the dunks started coming, the fans were like thirteen-year-old boys looking at porn for the first time, almost overwhelmed by the sight of everything. You had the decade's most memorable player facing off against a precocious upstart, with Thompson going right before Doc, firing up the crowd with a superb double pump, and finishing with an incomprehensible-at-the-time 360, playing the role of the talented young band that's too good to be a warm-up band. (Think Springsteen opening for the Stones in '75.) You had Doc dramatically measuring his steps from one basket to another as the crowd shuffled in anticipation and wondered what the heck he was doing, finally realizing, "Wait a second, is he going to dunk from the foul line?" Then you had the dunk itself: Erving loping toward the basket and exploding from the foul line, his oversized hand making the basketball look like a golf ball, carrying and carrying and finally *tomahawking* the ball through the basket as everyone lost their collective shit. Doc's dunk stands alone for originality, pent-up drama, sheer significance and lasting impact, even if he screwed up by not saving that dunk for last. Right guy, right place, right time, right moment. Basketball was starting to go up—literally—and it wasn't a bad thing.[67]

SUMMER OF 1976: THE MERGER

This gets my One of the Greatest Summers Ever vote: our two hundredth Independence Day, the Montreal Olympics, Randy "Pink" Floyd's class doing senior hazing at Lee High School, Mark Fidrych's apex and the ABA-NBA merger in the span of three months? Come on. The merger process was given a jolt when the ABA hired a dick-swinging antitrust attorney named Fred Furth, who had some world-class negotiating sessions with the NBA's bright assistant commissioner—wait for it . . . wait for it—Mr. David Stern![68] Here's what they settled, with my comments in parentheses:

1. Denver, New York, San Antonio and Indiana joined for a cost of $3.2 million per team. Those teams would not receive TV money for three years, could not take part in the '76 college draft and would be called "expansion teams," but they *were* allowed to keep their players. The Nets also had to pay the Knicks $4.8 million over ten years for violating their territory rights.

   (My thoughts: A bit of a raping so far, although it's nice that the Knicks got even more money to throw away at bad players. My biggest issue was the NBA excluding ABA teams from a deep '76 rookie draft in which Johnny Davis (number twenty-two), Alex En-

---

67. The Slam Dunk Contest is a hundred times better in person than on television. Even if there's only one memorable dunk the entire night, it's still worth sitting there for three hours enduring all the other crappy events. I was there for Dwight Howard's Superman dunk in 2008 and that was a *moment.*

68. My favorite *Loose Balls* anecdote that doesn't involve Barnes: the ABA fell behind in payments that summer to Furth, so when one executive mentioned that they'd take care of the fee soon, Furth told him, "I know you will, because if you don't have $25,000 on my desk by Friday, Julius Erving will be working in my garden." Classic! Long live the Furth!

glish (number twenty-three), Lonnie Shelton (number twenty-five) and Dennis Johnson (number twenty-nine) dropped to Round 2. Shows how little leverage the ABA had at the time.)

2. Kentucky owner John Y. Brown received $3 million for folding his franchise, then spent half that money to buy Buffalo. So the four ABA teams that joined the NBA got crushed financially, but Brown bought in and pocketed $1.5 million? Huh? Meanwhile, the St. Louis owners struck the greatest mother lode in professional sports history, folding their shitty franchise for $2.2 million and one-seventh of the TV money from the four remaining ABA teams—money they were guaranteed in perpetuity. In other words, they received four-sevenths of a cut of the TV contract every year *forever.* Through 2009, that cut was worth about $150 million. Just free money falling out of the sky, year after year after year after year.[69]

(My thoughts: The Nets won two titles with Doc, only the league's signature player and a big reason for the merger, then got shafted to the degree that they sold Doc before the '77 season just to keep their franchise afloat. The Spirits had a terrible team that would have folded anyway—no fan support, no assets that remotely compared to Doc, no appeal as an NBA market whatsoever—and they somehow finagled a deal that was a hundred times better than New Jersey's deal. Go figure.)

3. Players from folded ABA franchises would be auctioned off in a dispersal draft, with price tags assigned to each player and Chicago guaranteed the first pick (so they could take Artis Gilmore). The remaining picks were made in reverse order of finish during the '76 season, with Atlanta trading the number two pick to Portland for Geoff Petrie, then Portland landing the two biggest prizes (Maurice Lucas at number two and Moses at number five).[70] Also, Detroit paid a whopping $500,000

69. How many meetings do you think Stern had with high-powered lawyers from 1984 to 2010 where he tried to figure out ways to weasel out of the St. Louis pact, failed, then unleashed a parade of *f*-bombs and kicked everyone out of the conference room? The over/under has to be 39.5.

70. Portland also had the fifth pick that year, stupidly taking Wally Walker over Adrian Dantley in a typical "let's take the white guy, maybe he's not as good as the black guy, but our fans will love him" 1970s move. They could have landed Dantley, Malone *and* Lucas in the same summer; instead, they dealt Moses, botched the Walker pick and *still* won the '77 title.

for Marvin Barnes in an apparent attempt to get Bob Lanier to hang himself.

(My thoughts: In the Things That Would Have Been Much More Fun if They Happened Now department, can't you see ESPN televising the ABA dispersal draft at like 2:00 p.m. on a Tuesday afternoon as Ric Bucher breaks the Portland/Atlanta trade, Chad Ford laments the lack of European players and Jay Bilas spends ten minutes raving about Malone's rebounding skills and "second jumpability"? Alas.)

4. The NBA agreed to abolish the reserve clause and allow free agency for any veteran player with an expiring contract. This was the single biggest sticking point—the owners wanted compensation, the players did not—and it could have dragged on for another few years if not for a brainstorm by NBA Players Association head Jeff Mullins: give the owners compensation for four years because that's how long it would have taken for the case to reach the Supreme Court, anyway. Everyone agreed and that was that. Compensation would be awarded by O'Brien's office as long as the two teams involved didn't agree first.

(My thoughts: This was the single biggest NBA moment since the shot clock. Everything about the way players were paid and contenders were built was about to change. For good and bad. And for the first few years, it was mostly bad.)

What ensued was the single zaniest summer of player movement in NBA history. Chicago and Houston reinvented themselves with franchise centers (Gilmore and Malone). Portland landed a rebounding sidekick for Walton. The Nets sold Doc to Philly for $3 million and traded Brian Taylor with two number one picks for Tiny Archibald.[71] Philly suddenly had the '75 ABA co-MVPs (Doc and McGinnis) on the same team. Moses bounced around twice before landing in Houston. The Knicks bought McAdoo from Buffalo and lavished him with a five-year, $2.5 million deal,

71. This ranks up there in the Dumb Sequences pantheon: you sell Doc but mortgage your future for Tiny Archibald? Huh? Those picks turned out to be number two overall two years in a row (Phil Ford and Otis Birdsong). And with that, three-plus decades of Nets hell had begun!

killing his incentive to give a shit until 1982. Gail Goodrich became the Jackie Robinson of free agency, inadvertently murdering professional basketball in New Orleans for two solid decades (hold that thought). Red Auerbach refused to pay Paul Silas market value, shipped him to Denver for Curtis Rowe, then bought Sidney Wicks from Portland (and murdered Celtic Pride in the process). None of the top five teams from '76 (Golden State, Phoenix, Boston, L.A., Cleveland) improved itself in any conceivable way. Throw in the rise of cocaine, free agency and escalating salaries and you need to get emotionally prepared for the weirdest three-year stretch in NBA history.

1976–77: THE CANNONBALL

Brace yourself: this might be the only time in sports history that a professional sports league didn't expand enough. The NBA jumped from eighteen franchises to twenty-two but added *twenty-eight* quality players to its talent pool, including four franchise guys (Erving, Gervin, Gilmore and Thompson) and a potential franchise guy (Moses).[72] Throw in a loaded draft class (John Lucas, Dantley, English, DJ, Parish, Mitch Kupchak, Walter Davis . . .) and there were two quality newcomers for every franchise. Suddenly we had teams struggling with alpha dog battles (McAdoo-Haywood, Erving-McGinnis, Barnes-Lanier) and contrasting styles (old-school versus playground), certain teams quickly gelling into contenders (Portland, Denver) or falling off (Boston, Phoenix, Cleveland, G-State) and fans alternately delighted by the ABA's infusion of athleticism and appalled by high-priced guys playing so selfishly. And if that's not enough, cocaine and freebasing were taking the league by storm. Again, silliest year ever—like mixing up everyone's Madden rosters, restarting a franchise season and randomly giving drug problems to 25 percent of the players.

72. The others: 5 All-Stars (Ron Boone, Don Buse, Dan Issel, Bobby Jones, Billy Knight), 4 future All-Stars (Larry Kenon, Maurice Lucas, Dan Roundfield, James Silas), 14 valuable rotation guys (Mack Calvin, M. L. Carr, Don Chaney, Louie Dampier, Caldwell Jones, Swen Nater, Mark Olberding, Tom Owens, Billy Paultz, Ralph Simpson, Brian Taylor, Dave Twardzik, John Williamson, Willie Wise), and one high-priced head case (Marvin Barnes).

Even the records bore out the chaos: no team won more than 52 games and only one team won less than 28 (the Nets). Meanwhile, the "ABA was a quality league" argument gained steam when nine alumni became '77 All-Stars and five played prominent roles in the '77 Finals. The infusion of ABA blood made the league faster, deeper and infinitely more athletic; other than Bill Walton, the league's most thrilling players were ABA guys (Doc, Ice, Thompson and Moses). The days of a potbellied Nelson logging big minutes in the Finals were long gone, personified by Phoenix returning every key player and finishing 34–48. Still, it was an upheaval of sorts. Like watching the water in a pool thrashing around after a cannonball.

The water kept splashing the following summer, when eleven of the top eighteen draft picks switched by trade and two were repackaged a second time. Trading picks was a relatively recent trend; as late as 1971, everyone picked in their spots and that was that. All hell broke loose in 1977, with two trades netting Milwaukee the first, third and eleventh picks in a superb draft—and, of course, they botched two of them (Kent Benson and Ernie Grunfeld, back when teams could waste two top-twelve picks on slow white guys without getting creamed on the Internet and talk radio). Still, they were the first team to say, "We're going to rebuild with multiple picks," a relatively bold move in a league where nearly every franchise was losing money and worrying about its precarious relationship with fans.[73] We also had our first full-fledged free agency summer in 1977, with Jamaal Wilkes (Lakers), Gus Williams (Seattle), Truck Robinson (New Orleans), Bobby Dandridge (Washington), Jim Cleamons (New York) and E. C. Coleman (G-State) switching teams.[74] Usually teams banged out compensation themselves, with the most famous example happening in '79, when Boston signed Detroit's M. L. Carr and it ballooned into a larger deal: Carr and two future number one picks for McAdoo (used to land Parish and McHale a year later). When San Diego signed Walton that same summer, the teams couldn't agree and left it up to the league. The wackiest free agent transaction will always be the '79 Clippers signing Brian Taylor

73. This spawned a three-year trading frenzy that led to this startling fact: Chicago (number two) was the only top-fifteen team to pick in its assigned spot in the 1979 draft.
74. Coleman made first-team All-Defense in 1977 and was out of the league within 18 months. As far as I can tell, this is the most random thing that ever happened.

from Denver, then giving up two second-round picks, four kilos of cocaine and their best drug connection as compensation.[75]

Despite unprecedented upheaval, our first postcannonball Finals (Portland-Philly) made everyone happy: CBS (highest-rated Finals ever), the NBA (Bill Walton, backing up the "great white hope" hype), Brent Musburger (who nicknamed Walton "Mountain Man" and tried to become the Cosell to his Ali), basketball purists (delighted that Portland "saved" the league) and virulent racists (who enjoyed the way this series was "analyzed" by mainstream media). The Sixers were painted as a disorganized schoolyard team, a product of the ABA and its "look at me" culture, just a bunch of high-priced blacks who didn't care about making each other better. They had players with nicknames like "Jellybean"[76] and "World," their layup lines were more famous than any of their wins, and because everyone was out for themselves, Doc was unfairly considered to be more sizzle than steak. By contrast, Portland played like Russell's old Celtics teams and thrived on fast breaks and ball movement, with everything hinging on Walton's once-in-a-generation skills. They started three white guys, their best player had red hair and their point guard had a crew cut. Their deliriously happy fans filled a 12,666-seat bandbox and made every game sound like a mid-sixties Beatles concert. Even their rough but lovable bald coach barked out orders and looked like he should have been running one of those *Dead Poets Society*–type boarding schools. So when the Blazers swept the Lakers, then rallied back from a two-games-to-none lead by winning the next four from Philly, they defeated the NBA's two biggest quote-unquote problems in one fell swoop: Kareem (the surliest of superstars, someone who had just worn everyone out) and the overtly prejudiced belief that undisciplined, overpaid black guys really *were* ruining the game. That's why Portland's "quest" to save basketball made for ratings magic. As long as Walton and the Blazers were kicking some selfish black ass, the average white sports fan would pay attention to the NBA.

75. Be honest: part of you wanted to believe this.
76. That would be Jellybean Joe Bryant, or as we know him now, Kobe's dad. He was an unapologetic gunner who spent much of the '77 season demanding to be traded. Let's just say that the apple landed about 3 inches from the tree.

(And if the Blazers didn't keep kicking some selfish black ass? Then the NBA was in trouble.)[77]

1977–78: THE BLOWN TIRE

If '77 was the NBA's craziest season, then the '78 season had to be its most damaging. Let's rank the problems in order of least harmful to most harmful.

Crisis no. 1: the drive-by shooting of the Blazers. Walton went down with Portland sporting a 50–10 record and generating buzz that they might be the greatest team ever. In one fell swoop, the NBA lost its signature team, most visible white star, most compelling story line and most entertaining team not just for '78 but '79 and '80, too. Imagine Jordan breaking his foot during Chicago's 72-win season and disappearing for the next three years. How does that Heat-Sonics Finals in '96 grab you? Or consecutive Indiana-Utah Finals in '97 and '98? Get the idea? Walton's injury was practically a death blow until Larry and Magic showed up.[78]

Crisis no. 2: cocaine. Everywhere at this point . . . and nobody knew it was bad yet. I don't need to spell it out for you. Just watch *Boogie Nights*. You should, anyway. I made ten references to it already and could easily go for thirty more. Just rent it. It's a real film, Jack.

Crisis no. 3: consecutive Bullets-Sonics concussions. Do you realize the '78 and '79 Finals were the only NBA Finals of the past half century that didn't have a recognizable superstar or big-market team? The '78 Finals

77. I'm stating the *perception*, not the reality. It's sad that I have to clarify that. By the way, Jabaal Abdul-Simmons may have been the only white American outside Philly rooting for the Sixers in the '77 Finals. Every Doc dunk made me "*Gilligan's Island* is on!"–level happy. I was also fascinated by Lloyd Free and his jump shot; when he changed his name to World B. Free and averaged 30 a game in San Diego, I felt vindicated for jumping on the Free bandwagon so early. That was the perfect combo of talent and craziness that I was looking for in elementary school.
78. Let's say Walton stays healthy and Portland wins three straight titles. Our '80 Conference Final matchups: Philly-Boston and Portland-L.A. with Walton, Bird, Doc, Kareem and Magic. Wow.

stretched over eighteen agonizing days to accommodate CBS; Unseld won Finals MVP and a brand-new car, although the ceremony was marred when the distraught head of CBS asked if he could borrow Unseld's car to kill himself in it. The bad luck extended beyond Walton going down: the league barely missed out on a Sixers-Nuggets Finals in '78 ("Thompson versus the Doctor!") and a thoroughly entertaining Spurs-Suns Finals in '79 ("Davis and Westphal take on the Iceman!"). If Stern had been running the league in '78 and '79, you might have seen that decade's equivalent of Dick Bavetta or Bennett Salvatore reffing a few of those pivotal Spurs-Bullets, Sixers-Bullets and Nuggets-Sonics games. And you know it's true.[79]

Crisis no. 4: the CBS problem. A heated contract negotiation that spring resulted in a four-year, $74 million deal that the network tried to back out of even as it was signing it. As part of the deal (and we're using that word loosely), CBS was given carte blanche to run playoff games on tape delay, tinker with playoff dates/times and scale back on the number of Sunday telecasts. And cable TV hadn't taken off yet. Yikes.

Crisis no. 5: fighting. Fighting had always been considered part of basketball, an inevitable outcome of a physical sport (much like hockey). Willis Reed put himself on the map by cleaning out the '67 Lakers. Maurice Lucas made his reputation by dropping Gilmore. Dennis Awtrey lasted ten years because he was the Guy Who Once Decked Kareem. Ricky Sobers turned around the '76 Warriors-Suns series by socking Barry. Calvin Murphy had the league's most famous Napoleon complex, frequently beating up bigger guys and scoring a knockout over six-foot-nine Sidney Wicks. So when the Blazers and Sixers had their ugly brawl in Game 2 of the '77 Finals, nobody was really *that* appalled. It started when Darryl Dawkins tried to sucker-punch Bobby Gross (hitting teammate Doug Collins instead), then backpedaled right into a flying elbow from

---

79. Four perfect candidates: Seattle at Denver, '78 (Game 5, series tied at 2); Philly at Washington, '78 (Game 6, Bullets leading 3–2); Seattle at Phoenix, '79 (Game 6, Phoenix leading 3–2); Washington at San Antonio, '79 (Game 6, Spurs leading 3–2). The less sexy team won all four of those games.

Lucas,[80] followed by the two of them squaring off like 1920s bare-knuckle boxers before everyone jumped in. After getting ejected, Dawkins ended up destroying a few toilets in the Philly locker room. Was anyone suspended? Of course not! Not to sound like Grumpy Old Editor, but that's the way it worked in the seventies and we *loved it*! Portland swept the last four games and everyone agreed that Lucas' flying elbow was the turning point of the series. It was the perfect NBA fight for the times—no injuries, tremendous TV and a valuable lesson learned about sticking up for your teammates.[81]

Fast-forward to October: *Sports Illustrated* revolves its NBA preview issue around "the Enforcers," sticking Lucas' menacing mug on the cover and glorifying physical players in a pictorial ominously titled "Nobody, but Nobody, Is Gonna Hurt My Teammates." In retrospect, it's an incredible piece to read; the magazine took intimidating-looking pictures of each enforcer like they were WWF wrestlers, with Kermit Washington (gulp) posing shirtless like a boxer. Each picture was accompanied with text to make these bruisers sound like a combination of Clint Eastwood and Charles Bronson. An example: "Kermit Washington, the 6'8", 230-pound Laker strong man, is a nice quiet person who lifts weights and sometimes separates people's heads from their shoulders. In one memorable game last November in Buffalo, Washington ended an elbow skirmish with John Shumate by dropping the 6'9" forward with a flurry of hooks and haymakers. 'Shumate came apart in sections,' an eyewitness said."

Wow, punching people never sounded so cool! Since *SI* was the influential sports voice at the time—remember, we didn't have ESPN, *USA Today*, cable or the Internet yet—the tone of that issue coupled with kudos given to Murphy and Lucas the previous season may have inspired the violent incidents that followed. Lucas was a valuable player who wasn't good enough to command an *SI* cover unless it was for something

---

80. That was an "I'm standing up for my teammate" moment that ranks alongside Flatch punching the guy who cheap-shotted Jimmy Chitwood in the '54 North Sectional Regionals, then getting thrown into the trophy case and cutting his shoulder. *That's a gutless way to win! That's a gutless way to win!*

81. The NBA spruced up the fighting penalties after the '77 Finals, doubling the maximum fine ($10,000) and eliminating limits for game suspensions.

else . . . you know, like beating the shit out of someone. Was it okay to punch other players in the face? According to *Sports Illustrated*, actually, it was. As long as you had a good reason.

Fast-forward to opening night: Kent Benson sneaks a cheap elbow into Kareem's stomach, doubling Kareem over and sending him wobbling away from the play in obvious pain. An enraged Kareem regroups and charges Benson from behind, sucker-punching him and breaking his jaw.[82] Unlike other ugly NBA events from the past, this one had a black-guy-decking-a-white-guy clip playing on every local newscast around the country, with the black guy doubling as the league's signature player of the seventies. Uh-oh. The league decides against suspending Kareem, deeming it punishment enough that he's missing two months with a broken hand from the punch.

Fast-forward to December: Kermit gets belted by Houston's Kevin Kunnert after a free throw and they start fighting. Kareem jumps in to hold Kunnert back, Kermit nails Kunnert (who slumps over holding his face),[83] then Kermit whirls around, sees Rudy Tomjanovich running toward him and throws what Lakers assistant Jack McKinney later called "the greatest punch in the history of mankind," breaking Rudy's face on impact and his skull after it slammed off the floor. Kareem later described the punch as sounding like somebody had dropped a melon onto a concrete floor. Rudy rolled over, grabbed his face, kicked his legs and bled all over the court as everyone watched in horror. The final damage: two weeks in intensive care, a broken jaw, a broken nose, a fractured face and a skull cracked so badly that Rudy could taste spinal fluid dripping into his mouth.

Four forces were working against Kermit other than, you know, the fact he nearly killed another player. With Kareem's haymaker happening two months earlier, the combination of those punches spawned dueling epidemics of "NBA Violence Is Out of Control!" headlines and editorials

82. In *Giant Steps*, a book that will make you hate Kareem between 25 and 30 percent more by the last page, Kareem bitches about Awtrey making his reputation for sucker-punching him from behind, then neglects to mention that he did the same thing to Benson . . . and later brags about the Benson punch. He also suckered Happy Hairston during the '72 season (it's on YouTube).

83. The cameras missed it, but Kunnert got clocked—even when they're scraping Rudy off the floor, you can see Kunnert still wiping blood off his own face with a towel. Only 10 months later, Kunnert and Kermit were teammates on the Clippers, setting up one of the all-time awkward "Hey, good to see you again" moments in NBA history.

(with everyone forgetting that *SI* had glorified that same violence ten weeks earlier) and "Why do I want to follow a league that allows black guys to keep kicking the crap out of white guys when I'm a white guy?" doubts (the underlying concern that nobody mentioned out loud unless you were sitting in the clubhouse of a country club, as well as the subplot that scared the living shit out of CBS and the owners). Second, the only existing replay made Kermit seem like an unprovoked madman out for white blood, but the cameras missed Kunnert's initial elbow and the rest of their fight, catching the action only after Kunnert was sinking into Kareem's arms and Rudy was running at Kermit. Third, *Saturday Night Live* made light of the incident on "Weekend Update," showing the punch over and over again for a gag and giving it new life.[84] And fourth, with TV ratings faltering, attendance dropping and the league battling the "too many white fans, too many black players" issue, really, you couldn't have asked for worse timing. It was a best/worst extreme—the most destructive punch ever thrown on a basketball court, the perfect specimen to throw such a punch,[85] the worst possible result, the worst possible timing (CBS' contract was up after the season) and the worst possible color combination (a black guy decking a white guy). Kermit was suspended for sixty days without pay—no hearing, no appeal, nothing—losing nearly $54,000 in salary and becoming Public Enemy No. 1. (This went well beyond a few death threats. After Kermit returned from the suspension, police advised him against ordering hotel room service because they worried someone would poison him.) And Rudy eventually sued the league for $3 million, with his laywers portraying Kermit as a vicious Rottweiler who had been allowed off his leash by neglectful owners. Nothing good came from this incident. Nothing.

The Lakers coldly traded Kermit during his suspension, shipping him to Boston for my favorite Celtic at the time, Charlie Scott. Dark day in the Abdul-Simmons house. I remember attending my first Kermit/Celtics

---

84. This was a much bigger deal in 1977 because we only had a few channels and *SNL* averaged 30–35 million viewers. In the segment, Garrett Morris "defends" Kermit and says, "We blacks get blamed for everything. Look at this film. Why, he just grazed the cat. Whoops! Let's look at it from another angle . . ." One of his only funny moments ever.

85. In *Breaks*, Halberstam argues that it's the most devastating punch ever thrown—a chiseled specimen planting his feet and throwing a perfect right cross into the face of someone sprinting toward him. Or as Grumpy Old Editor calls it, a "cosmic accident." Ten years earlier, Willis Reed easily could have been Kermit during that '67 Lakers brawl.

game, seeking him out in warm-ups, finding him and thinking, "That's him, that's the guy," then watching him fearfully like he was like Michael Myers or something. He may have been the league's first pariah. But Kermit won Boston fans over immediately. Here was this tragic, forlorn figure carrying himself with undeniable dignity, attacking the boards with relentless fury, injecting life into Cowens like nobody had since Silas, throwing every repressed emotion into these games. Sometimes when the Garden was quiet—and that happened a lot, since we only won 32 games and fans were fleeing in droves—you could even hear Kermit grunt when he grabbed a ballboard: *uhhhhhhhhh.* Kermit averaged 11.8 points, 10.5 rebounds and 52 percent shooting in just twenty-seven minutes per game. By the end of the season, Kermit had become my favorite Celtic and I was convinced that Rudy's face had attacked Kermit's fist.

Of course, we traded him that summer. Go figure.[86] He moved to San Diego and then Portland, where Blazer fans embraced him the way the Boston fans had. When Halberstam wrote beautifully about him a few years later—really, one of the great character profiles ever written of an athlete—Kermit evolved into something of a victim, culminating in John Feinstein writing an entire book about the punch in 2002.[87] Maybe Rudy was in the wrong place at the wrong time, but so was Kermit. Like hundreds of NBA players before him, Kermit threw an angry punch with mean-spirited intentions . . . only this one connected. He became the league's Hannibal Lecter, the guy who threw The Punch and nearly killed someone. The NBA took violence more seriously after that, making fighting ejections mandatory and handing out longer suspensions, although it's turned into somewhat of an urban legend that Kermit's punch changed everything. The league didn't make a concerted effort to shed fighting completely until an ugly Knicks-Bulls brawl in the '94 playoffs

---

86. That was the year the Celtics fell apart and Hondo retired. When Irv Levin switched franchises with John Y. Brown and moved the Braves to San Diego, he took Kermit with him. I was crushed. Two favorites gone in 4 months.

87. It's really a long magazine profile, only Feinstein doubled the word count and repeated more than a few stories to stretch it into a book. Feinstein was a big influence on *The Book of Basketball* because he rushes his books to get to the next one. I want you to feel the opposite with mine. I want you to say, "Not only did I get my money's worth, but honestly, I'm burned out on Simmons for like 9 months, that book could have been about 200 pages less." Wait, you're already saying that? What the hell? We're not even at the halfway point yet! Get some coffee or something.

spilled into the stands with a horrified David Stern in attendance. *That* was the tipping point, not Kermit's punch.

1978–79: LIFE SUPPORT

Here's where the *perception* that the NBA was in trouble took hold, thanks to tape-delayed playoff games, declining attendance, star players mailing in games, Walton's continued absence, Buffalo's move to San Diego, Erving's disappointing play in Philly, a 75:25 black-to-white ratio and something of a smear campaign from various newspaper columnists and even *Sports Illustrated*. Since sports fans in 1978 and 1979 took their cue from *SI,* everyone was thinking the same thing: "The NBA is in trouble." Even if it wasn't necessarily true. With Boston already owning Bird's draft rights, Indiana State's undefeated '79 season assumed greater significance for NBA fans as it unfolded. Bird loomed as the potential savior of a floundering Celtics franchise, and when Bird battled Magic's Michigan State squad in the 1979 NCAA Finals, that boosted Magic's profile to savior status as well. By sheer coincidence, two of the league's three biggest markets (L.A. and Chicago) controlled the first two picks in the '79 draft. The Lakers won the coin toss and Magic, while Chicago's ensuing tailspin ended with Jordan saving them five years later. Throw in Boston signing Bird and everyone wins![88] Within a year, Bird saved the Celtics, Magic gave Kareem a pulse for the first time in five years, Philly finally built the right cast of role players around Doc, all three teams won 60-plus games and made the Conference Finals, and Magic put himself on the map with the clinching game of the Finals.

A bigger savior was coming that summer: cable. Just weeks after the NBA signed a three-year, $1.5 million deal with the USA Network for Thursday night doubleheaders and early round playoff games, ESPN launched the first-ever twenty-four-hour sports network on September 7, 1979, paving the way for *SportsCenter,* fun-to-watch highlights, and an eventual competitor for the league's cable rights. You couldn't

---

88. The Bulls passed up Sidney Moncrief for David Greenwood at number two. Ouch. In Magic's book, he writes that Jerry West wanted to trade down and pick Moncrief— remember, they already had Norm Nixon playing point—only Dr. Jerry Buss overruled him because he was buying the team and Magic was a bigger name.

find better advertising than slickly packaged game summaries that featured every exciting dunk, pass, and big shot and left out all the unseemly stuff. (You know, like fistfights, empty seats, utter indifference and players jogging around and looking spent for the wrong reasons.) David Stern believes the arrival of ESPN and cable TV had more to do with saving the NBA than Bird and Magic, although he feels like the whole "saving" part has been totally overblown.[89] Which it probably was. Remember, the Dallas Mavericks joined in 1980–81 for a cool expansion fee of $12 million, finishing 15–67 that season and spawning countless "Yeesh, maybe they should have had J. R. Ewing coach the team" jokes that were hysterically funny twenty-nine years ago. How bad could things have been if rich guys were throwing out $12 million checks to join the NBA?

Still, here's how much the NBA/CBS relationship had deteriorated: Despite being given two appealing Conference Finals in 1980 (Boston-Philly and L.A.-Seattle), CBS showed only three games live, broadcast another three on tape delay and completely ignored the other four (including a pivotal Game 4 in Phoenix).[90] When they landed Kareem, Magic and Doc in the Finals, they made the Lakers and Sixers play Games 3 and 4 back-to-back on a Saturday/Sunday, then gave affiliates the option of airing Game 6 (a potential clincher) either live or on tape delay at eleven-thirty at night. Since it was a Friday during May sweeps, nearly every affiliate opted for reruns of *The Incredible Hulk, The Dukes of Hazzard* and *Dallas,* with only the Philly, L.A., Portland and Seattle markets carrying the game live. That meant one of the most famous basketball games ever played (Magic starting at center in place of an injured Kareem, then carrying the Lakers to the title) happened well after midnight on tape delay in nearly every American city. Think how many young fans could have been sucked in for life. On the other hand, can you really blame the CBS affiliates there? I mean, both *The Incredible Hulk* and *The Dukes of Hazzard* plus *Dallas* to boot? That was a murderer's row! After a three-minute Googling frenzy, I can report that *Dallas* and *Dukes* were the top two shows in 1980; *Dukes* had about 21 million viewers and *Dallas* had a jaw-dropping

89. How do I know this? I called the commish and asked him. We talked for 35 minutes. Amazingly, he could still recall every detail and number off the top of his head 33 years later.
90. Incredibly, no tape exists of the four missing games, but you can buy the first two seasons of *Simon and Simon* on DVD. I don't get the world sometimes.

27 million. Obviously they weren't dumping those shows for an episode of *The League with Overpaid Black Guys Who Do Drugs*.[91] So yeah, it stinks that nobody watched Magic's famous 42-point game live. But it stinks more that the NBA screwed up by not scheduling that game for Saturday afternoon so everyone could see it.[92]

One year later, the unthinkable happened: even though a star-studded affair between Philly and Boston doubled as the greatest Conference Final ever played, CBS aired only nine of a possible fourteen Final Four games (six of those nine were tape-delayed) and showed four of the six '81 Finals games on tape delay (including the clincher). In a related story, the broadcast of the '81 Finals was the lowest-rated in history (6.7)[93] and an improbable '81 Western Finals matchup between the 40–42 Rockets and 40–42 Kings probably made CBS consider the first-ever tape delay of a tape-delayed telecast.[94] So yes, the NBA needed cable. Badly.

1979–80: THREEEEEEEEEEEEE!

Do you realize that it took the three-point line eight solid years to fully establish itself? A quick timeline:

1980. The old "dipping the toes in the water" mentality takes hold. Only Brian Taylor (239) and Rick Barry (221) attempt more than 200 threes,

---

91. Just stating the stigma, not the reality. Our top-ten TV programs in 1980: *Dallas, Dukes of Hazzard, 60 Minutes, M*A*S*H, Love Boat, The Jeffersons, Alice, House Calls, Three's Company, Little House on the Prairie.* You know it was a competitive TV year when *C.H.I.P.S.* was twenty-fifth.

92. Had Game 6 moved to Saturday, Game 7 could have moved to Tuesday and bumped CBS' worst night of the week: some rerun (extensive Googling couldn't figure out which one) followed by a "Movie of the Week." I did find that a show named *California Fever* held the 8:00–9:00 spot until December 10, 1979. IMDb.com's synopsis: "Vince and Ross are suburban L.A. teenagers enjoying disco, surfing, cars and the rest of the Southern California lifestyle." One of the show's stars? Lorenzo Lamas! I loved the late '70s.

93. CBS' ratings for every Finals from '76 to '90: 11.5 (Boston-Phoenix), 12.7 (Philadelphia-Portland), 9.9 (Washington-Seattle), 7.2 (Washington-Seattle), 8.0 (L.A.-Philadelphia), 6.7 (Boston-Houston), 13.0 (L.A.-Philadelphia), 12.3 (L.A.-Philadelphia), 12.3 (Boston-L.A.), 13.7 (Boston-L.A.), 14.1 (Boston-Houston), 15.9 (Boston-L.A.), 15.4 (L.A.-Detroit), 15.1 (L.A.-Detroit), 12.3 (Portland-Detroit).

94. "Wedman! Dunleavy! It's the Western Conference Finals on CBS!"

only twelve players attempt more than 100 for the season, only five players finish at better than 38 percent, and the average NBA game features fewer than six attempted threes. For the Celtics, I remember Chris Ford emerging as our "three-point threat" (nailing 43 percent of them) and feeling like this run-of-the-mill shooting guard suddenly had real value for us. Every time he made one, the crowd went crazy. So *something* was happening. We just weren't sure yet.

1981. A slight backlash. Mike Bratz leads the league with just 169 attempts; only Brian Taylor shoots better than 34 percent (38.3 percent to be exact); the league average drops from 28 percent to 24.5 percent; and attempted threes drop to four per game. Bizarre. Although we do have our first signature three: in Game 6 of the Finals, Bird nails a back-breaking three to clinch the title, then cements it with a joyous fist pump that was exciting even on tape delay when I was half asleep at one-thirty in the morning.

1982. Still nobody biting. Only four players attempt more than 100 threes. We did have another signature moment in Game 5 of the Celtics-Bullets series: Frankie Johnson and Gerald Henderson got into a fourth-quarter fight, then a pissed-off Johnson drained three treys (including a 30-foot bomb) to push the game into overtime before Boston prevailed in double OT. That game was televised live by USA, so it's the first documented time anyone went into eff-you mode with threes.[95]

1983. Crickets. Only four guys attempted more than 100 threes and the league's average was a paltry 24 percent. Of the leaders who qualified, Mike Dunleavy finished first (34 percent) and Isiah Thomas was second (28 percent), ironic since he's the worst long-range shooter of any modern point guard.

1984. There's a little traction when Utah's Darrell Griffith leads the league in attempts (252), makes (91) and percentage (36.1 percent). How's that for irony? A guy nicknamed Dr. Dunkenstein was keeping the three alive?

---

95. Remember the days when players could get in fights and remain in the game? Then the Kermit punch happened and everything changed . . . oh, wait, not true.

1985. Threes climb to 6.2 per game; the league's average climbs to 28.2 percent; fifteen players attempt 100-plus threes; four players break the 40 percent mark; and the three gains "cool" status when Bird adds it to his arsenal (making 42.7 percent and draining two memorable ones in his 60-point game).

1986. Our long-awaited breakthrough includes:

1. The first three-point contest at All-Star Weekend, which Bird wins handily after guaranteeing victory beforehand.[96]

2. The Legend getting inspired by his title and adopting the three as a weapon, ripping off a ten-game stretch later that month in which he made 25 of 34 threes. By season's end, he led the league in attempts (194) and makes (82) but finished fourth in percentage (42.3 percent). Beyond that, the Legend becomes the first to use threes as a psychological weapon, draining four in the fourth quarter of Boston's sweep over Milwaukee in the Conference Finals, then making the ludicrous "dribble out of the paint, dribble around three guys, find a spot in front of Houston's bench, and launch an Eff You Three" that nearly caused the Garden's roof to cave in during the clinching game of the '86 Finals.

3. Three-point specialists were emerging like Craig Hodges (45%), Trent Tucker (44%), Kyle Macy (41%), Michael Cooper (39%) and Dale Ellis (36%), guys who spread the floor and opened things up down low.

4. Three legitimately memorable threes: Doc banking a buzzer-beater to beat the Celtics on national TV; Dudley Bradley winning a playoff game over Philly with an improbable buzzer-beater; and Jeff Malone making the crazy "chase down the loose ball and falling out of bounds" three that they showed in "The NBA . . . It's FANNNNNtastic!" commercial for a solid year.[97]

96. Even better, they used the *Miami Vice* theme for everyone's turn. Two of my biggest heroes in the mid-'80s were Bird and Sonny Crockett—now they were basically teaming up? Throw in a girlfriend putting out right after the contest and that could have been the greatest night of my sixteen-year life. So close. I was one piece away.

97. My second-favorite three ever behind Bird's three in the 60-point game that didn't count and ended with him falling into the trainer's lap as the Hawks celebrated.

1987. Bingo! Threes climb to nearly 10 per game, the league's percentage climbs over 30 percent, eight players attempt 200-plus threes and twenty attempt at least 125 threes. And if Bird made that three to win Game 4 of the '87 Finals (page 26), we would have had ourselves the most famous three ever. Anyway, that's how the three became the *threeeeeeeeeeeee!* It was an eight-year process.

One other trend opened up offenses: a point guard boon. Of the twenty-two NBA teams in 1981, half employed true PGs: Magic Johnson/ Norm Nixon, Tiny Archibald, Mo Cheeks, Gus Williams,[98] Kevin Porter, Rickey Green, Johnny Davis, Eddie Johnson, Micheal Ray Richardson, John Lucas and Phil Ford. With Isiah Thomas and Johnny Moore joining the mix the following season, that's an inordinately high number of true points, isn't it? No wonder scoring and field goal percentages kept going up. The '78 teams averaged 108.5 points and 46.9 percent shooting; by '84, those numbers had risen to 110.1 and 49.1 percent (and those numbers would have been higher if everyone wasn't jacking up bad threes). The days of the '77 Lakers nearly making the Finals without a single ball handler were over, and if you ever see any of those Philly-Boston games from 1981, watch Tiny and Cheeks put on an absolute clinic—just two guys who knew how to run fast breaks, handle the ball, bang home 15-footers and penetrate whenever they needed to penetrate. What a pleasure.

1980–81: NOSE CANDY

Cocaine use went from recreational to potentially league-altering in 1980. Why do I know this? Because the following things happened:

• During a practice before the 1980 Finals, the Lakers were stretching when a coked-out Spencer Haywood simply passed out. He was excused for the rest of the postseason. Quickly. The Broken Mirror strikes again! It's amazing he wasn't on the floor for the Kermit-Rudy punch.

---

98. Technically, Gus wasn't running a team because his agent, Howard Slusher, foolishly advised him to hold out for the entire '81 season in a misguided effort to get a new deal. I think Slusher secretly advised the dolts running the Writers Guild during their 2007–8 strike.

- Utah's Terry Furlow was killed in a car accident just one week after the '80 Finals ended. Furlow was driving and his blood had traces of cocaine and Valium. Hmmmmmm.[99]
- In August 1980, spurred on by Richard Pryor setting himself on fire in a freebasing accident, the *L.A. Times* released an investigative feature about drug abuse within the celebrity culture and reported that cocaine and freebasing had become a borderline epidemic in the NBA, with then-Atlanta GM Stan Kasten estimating the number of players dabbling in drugs at 75 percent. Seventy-five percent!
- When *SI* wrote about David Thompson being his "old soaring self" in November of 1980, the piece included repeated references to cocaine rumors the previous season, with Thompson not really denying them by telling an acquaintance, "I'm not doing anything worse than what everybody else in the NBA is doing."[100]

Should we have been surprised? Look at what was happening in the late seventies and early eighties: widespread coke use had taken off within the music/movie/television industries, prep schools, discos, nightclubs and every professional sports league,[101] but everyone remembers the NBA struggling most because we could *see* the effects (bleary eyes, skinny bodies, inconsistent and lethargic play). There isn't a more naked sport than basketball. Nobody can deny that from 1977 to 1983, certain stars struggled as they should have been peaking; certain young stars openly battled personal issues; and certain veteran stars acted erratically, missed scores of practices, burned the candle at both ends and/or had their careers end abruptly. We learned the identity of some of them thanks to drug rehab

99. Former teammate Eddie Johnson later told *SI* that Furlow, his best friend, was a freebaser and "did a lot of things I didn't want him to do. I tried to get him to change, but Terry felt like he could conquer anything." You'll understand the irony within two pages.

100. Denver made Thompson take responsibility for the team's crappy '80 season by making him return $200K to help its financial troubles (which Denver loaned back with interest by 1983). Can you imagine the Players Association going for that now? Also, how big a favor did they inadvertently do for Thompson? That absolutely would have been coke money.

101. During this same stretch, the NHL suspended New York's Don Murdoch for 40 games for coke possession; baseball suspended Steve Howe; the NFL's "drug problem" appeared on the cover of *SI* in 1982; and Mackenzie Phillips tried to snort the entire cast of *One Day at a Time.*

stints and public admissions—Thompson, Walter Davis, John Drew, Richardson, John Lucas, Barnes, Bernard King, Eddie Johnson—and we'll always wonder about some of the others (including one of the era's biggest stars, someone who became infamous in NBA circles for his surreal ability to thrive even after he had used cocaine). Regardless, there were an inordinate number of "What the hell happened to him?" and "Why did his career inexplicably end?" guys for such a brief time frame; after Furlow's death and the *L.A. Times* report, it's hard to figure how two more years passed before the powers that be did anything.[102]

Some teams traded troubled players instead of helping them. The Knicks dumped Richardson, the Nets dumped Bernard, the Hawks dumped Drew; it's like they wanted to get *anything* of value before those guys snorted themselves out of the league. The '81 Warriors suspended Lucas for their last eight games while fighting for a playoff spot; then again, he didn't leave them much choice after no-showing six games and missing three team flights and over a dozen practices.[103] When Drew finally sought help in 1983, he admitted to the *New York Times* that he'd been freebasing for three years and snorting cocaine since 1978. You're telling me his teams didn't notice? Or that the Lakers didn't notice Haywood sniffling his way through the '80 season? (That same piece revealed that Buck Williams, speaking at an awards dinner that year, had estimated the percentage of NBA players using drugs as "maybe 20 or 30 percent," adding that the figure was much lower than he thought it would be. Much *lower*? Really?) It turned out to be a fairly wasted era for basketball; maybe it's good thing everything was tape-delayed.

What's the greatest NBA coke-era story that I can print? A 1982 *SI* feature about troubled Hawks guard Eddie Johnson casually included revelations that Atlanta had placed him in a psychiatric facility against his will, that Eddie had stolen a Porsche from a car dealer, that he'd been arrested for gun possession and cocaine possession in separate incidents and that he'd jumped out of a second-story apartment to evade drug

102. The '79 and '80 Hawks had Drew, Furlow *and* Eddie Johnson. I spent 20 minutes looking for a freebase pipe in their '80 team picture and couldn't find it.

103. In a June '81 *SI* piece, Lucas denied using coke and claimed he was suffering from depression, a diagnosis confirmed in the piece by his therapist, Dr. Robert Strange, or as he'd come to be known, "the worst therapist of all time." Within a few years, Lucas admitted to snorting everything in sight for most of his career. I love the "SI Vault."

dealers who were shooting at him.[104] (I vote for Don Cheadle to play Eddie in the movie.) And you know what? That's honorable mention. We have to give first prize to the Broken Mirror himself, Spencer Haywood. After Paul Westhead suspended him for the '80 Finals, Haywood wrote in his 1988 autobiography that he hired a Mafia hit man to kill his coach before changing his mind. I'm almost positive this would have marred the Finals. Also, that revelation led to my favorite quote from the coke era: Haywood remembering in the book, "I left the Forum and drove off in my Rolls that night thinking one thought—that Westhead must die." Now that's a great high school yearbook quote.

(One positive this season: free agent compensation was replaced by right of first refusal, so we didn't *really* have free agency, but we kind of did. Example: L.A. signs Mitch Kupchak, the Bullets agree not to match and Washington ends up with Jim Chones, Brad Holland and a 1983 number one pick for "not refusing." I like the right of first refusal; it's really too bad it can't extend to ex-girlfriends. "Yeah, you can date her, but only if you give me your iPod.")

1981–82:
THE PERILS OF OVERCOACHING

After everyone made a fuss about Bill Fitch (NBA title) and Cotton Fitzsimmons (Western Finals) doing terrific jobs in the '81 playoffs, the era of overcoaching kicked off when SI's subsequent NBA preview centered on the success of former college coaches in the NBA.[105] Suddenly coaches were frantically diagramming plays during time-outs, studying tape until the wee hours, hiring multiple assistants and pontificating about the sport like Henry David Thoreau, culminating in Hubie Brown getting hired by the Knicks (I love Hubie, but he's the ultimate "hey, look at me" coach) and paving the way for Rick Pitino's $50 million deal

104. Eddie's explanation to *SI:* "I was in the wrong place at the wrong time. I was at these chicks' house, and these guys busted in the door. I didn't know what was going on. I was just there. Then they started shooting at me." Oh.
105. One of the coaches featured in the article? Westhead, fired a few weeks later for clashing with Magic. See? Coaches ultimately don't matter except for a select few.

in Boston and Avery Johnson employing at least 375 assistants for the Mavericks during the 2007–8 season. The new wave of coaches made defenses sophisticated enough by 1981 that the league created an "illegal defense" rule to open the paint. Here's how referee Ed Rush explained it to *SI:* "We were becoming a jump-shot league, so we went to the coaches and said, 'You've screwed the game up with all your great defenses. Now fix it.' And they did. The new rule will open up the middle and give the great players room to move. People like Julius Erving and David Thompson who used to beat their own defensive man and then still have to pull up for a jump shot because they were being double-teamed, should have an extra four or five feet to move around in. And that's all those guys need."

Nice! That explanation actually made sense. But as the egos of coaches swelled, so did the egos of players who didn't feel like getting ordered around. One famous youngster battled injuries during his second season and threw up a series-losing air ball in a stunning Round 1 playoff upset. As the player headed into his third season, the team's owner handed him the biggest contract in sports history: $25 million for 25 years. When the team struggled coming out of the gate, the player told reporters that he couldn't play for his coach anymore and demanded to be traded. The coach got canned the following day. Now disgraced and considered a selfish jerk, the young player was booed at home and became the poster boy of the Too Young, Too Rich, and Too Immature NBA. One of his teammates wondered, "If he got mad at a player, would the player be gone the next day?" *SI* called him a "greedy, petulant and obnoxious 22-year-old" and decided he's "clearly a great player. Just as clearly, he's no longer a great guy."

The player? That's right . . . Earvin "Magic" Johnson.

Only after the '81 playoffs did people start believing that coaches could work wonders. I've purposely avoided them in this book for the following reason: there's no concrete evidence that they make a genuine, consistent difference except for a small handful of gifted leaders (Pat Riley, Gregg Popovich, Phil Jackson, Chuck Daly, Larry Brown, Jerry Sloan) and forward thinkers (Mike D'Antoni, Don Nelson, Jack Ramsay). Plenty of coaches understand The Secret; only a few can pass it along to players; even fewer can keep The Secret thriving with any type of roster. Daly spearheaded those terrific Bad Boy Pistons teams, failed to find the same success with two knuckleheads (Derrick Coleman and Kenny Anderson) in New Jersey, then suffered through the unhappiest of seasons with a petulant Penny Hardaway on the '97 Magic. Only a handful of coaches would have enjoyed the same success that Daly had with Detroit, just like the same handful would have failed to reach Coleman, Kenny and Penny. Which brings me back to my point: unless you're teaming an elite coach with a quality roster, coaches don't really matter. You have your top guys—usually three or four per year—and everyone else ranges between functional, overrated, replaceable, incompetent, "my God, what a train wreck" and Vinny Del Negro. Most of them tread water or inflict as much damage as good.

Look at the firing numbers over the past decade: eight to ten coaches get fired every year, none lasts more than three or four years, and there might be three or four quality coaches in any given season. Doc Rivers lost 18 straight games and won a title within a sixteen-month span. Hubie finished with a record of 424–495 and somehow became known as a memorably good coach in the process. Paul Westphal led the Suns to the '93 Finals; within eight years, nobody would hire him. KC Jones made the Finals four of five years in Boston, took two years off, then lasted 118 games in Seattle. We have amassed overwhelming evidence that coaches are exceedingly dispensable—they're only as good as their talent, with a limited number of exceptions. Occasionally they might stumble into the right situation, but ultimately, players win titles and coaches lose them. I am going to keep pining for the return of the player-coach (page 322) if it's the last thing I do. What's the difference? So it doesn't work and he gets fired? How is that different from what happens now? Maybe Red Auerbach knew what he was doing with a seven-play playbook, no assistants and a rolled-up program.[106]

One more thing: if you thought coaches were getting wacky, you should have seen the new slew of owners. Donald Sterling spent $13 million on the Clippers, watched the first home game from midcourt with his

---

106. All you need to know about NBA coaches: during every time-out, they huddle with their staff about 15 feet from the bench, allow the players to "think," then come back about a minute later with some miraculous play or piece of advice. "Hey guys, listen up—I think we just figured out how to stop LeBron!" I want to see an owner forgo a coach, put the players in charge of themselves and see if there's any difference . . . and with the $4 million they saved on coaches, they could knock down season ticket prices. I pray that Donald Sterling reads this.

shirt unbuttoned to his navel, then jumped in coach Paul Silas' arms and kissed him when they won; within a few months, he'd failed to make deferred payments to players, refused to pay operating expenses and owed over half a million to the NBA's pension fund and various creditors. Cleveland's Ted Stepien overpaid for free agents Scott Wedman and James Edwards, lost $5.1 million during the '82 season and traded away so many number one picks that the Association awarded the franchise compensatory picks when Stepien sold the team. (They also passed the Stepien Rule—teams weren't allowed to trade first-rounders in consecutive years. How many guys can say they owned an NBA team and had a rule named after them?) Philly's Harold Katz nearly caused an owner revolt when he offered Moses a then-record six-year, $13 million deal and gave Houston a number one pick and Caldwell Jones so they wouldn't match.[107] This launched a twenty-eight-year pattern of franchises stupidly overpaying for players, then warning the players' union it had to do something to keep the costs down. How could so many rich people be so dumb?

1982–83: THE CONNECTION

This was the year when everyone realized, "Hey, maybe we should do stuff to win the fans over!" That led to the following innovations and brainstorms:

1. Feeling frisky after inking a new four-year deal for $93 million, CBS unveiled an abnormally catchy intro that included computerized graphics of a basketball court, Brent Musburger's orgasmic narration, recaps of previous games and a signature hum-along song that everyone from my generation immediately loved: *"Dah-da-da-da do-do-do dooo do-do-do-doooo . . . (do-do-do-do) . . . dah-da-da . . . duhhh duhhhh duhhhhhhhhhhhhhhhhh . . . DAH-DA-DOOO!"*

2. The NBA created its NBA Entertainment division, which immediately launched an "NBA Action . . . It's FANNNNNN-tastic!" commercial campaign that can only be described as a watershed. *Wait, so you're*

107. You gotta hand it to Harold here—I mean, they *did* win the '83 title, right?

telling me it's fun *to attend an NBA game?* Paul Gilbert and his NBAE crew kept the first effort relatively simple: just happy eighties music with various shots of cheerleaders, cheering fans and even someone holding an I LOVE IT sign, along with action shots of Kareem reaching for a jump ball, Bird's reverse layup, Magic clapping and Doc's toma-hawk jam. After Don Sperling took over NBAE, the ads eventually peaked with three classics: the one with "I'm So Excited" by the Pointer Sisters that featured Isiah stomping his feet and doing a circle, Bernard winking on the bench and a smoking-hot Laker Girl blowing a kiss at the camera; the parade of buzzer-beaters that included Jeff Malone's aforementioned three (the greatest for all of eternity unless someone makes one with their dick); and an Oscar-winning sixty-second mon-tage that used Hall and Oates' "One on One" and featured a number of pretty passes, Jerome Whitehead stuffing a Tom Chambers dunk and James Worthy's gorgeous 360-degree layup in slow motion during the sax solo.[108] I can't emphasize this strongly enough: those ads had a gal-vanizing effect on kids like myself in the eighties—they made the NBA seem cool, made us look forward to the next one, and made it seem like *something* was happening with this league.

(A note that's too important to be a footnote: "I'm So Excited" also appeared in an unforgettable *Miami Vice* two-parter called "Return of Calderon," during the nightclub brawl in which Crockett and Tubbs thought they found the Argentinean assassin. The song played in *Va-cation* when Clark Griswold flirted with Christie Brinkley, as well as during a crucial scene in *Beverly Hills Cop II*. And it anchored the *Saved by the Bell* episode when Jessie became addicted to caffeine pills, leading to her famously ridiculous "I'm so excited . . . I'm so ex-cited . . . I'm so . . . scared" meltdown. There's a ton of hyperbole in this book, but the following statement does not qualify: no eighties

---

108. If I was putting together a cheesy-but-phenomenal '80s time capsule and could only use 30 minutes of material, I'd include the "We Are the World" video; the "One on One" NBA ad; the final training scene in *Rocky IV* when he climbs the 25,000-foot mountain in Russia wearing ski boots and a normal parka; Madonna's performance at the '85 MTV Video Music Awards; Journey's "Separate Ways" video; *The Karate Kid*'s "You're the Best" fight montage; the Super Bowl Shuffle video; and the *Beverly Hills Cop* scene where Axel Foley drives through Bev Hills for the first time. That's really all you need to know about the '80s. It's all in there.

song overachieved from a pop culture standpoint more than "I'm So Excited." See? That was important.)

3. Marvin Gaye's All-Star Game anthem doubled as the best moment in All-Star history, hands down; nothing else came close. Coolest singer alive at the time. The celebrity capital of the world (L.A.). Stars like Bird, Isiah, Magic, Kareem, Dr. J, Moses, Jack Sikma and Sikma's blondafroperm looking on. High expectations going in. And even though everyone had always sung the song in the most traditional way possible, Marvin sauntered out with dark, oversized "I might be coked up, I might not" sunglasses, gave the anthem his own little spin and absolutely *crushed* it. By the last fourth of the song, the entire Forum was clapping and swaying like it was the Apollo Theater. That performance will never be topped. Right year, right sport, right city. You could not have gotten that 150 seconds in any other sport, you have to admit.[109]

1983–84: WE'RE HERE

For better and worse, the NBA of the twenty-first century was shaped in what has to be considered the single greatest season in the history of professional sports, or at least one of the top five hundred. A closer look at each milestone:

The salary cap. In March '83, the league avoided a possible labor stoppage with a new CBA that guaranteed players 53 percent of the gross revenues in exchange for a cap that went into effect the following season ($3.6 million, climbing every year after), making players and owners revenue-sharing partners for better or worse.[110] Why did the owners want it? Because it put a lid on escalating salaries and gave them (relatively) fixed

---

109. Marvin's father murdered him just 14 months later. Don't forget to include Marvin Gaye Sr. on the Mount Rushmore of Worst Celebrity Dads along with Ryan O'Neal, the Great Santini and Jim Pierce.

110. Two key provisions: teams could exceed their cap to match offer sheets and use 50 percent of a retired/waived/injured player's cap figure to acquire another player. That kept the good teams good, if you catch my drift.

costs. Why did the players want it? Because it forced every team to spend money; that season, Philly and New York were spending five times as much as the Pacers. As the years went along, the cap became more and more elaborate and confusing, a luxury tax component was added and Larry Coon became an Internet hero for writing a forty-thousand-word FAQ that explained every conceivable cap/tax rule and loophole.[111] Coupled with overexpansion (still a few years away), the days of contenders going nine-deep with quality players and two franchise guys were almost over. We just didn't know it yet.

The drug policy. The new CBA agreement moved the league into "three strikes and you're out" mode. The first offense was a suspension with pay and rehab (paid by the league) as long as the player voluntarily came forward. Same for the second offense, although teams were given the option of waiving the player and replacing him on their cap. The third strike was a lifetime ban (reviewable every two years) regardless of whether the player came forward voluntarily or not.[112] Richardson, Drew and Lucas were the odds-on favorites to be banned first, with Sugar winning the snort race (he got kicked out in 1986).[113] The important thing to remember: not only was the NBA committed to cleaning things up, fans felt like the league had committed itself to cleaning things up. The days of bleary-eyed superstars drifting through games was almost over. At least until they switched to pot in the nineties.

The David Stern era. Fitting that he took over on February 1, 1984, one month into what would become the league's most important year. We don't need to waste words blowing Stern here. Just know that he's either

---

111. You can find that website at www.cbafaq.com. I'm convinced that Larry Coon is a stage name.

112. Any conviction or guilty plea involving a cocaine/heroin crime also resulted in an immediate ban. We never had a guinea pig for this one; just think, if someone like Richard Dumas had ever been caught selling 30 pounds of pot during his playing days, we'd be calling this the Richard Dumas Rule.

113. The complete list of players banned for at least one season: Richardson ('86), Lewis Lloyd ('87), Mitchell Wiggins ('87), Duane Washington ('87), Chris Washburn ('89), Roy Tarpley ('91), Dumas ('94, two-strike suspension), Stanley Roberts ('99) and Chris Andersen ('06). Nice nine-man rotation! The starters: Sugar, Lloyd, Dumas, Tarp and Roberts. The coach: Amy Winehouse.

the first- or second-best sports commissioner ever (depending on how you feel about Pete Rozelle); he was overqualified for the job (and still is); he had a dramatic impact not just on the league itself but also on the NBA's marketing/entertainment/legal/corporate staffs (having Larry O'Brien as a boss and then Stern was like jumping from single-A to the majors); he became the face of the Association almost immediately (and remember, it had never had one before); by December '89, the league had inked four-year deals with NBC and Turner for a combined $875 million; and Stern succeeded to the degree that he was earning more money than only a handful of players by the end of the decade. If that's not enough, he increased the entertainment level of every draft from 1984 to 2010 by approximately 24.7 percent. Maybe Stern didn't make the league take off, but he was flying the plane masterfully when it happened.

All-Star Weekend. When an NBA marketing adviser named Rick Welts lobbied O'Brien to turn the All-Star Game into an entire weekend, the commissioner's response was predictably grumpy and shortsighted. As Welts recalled three years later in the *New York Times,* "I wouldn't say it got a ringing endorsement. Larry said that, number one, it couldn't cost the league a nickel. We said we'd see what we could do." (Note: if someone ever writes O'Brien's autobiography—and really, the odds are 200 to 1— it would definitely *not* have a title like *Thinking Ahead* or *The Visionary.*) Welts and his marketing team quickly sold sponsorships for the Dunk Contest and Old-Timers Game, scheduled those events for Saturday in Denver and convinced TBS to televise it. And then something kooky happened: fans became legitimately excited about the Dunk Contest, especially when Doc agreed to appear and re-create the magic from his revered '76 performance (also in Denver).[114] The Old-Timers Game was surprisingly fun and loaded with legends (Hondo, Pearl, Pistol Pete, Barry, Unseld, Cowens, Heinsohn, even Johnny "Red" Kerr), with Pistol exploding for 18 points in 18 minutes and East coach Red Auerbach fuming after a

---

114. I can't speak for every other kid in the mid-'80s, but I remember counting down the days to two random events: the first Dunk Contest and WrestleMania I one year later. In a related story, there wasn't a girlfriend to be seen during that stretch. Not a one.

game-turning call in the final minute.[115] Even better, Heinsohn never coughed up a lung despite Vegas posting even odds for "Tommy Heinsohn will cough up a lung during the game."

The Dunk Contest contestants were Larry Nance, Edgar Jones, Dominique (the odds-on favorite), Ralph Sampson (as always, they had to have one "Why the supertall guy?" contestant), Clyde Drexler, Orlando Woolridge, Michael Cooper and two doctors (Dunkenstein and J). Wilkins, Nance and the Docs advanced to Round 2 (both Erving and 'Nique dunked two balls at once); Nance prevailed in the Finals because Erving blew his first dunk. Watching it twenty-five years later on tape, it's shocking how rudimentary the dunks were—only Doc's last dunk from the foul line (his entire foot was over) qualified as memorable, and Nance's Plastic Man performance (a variety of long-armed dunks with his hand way over the rim) seems pretty mundane. But at the time? Riveting! If you watch the YouTube clips, the pivotal moment happens right before the finals, when Doc crouches on the sidelines and diagrams potential dunks with his two young sons and teammate Andrew Toney (replete with different phantom dunk gestures); this was one of those rare "Wow, maybe these black guys aren't all on drugs; they actually seem like normal people" moments that the NBA needed so desperately in order to connect with secretly-still-a-little-racist America. Within two years, they added a Three-Point Contest (dramatically won by Larry Bird) and we were off and running.

One other note: the actual All-Star Game was fantastic. Doc had 34 points; Isiah won the MVP with 22 points and 15 assists; Magic had 22 assists in 37 minutes; the East won by a 154–145 score that doubled as the highest combined point total ever to that point;[116] and the supercompetitive game featured an inordinate amount of quality players (including

115. Red went ballistic after Thurmond blocked Barry's shot with 59 seconds left and got whistled for a cheap foul. Hissed Red afterward, "I don't mind getting beat, but my guys were playing for pride and to win the game, and [ref Norm Drucker] tried to make a joke out of it." Red was the best. The Old-Timers Game disappeared after Norm Nixon got seriously hurt a few years later. Nobody wanted to see someone drop dead during All-Star Weekend. Not even if it was Kareem.

116. The two sides took a staggering 241 shots and made 53 percent of them. As always, two great PGs make for a great ASG, and with Bird involved, it's even better. Everyone played at least 11 minutes except for the immortal Kelly Tripucka (6 minutes, 1 point), whose hair, mustache and teeth made him look like a mutant John Oates.

twelve Pyramid guys and five of the top twenty-five, a stat that will make sense in about 108 pages) actually giving a crap. Until the '87 Classic, this was the best All-Star game ever played. Again, only good came out of the '84 All-Star Weekend. Even Rick Barry's latest rug was a huge hit.

The birth of tanking. With Hakeem and Jordan looming as draft prizes, both the Rockets (blew 14 of their last 17, including 9 of their last 10) and Bulls (lost 19 of their last 23, including 14 of their last 15) said, "Screw it, we'll bastardize the sport," and pulled some fishy crap: resting key guys, giving lousy guys big minutes and everything else. Things peaked in Game 81 when a washed-up Elvin Hayes played *every minute* of Houston's overtime loss to the Spurs. Since none of the other crappy teams owned their picks, only Chicago and Houston controlled their destinies (hence the tanking). The worst teams in each conference flipped a coin for number one back then, so the 29-win Rockets "won" the toss and picked first; the 26-win Pacers "lost" and picked second (Portland by proxy); and the 27-win Bulls settled for third (winning the ultimate prize).[117] The unseemly saga spurred the creation of a draft lottery the following season. And even that didn't totally solve the tanking problem; Team Stern has changed the lottery system five times in twenty-five years, and we're probably headed for a sixth soon. My solution: every lottery team gets the same odds. What's wrong with keeping shitty teams shitty and improving mediocre ones? Why is this bad? You can't have great teams unless you have lousy ones. If that makes me an NBA Republican, so be it.

The 1984 Finals. Or, as it's more commonly known, the Single Biggest Break in NBA History. Two years after the NBA extended its season so CBS could show the Finals live (raising the very logical question that I pray you're asking: "Wait, what the hell took the NBA so long?"), the network finally obliged . . . and, of course, they hit the ratings jackpot. Not only did you have the rebirth of the league's most storied rivalry, you had

---

117. Indiana's pick went for Portland's Tom Owens in '81; Cleveland's went for Dallas' Mike Bratz in '81; and the Clips traded theirs for Philly's World B. Free in '78. Maybe coke infected not just players but owners and GMs. By the way, the Cavs beat Washington in game 82 for their twenty-eighth win, dropping their pick to number four and costing Dallas a shot at MJ. Ouch.

Bird versus Magic II; East Coast versus West Coast; Jack Nicholson versus Busty Heart;[118] Johnny Most versus Chick Hearn; the Garden versus the Forum; the two best passing teams of that decade; two loaded squads with eighteen quality guys (including eight future Hall of Famers); and a seven-game donnybrook that featured four ESPN Classic–caliber contests (including Gerald Henderson's steal saving a potential sweep in Game 2). Game 4 (Boston 129, L.A. 125 in OT) was probably the most entertaining/dramatic/physical/hostile/loaded Finals game to that point, an exceptionally played, hypercompetitive slugfest that featured Kevin McHale's series-turning clothesline on Kurt Rambis; Kareem nearly whistling an elbow off Larry's noggin and the two exchanging face-to-face eff-yous; Magic improbably falling apart in crunch time and OT; Bird just missing a desperation three to win it and McHale missing the bunny follow; Bird's backbreaking turnaround over Magic in OT; Maxwell walking across the lane and giving Worthy the choke sign after Big Game James clanged a huge free throw; and M. L. Carr's improbable steal/dunk to clinch it.

Here's why we will never see another basketball game like that: the rules don't allow it. You won't see that many great/good players on the same court in the salary cap era, and you won't see that level of hostility and passion because of the rules now in place against taunting and flagrant fouls. The NBA, where diluted pussyball happens! If you listen to me on anything, I hope it's this: just watch the damned game sometime. It's that good. Even as the Celtics were euphorically prancing off the court with McHale flashing his armpits, it felt like the axis for professional sports had been shifted a little. And when Boston prevailed in a heated Game 7 in equally dramatic fashion, the days of anyone wondering if the league was too black (or whether the league would make it, drugs were ruining the sport, or they might lose their TV contract) were finally over. So, um . . . yeah.[119]

---

118. Busty was a local stripper who became the Morganna of the Bird era. You know whose section she kept landing in? Mine! Busty, thanks to you and your mega-guns for helping me get through puberty. And to the guy who was sitting in front of me during Game 5—I'm sorry for standing up too quickly and knocking you unconscious with my boner. That was uncalled for.

119. In March '85, *SI* ran a feature about the decline of TV sports ratings but passed on its usual NBA-bashing, even admitting, "A kind of dry rot [for ratings] has set in for all major sports except pro basketball." My baby's all growns up! My baby's all growns up!

The 1984 draft. You will not find a bigger month for a sports league than June '84 for the NBA. Not only did the Finals revive the sport, not only did the world embrace the power of Stern's mustache, but Chicago stumbled into the future of professional basketball (Jordan) in a draft that included three other legends (Hakeem, Stockton and Barkley). When Nike signed Jordan to a then-mammoth $2.5 million deal during the same summer when Bird and Magic filmed their famous Converse commercial, the door opened for NBA players to cross over to mainstream advertisers and become their own mini-corporations. Jordan did it first with his posters, Air Jordan sneaker line and Mars Blackmon commercials; others like Magic and Bird quickly followed suit. The League That Was Too Black had become the League That Raked in Shitloads of Money, and it would never look back.

Anyway, that's how the hell we got here. And yeah, maybe we never covered overexpansion, JumboTrons, luxury boxes, skyrocketing ticket prices, the growth of sports radio and fantasy hoops, the influx of foreign players, the addition of a third referee, video games taking off, the underclassmen boon, the HIV scare, the impact of the Dream Team (and the negative impact of Dream Team II), RileyBall, the lottery changes, rookie opt-out clauses, Latrell Sprewell's choking habits, the '99 strike, the rookie salary scale, the ban on high schoolers, advances in ACL surgeries, the art of finding cap space, tattoos and baggy shorts, the marijuana epidemic (that's right, epidemic), the perils of overcoaching, KG's $120 million contract, the '99 lockout, Mark Cuban and the Maloofs, the Internet boom, Barkley's TV career, Moochie Norris' afro, the Artest Melee, the dress code, ESPN's Trade Machine, the Donaghy scandal, All-Star Weekend in Vegas, the scary stretch from 1994 to 2004 when defenses became too effective and games slowed down too much, or even the economy's recent collapse and its effects on a league that I nicknamed the "No Benjamins Association" in a February '09 column. For our purposes—figuring out who mattered and why—we got to where we needed to go. Just trust me.

FOUR

THE WHAT-IF GAME

MOSES MALONE ▪ F

WE SPEND AN inordinate amount of time playing the what-if game. *What if I never got married? What if I had gone to Harvard instead of Yale? What if I hadn't punched my boss in the face? What if I never invested my life savings with Bernie Madoff? What if I never walked in on my wife banging our gardener?* You can't go back, and you know you can't go back, but you keep rehashing it anyway.

There are three great what-ifs in my life that don't involve women. The first is, "What if I had gone west or south for college?" This haunts me and will continue to haunt me until the day I die. I could have chosen a warm-weather school with hundreds of gorgeous sorority girls, and instead I went to an Irish Catholic school on a Worcester hill with bone-chilling 20-degree winds, which allowed female students to hide behind heavy coats and butt-covering sweaters so thick it became impossible to guess their weight within a 35-pound range. That was a great idea.[1] The second: "What if I hadn't quit the *Boston Herald,* taken a year off from writing and tended bar in 1996?" You wouldn't be reading this book if that hadn't happened. I needed to recharge my batteries, stay up until 4:00 a.m., date the wrong women, smoke an obscene amount of pot and figure some shit out. That's what I needed at the time, and nobody can tell me different. And of course, the third: "What if I had tried to write this monstrosity of a book without the help of copious amounts of hard alcohol, cocaine, amphetamines, ADD medication, Marlboro Lights, coffee and horse tranquilizers?" I'll let you decide whether that decision worked out or not.

The what-if game extends to every part of life. For instance, I have three and only three favorite movie what-ifs. In reverse order . . . [2]

3. **What if Robin Williams played the Duke in *Midnight Run*?** He signed to play Jonathan "the Duke" Mardukas and backed out before shooting because of a scheduling conflict. The producers scrambled around for a replacement before settling on Charles Grodin, not exactly a scorching-hot name at the time. The rest is history. Maybe Williams would have taken things in a more frantic, slapstick direction—and that's saying something, since this was the same movie that broke the record for most guys knocked briefly unconscious by a punch—but it wouldn't have been a good thing. Grodin *nailed* the Duke. Understated, sarcastic, never flinched. Williams messes that movie up. I am convinced. And if you don't agree with me, I have two words for you: shut the fuck up.

2. **What if Leonardo DiCaprio did *Boogie Nights* instead of *Titanic*?** Leo had the choice, mulled it over, opted for *Titanic* . . . and ended up carrying that movie and becoming a superduperstar. (By the way, that movie bombs with anyone else.) But imagine if he played Dirk Diggler.

1. High schoolers, go west or south: Duke, Virginia, Vanderbilt, UNC, UCLA, Rollins, Pepperdine, Arizona, ASU, Miami and my personal favorite, UC Santa Barbara. Stay warm. Just trust me.
2. I threw this idea at William Goldman. His two favorites: George Raft turned down Bogie's part in *Casablanca,* and they went after Brando and Beatty for *Butch Cassidy and the Sundance Kid* before settling on Redford and Newman. "Nobody knows anything in Hollywood," he wrote me. "Never forget that." Sounds like the NBA.

Look, I liked Mark Wahlberg's performance in that movie. It's a solid B-plus and he didn't take anything off the table. But that could have been the defining part of Leo's career. To rank the best new actors of the past fifteen years, Leo and Russell Crowe are either one-two or two-one, Philip Seymour Hoffman is third and Matt Damon is fourth.[3] As much as I like Wahlberg, he's not on that level. Leo could have taken Dirk Diggler to new heights, which seems significant since *Boogie Nights* is already one of my ten favorite movies ever. I even think he could have pulled off the "Feel the heat" and "It's my dojo!" scenes.[4]

1. **What if Robert De Niro was hired for Michael Corleone instead of Al Pacino?** This almost happened. When Francis Ford Coppola screened them, he liked De Niro so much that he saved the part of young Vito for him in *The Godfather: Part II.* This will always be the number one movie what-if because it can never be answered: Pacino was tremendous in I and submitted a Pantheon performance in II. Could De Niro have topped that? Possibly, right? That character was in both of their wheelhouses. I guess it comes down to which guy was better, which is like the Bird-Magic debate in that there isn't a definitive answer and there will *never* be a definitive answer.[5] Now that, my friends, is a great what-if.

We should set some ground rules if we're extending the concept to the NBA, like avoiding injury-related what-ifs because injuries are part of the game. ("What if Bill Walton's feet had never broken down?" sounds fine on paper, but Walton never had a chance running around on those fragile clodhoppers. He was predisposed to breaking down, the same way someone like Kurt Cobain was predisposed to becoming a suicidal druggie maniac.) I also want to avoid fascinating-but-nonsensical what-ifs, like "What if Shaq and Kobe had been able to get along?" (those guys had

3. I would have thrown Billy Crudup in there, but he's like Vince Carter—all the talent in the world and he just didn't want it.
4. My friend Chris Connelly disagrees and believes that Leo didn't have the raw sexuality to pull off Diggler believably. This is a nice way of saying that Leo is too much of a skinny sissy.
5. I tried to answer it in a 2002 mailbag and even got my stepfather involved because he's watched *The Godfather* 25,712 times. We went with De Niro. Barely.

mammoth egos and were destined to clash),[6] as well as draft-related what-ifs unless the right decision was glaringly obvious even at the time and the team still screwed up. And I'm avoiding the "What if Jordan didn't retire for eighteen months?" question because that decision affected too many subsequent scenarios—it's like asking "What if Ali didn't lose four years of his prime?" or "What if Shawn Kemp used condoms?" And besides, it's not like he *willingly* retired, right? (Wink wink.) Everything else is fair game.

Here are the top thirty-three what-ifs in NBA history, in reverse order:

33. What if the '63 Royals never got switched into the Eastern Conference when the Warriors moved to San Francisco?

The '63 Royals dragged a Boston team with seven Hall of Famers to a seventh game, then peaked over the next three seasons (55, 48 and 45 wins), only they could never get past Russell's Celtics (and later Wilt's Sixers). Playing in the West, the Royals potentially could have made five straight Finals ('63 to '67); at the very least, they would have made the '65 Finals because Baylor missed the playoffs. And you know what? It's impossible to measure the impact of such a seemingly minor decision on Oscar Robertson's career. Here's the greatest point guard of the NBA's first thirty-five years and one of the ten best players ever, only he never reached the Finals in his prime simply because he switched conferences at the worst possible time. Would we remember Oscar differently had he been putting on a show every spring in the Finals on ABC? What if Oscar had shocked the Celtics on the biggest stage and won a title? Would his career momentum have built the way Jordan's did after his first title, like an invisible barrier had been broken down? Would we remember Oscar as the greatest or second-greatest player ever instead of a top-ten guy?

Now here's what *really* drives me crazy. In 1962, there were four Eastern Conference teams (Boston, New York, Philly and Syracuse) and five Western Conference teams (Los Angeles, St. Louis, Chicago, Detroit and

6. It's like the Lennon-McCartney problem—you can't have two alpha dogs in a band or a basketball team. It will implode. It will.

Cincy). When Philly moved to San Fran,[7] the conferences became imbalanced and one Western team had to move to the East. The Royals were a logical pick because they were located more east than anyone else. I get that. But one year later, Chicago moved to Baltimore and remained in the Western Conference.

Do me a favor and look at a map. Do it right now. I'll wait.

(Twiddling my thumbs.)

(Humming.)

Good, you're back. Now check out that map. I mean, What the hell? It's no contest! How could they keep Cincy in the East and Baltimore in the West when Baltimore was nearly a thousand miles farther east? How does this make sense? How?[8] From a commonsense standpoint, why weren't the NBA powers that be more interested in making it easier for Oscar to reach the Finals? Those shortsighted dopes robbed us of some potentially bravura playoff moments, including three or four Oscar-West playoff showdowns in their primes and at least one guaranteed Celtics-Royals Finals. And all because nobody running the NBA knew how to read a map.

(Amazingly, this wasn't the league's biggest geographical screw-up ever. After the ABA and NBA merged, Denver and Indiana were sent to the Western Conference while San Antonio and the Nets joined the East. For the '77 season, Houston and San Antonio played in the East while Milwaukee, Detroit, Kansas City and Indiana played in the West. Check out that map you just found, then explain to me how this made any sense whatsoever. I'll give you a thousand dollars.)

32. What if the Knicks chose Rick Barry over Bill Bradley in 1965?

A memorable college player and potential box office draw, Bradley graduated from Princeton and headed right to England, where he planned on

7. I love calling San Francisco "San Fran" even if everyone in the Bay Area bristles in disgust. Why should I have to keep typing "Francisco" when I can save 5 letters? What about my fingers? This book is 250,000 words! You can't give me the "San Fran" thing?

8. When the expansion Bulls joined in '67, they were placed in the West and Baltimore finally moved into the East. Although they did briefly consider keeping Chicago in the East and then moving Boston into the West.

spending two years on a prestigious Rhodes Scholarship at Oxford. There's a big difference between waiting for a franchise center for two years (like David Robinson) and waiting for a slow small forward, right? It's unclear if Bradley was a better prospect than Barry (a scoring machine at the University of Miami); maybe he was a bigger name and the Knicks desperately needed some star power, but that two-year wait nullified every Bradley advantage, in my opinion.[9] Had the Knicks taken Barry, maybe their feel-good '70 title season never happens, but maybe Barry never gets lowballed and makes his stupid jump to the ABA (or loses three years of his prime because of injuries and lawsuits).

And if you want to get technical, Barry was the second-best passing forward of all time behind Larry Legend; if anyone could have fit in seamlessly with those Knicks teams, it's him. One of two extremes would have played out: either Barry goes down as one of the twelve greatest players ever and a New York icon, or he goes down as a temperamental, annoying asshole whom everyone in New York despised before he finally got driven out of town for eyeballing Willis Reed after a dropped pass, then getting thrown into the fifteenth row at MSG by Willis. It's one or the other.

31. What if Detroit took Carmelo Anthony over Darko Milicic?

The Pistons landed the second pick in '03 and targeted Darko right away; they already had a keeper at small forward (Tayshaun Prince) and needed size because they were still eight months away from Danny Ainge gift-wrapping Rasheed Wallace for them. Of course, many thought they were making a franchise-altering mistake (including me), which opens the door for what-if potential. If 'Melo goes to Detroit, you know what happens? Detroit loses the '04 title. He screws up their chemistry and threatens Prince's confidence just enough that we wouldn't have seen the same Pistons team that fileted the '04 Lakers. Also, Brown coached 'Melo in the

---

9. According to Leonard Koppett, scouts worried that Barry was too skinny to handle the pro game. Even back then, scouts were dumb.

2004 Olympics and they loathed each other to the degree that a bitter 'Melo went into a yearlong tailspin. Do you really think these guys wouldn't have clashed in Detroit? Come on. Can't you see 'Melo pouting on the bench during an '04 playoff game while a confused Ben Wallace stands near him, wonders whether to say something, then just walks away?

The long-term effect: Brown quits; 'Melo or Prince gets traded; that Detroit nucleus of Hamilton-Billups-Wallace-Wallace never makes a Finals; Darko gets major minutes on a lottery team in his formative years and potentially turns into something other than a mopey dunk tank and I never write jokes like "Does anyone else think NBA Entertainment should make a DVD called 'Ultimate Darko,' featuring every garbage time minute that Darko played this season, plus some of his best high-fives and shoulder slaps on the Pistons bench, along with director's commentary from Darko, LaRue Martin, Sam Bowie and Steve Stipanovich?" Picking the wrong guy ended up *winning* Detroit that one championship. As for the "What if they had taken Bosh or Wade?" argument, there was a definitive top three at the time (LeBron, Darko and Carmelo), and Detroit would have been skewered for taking anyone else second. Those guys didn't have the same value. When I found Chad Ford's 2003 pick-by-pick analysis online recently,[10] I was reminded that (a) Miami stunned everyone by taking Wade at number five and (b) there was a real debate at the time whether Bosh would ever put on enough weight to be anything more than the next Keon Clark. So saying that they could have had Wade or Bosh with that pick is unfair unless you're making the argument Detroit should have traded down. There's no way Wade or Bosh was going second in that draft. None.[11]

---

10. Actual Chad quotes from that column: "Darko is really one of a kind"; "What sets Darko apart is his toughness in the post"; "[Carlos Delfino] reminds me of Michael Finley"; "I don't like [Kendrick Perkins] for the Celtics, I'm not sure how it helps them in the short term or the long term"; "[Maciej Lampe at number thirty is] the steal of the draft." I love the ESPN.com archives. As long as I'm not looking up my own humiliating predictions. (Emeka Okafor over Dwight Howard, anyone?) Then I hate them.

11. Had Detroit traded down and gotten Wade, now we're talking about multiple titles. That's not a fair what-if. Regardless, landing Darko in a top five with Bron, Wade, Bosh and 'Melo was like reaching into a brown paper bag filled with two checks for $100 million, two checks for $10 million, and a check for $10, and pulling out the check for $10.

30. What if the Mavs re-signed Steve Nash in 2004?

At the time, I defended Dallas for letting Nash leave because (a) he hadn't looked good in the previous two playoffs and (b) $60 million seemed like an obscene amount of money for a thirty-one-year-old point guard with back problems. What I didn't defend was Dallas subsequently using that found money (and more) to throw $73 million at Erick Dampier, who's such a dog that PETA monitors all Dallas practices to make sure he isn't mistreated. If you're throwing money around, throw it at Nash over Dampier, right?[12] Dallas also fatally underestimated the rule changes that transformed Nash into a two-time MVP. Had they kept Nash and Antawn Jamison (dealt for Jerry Stackhouse and Devin Harris) and still made the Antoine Walker/Jason Terry trade, that's suddenly a monster roster (Nash, Nowitzki, Jamison, Terry, Josh Howard, DeSagana Diop, Veteran Free Agent X and February Buyout Guy X year after year after year) as well as the league's single most entertaining team (and that's before we get to what-if number 13). Looking back, it's peculiar that Mark Cuban played the "fiscal responsibility" card with Nash right before spending recklessly on a thief like Dampier. I have a great deal of respect for Cuban as a businessman and a thinker, but other than passing on Nash, he spent the decade making it rain Pacman-style—only coming close to a title in 2006, when the Mavericks were robbed (page 464 the window closed with a nine-figure payroll and no hope for turning things around unless Jason Kidd gets placed on an accelerated HGH program while we're printing this book. Too bad. One of my "bucket list" sports goals in life was to watch a pissed-off David Stern hand Cuban the Finals trophy while Cuban sobbed like Rocky at the end of *Rocky II*.[P6]

12. Dallas got suckered by a textbook contract run: for the last 3 months of '04, Damp averaged a 13–13 and 2 blocks, highlighted by back-to-back 19–21 and 16–25 games in the final week. Take away '04 and his career average is a 7–7. Good guy.

P6. After a decade-long pattern of Dallas falling short in the playoffs and Cuban blaming everyone but his best players, I wonder if he's like an overly benevolent father of a rich prep school kid who showers the kid with too many gifts, hires him too many private tutors and gets a little too involved in his school, and every time things don't go his kid's way he makes excuses like "He got a B in English because his teacher didn't like him!" and "He wouldn't have gone 0-for-5 in the title game if the coach hadn't moved him down in the lineup!" Those kids always end up being pussies who keep waiting for their parents to save them. Maybe that's Dallas in the playoffs.

29. What if John Thompson never screwed up the '88 Olympics?

As the years passed, an urban legend was spawned about that defeat, something about "the team wasn't talented enough," which eventually led to the dawning of the original Dream Team in 1992. In the words of John McLaughlin, *Wrong!* They had a franchise center (David Robinson), a franchise forward (Danny Manning, the number one pick that year), two reliable shooters (Mitch Richmond and Hersey Hawkins) and two athletic swingmen who were perfect for international play (Dan Majerle and Stacey Augmon). But Thompson killed their chances by picking point guards Charles Smith (his own guy from Georgetown)[13] and Bimbo Coles over Tim Hardaway (my God), Mookie Blaylock, Dana Barros, Rod Strickland, Steve Kerr and even high schooler Kenny Anderson. He willingly sacrificed outside shooting and the slash-and-kick game (only two of the most crucial ingredients to international success) so he could play a pressure defense that fell right into the hands of the cagey Russians (who thrived on ball movement and open three-pointers). Savvy.

This was one of those rare miscalculations where everyone braced for a collapse well before it happened. I mean, we were *all* worried. And after Russia toppled us in the semis and we left Seoul with a bronze, everyone played the "Screw it, we need to send the pros!" card instead of blaming Thompson and saying, "Let's never give a coach that kind of roster power again."[14] But you know what? Thompson's incompetence spawned the first Dream Team—a transcendent summer for the NBA and a tipping point for international basketball—and everything that came afterward, including indefensible behavior by our boys in '96 and '02 and an embarrassing butt-whupping by Argentina that forced the powers that be to

13. Charles Smith played for Boston a year later and threw up enough bricks to build a three-bedroom condo in Charlestown. Another underrated mistake: cutting Glen Rice and Sean Elliott, which reared its ugly head when Hawkins got hurt in Seoul and Richmond was suddenly the team's only reliable shooter. And on top of it, they cut Kerr despite an international three-point line. John Thompson, everybody! ·

14. Let's chisel this on Thompson's Hall of Fame plaque: SCREWED UP '88 OLYMPICS, COST USA GOLD right above the spot where it says HAD MOURNING AND MUTOMBO AT SAME TIME, NEVER ADVANCED PAST ELITE EIGHT WITH THEM.

crack down on assholism and stop slapping together purposeless All-Star teams. Ultimately, it made our product better, and once foreign countries started catching up to us, how many fledgling careers were ignited in Germany, Spain, Argentina, Lithuania and everywhere else? All because John Thompson blew the gold medal. Thank you, John. I think.

28. What if Minnesota didn't piss off Kevin Garnett by quietly shopping him before the '07 draft?

Here's what happens: KG glumly returns to another crappy T-Wolves team for a few months (maybe more), opening the door for Boston to trump Los Angeles for Pau Gasol in February and team him with Paul Pierce, Rajon Rondo, Ray Allen and Al Jefferson. Not a Finals team . . . but not a bad team either, right?[15] Maybe the Celtics could have just made the KG trade in February using the same players, but would it have been as effective? Remember, Boston signed James Posey and Eddie House at discounts once KG was aboard—that's not happening without the trade— and would have had a near-impossible time pulling off a six-for-one deal midseason with both rosters already filled. Throw in KG's trade kicker and that deal doesn't happen until the summer. By that time the Celtics would have moved on Gasol or . . .

(Wait for it . . .)

(Wait for it . . .)

Kobe.

Remember Kobe's hissy fit before the '08 season that spurred the Lakers to shop him around, only nobody would meet their asking price (an

---

15. My favorite awful Chris Wallace moves: tying up Boston's cap space for three years with an alcoholic making the max (Vin Baker); taking Denver's eleventh pick in '01 when he could have kept rolling that pick over, then picking Kedrick Brown; trading a number one for Juan Carlos Navarro; trading Joe Johnson and a number one for Rodney Rogers and Tony Delk without signing Rogers to an extension first; picking Joe Forte over Tony Parker; spending $21 million on Darko Milicic; giving away Gasol in a garage sale and getting his younger brother, which was like trading Sly Stallone in 1988 for three young character actors and Frank; buying Broadcast.com from Mark Cuban for $3 billion. Yeah, I know he didn't do the last one, but it just *seemed* like something he would have done.

All-Star plus cap space plus picks)? If the Celtics hadn't traded for Garnett, they could have offered Paul Pierce, Theo Ratliff's expiring contract, their number one and their rights to a future Minnesota number one for Kobe and two relatively unfriendly contracts (Brian Cook and Vlad Radmanovic). Boston would have kept a foundation of Kobe, Ray Allen, Jefferson,' Kendrick Perkins and Rajon Rondo; the Lakers would have replaced Kobe with another All-Star and gotten three number ones (including Minnesota's future pick, which could have been valuable) and $20 million of expiring contracts with Ratliff and Kwame Brown (already on their roster) to make a run at Garnett or Gasol. Since Pierce outplayed Kobe in the 2008 Finals, can you imagine if this happened with Pierce (and maybe even KG) on the Lakers and Kobe on the Celtics?

Obviously I enjoy the way it worked out: Garnett revived basketball in Boston and won a title; Pierce redefined his career; Kobe won the MVP before gagging in the Finals; the Lakers hijacked Gasol and riled everyone up (I'm still riled, actually);[16] both Phoenix and Dallas panicked and made controversial "I'm going all in with these eights" trades for Shaq and Kidd (then imploded in the playoffs); Miami dumped Shaq's contract and kicked off Tankapalooza 2008; Shawn Marion became the first professional athlete to seem pleased going from a team with a .700 winning percentage to a team with a .200 winning percentage; and the Lakers and Celtics made ABC $325 billion by meeting in the Finals. And none of it happens if the T-Wolves don't piss off Garnett in the summer of '07.

27. What if Ron Artest never charged into the stands in Detroit?

I can't believe we made it this far in the book without paying homage to the most unfathomable NBA moment of the decade. Consider:

16. Hold on, I'm not done with Wallace. My buddy House and I ran into him in a Boston bar after I slammed the Baker deal on ESPN.com. He tried to explain the logic, which was nice of him—but the explanation ended up being so brainless that House pretended to go piss and never came back. The highlight: when Wallace claimed Shammond Williams was the key to the deal. When I asked why Wallace didn't at least swap first-rounders with Seattle once over the next five years—which they would have done because, you know, they were desperate to get Baker and all—Wallace briefly had a look on his face like, "Shit, why didn't I think of that?" It was surreal. Thank God I had a witness in House.

- It's the only sporting event from 1997 to 2008 that prompted me to write two separate columns within 36 hours. If we built a Hall of Fame for Jaw-Dropping TV Nights in My Lifetime, my original induction would include O.J.'s Bronco chase (the Babe Ruth of this idea), the first Tyson-Holyfield fight, Princess Diana's limo accident, Buckwheat's assassination by John David Stutts, the night Gordon Jump tried to molest Dudley and Arnold on *Diff'rent Strokes,* and the Artest melee. Those will always be the Big Six, at least for me.[17]

- The clip has been watched and rewatched almost as many times as the Zapruder film. It's also been removed from YouTube for violating copyright restrictions more than any other NBA-related clip other than Game 6 of the Lakers-Kings series.[18]

- Along with the Tim Donaghy scandal and the time Darius Miles gave Stern a full-body, genitals-to-genitals hug during the 2000 draft, it's the most traumatic event of David Stern's reign as commissioner (he even admits as much) and changed the rules about player-fan interactions for the rest of NBA eternity.

- From a comedy standpoint, it catapulted both Artest and Stephen Jackson into the Tyson Zone, gave us the phrase "pulling an Artest" for eternity and even allowed us to imagine what life would be like if Jermaine O'Neal could punch out Turtle from *Entourage.* Jackson ended up winning the Comedy MVP for somehow coming off crazier than the guy who charged into the stands, challenging the entire Pistons team, throwing wild haymakers in the stands and basically turning into the Token Crazy Guy in a Basebrawl Fight multiplied by 100. When Jackson left the arena waving his arms like a pro wrestler as people dumped beer on him, I think he shattered the My God, That Guy Is Freaking Crazy! record in professional sports.

17. How you know an event qualifies: Will you always remember where you watched it? (Check.) Did you know history was being made? (Check.) Would you have fought anyone who tried to change the channel? (Check.) Did your head start to ache after a while? (Check.) Did your stomach feel funny? (Check.) Did you end up watching about four hours too long? (Check.) Were there a few "can you believe this"–type phone calls along the way? (Check.) Did you say "I can't believe this" at least fifty times? (Check.)

18. That game is the NBA's version of the 18 missing minutes of the Watergate tapes. If you try to watch it, you could die like the characters in *The Ring.*

- From an I-knew-this-could-happen standpoint, put it this way: if you scrolled through the lineups of all thirty teams before the 2005 season, then asked yourself, "What pair of teammates would be the most likely candidates to start a fight in the stands, eventually leading to the ugliest sequence in NBA history?" the heavy favorites would have been Artest and Jackson in Indiana, with Zach Randolph and Ruben Patterson a distant second in Portland. Maybe it was a Hall of Fame TV night, but at no point did anyone who follows the NBA on a regular basis say to themselves, "I can't believe Ron Artest and Stephen Jackson are taking on Row 3 in the Palace right now!"
- Another underrated and slightly silly side effect: it was one of the most memorable moments in fantasy sports history. Imagine taking Ron with one of your top picks, then watching him charge into the stands a few weeks later. *Wait, Ron . . . Ron . . . noooooooooooooooo-oooooooooooooo!*
- Adam Carolla had a funny take: imagine being the first guy who was mistakenly attacked by Artest. You've been watching these guys for two hours, you're pretty buzzed, you're loving the seats . . . and then this fight breaks out, it's riveting as hell, it keeps going, and then suddenly Artest gets nailed by the cup and he's coming right at you. As Carolla said, it would be like watching *Captain Hook* in the movies for two hours, then Captain Hook comes right out of the movie screen and attacks you. Would you have blamed that first guy for soiling himself?

So you have *all* those things already in play, followed by the what-if potential that emerged afterward. Right before the melee, the Pacers had just finished throttling the Pistons and staking their claim as The Team to Beat in 2005. In the span of five minutes, everything went down the drain . . . and if you remember, the shoddy '05 Finals between San Antonio and Detroit ranks alongside the '94 Finals and the '76 Finals on the Wait, Are We *Sure* These Were the Best Two Teams? Scale. There's no way to prove it, but I will always believe Indiana had the best 2005 team even if they were predisposed to self-combusting. Whatever. From that moment on, professional basketball was effectively murdered in Indiana. Larry Bird probably feels like Artest and Jackson charged into the stands and started beating the hell out of him. That's basically what happened.[19]

26. What if Grant Hill never signed with Fila?

If you thought shoe companies signed NBA stars, designed cool-looking sneakers for them, mailed them those sneakers and that's it . . . you thought wrong. And until I visited Nike's Dr. Evil–like compound in November 2009, so did I. Turns out real science is involved. Nike brings many of its athletes to Oregon, pushes them through elaborate stress tests in the company's state-of-the-art training lab, breaks down their running mechanics and foot structure (and also how those two things relate), then builds the best possible shoe for them. Like how you'd build a mouthpiece for someone's specific mouth, only for feet, and only after measuring how someone talked and chewed food for an entire weekend. As they were explaining the process to me and bragging about their success rate with feet/ankle issues, one Nike executive casually mentioned, "Ask Grant Hill if he wishes he'd signed with Nike way back when."

Hmmmmmmm. In 1997, Fila signed Hill to a massive $80 million deal meant to splash the company into America's basketball sneaker market. With Nike and Reebok heatedly bidding for every name player, Fila strategically went the other way, throwing the bulk of its NBA budget behind the league's most likable young star. How good was Hill? He shared the Rookie of the Year award with Jason Kidd, averaged two straight 20-9-7 seasons (only LeBron has done it since),[P7] made five straight first or sec-

---

19. The lowlights: Reggie Miller retired; O'Neal morphed into an overpaid underachiever with a bad attitude and was sent packing to Toronto; Jackson and Jamaal Tinsley were peripherally involved in a strip club shooting; their fans grew to loathe the postmelee team so passionately that the Pacers panicked and sent Al Harrington and Jackson to Golden State for a Mike Dunleavy/Troy Murphy pu-pu contract platter; and they lost a reported $30 million in 2009 and might be a threat to relocate. Not even the Basketball Jesus can save them.

P7. In '96, Hill finished 19th in PPG (20.2), 13th in RPG (9.8) and 15th in APG (6.8). In '97, Hill finished 12th in PPG (21.4), 19th in RPG (9.0) and 12th in APG (7.3). He's the last guy to finish in the top twenty in all three categories for two straight years. Only KG ('03) has done it since. Had Hill stayed healthy, he would have transformed T-Mac's career and been a Level 3 or Level 4 Pyramid Guy (you'll understand what that means in about 100 pages).

ond All-NBA teams, averaged 25.8 points in his last pain-free season and even thrived after the media unfairly tagged him as The Next MJ. Really, Hill was the next Pippen—an evolutionary, more devastating version— until fracturing his left ankle during the 2000 playoffs, two months before he realized free agency. Undaunted, Orlando handed Hill a $92.7 million deal that summer, never imagining his troubled ankle could be headed for multiple surgeries, a steel plate and six screws. Just like that, Evolutionary Pippen 2.0's prime vanished into thin air. Could those Filas have contributed to his woes? Yes, Hill's injuries could be coincidence, and yes, Fila surely was careful in customizing its shoe for Hill. (Can you tell my lawyers encouraged that language?) But let's say you were spending $400,000 on a fancy sports car. Would you pick a new company just getting into the luxury sports car business and feeling its way, or would you pick Ferrari, a behemoth with deep pockets that's been cranking out high-caliber sports cars since forever? You'd go with Ferrari, right? It's also worth mentioning that Grant Hill now wears Nikes . . . and has for the past few years. Something tells me it's not a coincidence.

25. What if MJ never played with the Wizards?

In the big scheme of things, no biggie. But imagine how cool it would have been if Game 6 of the '98 Finals—MJ winning the title by himself and ending his career with the layup-steal-jumper sequence—was our last basketball memory of Michael Jordan. That Washington comeback made him seem mortal, cluttered our brain with a few unpleasant memories, hurt his career historically (even if we didn't realize it) and opened the door for a decade of ludicrous "Kobe/LeBron might even be better than MJ!" arguments. Which leads me to my world-renowned Kurt Cobain Theory: Part of the reason Nirvana gained steam historically was because Cobain killed himself at the perfect time, right after *In Utero* and the *MTV Unplugged* album, when he was hooked on drugs and slowly going insane. Had he hung around and survived, we would have been treated to a few rehab stints, some bizarre behavior, a messy/bloody/violent breakup with Courtney Love that would have landed one of them (or both) in jail, at least two incoherent albums that every annoying Cobain fanatic would have defended as "genius, man, pure genius," followed by a six-year disappearance and an eventual booking on *Celebrity Rehab* with Dr. Drew, where he definitely would have hooked up with Mariah Carey. He would have made Scott Weiland seem more bubbly than the dudes from Wham! After enduring his pathetic downfall for twelve or fourteen years, would we still be hailing Cobain as a musical genius and crediting him as the father of alternative music? No way! He would have been just another druggie musician who threw away his career.[20] If you don't believe me, look how we regarded Michael Jackson before he died—the freak of freaks, a celebrity cautionary tale, a creepy (alleged) child molester—even though as recently as 1987 we agreed that Jackson was the most talented pop artist ever. Or consider how Eddie Murphy would have been remembered historically had he perished in a plane crash two months after the 1988 release of *Coming to America*. Memories affect perceptions for better and worse. They do. Our last Cobain memory was that MTV special, just an anguished, captivating, overwhelmingly talented dude delivering the best *Unplugged* of all time. That's one of the things that helped him endure. And our last Jordan memory should have been the swipe of Malone and the jumper over Bryon Russell. Alas.

24. What if John Havlicek didn't get injured during the '73 Eastern Finals?

I know, I know . . . I promised that we would avoid injury-related what-ifs. The '73 Celtics finished 68–14 (the fourth-best record ever) and had their most dominant team of the Cowens/Havlicek era. Hondo separated his shooting shoulder in Game 3 of the Knicks series, missed the rest of that game plus the next one (both Boston losses) and played left-

20. A great parallel: Billy Corgan started out just as fast as Cobain; by 2001, he was an egocentric bald guy who made music nobody bought. Nobody cares that Smashing Pumpkins vs. Nirvana was a semilegitimate argument in 1994, or that the 12 best Pumpkin songs might be better than the best 12 Nirvana songs. The fact remains, Nirvana came first and paved the way. It's like comparing David Thompson to Dr. J. The stats might back you up, but you still can't do it.

handed for the last three, with the Celtics still stretching it to seven before the Knicks finally realized, "Wait, Hondo is playing with one hand—let's hound him every time he has the ball!" So the Celtics suffered their first-ever Game 7 defeat at the Garden, with the Knicks beating an aging Lakers team in the Finals. That trophy belonged to Boston; considering Hondo played 1,442 of a possible 1,475 games (including playoffs), the fact that his only major injury in sixteen seasons happened at that specific point in time ranks among the biggest flukes in NBA history. When an over-the-hill Celtics team stumbled into the '76 title, it was almost like the NBA gods were paying them back for robbing them in '73.[21]

Just know this was the only fluky post-shot-clock injury that almost definitely swung a title. Do the '58 Celtics beat the Hawks if Russell didn't sprain his ankle early in the series? Maybe . . . but we don't know. Do the '88 Pistons topple the Lakers if Isiah didn't sprain an ankle in the third quarter of Game 6? Maybe . . . but the Lakers still had home court in Games 6 and 7 (and Magic and Worthy in their primes). Do the '87 Celtics beat the Lakers if McHale didn't break his foot? Do the '83 Lakers hang with Philly if Worthy didn't break his leg? Could the '04 Lakers have held off Detroit if Karl Malone didn't hurt his knee? Do the '85 Celtics beat the Lakers if Bird didn't injure his shooting hand in a bar fight?[22] Would the '03 Mavs have won a title if Nowitzki didn't get hurt? What about the '99 Knicks with Ewing? Could the '96 Magic have hung with the Bulls if Horace Grant didn't get hurt in the first half of Game 1? Could the '62 Sixers have beaten Boston if Wilt didn't injure his hand

21. My dad still complains about the refs in Game 4, when the Knicks rallied from a 16-point deficit with help from Jack Madden and Jake O'Donnell and won in double OT. Heinsohn chased the refs into the MSG tunnel afterward. When Madden screwed the '91 Celtics on a bogus offensive goaltending call to end the Detroit series, my dad yelped, "Jack Madden hates us! He's been screwing us ever since you were born!"

22. This one gnaws at me. Bird was riding the biggest hot streak of his career: back-to-back buzzer-beaters in January, the 60-point game and memorable ass-whuppings of Cleveland and Detroit in the Playoffs. He showed up for practice before Game 3 of the Philly series with a heavily bandaged right index finger and started throwing up bricks. Averaging a 30–10 on 52 percent shooting before Game 3, the Legend floundered to a 21–7 with 40 percent shooting for his last 9 playoff games. Both the *Globe* and *Herald* connected the dots that summer, reporting that between Games 2 and 3 of the Philly series, Bird got into a fight at a Boston bar called Chelsea's and punched out a bartender named Mike Harlow (eventually settling out of court with him). So much for the '85 title. Mike Harlow came thissssssssss close to getting his own what-if in this chapter.

trying to punch Tommy Heinsohn (and hitting a teammate instead)? There are no definitive answers. We don't know. With the '73 Celtics, we know: they had the best team, the best player (Hondo) and the reigning MVP (Dave Cowens). Even getting half a series from Hondo (and 40 percent of Hondo when he played), that series still went seven. What does that tell you?

23. What if Wilt ended up on the Lakers instead of the Sixers in 1965?

We covered this story in the Wilt-Russell chapter. (And by "we," I mean me.)[23] Yup, Wilt, Elgin and Jerry could have become teammates four years sooner than it actually happened. And it didn't happen for a remarkable reason. Forget about the potential playoff ramifications; can you imagine how much damage Wilt would have done in Hollywood in his sexual prime? He would have been throwing his cock around like it was a boomerang. I'm almost positive that Elizabeth Taylor and Raquel Welch would have been clunked in the face with it. That probably happened anyway. Let's just move on.

22. What if Kobe signed with the Clippers in 2004?

The Clippers fervently believed Kobe was coming—remember, this was the same summer when Kobe was getting blamed by everyone for pushing out Shaq and Phil Jackson—until he broke their hearts by changing course at the last minute. Other than the Lakers offering an extra year and slightly more money, was anything else offered to help stop Kobe from joining a younger and more talented Clippers team? Are the rumors true that the Lakers illegally promised Kobe a postretirement piece of the Lakers?[24] Were the Lakers reluctant to pursue Kobe offers before the '08 sea-

23. I mistakenly attempted the "fourth person singular tense," as perfected by Will Leitch during his reign as *Deadspin* editor. We don't know why he wrote that way, but we always found it interesting.
24. The smoking gun: Kobe was represented by Rob Pelinka, who orchestrated Carlos Boozer's sleazy move from Cleveland to Utah.

son because of something promised during those '04 negotiations? It's all hypothetical, and we'll never know for sure until Kobe retires and we learn if he earned the Magic Johnson Memorial Ownership Discount from Dr. Buss. But everyone working for the Clippers feels like *something* happened to trump their offer beyond the dollar figures. They just don't know what.[25]

Regardless, this was the biggest moment in Clippers history, the time they came within a hair of stealing Kobe and completely changing the face of pro basketball in Los Angeles as we knew it. The second biggest moment was when they signed Bill Walton . . . who played 167 games in six years and topped 55 once. The third happened in the second round of the '06 playoffs, needing one stop to secure the series, when Mike Dunleavy stuck an ice-cold rookie named Daniel Ewing on Raja Bell and blew their one chance at an extended playoff run. The fourth was when they lost a deciding Game 5 in 1990 and ESPN Classic showed the game fifteen years later. (That's right, the Clips on ESPN Classic!) The fifth was a five-way tie between the times Marques Johnson, Derek Smith, Norm Nixon, Shaun Livingston and Danny Manning blew out their knees. And the sixth was when I nearly made a half-court shot at a Clippers game for *E:60*. Not a fun three decades for the Clips in California.

21. What if the Lakers picked Dominique Wilkins over James Worthy in the 1982 draft?

The defending champs were picking first thanks to a head-scratching trade with Cleveland.[26] Desperately needing young blood at the forward spot, the Lakers lucked into the perfect draft for that wish list—Worthy, Terry Cummings and 'Nique went one-two-three—ultimately opting for Worthy's all-around excellence and experience over 'Nique's upside and

25. Devil's advocate view: maybe Kobe just realized, "What the hell am I doing? It's the Clippers! Am I crazy?"

26. During the '80 season, idiot Cavs owner Ted Stepien traded Butch Lee and his '82 number one for an '80 number one (destined to suck since the Lakers were a top-four team) and Don Ford, a run-of-the-mill swingman who looked like a cross between Craig Ehlo and Ted McGinley. With the exception of Mike Bratz, there has never been a worse player traded for a franchise-altering number one.

explosiveness.[27] You know what's surprising? This wasn't a popular choice at the time. NBA fans were drooling at the thought of 'Nique (one of the most thrilling college players ever to that point) running the wing with Magic, Nixon and the Showtime Lakers. But an unhappy Wilkins could have imploded them and the Lakers didn't want to take the chance; he didn't help his cause by refusing to play for the Clips (picking second) or Jazz (picking third). Knowing what we know now, it's just far-fetched to imagine 'Nique giving up shots, deferring to Kareem and breaking a sweat on defense. Then again, maybe Riley and Magic could have changed his ways (after all, they salvaged McAdoo's career and he was infinitely more selfish than 'Nique), and had they done so, the ceiling of those Showtime Lakers teams climbs a level because 'Nique was such an electric player and unstoppable scorer. Beyond that, Magic would have made him better and they might have broken the record for Most Alley-Oops That Brought the House Down. Shit, we might have spent 1985 to 1993 having Jordan-Dominique arguments that centered around "Who's better?" instead of "Who's a better dunker?"

Had the Lakers taken Wilkins, his career would have been remembered differently: either better or worse, but definitely not the same. We can agree on that. We can also agree that Worthy would have been the big loser here: the Clippers would have taken him second, then Utah would have taken Cummings third because he could play both forward spots (in fact, they took Thurl Bailey the next year for the same reason). Instead, Worthy went first, Cummings went second and poor Utah had to trade number three to Atlanta for John Drew, Freeman Williams and $750,000 in a deal that seemed awful even before Drew entered rehab a few months later and admitted he'd been freebasing for three solid years. (Way to do your homework, Utah!) Has there ever been a best-case/worst-case draft scenario that rivals James Worthy landing on the '83 Lakers instead of the '83 Clippers? Instead of winning three rings, a Finals MVP and NBA's 50 at 50 honors, he would have joined a woeful Clippers team, fallen prey to the Clippers jinx, blown out his knee in twenty-nine places within three years

27. Worthy averaged a 16–6 and shot 57 percent as a UNC senior; Wilkins averaged a 21–8 and shot 53 percent as a University of Georgia junior. 'Nique got knocked out of the Final Four; Worthy shined in the title game with a 28–17.

and missed every one of Magic Johnson's postgame Laker orgies. We never would have uttered the words "Big Game James." Ever.[28]

20. What if Atlanta took Chris Paul with the number two pick of the 2005 draft?

We knew this was an Aretha Franklin–sized mistake at the time because Paul was the best player in the '05 draft and, more importantly, *Atlanta desperately needed a point guard!*[29] But with Paul turning into a franchise guy and Evolutionary Isiah, it's slowly becoming the poor man's version of Bowie-over-MJ for this generation of hoop fans, a relatively inexplicable decision that became between ten and twenty times more inexplicable as the years passed. With the supporting talent the Hawks already had in place (Joe Johnson, Josh Smith, etc.), you couldn't pick a better team for him. You really couldn't.[30] It's safe to say CP3 (and Deron Williams)will be haunting Atlanta fans for years to come. All 527 of them.

But here's what we haven't made enough of . . .

19. What if Portland took Chris Paul with the number three pick?

Ohhhhhhhhhhhhh . . . you forgot about this one, huh? Portland sent that pick to Utah for the number six pick (Martell Webster), the number twenty-seven pick (Linus Kleiza) and a 2006 number one (the number thirty pick, Joel Freeland). So let's say the Blazers had just kept number three and picked Paul, which would have made sense because, you know, he was the best player in the draft and all. They're still a lottery team the following season,

---

28. Worthy could have played with Bizarro Worthy (Tom Chambers) on the '83 Clips. I will explain on page 288.

29. Yes, I wrote this at the time. Repeatedly. For anyone reading this book from 2030 on, the guy Atlanta took instead was a forward named Marvin Williams who couldn't start for UNC the previous year. I thought this was a bad sign.

30. In consecutive drafts, Hawks GM Billy Knight took Marvin Williams over Paul and Shelden Williams over Brandon Roy. There's a 17 percent chance he just sold you this book at an Atlanta Borders or Barnes & Noble. Tall, late '40s, black, seemed sad . . . was that him?

although probably not quite as bad; maybe they end up with Rudy Gay at number eight instead of Aldridge at number four. They're definitely better in '07, maybe a fringe playoff team, so let's take Oden away from them and give them the number twelve pick (Thaddeus Young) that year. So which foundation would you rather have if you're a Portland fan?

> *Scenario A: Oden, Aldridge, Webster, Roy, Travis Outlaw, Jarrett Jack, Joel Przybilla, the rights to Rudy Fernandez and Paul Allen's billions*
> *Scenario B: Paul, Roy, Gay, Outlaw, Przybilla, Jack, Young, the rights to Rudy Fernandez and Paul Allen's billions*

Hmmmmmm. Paul and Roy as your backcourt for the next six to eight years?[31] Could that have worked when both guys need the ball in their hands? (Possibly.) Would they have had enough size? (From the looks of it, no.) Would they have played a more wide-open style and would it have worked? (With the talent on hand, I say yes.) Anyway, if Portland takes Paul, that sets off a crazy chain reaction: New Orleans ending up with Deron Williams instead of Paul; Utah never getting a franchise point guard; Oden and Aldridge landing in other cities; maybe Roy not turning into a franchise guard playing second fiddle to Paul; and maybe Paul not being quite as driven because he's not as ticked off for the next few years after three teams passed on him.[32] I like the way it worked out.

---

31. I would have said "next decade" but supposedly Roy's knee ligaments are made out of pages 41 and 42 of this book.[P8]

P8. In *TBOB*'s hardcover, the end of that footnote read, "There's a 98.5 percent chance that 'What if Portland had taken Durant over Oden?' will crack the *Second Book of Basketball* in 2016." I was off by six years and 1.5 percent. This will all make sense in exactly 1 page.

32. Remember when the Texans took Mario Williams over Reggie Bush and everyone gave them copious amounts of shit? It was the best thing that ever happened to Williams; he killed himself to prove everyone wrong. NBA examples along the same lines: Paul, Karl Malone, MJ, Paul Pierce, Rashard Lewis and Caron Butler. Most underrated example: Tom Brady.

18. What if the Knicks bought Julius Erving's contract from the Nets in 1976?

After the ABA merger happened, the Nets made an intriguing offer to the Knickerbockers: *He's yours if you waive our territorial penalty ($480,000 per year for ten years)*. Already saddled with the expensive Haywood contract, the Knicks turned them down and set their franchise back seven solid years.[33] Philly bought Doc for $3 million and poor Doc coexisted with overhyped guys, ball hogs, head cases and underachievers for the next three years, too dignified and too unselfish to fight them for shots. So really, this couldn't have turned out worse unless Doc also knocked up a white female sportswriter covering the Sixers and didn't publicly acknowledge their daughter until she became a tennis star sixteen years later.

(Hey, wait a second . . .)

One more wrinkle: the Nets settled that territorial fee two years later by swapping the fourth pick in the '78 draft (Micheal Ray Richardson)[34] and their number one pick in 1979 (eventually Larry Demic at number nine) for the thirteenth pick in 1978 (Winford Boynes), Phil Jackson, all of Phil Jackson's weed and a settlement for the remaining money. If you want to get technical, this had a double impact because, before the '83 season, the Knicks signed Bernard King to a $4.5 million, five-year offer sheet that Golden State matched, finally agreeing to send King to the Knicks for . . . (drumroll, please) . . . Micheal Ray Richardson![35] So maybe the Knicks screwed up by not getting Doc, but it led to two wildly entertaining Micheal Ray years, one "What the hell is wrong with Micheal Ray?" season, one extremely good Bernard season, then one and a half life-altering Bernard years. That's not so bad, right?

33. Even weirder: the Knicks bought Bob McAdoo from Buffalo 20 games into the season and gave him the same money they would have given to Doc. Huh? Wilt flirted with a Knicks comeback that same summer—potentially, the Knicks could have trotted out Wilt, Haywood, Doc, Frazier and Monroe.

34. This also ranks among the great what-ifs if you were a dealer living in Manhattan in the early '80s. No Micheal Ray in New York?

35. This was like Marbury for Kidd, only with the Russian roulette aspect of "each guy has battled serious coke/alcohol problems and will either make or break our franchise." And yes, the Warriors were broken. They dumped him to Jersey for Sleepy Floyd four months later.

17. What if Portland had taken Kevin Durant over Greg Oden?

Here's what we knew about Oden heading into the 2007 Draft: owned Ewing-like potential as a rebounder and shot blocker . . . struggled with a broken wrist during his freshman year at Ohio State . . . only played one "Wow!" game (the '07 NCAA Championship: 25 points, 12 rebounds, 4 blocks in defeat against Florida's Joakim Noah and Al Horford) . . . his right leg was one inch longer than his left leg (a red flag for potential knee/feet/back issues) . . . openly admitted that he didn't love basketball and once wanted to become a dentist . . . frightened everyone in Portland with a jittery pre-draft workout . . . looked and walked like a thirty-six-year-old man.[P9]

Meanwhile, Durant lived and breathed basketball, became a national phenomenon during his only Texas season, crushed his Portland work-out[P10] and had no conceivable offensive ceiling. Throw in Portland's tortured history with fragile centers and, as the years pass, it's becoming harder to fathom that the Blazers willingly decided, "Screw the sure thing, let's take the big guy with uneven legs who played one great college game." But that's what they did. Because we love revising history over time, owner Paul Allen and then–general manager Kevin Pritchard have been protected by the "Come on, anyone would have taken Oden, you always take a franchise center, it's not their fault he keeps getting injured" defense. That presumes Oden was considered a sure thing—like Kareem,

P9. When basketball players are dressed in everyday clothes, it's mesmerizing to watch them walk. Always bigger in person, they move so effortlessly that it feels like they belong to another species. Most tall people move gingerly, their posture sucks and everything about them says, "I wish I wasn't this tall." The best NBA athletes don't carry themselves that way. *They glide.* They never look gawky. So when I saw Durant shuffle effortlessly down a hallway before the 2007 ESPYs, I thought, "Good, I was right, that guy was born to play basketball." A few hours later, Oden walked down that same hallway looking like Redd Foxx in *Sanford and Son.* His posture was totally screwed up. If you saw him from behind, you would have thought it was a retired player. On that moment alone, I couldn't believe he went first. Oden walked like a guy whose infrastructure was out of whack. Had I been running Portland's 2007 Draft and seen him walk across a room even once, that would have been it for me. The great ones always glide. They just do.

P10. Pritchard after Durant's workout: "That was an incredible workout . . . I've seen probably, in this building, a couple hundred workouts, and that was as impressive as any workout that I've seen in here."

Ewing or Hakeem—and ignores those six months everyone spent wondering about him before the 2007 Draft. Like me, Boston GM Danny Ainge liked Durant as the top pick for one reason: *Durant* was the sure thing, not Oden. If you followed Durant in college (and Ainge fell head over heels for him, as did I), you knew about his work ethic, leadership, character and scoring DNA. I thought Durant was a genetic freak: like Tracy McGrady crossed with Plastic Man, someone God created to make baskets and get to the line. Oden left you hoping he stayed healthy, hoping basketball would become more important to him, hoping his spotty college year wasn't an aberration, hoping he developed a low-post game and a killer instinct . . . for a sure thing, you sure were doing a lot of hoping. How was that any different from the Bowie/Jordan dilemma twenty-three years earlier? When Durant became the youngest scoring champ ever and placed second in the 2010 MVP balloting—as Oden recovered from his second season-ending knee injury, no less[P11]—Portland's decision barreled into the what-if chapter six years earlier than expected.

So what if the Blazers picked Durant instead of Oden? They become the fledgling Western Conference juggernaut of the 2010s (not Oklahoma City); Portland becomes a legitimate 2010 destination for LeBron; any successfully unconventional decision would be called "a Pritchard"; and everyone in Portland would be so perpetually happy that it would never rain there again. Instead, we have to start bracing for the 2029 or 2030 draft, when Portland wins another lottery and finds itself stressing between Sure Thing Potential Superstar Scorer X over Possibly Fragile Franchise Center X as everyone else wonders, "Wait a second, we're doing this *again*?" One of these generations, the Blazers will get it right.

P11. Oden also suffered an embarrassing Internet scandal in the winter of 2009, when an ex-girlfriend leaked naked cell phone photos that Oden had taken of himself two years earlier. Although "embarrassing" might be misleading, because after seeing the awe-inspiring size of Oden's dong, everyone realized his legs really *were* different sizes. Important note: I refused to look at the pictures; I made it through 2010 without seeing Oden's dong or *Avatar*.

16. What if Kobe was convicted of sexual assault instead of settling with his accuser out of court for big bucks?

Whoops, I forgot that in 2005 everyone in the Los Angeles area agreed to pretend this never happened. Now they act perturbed if anyone else brings it up (or broaches it). I live in L.A. right now, so unfortunately, I have to follow the code. When I move back East someday, we'll update this section in the next printing. Stay tuned.

15. What if the Suns didn't screw up a potential Nash dynasty with some of the cheapest and most perplexing moves ever made?

I wanted to avoid playing the "What if the front office did this instead of this?" game because it's so subjective, but Phoenix's wretched game plan from 2004 to 2008 had to be commemorated in some way. Here's a detailed look.

1. During the same summer they signed Nash, Phoenix traded the seventh pick in the '04 Draft (and a chance to take either Luol Deng or Andre Iguodala) to Chicago for $3 million and a 2006 number one. One week later, they signed Quentin Richardson to a six-year, $42.6 million deal, even though they could have drafted Deng or Iguodala and paid either of them one-third what Richardson was getting. They kept Richardson for one year before swapping Q and their twenty-first pick (Nate Robinson) in the '05 draft to the Knicks for Kurt Thomas. Two summers later, they dumped Thomas on Seattle along with two number ones just to shed him off their cap for tax purposes. As astounding as this sounds, Bryan Colangelo's decision to sign Richardson instead of just drafting Deng or Iguodala—which was dumb at the time, by the way—ended up costing them four first-round picks![36]

36. Hold on, this gets better. Your 2005 NBA Executive of the Year? That's right, Mr. Bryan Colangelo! I love the NBA.

2. Phoenix lowballed Joe Johnson so insultingly that he asked them not to match Atlanta's $70 million free agent offer, leading to Phoenix accepting Boris Diaw and two future first-rounders for him. The Suns had just come within two wins of the '05 Finals and built a run-and-gun identity; suddenly they were dealing a twenty-four-year-old potential All-Star, the perfect swingman for their system and a deadly shooter who could even play backup point guard, and they were only getting back a bench player and two future picks? With Nash, Amar'e, Marion and Johnson, you're set for the rest of the decade. Surround them with role players and veteran buyout guys and you're contending until Nash breaks down, and even then, you can just shift the offense over to Johnson as the main creator. *How can you give that guy up?* So what if he's insulted and doesn't want to come back? He'll get over it! You're paying him $14 million a year and he gets to play with Steve Nash! Arrrrrrrgh.[37]

3. Instead of picking Rajon Rondo with the twenty-first pick in '06 (the pick acquired from Chicago), they shipped his rights to Boston for Cleveland's 2007 number one and $1.9 million. A few weeks later, they gave Marcus Banks $24 million. Would you rather have a potential up-and-comer like Rondo for cheap money or a proven turd like Banks for five times as much? Tough call. If you just had a head injury.[P12]

4. They gave Diaw a five-year, $45 million extension that summer, which meant the Diaw/Banks combo now earned as much money every year as Joe Johnson. Awesome.

5. So the Iguodala/Deng/Rondo pick became number twenty-four in the '07 draft . . . and naturally, the Suns sold it to Portland for $3 million. Why didn't they just take Spanish star Rudy Fernandez (Portland's pick)? You can't play the luxury tax card because Fernandez wasn't planning on joining the NBA for at least a year; it would have been

37. I'm not totally absolving Johnson here. So they dicked him around a little. When you're playing with Steve Nash, do you know what that means? *You're playing with Steve Nash!* Why give that up unless you have to?

P12. Rondo evolved into an electrifying guard—like Fat Lever crossed with an alien—outplayed LeBron in a Playoff series (2010, second round) and became the best player on a Finals team. Normally this would have driven all of Phoenix to hard drugs and possibly crystal meth, but the Hoop Gods gave them an endearingly entertaining '10 season (Western Finals, fantastic chemistry, fun to watch). No way Rondo blossoms quite like that behind Nash. We're all winners.

savvy if Phoenix had stashed him in Europe as an asset down the road. Instead, owner Robert Sarver announced to his fans, "Screw you, I'd rather have the $3 million, I'm taking the cash." One year later, Fernandez would have been a top-ten pick after lighting it up in Spain; he even gave the Redeem Team everything it could handle in the 2008 Olympics. Can you quantify the damage there?[38]

I hate delving into the Marty McFly Zone when many of the aforementioned screwups were interrelated, but let's figure out how the Suns could have turned out if cheapskate owner Sarver didn't sign off on the aforementioned game plan in 2004. They could have had a six-man nucleus of Nash, Marion, Stoudemire, Johnson, Leandro Barbosa and Deng/Iguodala from 2004 to the present that shouldn't have been touched; now add first-rounders in '05, '06 and '08 for tax purposes. Even if they surrounded that nucleus with draft picks, minimum-wage veterans and February buyout guys and did nothing else, wouldn't they have been positioned for the short term and long term better than any franchise in the latter half of this decade? The bigger question: why own an NBA team if you're going to cut costs? What's the point? Why would that be fun? So people could stare at you during dinner and whisper, "Hey, that's the cheap-ass who owns the Suns"? This pisses me off. What a wasted chance, and what a waste of Nash's prime.

(Note to the Phoenix fans: you can now light yourselves on fire.)

14. What if Orlando had kept Chris Webber's draft rights instead of trading him?

Remember when the Magic defied 1-in-66 odds to win the '93 lottery, giving them the number one pick for the second straight year in maybe the biggest stroke of luck in NBA history? Since Webber was the ideal complement to Shaq (a great passer who could play the high post, crash the boards, run the floor and defend the rim), we spent the next few weeks wondering how any-

---

38. They downgraded from Deng or Iguodala to Rondo to Fernandez to nothing . . . which means they traded a number seven pick in a loaded draft for $4.9 million, less than they paid Banks to sit on their bench in '07.

one could match up with Shaq, Webber, Nick Anderson, Dennis Scott and Lord knows who else over the next ten to twelve years. Magic GM Pat Williams had other ideas: he was swayed by Penny Hardaway's workout right before the draft, which Williams described afterward by saying, "I've never seen someone come in and do the things that Penny Hardaway did in that workout."[39] On draft day, Williams shocked everyone by swapping the first pick to Golden State for the third pick overall and first-rounders in '96, '98 and '00, a move that was widely panned at the time and nearly caused a riot in Orlando. No NBA trade received more attention, went in more directions over a ten-year span and spawned more what-ifs. Webber battled with Warriors coach Don Nelson constantly as a rookie (Webber wanted to play forward, Nellie wanted him to play center) during a 50-win season in which Tim Hardaway was recovering from a torn ACL. The following year, Hardaway returned with C-Webb, Latrell Sprewell (first-team All-NBA in '94), Chris Mullin (just past his prime), Rony Seikaly, Avery Johnson and Chris Gatling . . . I mean, that's a pretty nice top seven, right? Webber didn't care; he had an opt-out clause and wanted out. Stuck between a rock and Shawn Kemp's boxers, the Warriors swapped him to Washington for Tom Gugliotta and three number ones and inadvertently damaged his career (see page 377 for the grisly details). Meanwhile, Hardaway exceeded everyone's expectations, led Orlando to the '95 Finals and made an All-NBA first team—and then he clashed with Shaq (Shaq bolted for L.A.), devolved from an unselfish playmaker to a me-first scorer and blew out his knee in Phoenix. Bad times all around.

So what if Orlando just kept Webber? Does Shaq still leave after the '96 season? (Impossible to say.) Would Webber have thrived as the Robin to Shaq's Batman? (I say yes.) Who would the Magic have targeted with their '94 cap space instead of Horace Grant?[40] (My guesses: Detlef Schrempf and Steve Kerr.) Would they have made the '95 Finals with Shaq, C-Webb, Scott, Anderson, Brian Shaw and my two free agent guesses? (I say yes.) Would they have had a better chance against the '95 Rockets with that team? (Actually, yes.) As for Penny Hardaway, he takes

39. My buddy JackO and I have been joking about that workout for years. Unless Penny was making half-court shots while stepping on broken glass and swinging his genitals like a lasso, there's no effing way that one workout should have swayed the Magic from a Webber/Shaq combo. None.

40. I hate the Magic, Jazz, the Heat and everyone else for the whole "It feels funny using 'they' when you write about a team whose name doesn't end in an *s*" conundrum.

Tim Hardaway's minutes on that aforementioned 50-win Warriors team, thrives in Nellie's offense with Spree, Mullin and Owens flanking him, and potentially becomes a Hall of Famer for all we know. Just remember, C-Webb and Penny were both top-forty talents who never reached their potential for reasons that aren't entirely satisfying. Had the trade never happened, maybe one of them (or both of them) would have reached that potential. Let's give them starting spots on the What-If All-Stars.

13. What if Anthony Carter's agent never messed up?

A forgotten footnote in NBA history: when Anthony Carter's agent (Bill Duffy) never faxed Miami a letter exercising Carter's $4.1 million player option for the 2003–4 season.[41] After the deadline passed, Carter became a free agent (whoops!) and Miami suddenly had enough cap space to throw a $60 million, six-year offer at Lamar Odom. One summer later, they packaged Odom, Caron Butler, Brian Grant's cadaver and a 2006 first-rounder to L.A. for Shaq. Two obvious repercussions here: First, Miami never wins the 2006 title if Duffy doesn't screw up. Second, since Miami couldn't have gotten Shaq without Duffy, where else could Shaq have landed when the Lakers *had* to trade him?[42] Could Dallas have stolen him for something like Michael Finley, Devin Harris, Alan Henderson's expiring contract and a number one pick? Would Denver have offered Marcus Camby, Nene Hilario and Voshon Lenard? Could the Bulls have hijacked him for Eddy Curry (a free agent after the season), Antonio Davis (expiring) and a first-round pick? I say Dallas had the best chance, which means they would have avoided that crippling Dampier move, gotten Shaq, and kept their best four guys (Nowitzki, Howard, Stackhouse

41. Poor Carter ended up signing a two-year, $1.5 million deal with San Antonio, with Duffy's agency repaying Carter the lost wages from the Miami deal. One of my top-twelve can't-be-proven NBA conspiracy theories ever: Miami paid Duffy to "forget" to send that letter.
42. When the Lakers re-signed Kobe that summer, a secret handshake promise to trade Shaq ASAP was part of the deal. I know this for a fact. Let's just say I had a few drinks with the right person once.

and Terry). How many titles are we thinking there? Two? Three? When I emailed him about this last summer (subject line: "Insanely Random Question"), Cuban responded, "[I have] no idea if we would have gotten him, but I know Shaq wanted to come."

You know what that means? If we're making the list of Guys Who Prevented Us from Seeing a Pissed-Off Stern Hand a Sobbing Cuban the Lawrence O'Brien Trophy, here's the top five in no particular order: Dwyane Wade, Bill Duffy, Bennett Salvatore, Don Nelson and Isiah Thomas (for stupidly taking Penny's contract in the Marbury deal and giving Phoenix enough cap space to woo Nash the following summer).

Hey, speaking of Isiah . . .

12. What if the Knicks never hired Isiah Thomas?

This could have been its own bizarro "Where Amazing Happens" NBA commercial called "Where Isiah Happens."

(Cue up the annoying piano music that haunted me every time I tried to fall asleep after hearing it for six straight months during the '08 season.)[43]

Picture: The '05 Suns celebrating after a playoff win.
Caption: Where Phoenix dumps the Stephon Marbury and Penny Hardaway contracts on some unsuspecting sucker and remakes its team into a contender happens.

Picture: The '07 Bulls celebrating after a playoff win.
Caption: Where Chicago dumps Eddy Curry and his gigantic ass for two lottery picks and copious amounts of cap space happens.

Picture: The '07 Raptors celebrating after a playoff win.
Caption: Where Toronto finds some dummy to take Jalen Rose's contract off their hands and aid its rebuilding process happens.

---

43. I took this section from a February '08 column. Within ninety minutes of it being posted, an enterprising reader made a homemade version of the ad and posted it on YouTube. I've never been prouder.

Picture: San Antonio's 2005 trophy celebration.

Caption: Where San Antonio dumps Malik Rose's contract for a cap-friendly center who helps them win the title happens.

Picture: Steve Francis sitting glumly on the Knicks bench.

Caption: Where Orlando finds someone to take Steve Francis' horrendous contract so they can free up $15 million in cap space happens.

Picture: The '08 Blazers celebrating after a last-second win.

Caption: Where the 2008 Blazers become the NBA's most likable young team because they found a taker for Zach Randolph happens.

Picture: Anucha Browne Sanders celebrating on the courthouse steps.[44]

Caption: Where a humiliating $11 million sexual harassment settlement happens.

Picture: A white SUV.

Caption: Where a Truck Party happens.[45]

Picture: Curry and Randolph looking overweight, like they just barbecued Nate Robinson on a grill and ate him.

Caption: Where an NBA frontcourt that includes two C-cups happens.

Picture: Utah rookie Gordon Hayward.

Caption: Where trading away a future number-one pick in 2004 that becomes a top-ten pick in 2010 happens.

Picture: A mostly empty Madison Square Garden.

Caption: Where a sixty-year tradition of professional basketball going down the tubes happens.

---

44. Browne Sanders was the fellow Knicks employee who sued Isiah for sexual harassment and won. Isiah could have settled out of court but couldn't even pull that deal off.

45. During the Browne Sanders lawsuit, it was revealed that Stephon Marbury had boinked a female MSG intern named Kathleen Decker outside a strip club in his SUV. *The Daily News* showed a picture of the SUV on its front page with the headline, "Truck Party!" Basically, the name for my 2007–8 fantasy hoops team fell out of the sky. Also, Decker's father won the 2007 Most Horrified Dad ESPY.

Picture: Isiah sitting on the bench with that frozen, blank look on his face like he's either flatlining or planning to kill everyone in the locker room after the game.

Caption: Where Isiah happens.

(Follow-up note: Has any GM in NBA history ever directly altered the fortunes of seven franchises for the better? Portland, San Antonio, Phoenix, Toronto, Orlando, Chicago, New York . . . that's nearly 25 percent of the league! He is missed. By the other GMs.)[P13]

11. What if Maurice Stokes never went down?

Not an injury what-if because the Royals star technically didn't get injured playing basketball; he contracted encephalitis, a fluke of an illness that happens only if an undiagnosed bacterial infection or undiagnosed brain trauma is left untreated, worsens and eventually causes brain damage. Poor Stokes banged his head in the final game of the '58 season against Minneapolis, flew back to Cincinnati that night, never got treated over the next three days, flew to Detroit for a playoff game and played sluggishly, then finally collapsed on the plane home. So a fluky combination of factors—poor medical treatment, multiple flights (the last thing you want to do with brain trauma) and poor Stokes gutting out a playoff game when he felt terrible—led to brain damage and Stokes spending the rest of his shortened life in a wheelchair.

How good was Stokes? He averaged a 17–16, 16–17 and 17–18 in his only three seasons as the NBA's first ahead-of-his-time power forward, like a taller Charles Barkley, a six-foot-seven 275-pounder who pounded the boards, handled the ball full-court, and had a variety of Baylor-like moves around the basket (scoop shots, finger rolls and the like). Had he avoided gaining weight in his late twenties (you never know with this

P13. When Knicks owner James Dolan nearly rehired Isiah as a consultant in 2010, a Knicks buddy asked me "if it's ever revealed that Dolan was mentally ill while he owned the Knicks, would the NBA feel bad and compensate us with extra no. 1 picks?" He was serious.

stuff), Stokes would have been a mortal lock for the NBA's 50 at 50. Given that Oscar was a future territorial pick for the Royals, we can safely assume that an Oscar-Stokes combo would have altered the course of a Finals or two in the sixties. From a big-picture standpoint, the NBA lost its most charismatic black star of the fifties *and* sixties. What a shame. There wasn't a single silver lining except for an improbable, feel-good human interest story that we'll continue in the Jack Twyman section of the Pyramid.[46]

10. What if Memphis instead of Cleveland landed LeBron?

Take a trip back to the 2003 lottery with me. We're down to Cleveland and Memphis in the final two. If the Grizzlies draw number two, they turn the pick over to Detroit because they stupidly traded a conditional number one for Otis Thorpe five years earlier (a pick that only had top-one protection in 2003).[47] If the Grizz draw number one, then they keep the pick and get LeBron. Suddenly we're presented with the greatest hit-or-miss moment in the history of professional sports—like going on *Deal or No Deal,* getting down to two suitcases and having a 50/50 chance of winning $500 million. For a few seconds, ESPN's camera shows Jerry West, who has the same look on his face that Forrest Gump had when he groped Jenny's boobies for the first time. If Jerry had dropped dead right then and there, nobody would have been surprised. Well, we know how it turned out: Cleveland got the first pick, Memphis got nothing and a heartbroken West retired and eventually disappeared off the face of the earth, presumably to spend the next few years playing Russian roulette in Southeast Asia

---

46. "Wait a second, there's a Jack Twyman section?" you ask. You're fuckin'-A right there's a Jack Twyman section!

47. You have to love a draft that had two of the top 20 what-ifs playing off the same scenario. I hope you fledgling GMs learned something in this chapter: don't trade number one picks five years down the road for guys like Don Ford and Otis Thorpe. By the way, the guy who made those trades and helped kill professional basketball in Vancouver—Stu Jackson—was improbably hired by Stern and given a perplexing amount of power this decade. I had two different connected NBA friends inadvertently make the same joke: if Stern is Michael Corleone, Stu is definitely Fredo. In Fredo's defense, I don't think even he could have ruined basketball in Vancouver that quickly.

like Christopher Walken in *The Deer Hunter.* (Sorry to throw consecutive movie references at you, but the situation demanded two of them and that's that.) Now look at the domino effect over the next five years if Memphis gets that pick:

1. LeBron joins a deep Grizzlies team (Pau Gasol, Shane Battier, Mike Miller . . .) that won 50 games despite getting nothing from that '03 draft. A little better than starting out on a lottery team with knuckleheads like Ricky Davis and Darius Miles, right?

2. Picking second, Cleveland takes Carmelo and builds around 'Melo, Carlos Boozer and Carlos Boozer's chest hair. Since Denver GM Kiki Vandeweghe took Nikoloz Tskitishvili over Amar'e Stoudemire in 2002, it goes without saying Kiki would have been stupid enough to take Darko at number three over Chris Bosh. The rest of the draft probably unfolds the same way, although Chad Ford still probably has the immortal Maciej Lampe going ninth to the Knicks.

3. What are the odds LeBron stays in Memphis after his rookie contract ends? I'm going with between 0.000001 and 0.009 percent. And that might be high. Which means he becomes a free agent following the 2007 season, leading to numerous lousy teams devoting their '06 and '07 seasons to carving out enough cap space for him, as well as Isiah failing to plan ahead, inadvertently knocking New York out of the LeBron sweepstakes and a summer of rioting in the streets of Manhattan the likes of which we haven't seen since the '77 blackout and the Son of Sam murders. Also, LeBron's departure swiftly kills basketball in Memphis, with the Grizzlies moving to England and becoming the London Hooligans. (Actually, what am I saying? That still might happen.) And every title from 2008 to 2022 might look different. That's about it.

9. What if Ralph Sampson entered the 1980 draft?

In April 1980 the rejuvenated Celtics were coming off 60 wins and preparing for a bloodbath with Philly in the Eastern Finals . . . and as this was happening, they won the coin flip giving them the number one pick (thanks to the McAdoo trade one year earlier). The seven-foot-four Sampson was finishing a much-hyped freshman year at Virginia (15–11, 5 blocks a game); we forget this now, but Sampson ranked right up there with Walton, Kareem and Wilt once upon a time on the This Guy Is Going to Join the NBA and Obliterate Everyone Scale.[48] The Celtics quietly started lobbying him: *Come play with us. You'll compete for a title right away with Bird, Cowens, Maxwell and Tiny on the greatest franchise ever. Why risk getting hurt? You and Bird could own this league for the decade.* When Sampson improbably turned them down, they settled on plan B: trading that pick (along with number thirteen) for Robert Parish and number three (Kevin McHale), then winning three titles within the next six years.

Do they win those trophies with Sampson? That depends on how you project his career had he skipped those last three college years—in which he never improved playing with inferior teammates while facing slow-down tactics and triple-teams—and got thrown into the fire at the highest possible level on a contender. In 1980, Auerbach believed that Sampson had the athletic ability and instincts to become the next Russell. I always thought Sampson was like a postmerger Kareem sans the sky hook: same height, same body, slightly disappointing rebounder and shot blocker (though still solid in both departments), but a mismatch for nearly everyone because of his size and quickness. Those last three college years significantly damaged his ceiling. He never developed a money-in-the-bank shot; if anything, he bought into the whole "Sampson is a guard in a big man's body" hype, started screwing around 20 feet from the basket and tried to run fast breaks like a mutant Bob Cousy. Throw in a dreadful Houston team in his rookie season and that's *four* wasted seasons in his formative years. He never recovered. Imagine Ralph learning the ropes in Boston, mastering the rebounding/shot-blocking thing, playing high-pressure playoff games, running the floor with a great fast-break team and getting fed easy baskets from Bird from 1980 to 1984. On paper,

---

48. In retrospect, we should have known that a guy named Ralph wasn't going to be one of the best centers ever. Had he embraced the Muslim faith and changed his name to Kabaar Abdul-Sampson or Raheem Sampson, he'd have been unstoppable. Look at the names of the best players ever: they're all great names that you'd give a sports movie character. Michael Jordan. Bill Russell. Magic Johnson. Jerry West. Larry Bird. Moses Malone. You'd never name the lead of a sports movie Ralph Sampson or Darko Milicic.

that would have been the cushiest situation in NBA history for a franchise center.[49] Would that have been better than a McHale/Parish combo? Depends on how you feel about Auerbach's "next Russell" assessment. Red flipped out publicly after Sampson turned them down, hissing that Ralph was being "hoodwinked by glad-handers" and adding, "The people who advised him to stay in school will have trouble sleeping nights. They're taking away earning potential he'll never get back, and they're forgetting that if he gets hit by a car, it's the end of the line. It's ridiculous. If he were an intellectual genius and was planning on being a surgeon, you could see him wanting to go to school." Considering Sampson only played four healthy NBA seasons and filed for bankruptcy a few years later, maybe Red knew what he was talking about. (Whether he assessed Ralph's ceiling correctly is another story.) But Ralph stayed in school, leading to . . .

8. What if the '86 Rockets never fell apart?

Magic's Lakers won titles in '80, '82 and '85 and were demolished by the '86 Rockets. Bird's Celtics won titles in '81, '84 and '86 and held the number two pick in a seemingly loaded '86 draft. So who ended up squeaking out two more titles and becoming the Team of the Decade? The Lakers. Why? Because of our number two what-if (sigh), as well as the untimely, unseemly, unprecedented, unfathomable, un-(fill in any other negative word) demise of the promising Sampson-Hakeem era.

We always hear about the tragic falls of Doc and Darryl, the two Coreys, Mike Tyson, Len Bias and about fifty different bands and singers from the eighties, but nobody ever remembers to include the team Pat Riley once called "the Team of the Future." For historical purposes, Houston's "upset" of the '86 Lakers was eventually dismissed as something of a fluke; during a fifty-month stretch from April '85 to June '89 in which we changed presidents, watched Rocky single-handedly end the Cold War,

49. Two of Sampson's three defining moments involved Boston anyway: his scary fall in March '86 (it happened in the Garden, so it makes you wonder if ghosts were involved) and the punch he threw at six-foot-one Jerry Sichting in Game 5 of the '86 Finals, leading to Boston's fans rattling his confidence in Game 6 (and the debut of the Ralph Sampson "I hope I get out of here alive" face).

became terrified of cocaine and unprotected sex, lost the ability to pro-
duce decent music, made a former Austrian bodybuilder the biggest
movie star alive, learned how to market black athletes, looked on sadly as
Eddie Murphy lost his sense of humor and Michael Jackson transformed
from biggest star on the planet to full-fledged freak and cautionary tale
and set the table for Jay Leno and Jerry Seinfeld to become the richest comedians of all time, the Lakers lost only one of their eighteen playoff
series . . . only it was to an upstart Rockets team who fell off the face of the
earth almost as quickly as they showed up. So naturally, it must have been
a fluke. Right?

Here are the facts: The Rockets lost Game 1 and swept the next four,
clinching at the Forum even after Hakeem got thrown out with six minutes remaining for fighting with Mitch Kupchak. (This one ended with
Sampson famously making his miracle buzzer-beater and Michael
Cooper sinking to the floor in disbelief, adding to the whole "what an
upset" myth.)[50] If you watch that series carefully, Houston couldn't have
been a worse matchup for the Lakers, whose major weaknesses were rebounding and defending elite low-post scorers. That Sampson-Hakeem
combo was their Kryptonite.[51] Watching Kareem "try" (repeat: "try") to
defend the impossibly quick Hakeem was like watching one of those slow
thirty-five-year-old linebackers (think Ray Lewis) getting stuck covering a
quick running back (think Darren Sproles) on a swing pass in the open
field without help. Mr. Ninny just had no chance. If they switched him to
Sampson (playing the high post), that pulled him away from the rim,
robbed the Lakers of their only shot blocker, and allowed Ralph to beat
him off the dribble . . . and that's before we get to the nightmare of undersized or athletically challenged forwards like Kupchak, A. C. Green or
James Worthy trying to handle Hakeem on the low post. If that weren't

50. This was the second-best buzzer-beater other than Jerry West's half-court shot in the
1970 Finals. How many series end on a twisting, 180-degree fling shot that happens in
under a second? And they diagrammed it in a huddle to boot!
51. Houston won Games 2, 3 and 4 by 10, 8, and 10, with Hakeem scoring 75 in Games
3 and 4. Pat Riley later lamented, "We tried everything. We put four bodies on him. We
helped from different angles. He's just a great player." The Rockets badly outrebounded
L.A. in their four wins. As SI's Jack MacCallum wrote afterward, "The Rockets headed
into [the Finals] secure in the knowledge that they had gone over, around and through
the Lakers. And everybody else knew it, too."

enough, Houston was blessed with lanky, athletic perimeter guys (Robert Reid, Lewis Lloyd,[52] Rodney McCray) who could rebound and cause problems for Magic. In retrospect, the only thing Houston was missing was a coaching staff of female call girls who could have seduced the Lakers after games and gotten them into trouble. That's how good the matchup was for Houston. Throw in pesky point guard John Lucas (who suffered a drug relapse two months before the playoffs) and they were put on the planet to beat up on those mid-eighties Lakers teams.

Still not sold? Hakeem and Ralph were the first picks in consecutive years ('83 and '84) and, along with the McHale/Parish combo in Boston, caused such a panic that every mid-eighties team became obsessed with adding size, leading to our number one what-if (hold tight), Joe Kleine and Jon Koncak getting picked ahead of Karl Malone, lottery teams rolling the dice with troubled losers like Chris Washburn and William Bedford and everything else. Suddenly the poor Lakers were a smallball team trapped in a big-man's league; with Kareem's rebounding/shot-blocking numbers in free fall, after Houston laid the smack down on them, everyone assumed the Magic-Kareem era was over. We never could have guessed that the promising Hakeem-Sampson era *had already peaked* in those four games. The following year, they battled the Disease of More (both Sampson and Hakeem wanted new contracts), lost Lucas to Milwaukee (he needed a fresh start) and suffered the double whammy of cocaine suspensions for Lloyd and Mitchell Wiggins (before the '87 All-Star break, Houston's three best guards were gone), and while all of this was happening, the effects of a harrowing Sampson fall at the Boston Garden in '86 started to surface: after injuring his back and hip in the plunge,[53] he started running differently to take pressure off his back and

---

52. Lloyd was devastating in transition and startlingly efficient: from '84 to '86, he averaged a 16–4–4 on 53% shooting. He's also the starting two-guard on the "Now that I'm watching this game 20 years later on ESPN Classic, I can totally see him failing a drug test—he's got crazy eyes!" All-Stars.

53. Sampson went up for a dunk, got blocked, got twisted awkwardly and crashed to the ground so violently that the Garden made an *ohhhhhhh* sound and went deathly quiet. He landed right on his head and back, almost like he fell out of a bunk bed while sleeping. They carried him off on a stretcher a foot too short, so his mammoth legs dangled off it. Here's how bad the injury looked when it happened: I actually remember where I was when I watched it live (my mom's bedroom—she had a great TV). You know it's a watershed moment when you can remember where you watched it.

wrecked his knees. Golden State acquired him during the '87–'88 season for (hold your nose) Joe Barry Carroll and Sleepy Floyd. So much for the Next Great Team in the West. Only recreational drugs and a fluke fall could stop them.

Here's the best way to put Houston's demise in perspective. Let's say the Pistons fell apart after the '86 playoffs because Isiah's knee betrayed him and Dennis Rodman, Vinnie Johnson, and John Salley were all kicked out of the league for cocaine. What happens to that void in the Eastern Conference? At the very least, the Celtics play in two more Finals ('87 and '88) and possibly steal one or both because they aren't worn down from battling the Pistons. Maybe Jordan wins eight titles instead of six. Maybe Dominique and the Hawks sneak into the Finals one year. Maybe the Blazers win the 1990 title and Clyde Drexler's career unfolds differently. Who knows? For the Lakers, having the Hoops Gods knock that Rockets team off—just vaporize them, basically—was almost as big a gift as that 1979 number one pick from New Orleans. And wouldn't we remember Hakeem's career differently had he been sticking it to Kareem and the Lakers for the rest of the eighties? What if he won four or five titles instead of two? Would that propel him past Kareem and make him the second greatest center of all time? It's safe to say that the '86 Rockets were the signature what-if team in NBA history.[54] Twenty years later, the *Houston Chronicle*'s Fran Blinebury wrote a column about them called "The Lost Dynasty" that included this quote from Lucas: "When I walk around Houston now and I hear people talk about winning those championships in '94 and '95, I just shake my head. I tell them, 'You've either forgotten or you have never seen the best Rockets team. I know. I was a part of it. And I was a big part of bringing it down.' . . . You look at most teams that are put together like that one and they get about an eight- to 10-year window. We didn't know it, but our window was right there, and then it slammed shut."

Allow me one last Ralph-related note because we can't have a what-if chapter without him. Only seventeen NBA rookies were considered sure-thing franchise guys in the past fifty years: Elgin, Wilt, Oscar, Kareem,

---

54. Personally, I think the Lakers should retire the number of Houston's coke dealer, as well as the Celtic who fouled Sampson in that '86 game in Boston.

THE BOOK OF BASKETBALL

Maravich, Walton, Bird, Magic, Sampson, Hakeem, Jordan, Ewing, Robinson, Shaq, Webber, Duncan and LeBron.[P14] Eleven of those sure things cracked the top twenty of my Hall of Fame Pyramid (coming shortly). Only Sampson and Webber will miss the Hall of Fame. Only Sampson and Walton failed to play more than four quality seasons, although Walton did win an MVP and Finals MVP and reinvent himself as the sixth man on an iconic team. When you look at Ralph's career compared to every other sure thing, it has to be considered one of the biggest flukes in sports history—a combination of bad luck, the wrong situation, and a player who was slightly overrated in the first place. Sampson flamed out as quickly as Bo Jackson or Dwight Gooden, only without the fanfare and legendary stories to keep his historical fire burning. He didn't just fade away; there's no trace of him. He left footprints like the kind you'd see on a beach. He didn't even inspire a "Whatever Happened to Ralph Sampson?" documentary that would have cruised to a sports Emmy in the right hands. If there's a lesson with all of this, I haven't found it yet. Just know that Magic, Kareem and Riley probably wipe their foreheads and say "Phew!" every time somebody brings up the '86 Rockets. And they should.

7. What if Julius Erving played with Pete Maravich?

Oh, wait, he did! For two exhibition games . . . but still. Before the '72–'73 season, Erving signed with Atlanta and jumped to the NBA for two exhibition games before the ABA legally blocked the move and forced him to play another season in Virginia. In retrospect, Doc's biggest mistake was jumping to the wrong team; Milwaukee held his NBA draft rights but Atlanta thumbed their noses at the Bucks and signed Doc, with the ensuing legal battle involving two professional teams separately suing the Hawks.

P14. Even though I would have bet anything on Durant becoming one of the best offensive forwards ever (barring injury), others were concerned about his build (too skinny) and defense (specifically, what position he might play). My counter at the time: if someone's ceiling is ten scoring titles, 38 points a game for one season and 50–40–90 career percentages, he's a sure thing. And I was right. For once.

Everything was held up for one year before Nets owner Roy Boe paid off the Hawks *and* Squires to bring Doc to New York.[55] Four absorbing wrinkles here:

1. The ABA without Doc for its last three seasons? One word: catastrophe.
2. In the past fifty-five years, the three most boring NBA seasons were 1974, 1975 and 1976. Let's just say that Doc would have helped.
3. Had Doc ignored Atlanta and concentrated on joining Milwaukee (not far-fetched since Doc wasn't a superstar yet and other ABA stars were jumping leagues),[56] Doc and Kareem potentially could have been teammates before either turned twenty-six. And not just that, but an aging Oscar would have been there, and Bobby Dandridge, too. Forget about altering the NBA landscape from 1973 to 1976; once Doc started coming into his own, the '74 Bucks could have won 70-plus games in a diluted NBA. Don't you love the what-if game?
4. If everything worked out and Doc jumped to the '73 Hawks, he would have gone to a team that won 46 games with Maravich, Lou Hudson and Walt Bellamy. Imagine adding Doc to the mix. And what about Young Doc and Young Pistol playing on the same team? I think the pilot just turned off the NO RIDICULOUS ALLEY-OOPS sign. A Doc-Pistol alliance would have pushed YouTube to another level, transformed Maravich's career, caused Brent Musburger to ejaculate on live TV and made Atlanta the league's biggest box office draw. Also, the ABA would have folded within two years and never merged with the NBA. And we'd have copious amounts of game film of the Doctor at his high-flying, mushroom-afro-wearing apex instead of just eyewitness accounts and possibly apocryphal stories. Damn it all.

55. It's really too bad that ESPN legal analyst Roger Cossack wasn't around then—he would have been more visible than Mel Kiper Jr. during the month of the NFL Draft.
56. Charlie Scott and Mel Daniels bailed on the league *during* the '73 season and got away with it. So it did happen. The ABA only had the legal resources to pick their spots and block bigger stars like Rick Barry.

6. What if New Orleans kept the rights to Moses Malone?

And you thought this one was going to be "What if the '77 Blazers hadn't traded Moses?" Ha! Too easy. This decision affected the fortunes of six franchises, swung six MVP votes and at least six titles (possibly more), robbed us of a potential Greatest Team Ever and set the tone for three decades of Clippers futility. The story starts in December 1975: Anticipating a merger, the NBA held a supplemental draft for recent undergraduates who signed with the ABA but didn't have an official NBA draft class. Lord knows how they came up with the rules for this thing, but five players were drafted (Moses, Mark Olberding, Mel Bennett, Charles Jordan and Skip Wise) and two of the selections cost teams their 1977 number one picks (New Orleans with Moses, the Lakers with Olberding). The following summer, the Jazz decided that they would rather have that number one pick back over keeping Malone's rights, so Moses was tossed into the ABA/NBA dispersal draft and assigned a price tag of $350,000.[57]

Now you're asking, "Wait, Moses was only twenty-one years old. Why didn't the Jazz just keep him? Wasn't he better than a future number one pick?" They might not have realized how good he was since Moses broke his foot the previous season and played just 43 games (averaging a 14–10), but the reason was much less defensible. The Jazz were enamored of free agent Gail Goodrich and needed that 1977 number one as part of a compensation package to sign him away from Los Angeles. How can we explain the idiocy of a floundering team deciding, "Let's team up a twenty-eight-year-old shooting guard who doesn't play defense with a thirty-three-year-old shooting guard who doesn't play defense; we'll score more points and the fans will love it"? That's just how the NBA worked

---

57. You have to love the way the NBA operated in the mid-'70s. The Jazz said, "Um, hey, we've been thinking about it—we'd love a mulligan on that Moses decision," and Commissioner O'Brien's office said, "No problem—here's your number one back!" Given how haphazardly things were run back then, it makes you wonder if they called O'Brien, he was on the other line, his secretary asked what the call was about, the Jazz told her, she said "Hold on" and passed the message on to O'Brien, and he waved her off by saying "Fine, fine, just tell them yes" before getting back to his phone call with Ben Bradlee or Walter Mondale.

back then. *Sports Illustrated*'s Jerry Kirshenbaum wrote a November feature about the trade that included this section: "Goodrich had been signed earlier by the New Orleans front office with the blessing of Coach Butch van Breda Kolff, who had him for a while during his two-year stint as Laker coach in the late '60s. Van Breda Kolff thinks Goodrich wears his years well, just as he himself does. Now in his fifth pro coaching post, the Jazz boss has a foghorn for a voice, shows up for games in what might be called casual clothes and enjoys the kind of stamina he demonstrated during a nine-hour pub crawl the other day to commemorate his 54th birthday. It was a celebration broken only occasionally by talk of basketball."

Ladies and gentlemen, your 1976–77 New Orleans Jazz! *So what if Gail Goodrich is thirty-three and has eleven years on his NBA odometer? He wears his years well! Who wants to do a shot?* And you wonder why Red Auerbach dominated the NBA for thirty years; maybe he was just the only GM with an IQ over 100 who wasn't drunk all the time. Goodrich suffered an Achilles tendon injury, played just 27 games and retired two years later. So much for wearing his years well. It's also strange that the Jazz decided Malone's young legs and voracious rebounding wouldn't come in handy when Rich Kelley, Ron Behagen and Otto Moore were their incumbent big guys. Remember, Malone's talent wasn't exactly a secret; one of the most famous college recruits of all time, Moses became the first player to jump directly from high school to the pros in 1974. The Jazz didn't care. We can only guess that van Breda Kolff said something like, "I don't care if he's talented; supposedly the guy is as dumb as a rock. I want Goodrich!" So not only did the Jazz relinquish the rights to a future three-time MVP, they packaged their 1977, 1978 and 1979 number one picks and a 1980 second-rounder for Goodrich and L.A.'s 1978 number one pick. The Lakers ended up picking number six in '77 (Kenny Carr), number eight in '78 (sent to Boston for Charlie Scott) and (wait for it . . . wait for it . . . wait for it) number one in 1979 (Magic Johnson). Incredibly, unfathomably, unbelievably, inconceivably, an already moronic decision to overpay Goodrich (just about washed up at that point) ended up costing New Orleans Moses *and* Magic.[58]

---

58. Yes, the Jazz probably wouldn't have earned the number one overall pick three years later had they just kept Moses, since he won the MVP three years later. That "Moses and Magic" line just looked imposing on paper, you have to admit.

Hold on, we're not close to being done. Portland picked Moses fifth in the ABA dispersal draft purely for trading purposes, wanting no part of his $300,000-per-year contract. According to *Breaks,* Moses struggled in training camp for understandable reasons: Portland had a hyperintelligent offense with a hands-on coach and Moses had never been coached before; this was his third team in three seasons; his skills were extremely raw at this point (just a straight rebounder/banger with great footwork and that's it); and since he was already on the trading block and backing up both Walton and Maurice Lucas, Moses wasn't exactly invested. As the situation devolved into a fire sale, Moses unleashed holy hell in one exhibition game, with players and coaches collectively realizing, "Holy shit! This guy is a prodigy!" They had no idea that the team had already agreed to trade him to Buffalo for a 1978 number one pick and $232,000,[59] creating . . .

5. What if the '77 Blazers didn't trade Moses Malone?

Put it this way: they ended up winning the title *without* him and started out 50–10 the following year before Walton's feet fell apart. Within a year, Walton had signed with the Clippers and their championship window had closed. Had they kept Moses, maybe Walton doesn't keep playing in pain, maybe they don't rush Walton back for the '78 playoffs, maybe Walton's feet don't fall apart, maybe Walton doesn't have the falling-out with their medical staff . . . for all we know, maybe Walton plays 400–500 more games in Portland with shortened minutes thanks to Moses. Throw in the way Moses matured in '77 (averaging a 13–13 in just 30 minutes), '78 (19–15) and '79 (25–17, MVP) and who knows how many championships were swung? Think of that vacuum of good teams in the late seventies—could the Blazers have won three in a row had Walton stayed healthy? Four? Five? And what would have happened to *Breaks of the Game*? Would Halberstam have picked another team? This trade didn't

59. This part kills me. How did they decide on $232,000? Somebody needs to write a book detailing every fucked-up thing that happened in the NBA in 1976. It could be 1,200 pages.

just swing NBA titles, it swung the Greatest Sports Book Ever title! My head hurts.[60]

And we're not even done, because poor Moses played in Buffalo for exactly six days before they shipped him to Houston for *two* number one picks in '77 and '78, hammering home Portland's screw-up since Buffalo basically swapped a number one for two number ones. Don't worry, this worked out just as badly for them as it did for everyone else: Moses only played six minutes in two games for the Braves because, hey, when you already have John Shumate and Tom McMillen at power forward, why see what you might have with the most ballyhooed high school recruit since Lew Alcindor?[61] That '77 pick from Houston ended up being number eighteen (somebody named Wesley Cox) because Moses ignited the Rockets and propelled them to a division title. When the Rockets struggled the following season (a combination of Moses missing 23 games and the harrowing aftereffects of the Tomjanovich/Washington incident), their 24–58 stink bomb netted Buffalo the number four overall pick—only the Braves had already traded it away (along with their 1979 number one) in the disastrous Tiny Archibald deal.[62] Buffalo moved to San Diego that summer, so if you're scoring at home, technically, the fact that they dumped Moses for nothing could qualify as their "curse of the Bambino" moment; from that day on (October 24, 1976), only horrible things happened to them. And deservedly so. What I can't understand: with unhappy Buffalo star Bob McAdoo grumbling about a new contract all summer, why didn't they keep Moses around as insurance when it looked like they might be trading their star center? Six weeks after the Moses deal, they sent Big Mac packing for John Gianelli

60. The Buffalo pick ended up being number three overall in '78: Portland sent it to Indiana along with Johnny Davis for the number one overall pick, taking Mychal Thompson as Walton insurance. Maybe Thompson wasn't a Pantheon center, but he was good enough to get his own goofy Nike poster: just Thompson wearing a Hawaiian shirt and holding a parrot while sitting by a tropical pool. The implication being . . . I don't know.

61. On January 25, 1977, one week after *SI* wrote a "Look at how Moses has ignited the Rockets" feature, Tates Locke (the guy who quickly buried Moses in Buffalo) was fired as the Braves' head coach. This was not a coincidence. For the *Lost* fans out there, three-plus decades of bad luck for the Braves/Clippers started right after they fired Jack and replaced him with Locke.

62. New Jersey traded the pick a fourth time, leading to the Micheal Ray era in New York. Sadly, I am out of cocaine jokes. I'm tapped.

and cash. And the seeds of three-plus decades of Clippers futility were planted.[P15]

So if you're scoring at home, Moses Hot Potato ended up swinging the destinies of six franchises in fewer than five months: New Orleans (never recovered, moved four years later); Los Angeles (landed Magic, won five titles with him); Portland (gave away Walton insurance and God knows how many titles); Buffalo (never recovered, moved within two years, jinxed even today); Houston (made the '81 Finals with Moses, eventually traded him to Philly, and made the Hakeem-Sampson era possible); and Philly (acquired Moses in '82, won a title with him). We also nearly witnessed the destruction of one of the most talented players ever: by all accounts, Moses moved so many times from 1974 to 1976 that he was practically broken by the time he reached Houston; it took the Rockets an entire season to rebuild his confidence. Eventually he became a Hall of Famer and haunts three teams to this day. And to think, it all started because Butch van Breda Kolff decided that Gail Goodrich wore his years well.

4. What if the 1960 Lakers hadn't crashed in the perfect cornfield?

January 18, 1960. The Lakers are flying back to Minneapolis after a day game in St. Louis. They're riding in their own DC-3. It starts to snow. The plane loses its power. The heat goes off. The pilots can't communicate with anyone. The plane bounces around in the snow for a few hours, with the pilots opening a side window every few minutes to scrape snow off the windshield so they can see. They have about thirty minutes of gas left and can't find an airport, so finally they decide to land the plane on the best available cornfield in Carroll, Iowa. They keep trying to land but can't find

P15. After Blake Griffin pooh-poohed the notion of a Clippers curse before the '09 draft, I wrote him an open letter (as a column) documenting every crazy/freaky/cursed Clipper moment since the Braves ditched Buffalo, with the implication being "Look, buddy, you don't know what you're getting into here." Four months later, Griffin fractured his patella in their final exhibition game (killing his rookie season). I felt terrible. At the same time, this is bigger than all of us. What's a frequent plot in horror movies? Indian burial grounds. What's the most sacred animal to Indians? Buffalo. Did you really think a team could stab *Buffalo* in the back and get away with it?

an area that isn't flanked by power lines, so the pilots keep having to jerk the plane up and try more attempts. At this point, police cars, fire trucks and even the town's mortician are doing their best to follow a plane they can barely see. Finally, the pilots find the perfect snowy cornfield, cut the engines and land the plane smoothly on about four feet of snow. Everyone cheers. To this day, it's the closest we've ever come to losing a professional sports team.[63]

It would have been the biggest tragedy in NBA history and a crippling blow to a league barely making it at the time. And that's just the start of it. We lose one of the fifteen greatest players ever (Elgin Baylor) midway through his sophomore season, as well as the most athletic forward of that era and someone who was in the process of knocking down the "basketball can also be played in the air" door. The Elgin/Jerry era never happens. We endure roughly five hundred documentaries, TV features, books and magazine features about that fateful night had it turned out morbidly.[64] The '60 Lakers either fold immediately or suspend play, then regroup for the '61 season after filling out their roster with expansion players and extra draft picks . . . which only means we're now redoing every part of NBA history from 1961 to 2010, including sixteen different Finals. Finally, another owner grabs that Los Angeles market if the Lakers fold. Would we be watching the Los Angeles Warriors right now? What about (gulp) the Los Angeles Celtics? In the biggest understatement of this entire book, I say it's a good thing that the plane landed safely.

3. What if ABA commissioner George Mikan didn't screw up the Lew Alcindor sweepstakes?

When Alcindor finished his UCLA career in the spring of 1969, his family assembled a team of agents and advisers and spent the next few months debating between the ABA and NBA. Both leagues needed him desper-

---

63. Nowadays, we have a Catastrophe Rule: an emergency expansion draft in which every team can only protect four or five guys. Then that team gets the top pick of the next draft (plus its own pick). It's a good thing this isn't widely known because an irate Knicks fan would have tampered with the team's charter during the Isiah era.

64. And one sappy Disney movie in the late '90s with Samuel L. Jackson playing Elgin and Matthew McConaughey playing Hot Rod Hundley in a film called *Cornfield of Dreams* or *Final Flight*.

ately: the NBA because he was the biggest star to enter the league since Oscar Robertson, the ABA because Big Lew would have legitimized their league, gotten them a TV contract, and forced a merger down the road. If anything, the ABA should have overpaid for Alcindor and hoped to recoup the money with ticket sales and TV money.

Now here's where it gets crazy. Without ever tipping his hand publicly, Alcindor decided privately that he wanted to play in the ABA. Milwaukee held his NBA rights, but Big Lew was more interested in the Nets; he grew up in New York, loved the idea of playing near family, found the city's Muslim population appealing and understood the value of a big market. Milwaukee did nothing for him. How do we know this? He confessed as much in his 1983 autobiography *Giant Steps*[65]—everything I just told you—and fled Milwaukee as soon as a window opened after the '75 season. He wanted to play for the Nets. But he wasn't interested in spending the summer playing the leagues against each other, so Big Lew's team told the ABA and NBA the same thing: *We will meet you once, we will listen to one offer, and that's that. Do not lowball us. Give us your best possible offer first.* The jackasses running the ABA somehow came up with one of their only shrewd ideas: *When we meet Alcindor, we'll give him a certified check for $1 million up front as part of whatever offer we make. Not only will that check prove that we're serious and we don't have financial troubles, but it will burn a hole in his pocket and he'll eventually say yes.*

You have to admit, that's a great plan. Desperate, but great.

Okay, so the NBA goes first and makes an offer that Kareem would later call "extremely good" in *Giant Steps*. Mikan met Alcindor's people next. They talk numbers. They talk about sticking Lew in New York and maybe even flanking him with a few UCLA teammates. Money gets discussed. Some figures are thrown around. For whatever reason, Mikan never gives Alcindor that check. *It stays in his pocket!* Either he freezes or he forgets. There's no in-between.[66] On top of that, they lowball him with a shitty

---

65. I bought this book for $6 online; the highlight was reading it, gleaning all the information I needed, then starting a bonfire with it in my backyard. In the words of Marv Albert, "Kareem Abdul-Jabbar is *on fire!*"

66. Looking back, it's the biggest NBA turnover ever other than Isiah's pass that the Legend picked off (1987) and Karl Malone getting stripped right before Jordan's last shot (1998). It's too bad the ABA didn't have George McGinnis hold the check; he would have turned it right over.

offer. So Alcindor's team leaves the meeting wondering why the ABA didn't totally step to the plate. Alcindor feels insulted and vows never to play in the ABA. The ABA owners flip out when they realize that Mikan never gave him the check. Milwaukee swoops in and signs Alcindor for a record $1.4 million. And Mikan gets canned within a year. As Kareem wrote later, "The Nets had the inside track and had blown it."

Let's say Mikan didn't mess up and Big Lew signed with the Nets. Maybe he steals New York thunder from the '70 Knicks. Maybe the Nets trade for Rick Barry one year later and become a superpower. Maybe the merger happens sooner than later, maybe the Nets become the team of the seventies, and maybe Lew/Kareem never ends up playing with Magic and the Lakers. Three things definitely don't happen: the Bucks don't win the '71 title, Oscar never ends up in Milwaukee, and we have NBA MVPs in '71, '72 and '74 not named Alcindor or Abdul-Jabbar. I mean, George Mikan could have gone on the *Tonight Show*, thrown on his goggles and sodomized Johnny Carson on live TV and not done more damage to the ABA than he did by not giving Alcindor that check. My head is spinning.[P16]

2. What if Len Bias hadn't overdosed?

I still haven't gotten over this one. How can you calculate the short-term and long-term damage? The Celtics had just finished one of the greatest seasons in NBA history and were *adding* Len Bias. You couldn't have drawn up a better young forward for that particular team, someone who played like a more physical Worthy, but with Jordan's athleticism, if that makes sense. (Other than MJ and 'Nique, no eighties player attacked the

P16. A crazy Kareem-related what-if surfaced on YouTube: Before the 1982 Draft's coin flip, when Ralph Sampson (a UVA junior) had a deadline to enter or withdraw, CBS' Brent Musberger reported that the Lakers (already guaranteed number one or number two) had frantically tried to pull off a four team deal sending Kareem to the Knicks, Bill Cartwright to Utah, Micheal Ray Richardson to an unnamed fourth team and Utah's pick (the other half of the coin flip) along with something else to the defending champs (who would've taken Sampson first and Worthy second). Said Musberger, "With so many players involved and so many agents, it was impossible to get the approvals needed." Sampson withdrew, Kareem stayed and the Lakers won three more titles. Holy schmoley.

basket like a young Len Bias.) If you sat down on June 19, 1986, right after the Celtics thrashed Houston for the title, and drew up a wish list for the perfect rookie to add to the '87 Celtics, you would have come up with five wishes: an elite athlete capable of playing either forward spot; an over-competitive MFer with a mean streak; a scorer capable of carrying Boston's offense for extended stretches off the bench; a rebounder who could bang with young bucks like Barkley and Malone; and just for the hell of it, someone who loved ramming home alley-oops as Bird's new toy. You would have settled for a forward who hit three of those check marks; four would have had you high-fiving yourself; five would have made you pass out.

Well, this was too good to be true. Bias dropped dead within forty-eight hours of the draft. Coke. And this is one of those what-ifs where the damages are easy to define. You can see them clearly. They stand out. The NBA lost a potential signature player and faced its biggest drug crisis yet. The Celtics wouldn't fully recover for another twenty-one years. Long-term, they were just *screwed*. Pull Pippen from the '87 Bulls, Malone from the '85 Jazz or Duncan from the '97 Spurs—just make believe they never played a game—and that's how much Bias' death meant.[67] Short-term, we missed out on seeing an '87 Celtics team that would have been the great-est of all time. One of the three greatest teams ever with one of the five best players ever and the greatest front line ever was adding one of the three best forwards of that decade? That's a lot of greatests and bests. Medium-term, Bird and McHale were forced to play big minutes without Bias; neither of them would be the same after killing themselves that sea-son. Bird's body finally gave out a year later (first the heels, then the back); McHale injured his foot before the '87 Playoffs, came back too soon be-cause they didn't have anyone else, broke the foot, kept playing on it and never really recovered. Bias cuts down everyone's minutes, keeps everyone from playing injured, makes the actual games easier . . . it would have been the difference between Bird and McHale traveling 200,000 hours a year in coach or 125,000 a year in first class.

67. Remember, Bias was supposed to take the torch from Russell, Havlicek and Bird. That's how good he was. Also, there was a cap in place by '86 and owners like Ted Stepien weren't stupidly giving away number one picks anymore. It was significantly tougher to improve. Fuck.

Some other things we missed: a sneering Bias banging bodies with the bad-boy Pistons from '87 to '92; a fascinating three-headed Barkley-Malone-Bias rivalry; Bias upping the stakes in any playground game against the Blazers and Hawks; Bird treating Bias like his prized new toy and tossing him as many alley-oops as humanly possible;[68] the Celtics improbably becoming "cool"; and an Eastern Conference star who would have stood up to Jordan without blinking or being intimidated. It's the last point that hurts the most. There was a particular brashness about Bias, a swagger, a playground vibe that nobody else had. These were still the days of tight shorts and awkward high fives; few players were cool and the ones who were ('Nique, Worthy, Jordan, Bernard) kept their emotions in check for the most part. Jordan might have embraced that playground demeanor had he attended a school other than North Carolina, where Dean Smith frowned on anything that could be perceived as showing up the opposition, but the Carolina influence tempered his bluster to some degree. Maybe Jordan landed the sneaker commercials and posters, but Bias was the one who brought the streets to big-time hoops. He resonated with black fans much the way Hawk, Pearl and Doc did back in the day.

When Len's playground swagger became more fashionable in the '90s—thanks to UNLV and the Fab Five, postdunk woofing, baggy shorts, trash talk and everything else—that style seemed more contrived, like the players were doing it only to say "Hey, look at me!" Trust me, nothing about Len Bias was contrived. He went out of his way to dunk on people, not because it made him seem cool but because it sent a message and established a tone for the game. He grabbed rebounds in traffic and spat out an occasional "Arrrrrrgggggggghhhh!" just to make sure everyone knew who was boss. He barked at teammates, referees and opponents alike. If fans booed Maryland during a road game, he fed off that noise like so many other greats and learned to channel it to shut them up, then thrived on that respectful silence when the game was wrapping up. He played with passion and heart. He showed a mean streak at times but never made

---

68. I know I mentioned this twice but it continues to kill me. Remember, Bird routinely got bored during games, spent entire halves shooting left-handed and once played an '86 game where he and Walton tried to figure how many different ways they could run a play where Bird threw it in to Walton, then cut toward the basket and caught a return pass from Walton. You're telling me he wouldn't have said, "I want to see if I can get Len 15 alley-oops tonight"? I am shaking my head.

you feel like he didn't give a shit. Quite simply, he stood out. If Bias had arrived on the scene seven or eight years later, I'm sure he would have been wearing baggy shorts and woofing it up just like everyone else, but that's the beautiful thing: not just that Bias made it big when he did, but that he *wasn't* contrived. We spent so many years searching for an archrival for Jordan—the Frazier to his Ali, someone who'd bring out the best in him—when really, that player was probably Len Bias. We were robbed. And so were the Celtics.

(The good news: Bias' overdose combined with Robert Downey Jr. performing gay tricks for his coke dealer in *Less than Zero* fostered a fear of cocaine in nearly every American male growing up between 1986 and 1994. To this day, I haven't tried cocaine or even thought about trying it. Just would have been hypocritical, you know? I guess that's a silver lining. No pun intended.)

1. What if the 1984 draft turned out differently?

Oh, and you thought no. 1 would simply be "What if Portland had taken MJ over Bowie?" This draft was so complicated that it inspired Houston and Chicago to create the concept of "tanking" during the regular season (page 154). Once Houston won the coin flip and locked into Hakeem, all hell broke loose. Here's what we know for sure:

1. Both Portland (second) and Chicago (third) would have swapped their picks for Sampson, although that wouldn't have been enough of a return for a much-hyped rookie center who possessed the third-highest trade value behind Magic and Bird that summer.[69] Years later, Dr. Jack Ramsey told Sam Smith, "We had to have a center. We would have done that [trade]." I sure hope so. In his 1996 autobiography *Living the Dream*,[70] Hakeem claims that Houston nearly traded Sampson to Portland for

69. My hypothetical top ten: Bird, Magic, Sampson, Isiah, Bernard, Moses, 'Nique, Moncrief, McHale, Buck Williams.
70. I found this information online—I refused to buy *Living the Dream* because it sounded so awful. A strong statement from someone who bought *Give 'Em the Hook* by Tommy Heinsohn.

Drexler and the number two pick, writing, "From 1984 until today, the Rockets could have had a lineup with me, Clyde Drexler and Michael Jordan, developing together, playing together, winning together. But the Rockets never made the move." Whether that's true or untrue, I don't blame Houston for turning that down because Drexler hadn't exactly lit the NBA on fire as a rookie. Still, Hakeem, Jordan and Drexler playing their entire careers together? Just staggering. It's like imagining what would have happened if Microsoft and Apple had merged in 1981.

2. The sharks circled a crappy Chicago team for Jordan, giving credence to the "Portland seriously blew that pick" argument. Dallas offered Mark Aguirre straight up for the pick. Philly offered an aging Doc straight up for the pick; they also offered the number five pick plus Andrew Toney. Trades with Seattle (Jack Sikma) and Golden State (Joe Barry Carroll) were discussed. Eventually, the Bulls started feeling like they were sitting on a winning lottery ticket. And they were.[71]

3. Patrick Ewing nearly entered the draft before changing his mind and returning to Georgetown. Had Ewing thrown his hat in the ring, he would have gone first, Hakeem second (to Portland) . . . and then—Bulls GM Rod Thorn told Flip Bondy that Chicago had Jordan rated higher than Bowie because they were afraid of his injury track record.[72] Obviously if Hakeem had landed in Portland, we'd enter the Marty McFly Zone and have to reconceive everything that happened in the NBA from 1985 to 1998 (different Finals, different champs, no Ewing in New York, etc. etc.). I started trying to figure it out and my nose started bleeding. I took this as a sign to stop.

4. Jordan's potential was unclear because he played for Dean Smith in the pre-shot-clock era. Everyone knew he was good, but how good? His ceiling didn't start leaking out until the '84 Olympic tryouts, which Jordan dominated to the point that U.S. coach Bobby Knight called his buddy Stu Inman (Portland's GM) and *implored* him to

71. Philly's offer never became public. Owner Harold Katz also tried to swap Doc for Terry Cummings before Doc called him out and the entire city of Philadelphia turned on him. Although that's not saying much. Philly would turn on me just for making fun of them in this footnote. Crap, there goes another book signing.
72. They had just been burned by two questionable high draft picks: Ronnie Lester (bad knees) and Quintin Dailey (bad soul). They wanted a sure thing.

take Michael.[73] When Inman demurred and said that Portland needed a center, Knight reportedly screamed, "Well, play him at center, then!" We also know that Nike (based in Portland) built an entire sneaker line around Jordan before he played an NBA game. So for anyone to play the "We didn't know how good Jordan would be" card just isn't true.

5. It's a myth that Portland "desperately" needed a center. A 48-win team with a perfectly decent center combo—Mychal Thompson (16–9 in 33.5 minutes) and Wayne Cooper (10–6 in 20.5 minutes)—they also possessed trade chips like Drexler, Jim Paxson (second-team All-NBA and a restricted free agent), Fat Lever (an up-and-coming point guard), Calvin Natt (a bulldog forward) and Cooper. What they really needed was a rebounder; Natt and Kenny Carr were both undersized power forwards. For instance, San Diego shopped scorer/rebounder Terry Cummings all summer and finally dealt him for Marques Johnson after the draft. Why didn't Portland overwhelm the Clippers with a Cummings offer (like a Drexler-Natt package) and take Jordan second? You got me.[74] Instead, they sent Lever, Cooper, Natt and their '85 first-round pick to Denver for Kiki Vandeweghe, an accomplished scorer (29.8 PPG in '84) who also happened to be the worst defensive player alive. Here's how lopsided and shortsighted that deal was: Denver jumped from 38 wins to 52 wins and the '85 Western Finals solely because of that trade. As for Portland, they probably met in the first week of June and debated two potential courses of action:

Door No. 1: Jordan (most exciting college guard of the decade), Lever (twenty-three, named second-team All-NBA just two years later), Cooper (twenty-seven, averaged a 13–8 the next two years in Denver), Natt (averaged a 23–8 in '85) and an '85 number one pick (ended up being fifteenth)
Door No. 2: Vandeweghe and Bowie

---

73. The two best players in prolonged tryouts that included every relevant name from the '84 and '85 drafts? Jordan and Barkley. Chuck ended up getting cut after Knight told him to lose weight and Barkley went the other way. Other cuts: Malone, Stockton, Joe Dumars and Terry Porter. Guys who made it: Jeff Turner, Joe Kleine, Steve Alford and Jon Koncak. I think Chris Wallace and David Duke were advisers to Knight that summer.
74. Or they could have overwhelmed Houston for Sampson: the number two, Drexler *and* Fat Lever.

Anyone in their right mind goes with Door No. 1 unless they're reasonably certain that (a) Bowie was a sure thing and (b) Jordan wouldn't come back to haunt them. I am assuming that Portland's brain trust felt "reasonably certain" of those two things. And to hammer home how dumb, indefensible and reckless that feeling was, let's bang out a retroactive diary of the first twenty-two minutes of the '84 draft. Our announcers? Al Albert and Lou Carnesecca for the USA Network.

0:02. Albert hypes the proceedings by claiming there are "six bona fide superstars" ready to get picked. Apparently he's counting 296-pound Charles Barkley twice.

0:03. Peering over a pair of black eyeglasses, Carnesecca fidgets with a pen, rambles uncomfortably for forty solid seconds and does everything possible not to look at the camera. He looks like a priest being questioned by police about an assault on an altar boy. Glad he's here.

0:07. USA scrolls the order of the entire first round accompanied by some phenomenal eighties porn music. I half expected them to come out of that scroll with Ginger Lynn riding Al Albert on a waterbed. That's followed by David Stern stepping to the podium for his first NBA draft, only he's wearing Gabe Kaplan's mustache from the 1977 season of *Welcome Back Kotter.* Forget about NBA TV—why don't they rerun this draft on Comedy Central?

0:10. One of the two guys sitting at Houston's draft table has a mullet and a bushy mustache. Gotta love the eighties. As we watch them gabbing on the phone, the following exchange happens:

AL: The Rockets timing has been impeccable. Last year, number one with Ralph Sampson coming out; this year, Hakeem Olajuwon decided to come out early, and that's just in time for Houston.

(Three seconds of silence pass.)

LOU *(barely audible)*: The postman did ring twice.

0:11. Hakeem goes first, although he spelled it "Akeem" back then. He's rocking the low-cut Jheri curl, a black tuxedo and a maroon bow tie. Fantastic.[75]

0:12. Eddie Murphy borrowed his accent for Prince Akeem in *Coming to America* from the draft interview Akeem just did with Bob Doucette. There is no doubt in my mind. He even named the character after him.

0:16. Stern utters one of the most unforgettable sentences in NBA history—"Portland selects Sam Bowie, University of Kentucky"—as the camera shows the reps at Portland's table with dueling "Yikes, I hope we didn't fuck that up" looks on their faces.[76] That's followed by Bowie ambling to the stage as Al narrates, "Sam Bowie, the young man who came back from a stress fracture injury, the left shinbone, he was out for two seasons, redshirted, he has come back, he returned strong at Kentucky."

(So a team that just lost its franchise center six years early with repeated stress fractures in his feet just took another center who missed two full college seasons because of his stress fractures? And he's three years older than the sure thing about to get picked right after him? Sounds encouraging!)

0:17. During a less than enthralling package of Bowie highlights, Al tells us again that Sam has recovered fully from his stress fractures before adding unironically, "He passed up the Olympics." High comedy. Every major college player tried out for that team except for Sam. Seem like a red flag to you? Nahhhhhhhh.

0:18. The Bowie highlight package finishes with a frozen picture of Bowie and a graphic with his '84 stats: 10.5 points, 9.2 rebounds, 52% FG, 72% FT. In other words, his college stats were worse than Mychal Thompson's

---

75. You know what's interesting? Houston just passed up the greatest player ever and I *still* feel like they made the right pick. You always go with a sure-thing center over a sure-thing guard. Always.

76. Stern always said the entire franchise's name during this draft except this one time: He skipped the "Trail Blazers" part, like he was trying to get off the stage as fast as possible. You can't blame him.

NBA stats. What an upgrade![77] Meanwhile, Al and Lou have the following exchange:

AL: And Lou, what do you say for a young player who sat out two formative years and has come back to regain it?

ME: "Don't pick him"?

LOU: Well, I think it shows the type of perseverance that he has, that he was able to withstand all that misery and come back and perform, and look where he is now.

(Note: nothing gets fans more fired up than words like "perseverance" and "withstanding all that misery." Screw that Jordan guy and his stupid dunking!)

0:18. Doucette interviews Bowie, who seems like a tragic figure in retrospect; it's like watching Jackie Kennedy at LBJ's swearing-in with JFK's blood all over her dress. Their first exchange:

DOUCETTE: Sam, um, courage has been your middle name, you've had to really fight back from some adversity, and I know a lot of folks particularly yourself are happy to see this day arrive.

SAM: Right, I had a two-year layoff with my leg injury, but if I didn't have the support of the community of Lexington and the state of Kentucky, I don't know if I would have been able to do it without their help.

(Imagine being a Blazers fan and watching this. Mad props to Sam for defying the odds and coming back, but why take a "defying the odds" guy

---

77. Did Bowie's staggeringly unstaggering college stats remind you of anyone else? I'm thinking an OSU center, number one pick, looked twenty years older than his age, also played for Portland . . .[P17]

P17. I wrote that footnote for the hardcover. When Oden fractured his patella one month after TBOB came out, both Clippers and Blazers fans were blaming me for season-ending injuries to their best young players. Did you know I have the power to break patellas? Me neither. While we're here: I turned my man cave into an homage to 1976–1986 hoops (my favorite NBA stretch) since that's where I spent the most time writing this book. I collected/framed 20+ posters from that stretch, including a rarely-seen Nike poster of a smiling, oversized Sam Bowie standing in Portland's skyline alongside the other "buildings." If we ever have an earthquake in L.A., you know that's the framed poster that will fall off the wall and break into fifty pieces.

with a sure thing on board? Why even risk it? Why? Why? *Answer me! Why?*)

0:19. It's only getting better . . .

DOUCETTE: [The Blazers] tell me that they put you through an extensive physical before they made a decision on you. And the end result was a good one?

SAM (*smiling sheepishly*): Well, I went up to Portland and they gave me about a seven-hour physical, they didn't let anything out, so, uh, I don't know if that's referring back to the Bill Walton situation, I know he had a stress fracture, but as far as I'm concerned I'm 100 percent sound.[78]

(Waitasecondwaitasecondwaitasecond . . . a *seven-hour* physical? This is like watching the *Hindenburg* take off.)

0:20. Cut to both Chicago reps smiling happily at Chicago's table[79] as Al sets up number three by taking a dramatic pause, lowering his voice and finally saying, "Michael Jordan seems to be the next one up." For the first time in twenty minutes, Lou seems like he might be awake: "Mmmmmm, everyone's excited about that one. He really captures the imagination." Then again, you could say the same about a seven-hour physical.

Now it gets really good . . .

AL: You know, there was a question a little earlier perhaps, Portland toying with the idea of the great, can't-miss talent of Michael Jordan against Sam Bowie, who, uh, who of course, coming off the injury, he says he is sound, Portland has checked him out through a seven-hour test, but the question is Bowie going now over the course of an 82-game schedule.

LOU (*nodding*): It is a calculated risk.

---

78. Worth mentioning: Sam was extremely polished and handled himself well. I feel bad for the guy. I mean, it's not his fault they drafted him over Jordan, right? And he was a quality center when he was healthy. Which was only 54 percent of his career, but still.

79. If you ever get a chance to watch this clip, check out the look on the guy who's on the phone for Chicago—he's so delighted, it looks like he's getting blown under the table. We'll never know for sure.

(Note: At this point, every Blazers fan in 1984 had thrown up in their mouth at least a little.)

0:22. A giddy Stern: "The Chicago Bulls pick Michael Jordan, from the University of North Carolina."

The crowd applauds and cheers. They know already. That's followed by a montage of exciting early MJ highlights with Al telling us, "This man is a can't-miss" and a suddenly lively Lou adding, "You know, he makes them when they count, he can do it in traffic, he can do it under tremendous control, he's a great, great creator, in the mold of a Dr. J, not as big, but is in that class, Michael is gonna make a great, great player, he's what you call the People's Player, people love to see this young man perform." Al caps it off by saying, "He is star material, a great shooter, superb athletic ability, there are many teams that tried to pry that third pick from Chicago."

I mean . . .

Just read everything from 0:16 to 0:22 again. We've seen a revisionist history in recent years that Bowie's selection was defensible because the NBA was size-obsessed back then. But how can any team roll the dice with red flags like "calculated risk," "seven-hour physical," "two-year layoff" and "adversity/courage/perseverance" and pass up white flags like "can't-miss talent," "great, great player," "star material," "sure thing," "in the mold of a Dr. J," "great, great creator" and "People's Player"? Incomprehensible. Totally, completely incomprehensible.

Which brings us to a special bonus what-if. On the day of the draft, what if Portland's decision makers took a collective breath, said to each other, "Wait, are we crazy?" and reconsidered everything one last time? It's like the second-to-last scene in *All the President's Men*, when Woodward and Bernstein wake up *Washington Post* editor Ben Bradlee in the middle of the night to urge him to run their controversial report about corruption spreading all the way through Richard Nixon's White House. Afraid that Bradlee's house has been bugged, they bring him outside and fill him in on the front lawn.[80] The boys haven't slept in two days; Bradlee is wear-

---

80. Jason Robards won a Best Supporting Actor Oscar as Bradlee in one of my favorite performances ever. He owns every scene of a movie with Redford and Hoffman in it. Within seven years, he was playing the lead in *Max Dugan Returns*. I don't get Hollywood.

ing a bathrobe and looks pissed off since they just screwed up the same story a few days before. Finally Bradlee lets them write the story, but not before telling them, "You guys are pretty tired, right? Well, you should be. Go on home, get a nice hot bath, rest up, fifteen minutes. Then get your asses back in gear. We're under a lot of pressure, you know, and you put us there. Nothing's riding on this except the First Amendment, the Constitution, freedom of the press, and maybe the future of the country. Not that any of that matters, but if you guys fuck up again, I'm gonna get mad. Good night."

If Ben Bradlee had owned the Blazers in 1984, he would have put the fear of God in everyone deciding on that pick and they would have gravitated toward the sure thing. Blazers owner Larry Weisberg was reportedly enamored of Jordan, but he was also an unassuming, low-key real estate tycoon who didn't evoke that same Bradlee-like trepidation in his staff. They weren't afraid of him, and they weren't afraid of the repercussions. That's why the Blazers plowed ahead with Sam Bowie . . . and that's why they fucked up. But hey, nothing was riding on it except for the future of the NBA, hundreds of millions of dollars in lost revenue, somewhere between four and ten squandered championships and a lost opportunity to employ the greatest basketball player of all time.

FIVE

MOST VALUABLE CHAPTER

BILLY CUNNINGHAM
forward

PHILADELPHIA

SAY WHAT YOU want about the NBA, but fifteen of its running features and subplots distinguish it from every other professional sport (in a good way):

1. A wildly entertaining rookie draft that helped calibrate my Unintentional Comedy Scale. Things settled down over the last few years when agents and PR people realized things like, "Maybe we shouldn't send him to the Draft dressed like a pimp" and "Maybe it's not a good idea to give David Stern a full body, genitals-on-genitals hug after you get picked," but it's still one of my favorite TV nights of the year, if only because Jay Bilas has a ton of length and a ridiculous wingspan.

2. A dress code for injured players that, after an adjustment period, ultimately led to fashionably dressed scrubs hopping onto the court after time-outs to dole out chest bumps and high fives. We witnessed a blos-

soming of the Overexcited Thirteenth Man in the '08 Playoffs; if Walter Herrmann was the Jackie Robinson of this movement, then Brian Scalabrine was Larry Doby and Scot Pollard was Don Newcombe. Where else can you see a $2,000 leather jacket get stained with sweat by a chest bump?

3. Courtside seats that serve a double purpose: First, they're hard to get without connections or unless you have six figures sitting around for season tickets. If you're sitting in them, your success in life has been validated in some strange way, even if everyone sitting in every non-courtside seat probably thinks you're an asshole. (It's the same phenomenon as sitting in first class and watching everyone else size you up in disgust as they're headed to coach, multiplied by fifty.) And second, it's the best possible seat in any sport. You're right on top of the court, you hear every order, swear, joke, insult or trash-talk moment, and if you're lucky enough to be sitting right next to one of the benches, you can hear them discussing strategy in the huddle.[1] There isn't another sports fan experience like it. I'd even argue that the twelve seats between the two benches—six on each side of the midcourt line, or as they're commonly known, the Nicholson Seats—are the single greatest set of seats for any professional sport.

4. Cheerleaders dressing like hookers and acting like strippers. Can't forget them.

5. Foreign players entering the NBA with heavy accents, then picking up a hip-hop twang over the course of a few seasons from being around black people all the time. I call this "Detlef Syndrome" because Schrempf was the ultimate example; by the halfway point of his career, he sounded like the German guys in *Beerfest* crossed with the Wu-Tang Clan. It's just a shame that Arnold Schwarzenegger didn't train at an all-black gym in the seventies; we really could have seen something special.[2]

1. Or at a Lakers game, where you can hear Kobe bitching out teammates and coaches! That reminds me of the highlight of the '08 Finals: Matt Damon cheering the Celts in Game 5 when Phil Jackson turned and hissed, "Sit down and shut the fuck up!" Had they won, I think I would have sacrificed a pinky for Damon to snap into Will Hunting mode and pull the "Hey, Phil, you like apples? . . . How 'bout them apples?" routine.
2. Another classic example: Olajuwon sounded like Prince Akeem in *Coming to America*, only if he hung out in downtown Oakland for ten years.

6. An even weirder phenomenon than Detlef Syndrome: for reasons that remain unclear, the NBA causes some journalists to write NBA-related columns or features like they're "writing black." Unquestionably, it's the worst journalistic trend of the last twenty years other than the live blog. I never understood the mind-set here: *There are a great many black players in this sport; therefore, I must make my prose a little more urban.* Really? That's logical? I don't get it. You feelin' me? Word. This is one phat book I'm writing, yo. Recognize.

7. Real fans yanked from the stands to shoot half-court shots for cars, money or whatever else is being offered. What other sport allows fans to become part of the action like that? Of course, they never come close because of the little-known rule that only unathletic people, females or people weighing over three hundred pounds are chosen for the half-court shot. But still, at least it's exciting.[3]

8. The most simple yet revealing statistics in any sport: points, rebounds, steals, blocks, assists, free throws, field goals, threes and turnovers. Over the past ten years, a series of stat freaks inspired by the baseball revolution pushed a variety of convoluted statistics on us, but really, you can determine the effectiveness of nearly any player by examining an NBA box score. Rarely does a post-1973 box score deceive, although a few subtle stats could be created to make things even better. We'll delve into this during the Wes Unseld section.[4]

9. What other sport offers the broken-nose mask that Rip Hamilton popularized? For how prevalent these things have been for the past thirty years, I can't believe we never came up with a nickname for it. A few years ago I launched an unsuccessful movement to name it "the Schnozzaroo." Never caught on. What's strange is that they're such an afterthought for players who care deeply about their postgame

---

3. The half-court shot is my lifelong passion. It should only be shot one way—a three-step start, followed by a heave from under your collarbone. After spending fifteen years watching fans shoot it like a free throw or whip it like a baseball, I asked the Clips to let me shoot one for an ESPN segment. That morning, they let me practice at the Staples Center and it took twenty minutes to adjust to the glass backboard and the rows of seats behind it (you have to shoot it two feet farther than you'd think). By game time, I was ready but had too much adrenaline and banked it off the front of the rim—one inch lower and I would have banked it home. Story of my life. Here's why I'm telling you this: if you ever get picked, do the three-step heave and aim two feet farther than you think.

4. Let's hope that's the first and last time anyone writes that sentence.

wardrobe, their appearance, their shoes—and yet they'll slide on these homely, bland plastic masks without sprucing them up. Shouldn't they be painting them the way goalies decorate their masks in hockey, or maybe even wearing an intimidating, Hannibal Lecter–style mask for a big playoff game? What about putting advertising on it (like the Nike logo)? We need to spruce up the Schnozzaroos. You have to love a league that just spawned this paragraph.

10. Telecasts with Hubie Brown, a man who mastered the hypothetical first-person plural tense over the past twenty-five years and transformed it into a common conversation device. What would our lives have been like without Hubie? I wish Paul Thomas Anderson had cast him as Jack Horner's assistant director in *Boogie Nights,* just so we could have had a moment like this one during the filming of *Spanish Pantalones*: "Okay, let's say I'm Dirk Diggler in this scene. I'm hooking up with Rollergirl, I'm on a waterbed, I'm horny as hell, I'm Spanish, I'm hung like a horse and my pants are *on fire.* Now I'm thinking about rolling Rollergirl over from missionary to doggie style because I know that I'm keeping my options open and I can go right from doggie into another position. I also know that I should be *thinking* about using a Spanish accent. . . ."

11. The unique-to-the-NBA phenomenon where a traded player looks dramatically different in his new uniform. Sometimes it looks like he's been reborn, sometimes it's like he's finally found the perfect color/style, sometimes he looks like something's drastically wrong, and in rare cases the uniform makes him look slower, fatter and less athletic (like Shaq when he joined the Suns). I remember when Kwame Brown got traded to the Lakers and looked magnificent in his new duds: his arms looked bigger, he seemed more imposing and he carried himself differently. For all we knew, he had transformed into Jermaine O'Neal. But absolutely *nothing* had changed talent-wise except that he turned a Wizards jersey into a Lakers jersey. As we soon found out. Because Kwame Brown sucks. Still, for those first few Lakers games, he looked pretty damn good. It's just unfortunate that actors, politicians and singers can't take advantage of the new-uniform phenomenon; people like Jakob Dylan, Matt LeBlanc, Joe Biden and Adam Duritz could have remade their careers.

12. In my lifetime, David Stern narrowly edges Pete Rozelle as the com-

missioner with the most dominant personality, someone who always kept his league in complete control, gained such power and prominence that we actually wondered if he had fixed certain games or banned certain superstars without telling us, spawned a generation of legendary, Bill Brasky–like "Did you hear about the time Stern spent twenty minutes f-bombing _____ [name at least two executives from any company, sponsor, network or the league itself from the past twenty-five years]?" stories and anecdotes, and left such a legacy that he inspired one writer (in this case, me) to make a semiserious case in one column for why David Stern should be our next president. Just like there will never be another Magic, Michael or Larry, there will never be another David Stern.[5]

13. Mothers who show up for home games, go overboard supporting their sons and sometimes make fools out of themselves. Every time I think back to a Sixers game during the Iverson era, it makes me jealous that I can't write this book right now with twenty thousand fans cheering me on as my mom sits in the front row wearing a Simmons jersey, whooping it up and holding a sign that says, MY BABY IS THE SPORTS GUY AND HE'S ALL THAT!

14. Tattoos. Tons and tons of tattoos. No other sport has you saying things like, "I wonder what those Chinese characters stand for" and "Wait a second, is that Notorious B.I.G.'s face on the point guard's right arm?" My buddy JackO has been arguing for years that, along with a game program, home teams should hand out a tattoo program that explains the origin of every tattoo on both teams (complete with pictures). Like you wouldn't thumb through it during time-outs?

15. The Most Valuable Player award that matters the most.

5. My favorite Stern story: he held up the 30th pick in the '08 draft for four full minutes to ream ESPN officials for reporting rumors about Darrell Arthur's supposedly problematic kidneys, dropped roughly 800 f-bombs, put the fear of God into everyone and then calmly strolled out and announced Boston's pick. The man has no peer.[P18]

P18. My second-favorite Stern story: At the Commissioner's Party after the 2010 Slam Dunk Contest in Dallas, a connected NBA friend of mine kept passing up appetizers because he was waiting for pigs in a blanket. My friend claimed they were Stern's favorite food; they make an appearance at every NBA party; they're always high caliber; and when the NBA had recently thrown a party without them, Stern flipped out. My friend then wagered "any amount of money" that pigs in a blanket would come out. A few minutes later? A waiter walked out with pigs in a blanket. And they were delicious. Actually, that might be my favorite Stern story. I need to think about this some more.

THE BOOK OF BASKETBALL   223

(Sound of a record screeching to a halt.)

Wait, you don't believe me? Can you name the last ten NFL MVPs? You can't. Can you name the last ten MVPs in each baseball league, then definitively say which guy was better each year? Nope. Do you even know the name of the NHL MVP trophy, much less the last ten winners?[6] Unless you're Canadian, probably not. Only the NBA taps the full potential of the Most Valuable Player concept: everyone plays against each other, it's relatively simple to compare statistics, and if you watch the games, you can almost always figure out which players stand out. You only have to follow the season. If you combine the MVP voting with the All-NBA teams, the playoff results, and individual statistics, you end up with a reasonable snapshot of exactly what happened that NBA season, much like how the four major Oscar awards reasonably capture what happened in Hollywood from year to year.

Of course, there are exceptions. Charles Barkley won the '93 MVP even though Jordan was the best and proved it authoritatively in the Finals. You know whose name sits next to "1993 NBA MVP" for the rest of eternity? Barkley. That's just the way this crap works. One year later, *Forrest Gump* won Best Picture over *The Shawshank Redemption* and *Pulp Fiction*. If you could only watch one of those three movies again, which one would you pick? I bet you're not picking *Gump*. If you're old enough to remember walking out of the theater after those three movies in '94, which one left you the most blown away? Again I bet you're not picking *Gump*. I remember seeing a *Shawshank* matinee with my girlfriend at the time,[7] limping out of the theater in disbelief, then sitting in her car afterward having an "I can't believe how freaking amazing that was" conversation and not departing the parking lot for fifteen solid minutes. That definitely didn't happen when I walked out of *Gump*. Although I do remember wondering how Jenny Gump died of AIDS when it hadn't been created yet.

So why didn't *Shawshank* win the Oscar? Because it had a crappy title.[8]

6. It's the Hart Memorial Trophy, named after Dr. David Hart, the father of Cecil Hart (coach and GM of the 1924 Canadiens). Dr. Hart donated the trophy that year to the league, so they named it after him. I'm not making this up.

7. You know it's a memorable flick when fifteen years later you can remember exactly where you saw it. I saw *Shawshank* in Braintree and *Pulp Fiction* at a scummy Loews Theater in Somerville. (Whoops, cue up the porn music.) "Bow-cha-cha bow-bow-bow . . . thank you for coming to Loews . . . sit back and relax . . . enjoy the *show!*"

8. The only way that title could have been worse was if they called it *500 Yards of Shit-Smelling Foulness.*

If they had gone with a generic Hollywood title like *Hope Is a Good Thing* or *Crawling to Freedom,* more potential moviegoers would have understood the premise and seen it. When flipping through movie times in a 1994 newspaper, you weren't gravitating toward the prison movie with the confusing title and a douche like Tim Robbins in the leading role. Believe me, I was nearly one of those people. I specifically remember *not* wanting to see *Shawshank* until my dad (an early *Shawshank* lover) told me something crazy like, "Look, if you don't see this movie within the next forty-eight hours, I'm coming over and severing your carotid artery." Now? It's one of the greatest titles of all time. I wouldn't change a thing about it. Back then, it probably cost that movie $75 million and the Oscar. As for MJ, he didn't win the '93 MVP because everyone was tired of voting for him. That's the only reason. And it's a shitty one.

Since the MVP means more to the NBA than any other sport, and since we're headed for a mammoth "Evaluating the Best Players Ever" section in a few pages that involves an Egyptian pyramid—no, really—I thought we'd travel back in time and correct every mistake or injustice in MVP history. I'm also creating a playoffs MVP because it's nonsensical that we have awards for the regular season and Finals, but nothing covering every play-off series including the Finals. For example, the 2007 Spurs wouldn't have won without Tim Duncan, their entire low-post offense, best defender, best rebounder, best shot blocker and emotional leader. With nearly eight hundred games (including playoffs) and one knee surgery already on his odometer, Duncan had learned to pace himself during the regular season by then, concentrating on defense and rebounding and saving his offensive energy for message games and playoff games. In the regular season, he played 80 games and finished with a 20–11–3, shooting a career-high .546 from the field and making first-team All-NBA. Then he averaged a 22–12 and blocked 62 shots in 20 playoff games as the Spurs swept Cleveland in the Finals. So what happened? A French guy (Tony Parker) stole Finals MVP honors for lighting up a particularly poor group of Cleveland point guards, averaging a 30–4 in the sweep and shooting .568 from the field.[9]

9. The Cleveland crew: Daniel Gibson, Damon Jones and Eric Snow, whose shooting prowess I described in 2007 by writing, "If my life were at stake and I had to pick any NBA player to miss a 20-footer that he was trying to make, or else I'd be killed, I'd pick Snow and rejoice as he bricked a set shot off the side of the rim."

Let's say your great-grandkid looks back at that season sixty years from now. Dirk Nowitzki won the MVP, Tony Parker won the Finals MVP . . . and other than his first-team All-NBA spot and solid playoff numbers, how would you discern that Duncan, *by far,* was the crucial player on the best team of the 2006–7 season? You couldn't. That's why there should be a regular-season MVP, a Finals MVP *and* a playoffs MVP, and that's why I'm handing out my imaginary playoffs MVP, creating a universal definition for regular-season MVP and settling every erroneous pick since 1956. But before we get there, three crucial MVP wrinkles have to be mentioned:

Wrinkle no. 1. The first award was given out for the 1955–56 season, with players controlling MVP votes and writers handling All-NBA first and second teams. (Only one rule: players couldn't vote for anyone on their own team.) Given the racial climate of the fifties and the general resistance to the influx of black players, how could anyone have expected a fair vote when 85–90 percent of the players were white? Wasn't it more of a popularity contest than anything? When you apply the "best player is decided by his peers" concept to modern times, you can see its inherent dangers and potential for a lack of objectivity. Critics are critics for a reason—it's their job to objectively evaluate things. You can't expect players to suddenly become impartial reviewers. For instance, let's say the 2008 players considered Kobe to be a world-class bully, egomaniac and phony.[10] Under this scenario, if they were voting for the 2008 MVP, would Kobe have had any chance of pulling it out over Chris Paul?[11] And considering the Hornets loved Paul and wanted him to win, wouldn't they have voted for someone without a real chance like LeBron? NBA players should only be voting for things like Worst B.O., Guy You Don't Want to Leave Alone with Your Girlfriend, Least Likely Star to Pick Up a Check, Toughest Poker Competitor, Ugliest Player and Craziest Mothafucka You Don't Want to Cross.

10. This is a hypothetical example. As far as you know.
11. Actually, with the way the NBA works now—players from different age groups bonding by coming through the ranks at the same time and, in some cases, knowing each other since AAU ball—it's not far-fetched to think that there'd be more politicking now. The whole Bron-Melo-CP generation loves each other. Wouldn't those guys have swung 2008 votes behind Paul? Wouldn't the older guys have gravitated toward KG?

Wrinkle no. 2. Starting with the 1979–80 season, a handpicked committee of journalists and broadcasters was given the voting reins, creating more problems for obvious reasons (some might not follow the entire league, some might be biased toward the guy they're watching every night, some might be dopes about the NBA) and less obvious ones (recognizable stars now had an advantage, as did someone without a trophy competing against a previous winner). Starting in the early nineties, a more subtle problem developed: a group almost entirely composed of middle-aged white journalists who couldn't identify with the current direction of the league, missed the access they once had and openly despised the new generation of me-first, chest-pounding, posse-having, tattoo-showing, commercial-shooting overpaid stars were being asked to objectively decide on the MVP. I'd say that's a problem. I once asked a well-known basketball writer if he had DirecTV's NBA Season Pass, and he recoiled in disgust, like I had asked him if he'd ever been to a sex club and banged someone through a glory hole or something. And this was a guy with an MVP vote. Can we really rely on the over-fifty, "I used to love the NBA before the league went to hell" demographic to make the right decisions?

Wrinkle no. 3. Current voters openly confess to being confused about the voting criteria, mainly because the NBA powers that be willingly facilitated that confusion by never defining the term "valuable." They *like* when radio hosts and writers get bent out of shape about it. They *want* voters to wonder if it's an award for the best player or the most valuable one, or both, or two-thirds one part and one-third the other part, or whatever ratio someone ends up settling on. We only know the following:

1. It's an award for the regular season only.
2. Candidates have to play at least 55 games.
3. Whoops, that's all we know.

See how we might have trouble coming up with the right pick annually? That's why I pored through every season making sure that every choice was either completely valid, relatively valid or invalid, applying my own definition of the MVP, a formula I have been revising and redefining for an entire decade before finally settling on the language for life last summer.[12] My definition hinges on four questions weighted by importance (from highest to lowest):

Question no. 1: If you replaced each MVP candidate with a decent player at his position for the entire season, what would be the hypothetical effect on his team's records? You can't define the word "valuable" any better. Say you switched Rasual Butler for Kevin Durant during the summer of '09. How would Oklahoma City's 2009–10 season have turned out? They grabbed the eighth seed in a wicked conference thanks to Durant, a beloved leader, teammate, spokesman and crunch-time guy for the youngest roster in the league. Switch him with Butler and the Zombie Sonics probably finish 23–59 instead of 50–32. Ranking the 2010 MVP candidates by this question alone, LeBron ranks first, Durant ranks second, Dwyane Wade third, Dwight Howard fourth and Eddy Curry last.

Question no. 2: In a giant pickup game with every NBA player available and two knowledgable fans forced to pick five-man teams, with their lives depending on the game's outcome, who would be the first player picked based on how everyone played that season?[13] Translation: who's the alpha dog that season? The Finals answer this question many times . . . but not *every* time. We thought Kobe was the alpha dog in 2008, but after watching him wilt[14] against Boston in the Finals—compared to the way LeBron carried a crappy Cavs team to seven games against Boston and nearly stole Game 7—it's unclear. This question reduces everything to the simplest of terms: we're playing to 11, I need to win, I can't screw around with this choice, and if I don't pick this guy, he's gonna get pissed and kick our asses as the second pick. I mean, imagine the look on '97 MJ's face if someone picked '97 Karl Malone before him in a pickup game. It would have been like Michael Corleone in *Godfather Part II* when Kay informed him about her abortion.

---

12. That's not a lie. I spent as much time working out the kinks for this MVP theory as Jonas Salk did on the polio vaccine.
13. I think this is how the annual Rucker League tournament works in Harlem. I'm not kidding.
14. Do you think they created the verb "wilt" because of Wilt Chamberlain? It's an honest question.

Question no. 3: Ten years from now, who will be the first player from that season who pops into my head? Every season belongs to someone to varying degrees. Why? Just like the political media can affect a primary or a presidential campaign, the basketball media can swing an MVP race. They shape every argument and story for ten months, with their overriding goal being to discuss potentially provocative angles, stories or controversies that haven't been picked apart yet. There's no better example than the '93 season: Jordan was still the best, but the controversial Barkley had just been swapped to Phoenix, then made a leap of sorts at the '92 Olympics, emerging as the team's most compelling personality and second-best player. Pigeonholed during his final Philly years as a hotheaded, controversial lout who partied too much and showed truly terrible judgment— epitomized by the incident when he accidentally spat on a young fan, followed by the story being twisted around to "Barkley spits on young fan!"—suddenly everyone was embracing Chuck Wagon's humor and candor. Once he started pushing an already good Suns team to another level, Barkley became *the* story of the '92–'93 season, a bona fide sensation on Madison Avenue and the most charismatic personality in any sport.[15]

Should that "transformation" have made him the most valuable player in 1993? Well, the '92 Suns won 53 games, shot 49.2 percent from the field, scored 112.7 points per game and gave up 106.2. The '93 Suns won 62 games, shot 49.3 percent, scored 113.4 and gave up 106.7. They rebounded better with Barkley but he weakened them defensively. Maybe they had a better overall team in '93, but didn't free agent pickup Danny Ainge, rookies Oliver Miller and Richard Dumas, emerging third-year player Cedric Ceballos and new coach Paul Westphal deserve a little credit? You also can't discount what happened in the Western Conference: following a particularly strong '92 campaign that featured four 50-win teams and nine above-.500 teams in all, only six '93 teams finished above .500 and the eighth playoff seed went to a 39-win Lakers team. Barkley's regular-season impact, purely from a basketball standpoint, wasn't nearly as significant as everyone believed. Admittedly, he injected that franchise

15. The NBA definitely needed a Barkley charisma injection that season. Look at the elite veterans other than MJ: Malone, Stockton, Ewing, Hakeem, Dumars, Drexler, Mullin, Pippen, Robinson, Brad Daugherty, Mark Price. All nice guys, but would you want to spend the weekend in Vegas with any of them?

with swagger, gave them a proven warrior and inside force, boosted home attendance, helped turn them into title favorites and pushed a very good team up one level. For lack of a better word, he owned that season. When you think of '92–'93, you think of Barkley and the Suns first; then you think, "Wait, wasn't that the year Chicago pulled out the Charles Smith Game and then MJ single-handedly destroyed Phoenix in the Finals?" Still, ownership of a season shouldn't swing the voting. In '93, it did.

Question no. 4. If you're explaining your MVP pick to someone who has a favorite player in the race—a player that you didn't pick—will he at least say something like, "Yeah, I don't like it, but I can see how you arrived at that choice"? I created this question after what happened with my '08 MVP column, when I picked Garnett and found myself deluged with "You're a homer, you suck!" emails from fans of other candidates. I expected the choice to be unpopular, but *that* unpopular? Did I make a mistake? I rehashed my thought process and realized that my logic was sound and (seemingly) unbiased: I'd abided by the same reasons for which I picked Shaq in '05—namely, that Garnett transformed the Celtics defensively and competitively, turned the franchise around, gave it leadership and spawned a record 42-win turnaround—and included a few I-saw-this-happen examples to bang my logic home. Still, I *was* biased for one reason: I had watched nearly every minute of that Celtics season, whereas I had only seen pieces of 25–30 Hornets and Lakers games. My affection for the Celtics didn't taint my opinion but my constant exposure to them did. Did I know *exactly* what Chris Paul did for the Hornets?[16] Not really. Had I grown up a Hornets fan and diligently followed their miraculous transformation I inevitably would have ended up arguing Paul's merits.[17] The crucial variable: any Lakers fan would disagree with Paul over Kobe, but at the very least they would have understood the logic. They wouldn't have agreed with it, but they would

16. I keep typing "Chris Paul" because he's one of those guys whose name has to be said all at once. It's weird to call him "Chris" or "Paul." He's like my friend Nick Aieta in this respect.
17. The same phenomenon happens with parents: they spend so much time with their kids that they begin to think, "There are no other kids like this!" and "He's so far advanced over every baby his age!" By the way, you should see my daughter run. Fast jets, phenomenal balance. Much better than the other five-year-olds.

have understood it. Well, they didn't understand the wisdom of the Garnett pick. At all. And that's a problem.

Lump those questions together like MVP Play-Doh and suddenly we have a trusty formula. Ideally, I want a player who can't be replaced, then an alpha dog, then someone who owned that season to some degree, then a pick who doesn't need to be overdefended to a prejudiced party . . . and after everything's said and done, a choice who vindicates my support by kicking ass in the playoffs. Although it sounds great on paper, it doesn't happen every year, as you're about to see. For reference purposes, here's the complete list of NBA alpha dogs in the shot-clock era, along with the actual MVP winners and my choices for Playoffs MVP. I put in boldface the MVP winners who, after much research and deliberation, I signed off on as a valid choice that can't be debated.

Alpha Dog (1955): Dolph Schayes
MVP: **Bob Cousy**[18]
Playoffs MVP: Schayes

Alpha Dog (1956–57): Bob Pettit
MVP: **Pettit ('56), Cousy ('57)**
Playoffs MVP: Paul Arizin ('56), Russell ('57)

Alpha Dog (1958–65): Bill Russell
MVP: **Russell ('58, '61, '62, '63, '65)**; *Pettit ('59),* **Chamberlain ('60),**
   Robertson ('64)
Playoffs MVP: Pettit ('58), Russell ('59–'65)

Alpha Dog (1966–68): Wilt
MVP: **Wilt ('66, '67, '68)**
Playoffs MVP: Russell ('66), Chamberlain ('67), Russell ('68)

Alpha Dog (1969–70): West
MVP: Wes Unseld ('69), Willis Reed ('70)
Playoffs MVP: John Havlicek ('69), Walt Frazier ('70)

18. They didn't hand it out this year, but Cousy averaged a 21–8–6 and finished second in scoring and first in assists. He was the Imaginary MVP.

Alpha Dog (1971–74): Kareem
MVP: **Jabbar** *('71, '72, '74), Cowens ('73)*
Playoffs MVP: Kareem ('71), West ('72), Frazier ('73), Havlicek ('74)

Alpha Dog (1975): Rick Barry
MVP: Bob McAdoo
Playoffs MVP: Barry

Alpha Dog (1976–78): Unclear[19]
MVP: **Kareem** *('76–'77), Walton ('78)*
Playoffs MVP: Cowens ('76), Walton ('77), Bobby Dandridge ('78)

Alpha Dog (1979–83): Moses Malone
MVP: **Moses** *('79, '82, '83),* **Kareem** *('80), Erving ('81)*
Playoffs MVP: Dennis Johnson ('79), Kareem ('80), Bird ('81), Magic ('82), Moses ('83)

Alpha Dog (1984–86): Bird
MVP: **Bird**
Playoffs MVP: Bird ('84, '86), Kareem ('85)

Alpha Dog (1987–88): Bird/Magic (tie)
MVP: **Magic** *('87),* **Jordan** *('88)*
Playoffs MVP: Magic ('87–'88)

Alpha Dog (1989–90): Unclear[20]
MVP: **Magic** *('89, '90)*
Playoffs MVP: Isiah Thomas ('89, '90)

Alpha Dog (1991–93): Jordan
MVP: **Jordan** *('91, '92), Barkley ('93)*
Playoffs MVP: Jordan ('91–'93)

19. Kareem was a wash with McAdoo in '76 and Walton in '77–'78.
20. Can't pick between Magic and MJ in '89–'90. Impossible.

Alpha Dog (1994–95): Olajuwon
*MVP: **Hakeem ('94), David Robinson ('95)***
Playoffs MVP: Hakeem ('94, '95)

Alpha Dog (1996–98): Jordan
*MVP: **Jordan ('96, '98)**, Karl Malone ('97)*
Playoffs MVP: Jordan ('96–'98)

Alpha Dog (1999): Haywood Jablome[21]
MVP: Malone
Playoffs MVP: Duncan

Alpha Dog (2000–2): Shaq
*MVP: **O'Neal ('00)**, Iverson ('01), **Duncan ('02)***
Playoffs MVP: Shaq ('00–'02)

Alpha Dog (2003–5): Duncan
*MVP: **Duncan ('03)**, Garnett ('04), Nash ('05)*
Playoffs MVP: Shaq ('02), Duncan ('03, '05), Ben Wallace ('04)[22]

Alpha Dog (2006): Kobe
MVP: Nash
Playoffs MVP: Dwyane Wade

Alpha Dog (2007–10): LeBron/Kobe
MVP: Nowitzki ('07), Bryant ('08), LeBron ('09, '10)
Playoffs MVP: Duncan ('07), Paul Pierce ('08), Bryant ('09, '10)

That leaves a whopping seventeen MVP seasons needing to be hashed out: 1959 (Pettit), 1962 (Russell), 1963 (Russell), 1969 (Unseld), 1970 (Willis), 1973 (Cowens), 1978 (Walton), 1981 (Doc), 1990 (Magic), 1993 (Barkley), 1997 (Mailman), 2002 (Duncan), 2005 (Nash), 2006 (Nash),

---

21. I hated the 50-game, strike-shortened season when everyone was out of shape. I refuse to pick an alpha dog. You can't make me. It's like choosing between syphilis and anal warts.
22. The case for Wallace: 23 games, 10.3 PPG, 14.3 RPG, 100 combined blocks/steals, excellent D on Shaq in the Final, and a splendid afro.

2007 (Nowitzki) and 2008 (Kobe).[23] We're separating them into three categories: fishy choices that were ultimately okay, fishy choices that were
proven to be stupid and outright travesties of justice that should have resulted in arrests and convictions. Before we rip through them, I urge you
to pour yourself a glass of wine, put on some John Mayer and maybe even
don a smoking jacket.

(Waiting . . .)

(Waiting . . .)

All right, let's do it.

CATEGORY 1:
FISHY BUT ULTIMATELY OKAY

Bill Russell (1962)

Already the two-time defending MVP (shades of MJ in '93), Russell
peaked statistically in '62 like so many others, averaging a 19–24–5 for a
60-win Boston team and providing typically superhuman defense. If the
media were voting, Russell would have gotten boned because of the "You
already won a few times and it's time for some new blood" corollary
(shades of MJ in '93), and either Wilt (50–25, first-team All-NBA) or
Oscar (the league's first triple double) would have prevailed. They were
the season's dominant stories other than pinball-like scoring and Elgin
Baylor getting saddled with military duty and only playing 48 games—all
on weekends, all without ever practicing with the Lakers—but somehow
averaging an ungodly 38–19–5.[24]

I would argue that Elgin's 38–19–5 was more implausible than Wilt's 50
a game or Oscar's triple double. *The guy didn't practice! He was moonlighting as an NBA player on weekends!* Wilt's 50–25 makes sense considering the feeble competition and his gratuitous ball hogging. Oscar's

23. Again, I'm ignoring the '99 season. I went to most of the Celtics games that year because my dad never wanted to go—the lockout ended too abruptly and three-fourths of
the league was out of shape. Awful season. No award should have been given out other
than the Eff You Award. Which, by the way, would be an awesome award. "Ladies and
gentlemen, our five-time Eff You MVP, Mr. Vince Carter."
24. Goes to show you where the league was in 1962—it couldn't even pull some strings
to get its most exciting player out of military duty.

triple double makes sense considering the style of play at the time. But Elgin's 38–19–5 makes no sense. A United States Army Reservist at the time, Elgin worked in the state of Washington during the week, living in an army barracks and leaving only whenever they gave him a weekend pass. Even with that pass, he had to fly coach on flights with multiple connections to meet the Lakers wherever they were playing, throw on a uniform and battle the best NBA players, then make the same complicated trip back to Washington in time to be there early Monday morning. That was his life for six months. The only modern comparison would be Kobe's '04 season, when he was accused of rape[25] and flew back and forth between Colorado (where the hearings were taking place) and either Los Angeles or wherever the Lakers happened to be playing, and everyone made an enormous deal about Kobe's "grueling" season even though he was flying charters and staying at first-class hotels. Can you imagine if Kobe had been reenacting Elgin's '62 season? The world would have stopped. We would have given him a Nobel Prize. And yet I digress.

In the sixties, first-place votes counted for 5 points, second place for 3 points and third place for 1 point. You could only vote for three players. The '62 MVP voting broke down like so:

Russell: 297 (51–12–6)[26]; Wilt: 152 (9–30–17); Oscar: 135 (13–13–31); Elgin: 82 (3–18–13); West: 60 (6–8–6); Pettit: 31 (2–4–9); Richie Guerin: 5 (1–0–0); Cousy: 3 (0–0–3).

You're not gonna believe this, but I have a few thoughts. First, Elgin's season was so freaking amazing that he missed 40 percent of the season and still finished fourth (even grabbing three first-place votes). Second, Wilt's "legendary" season impressed his peers so much that only nine players (10 percent of the league) gave him a first-place vote, proving how silly the '62 statistics were (as well as the level of Wilt's selfishness).[27]

---

25. Kobe settled with the alleged victim for a significant amount of money before the case went to trial. We never heard from her again. You could have a good "Has anyone ever paid more money for one sexual encounter that we know about because of ensuing legal arguments?" argument between Kobe and Michael Jackson.

26. Those numbers stand for first-, second- and third-place votes. Russell's 51–12–6 means he had 51 firsts, 12 seconds and 6 thirds.

27. The '62 Knicks were outraged by his 100-point game against them, specifically how Wilt hogged the ball and the Warriors fouled near the end to get him the ball back. It's safe to say he didn't get any of their votes.

Third, West, Pettit, Guerin and Cousy grabbed as many first-place votes as Wilt and stole another twelve second-place votes and fifteen thirds. West averaged a 30–8–5 and wasn't the best guy on his own team; Pettit averaged a 31–19 for a 29–51 Hawks team; Guerin averaged a 30–7–6 for a 29–51 Knicks team; and Cousy had his worst season in 10 years (16–8–4) and only played 28.2 minutes a game. Should any of them have sniffed the top three? You could say they split the "I hate blacks and they're ruining our league" vote. Anyway, I'm fine with the Russell pick: he was the dominant player on the dominant team. Thirty years later, Wilt or Oscar would have won and I'd be ranting and raving about it. Let's move on.

Bill Russell (1963)

Great two-man race between Russell (17–24–5, superhuman defense for a 60-win Boston team) and Baylor (34–14–5 for a 53-win Lakers team). Both legends were at the peak of their respective powers, which seems relevant because Russell was valued a little more highly than Baylor at the time.[28] Here's how the voting broke down: Russell: 341 (56–18–7); Elgin: 252 (19–36–18); Oscar: 191 (13–34–21); Pettit: 84 (3–14–27); West: 19 (2–1–6); Johnny Kerr: 13 (1–1–5); Wilt: 9 (0–2–3); Terry Dischinger: 5 (1–0–0); John Havlicek: 3 (0–1–0); John Barnhill: 1 (0–0–1);[29] Walt Bellamy: 1 (0–0–1). Good God! The NBA logo in '63 should have had a Ku Klux Klan hood on it. The votes for Dischinger (26–8–3 in just 57 games for a 25-win Chicago team) were particularly appalling. Even if some votes were strategic—no Laker was voting for Russell, no Celtic was voting for Elgin, and maybe no Royal was voting for Elgin or Russell—it's telling that inexplicable votes always seemed to be for white guys.

Back to Elgin and Russell. In modern times, Elgin would cruise to the MVP for the typical bullshit reasons of "He's never won it before" and "He's overdue and we need to recognize him." That same faulty logic led

28. Here's how we know this: If Boston called L.A. and proposed a Russell-Elgin trade, L.A. would have initially thought, "Wow, Russell is available?" and maybe even had a meeting. If the Lakers proposed the same trade, Auerbach would have hung up on them.
29. Barnhill was a rookie guard for St. Louis who averaged a 12–5–4 and didn't make the '63 All-Star team, but somebody gave him a third-place vote. Inexplicable. His nickname was "Rabbit." Don't you miss the days when athletes had animal nicknames?

to many of the egregious MVP crimes on this list (we'll get to them), as well as Marty Scorsese finally winning an Oscar for a movie that ended with a rat crawling on the balcony as a big neon SYMBOLISM! SYMBOLISM! sign flashed in the background. So I can't endorse Elgin's candidacy here. With that said, of every "He's overdue and we need to recognize him with an MVP" season in NBA history, '63 Elgin ranks right up there. It's an absolute shame that he never won the award.

(And if the Lakers had won the '63 Finals, then I'd be pleading his case. But they didn't.)

Kareem Abdul-Jabbar (1972)

Here we have the league's reigning alpha dog and MVP averaging a career-best 34.6 points, 16.8 rebounds and 4.6 assists per game for a 63-win team. From 1969 to 2008, that's the single greatest statistical season by a center; Young Kareem was also the best defensive center of that decade other than Nate Thurmond. So I can't kill this pick. But we should mention—repeat: *mention*—that the Lakers broke two records (69 wins, 33 straight) en route to Jerry West's first championship. Unfortunately, nobody could decide which Laker was more responsible: West (26–4–10, led the league in assists) or Wilt (15–19–4, 65% FG, led the league in rebounds)? Check out the bizarre voting, the only time that one team placed two of the top three: Kareem: 581 (81–52–20); West: 393 (44–42–47); Wilt: 294 (36–25–39).

This raises an interesting question: Should a special "co-champs" choice be added to the ballot for every season with a memorable team that didn't have an identifiable alpha dog? The '58 Celtics (Cousy and Russell), '70 Knicks (Reed and Frazier), '72 Lakers (West and Wilt), '73 Celtics (Hondo and Cowens), '97 Jazz (Stockton and Malone), '01 Lakers (Shaq and Kobe), '05 Heat (Shaq and Wade) and '08 Celtics (Pierce and Garnett) all qualify and solve many of the problems in this chapter. The '72 season was the ultimate example: Kareem was the singular MVP and West and Wilt were co-MVPs. Right? (You're shaking your head at me.) Fine, you're right. Dumb idea.

Bill Walton (1978)

Even an unbiased observer would admit that for the eleven months stretching from April '77 through February '78, the Mountain Man was the greatest player alive and pushed that Portland team to surreal heights.[30] Right as that team was cresting, the February 13, 1978, *Sports Illustrated*—one of the watershed issues of my childhood because of an insane Sidney Moncrief tomahawk dunk on the cover—ran an extended feature on the Blazers in which Rick Barry called them "maybe the most ideal team ever put together." Everything centered around Walton (19–15–5, 3.5 blocks), the next Russell, an unselfish big man who made team-mates better and even shared killer weed with them. Two weeks after the *SI* story/jinx, the big redhead injured his foot and didn't return until the playoffs, when he fractured that same foot in Game 2, killing Portland's playoff hopes and leading to his inevitable messy departure.[31]

Now . . .

It's hard to imagine anyone qualifying for MVP after missing twenty-four games, much less taking the trophy home. But we're talking about an especially loony season, as evidenced by our rebounding champ (Mr. Leonard "Truck" Robinson) and assists champ (the one, the only, Kevin Porter). Kareem sucker-punched Kent Benson on opening night, missed 20 games and struggled for the remainder of the season. Erving submitted a subpar (for him) season.[32] The strongest candidates were George Gervin (27–5–4, 54% FG) and David Thompson (27–5–5, 52% FG), both leading scorers for division winners who weren't known for their defense. Guards weren't supposed to win MVPs back then; only Cousy and Oscar had done it, and as much as we loved Skywalker and Ice, they weren't Cousy and Oscar. So Walton drew the most votes (96), Gervin finished second (80.5),

---

30. I am not an unbiased observer. Wait until we get to the Pyramid section; I do every-thing but splooge on Walton's '77 Topps card.

31. "Messy" is an understatement: Walton demanded a trade, filed a medical malpractice suit, lost some friendships and signed with the Clips in 1979. One of the ugliest sports divorces ever.

32. That was also the year he cut down his afro. Big mistake. That afro made him look six foot ten and added at least a foot to his vertical leap.

Thompson third (28.5) and Kareem fourth (14); a dude from Venice named Manny, the league's unofficial coke dealer, finished fifth (10).[33]

The case for Walton: He played 58 of the first 60 games and the Blazers went 50–10 over that stretch. He missed the next 22 games and the Blazers stumbled to an 8–14 finish (hold on, huge "but/still" combo coming up), *but* they *still* finished with a league-best 58 wins and clinched home court for the Playoffs. So yeah, Walton missed 24 games *and* had an abnormally profound impact on the regular season, winning 50 games during a season when only two other teams finished with 50-plus wins: Philly (55) and San Antonio (52).

The case against Walton: Borrowing the Oscars analogy, would you have accepted the choice of *No Country for Old Men* for Best Picture if the movie inexplicably ended with thirty-five minutes to go? (Actually, bad example—that would have been the best thing that ever happened to *Old Men*. I hated everything after we didn't see Josh Brolin get gunned down.[34] You're never talking me into it. I hated English majors in college and I hate movies that are vehemently defended by English majors now. The last twenty minutes sucked. I will argue this to the death.) Take two: Would you have accepted *The Departed* as Best Picture if the movie inexplicably ended with thirty-five minutes to go and you never found out what happened to DiCaprio or Damon? No.

Ultimately it comes down to one thing: even if Walton and the Blazers only owned 70 percent of that season, still, they *owned* it. Nobody else stood out except Kareem (for clocking Benson), Kermit Washington (for clocking Rudy T.), Thompson/Gervin (for their scoring barrage on the final day), the Sonics (who started out 5–22 and staged a late surge to make the Finals) and Manny (the aforementioned coke connection that I

---

33. I have no clue what the scoring system was this season; all they released were final points. For all we know, the players voted right after plowing through a pile of cocaine the size of a Gatorade bucket. I can't make enough coke jokes about this era.

34. If I ruined the movie, too bad—it's been out for two years. That reminds me: at a New Year's Eve party in '95, my buddy JackO told me that he hadn't seen *The Usual Suspects;* I had a few in me and blurted out, "Kevin Spacey is Keyser Söze." He's still pissed fourteen years later. And you know what? I don't care. If you haven't ruined a movie twist for a friend as a way to bust his balls, you're missing out in life. I'm telling you. We've had probably a hundred hours' worth of conversations about me blowing *The Usual Suspects* for him. Even right now, he's fuming. This is great.

made up, as far as you know). That's good enough for me—I'll take 70 percent of a Pantheon season over 100 percent of a relatively forgettable season. I'm signing off. We'll make an exception here with all the missed games. Just this once.

Tim Duncan (2002)

The '02 season featured a ballyhooed battle between Duncan (a career year: 25–13–4 plus 2.5 blocks and superb defense) and Jason Kidd (15–7–10 and superb defense), with Kidd owning the season because of a much-argued-about trade the previous summer, when Phoenix swapped Kidd to New Jersey for Stephon Marbury a few months after Kidd was charged with domestic assault.[35] Energized by the change of scenery, Kidd led the perenially crappy Nets to 52 wins, swung the New York media behind him and stood out mostly for his unselfishness and singular talent for running fast breaks, as well as for his attention-hogging wife, Joumana, who brought their young son courtside and seemingly knew the location of every TV camera.[36] Maybe Kidd's '02 season didn't match his '01 season in Phoenix (17–6–10, 41% FG), but mostly by default, Kidd became the featured story in a historically atrocious Eastern Conference,[37] leading to one of the closest (and dumbest) MVP votes ever: Duncan: 952 (57–38–20–5–3); Kidd: 897 (45–41–26–9–3); Shaq: 696 (15–38–40–25–5); T-Mac: 390 (7–5–28–45–10).

Um . . . why was this close? Duncan topped 3,300 minutes, 2,000 points, 1,000 boards, 300 assists and 200 blocks, carried the Spurs to a number two seed in the West, didn't miss a game and had a greater effect on his teammates than anyone but Kidd. His supporting cast: Bruce Bowen, Antonio

35. Anytime "he smacked his wife, let's get him the hell out of here" is the only reason for dealing one of the best top-ten point guards ever, I'm sorry, that's a shitty reason. By the way, this footnote was written by Ike Turner.

36. This backfired when Kidd dove into the stands for a loose ball, landed on his son and broke his collarbone. Karma is a bitch, isn't it? No young child should be allowed to sit courtside or in the first few rows of a basketball game. It's too dangerous and any worthy parent would know that. I never liked Joumana after that. Hold on, I have to get off my high horse.

37. Ironically, Kidd had a career year in '03 (19–9–6, 41% FG) and finished ninth in the voting because everyone was still mortified by how '02 turned out.

Daniels, Tony Parker, Malik Rose, Danny Ferry, Charles Smith, a past-his-prime David Robinson, a pretty-much-past-his-prime Steve Smith and a past-being-past-his-prime Terry Porter. That's a 58-win team? Had you switched Duncan with someone like Stromile Swift, the Spurs would have won 25 games. Meanwhile, the Lakers swept the Nets in the Finals in a mismatch along the lines of Tyson-Spinks, Ryan-Ventura and any *Sopranos* cast member acting in a scene with AJ.[38] That's when we all realized, "We knew the East was bad, but we didn't know it was *that* bad!" That a 39 percent shooter for a 52-win team in a brutal conference nearly stole the MVP from the greatest power forward ever during his finest statistical season for a 58-win team . . . I mean, you can see why I don't trust the MVP process so much.

(By the way, Shaq retained alpha dog status this season, remaining on cruise control for 82 games—partially because he was lazy, partially because this was the year when he fully embraced his abhorrence of Kobe—before turning it on for the playoffs and averaging a 36–12 in the Finals. From there, he spent the entire summer eating. In fact, I think he grilled one of the Wayans brothers, covered him in A-1 sauce and ate him at one point.)

CATEGORY 2:
FISHY AND ULTIMATELY NOT OKAY

Bob Pettit (1959)

Again, any time you're putting the MVP in the hands of mostly white players competing in an era marred by racism and resentment toward black athletes, you're definitely hitting a few speed bumps. The league had an unwritten "only one or two blacks per team and that's it" rule in the fifties; even as late as 1958, the Hawks didn't have a single black player. So it's a little suspect that Pettit (a white guy) won the '59 MVP award in a landslide over the league's reigning MVP and most important player (Russell, a black guy) when 90 percent of the votes were from whites. Check out their numbers during '58 and '61 (when Russell won) and '59 (when Pettit

---

38. You can still find pieces of Todd MacCulloch's body sticking to the ceiling of the Staples Center after Shaq ripped him apart like a pit bull.

won), factor in their defensive abilities (Pettit was mediocre; Russell was transcendent), then help me figure a coherent explanation for Pettit nearly tripling Russell in the '59 voting that doesn't involve a white hood.

Here are the numbers:

NAME	YEAR	PPG	RPG	APG	FG	REC	MVP	FINALS
Russell	1958	16.6	22.7	3.2	44%	49–23	First	Runner-up[39]
B. Pettit	1958	24.6	17.4	2.2	41%	41–31	Fourth	Champ
Russell	1959	16.7	23.0	3.2	46%	52–20	Second	Champ
B. Pettit	1959	29.2	16.4	3.1	41%	49–23	First	Runner-up
Russell	1961	16.9	23.4	3.4	43%	57–22	First	Champ
B. Pettit	1961	27.9	20.3	3.4	45%	51–28	Second	Runner-up

Here's how the '59 voting shook out: Pettit: 317 (59–7–1); Russell: 144 (10–25–29); Elgin: 88 (2–20–18);[40] Cousy: 71 (4–11–18); Paul Arizin: 39 (1–7–13); Dolph Schayes: 26 (1–6–3); Ken Sears: 12 (1–1–4); Cliff Hagan: 7 (1–4–0); Jack Twyman: 7 (0–1–4); Tom Gola: 3 (0–1–0); Dick McGuire: 3 (0–1–0); Gene Shue: 1 (0–0–1).

Here's what happened in the '59 playoffs: Elgin's 33-win Lakers team shocked Pettit's Hawks in the Western Finals, then were swept by the Celtics in the Finals.

You know how the host of *The Bachelor* always says going into commercial, "Coming up, it's the most dramatic rose ceremony *ever*"? Well, this was the most racist MVP voting year *ever*. You had Pettit's bizarre landslide win (six times as many first-place votes as Russell?), half the league ignoring Elgin, the Cooz stealing four of Russell's first-place votes and four other white players (Arizin, Schayes, Sears and Hagan) unaccountably earning first-place votes. You can't play the "Pettit was a sentimental choice" card

39. Russell sprained his ankle in Game 3, missed two games and was never the same that series. What's strange is that the Celtics were sidelined by only *one* crucial injury over a 13-year span—during an era with inferior sports science, exercise routines, equipment and doctors—whereas the 1980s Celtics and 1980s Lakers probably had nine killer injuries between them.

40. Elgin won Rookie of the Year and finished with a 25–15, yet earned as many first-place votes as Sears and Schayes combined. Huh?

because he'd already won in '56. And if you're not buying the race card, re-member the times (pre-MLK, pre-JFK, pre-Malcolm, pre-desegregation), the climate (in baseball, the Red Sox signed their first black player in '59: the immortal Pumpsie Green), and stories like the following one from *Tall Tales* (pages 72–73) about the Lakers playing an exhibition game in Charleston, West Virginia. Their three black players (Baylor, Boo Ellis and Ed Fleming)[41] were not allowed to check into their hotel or eat anywhere in town except for the Greyhound bus station. Here's how Hot Rod Hundley and Baylor remembered the incident:

Hundley: "The people who put on the game wanted me to talk to Elgin about playing. After pregame warmups, I went into the dressing room and he was sitting there in his street clothes. I said, 'What they did to you isn't right. I understand that. But we're friends and this is my hometown. Play this one for me.' Elgin said, 'Rod, you're right, you are my friend. But Rod, I'm a human being, too. All I want to do is be treated like a human being.' It was then that I could begin to feel his pain."

Baylor: "A few days later, I got a call from the mayor of Charleston and he apologized. Two years later, I was invited to an All-Star Game there, and out of courtesy I went. We stayed at the same hotel that refused us service. We were able to eat anywhere we wanted. They were beginning to integrate the schools. Some black leaders told me that they were able to use what had happened to me and the other black players to bring pres-sure on the city to make changes, and that made me feel very good. But the indignity of a hotel clerk acting as if you aren't there, or people who won't sell you a sandwich because you're black . . . those are the things you never forget."

So yeah, things eventually did change; some of those changes were al-ready in motion in 1959. But Russell and Baylor were pushing the sport in a better direction and some of their peers weren't, um, *down* with the new movement yet. That's the only explanation. I don't mean to come off like

41. Totally underrated sports nickname: "Boo." When I'm the tsar of sports, I'm going to demand that we always have athletes nicknamed "Boo," "Goo," "Night Train," "Blue Moon," "Goose," "Rabbit," "Cool Papa," "Turkey" and "Bad News."

Sam Jackson screaming, "Yes, they deserved to die and I hope they burn in hell!" in *A Time to Kill*, but at the same time, bigotry affected the '59 vote and that's that. Russell was the MVP.

Wes Unseld (1969)

As a rookie with the Bullets, Unseld made a name for himself with bone-crushing picks and crisp outlet passes, averaging a 14–18 and shooting 47% for a 57-win team. Willis Reed played a similarly valuable role in New York, averaging a 22–14 and shooting 52% for a 54-win Knicks team, but Unseld's total in the MVP voting more than doubled Willis (310 to 137) and Unseld grabbed first-team All-NBA honors. In the first round of the '69 playoffs, Reed and the Knicks swept Baltimore and everyone felt stupid.[42]

Here's my problem: if you're giving the MVP to the fifth-best rebounder in the league and he's only responsible for 20 points a game (in this case, 14 points and 3 assists), he'd better be a cross between Russell and Dikembe Mutombo on the defensive end. Poor Unseld was only six foot six and eventually grew a Fletch-like afro to make himself look taller—shades of Tom Cruise wearing sneakers with four-inch lifts—and it's not like he was defending the rim and spraying shots everywhere. If anything, his value lay in subtle talents like outlets and picks. Maybe Big Wes was a wonderful role player, the perfect supporting piece for a contender, someone who made his team better (and eventually other teams better when he made a brief run at being the worst GM ever). But he was never a *dominant* player, you know?

No matter. By the holidays, everyone had decided that something special was happening with this Unseld kid; in the simplest terms, he stood out more than everyone else. His outlets were fun, his picks were fun and his rebounding stats were good enough that you could sell him as MVP and not get laughed out of the room. That doesn't mean he was more valuable than Willis, Billy Cunningham (a 25–13 for a feel-good Sixers

---

42. The Bullets were weakened before the playoffs when Gus Johnson blew out his knee, but still . . . an MVP can't get swept in the first round, right? Grumpy Old Editor says Bullets coach Gene Shue blew that series with the not-so-brilliant idea of having Unseld bring the ball up like a point guard. The ruining-to-helping ratio over the course of history with NBA coaches has to be 8:1.

team that overachieved) or even a stat-monger like Wilt (21–21 plus shot blocking and 59% shooting). Much like Steve Nash in '05 and '06, this was the proverbial "nobody else jumps out, I really like watching this guy . . . fuck it" vote. You felt good about yourself if you voted for Wes; it meant you knew your hoops and appreciated the little things about basketball. The following year, Unseld had an even better season (16–17 with 52% shooting) for another good Bullets team, only they left him off the '70 All-Star Team and both All-NBA teams. In fact, he never made a first or second All-NBA team again and only played in four more All-Star Games. You know what that tells me? That everyone felt like they got a little carried away with the '69 MVP award—like sending a girl a dozen roses after the first date or something.[43]

Here's how the voting went down: Unseld: 310 (53–14–8); Reed: 137 (18–11–14); Cunningham: 130 (15–16–8); Russell: 93 (11–8–22).[44] I thought Cunningham earned the MVP and here's why: even after dumping Wilt to L.A. for 45 cents on the dollar, Philly rallied for 55 wins and second place in a ferociously competitive conference. The key to everything? Cunningham. After rugged rebounder Luke Jackson blew out his knee in Game 25, Dr. Jack Ramsey's '69 Sixers willingly embraced smallball, moving Cunningham to power forward along with guards Archie Clark, Hal Greer and swingman Chet Walker, pressing all over the court and running as much as they could. Their chances hinged solely on Billy C. playing bigger than his size (six foot six), logging gargantuan minutes (82 games and 3,345 minutes in all) and battling the likes of Hayes, Lucas, Johnson and DeBusschere every night. Not only did he pull it off, he finished third in scoring and tenth in rebounds. In a transitional season devoid of an alpha dog, it remains the league's single most impressive feat. For whatever reason, everyone was more interested in Wes Unseld's picks and outlets. My vote goes to Billy C.

---

43. As a freshman in college, I made the rookie mistake of buying Janine Cunningham a half dozen roses after sucking face with her a few nights before. She left treadmarks running the other way. I could have given her a handful of plutonium and it would have gone better. And she was a cool chick. I guarantee she loves being referenced in this book. The point is, don't overreact with women or MVP votes.
44. The real outrage was that Russell didn't win Coach of the Year. Name me another coach who was also playing 45 minutes a game.

Bob McAdoo (1975)

One of the top twenty-five players ever (Rick Barry) peaked during the regular season (31–6–6, league leader in steals and FT%) for a team that finished first in the West, then carried his underdog Warriors over Washington in the Finals with a vintage performance (28–6–6, 50 steals in 17 playoff games). One of the top sixty-five players ever (McAdoo) peaked during that same season (35–14, 52% shooting, 3,539 minutes) for a team that finished third in the East, then lost in the first round in seven games to Washington (whom Golden State eventually swept).[45] McAdoo may have been an ahead-of-his-time offensive player enjoying a banner year, but Barry's passing, unselfishness and overall feel separated him from everyone else. Unfortunately, we were still stuck in the Look, Big Guys Are More Valuable Than Anyone Else and That's *That* era, a mind-set that wasn't helped by the lack of titles for Oscar and West in the sixties and never changed until Bird and Magic showed up.

But that's not what was so galling. Here's the one time where we can definitively say, "The other players stuck it to Player X." Check out the top five: McAdoo: 547 (81–38–28); Cowens: 310 (32–42–24); Hayes: 289 (37–26–25); Barry: 254 (16–46–36); Kareem: 161 (13–21–33). So Barry was the league's best player and proved as much in the playoffs . . . and he finished *fourth*? What happened? Barry was the Association's most despised player, someone who whined about every call, sold out teammates with a variety of eye rolls and "why the hell did you drop that" shrugs and shamelessly postured for a TV career (even moonlighting for CBS). We can't discount residual bad blood from Barry jumping to the ABA, as well as his reputation for being a gunner and not clicking off the court with black players.[46] So what if he turned his career around, became a team captain, led the league in

45. In fairness, Mac had a monster series, averaging a 37–13 in a whopping 327 minutes and even interacting with a teammate two different times.

46. Barry defended himself from this rap in a December 1974 *SI* feature with this eye-popping quote: "We like each other for what we are, not for the color of our skins. I was kidding Charlie Johnson the other day, saying, 'Don't tell me about you guys being put down. You had all the great detectives, didn't you? There was Boston Blackie, Sam Spade, The Shadow . . . ' It's a great atmosphere." Yikes! Cut off his mike! Imagine if somebody said that now. ESPN would have a twelve-hour town hall meeting about it. I think Rick Barry made this book 3 percent better. I really do.

steals and free throw percentage, finished second in points, finished with most assists (492) of any forward ever and led his team in every relevant statistical category except for rebounds? Rick Barry didn't have a snowball's chance in hell with the other players voting. They thought he was a dick. That may have been true, but nobody was more valuable in 1975.

Julius Erving (1981)

This season featured a two-man jog[47] between division rivals Erving (25–8–4 for a 62-win Philly team) and Bird (21–11–6 for a 62-win Celtics team that clinched home court by beating Philly in Game 82). Doc became the "sexy" media story that season because Philly blossomed as an unselfish team, so everyone collectively decided at the halfway point, "Okay, this is Doc's year." Meanwhile, Bird quietly gained steam as the season went along, putting up a series of 20–20 games (36–21 at Philly, 35–20 in Chicago, 21–20 in Cleveland, 28–20 in New York) during an absurd 25–1 streak before suffering a painful thigh bruise, playing in pain for a month and healing in time for a February West Coast trip in which he tossed up a 23–17–8 with 4 steals in Seattle, then a 36–21–5 with 5 steals and 3 blocks in Los Angeles less than twenty-four hours later (with an injured Magic watching from the sidelines). By the last month of the season, everyone should have agreed that (a) Bird and Doc were dead even and (b) the guy whose team clinched home court should get MVP. Didn't happen. In that eighty-second game in Boston, Bird scored 24 in the victory and was all over the place—5 steals in the first quarter alone—while Erving struggled to tally just 19 points. When the Sixers and Celtics met in the '81 Eastern Finals, Philly self-destructed with a three-games-to-one lead and Bird banked home the game-winning shot in Game 7. Bird for the series: 27–13–5. Doc for the series: 20–6–4. Two weeks later, the Celtics captured the title in Houston. So much for it being "Doc's year."

Does that mean Bird was the league's best player? Not necessarily. You could make a strong case for Moses, the league's best center from 1979 through 1983, only Moses was toiling away on a subpar Rockets team that finished 41–41 in 1980 and 40–42 in 1981. (It's hard to argue anyone was

47. You couldn't really call it a "race" because neither guy was at his peak.

supremely valuable when he couldn't drag his team over .500.) So if we're giving the MVP to someone who wasn't the alpha dog, then it'd better be a great player having a career year—again, not in play in 1981—which means the time-tested "best guy on the best team" theory comes into play. And that was Bird.

Now, you might be saying, "Screw it, there was no clear-cut MVP that year and everyone knew Bird would get one eventually, so I'm glad Doc got it because he meant a lot to the league." First of all, you're a sap for thinking that; we showed Doc how much he meant six years later when he got showered with gifts during his retirement tour. Second, the MVP trophy isn't a token of our affection—it's not a diamond ring, a plasma TV or even a cock ring. What is it? An honor that says definitively, "The majority of us agreed that this guy was the most important player of this particular season." And since that's the case, everyone screwed up because four months after the '81 playoffs ended, Bird graced the cover of *SI* for a feature titled, "The NBA's Best All-Around Player." Why didn't they realize that when he was tossing up 20–20's? You got me. But if Bird was considered the NBA's best all-around player during a year without a definitive MVP and his team won the title, and we gave the award to someone else, then we made a mistake and that's that.[48]

Dirk Nowitzki (2007)

An edited-for-space version of what I wrote in my 2007 MVP column after realizing that Nowitzki didn't qualify under any of my three MVP questions[49] but remained the consensus choice:

Statistically, Nowitzki submitted superior seasons in 2005 and 2006, and his 2007 stats ranked behind Larry Bird's best *nine* seasons, Charles

48. I made that decision using the same facts, theories and rules of thumb that govern every other inch of this chapter. If you still think I'm a homer, then allow me to introduce you to my law firm, Buh Low Mee. P.S.: Bird got screwed out of the '81 Finals MVP as well; Cedric Maxwell won by a 6-to-1 margin in a Duncan/Parker-type situation. I think people were just excited to vote for someone nicknamed "Cornbread."

49. The answers: Gilbert Arenas (question 1); Kobe (question 2); either Nash, T-Mac or LeBron (question 3). As I wrote, "Usually, the most logical MVP candidate owns two of those questions (and ideally, three). Not this season." Question 4 hadn't been created yet.

Barkley's best *10* seasons and Karl Malone's best *11* seasons. Nowitzki's shooting percentages were remarkable (50 percent on field goals, 90 percent on free throws, 42 percent on 3-pointers), but his relevant averages (24.6 points, 9.0 rebounds, 3.4 assists) look like a peak season from Tom Chambers. If you're giving the MVP to someone because of his offense, he'd better be a killer offensive player. You can't say that about the 2007 Nowitzki.

The argument *for* the big German is simple: He's the most reliable crunch-time scorer in the league and the best player on a 66-win team. Of course, when the '97 Bulls won 69 games, you could have described Jordan the exact same way . . . and he finished second to Malone. Then again, maybe we should scrap the historical comparisons after Steve Nash's back-to-back trophies transformed the award into what it is now: a popularity contest. It's a 900-number and Ryan Seacrest away from becoming a low-key version of *American Idol.* And since people want the big German to win the award this year, he's going to win it. In the irony of ironies, Nash played his greatest season at a time when everyone took him for granted and paid more attention to Nowitzki. . . . You could have switched Dirk with Duncan, KG, Bosh, Brand or any other elite forward and the Mavs still would have won 55–65 games. But the 2007 Suns were built like a complicated Italian race car, with specific features tailored to a specific type of driver, and Nash happened to be the only person on the planet who could have driven the car without crashing into a wall. The degree of difficulty was off the charts. So yes, this was my favorite Nash season yet.

Did I vote for him? In a roundabout way, yes—Nash earned my vote for second place (I couldn't give my MVP vote to a total defensive liability) and the fans earned MVP because we had endured one of the least entertaining seasons ever. I know, I know, lame.[50] I wish we handled MVP awards, the Oscars and the Emmys the same way—if there's no deserving candidate in a given year, let's roll the award over to the following year and

---

50. It was part protest (for the shitty season) and part parody (because *Time* magazine had named "You" the 2007 Man of the Year). One of my dumbest ideas ever. It almost caused an Internet riot. I still get emails about it.

make it worth two awards, kinda like how golfers roll over a tie in a skins match and count the next hole for twice as much. An award should be earned, not handed out.

Anyway, you know how the Dirk debacle turned out: Golden State shocked Dallas in one of the biggest NBA upsets ever, although it stopped being so unrealistic right as the Warriors were butchering the Mavs in Game 3 in front of a frenzied G-State crowd. Here's what I wrote between Games 4 and 5, when it became apparent that so many had made such an enormous mistake vouching for the MVP-ness of Mr. Nowitzki:

We're headed for the most awkward moment in NBA history within the next 10 days. Here's how it will play out:

(We see Jim Gray, David Stern and Dirk Nowitzki standing awkwardly in front of a single camera at halftime of a Round 2 playoff game.)

GRAY: Now to present the 2006–7 Most Valuable Player Award, NBA commissioner David Stern.

STERN: Leave. Now.

(Gray slinks off.)

STERN: Well, Dirk, maybe the playoffs didn't turn out the way you planned, but for 82 meaningless games during one of the worst seasons of my 23-year tenure, you were the best player in a terrible league. Unfortunately, voting for the award happens right after the regular season, so voters weren't able to factor in your complete meltdown in Round 1 against Golden State. You didn't just fail to step up like an MVP should, you whined and complained the entire series, disgraced your teammates and embarrassed your fans. Not since David Hasselhoff has America been so embarrassed by someone with a German-sounding name. I don't know whether to hand you this trophy or smash it over your head. Lucky for you, this is being televised, so I can only hand you the trophy and congratulate you on the 2006–7 Most Valuable Player Award. I'm going to leave now so I can throw up.

DIRK NOWITZKI (*taking the trophy*): Thank you, Mr. Commissioner.

(*Stern waves disgustedly at him and walks away.*)

And . . . scene!

That's pretty much what happened. Never before had a so-recently-disgraced player accepted the trophy in such awkward fashion. Poor Dirk ended up fleeing to Australia to clear his head like Andy Dufresne or something. Now that we're examining this stuff retroactively, if you're ignoring my skins match suggestion, then Nash gets the '07 MVP because he shouldn't have won in 2005 or 2006 (we'll get to that), so in a weird way, he was due even though he *wasn't* due. I know it's like voting for a DH to win a baseball MVP, but there's no other option. You have to believe me.[51]

CATEGORY 3:
OUTRIGHT TRAVESTIES

We're counting these down in reverse order from eight to one:

8. Kobe Bryant (2008)

He bitched for a trade and disparaged teammates before the season started. He spent the first few weeks on businesslike cruise control before

---

51. Nash and the Suns nearly toppled the San Antonio Donaghys in the playoffs. By the way, the MVP debate should have been decided by a Dallas-Phoenix game in mid-March when Nash emerged as the top dog, notching a 32–8–16 and nearly every clutch play in a double-OT victory. I watched the game with House and JackO and we agreed that it was a seminal moment of the 2007 season; Nash just wanted it more than Nowitzki did. You could see it. I still remember House hissing, "So much for the MVP race." How did Dirk end up winning? I have no idea. The one silver lining: when we learned in 2009 that Dirk was engaged to a thirty-seven-year-old former stripper with eight aliases and outstanding warrants for credit card fraud, I spent a solid week refreshing eBay hoping she put his 2007 MVP trophy on there.

"embracing" his teammates, then fully committing himself after the Gasol trade. From there, we spent the next two months hearing that it was Kobe's year, that he was finally "getting it," that this was the best all-around ball he'd ever played, that he was becoming a leader on and off the court, that he was even going out to dinner with his teammates and picking up checks. This revisionist fairy tale gained steam through the first three rounds before going up in flames during the Finals, when Kobe didn't play a single great game and stink-bombed a must-win Game 6 (going down with surprising meekness). The Lakers splintered as soon as things got rough, proving something I had been arguing all along: the whole "Kobe is a leader" thing was still a work in progress.

This should have been Chris Paul's trophy—nobody meant more to his team or his city—and if not him, then Garnett. I still can't believe everyone bought into Kobe's Bee Ess. As it turned out, they were one year early.

7. Steve Nash (2005)

A baffling choice that gets more baffling with time. When they changed the hand check rules and ushered in the "let's make basketball fun again" era, Nash jumped out as Phoenix's quarterback of a thrilling offense. Everyone (including me) was enthralled that someone had revitalized the Cousy-like potential of the point guard position; at some point, things escalated and writers started throwing him out as an MVP candidate, which initially seemed preposterous because it would have been the first time (a) a table setter won the award; (b) a non-franchise player won; and (c) a defensive liability won. Those are three pretty big leaps.

Were there racial implications to the Nash/MVP bandwagon? In a roundabout way. It was *fun* to root for Nash. Here was a Canadian dude with floppy hair and a nonstop motor who looked like Kelly Leak, made throwback plays (like his trademark running hook), knew how to handle a fast break, made teammates better and always handled himself with class. His style (unique, exciting) and color (white in a predominantly black league) made him stand out more than anyone else in any given game. Beyond that, he was the league's biggest new wrinkle and a "Steve Nash is fun to watch, why can't he be the MVP?" column or radio angle stood out.[52] Everything snowballed from there. When Shaq battled minor injuries and Dwyane Wade escalated his game to "poor man's MJ" heights, there were just enough cracks in Shaq's MVP campaign that the door opened for Nash, colored by a slew of "It's been such a delight to watch someone this unselfish who handles himself with so much class" media comments (in columns or on radio), a nice way of saying, "I'm glad he's not one of those me-first black guys with tons of tattoos who pounds his chest after every good play." By then, the Nash bandwagon was running amok like the runaway train that freed Dr. Richard Kimble. Throw in the NBA's vested interest in pushing Nash—remember, the guy considered to be the future of the league had been dealing with a rape trial just twelve months before—and as soon as the "nobody else jumps out, I really like watching this guy . . . fuck it" logic came into play during awards time, just enough people were feeling that way that poor Shaq ended up getting robbed.[P19] Our final voting for 2004–5: Nash: 1,066 (65–54–7–1–0); Shaq: 1,032 (58–61–3–3–1); Nowitzki: 349 (0–4–43–30–16); Duncan: 328 (1–0–40–13–19); Iverson: 240 (2–4–20–20–23).[53]

My vote went to Shaq because of a simple mathematical exercise revolving around two indisputable facts:

1. The Lakers won 57 games in 2004 and 34 games in 2005.
2. Miami won 42 games in 2004 and 59 games in 2005.

I'm no Bill James, but even I can crack those numbers: Shaq caused a 40-game swing, shifted the balance of power from West to East and would

---

52. That's not a racial argument. The same process would have happened had he looked like Earl Boykins. People will *always* gravitate toward an underdog, especially if he has bad hair.

P19. Shaq got his revenge while playing with the '09 Suns, when he reportedly stole Nash's reality show idea in which Nash planned on competing against other great athletes in their specialty sports. Nash hired an entertainment lawyer, threatened to sue Shaq and eventually secured an exec producer's credit. And they were teammates the entire time! You're not gonna believe this, but the '09 Suns missed the playoffs.

53. My favorite MVP voting fact of 2005: some idiot gave a first-place vote to Amar'e Stoudemire, whose career had been invigorated and reinvented by Nash. That's like giving your vote for the Nobel Prize in Medicine to Frankenstein's monster instead of Dr. Frankenstein.

have won the title had Wade not gotten injured with a three-games-to-two lead in the Eastern Finals. As I wrote at the time, "This year has been special in the sense that people *get him* now—he's had a breakout season, only in the personality sense. Now there isn't a more beloved, charismatic, entertaining athlete in any sport. When I think of the 2004–2005 season, I'm going to think of Shaq first . . . and that's the very definition of an MVP. At least to me." I still feel that way.

6. Magic Johnson (1990 MVP)

If you ever run into Charles Barkley for any social reason—at a blackjack table, boxing match, Gambler's Anonymous, wherever—bring up the 1990 MVP race and watch him go. Here's what he'll say: "I had the most first-place votes! That's the only time that ever happened! First of all, I wanna know how I could get the most first-place votes and not win the award! I think you should only vote for one guy—I don't get why you have to rank the votes. Number one, they don't do the Oscars that way. And first of all, either you're the best guy or you're not. So number one, if the most people thought I was the best guy, then that makes me the MVP. First of all, if I'm the best guy, then I'm the MVP, anyway. So number one, I should have been the MVP. And second, Magic should give me that damned trophy!"

Here were the three candidates:

Magic: 22–12–7, 79 games, 2,937 minutes, 63 wins . . . a world-class defensive liability by this point . . . received credit for keeping L.A. going without Kareem even though they were better off with the Vlade Divac/Mychal Thompson combo . . . best four teammates: James Worthy, Byron Scott, A. C. Green, Divac . . . Playoffs: 25–6–13, 49% FG (9 games, second-round loss) . . . the weakest of his three MVP years.

Barkley: 25–12–4, 1.9 steals, 60% FG, 79 games, 3,085 minutes, 53 wins . . . below-average defender . . . best four teammates: Johnny Dawkins, Rick Mahorn, Hersey Hawkins, Mike Gminski . . . Playoffs: 25–11–6, 54% FG (10 games, second-round loss) . . . best all-around year to that point.

Jordan: 34–7–6, 2.8 steals, 53% FG, 82 games, 3,197 minutes, 55 wins ... league leader in scoring and steals ... first-team All-Defense ... best four teammates: Scottie Pippen, Horace Grant, Bill Cartwright, John Paxson ... Playoffs: 37–7–7, 51% FG (18 games, Eastern Finals loss)

And the voting: Magic: 636 (27–38–15–7–4); Barkley: 614 (38–15–16–14–7); Jordan: 571 (21–25–30–8–5).

Everyone remembers Barkley getting screwed when Jordan had a bigger gripe. Look at his superior offensive numbers and remember that (a) he was the league's best defensive noncenter and (b) Barkley/Magic couldn't guard anyone.[54] Why didn't Jordan cruise to the award? First, the media kept perpetuating the bullshit that Bird and Magic "knew how to win" and Jordan "didn't know how to win yet." (What a farce.) Second, Barkley emerged as somewhat of a hip choice, becoming the Man on a raucous Sixers team that memorably brawled with Detroit on the final night of the season. And third, MJ was still facing a "selfish" rap even though he was making 53% of his shots. Wouldn't you *want* him shooting as much as possible? When everyone was calling him a ball hog in '89 and '90, MJ averaged a combined 7.2 assists, 23.2 field goals and 8.5 free throws per game. In '93, when everyone claimed he embraced the triangle and trusted his teammates, he averaged 5.5 assists, 25.7 field goals and 7.3 free throws per game. I'd argue that Jordan started cresting in '88 and it took his underwhelming supporting cast three full years to stop murdering him every spring. He's my '90 MVP.

5. Dave Cowens (1973 MVP)

Four factors collided this season: Boston nearly broke the record for regular-season wins by going 68–14 (so everyone felt obligated to vote for a Celtic); Kareem won in '71 and '72 (so everyone felt obligated to

---

54. The Lakers were shocked by Phoenix in the '90 playoffs mainly because Kevin Johnson ripped them to shreds. Put it this way: if you were a speedy point guard from 1987 to 1991 and you *couldn't* light up the Lakers, you really needed to reevaluate things.

vote for someone else); the league was heading into the "everyone's over-paid and doesn't give a shit" era (so someone as intense as Cowens stood out); and the players (still voting) didn't realize that Boston shared a division with 21–61 Buffalo and 9–73 Philly (padding their record by going 14–0), whereas Milwaukee finished 60–22 in a tougher division and had the same point differential as Boston. Besides, you couldn't really pick a best player on those Celtics teams—Cowens (21–16–4 and the rebound-ing duties), John Havlicek (24–7–7 and the crunch-time duties) and Jo Jo White (19–6–6 and the ballhandling duties) were equally indispensable. It's hard for me to believe that Cowens was *more* valuable than Havlicek. Even the voting reflects this: Cowens: 444 (67–31–16); Kareem: 339 (44–24–27); Nate Archibald: 319 (44–24–27); Wilt: 123 (12–16–15); Havlicek: 88 (12–16–15).

Sounds like we needed a co-MVPs choice on the '73 ballot. Meanwhile, the league's best player (Kareem) averaged a 30–16–5 and provided supe-rior defense for the troubled Bucks (other than a slew of injuries and a suspicious Wali Jones meltdown that led to his release,[55] the Big O became the Really Big O), also suffering a personal tragedy when seven coreli-gionists living in his Washington, D.C., house were murdered by a rival Muslim faction. (A February 19 *SI* feature about Kareem was even head-lined "Center of a Storm.") And you know what? The Bucks *still* won sixty. Kareem's candidacy was crippled by dubious support for Archibald, the first player to lead the league in points and assists—and beyond that, min-utes (a jaw-dropping 3,681), field goals, free throws, field goal attempts and free throw attempts—for a 36-win team that missed the playoffs. Can you really be "most valuable" when your team lost 46 freaking games? And don't get me started on the foolishness of a point guard averaging nearly 27 shots and 10 free throw attempts per game. Isiah could have hogged the ball like that; same for Chris Paul, Kevin Johnson or Tim Hardaway before he blew out his knee. None of them did it. Why? *Because it would have killed their teams! They were point guards!* We haven't seen anything like

---

55. The Bucks believed Jones was using drugs, hired PIs to follow him, placed him on medical suspension for "loss of weight and stamina" and finally fired him. Jones pro-fessed his innocence and sued the Bucks for the rest of his owed salary, getting his money when Milwaukee's "Any time someone loses weight and acts irrationally they're on drugs" defense held about as much legal weight as the "She was asking for it" defense.

Tiny in '73 before or since and it's definitely for the best. Anyway, Kareem got robbed.

4. Charles Barkley (1993 MVP)

If any of the four media members who gave their '93 first-place votes to Patrick Ewing are reading right now, please put down this book and spend the next hour trying to ram your head up your ass. You did it in 1993; I want to see you do it again. How can you live with yourself? The quality of the top three in '93 ranks up there with the races in '62, '63 and '64, as well as the back-to-back Bird-Magic-MJ battles in '87 and '88.[56] Check out these numbers:

Barkley: 835 votes (59–27–10–2–0): 26–12–5, 52% FG . . . 62 wins . . . his greatest all-around season.

Hakeem: 647 (22–42–19–12–2): 26–13–4, 53% FG, 150 steals, 342 blocks (league leader) . . . first-team All-Defense . . . 55 wins . . . his greatest all-around season to that point.

Jordan: 565 (13–21–50–12–2): 33–7–6, 50% FG, 221 steals (league leader) . . . first-team All-Defense[57] . . . 57 wins . . . retains alpha dog status for the season.

That's right, signature seasons from three of the best twenty players ever! Unfortunately, eighty-six voters overlooked the fact that Jordan and Hakeem were two of the most destructive defensive players ever and Barkley couldn't guard Ron Kovic. Don't you have two tasks as a basket-

---

56. I say '87 was the best modern race. Magic finished first with a remarkable 24–12–6 and finally seized control of L.A. from Kareem. MJ averaged 37 a game, officially became the Next Great Player and finished second. And Bird submitted his finest season ever (28–9–8, 53% FG, 40% 3FG, 90% FT and a superb blondafroperm) and finished a distant third only because everyone was tired of voting for him. When you get career years from the greatest forward and point guard ever, along with a breakout year for the best player ever, that's pretty good.

57. This had to be the greatest first-team All-D ever: Pippen, Hakeem, Rodman, Jordan and Dumars, all in their primes. Wow. Not a bad Best Starting Five of the '90s if you wanted to kick ass defensively.

ball team: to score and to stop the other team from scoring? At the time, I would have voted for MJ first, Hakeem second and Barkley third. And I would have been vindicated because Jordan *cremated* the Suns in the '93 Finals. So there.

3. Steve Nash (2006 MVP)

I picked Nash fifth in my '06 MVP column, writing, "A cute choice last season, mainly because none of the other candidates stood out and I could see why someone would have been swayed. (Like ordering one of those fancy foreign beers at a bar, the ones in the heavy green bottles with the thirteen-letter name that you can't pronounce, only someone else is drinking it, so you say to yourself, 'Ah, screw it, I'm tired of the beer I always drink, lemme try one of those.') But this year? I'm not saying he should be ignored, but if you actually end up picking him, either you're not watching enough basketball or you just want to see a white guy win back-to-back MVP's."

Here's what I wrote in that same column after picking Kobe (edited for space):

> You don't know how much this kills me. Actually, you probably do. But Mamba passes all three MVP questions . . . [58]
>
> **Answer for Question No. 1**
>
> Kobe. The dude scored 62 in three quarters against Dallas, then 81 against Toronto a few weeks later. He's about to become the fifth player in NBA history to average 35 points a game (along with Wilt, MJ, Elgin and Rick Barry). He made up with Shaq. He made up with Phil. He made up with Nike. He appeared on the cover of *Slam* magazine with a mamba snake wrapped around him. He did everything but make the obligatory cameo on *Will and Grace*. No player took more abuse from writers, broadcasters and radio hosts this season, but Kobe seemed to feed off that negative energy. It was almost Bondsian. And just when it kept seeming like he might wear down, he'd toss up another 50 just to keep you on your

---

58. He also passed question 4: none of the fans from opposing teams would have been outraged by a Kobe pick.

toes. Kobe was relentless. That's the best way to describe him this season.[59]

Answer for Question No. 2

Kobe. He's the best all-around player in the league, the best scorer, the best competitor and the one guy who terrifies everyone else. Plus, if you *didn't* pick him, he would make it his mission to haunt you on the other team.

Answer for Question No. 3

If you replaced Kobe with a decent 2-guard (someone like Jamal Crawford) for the entire '06 Lakers season, they would have won between 15 and 20 games. I can say that in complete confidence. Terrible team. When Smush Parker and Kwame Brown are your third- and fourth-best players, you shouldn't even be allowed to watch the playoffs on TV. Throw Kobe in the mix and they're headed for 45 wins. So he's been worth 25 victories for them. Minimum.

Here was the voting in 2006: Nash: 924 (57–32–20–8–6); LeBron: 688 (16–41–33–23–7); Nowitzki: 544 (14–22–25–36–17); Kobe: 483 (22–11–18–22–30); Chauncey Billups: 430 (15–13–22–18–25).
(Translation: I give up.)

2. Willis Reed (1970 MVP)

With Russell retired and the Celtics floundering, the Knicks took command of the East, won a league-high 60 games, ignited Manhattan and became the media darlings of the '70 season. Their two best players were Reed and Frazier: Reed averaged a 22–14, shot 50 percent and protected his teammates; Frazier averaged a 21–6–8, ran the offense, guarded the best opposing scorer and would have led the league in steals had they kept track. If there was ever a season for co-MVPs, this was it. Since the belief was that centers were

---

59. His stats: 35.4 PPG, 5.3 RPG, 4.5 APG, 45% FG, 27.2 FGA . . . and he won 45 games with Smush, Kwame, Brian Cook and Chris Mihm playing big minutes—or, as Lakers fans called them at the time, the Shit Sandwich.

more valuable than non-centers, Reed (498 votes, 61–55–28) squeaked by Jerry West (457 votes, 51–59–25). And nobody ever thought about it again.

Check out West's season again. He averaged a 31–5–8 for a 46-win Lakers team that lost Wilt at the 12-game mark with a torn knee (he never returned in the regular season) and had its other two top players (Baylor and Happy Hairston) miss 55 games combined. The next four best players on that team? Mel Counts, Dick Garrett, Keith Erickson and Rick Roberson. Even Charles Manson had a better supporting cast than the Logo that year. Somehow the Lakers finished second in the West, then Wilt returned for the playoffs and they rallied to make the Finals. Statistically, this was West's finest year: he led the league in points, finished fourth in assists and shot 50 percent from the field and 83 percent from the line. From a big-picture standpoint, West carried the Lakers all season and dragged them to within one victory of the title. From an alpha dog standpoint, if you had to pick someone who bridged the gap between Russell's retirement and Kareem's ascension, you'd pick West. And he's one of the best eight players ever, as well as the guy they selected for the freaking NBA logo, only he never captured an MVP. So why wasn't this his year? Because the New York media were too busy losing their minds over an admittedly entertaining Knicks team. This was an eight-month circle jerk that eventually led to something like seventeen books being written about that season.[60] A Knick was getting the MVP and that was that. The Logo never had a chance. Just know that the trophy was pilfered from him.

1. Karl Malone (1997 MVP)

This wasn't an MVP race, it was a crime scene. The previous season, Jordan averaged a 30–7–4 for a 72-win team, finished with 109 first-place votes and would have been the unanimous MVP if not for the four morons who voted for Penny Hardaway, Hakeem and Malone.[61] During the '97 sea-

60. Shades of the '04 Red Sox here: the event itself was eventually exceeded by the media and fans telling everyone how great it was and desperately trying to put everything in perspective. By the way, I include myself—my Red Sox opus was called *Now I Can Die in Peace*. Still in bookstores with a third edition!

61. That's reason number twenty-five why MVP votes need to be made public: if you make a pick *that* dumb, you should be obligated to defend it. I'm against anonymous incompetence in all forms.

son, Jordan's credentials "dropped" to 69 wins and a 30–6–4—in other words, he was 98 percent as good as the previous season—only Malone stole the award with a 27–10–5 for a 64-win Jazz team. Here's the voting from that year:

Malone: 986 (63–48–4–0–0)
Jordan: 957 (52–61–2–0–0)

Look, I was there—this was inexplicable as it was happening. We'll cover Malone's inadequacies in a later chapter, but here's the best analogy I can give you: For my buddy House's bachelor party in 2008, a group of us trekked to Vegas for four days and landed at the world-renowned Olympic Garden one night. Normally in strip joints, I suggest we find a corner and surround ourselves with those big comfy chairs—I call it the "Chair Armada"—so we aren't continually approached by below-average strippers trying to pull the "Maybe if I plop right down on his lap, he'll feel bad for me and buy a lap dance" routine. There wasn't a corner this time around, so we grabbed a few chairs facing the stage and it worked almost as well. Unable to dive-bomb us from behind, the strippers settled for circling repeatedly and trying to catch our eyes. This strategy could have worked if most of them didn't look like Hedo Turkoglu. One probably circled us twenty times in two hours—never drawing an extended glance from any of us—before our buddy Monty checked her out on the twenty-first approach, gave up on finding a more appealing option, and said, "Fuck it." And off they went. When we made fun of him the next morning, he said simply, "It was getting late."

What does that have to do with Karl Malone? Just like Monty's stripper, the Mail Fraud circled the MVP voters for ten solid years and never finished higher than third. Meanwhile, the NBA was becoming more and more diluted—expansion had ravaged the league, some younger stars (Shawn Kemp, Penny Hardaway, Larry Johnson, C-Webb, Kenny Anderson, Derrick Coleman) weren't panning out, and Hakeem, Barkley, Robinson, Drexler and Ewing were past their primes—which meant Utah, a team that was worse in 1997 than they were in 1988 or even 1992, suddenly became a juggernaut in the West.[62] There also wasn't a dominant story in '97. Everyone was Jordaned out. The "Shaq goes to Hollywood" and "Here comes Iverson" stories had been beaten to death. So had the "Hakeem, Drexler and Barkley are three future Hall of Famers and they're all playing together" story. Latrell Sprewell hadn't strangled P. J. Carlesimo yet (although he'd definitely considered it). The Grizzlies, Spurs, Celtics and Nuggets spent the last two months desperately trying to outtank each other for Duncan. By mid-March, once everyone realized that the Bulls couldn't win 73 games, we were just plain bored and awaiting the playoffs. Then *SI*'s Jackie MacMullan wrote the following piece for her March 19 column:

Headline: "The Jazz Master"

Subhead: "Malone is playing like an MVP—not that anyone has noticed."

First sentence: "Jazz forward Karl Malone knows Michael Jordan will win the league MVP trophy again."

You get the idea. You can't blame Jackie for looking for a cute angle—she spent about 800 words talking about how underappreciated Malone was

62. I'm springing one of my favorite theories here: the Tipping Point Friend. Every group of female college friends goes between eight and twelve girls deep. Within that group, there might be three or four little cliques and the backstabbing is through the roof, but the girls get along for the most part and make a big deal about hanging out, doing dinners, having special weekends and everything else. Maybe two of them get married early, then the other ones start dropping in their mid-twenties until there's only five left—the cute blonde who can't get a boyfriend because she's either a drunk, an anorexic or a drunkorexic; the cute brunette who only attracts assholes; the 185-pounder who'd be cute if she lost weight; the not-so-cute one with a great sense of humor; and the sarcastic chain-smoker with 36DDs who isn't quite cute enough to land anyone but hooks up a lot because of the 36DDs. In this scenario, the cute brunette is the Tipping Point Friend—as long as she's in the group, guys will approach them in bars, clubs or wherever. Once she settles down with a non-asshole, now all the pressure is on the drunkorexic and if she can't handle it, then the girl with 36DDs has to start wearing crazy shirts and blouses to show off her guns. My point is this: the Jazz were the sarcastic chain-smoker with 36DDs who hooked up often but never found a serious suitor. By 1997, their competitors had dropped out and they were suddenly the hottest friend in their group. Does that mean they were hot? No!!! No!!!!!!!!! For the love of God, no!!!!!!!!!

over the years. (Which was true, to a degree.) That got the ball rolling, and within a couple of weeks, this became the cute story du jour. Why *couldn't* the Mailman win the MVP? I hadn't started my old website yet but remember thinking, "Why couldn't he win the MVP? Because MJ is in the league! How 'bout that reason?" I just thought this was the dumbest thing ever. I couldn't believe it. So the playoffs rolled around and fifty-three voters turned into Monty at the OG: Malone strolled by them for the umpteenth time, they shrugged, stood up and brought him into the VIP room. And that's how Michael Jordan got robbed of the '97 MVP. Fortunately for us, he exacted revenge in the Finals over (wait for it) Karl Malone and the Utah Jazz! In Game 1, after Malone missed two go-ahead free throws in the final 20 seconds, Jordan swished the game-winner at the buzzer, turned and did a clenched-fist pump, a move that Tiger Woods later would hijack without paying royalties.[P20] And that's when everyone who voted for the Mailman felt really, really, *really* dumb. I love when this happens.

P20. MJ got his revenge—inadvertently, but still—by taking Tiger under his debauchery/ gambling/carousing wing and aiding Tiger's fall from grace, nine-figure divorce, public humiliation and probable banning from the Sports Legend Mount Rushmore (next to Ali, Jordan and Ruth). Consider those royalties paid, MJ.

SIX

THE HALL OF FAME PYRAMID

WALT BELLAMY
HAWKS' CENTER

BY NOW, YOU'VE probably figured out that I love basketball. When you love something unconditionally, does that mean it's perfect? Of course not. I find myself tinkering with ways to improve my favorite sport all the time, constantly asking, "Why don't they do that?" or even better, "Why *wouldn't* they do that?" Here, off the top of my head, are thirty-three suggestions to improve the NBA.

1. I wish the Finals would go back to the 2–2–1–1–1 format.
2. I wish we'd make a pact to agree that (a) there will never be another MJ, and (b) we're not allowed to compare anyone to him anymore.
3. I wish we would change the NBA trade deadline to 4:00 a.m. on the Saturday night of All-Star Weekend, just so we'd have at least one megadeal per year consummated after twenty Jack-and-Cokes in the wee hours. Imagine seeing this scrolling across the ESPN news ticker in the wee

hours: *ESPN's Ric Bucher reports that Knicks GM Donnie Walsh and Dallas owner Mark Cuban just finished Patrón shots at the Dallas Ritz-Carlton's main bar and made the bartender call up ESPN.com's trade machine.*

4. Borrowing this idea from a Philly reader named Mike: I wish we'd abolish those hideous in-game coach interviews, simply because I can't handle hearing someone like Nancy Lieberman get stoned by another coach after she asks what they have to do to stop the other team's best player. They are running out of ways to say, "I have no idea, Nancy. If I knew that, we'd be winning the game."[1]

5. Come to think of it, I wish we didn't have NBA sideline reporters. But if we *have* to have them—and really, I don't see why—I wish we hired casual female fans like my wife. Why? Because casual female fans notice things during sporting events that nobody else notices. My buddy Strik once sent me a "Bruce Willis in da house!" text during a Clips game—I quickly relayed this information to the Sports Gal, who scanned the lower sections of the arena with the intensity of Jack Bauer looking for a terrorist in a crowded mall. Within about ten seconds she found Bruce sitting courtside to our right, like she had a homing device in her head. Then she spent the next thirty minutes watching him and making comments like "He seems nice" to the lady sitting next to her. So why couldn't someone like my wife become a sideline reporter? Why pretend this is a serious gig? My wife would file reports from the Blazers' huddle like, "Guys, Greg Oden seems sad, he just seems sad to me, I hope everything's okay," or "Phil Mickelson and his wife are sitting courtside, and guys, I do *not* like her roots," or even "Guys, I'm still trying to get an answer as to why Amar'e Stoudemire is wearing that suit. Lime green is *not* his color, as we all know."[2]

---

1. When I'm running ESPN in a few years, I'm going to bring back Roy Firestone's old half-hour interview show and hire Nancy to host it. The show will be called *Up Close and Uncomfortable with Nancy Lieberman.* You're gonna love it.
2. You know how horse racing always has the best postgame interviews because the reporter has to ride next to the winning jockey? Takes a certain amount of skill to juggle two things at once, right? I wish there was a way to incorporate that in the NBA. I also wish we made foreign players live up to the stereotypes of their respective countries. For instance, after Michele Tafoya grabs Tony Parker, he should quickly slip on a beret, start chain-smoking and say rude things to her.

6. I wish Utah and New Orleans would switch last names so New Orleans could be the Jazz again. Let's do the right thing here.

7. I wish WNBA scores and transactions would be banned from all scrolling tickers on ABC and ESPN. I'm tired of subconsciously digesting tidbits like "Phoenix 52, Sacramento 44 F" and thinking, "Wait, that was the final score?" before realizing it was WNBA. Let's just run their scores on NBA TV with pink lettering. And only between the hours of 2:00 a.m. and 7:30 a.m.

8. I wish we could agree on a universal fantasy league scoring system that everyone used. Here's my vote: has to be auction style; eight categories and double weight for points-rebounds-assists; $50 total for weekly free agent claims (highest bid wins each player); twelve-player roster with one injury spot; you have to start a PG, SG, SF, PF and C, with four extra starting spots for a guard, SG/SF, PF/C and a ninth man; extend fantasy through the real NBA playoffs, with weekly head-to-head play wrapping up at the end of the regular season (winner taking home 35 percent of the pot and second place getting 15 percent), then the top four advance to the playoffs (same 35/15 payout), keep six players and fill out their rosters with players from other fantasy teams that didn't make it in a straight draft (with number one drafting first each round). Not only did I just solve fantasy basketball in one paragraph, but as the postseason drags on and teams drop out, by the NBA Finals, it would be like the last scene of *Rollerball:* just a few fantasy owners heroically skating around and trying not to get struck by a flaming motorcycle. You have three Lakers, I have two Celtics, let's fight to the death. It also brings us closer to our ultimate goal as fans: playing fantasy 365 days a year. Yes, we can.[3]

9. I wish we could choose two teammates to combine for fantasy purposes every season. Back when they played on the Pacers together, I always wanted to combine Antonio Davis and Dale Davis into one roto monster called Über-Davis for my fantasy league. Now I'm thinking that, before every season, we could vote on ESPN.com for a pair of teammates to be combined for fantasy purposes to make drafts more

---

3. The biggest problem this system solves: you won't lose your fantasy playoffs because someone suffered a dumb injury in April, or because the other guy's team had four more games than you. How is that skill?

interesting. For instance, Oden and Joel Przybilla could have become "Joreg Pryzboden" with an '09 average of 14–16 with 2.4 blocks. You wouldn't have enjoyed rooting for Joreg Pryzboden?[P21]

10. I wish every vote for the major awards and All-NBA teams would be made public. Again, I am against anonymous incompetence in all forms.

11. I wish all footage from the lockout season would be destroyed. As well as tapes of every Knicks-Heat playoff game from the nineties. And any Pistons-Nets playoff game from 2000 on. I am against celebrating bad basketball in all forms.

12. Stealing a premise from Rasheed Wallace, I wish the defending champion's coach would wear a WWE-style championship belt to every game. If his team loses the title at the end of the season, the incumbent would then hand over that belt to the winning coach (hopefully sobbing like Johnny Lawrence at the end of the 1984 All-Valley Karate Tournament).

13. Remember my wish for a program that explained the origin of every NBA tattoo? I also wish the league would designate tattoo shops in every NBA city as an "Official NBA Tattoo Store," load those stores with cameras, then require players to get inked *only* in those thirty stores. Why? For our new NBA TV reality show, *Where Ink Happens.* This can't miss. "Coming up on *Where Ink Happens,* Michael Beasley stops by to get 'Beas Breeze' tattooed on his neck!"

14. I wish teams weren't allowed to play music during game action. I don't need to hear the *Jaws* theme as the Spurs are trying to stop Kobe with two minutes to go. I really don't. Also, if your announcer feels obligated to pump up fans with in-game comments like "Get on your feet!" or "Lemme hear it—*deeee*-fense! *Deee*-fense!" then you shouldn't have a basketball team. It's really that simple.

15. I wish we would change the NBA's championship trophy back to a hockey-like cup (which was the case through the late seventies). I also wish we wouldn't name that trophy after Larry O'Brien, who was so shortsighted that his staffers had to talk him into the Slam Dunk Con-

P21. Pryzbilla blew out his knee early in the 2009–10 season. *TBOB* racked up bodies like Jigsaw in *Saw.*

test. Screw him. Let's make it a cup and call it the David Stern Cup. He carried O'Brien for those last few years, anyway.

16. You know how every member of an NHL champion team gets to spend one day with the Stanley Cup during the summer? I wish every member of an NBA championship team spent one day with the David Stern Cup. Talk about a mortal lock for potential comedy . . . can you imagine certain NBA troublemakers in brief control of the Stern Cup? Would the thing even come back in one piece? Would they lose it? Would they try to smoke pot from it? Who would be the first guy to lose it for a few hours?

17. During the first three quarters of NBA games, I wish all made baskets from midcourt and beyond were worth four points. Give me one reason why this shouldn't be a rule. You can't.

18. I wish we would blow up the NBA draft telecast. Every entertaining quirk (uncertainty of picks, hideous suits, lack of hard information, stammering interviews, sobbing mothers, overexuberant posse members, rookies drafted twenty picks later than they thought and slowly turning green as it happened) was slowly drummed out last decade by wily agents, enterprising Internet reporting, 24/7 news coverage and an acquired sophistication among prospects who grew up watching the Unintentional Comedy Scale shattered during every draft. So we need to create the comedy. Let's have three gregarious veterans (I'm thinking Dwight Howard, Nate Robinson and Grant Hill) conduct every postpick interview to loosen up kids who just got drafted (like an NBA version of *The View*). Let's have two funny NBA players (I'm thinking Jared Dudley and Chris Kaman) rate everyone's suits as the draft goes along. Let's put a tiny camera on David Stern's tie (the Stern Cam!). Let's add one ESPN analyst with a snarky sense of humor, someone who will say things to Jay Bilas like "You hate short wingspans more than Lindsay Lohan hates dignity." (Fine, fine, I'll do it. Count me in.) And let's make Ron Artest our sideline reporter. Who's a bigger attention hog than him? You're telling me he wouldn't love prowling the crowd and interviewing parents, fans and coaches? Didn't we learn from the 2010 Finals that you can never have enough of this formula: "Ron Artest + live microphone"?

19. I wish NBA cameras would no longer be allowed to zoom in within eighteen inches of somebody's face. I don't need any more unpopped whiteheads, acne scars and dangling nose hairs in my life.

20. I wish Allen Iverson would start a charity so he can hold a celebrity golf tournament. Why? Because what would be more entertaining than the First Annual Allen Iverson Celebrity Golf Tournament? Anything? Anything at all? Imagine AI showing up five hours late for his 9:00 a.m. tee time. How would he be dressed? How would he react if he missed a four-foot putt? Or imagine a terrified Kyle Korver in a foursome with 50 Cent, Ron Artest and Ice Cube. What about Jim Nantz saying, "Let's go to Verne Lundquist on sixteen, where there's apparently been some gunfire again"? I might devote the rest of my life to making this tournament happen. If Michael Douglas can have a celebrity golf tournament, why can't Allen Iverson?[4]

21. For the NBA League Pass package, I wish we always had the option of watching our favorite team's telecast with our favorite team's announcers and local commercials. What's the point of shelling out two bills a year for the NBA or baseball and not getting your own guys every game? I want Tommy Heinsohn screaming after every call that goes against the Celtics. I want the Foxwoods and Giant Glass commercials. *Don't deprive me!*

22. I wish that if a parent brings a young child to courtside seats at an NBA game and that poor kid subsequently gets trampled by a gigantic basketball player diving for a loose ball, then that parent should lose parental rights and Angelina Jolie or Madonna gets to adopt the kid.

23. I wish we would dump double technicals. If two players have a non-punching altercation, or they keep jawing at each other to the point that they have to be separated and the referees can't keep the game moving . . . yes, I can see it. But NBA refs hand out double technicals if two players look cross-eyed at each other.[5] What's wrong with allowing

4. Douglas' tournament gave us some of the funniest moments of the last decade: Douglas high-fiving with a grown-up Haley Joel Osment after big putts. They made Tiger's high-fives with his caddies look smoother than LeBron and Mo Williams celebrating something.

5. Riley's Knicks went overboard with trash-talking MJ's Bulls, everyone followed their lead, and Team Stern had to step in before we had the first-ever locker room drive-by shooting. Now players can't talk shit anymore. So sad. Nearly every problem that plagued the NBA in the past two decades, minor or major, can somehow be traced back to Riley's Knicks. I am convinced.

the competitive juices to flow? Isn't a reasonable amount of trash-talking part of what makes the NBA so much fun?

24. For NBA All-Star Saturday, I wish we had a H-O-R-S-E contest, a half-court shot contest and a dunk contest with a rim that keeps rising like a high-jump bar.

25. I wish we had the option of dumping the Evil Box. Other than Viagra and the Internet, the most dangerous development for marriages in the past two decades has been the Evil Box—that constant score/time box that remains in the corner of our TV screens during games. Once upon a time, you could just tell your wife/girlfriend, "Two more minutes, the game's almost over" and she'd be totally fooled. It could have been the start of the fourth quarter and she'd never know, except for those dreaded moments right before a commercial when the huge score graphic would come flying out of nowhere. Now? When you pull the "two more minutes" routine, they immediately glance at the Evil Box and know you're lying. The whole thing sucks. As soon as technology advances to the point that our Internet service is connected to our televisions and everything is controlled by one remote, I'm giving viewers the option to dump the Evil Box if they're trying to deceive their ladies.[6]

26. I wish the *South Park* guys (Matt Stone and Trey Parker) would purchase an NBA team. We need them in the league for comedy's sake. Let's give them the Nuggets at a steep discount.[7]

27. Stealing this idea from Louisville reader Jason Willan: During the lottery, I wish every team sent a representative who makes no basketball sense but has an obscure tie to the city or franchise. *Representing the Memphis Grizzlies . . . Lisa Marie Presley! Representing the New Jersey*

6. Interesting note here: when a guy tells a girl, "There's only two minutes left" (and it's actually fifteen minutes in real time), that equals the same amount of time as when a girl tells a guy, "I'll be ready in five minutes" (and it's really fifteen).

7. Matt's response (via email): "We'd only be able to afford a minority share unless there is a foreclosure on the Grizzlies soon. And I'd have to talk Trey into it because he's more of a football fantatic. Just know that we would be *way worse* than [Mark] Cuban as far as mouthing off about refereeing and other shit and we'd average 400K a week in fines. There is just no way me and Trey can keep our mouths shut. Good for the league, bad for our wallet. So it probably can't happen." The good news? I think I just gave them an idea for *BASEketball II*.

Nets . . . Joe Piscopo![8] *Representing the Miami Heat . . . Philip Michael Thomas!*"[9]

28. I wish we'd dump the rule that teams can call another time-out following a time-out, since the last three minutes of a game shouldn't take twenty-five minutes. Why not prevent teams from calling consecutive time-outs unless the ball has been inbounded? Wouldn't that reward good defense and penalize offenses too inept to call a good play? Wouldn't the games flow much better? I also wish we made a rule that no team could call time trailing by more than six points with less than 20 seconds left.

29. I wish the All-Star Game would be changed to the following format: best two players in the league buck up for first choice, then proceed to pick their teams like they're on a playground. Same goes for the NBA playoffs: you win the number one seed in your conference, you get to pick your opponent for the first round; then number two makes a pick; then number three. Imagine the bad blood that could transpire.

30. I wish NBA TV would buy the rights to *SNL*'s "Referee Pittman Show" sketch and bring it back with various NBA referees—just a half-hour show of a serious studio audience asking Dick Bavetta and Bennett Salvatore matter-of-fact questions like "What's it like to referee with your head all the way up your butt?" and "My boy and I were wondering—we know you have no soul, but what takes its place? Is it human excrement or dog excrement?"

31. I wish we would give out the Mokeski, given annually to the best American-born white player in the league. Last year's winner would have been . . . David Lee? See, you'd be fascinated by the Mokeski award.[10]

32. I wish we would shorten the regular season by six games, guarantee the top six seeds in each conference, then have a double-elimination tour-

8. The Nets used Piscopo as their PA announcer for a 2002 Finals game, leading to my favorite running streak in sports: no NBA team that ever used Joe Piscopo as an announcer in the Finals has gone on to win the title.

9. Miami should do this, anyway. Imagine Thomas sitting between Joe Dumars and Larry Bird at the lottery in a white linen suit with a huge smile on his face.

10. And don't forget about my Eff You Award (page 233). I love that one. The winner of the 2009 Eff You Award was definitely Elton Brand. For 2010? Gilbert Arenas!

ney for the seventh and eighth seeds between the remaining eighteen teams. I suggest this for five reasons. First, it would be entertaining as hell. In fact, that's what we'll call it: the Entertaining-as-Hell Tournament. Second, I'm pretty sure we could get it sponsored. Third, the top twelve teams get a reward: two weeks of rest while the tournament plays out. Fourth, a Cinderella squad could pull off some upsets, grab an eighth seed and win fans along the way. And fifth, with the Entertaining-as-Hell Tournament giving everyone a chance, no team could tank down the stretch for draft picks without insulting paying customers beyond repair. Why are we paying full price to watch forty-eight minutes of garbage time as four starters pretend to be injured on the bench?[P22]

33. I wish we could blow up the Basketball Hall of Fame and start over.

I care about the thirty-third wish more than the other ones. Why? Because I despise the following argument: *Come on, that's the way we've always done it!* When those nine words become the sole reason for keeping something intact, it's a bigger red flag than the one Nikolai Volkoff waved. Change is good. Change leads to hockey masks for goalies, wheels for suitcases, baby seats for little kids and seats atop the Green Monster. Change leads to iTunes, Madden video games, Tommy John surgery, plasma televisions, BlackBerrys, podcasts and JetBlue. Change leads to Vegas casinos making decisions like "What if we put a blackjack section outside next to a topless pool?" If you don't keep moving, that means you've stopped.

With the Basketball Hall of Fame, we stopped. The place doesn't work. It's been a failure for twenty-five years and counting. Consider the following true story: Of all my friends, only my buddy House loves the NBA as much as me. We've been buddies since my freshman year in college, road-tripped numerous times, smelled each other's farts, eaten hundreds of meals together, had thousands of inane sports calls . . . hell, we even ran the high screen like Stockton and Malone once upon a time. We're proba-

P22. This idea gained enough momentum that the NBA's Competition Committee had a spring 2010 meeting about it. Although the guy running the meeting inexplicably blew out his patella halfway through and had to be carried out. Just kidding.

bly in the top 0.0000000000000001 percent of NBA fans, as evidenced by me writing this book and House owning game-worn jerseys of Tom Gugliotta, Manute Bol and Bobby Sura.[11] If two college students in Massachusetts ever would have declared, "Screw class today, let's road-trip to Springfield," it would have been us. Even after college, when I lived in Boston for the next decade, House visited me twice a year and we were only a brisk ninety-minute drive from Springfield.[12]

Well, from 1988 to 2002, guess how many times we went to Springfield together? Zero. Zero! We didn't go once!

You know what that tells me? That the Basketball Hall of Fame doesn't work. Cooperstown works because of the gorgeous drive through upstate New York, a throwback trip that makes you feel like you're traveling in a Volkswagen Bug with Ray Kinsella and Terence Mann. The trip works because there's no easy way to get there; the closest airport is an hour away, making it more rewarding since it's a sacrifice just to get there. It works because they built a gigantic hotel in Otsego, New York, and flanked it with a fantastic golf course. It works because of 150 years' worth of baseball memories and memorabilia, and because of the generational twinge with any Cooperstown trip. *My dad took me there because his dad took him there, and now I'm taking my son there.* You know, the whole *Field of Dreams* angle. If you're fortunate enough to sire a son, you'd feel like an inadequate father if you didn't take him to Cooperstown. Like you were cheating him.

Springfield doesn't work that way. There's no father-son angle because the NBA hasn't been popular long enough. There's no beautiful ride, just a bunch of ugly highways and a downtrodden city that battles a complex

---

11. That wasn't a joke. One of House's biggest regrets in life: *not* winning a bid for a Lloyd Daniels game-worn.

12. That's a two-hour drive unless I'm behind the wheel. Ask any of my friends: if they're two hours from a destination, need to arrive in ninety minutes and could pick one friend to drive, they'd pick me. I'm the same guy who once drove from my dad's old house in Wellesley to my mom's house in Stamford in 2:04—that's a 185-mile drive with a toll booth stop and ten minutes of back roads. I was four minutes away from becoming the Roger Bannister of that drive. By the way, this was my life highlight of 1995 other than sucking face with Lizzie Baker, writing a back-page story for the *Boston Herald* and buying my first bong. Not a strong year.

about being the poor man's Hartford.[13] The Hall itself is constantly being renovated and re-renovated; because it attempts to "celebrate" the history of basketball, college basketball *and* professional basketball, the end result feels like three different agendas competing at once. Back in 2002, they opened a $45 million, 80,000-square-foot home near the old one—the third by my count—and surrounded it with retail stores and restaurants. Did it work? Maybe. I don't know. I've never been there. There's been too much residual damage, like a restaurant that burned its customers with too many bad meals over the years . . . and now they've reached a point where they could hire the best chef on the planet and it wouldn't make a difference for me. So why hasn't the NBA dumped Springfield and built its own Hall of Fame? *Because that's the way we've always done it!* Hence the problem: what you're about to read, for all intents and purposes, is a pipe dream. It will never happen. The NBA would never do it—they're too invested in the Springfield location, just like they're too invested in the WNBA.[14] This is the closest you will ever come to a pure NBA Hall of Fame: a pipe dream.

How would it work? Well, we need the right location. Only one place works. Only one.

(Think about it.)

(Keep thinking, it will come.)

(And . . . time!)

Indiana.

Has to be Indiana, right? That's the basketball capital of the world. They filmed *Hoosiers* there. The Basketball Jesus grew up there. Bobby Knight coached there. They have the most rabid basketball fans on the planet. If you're looking for the same elements that make Cooperstown work—an out-of-the-way destination, the *Field of Dreams* drive, a sense that basketball matters more than anything else—then Indiana should be the place. Personally, I'd stick it in French Lick. Bird grew up there, they al-

---

13. Before you say "So long to your Springfield book signing," I am pro-Springfield and my dad's best friend (superhero lawyer Roy Anderson) lives there. I will always defend Springfield and Worcester. I just think the Hall of Fame needs a fresh start.

14. And we're stuck with the WNBA, too.

ready have a casino[15] and there's something exciting about road-tripping to a place named French Lick. It just feels right. All of it. The heart of Indiana doubles as the heart of basketball. That's where the NBA Hall of Fame should be.

We also need a hook that separates it from Springfield and every other Hall of Fame before it. That brings me to an idea that first trickled into my columns in 1997, the same year baseball launched interleague play, when I drove to Shea Stadium for the first ever Red Sox–Mets regular-season series with my buddy Gus Ramsey and his father, Wally (two die-hard Mets fans whom I've known forever). On the way to the game, Wally came up with a brainstorm to inject some much-needed life into baseball's Hall of Fame voting.[16] Ideally, the Hall of Fame should be a place where someone could stroll in, spend weeks walking around and absorb everything about the game; by the time they departed, they would know *everything there is to know* about that particular sport. Cooperstown, Springfield and Canton are more interested in showcasing as much stuff as possible; even their Hall of Famer plaques are randomly showcased with no real thought given to each player's specific place in history. It's like having a Hall of Fame for models and putting the plaques for Gisele Bundchen and Christie Brinkley right next to the one for the "before" model from the first "before/after" Weight Watchers ad. Shouldn't careers be weighted in some way? We spent the rest of our ride figuring out the number of levels (settling on five in all, with Level 5 being the highest) and arguing topics like "Was Koufax an L4 or an L5?" and "Was Nolan Ryan even an L2?" That's when I knew the Pyramid idea could work. Anytime a brainstorm immediately leads to heated arguments in a sticky rental car, and any time cool abbreviations manifest themselves organically like "L4" and "L5," you know you're on to something. So screw it— if we're building an NBA Hall of Fame from scratch, why not make it a

15. You know how casinos can only be built in Nevada, in Atlantic City or on Indian reservations if they're on land, but you can have gambling as long as there's water around? In French Lick, they built a casino with a manmade mini lake around it; you go inside by walking over a moat. And you thought people in Indiana were dumb.

16. We didn't realize we were inadvertently borrowing Bill James' plan to redefine Hall of Famers and weight them for importance. Regardless, I'm 100 percent positive that Wally invented the Pyramid concept in that day. I came up with the part where it would look like a mini Luxor. And Gus just did a lot of nodding.

five-level pyramid (like a mini-replica of the Luxor casino in Las Vegas,[17] only without cigarette burns on the carpets) where great players aren't just elected to the Hall of Fame but elected to a particular level depending on their abilities?

Pour yourself some scotch and break out a stogie . . . this is about to get good. Imagine you fly to Indiana, rent yourself a car and make the ninety-minute drive to French Lick. You check into the Larry Bird Luxury Golf Resort, drop your stuff off, head over to the Pyramid and buy your ticket. They direct you to the second floor of the basement (everyone starts their tour there), where you can find relevant memorabilia from seven NBA decades: old jerseys and exhibits, seats from the old Madison Square Garden, pieces of the parquet from the Boston Garden, all the different basketballs and sneakers used over the years, the first 24-second shot clock, the evolution of NBA video games and everything else of that ilk. Consider this the most historical floor on the building. From there, you take the escalator up to the top floor of the basement, where you find special sections devoted to the greatest games and playoff games, as well as plaques to recognize five distinct groups of players. None would be considered Pyramid guys, but we couldn't have a Hall of Fame without them. Remember, the goal is to learn everything you possibly can about the history of the NBA, as well as who mattered and what happened.[18] So here are those five groups:

GROUP 1: THE PIONEERS

Celebrating the greats who launched their careers between 1946 and 1956, when the league was still evolving into what it eventually became. Think George Mikan, Bob Cousy, Joe Fulks, Bill Sharman, Dolph Schayes, Bob Pettit, Arnie Risen, George Yardley, Vern Mikkelsen, Dick McGuire, Harry

---

17. The Luxor pisses me off. How do you turn a sleek Egyptian pyramid into White Trash Central? They had the second-best casino concept (topped only by Caesars Palace) and completely fucked it up.

18. This is what pisses me off about Pete Rose's ban from Cooperstown. It's a museum. The goal is to teach people about baseball history. Just put on Rose's HOF plaque: GAMBLED ON BASEBALL WHILE MANAGING THE REDS, DISGRACED OUR SPORT. What's the big deal?

J. Gallatin, Ed Macauley, Buddy Jeanette, Larry Foust, Cliff Hagan, Neil Johnston, Bobby Wanzer, Clyde Lovellette, Al Cervi, Tom Gola, Slater Martin, Johnny Kerr, Jim Pollard, Bob Davies, Richie Guerin, Bob Feerick and Max Zaslofsky.[19]

GROUP 2: THE HARLEM GLOBETROTTERS AND OTHER AFRICAN AMERICAN PIONEERS

I'm not nearly black enough to write this paragraph. But here's what I'm thinking: tributes to pioneers like Sweetwater Clifton, Chuck Cooper, Ray Felix, Cleo Hill, Don Barksdale and Earl Lloyd; a "History of the Globetrotters" memorabilia section and video room; talking holograms of President Obama, Charles Barkley, Magic Johnson and others discussing the effects of the pioneers on their games and their lives; and Dan Klores' documentary *Black Magic* playing on a twenty-four-hour loop. Also, we could probably hire down-on-their-luck stars from the sixties, seventies and eighties like Marvin Barnes and Spencer Haywood to work there as congenial ushers and pay them an obscene rate like $50 an hour. This would clearly be Jabaal Abdul-Simmons' favorite floor in the Pyramid.

GROUP 3: GREATEST ROLE PLAYERS

Celebrating underrated players with specific skill sets who were inordinately valuable for good playoff teams. I'd start with these twenty-six: Michael Cooper, K. C. Jones, Frank Ramsey, Horace Grant, Bobby Jones, George Johnson, Don Nelson, Satch Sanders, Al Attles, Ben Wallace, Eddie Johnson, Vinnie Johnson, John Paxson, Bill Laimbeer, Bill Bradley, Kurt Rambis, Paul Pressey, Ricky Pierce, Bruce Bowen, Steve Kerr, Paul Silas, Derek Fisher, Rudy LaRusso, James Posey, Downtown Freddie Brown and

---

19. A few of these players also crack the Pyramid as true Hall of Famers. Stay tuned.

Jack Haley.[20] We could vote a new one in every three years. Also, Bowen's plaque could come with a device that accidentally trips people as they walk by.

GROUP 4: THE RECORD HOLDERS

Guys like Scott Skiles (dished out a record 30 assists in one game), Elmore Smith (a record 11 blocks), Larry Kenon (13 steals), Frank Layden (58 nose picks), Rasheed Wallace (41 technicals) and Wilt Chamberlain (20,000 sexual partners) get their due.

GROUP 5: THE COMETS

Potential Hall of Famers who suffered a career-crippling injury or were derailed by personal problems, extenuating circumstances or even death. I'd start with these eighteen: Micheal Ray Richardson, Andrew Toney, Penny Hardaway, James Silas, Marvin Barnes, Gus Johnson, Ralph Sampson, Brad Daugherty, Maurice Stokes, John Lucas, Sam Bowie, Terry Cummings, Roy Tarpley, Reggie Lewis, Grant Hill, Alonzo Mourning, Drazen Petrovic and Tim Hardaway.[21] We're leaving out Lenny Bias only because I'd end up staring sadly at his plaque and screaming, "Why? Whyyyyyy?" for ten to twelve hours before security pulled me away.

Okay, we're done with the basement. After wading through the lobby on the ground floor—which features an oversized NBA Pro Shop; Bennett Salvatore's new steakhouse, Two Shots for Wade; Rik Smits' Dutch Oven

20. Haley created the Overjoyed and Oversupportive High-Fiving Twelfth Man role that became a staple on NBA benches in the 1990s and 2000s, leading to someone deciding that it would be a good idea to make Mark Madsen and Brian Scalabrine multimillionaires.

21. I love this idea: anytime a star player or troubled draft pick is suffering from personal problems, we could make "The only way they're making the Hall of Fame is the Comets section" jokes.

Pizza; and an NBA-themed diner owned by Hubie Brown called the Tremendous Upside Café—we start climbing the levels of Pyramid guys. Please pay attention because this is super-duper important. Here are those five levels:

LEVEL 1 (GROUND FLOOR)

Just-made-it Hall of Famers or better, either because of the David Thompson Factor (great career, not long enough), the Dan Issel Factor (very good for a long time, never great) or the Pete Maravich Factor (memorable career, never won anything). This will all make sense in a few pages.

LEVEL 2 (SECOND FLOOR)

No-doubt-about-it Hall of Famers who couldn't crack Level 3 for one of five reasons: they never won a title as an elite guy; something was missing from their career totals; they never peaked for two or three years as a top-five guy; at least two or three guys played their position at the same time and were better; or their careers were shortened by injuries and/or rapidly declining skills. To fill out this floor, we're adding sections devoted to the twelve greatest teams of all time (as voted by our Hall of Fame Committee), along with screening rooms so fans could sample our extensive video library.[22] We'll also have a giant section devoted to everything you ever wanted to know about the ABA.

---

22. I also want dorky teenage video clerks like the ones that work in Blockbuster, only they'll all be six foot four with oversized appendages, as if they just had a growth spurt the night before. And we'll make them wear referee uniforms like they're working at Foot Locker. That's an essential.

LEVEL 3 (THIRD FLOOR)

No-doubt-about-it Hall of Famers who ranked among the best for a few years with every requisite resume statistic to match; no MVP winner can drop below Level 3 unless there is a *fantastic* reason. To fill out this floor, we're adding sections devoted to influential coaches, referees, writers, owners and innovators. That's right, Danny Biasone and Borsalino hats finally get their due! Maybe we can even hand out complimentary $24 bills with Biasone's face on them. In fact, let's do this. It's my elaborately fake idea that will never happen. Done and done.

LEVEL 4 (FOURTH FLOOR)

Basically L3 guys, only there's something inherently greater about them. Possible tip-offs: Do they have to be considered in any "best of all time" discussion? Did they have transcendent games or memorable moments? Were they just *dominant* at times? Will you always remember watching them play, even when you're ninety years old and peeing on yourself? Are they in the mix for some all-time benchmarks? To fill out this floor, we're also throwing in sections devoted to the four NBA commissioners— Kennedy, Maurice Podoloff, O'Brien and Stern—as well as the Scottie Brooks Hadlen Memorial Library and Bookstore featuring every relevant NBA-related book ever written. Including this one. On its own shelf. Just dozens and dozens of copies. And maybe even a six-foot cardboard cutout of me. What, you're going to deny my self-serving participation in my own fake idea? How dare you!

THE PANTHEON (PENTHOUSE)

Take a deep breath. We're at the top of the Hall of Fame Pyramid, literally and figuratively. These are the twelve greatest players of all time, the best of the best . . . the Pantheon.[23] There would be windows on all sides, a few balconies and maybe even a view of lovely Indiana from all directions. I'd have a conference room with seats where famous people could give speeches or presentations, or even a Q & A, just so they could make announcements like "Ladies and gentleman, just a reminder, Elgin Baylor will be taking questions on the Pantheon Floor at three o'clock." We also need a bar that opens at five every night (with a Happy Hairston Hour) and eventually turns into a hopping nightclub called Pantheon, equipped with one of those special elevators that take you from the ground floor right to Pantheon (like they have in the Palms). All right, I'm getting carried away. But here's what I love about the Pyramid model:

- Fans and writers would (I hope) argue about which players belong on which levels; it would become the "Jessica Biel vs. Jessica Alba" of sports debates. Is Shaq an L4 or a Pantheon guy? Does Reggie Miller make it past L1? Does Kobe crack L4? Where does Elgin land since he never won a title? What about Oscar, the greatest guard before MJ and Magic? Was Cousy great enough to be an L4? You get the idea.
- After we decide on the Pyramid guys—remember, we're dumping some current Hall of Famers into the basement in the "Pioneer," "Role Player," and "Comet" exhibits—a special selection committee would reassign levels to every player who made the cut. Let's say the committee features fifty well-known former players, journalists and broadcasters. Each would vote on levels for every existing Hall of Fame member from 1 (lowest) to 5 (highest); the average score for each member (rounded up) would determine his level; and each person would have to vote for twelve players (no more, no less) for the top level of the Pyramid. Makes it a little more interesting, no? Especially when we make the votes public. If you're the dimwit who kept Scottie Pippen from being an L3 because you voted for him as an L1, everyone needs to know you're a dimwit.

23. I thought about making the Pantheon a twelve-man roster and leaving it open so we could add LeBron someday and kick out one of the original twelve like it's a *Bachelor* episode. But that wouldn't be fair.

- The Pyramid structure would *look* cool. Besides the aesthetic benefits of a five-story building housing every meaningful nugget of NBA history and resembling an actual Egyptian pyramid, can you imagine climbing each level as the floors get smaller and smaller . . . and finally reaching the Pantheon? I'm getting chills just thinking about it.[24] Even if it can never happen, that's the great thing about pipe dreams . . . you can still have fun with them, right?[25] So here's how my levels would break down and why, and if you think this wasn't a convoluted excuse to rank the best NBA players in reverse order from 96 to 1, well, you don't know me well enough. These rankings were weighed by the following factors:

1. How well did he grasp The Secret?
2. Did he make a difference on good teams? Did he get better when it mattered? If your life depended on one game, would you want him out there trying to win it for you? Would you trust him completely in the final two minutes of a do-or-die game? In short, would you want to be in an NBA foxhole with him?
3. Would he have been not-so-fun, semifun, fun or superfun to play with? We'll explain in the Nash section.
4. Did he get traded at any point in his prime? If so, why? This doesn't matter as much with Level 1 or Level 2, but I need a *really* good reason to forgive trading a Level 3, 4 or 5 guy in his prime.
5. As a personal preference, I value someone who was great for a short period of time over someone who was good for a long period of time. Give me two transcendent years from Bill Walton over fourteen non-

24. The NBA won't sell sponsorship banners on my Pyramid because it's in bad taste. In real life? You'd be visiting the Volkswagen Touareg NBA Pyramid or something. Just shoot me.

25. One good thing about pipe dreams: there's always a 0.0003 percent chance they can come true. In the late '90s, I forget what sparked this—maybe it was a *Friends* episode—but every couple in America made their top-five lists for Celebs You'd Let Me Sleep with if I Had the Chance. Tiffani Amber-Thiessen was number one on my list. We moved to L.A. a few years later and my wife befriended a friend of T.A.T.'s. For our five-year anniversary, she got me a signed T.A.T. photo that read, "I heard I'm on your list, too bad you're married." I called T.A.T. to thank her, one thing led to another and we ended up banging in the back room at Mel's Diner because it was the closest thing to the Peach Pit. Okay, I made that last part up. The point is, you never know with pipe dreams.

transcendent years from Walt Bellamy. I'm not winning a championship with Bellamy; I'm winning one with a healthy Walton. So I'd rather have two great Walton years and twelve years of patchwork nobodies than fourteen straight Bellamy years, if that makes sense.

(Note: Bellamy's career exemplifies why we need the Pyramid. He averaged a 29–17 during his first three seasons—1961–63, before the league changed color and got bigger—and never made another All-Star team after '64. He's one of nine players to finish with 20,000 points and 14,000 rebounds, only Wilt owned him to the degree that the Dipper once shook his hand before an opening tip, promised Bellamy that he would get demolished, destroyed him for an entire half, then told him before the second-half tip, "Okay, now you can score." His teams never won—in fact, Bellamy's teams won just two playoff series and dealt him twice in his prime. When the '68 Knicks traded Bellamy and Howie Komives for Dave DeBusschere, the deal quickly turned them around and ushered in a six-year run of contention. The great George Kiseda[26] even wrote, "Walt Bellamy is the skeleton in the closet of the 20,000-Point Club." Clearly, Bellamy missed his calling—if he'd come along thirty years later, he would have been revered by fantasy owners and remembered in an entirely different light. Same for Jerry Lucas.)[27]

6. How deceiving were the guy's stats? Issel's numbers look fantastic until you remember that he couldn't have guarded the best guy on a WNBA team.[28] Karl Malone's gaudy stats don't reflect how his face looked like he'd been given a monster Botox injection at the end of every big game. You *have* to factor this stuff in. Statistics are extremely helpful, they fill in a lot of holes, but that's it. Beyond that, how much did the

26. Kiseda was the first great NBA writer; he covered the league for its first 20 years before becoming sports editor for the *L.A. Times.* Tragically, he never wrote an all-encompassing NBA book. Even weirder, the next great NBA writer (Bob Ryan) hasn't written a great one either. But hey, when you can spend your Sundays arguing with Mitch Albom and Mike Lupica in HD instead of writing a book, I guess you have to do it.
27. Grumpy Old Editor (GOE): "Walt Bellamy had the smallest head of any seven-footer ever. He was built like the Washingon Monument. And played that way."
28. That should have read "best girl." Wanted to make sure you were paying attention.

guy's era affect his stats? Remember the lessons from the "How the Hell?" section.

7. Did he have at least two memorably remarkable qualities about his game? We'll explain in the Pippen section.

8. Was he a great teammate, a decent teammate, a forgettable teammate or a gaping asshole? We'll explain in the GP section.

9. Did he make at least one first or second All-NBA team in his career? If the answer is no, we need a reason that makes sense, like Nate Thurmond falling short only because Kareem, Wilt, Cowens, Unseld and Reed peaked during his prime. We'll call this the Bill Laimbeer Corollary because I was looking for any possible reason to keep him out of the Pyramid—after all, he was a world-class douche and that was the best reason that worked. Screw him.[29]

10. Did he resonate on a level beyond stats? Did he connect with fans on a spiritual level or an "I've never seen anyone in my life like this guy" level? Was he an original prototype? Could he ever be re-created? Think Earl the Pearl.

11. If it's a player from 1946 to 1976, how well could his game have translated to the modern era?

That last question is a biggie. Say we brought '61 Wilt to 2009 and matched him against a slew of modern athletes with strength and speed. Wouldn't they handle him or slow him down? He might average a 20–10 or even a 25–14 nowadays, but with superior talent, smarter defenses, complex coaching strategies and unfavorable-for-him rule changes, hell would freeze over before '62 Wilt scored 100 in a single game.[30] From the tapes I watched, Wilt notched such brow-furrowing numbers mainly because he was a superathletic big man feasting on undersized, overmatched stiffs. You could say he was before his time physically. Do we credit him for

29. Other reasons: he only had 7 double-double seasons; he couldn't pass, run, jump or dribble; and again, he was a douche bag. With that said, I would have loved him if he'd played for the Celtics.

30. GOE claims, "Today, Wilt would be like one of those hapless Georgetown centers throwing up bricks and racking up dumb fouls (except, of course, when he got four and went to sleep). Without an offensive game more than five feet from the hoop, he'd be lucky to rack up 12 and 9." Yeesh.

that? Do we ignore the fact that 2000 Shaq may have surpassed Wilt's stats in 1962? Was Wilt fortunate for not having been born ten years later? Russell had a much better chance of thriving in 2009 because of his competitiveness and defensive instincts, even if he was built like Thaddeus Young. Would he dominate like he did in 1959? Of course not. You can't forget that twenty-first-century stars are evolutionary versions of the best guys from the fifties and sixties. Take Steve Nash and Bob Cousy. (Note: let's make sure that there is a team of doctors surrounding Tommy Heinsohn before he reads these next few lines.) Nash is a much better shooter, he's in better shape, he plays harder, he tries harder on defense, he's more technically sound . . . he's just *better*. But he didn't have anything close to Cousy's career, nor did he match Cousy's impact on his generation (as a player, personality, winner and innovator). So how do we judge which guy mattered more? Really, it's like comparing an '09 Porsche with a '62 Porsche: the '09 would easily win a race between them, but the '62 was a more groundbreaking car. So the Nash model wins the "Who were the most talented players ever?" question, but the Cooz model wins the "Who were the most groundbreaking players ever?" question. And both matter.

That's why I made the following decision: you can't effectively compare players from different eras unless both players thrived after 1976, when basketball fully evolved into the sport we're watching now. A few early stars would be effective today, but too many would flounder to the degree that it's difficult to project them being better than eleventh or twelfth men (if that). Take Dolph Schayes, the best player on Syracuse's '55 title team and a member of the NBA's Silver Anniversary Team. Could a slow white guy who played below the rim and lived on a deadly *set shot* succeed at a high level in 2010? Would Dolph be more useful in 2010 than Steve Novak? Um . . . I don't know. I really don't. After careful deliberation, I bumped nearly every pre-Russell star from the Pyramid for two big reasons. First, basketball didn't totally become basketball until they created the shot clock in 1954. Second, there was a center in the fifties named Neil Johnston who finished with the following resume:

Eight years, 6 quality, 6 All-Stars . . . top 5 NBA ('52, '53, '54, '55), top 10 ('56) . . . second-best player on champ ('56 Sixers), averaged a 20–14

(10 games) . . . 4-year peak: 21–12 . . . season leader: points (3x), rebounds (1x), minutes (2x), FG percentage (3x)

Pretty good, right? For the league's first decade, Johnston was its most
effective all-around center other than Mikan: a six-foot-eight 210-
pounder who thrived as long as everyone played below the rim and you
could unleash clumsy hook shots without getting them swatted away.
Then Russell showed up and ruined everything. Satch Sanders jokes that
Russell terminated the careers of Johnston, Harry Gallatin, Ed Macauley,
Charlie Share and every other old-school center (translation: white guy).
Sifting through the stories and anecdotes, unleashing Russell in the mid-
fifties sounds like what might happen if Dwight Howard joined the
WNBA. (By the way, this is the only scenario that would get me watching
the WNBA other than my daughter joining the league someday. It's really
those two and that's it.) Send the likes of David West or Hedo Turkoglu to
the early fifties in Doc Brown's time machine and they'd win four straight
MVPs. Sorry, every reader over sixty years old, but it's true. Also, remember not to get carried away with scoring/rebounding stats from 1959 to
1967, or how they allowed variations of offensive goaltending until 1966.
(FYI: When Wilt dropped 73 on the '62 Knicks, the Dipper got himself an
extra 22 points and 13 rebounds just from offensive goaltending and redi-
recting shots.)[31] And all information from 1970 to 1976 (stats, All-Star
nods, All-NBA nods) should be taken with three hundred grains of salt
(page 115), so if you're wondering why someone like Spencer Haywood
(two top fives, two top tens, a five-year peak of 24–12) or Lou Hudson
(four-year peak: 25–6–4, 51% FG) didn't make the cut, or why Bob
McAdoo and Tiny Archibald are ranked as L1 guys . . . well, that's why.[32]
Last thought: I kept the cutoff at ninety-six players for this edition

31. Trust me, I watched the tape. Every "big" Knick looked like a prehistoric version of
Brian Scalabrine. Do you think Dwight Howard could score 73 points in one game if of-
fensive goaltending was allowed, if he shot 50 times and if he was being guarded by pre-
historic Scalabrines? I say yes. Also, I'm naming my next fantasy team the Prehistoric
Scalabrines.
32. My toughest cuts: Walter Davis, Mitch Richmond, Gus Johnson, Laimbeer, Hudson,
Chet Walker, Chauncey Billups, Tom Gola, Alonzo Mourning, Tim Hardaway, Jack
Sikma, Paul Silas, Gus Williams. Toughest cut: Sikma. Easiest cut: Chuck Nevitt.

(both hardcover and paperback) so I could stretch the Pyramid to one hundred in 2016's *The Book of Basketball, Second Edition: A Quick Influx of Cash.* Odds for current stars to grab one of those four spots: Kevin Durant, -700; Pau Gasol, even; Carmelo Anthony, +250; Derrick Rose, +300; Deron Williams, +300; Rajon Rondo, +350; Chauncey Billups, +400; Manu Ginobili, +500; Chris Bosh, +750; Amar'e Stoudemire, +900; Brandon Roy, +1,200; Stephen Curry, +1,500; Tyreke Evans, +2,500; Ricky Rubio, +3,000; Joakim Noah, +4,000; Brook Lopez, +5,000; DeMarcus Cousins, +5,000; Yao Ming, +7,500; Greg Oden's penis, +10,000.

I'd wager on Durant (a lock), Gasol (second banana for consecutive champs, most skilled offensive big man right now), Rondo (averaged a 16–8–10 in his last 38 playoff games) and Anthony (24.7 career PPG, 15th all-time) for those four spots. (And really, it's too bad I can't wager on this since I control the Pyramid. I'm almost positive I would win.) For now, we're sticking with ninety-six Pyramid Guys only. Let's count them down in reverse order, starting at the lowest level and going up.

SEVEN

THE PYRAMID: LEVEL 1

96. TOM CHAMBERS

Resume: 16 years, 10 quality, 4 All-Stars . . . top 10 ('89, '90) . . . '87 All-Star MVP . . . 2-year peak: 26–8–3 . . . 2-year Playoffs peak: 24–9–3 (28 G) . . . played for 1 runner-up ('93 Suns) . . . 20K Club

YET ANOTHER THING that bugs me about Hall of Fames: they refuse to weigh the impact of each inductee, so there's never a cutoff guy for each position—aka the guy who barely made it, the "wall" everyone else needs to climb—so you can't evaluate a power forward's candidacy simply by asking, "Was he better than Tom Chambers?" Along with the next four guys for their respective positions, we're using Chambers to create the line for power forwards. Even though his eighties hairdo (blondish brown hair parted in the middle with some girth in the back) made him look like a cross between Paul "Mr. Wonderful" Orndorff and every women's softball player from 1985 to 1989, and even though he was so bland that he never earned himself a nickname,[1] Chambers filled the wing splendidly on fast breaks, scored effectively in the half-court, and shone during the single most competitive stretch in NBA history ('86 to '93, an era that included twelve of the top twenty-four guys on this list and nineteen of the top fifty) as the go-to guy on three conference finalists ('87 Sonics, '89 Suns, '90 Suns). Even on his last legs, he played crunch time for the '93 Suns, quite possibly the best single-season team that didn't win a title post-merger. Despite his notoriously uninspired defense,[2] Chambers deserves bonus points for two things:

1. He's the starting power forward on the White Guys Who Played Like Black Guys Team. Of the ten greatest in-game dunks ever, Chambers is the only white guy who makes the cut: for the two-hander where he dunked over Mark Jackson, got propelled upward, ended up on Jackson's chest and looked like he was throwing down on an eight-foot rim.[3]

2. Not only was Chambers named MVP of the greatest All-Star Game ever (1987), scoring 34 and outscoring MJ, 'Nique, Barkley and Hakeem combined, but Magic kept pick-and-rolling with him down the stretch and the Eastern stars couldn't stop it. Now I'm wondering what would have happened if Chambers and Worthy had switched teams in 1982 and Chambers had spent the ensuing decade playing with Magic. Would he have taken the '88 Finals MVP, made the Hall of Fame and cracked the NBA's top fifty instead of Worthy? It's not inconceivable, right?[4]

1. I would have gone with Tom "the Middle Part" Chambers, eventually shortened to just "the Part."

2. Bird delighted in torching Chambers, Alex English, Kelly Tripucka and Kiki Vandeweghe. If he had played for a West Coast team in the mid-'80s, you could have added 3 PPG to Bird's averages from those four guys alone.

3. His character had an unstoppable dunk move in the Lakers vs. Celtics video game, which counts for . . . something. Not sure what.

4. Worthy's career stats: 17.6 PPG, 5.1 RPG, 52% FG, 77% FT, two third-team All-NBAs. Chambers' career stats: 18.1 PPG, 6.1 RPG, 47% FG, 81% FT, two second-team All-NBAs. I'm just sayin'.

95. JO JO WHITE

Resume: 12 years, 7 quality, 7 All-Stars . . . '76 Finals MVP . . . Top 10
('75, '77) . . . 3-year peak: 22–5–5 . . . Playoffs: 22–5–6, 83% FT, 42.9 MPG
(80 G) . . . 3rd-best player on two champs ('74, '76 Celtics)

A postseason ace whose career playoff averages exceeded his three-year
regular season peak, Jo Jo finished as the best guard on two title teams plus
a 68-win team. Two things stood out other than his playoff heroics and
overwhelming evidence that he may have knocked up Esther Rolle to create David Ortiz. First, he logged seven straight regular seasons of 3,200-
plus minutes *and* averaged 600 playoff minutes from '72 to '76.[5] From '72
to '77, Jo Jo averaged 43 minutes while playing 90, 95, 100, 93, 100, and 91
games. No wonder his legs gave out and robbed him of two or three twilight years of stat padding. And second, Jo Jo finished with a 33–9 in the
legendary triple-OT game, played an obscene 60 minutes and sank one of
the most dramatic free throws ever.[6] Right after Havlicek "won" the game
in double overtime with his running banker, everyone charged the court
and the happy Celtics hopped to their locker room. Even as a full-scale
celebration/riot was unfolding around them, the referees decided that one
second remained on the clock. By this time, Jo Jo had already taken off his
uniform and removed the tape from his ankles. After everyone returned
to the court, Paul Westphal hatched the brilliant idea to call an illegal
time-out, sacrificing a technical but allowing Phoenix to inbound the ball
from midcourt—meaning a cooled-down Jo Jo had to sink the technical
after a fifteen-minute delay in which everyone already thought they won,
with nobody else on the floor and a mob of drunken maniacs crammed
around the court. If he missed that freebie, the Celtics would have lost on
Gar Heard's ensuing miracle turnaround at the buzzer. Nope. Swish. All
things considered, that has to be one of the ballsiest free throws ever

5. No guard played more than 30 playoff games and averaged more minutes than Jo Jo's
42.9 except Allen Iverson, who averaged 45-plus but only played 10-plus playoff games
twice.
6. In Game 6 of a '74 series in Buffalo, Jo Jo got fouled at the buzzer of a tie game, then
calmly drained the winning FT (and another for good measure) to clinch the series.
Only a Buffalo team could lose like that.

made. Jo Jo also sank the clinching freebies in the third overtime, even though he was so exhausted by that point, he was *sitting down on the court* when Phoenix shot free throws. If your life depended on it, you wanted Jo Jo out there. Period.

(His biggest problem in retrospect: it's tough to take a grown man named Jo Jo seriously as one of the greatest players of his era. If his name were Luther White or Julius White, he'd be remembered the same way Walt Frazier was remembered. Instead, he sounds like one of LC's catty friends in *The Hills*.)

94. JACK TWYMAN

Resume: 11 years, 7 quality seasons, 6 All-Stars ... top 10 ('60, '62) ... season leader: FG% (1x), FT% (1x) ... 3-year peak: 29–9–3 ... 3-year Playoffs peak: 20–8–2 (26 G)

One of my favorite random moments writing this book: spending a solid hour picking between Cliff Hagan and Twyman for the "white forward from the fifties and sixties" cutoff spot, then deciding Hagan was slightly better because he won a title and was elected to the Hall five years before Twyman in 1978 (even though he retired four years *after* Twyman). Honestly, those were my only two reasons. Twyman's finest contributions came off the court: after teammate Maurice Stokes was felled by a career-ending illness, Twyman's family took Stokes in, cared for him, raised money to pay his bills and was eventually immortalized in the 1973 movie *Maurie*, as well as a phenomenal Twyman/Stokes video exhibit in Springfield that I watched during every visit as a kid.[7] Throwing in the racial wrinkle (Twyman was white, Stokes was black) and social climate at the time, this has to rank among the better feel-good sports stories. So how does everyone remember *Brian's Song* and nobody remembers *Maurie*? Well, one movie had Billy Dee Williams and James Caan; the other had

---

7. Back in the late '70s, this was the single best exhibit in the Hall of Fame, as well as the precursor to Chris Connelly's tearjerker features on *SportsCenter*. Let's hope I didn't give Connelly any ideas. Uh-oh, he's driving to the cemetery to interview Maurice Stokes' coffin . . . *somebody stop him!*

Bernie Casey and Bo Svenson. 'Nuff said.[8] Twyman also became the league's first recognizable former star turned below-average TV analyst—I mean, when you're the first on that storied list, you know you've had an impact, right? The man paved the way for Russell, Magic, Isiah, and everyone else. Although he *was* fortunate enough to interview Russell right after the '69 Finals, when Russell couldn't answer "How does it feel?" and eventually just broke down. Since it's my single favorite championship moment other than Boston mayor Ray Flynn's teenage son somehow interjecting himself in the middle of the entire '86 trophy celebration,[9] you have to give Twyman credit for being involved.

93. KEVIN JOHNSON

Resume: 12 years, 7 quality, 3 All-Stars . . . top 10 ('89, '90, '91, '94), top 15 ('92) . . . 4-year peak: 22–4–11 (50% FG, 85% FT) . . . 2-year Playoffs peak: 22–4–11 (28 G) . . . 2nd-best player on one runner-up ('93 Suns) . . . 5th in most Playoffs assists (8.9 APG, 115 G)

My father and I attended a Cavs-Celts game during Johnson's rookie year when KJ played like a terrified ninth-grader bombing in a varsity game. Given that he was the seventh pick, we were stunned by how helpless he looked compared to teammate Mark Price.[10] A few months later, we thought Cleveland fleeced Phoenix when they swapped KJ in a megadeal for Larry Nance. *How could they turn that stiff into Larry Nance?* KJ transformed Phoenix into a playoff contender within a year, leading them to the '89 Western Semis and the '90 Western Finals and matching nearly everything we've seen from Chris Paul these last four years. And that's how my father and I learned never to give up on

8. You might remember Svenson starring as vigilante sheriff Buford Pusser in the classic '70s action trilogy, *Walking Tall.* Or maybe you don't. I just felt like writing the name Buford Pusser.

9. This kid was the real-life Spaulding Smails. There's a significant chance he drove his family's boat into a Charlestown pier later that night.

10. Price would have been a potential Pyramid guy if he hadn't blown out his knee. Even then, he still made a top five and three top fifteens and brought the Cavs within two wins of the Finals. He gets my vote for Most Underrated Guy of the Nineties.

young point guards.[11] Two things submarined KJ historically. First, he couldn't stay on the court, missing 15-plus games in five of eleven seasons and sparking rumors that his dysfunctional hammies were made out of papier-mâché. (Important note: If there was a Fantasy Hall of Fame for the most frustrating roto basketball players ever, he'd be the point guard. By the mid-nineties, if you took KJ in the first five rounds of your draft, the other guys openly mocked you. Soon only a rookie franchise would pick KJ within the first ten rounds of a fantasy draft, and whenever it happened, everyone else would smile knowingly. KJ was like the high school slut who spends time with everyone on the football team . . . then a new transfer comes in senior year, starts dating her and everyone on the team gets a big kick out of it. That's what KJ was like. We all went a few rounds with KJ. I miss having him around for comedy's sake.) And second, he helped blow the '93 Finals by choking so memorably during Phoenix's first two home games, Suns coach Paul Westphal actually had to bench him for *Frankie Johnson* in crunch time at the end of Game 2. By the time KJ pulled it together in Game 3, the Suns had squandered their home-court advantage and had no realistic chance of coming back—nobody was beating MJ in four out of five games during Jordan's apex.

Now, many have gagged in the Finals (John Starks in '94, Nick Anderson in '95, Magic in '84, Elvin in '75, Dirk in '06, etc.), but I can't remember someone melting down to the degree that it seemed as if he was throwing the game like Tony in *Blue Chips*. Since it happened during his defining showcase as a player, we have to penalize him for it. On the other hand, no point guard brazenly attacked the basket, dunked on bigger guys and destroyed guys off the dribble quite like KJ in his prime; it wasn't that opponents couldn't stay in front of him as much as how they instinctively backed up before he made a move. Had KJ peaked post-2004—when they started whistling hand check fouls, stopped whistling moving screens and made it so much easier for guards to get into the paint—he would have averaged a 30–15 and beaten out Steve Nash for consecutive MVPs. Well, unless his hammies exploded first.

11. One of my great regrets in life is that I never had a chance to tell Rick Pitino this story when he was thinking about trading Celtics rookie Chauncey Billups after *fifty fucking games.*

92. BOB LANIER

Resume: 14 years, 8 quality, 8 All-Stars . . . 4-year peak: 24–13–4 . . .
Playoffs: 19–9–4 (67 G) . . . won 2 Playoffs in his prime . . . 20K Point Club

Lanier and his size 21 sneakers narrowly edge Sikma[12] and his kick-ass blondafroperm for the cutoff center spot, only because Sikma was blessed with talented Seattle/Milwaukee teams and poor Lanier was stuck in NBA hell (Detroit) for the entire seventies. He even introduced Dick Vitale to friends as "my coach and GM" for two especially putrid years.[13] By the time Milwaukee traded for Lanier during the '80 season, the NBA community reacted the same way Texans react after a trapped child is rescued from a well. The Lanier-Sikma battle comes down to this: Both were traded to Milwaukee right after their primes. Lanier's price was Kent Benson (the number one pick in '77) and a 1980 number one; Sikma's price was Alton Lister and number ones in '87 and '89. In other words, Lanier was worth more. But not by much. We'll remember Lanier for his tough lefty hook, his sneaky fall-away, those giant sneakers and how he replaced Willis as the league's premier "I'm a nice guy, but if you cross me, I will beat the living tar out of you in front of everyone" center.

(To recap: Our Hall of Fame cutoff guys are Chambers, Jo Jo, Twyman, KJ and Lanier, or as they're known from now on, the Cutoff Guy Starting Five. For future generations arguing about this stuff, make sure any potential Hall of Famer was at least 0.000001 percent better than these five guys. Thank you.)

12. Sikma's resume: 14 years, 10 quality, 7 All-Stars; starter on 1 champ ('79 Sonics) and 1 runner-up ('78); 5-year peak: 19–11–4; '79 playoffs: 15–12–3 (17 G); fourth-best blondafroperm behind Ian Ziering, Larry Bird, and Tweety's buddy in *Bad Boys* (narrowly edging Dan Gladden, Wally Backman, and Sid Vicious). When Glenn Close wore a blond perm for *The Big Chill*, she told her hair stylist, "Give me the Sikma."
13. Dickie V. holds a special place in Celtics lore after trading M. L. Carr and two number ones for Bob McAdoo before the 1979–80 season. Boston ended up with the number one overall pick and shipped it to Golden State in the famous Parish/McHale trade. OHHHHH! OHHHHHHHH! THAT TRADE WAS AWESOME, BABY! OHHHH-HHH!

91. BAILEY HOWELL

Resume: 12 years, 10 quality, 6 All-Stars . . . top 10 ('63) . . . 4-year peak: 22–12–2 . . . started for 2 champs ('68 and '69 Celts)

A physical small forward (like a more efficient Ron Artest, without the crazy), Howell made six straight All-Star Games and played a pivotal role on Boston's last two title teams. Of players who logged 400-plus games in the sixties (starting in '60 and ending with '69), Howell finished fifth in field goal percentage (48.4%), eighth in scoring (20.2) and thirteenth in rebounding (10.7). I stuck him too high in the hardcover (no. 80), chewed on it for a few months, didn't feel great about it and rectified it here. Although it's funny to think of Bailey flipping through the paperback in a bookstore, seeing his ranking, then screaming, "Wait a second, I dropped eleven spots? What could I have possibly done? I've been retired for forty years! *Fuck you, Simmons! Fuck you!*"

90. CHRIS PAUL

Resume: 5 years, 4 quality, 3 All-Stars . . . top 5 ('08), top 10 ('09) . . . Simmons-approved MVP ('08) . . . MVP runner-up ('08) . . . 2-year peak: 21–5–11, 2.7 stl, 49% FG, 4:1 asst/TO ratio . . . All-Defense (2x) . . . leader: assists (2x), steals (2x) . . . '08 Playoffs: 24–5–11, 50% FG (12 games)

The Evolutionary Isiah. Although Paul struggled through an unhappy '10 season (the lowlights: a torn meniscus, a fired coach, declining attendance and a lottery appearance), his '08 and '09 seasons remain the best two-year statistical stretch by any point guard since Oscar.[14] Paul played the

---

14. In 2009, CP became the first top-ten scorer to lead the league in assists/steals and came within 12 points of becoming the fourth player to average 23-plus points and 11-plus assists in one season. Only 5 players led the NBA in steals and assists since 1974; he did it in consecutive years. In 2009, he even shot 50 percent from the field and 87 percent from the line. If he stays healthy, he could have a 25–12 season with a steals title and 50–40–90 percentages in him. It's in play.

position with particular pizazz, controlling the tempo of every game, reaching any spot he wanted and converting a dizzying number of high-degree alley-oops. (Nobody meant more to his teammates. When Paul appeared on Kimmel's show in 2008, the other Hornets sat in the audience. After the show, when Kimmel asked him to film a comedy bit and Paul agreed, his teammates tagged along instead of hitting Hollywood for a night out. They all left together. These are the stories I want to hear about my Pyramid Guys.) Of the current stars, he's trapped in the toughest situation: lousy supporting cast, clogged salary cap, franchise instability, competitive conference . . . and he can't flee for greener pastures until 2012. During the tumultuous summer of 2010, there were persistent rumors that New Orleans was shopping Paul to big-market teams along with Emeka Okafor's massive contract (like a Chris Paul tax), which would have chopped payroll but effectively assassinated professional basketball in N'Awlins. Wisely, they backed off. And Paul couldn't demand a trade to a contender, not after BP's oil spill left his hurricane-battered city on life support. He's stuck there. Evolutionary Isiah needs an Evolutionary McCloskey to save the troubled Hornets. And soon.

89. VINCE CARTER

Resume: 12 years, 10 quality, 8 All-Stars . . . '99 Rookie of the Year . . . top 10 ('01), top 15 ('00) . . . 3-year peak: 26–6–4 . . . 10 straight 20+ PPG seasons . . . Playoffs: 23–6–5 (56 G) . . . Playoffs record: most threes in one half (8)

I've never been a fan of gifted offensive stars who couldn't defend anyone, screwed over entire cities and thrived in dunk contests versus playoff games. In a related story, Vince has played eleven years without making it past the second round. Even weirder, his cousin Tracy McGrady never made it past the *first* round. No truth to the rumor that their annual family softball game only goes six innings before it abruptly stops. But Vince's career has been particularly annoying for a variety of reasons. His most famous moment? The time he leapfrogged Frederic Weis for a monster throwdown in the 2000 Olympics. (Anytime someone's career highlight

involves Fred Weis, really, what more can be said?)[15] His breakout playoff
season? The spectacular '01 showdown against Allen Iverson, when they
swapped 50-point games in Games 3 and 4 and the series came down to
Vince's missed three at the buzzer in Game 7. (That was the same day that
Vince chartered a plane so he could attend his UNC graduation in person,
then flew back to Philly afterward. It's the perfect Vince Carter story—he
put himself ahead of his team. And they lost.) His enduring trait? He
milked injuries and collisions like nobody we've seen and brought the
phrase "acting like he just got shot" to another level. (Nobody in NBA history had the words "Get up, you pussy!" screamed at him by more fans.
Nobody.) His legacy? He's the premier "so talented, shoulda been so much
better" guy of his generation.

Whatever. That's not what turned me against him for life. During the
'05 season, a disenchanted Vince tanked so hellaciously in Toronto—
killing his trade value for reasons that remain unclear—that the Raptors
were forced to settle for Jersey's offer of Alonzo Mourning (who had to be
bought out), Eric Williams, Aaron Williams and two nonlottery picks. You
could have predicted when it happened (and by the way, I did) that
Toronto damaged its future by not clearing cap space or getting any quality youngsters or picks back.[16] But that's how desperate they were. Rarely
has a professional athlete shown more callousness toward his fans.

Three months later, Vince hooked himself up to the Juvenation Machine in Jersey and admitted that he had stopped trying for Toronto—
no joke, he admitted this—presumably to force a trade, which had to
have been one of the most depressing revelations in recent sports history.[17] Anyway, that's one of the reasons I wanted to write this book: fifty

---

15. We knew we were in trouble when former teammate Keon Clark called Vince overrated and pointed out that the '02 Raptors played best without him (a fact, by the way).
It's not like Keon was sitting around taking shots at people; he barely knew where he was
half the time. This is the same guy who got arrested for marijuana possession during the
summer of '02, leading to one of my favorite conceivable NBA scenarios ever: Keon's
agent juggling $20 million free agent offers, then getting a phone call from Keon, who
tells him, "Um, this is my one phone call, so don't hang up . . ."

16. You're not gonna believe this, but GM Rob Babcock was fired shortly afterward.

17. Right before the playoffs, I wrote the following: "My buddy Gus asked the other day,
'Has anyone ever won the Comeback Player of the Year award for their performance in
the same season?' I say we give him that award, along with the Most Sobering Reminder
That We're Idiots for Caring About Professional Sports award."

years from now, we wouldn't want an NBA fan to flip through some NBA guide and decide that Vince Carter was a worthy basketball star. He wasn't.[P23]

There's a happy ending to this story. Every time Vince plays in Toronto, they boo him like it's Bernie Madoff returning to ring the bell of the NYSE. They boo him for the whole game. They never stop booing. For whatever reason, this brings out the best in Vince—he plays with passion and pride and even sank a few game-winners against them. It's the perfect epitaph for his career—the guy who could only get inspired by a fan base that actively detests him—along with the fact that Vince got an enormous amount of respect from other players, not for what he delivered but for his gifts themselves. Of anyone in the league over the past fifteen years, his peers felt like Vince Carter was the one who could do anything. Well, except give a shit on a consistent basis. You will regret what happened one day, Vince. You will.[18]

88. SHAWN KEMP

Resume: 14 years, 8 quality, 6 All-Stars . . . top 10 ('94, '95, '96) . . . 3-year peak: 19–11–2–2 . . . '96 Playoffs: 21–10–2–2, 57% FG . . . '96 Finals: 23–10, 55% FG . . . second-best player on 1 runner-up ('96 Sonics)

We thought Kemp would end up on thirty different posters. Instead, he became the poster boy of an unlikable era defined by overpaid, overhyped black superstars who grabbed their crotches after dunks, sneered after blocks, choked coaches, quit on teams, sired multiple kids by multiple women and didn't seem to give a shit. (Important note: I'm just stating the

P23. Any remaining doubts about Vince's legacy were erased on the 2009–10 Magic (his best team ever). Vince struggled all year, no-showed the East Finals and even provoked the ire of ESPN's Jeff Van Gundy (who carved him up during a Game 3 blowout in Boston). His Boston series was so poor that a few ESPN.com readers begged me to boot him from the Pyramid. Dropped him seven spots instead.
18. During the '09 season, I attended a Clips-Nets game with my buddy Sal. Vince came out like gangbusters and finished with 42. At one point Sal said matter-of-factly, "Wow, Vince is trying tonight." When fans *notice* if you're trying, there's a 100 percent chance you failed to reach your potential as a player.

unfair general perception, not the reality. Although Kemp's generation *did* have a knack for turning off casual fans.) When you mention Kemp's name to most NBA fans in twenty years, they will remember the way he dunked in traffic, how personal problems (drugs, alcohol and conditioning) side-tracked a potential Hall of Fame career, and the "seven kids by six different women before he turned 30" revelation (a bombshell at the time that pro-vides comedic mileage to this day).[19] Here's what they won't remember:

1. After Moses Malone, another fourteen years passed before another high schooler thrived in the NBA without playing college ball.[20] You could say Kemp paved the way for KG, Kobe, LeBron and everyone else. He even paved the way for Ndudi Ebi.

2. With the notable exceptions of Howard and Young Shaq, there hasn't been a force of nature like Young Kemp: he ran the floor better than any big man ever, finished off alley-oops from every conceivable angle (and some that hadn't been conceived yet) and dunked on everyone in sight (his '92 playoff dunks on Alton Lister and Chris Gatling reside in the Dunk Pantheon). We haven't seen anyone like him before or since. He also had one of the better nicknames of the past thirty years: "Reign Man," definitely the name of his sex tape had he ever released one.[21]

3. Kemp was Seattle's dominant big man on teams that averaged 58 wins from '93 to '97, including a '93 team that lost Game 7 of the Conference Finals when Phoenix shot 68 free throws (Tim Donaghy alert!), as well as a '96 team that won 64 games and lost to Chicago in the Finals. In the '96 playoffs, he outplayed Hakeem in a sweep of Houston, bested Mail-man in the Jazz series, and thrived in the Finals against Dennis Rod-man. Then Seattle signed semi-stiffy center Jim McIlvaine, for the reprehensibly dumb figure of $33 million. Kemp was saddled with a

19. If Kemp was like Roger Bannister breaking the four-minute mile, then Travis Henry brought the sports fertility record down to the 3:35 range when we learned that he'd sired 9 kids by 9 different women, the highest kids-per-partners rate (100.0) for anyone with more than 7 kids since Elias Sports Bureau started keeping track of this stat in 1973. I'm rooting for 10-for-10 because it would give him a double double.

20. Moses stopped at the ABA for a year: Kemp enrolled in community college for a year, but too late to play in games.

21. I just became the first writer ever to use the word "conceived" in a paragraph about Shawn Kemp without mentioning his kids. Thank you.

crummy contract and coming off a breakthrough spring in which he nearly busted down the Pyramid door like a SWAT cop. Instead of using excess cap space to fix Kemp's deal, Seattle paid a backup center twice as much. A bitter Kemp wiped the gym every day with the much wealthier McIlvaine, eventually falling into a drugs/weight/bad attitude spiral and prompting Seattle to swap him for Vin Baker.[22] I doubt that McIlvaine's contract single-handedly turned Kemp into a VH1 special. But it didn't help.

Whatever. Just watch a game from the '96 Finals sometime. During MJ's title run ('91–'93 through '96–'98), Kemp gained steam as the series went along (remember, Seattle won Games 4 and 5) and caused Sonics coach George Karl to proclaim afterward, "He was the best player on the court. No one can say otherwise." So if we're giving players like Bill Walton the benefit of the doubt in this Pyramid from a "what could have been" standpoint, Kemp deserves the same courtesy even if he was probably predisposed to losing his marbles. Really, the late-nineties Sonics should have controlled the West just like the Sampson/Hakeem Rockets should have controlled the late eighties. Then the McIlvaine signing sent Kemp into the tailspin, Houston's teams with Barkley and Hakeem never quite gelled, Shaq's Lakers didn't put everything together yet . . . and suddenly those Stockton-Malone teams were title contenders. Ridiculous. Kemp and GP should have played in four or five straight Finals together. These are the dopey realities that keep me awake when I'm watching ESPN Classic at two-thirty in the morning.[23]

22. In retrospect, trading Kemp for Baker was like trading Six Flags stock for AOL stock in 2006. What a debacle.

23. Poor Kemp went off the deep end Gary Busey–style in Portland. Here's how I described him in December '01: "With all the weird faces and gestures Kemp makes, it's like a constant cry for help. Have you ever been riding the subway when a crazy person jumps on and starts doing Crazy Guy things—loud whoops, deranged eye contact, inexplicable pointing and so on—and everyone moves to the other side of the subway car to get away from him? That's what Shawn Kemp does during Blazers games. He acts like the crazy guy on the subway."

87. GAIL GOODRICH

Resume: 14 years, 8 quality, 5 All-Stars . . . top 5 ('74) . . . 3-year peak: 25–3–5 . . . 2-year Playoffs peak: 25–3–5 (27 G) . . . leader: FTA (1x) . . . 3rd-best player on 1 champ ('72 Lakers) and 1 runner-up ('73 Lakers) . . . left unprotected in '68 expansion draft

One of the better-scoring guards from the confusing ABA/NBA era, the crafty southpaw gets bonus points for being a top-three player on a 69-win Lakers team and abusing Earl Monroe in the '72 Finals, as well as having an unorthodox low-post game, punishing smaller guards down low, and attacking the rim like a crazed Manu Ginobili (attempting 550-plus FTs four different times). Near the tail end of his prime, Goodrich carried enough weight that New Orleans forked over number ones in '77 and '79 to team him with Pete Maravich.[24] Since the Lakers grabbed Magic with one of those picks, Goodrich was actually responsible for *six* Laker titles, as well as the incredible game of Moses Hot Potato detailed on page 199. Part of me wonders if we never took him that seriously from a historical standpoint because his name made him sound like an LPGA golfer. But if we ever slapped together an all-time team of lefties, he edges Ginobili as the shooting guard.[25]

86. CONNIE HAWKINS

Resume: 9 years, 4 quality, 5 All-Stars (1 ABA) . . . ABA MVP ('68) . . . top 5 NBA ('70) . . . 3-year NBA peak: 23–9–4 . . . best player on ABA champ ('68 Pipers), 30–12–5 in Playoffs (14 G)

24. Hundreds of horrible contracts and free agency decisions followed, and yet it's weird that we never topped "Let's dump Moses so we can sign an aging Goodrich and give up two picks, one of which will turn into Magic."

25. Fine, I'll do it. Russell, David Robinson, Cunningham, Goodrich, Tiny Archibald (starters); Chris Mullin (sixth man); Cowens, Willis Reed, Lamar Odom, Sarunas Marciulonis, John Lucas, Manu Ginobili (bench). I always wanted a GM to intentionally build a left-handed team because opponents *always* have trouble remembering that a guy is left-handed. Always. It would be a 25-point advantage each game.

85. ARVYDAS SABONIS

Resume: 7 years, 1 quality, 0 All-Stars . . . 1-year peak: 16–10–3 . . .
2-year playoff peak: 11–8–2 (29 G) . . . career threes: 135–415 (33%) . . .
best player on Russia's '88 Gold Medal team . . . four-time European
Player of the Year

We're exercising the "what could have been" clause here. Eligible for the
'63 draft, Hawkins didn't join the NBA until the '69–'70 season because of
a college fixing scandal back in 1961, when the NBA dubiously banned
everyone involved under their "no taint" rule (even a misguided soul like
Hawkins, who never actually fixed a game). Hawkins spent the next few
years toiling away in failed pro leagues, minor leagues and playground
games before becoming the ABA's first superstar and suing the NBA for
blackballing him. When writer David Wolf (who eventually released *Foul!*,
a superb account of Connie's ten-year odyssey to make the NBA) wrote
about his plight for *Life* magazine in 1969, public sentiment swung behind Hawkins and the league settled for the startling sum of $1 million,
then assigned him to Phoenix, where he peaked by making first-team All-
NBA in 1970.[26] Although we'll never know how good Hawkins could have
been, he was the first modern power forward with athleticism and length
(a good seven to ten years ahead of Gus Johnson and Spencer Haywood),
a prototype for the Kemps and Garnetts, someone who played above the
rim before his knees started going on him. His freakishly large hands allowed him to palm basketballs like tennis balls; Hawkins waved the ball
over his head and found cutters with laser passes, and when he drove to
the basket, nobody stripped him because the ball was embedded in his
giant paw. But Connie's lack of college coaching and skinny body (he
weighed 200–205 pounds in his prime) led to effort/defense issues at
every stage of his career, so his game couldn't have translated to success in
the Playoffs unless he played with a shot blocker like Russell or Thurmond. Had he played a full NBA career, it probably would have resembled

26. Walter Kennedy handled this situation appallingly. The commish didn't investigate
Connie's "involvement" in the scandal (which amounted to him being given $200, then
giving it back) and blindly assumed he was a crook.

what Adrian Dantley or Alex English did: big offensive numbers, more than a few first-round Playoff exits. Regardless, it's all so tragic. Connie's whole career played out like a bad *White Shadow* episode.

You can't play the what-if game with Hawkins without bringing up Sabonis, potentially one of *the* great centers if his legs hadn't betrayed him. By 1995, poor Sabonis ranked just behind Artis Gilmore on the Moving Like a Mummy Scale. Thank God for YouTube, where a young and healthy Saba lives on breaking backboards, draining threes and throwing no-look passes; there's a reason everyone compared him to Walton with 25-foot range.[27] You might remember a twenty-three-year-old Sabonis carrying the Soviets to the 1988 gold medal (even though he was recovering from a ruptured Achilles tendon), outplaying David Robinson in the semifinals, controlling the game on both ends and putting himself on the map as an "all right, they weren't kidding when they said he was great" guy. Portland took a first-round flier on him in 1986, then spent an eternity luring him over before succeeding in 1995 (well after knee/foot injuries sapped his quickness). Lumbering up and down the court in what looked to be concrete Nikes, Sabonis still played a key role on a '00 Blazers team that choked away a potential championship. Considering he couldn't run or jump and remained effective, imagine how great he could have been in his prime. In fact, that nearly made the what-ifs chapter: what if Portland had signed Sabonis in '89, once Russia fragmented and he was allowed to leave the country, when he shockingly signed with Spain over joining the Blazers? Remember, Portland made the Finals in '90 and '92 and the '91 team won 63 games with Kevin Duckworth starting at center. Imagine swapping Duck for one of the best centers of that era. If Hawkins makes it on the coulda-been premise, then we can't leave out the Cold War–thwarting Saba.[28]

---

27. Casual NBA fans remember Saba for two things: his unbelievably gigantic head, which made him look like a pro wrestler, and his wife getting two DUIs during the height of the Jail Blazers era, allowing everyone to make the "Even the spouses of the players get in trouble on this team!" joke.

28. Dino Radja's take in '95: "Without his injuries [Saba] would have been better than David Robinson. Believe me, he was that good. In 1985, he was a beast. He ran the floor like Ralph Sampson. Could shoot the three, dunk. He would have been an NBA All-Star 10 years in a row. It's true, I tell you." Okay, Dino, okay! Settle down.

84. ROBERT HORRY

Resume: 16 years, 0 quality, 0 All-Stars . . . 4-year peak: 10–5–3 . . .
2-year Playoff peak: 13–7–3, 40% 3FG, 78 threes (45 G) . . . played for
7 champs ('94, '95 Rockets, '00, '01, '02 Lakers, '05, '07 Spurs) . . . leader:
Playoffs games (244) . . . played for ten 55-win teams and eight teams
with a .700-plus winning percentage . . . played for 1 team that won
fewer than 47 ('97 Suns, 40–42)

We can't leave Big Shot Rob out of any Pyramid hinging on The Secret.
His defining game happened in the 2005 Finals, about ten defining games
after we thought he'd already had his defining game. (Shit, I had written
"Somebody needs to go through Robert Horry's playoff games, pluck out
all the big plays and shots, then run them in sequence for like ten straight
minutes with a song like Aerosmith's 'Dream On' playing" two seasons
earlier.)[29] It would demean what happened to say Horry made "some huge
three-pointers" or "a number of game-saving plays." Considering the situation (a budding Spurs collapse), the circumstances (no teammate was
stepping up) and the opponent (a supposedly brilliant defensive team
playing at home), Horry's Game 5 (21 of the last 35 points, five threes)
ranks alongside MJ's final Bulls game, Frazier's Game 7 in 1970 and every
other mega-clutch Finals performance. Horry saved the season *and* Tim
Duncan's "Best Power Forward Ever" title. Had the Spurs blown that Finals, everyone would have blamed Duncan (20–14, 42% FG, 64% FT) for
falling short. Now he's just another legend who once struggled at the
wrong time with no real repercussions (like Kobe in the 2010 Finals, actually). That's the power of Big Shot Rob.[30]

My favorite thing about Game 5: When Horry drained a go-ahead

29. Later, Horry made the pivotal play of the '07 Suns-Spurs series by knocking Nash
into the press table at the end of Game 4, leading to suspensions for Amar'e Stoudemire
and Boris Diaw (for coming off the bench). Even washed up, Horry could turn a series
around.
30. Detroit's defense (and the Wallaces) had something to do with Duncan's poor performance. With the exception of Game 5, all tapes of this series should be destroyed.
Like, right now.

three late in the third quarter, it was like watching a poker legend who spent the last hour playing possum, then suddenly pushed a stack of chips into the middle. *Uh-oh. He's making his move.* After a few timely threes and an astounding lefty dunk in overtime, everyone realized the game's fate would somehow end up in Big Shot Rob's hands. Well, everyone but Rasheed Wallace. We're always quick to demolish athletes who screw up in big moments, but Sheed's incredible decision to leave a scorching-hot Horry—again, Robert Horry!!!—to double-team Ginobili in the final nine seconds was the single dumbest brain fart in NBA Finals history. For sweeping significance and staggering inexplicability, it cannot be topped. How could you leave Robert Horry alone in a big game? How?[31]

Like a peanut butter and jelly sandwich, Horry was always there if you needed him. He was a terrific help defender who constantly covered for teammates: big enough to handle low-post players, quick enough to handle perimeter scorers. He only asserted himself when his team truly needed him, never caring about stats or touches—giving him something in common with maybe 1.87 percent of the league—and routinely getting better when it mattered. What more would you want from a supporting player? Like Nate Dogg and John Cazale,[32] he flew under the radar and always ended up in the right situations.[33] For a mailbag, a reader asked me once if I would rather have Horry's career (seven rings and rich) or Barkley's career (no rings and obscenely rich). I picked Horry without blinking. Imagine playing on seven champions, ending up with a cool nickname, earning $55 million and the everlasting respect of everyone who ever played with or against you . . . and never dealing with any resid-

31. Rasheed is a great example of the *Sliding Doors* analogy. If he hadn't landed on the Pistons, he'd be remembered for clashing with referees, starring on those loony Jail Blazers teams and being a classic Shoulda Been Much Better guy. And if the Pistons hadn't won the year before, he'd be remembered for leaving Big Shot Rob open.

32. Cazale played Fredo Corleone and had crucial roles in five movies before dying of cancer: *The Godfather, Godfather II, The Deer Hunter, The Conversation,* and *Dog Day Afternoon.* Would you rather have Cazale's career or be a bigger star that wasn't respected as much (someone like Patrick Swayze or Rob Lowe)? For me, it's no contest—I would rather be Cazale (except for the cancer part), and I would rather be Horry than Karl Malone. Just like Cazale, nobody would have fit in with those Rockets-Lakers-Spurs teams like Horry did, and only true fans appreciate him. So there you go.

33. Some other members of the Horry/Dogg Hall of Fame: Mario Elie, Danny Ainge, Joe Pantoliano, Claude Lemieux, Don Cheadle, Johnny Marr, Emanuel Steward.

ual superstar BS? Have a great game, everyone notices you. Have a terrible game, nobody notices you. Is there a better gig? In a league loaded with players who have a distorted belief in their own talents, Horry understood his own limitations better than anyone. That's what made him great. And that's why I like the poker analogy for him. He sat there quietly with a towering stack of chips, never chased a bad hand and made your heart pound as he stared you down. You couldn't remember the pots he squandered, only the ones he raked in. And when he finally cashed out for the night, you hoped you would never see him again.

Should that earn him a Hall of Fame spot someday? I say yes. He won't get it. As a consolation prize, he lives here in the Pyramid. And here's my defense above everything else: if I called House one night to alert him, "Turn on NBA TV, they're showing the Robert Horry game," his response would be, "Which one?"

83. CLIFF HAGAN

Resume: 13 years, 7 quality, 6 All-Stars (1 ABA) . . . top 10 ('58, '59) . . . 4-year peak: 23–10–4 . . . 2nd-best player on 1 champ ('58 Hawks) and 2 runner-ups ('60, '61) . . . '58 Playoffs: 28–11, 50% FG (11 G) . . . 5-year Playoffs peak: 23–10–3

A valuable playoff piece for St. Louis during their underrated playoff peak (one title, four Finals appearances). If you played for ten years in the fifties and sixties, peaked for five, and starred for a champion and a couple of runner-ups, that was a *really* good career during the *Mad Men* era, when everyone traveled coach, shared hotel rooms with roommates, smoked butts and drank coffee, got plastered after games, didn't work out, didn't eat right, didn't take care of their bodies and banged bodies like they were playing rugby. One positive for the Hagan Experience: If the *Best Damn Sports Show Period*[34] ever did a countdown of the top fifty racists in sports history, Hagan's Hawks teams would have ranked up there with Jimmy

34. This is a Fox Sports cable show helmed by Chris Rose, a likable talent saddled with a worse supporting cast than Moses with the '81 Rockets. Usually they give up and just start counting shit down. Wise move.

the Greek, Al Campanis, Dixie Walker, Tom Yawkey and everyone else.[35] In an extended section about Lenny Wilkens in *Breaks of the Game,* it's revealed that Hagan was the only Hawks teammate who reached out to Wilkens and treated him like an equal. As Chris Russo would say, "That's a good job by you, Cliff!" Twyman and Hagan were definitely the starting forwards for the twentieth-anniversary White Guys You Would Have Wanted on Your Team if You Were Black team in 1966.

82. CHRIS MULLIN

Resume: 16 years, 8 quality, 5 All-Stars . . . top 5 ('92), top 10 ('89, '91), top 15 ('90) . . . 4-year peak: 26–5–4 (52% FG, 88% FT) . . . 2-year Playoffs peak: 27–7–4, 54% FG (16 G) . . . league leader: minutes (2x), 3FG% (1x) . . . member of '92 Dream Team

After throwing away his first three NBA years because of a drinking/ weight problem, a postrehab Mullin shaved his hair into a military flattop, got himself into sick shape and embarked on a rollicking five-year peak before a variety of injuries sidetracked him. Even though he crested a little late, few modern players were more entertaining or intelligent on the offensive end; he was like a left-handed, miniature version of Larry Bird, only with worse hair, paler skin and an accent that made him sound like a cross between Boston Rob and Mike Francesa. You couldn't hide him defensively, but at least he wreaked havoc from the blind side and jumped passing lanes like Bird, averaging 2-plus steals three different times. He's also on the all-time team of Modern Guys Who Seemed Like They Were the Most Fun to Play a Game of Basketball With (along with Bird, Magic, Nash, Walton, Duncan, Kidd, Pippen, Stockton, Horry, Bobby Jones and C-Webb).[36] According to Cameron Stauth's underrated *Golden Boys,* after

35. The famous racist Hawks story: Southerners Pettit and Clyde Lovellette froze out college legend Cleo Hill so blatantly that coach Paul Seymour got fired for standing up to them. Hill was eventually blackballed from the league. See *Black Magic* for the details.
36. Underrated playoff game: Magic and Mullin "guarding" each other in Game 2 of their '91 series, with Magic dropping 44 and Mullin getting 40 as both teams said, "Screw it, they'll cancel each other out." G-State prevailed, 125–124, in the last great moment of the TMC era.

Chuck Daly was selected to coach the Dream Team, his wish list for a roster looked like this (in order): Jordan, Magic, Robinson, Ewing, Pippen, Malone, Mullin. So the NBA's top coach at the time ranked Mullin behind Jordan and Pippen as the third-best perimeter player during the deepest run of talent in NBA history. The selection committee eventually sent out eight initial invites: Bird/Magic/MJ (locks to launch the team as a threesome), Pippen, Robinson, Malone, Ewing and Barkley. Mullin received the ninth invite. John Stockton was tenth. (Drexler and Christian Laettner[37] weren't added until the following spring.) Here's the point: Chris Mullin was *really* freaking good.

81. DAVE BING

Resume: 12 years, 8 quality, 7 All-Stars . . . '67 Rookie of the Year . . . top 5 ('68, '71), top 10 ('74) . . . 4-year peak: 25–5–6 . . . leader: scoring (1x) . . . never won a Playoff series

Bing rode the ABA/expansion statistical surge and put up impressive numbers during his offensive peak ('67 to '73), when he played with the likes of Dave DeBusschere and Bob Lanier and only made the playoffs once. Following his eighth season (19.0 PPG, 7.7 APG in '75), Detroit traded him to Washington along with a future first-rounder for Kevin Porter. Kevin Porter? How good a player could Bing have been? And how could he possibly make the NBA's 50 at 50 in 1996 over nos. 53, 57, 58, 63, 64, and 65 on this list? Because he was a good guy.[38] Call it the Bob Lanier Corollary: if someone is loved and respected *as a person* by fellow players and media members, his actual talents rarely match the way he's evaluated. Bing's two first-team All-NBAs help his historical cause more than anything, but both were dubious: in '68, Bing slipped in because Jerry West missed 31 games;

37. *Golden Boys* is worth a read if only for the no-holds-barred "Is this dude gay or what?" section on Laettner, which almost seems brazen now. I don't think Laettner was gay; he just went to Duke.
38. Bing took care of himself, dealt wonderfully with the media, did a ton of charity work, became one of the country's leading black businessmen, founded the NBA Retired Players Association and was named Detroit's Humanitarian of the Year in 1985.

in '71, Bing made it over Walt Frazier, who only tossed up a 21–7–7 on a 52-win Knicks team and doubled as the league's best defensive guard. Given a choice between Bing in his absolute prime (playing on a fifth-seeded team in the West), versus Clyde in his absolute prime (playing on a number one seed in the East) . . . the voters chose Bing. Absurd. Was Bing even better than Sweet Lou Hudson? They both peaked from '67 to '76 and finished with similar career numbers (a 20–4–3 with 49% FG for Hudson, a 20–4–6 with 44% FG for Bing), but Hudson played for seven straight teams that made the playoffs ('67–'73) and Bing made the playoffs once in that stretch. Who was more effective? I couldn't tell you because I wasn't there. I just know that Bing shouldn't have made the top fifty.[39]

80. BOBBY DANDRIDGE

Resume: 13 years, 9 quality, 4 All-Stars . . . top 10 ('79) . . . 5-year peak: 20–7–3 . . . 2-year Playoffs peak: 22–7–5 (38 G) . . . starter on 1 champ ('78 Bullets) and 2 runner-ups ('74 Bucks, '79 Bullets), 3rd-best player on 1 champ ('71 Bucks) . . . career Playoffs: 21–8–4 (98 G)

Dandridge remains my favorite "lost great" from the seventies, a small forward who played bigger than his size, lacked any holes and drew the following compliment from *SI*'s Curry Kirkpatrick in 1979: "All Dandridge is—a fact known to his peers for a couple of years now—is the best all-round player at his position." You could call Bobby D. a cross between Caron Butler and Big Shot Brob, someone who did all the little things, drifted between three positions, defended every type of forward (famously outdueling Julius Erving in the '78 Playoffs) and routinely drained monster shots (like the game-winner against a triple-team in Game 7 of the '79 Spurs series, which happened after he had been switched to a scalding-hot George Gervin and shut Ice down for the final

---

39. Bing battled eyesight problems and eventually went legally blind in one eye. Spike Lee claims in his NBA memoir that Bing measured jump shots not by looking at the basket but by glancing down at his position on the court because he couldn't see the rim. Seems more far-fetched than the ending of *He Got Game*.

few minutes). Unquestionably, he was the fourth-best small forward of the seventies behind Erving, Rick Barry and John Havlicek, as well as one of the signature greats from an all-black college who made it big in the pros.[40] The late Ralph Wiley wrote that while Hayes and Unseld were widely remembered for winning Washington the '78 title, "it was the sweet j of Sweet Bobby D. *true* aficionados recall," calling him a "grizzled, bearded, incommunicado jazz soloist" and adding that Bobby D.'s "sweet j ranks with Sam Jones, Dave Bing, Lou Hudson, Jerry West and Joe Dumars." I'm guessing that Ralph would have had Bobby D. in his top seventy-five.

79. PAUL WESTPHAL

Resume: 12 years, 5 quality, 5 All-Stars . . . top 5 ('77, '78, '80), top 10 ('79) . . . 5-year peak: 23–3–6, 52% FG . . . best player on 1 runner-up ('76 Suns), averaged 21–5–3, 51% FG (19 G)

Red Auerbach was the most successful NBA GM ever, so take the following with a grain of salt because it's impossible to nail *every* major roster decision. (Or in Billy King's case, any of them.) But Red gave away at least one title with two boneheaded decisions: swapping Westphal for Charlie Scott before the '76 season and replacing Paul Silas with anti-Celtics Sidney Wicks and Curtis Rowe before the '77 season. Both were financially motivated moves by a stubborn guy who couldn't accept where the league was headed yet. Had Red kept Silas and Westie, Boston could have won in '77 and possibly '78. But here's why Red was the luckiest bastard ever (and I mean that as a compliment): As the '77–'78 team was self-combusting in Havlicek's final season, Auerbach swapped Scott for Kermit Washington, Don Chaney and a number one pick. A few months later, Boston had the number six and number eight picks in the '78 draft. With their own pick

40. Bobby played at Norfolk State with Pee Wee Kirkland, Hooker Grant and Mad Dog Culpepper. Have there ever been three greater nicknames on the same team? What chain of events needs to happen for someone to earn the nickname "Hooker" again? And how can I help?

(number six), they rolled the dice on a junior-eligible named Larry Bird. With KC's number eight pick, they took a prolific scorer named Freeman Williams to replace Havlicek.[41] Without that extra pick, would Red have "wasted" the number six pick on someone who couldn't play in Boston for a year? *Getting the number eight pick in the Scott trade allowed him to use the number six pick on Bird.* Like always with Red from 1950 to 1986, even when something like the Westphal/Scott trade didn't work out, eventually it worked out.[42]

Westphal would have been just another forgotten great player if not for a heroic performance in the triple-OT game—a game that lives on forever on ESPN Classic and NBA TV—when he single-handedly saved the Suns more than once with a superhuman performance (crazy steals, ludicrous reverses for three-point plays and his trademark 360 banker, when he drove left at breakneck speed, planted about 8 feet from the basket, then did a 360-degree twirl and banked it home as his incredulous defender was twisted in nine different directions). If Havlicek had missed that running banker in the second OT, Phoenix could have clinched the title at home and Westphal could have joined the hallowed list of Best Guys on a Championship Team (and jumped thirty spots on this list). Instead, he's remembered as the league's best guard for five years ('76 to '80), as well as a memorably entertaining All-Star Game performer and the starting two-guard on the White Guys Who Played Like Black Guys team (don't worry, we're getting there).

41. Owner Irv Levin swapped franchises with John Y. Brown that summer, sending Washington, Wicks, Kevin Kunnert, and Williams's rights for Marvin Barnes, Billy Knight, Tiny Archibald and two second-round picks without telling Red, a colossally one-sided deal that, as always, somehow worked out for Red: Williams was a bust, Archibald revived his career, one second-rounder became Danny Ainge, and Red dealt Knight for Rick Robey, who eventually netted Dennis Johnson. So in a roundabout way, the awful Westphal trade was responsible for Bird, Ainge, Tiny and DJ becoming Celtics.

42. If Boston passed on Bird, Portland was picking next, then the Lakers. Let's say Portland passed on Bird because they wanted immediate help given Walton's uncertain injury status. Had the Lakers taken Bird and waited for him—a good possibility with Jerry West in charge—they would have landed Magic a year later and had Bird, Magic *and* Kareem. *Holy shit.*

78. DWIGHT HOWARD

Resume: 6 years, 5 quality, 4 All-Stars . . . top 5 ('08, '09, '10), top 15 ('07) . . . MVP runner-up ('10) . . . 3-year peak: 20–14, 2.6 blocks, 59% FG . . . '08 + 09 Playoffs: 20–16, 2.9 blocks (33 G) . . . Defensive Player of the Year ('09, '10) . . . All-Defense (3x) . . . leader: rebounds (4x) . . . career RPG: 12.7 (highest since Rodman and Moses) . . . best player on runner-up ('09 Magic)

Our most important under-thirty center right now, our only "Good God, that guy is a freaking specimen!" big man . . . and if T-Mac and Vince were the most polarizing superstars of the last decade, then Howard already has this decade sewn up. You might think I'm picking nits with someone gifted enough to lead the NBA in rebounding/blocks for two straight years[P24] and anchor a 2009 Finals team, but I can't shake stories like this one: at halftime of Game 1 of the 2010 Eastern Finals, ABC ran a pre-taped interview of Dwight Howard (dressed like Clark Kent) interviewing Dwight Howard (dressed like Superman).[P25] This would have been fine except for one thing: Boston was kicking Orlando's ass and stealing home court advantage at the time. Four wins away from a Lakers rematch and you're interviewing yourself as a goofy lark? What?????? If Jordan was consumed by winning, then Howard is consumed by winning people over. He's too nice a guy. It's his fatal flaw as a superstar, the same issue that doomed David Robinson until Tim Duncan fell into his lap. Gentle giants don't win titles. They only bring you close enough to break your heart.

If you ever played basketball, you know there's one rule with big guys: make sure they touch the ball enough. When big guys don't get enough

P24. Howard's rebound totals skew high because he's the only big guy on a smallball team. Orlando's second-leading rebounders in '08, '09 and '10? Hedu Turkoglu, Rashard Lewis and Matt Barnes. Come on. If there are 40–45 available rebounds per game, *Somebody* has to get them, right? It's the same reason Shawn Marion averaged 11.8 RPG in '06 and Gerald Wallace averaged 10.0 RPG in '10.

P25. My least favorite thing about Howard: he blatantly and unapologetically ripped off Shaq's Superman gimmick. When LaDainian Tomlinson hijacked "LT" from Lawrence Taylor, at least those were Tomlinson's inititals, and at least Taylor was retired. Howard stole Shaq's nickname with Shaq still in the league! Even better, Shaq hates him for it. There's a 15.3 percent chance they might have the greatest fight in NBA history.

touches, they get cranky. They stop running the floor. They stop setting good picks. They stop crashing the boards. Big guys are like women—they need affection, they need to be stroked every so often, and if you ignore them, they start resenting you. Except in Dwight Howard's case. See, nobody in Orlando ever has to worry about keeping him happy. He's always happy! *I didn't take a single shot in that quarter? That's okay!* In a roundabout way, his congenial nature allows him to avoid the night-to-night responsibility of carrying Orlando's offense. During the 2009–10 regular season, when so few teams employed a big man who could muscle Howard down low, he averaged just 10.2 field goal attempts (fourth on the team) and 10 free throw attempts per game. Let's put that in perspective:

Ewing, Year 6: 20.3 FGA, 7.7 FTA

Hakeem, Year 6: 19.6 FGA, 6.5 FTA

Shaq, Year 6: 19.1 FGA, 11.4 FTA

Moses, Year 6: 18.9 FGA, 9.5 FTA

Robinson, Year 6: 18.4 FGA, 10.5 FTA

Howard, Year 6: 10.2 FGA, 10.0 FTA

Mutombo, Year 6: 9.0 FGA, 5.4 FTA

So maybe that's our Howard comp: Dikembe Mutombo 2.0. Zeke only wanted to grab rebounds, throw some elbows, challenge shots and wag his finger like a scolding parent after every block. Howard only wants to run around, jump over guys, ram a few dunks home, block a few shots out of bounds, flex his muscles, smile to the crowd and interview himself during halftime shows.[P26] Of course, he will *never* get better this way, and if you look closely at his numbers these past three years (18–19 points, 13–14 rebounds, 3 blocks, 59 percent from the field, 59 percent from the line), it's hard to imagine him getting any better . . . even though he's only twenty-five years old. Alpha dog pedigree, sidekick mind-set. Too bad.

P26. For all his athletic ability, he's not a natural scorer, struggles with foul trouble and might be number one on the Dumbest Possible Foul at the Worst Possible Time leaderboard. Watching him is like watching a great college football lineman dabble in intramural hoops—maybe the tools are there, and maybe he's physically imposing, but he can never quite harness everything. Put Bill Russell's brain in Dwight Howard's body and they'd have to fold the NBA.

77. TRACY MCGRADY

Resume: 13 years, 7 quality, 7 All-Stars . . . top 5 ('02, '03), top 10 ('01, '04, '07), top 15 ('05, '08) . . . 4-year peak: 28–8–5 . . . leader: scoring (2x) . . . '03 season: 33–7–6 . . . Playoffs: 29–7–6, 43% FG (38 G) . . . never won a Playoff series

A resume jarringly similar to Pete Maravich's even if McGrady was significantly better defensively. Both were better known by nicknames ("T-Mac" and "Pistol"). Both carried lousy teams for much of their primes. Both were ridiculously gifted offensive players who had unusual weight with their peers, although McGrady was never discussed reverentially like Maravich was and is. Both suffered bad luck at pivotal points of their careers—Pistol not getting Doc as a teammate, T-Mac losing a hobbled Grant Hill for his entire Orlando tenure. Both were traded in their primes, although Houston underpaid for T-Mac and New Orleans overpaid for Maravich. Both were original prototypes: T-Mac was the first six-foot-eight guard with three-point range (an Evolutionary Gervin crossed with a touch of Dr. J); Pistol was simply unlike any guard before or since. And honestly? Both of them were ten to twelve spots too high on this list until the last stages of this book-writing process, when McGrady tarnished his legacy so badly during the 2008–9 season that I had to drop him seven spots. Originally I had projected the rest of his career and assumed he would enjoy two or three more quality seasons, even if the words "never won a Playoffs in his prime" stick out more egregiously than Jaye Davidson's dick in *The Crying Game*.[43] It was hard to imagine anyone ever taking his career *that* seriously if he never played in a second-round game, right? Then he murdered the '09 Rockets so completely and totally that he prompted me to craft this one-paragraph drive-by shooting in a February column about the collapsing NBA economy (and I stand by the venom):

43. Through 2008, T-Mac ranked fourth in career playoff scoring, at 28.5. Not as good as it sounds. His career playoff record: 16–27.

Nobody loves basketball more than me. I mean, *nobody*. But when an NBA player with two years remaining on his contract for a total of $44 million shows up for the season out of shape, complains most of the year, lets down his teammates and fans again and again, lands in some trade rumors and decides, "Instead of getting traded to a team I don't like, I'm going to announce that I'm getting microfracture surgery four days before the trade deadline and kill any potential trade, and even better, I'll be healed by next spring, just in time to showcase myself for another contract," and successfully pulls this off—with no repercussions from anybody—then yes, the system is broken and needs to be fixed. Because that was disgusting. Tracy McGrady, you are officially indefensible for the rest of eternity. Even your cousin Vince wouldn't have done that. And that's saying something.[P27]

76. DAN ISSEL

Resume: 15 years, 13 quality, 7 All-Stars (6 ABA) . . . top 5 ABA ('72), top 10 ABA ('71, '73, '74, '75, '76) . . . 3-year peak: 29–11–2 . . . ABA leader: scoring (1x) . . . ABA Playoffs: 24–11–2 (80 G) . . . 2nd-best player on ABA champ ('75 Colonels) . . . 25K-10K Club (25K-plus points, 10K-plus rebounds)

75. ARTIS GILMORE

Resume: 17 years, 12 quality, 11 All-Stars (5 ABA) . . . '72 ABA MVP and Playoffs MVP . . . '72 ABA Rookie of the Year . . . top 5 ABA ('72, '73, '74, '75, '76) . . . 5-year peak: 22–17–3 (ABA) . . . season leader: rebounds

P27. I dropped him from no. 75 (hardcover) to no. 77 (paperback) after T-Mac returned from knee surgery in November 2009 and demanded starter's minutes, then sulked when the '10 Rockets brought him off the bench. Houston sent him away until it could trade his expiring deal . . . which took three solid months. They paid him to go away. Maybe my NBA Hall of Fame should have an I Hate You for Underachieving, You Fucking Blew It wing.

(4x), FG% (6x), mins (3x), blocks (2x) . . . all-time NBA/ABA leader, FG% . . . best player on one ABA champ ('75 Colonels) . . . 20K–15K Club

I couldn't put Issel ahead of Artis for one reason: After Kentucky won the '75 ABA title, the Colonels needed to trade a big guy (Gilmore or Issel) to save money. Which one did they keep? Gilmore. So that settles that. Issel thrived for six ABA seasons but only made one NBA All-Star team after the merger. That's a little telling. Still, there's something to be said for a perimeter center who never missed games and gave his teams somewhere between a 19–8 and a 25–11 every night, averaging 29.9 points as a rookie in '71 and 19.8 as a fourteen-year veteran in '84. You can't blame Issel for a lack of NBA playoff success because the '78 Nuggets came within two games of the Finals (losing to Seattle), then fell apart because of David Thompson's drug problem and one of the single dumbest trades in NBA history: Bobby Jones straight up for George McGinnis.[44] On a personal note, Issel was one of my favorite visiting players because he was missing his front four teeth—every time he walked by us in the Garden tunnel, he looked like a vampire. These are the things that delight you when you're eight.

Meanwhile, Artis would have started at center for the Looks Better on Paper All-Stars if not for Bellamy. I'm barely old enough to remember Artis in his NBA prime, when he was a mountain of a man (seven foot two, 300 pounds) with a mustache/goatee combo that made him look like a half-Chinese, half-black count.[45] He looked intimidating until the game started and you realized that (a) his reactions were a split second slow (eventually earning him the nickname "Rigor Artis"), (b) he only took shots he could make (dunks, layups, and a lefty jump hook), and (c) it was unclear if he had a pulse (Artis made Kareem look like Kevin Garnett after

44. That type of trade happened routinely in the '70s and '80s: a team stupidly deciding, "Hey, let's trade our best all-around player and the heart of our team for an overrated star who's a bigger name and might be able to sell more tickets." Now teams just wait until the overrated star becomes a free agent, then they overpay him and kill their cap space. This counts as progress in the NBA.

45. Fun Artis fact: after Kentucky signed him, they measured him for reporters at the press conference. Artis was seven-foot-eight when they included his mammoth afro. Seven-foot-eight!

twenty Red Bulls). Artis grew up so poor in Florida that he wore sneakers two sizes too small in high school, so there was always something beaten-down about him, like his confidence didn't match his physique. Fans believed he should dominate more than he did and tougher players pounded him with no repercussions.[46] Without any big rivals who could handle him in a quicker ABA, Artis dominated just like the token tall guy dominates an intramural game in college. He never enjoyed the same success in the NBA, but there are worse things than a center giving you a 20–12 every night, clogging the paint, shooting 60 percent and looking like he's about to film a *Dracula* movie. If that's not enough, he appeared in the opening credit sequence of *The White Shadow*. Top that, Issel.

74. JOE DUMARS

Resume: 14 years, 7 quality, 6 All-Stars . . . '89 Finals MVP . . . top 10 ('93), top 15 ('90, '91) . . . All-Defense (5x) . . . 4-year peak: 21–2–5 . . . 2nd-best player on two champs ('89, '90 Pistons)

73. SIDNEY MONCRIEF

Resume: 11 years, 5 quality, 5 All-Stars . . . top 5 ('83), top 10 ('82, '84, '85, '86) . . . All-Defense (5x) . . . Defensive Player of the Year ('83, '84) . . . 4-year peak: 21–6–5, 51% FG, 83% FT . . . 3-year Playoffs peak: 21–6–5 (33 G)

Here's why we need a new Hall of Fame, Part XXXVII: The real Hall inducted Joe D. in 2006 even though Westphal, Moncrief and Dennis Johnson hadn't made it yet. Why Dumars and not the others? Because of the Lanier Corollary: Dumars was the one decent soul on those bad-boy squads, a splendid team player who lifted his game when it mattered, a

---

46. Artis snapped at Maurice Lucas once and chased him across the court, cornered him, then got decked by a roundhouse right. The punch put Lucas on the map and reinforced the whole "Artis is a big pussy" argument.

gifted defender who handled MJ better than anyone except John Starks. When the Association struggled with character issues in the mid-nineties, Joe D stood out for his class and professionalism. Watching him coexist with the crotch-grabbing jerks on Dream Team II was like seeing Nic Cage stuck traveling on the *Con Air* plane. (There was a famous story about two of the Dream Team IIers—definitely Shaq and someone else, I can't remember the second guy—pulling the players together before a key game and Dumars thinking, "Great, they're finally going to take this seriously." Then the two guys started singing a rap song they had written for the game. Poor Dumars.) And after his career, Dumars remained in the limelight by building Detroit's '04 championship team, remaining classy and manipulating the media as well as anyone except Donnie Walsh.[47] But Dumars was never a franchise player or a transcendent one (again: left off the Dream Team), and that '89 Finals MVP happened after a four-game sweep against an aging Lakers team that lost Magic and Byron Scott midway through the series. During certain pivotal playoff games (Game 5 of the 1990 Finals, for instance), Dumars sat for Vinnie Johnson in crunch time. When the Pistons aged so quickly after the '92 playoffs, Dumars became the alpha dog on teams that won 40, 20 and 28 games. There's no possible way, under any criteria, that anyone can prove Dumars was superior to Moncrief or Dennis Johnson. In my opinion, he was the worst of the three. But the other two have been rejected by the Hall. Repeatedly. Which is why we need to blow that baby up.[48]

Meanwhile, Moncrief was one of the defining what-if guys. If not for chronic knee problems that eventually derailed his career, Moncrief would have been the best all-around guard of the eighties and one of the top forty-five Pyramid guys. Before the days of arthroscopic surgery and ligaments that could be transferred from corpses, you were never the same after an ACL tear and that was that. In Moncrief's case, he jumped

47. Walsh's close friends include Peter Vecsey and Dan Klores (the latter a documentary filmmaker and formerly powerful PR guy in New York). There's a reason you've never read a negative Donnie Walsh piece.

48. Now you're asking, "Why put Dumars at no. 75, then?" Because he was a winner, he was clutch, and he would have been fun to play with. By the way, the Pistons took him 18th in the '85 draft, one spot ahead of Boston. The Celts were one Detroit brain fart, one coke binge and one heart malfunction away from getting Dumars, Lenny Bias and Reggie Lewis in consecutive drafts and dominating the '90s. Alas.

out of the building to the point that he gave us my beloved *Sports Illustrated* cover (the tomahawk dunk from Arkansas), but by the time the '87 playoffs rolled around, he was limping around on one leg like a war veteran. Too bad.[49] A healthy Moncrief would have been a more polished, less combustible version of Dennis Johnson. And that's saying something. Instead, he'll have to settle for no. 74, as well as being the second-greatest Sidney of all time—just behind Sidney Crosby and just ahead of Sydney the whore from *Melrose Place,* Sidney Rice and Sidney the lawyer from *Midnight Run. Sidney, siddown, relax, have a cream soda, do some fuckin' thing.*

72. CHRIS WEBBER

Resume: 14 years, 6 quality, 5 All-Stars . . . '94 Rookie of the Year . . . top 5 ('01), top 10 ('99, '02, '03) . . . 3-year peak: 25–11–5 . . . leader: rebounds (1x) . . . '02 playoffs: 24–11–5 (16 G) . . . played 70 or fewer games in 9 seasons, missed 294 games total

Of all the great talents who never fulfilled their promise, Webber was the only NBA player without a legitimate excuse. On paper, he had everything you'd ever want from a power forward: superior athletic ability, great footwork on the block, soft hands, the rebounding gene, even the passing gene. His background couldn't derail him because Webber hailed from a middle-class, two-parent family, attended a respected Detroit prep school, and learned quickly how to juggle a Jonas Brothers–like public persona with a much more urban private persona. He shone in the biggest spotlight possible at Michigan and helped create the iconic "Fab Five," who became genuine trendsetters with their chest thumping, yelping, baggy shorts and everything else. Everything that happened during his first twenty years seemed to be shaping an influential and successful professional career, a sure thing along the lines of Shaq, Ewing and Robinson.

---

49. Tim Hardaway was the first perimeter guy who blew out his knee and came back relatively the same. Nobody before him ever fully recovered. The seven most tragic examples: Billy Cunningham, Marques Johnson, Bernard King, Maravich, Gus Johnson, Moncrief and Elgin Baylor.

So what happened? You wouldn't say C-Webb had an atrocious career or anything. He made five All-Star teams, an All-NBA first team and three All-NBA second teams. He won Rookie of the Year and a rebounding title. Starring for a series of memorably entertaining Sacramento teams from 1999 to 2003, he was the league's second-best power forward and submitted a three-year peak of 25–11–5. He also earned a staggering amount of money; the Warriors, Bullets, Kings and Sixers paid him more than $185 million combined, more money than anyone other than Jordan, Shaq or Kevin Garnett. But like with Billy Corgan and Michael Keaton,[50] we'll always wonder why his career didn't turn out differently. During his prime (1994 to 2004), he played 70 games or fewer in nine different seasons, missed 283 of a possible 850 games and battled a never-ending assortment of injuries, culminating with a knee tear in Sacramento that robbed him of his explosiveness and forced him to change his style on the fly (although he remained relatively effective). Webber left us with two mildly fascinating what-ifs beyond the obvious "What if he stayed healthy?" question. We already covered "What if Orlando had just kept his rights?" Here's a smaller-scale one: "What if the Warriors hadn't stupidly given C-Webb a massive contract with an opt-out clause after one year?"

Webber entered the Association just when it stupidly started giving youngsters too much negotiating power (the era when inmates were running the asylum), a few years before the powers that be smartened up and pushed for a rookie salary scale. Although many promising careers were affected—including those of Kenny Anderson, Coleman, Vinnie Baker, Larry Johnson, Glenn Robinson, Juwan Howard, Rasheed Wallace, Jason Kidd, Marcus Camby, Antoine Walker, Stephon Marbury and Tim Thomas—Webber remains the biggest and most disappointing casualty. Armed with that opt-out clause, he wanted no part of Don Nelson's abrasive style[51] even though there's never been a better big man for Nellieball.

50. Remember, Keaton had a slight lead over Tom Hanks heading into their second decade of the Funny/Cool/Hip Guy Who Can Also Get Serious competition; then poor Keaton fell off the face of the earth and Hanks started winning Oscars. Now Hanks looks at him like Mariah Carey looks at Whitney Houston: "Yeah, maybe you won the first battle, but I won the war. Handily. *Now go do some more crack, bitch!*"
51. Poor Nellie learned a valuable lesson: you can't ride rookies when they're making ten times as much money as the coach.

When Webber threatened to opt out of his contract and sign somewhere else, the Warriors panic-traded him for Tom Gugliotta and three number ones. Webber found himself carrying a way-too-young Bullets team, developed bad habits and a lousy attitude, injured his knee, missed 116 games in four years and got shipped to Sacramento in a "don't let the door hit you on the way out" deal for Mitch Richmond and Otis Thorpe.[52] When he finally found another freewheeling offensive team, he was twenty-six years old. What a shame.

Much of his career came down to bad timing: seven years earlier or seven years later, a conventional rookie contract would have trapped him on the Warriors (where he belonged all along). His Kings teams had the misfortune of peaking during the apex of Shaq, Duncan and KG, respectively, suffering crushing Game 7 defeats in '02, '03 and '04, and if there's a complaint against Webber, it's this one: he wanted no part of the ball in big moments. Here's what I wrote about Webber after Sacramento's meltdown against the '02 Lakers, when every King except for Mike Bibby looked more terrified than the camp counselors at Crystal Lake:

> Webber officially grabbed the torch from Karl Malone, Patrick Ewing, Ralph Sampson and Elvin Hayes as "The High-Priced Superstar Who's Great to Have on Your Team Unless There's Three Minutes Left in a Big Game." None of this was really a surprise, but watching C-Webb figure out ways to eradicate himself from crunch-time possessions was the most intriguing subplot of the playoffs. Didn't it crack you up when Webber would receive a high-post pass, spin 180 degrees so his back could face the basket—*Don't worry, I'm not shooting, have no fear!*—then desperately look to shuffle the basketball to the nearest available King? Has anyone even played Hot Potato to that degree?

So how will we remember Webber? Ever since Calvin Schiraldi and Bob Stanley self-destructed in Game 6 of the '86 World Series, I've been a big believer that microcosms mean more than you think in sports. Yeah, the Red

---

52. I went to one Bullets-Celtics game where we seriously wondered if C-Webb was stoned during the game. I was with a buddy who was smoking a ton of pot at the time and he felt the same way; you tend to notice when other people seem high. It's like being in your own personal ESP Club.

Sox might have been one more out and fourteen different pitches away from winning the title—hold on, I'm gonna slam my head against the desk for old times' sake (owwwwwwwww!)—but Boston's cruddy relievers tortured Sox fans all season. Losing the title because the bullpen collapsed wasn't exactly a shock to any Red Sox fan. And when you examine what happened in the 2002 Western Finals with a superior Kings team playing the increasingly dysfunctional Lakers, you see that the series hinged on three games: Game 4 (when Horry made a game-winning three-pointer because nobody on the Kings grabbed the initial two rebounds), Game 6 (the worst and most unfairly officiated game of this decade), and Game 7 (when the Kings had multiple chances to close the game and couldn't get it done). Webber couldn't have done anything about Game 6 short of killing Dick Bavetta with his bare hands, but he didn't exactly dominate those last two games. Presented with a chance to define his career once and for all, he couldn't get it done. It just wasn't in him. Did he lose his confidence in big games after the infamous "time-out" game in college? Did his unhappy Bullets tenure prevent him from developing the necessary crunch-time chops until it was too late? Did he lack killer instinct in the first place? We'll never know.

If Webber's career were a video game, I'd love to press the reset button, start over with Orlando never making that risky trade and see what happens. But that's the thing about real life: you don't have a reset button, and if you make a couple of poor decisions along the way, those decisions sometimes end up shaping the player or person you become. We will remember Webber as one of the best seventy-five NBA players ever, but we'll also remember the potential for so much more.[53] In an interesting twist, Webber retired and quickly emerged as a special talent for TNT and NBA TV: candid, handsome, eloquent, passionate, funny, capable of sounding "blacker" or "whiter" depending on his supporting cast. I remember watching one of his first appearances after he signed with TNT in 2008 and thinking, "Holy crap, C-Webb could be a fantastic TV guy!" And I was

---

53. Considering Webber earned nearly $200 million, can you call him disappointing? He ended up being no. 72 instead of no. 28 . . . is that the worst thing in the world? I think it comes down to one issue: You know when you go to a car wash and they offer you the "everything" package? Only a few NBA players are chosen every generation for the "everything" package. If they fuck it up even a little, it's disappointing. So yeah, Webber finished no. 72. But he still goes to sleep every night knowing he could have been forty or fifty spots higher. And if he doesn't think about it, then that explains everything.

right. Although it was fitting that, right after Chris Webber retired, people were still wondering about his potential.

71. LENNY WILKENS

Resume: 15 years, 9 quality, 9 All-Stars . . . '68 MVP runner-up . . . leader: assists (1x) . . . 4-year peak: 21–5–9 . . . Playoffs: 16–6–6

We can only place so much stock in All-NBA teams; after all, Latrell "Future Coach Choker" Sprewell goes down in history as one of the five best players in 1994. But how could Wilkens finish second in the '68 MVP voting without making first- or second-team All-NBA that same season? Isn't that impossible? I caught a few of Lenny's games on tape (mostly All-Star contests back when everyone tried) and thought he had a fine command of those games, but they also illuminated why he's the only NBA 50 at 50 member who failed to make an All-NBA team, or why he missed the playoffs for each of his last seven seasons. Wilkens was very good and not great. The statistics and win totals back that up, and that's before we tackle how the ABA/expansion dynamic skewed everyone's stats from 1969 to 1976. Check out Lenny's career arc and remember that he turned thirty right before the '67–'68 season:

Wilkens ('66–'68): 18–5–7, 43%
Wilkens ('69–'73): 20–5–9, 44%

So wait . . . from age thirty-one to age thirty-five, Lenny got slightly *better*? I doubt it. If Lenny was a B-plus for eight years, he jumped to an A-minus in a depleted/diluted league. Which is fine. But he shouldn't have made 50 at 50 over Dennis Johnson, a better all-around player who achieved more success in a tougher era. If you're giving him credit, congratulate Wilkens for being the last effective player-coach; he pulled double duty for the Sonics in his prime and led their '72 team to 47 wins as their second-best player. Which leads us to a tangent: why hasn't a team tried a player-coach since Dave Cowens did double duty on the '79 Celtics? I believe it could work for four reasons. First, real coaches get fired all the time, relentlessly, over and over again. So we're doing *something* wrong. (Hire an NBA coach and there's an overwhelming chance he'll be gone within three years.[54] Just a few stand out every season: usually Gregg Popovich, Jerry Sloan and two other guys. Eighty percent of the coaching fraternity always seems interchangeable, ranging from half decent to "I wouldn't hire that guy to manage a McDonald's.") Second, Russell won two titles as a player-coach so it can't be that hard. (Sure, the game is more technical now and you have to break down game film and scouting reports. But couldn't quality assistants handle 90 percent of that? It's not football; only five guys play, game plans are fairly simple, and common sense usually prevails. Look at Phil Jackson: he's been more spiritual adviser/caretaker/relationship therapist than X's-and-O's teacher and the dude has eleven rings. The best NBA coaches don't overthink things, which is perfect for a player-coach since you don't have time to over-think.) Third, coaches usually get fired because they "stop reaching their players" or because "the team needs a spark." Would a player ever tune out one of his best teammates, someone who leads by example on the floor each night? It's the foundation of all teams: two or three players rising as alpha dogs, everyone else falling in line. Who knows the strengths and weaknesses of players better than someone playing with them? It's no different from George Clooney directing a movie, right? And even though the CBA prohibits teams from paying a player for a nonplaying job, a team could convince a player to coach for free and make the "real" head coach his lead assistant.

The fourth and last reason is simpler: what better way for a moribund franchise to get their fans talking? No random coaching move would get a run-of-the-mill team more publicity and attention short of hiring Whoopi Goldberg or reuniting Spree and PJ. Besides, is it really dangerous to experiment with a job that already carries an 80–85 percent rate of failure? Of all the kooky NBA nuances that long ago disappeared—players smoking at halftime, players on the floor when they're coked up, players

---

54. My funniest example: Orlando fired Brian Hill in 1997. Vancouver hired him and he led them to a sizzling 31–123 record before getting fired in 2000. Five years later, you know who hired him again? Orlando! The NBA coaching situation is so abysmal, teams rehire guys they already fired. Does that happen in any other walk of life? That's like CBS announcing in 2013 that they've decided to give Craig Kilborn his own late night show.

inexplicably punching each other in the face—the player-coach is the one that should have endured. As soon as some billionaire reader buys me an NBA team to run, I'm bringing it back.[55]

70. DAVID THOMPSON

Resume: 9 years, 5 quality, 4 All-Stars (1 ABA) . . . top 10 ABA ('75), top 5 NBA ('76, '77) . . . 2 All-Star MVPs . . . 3-year peak: 26–5–4 . . . best player on ABA runner-up ('76 Nuggets), averaged a 26–6–3 (11 G)

Lacks a conventional resume but aces the "Did he connect with fans on a spiritual level?" and "I've never seen anyone in my life like this guy!" tests. I remember attending a postmerger Nuggets-Celtics game and being so blown away by Thompson that my father's innocuous comment, "Too bad we only get to see him once a year," left me profoundly disappointed. Since we didn't have *SportsCenter* or DirecTV back then, for all I knew, Thompson was dunking on everyone's head ten times per game and I was missing it.

We'll remember Thompson as the Intellivision to Jordan's PlayStation 2, an original prototype for every high-flying two-guard who followed. Blessed with a lightning first step, a reliable jump shot, and a 44-inch vertical leap that had him handling jump balls for North Carolina State (not strange until you remember that seven-foot-four behemoth Tom Burleson played for them), Thompson had everything you'd want in your shooting guard except height. Listed at six foot four, Thompson was closer to six foot two and looks noticeably shorter than his contemporaries on tape.

---

55. I love this fourth argument. It's the same reason why Milwaukee should have hired me as its GM in 2008, or why the Clips should have done the same in 2009. Why the hell not? You're going nowhere anyway! Why not make the fans feel like they have a man of the people in charge? Why not get people talking? What's more likely to lead *PTI* for a week in May: "Bucks Hire John Hammond as GM" or "Bucks Hire ESPN Columnist as GM"? Wouldn't that become one of the biggest sports stories of the year? Now that's a hiring that definitely passes the Mom Test.[P28]

P28. Hammond was named 2009-10 Executive of the Year for building Milwaukee's entertaining "Fear the Deer" team. Did better than I ever could have. Although my theory wasn't wrong: one summer later, I campaigned for Timberwolves GM but they gave it to David Kahn, who's been the Bizarro Hammond and made so many mistakes that he was briefly blamed for the BP oil spill.

Didn't matter. The dude soared through the air like a Bud Light daredevil bouncing off a trampoline.[56] What really separated him was his zero-to-sixty explosiveness in traffic. Surrounded by four or five taller players, time and time again Thompson took your breath away by springing four feet to block a shot or dunk on someone's head. He didn't need a running start and didn't need to bend his knees. Honestly, it was like watching a squirrel, or a lousy sports movie with bad special effects where the lead character gets magic sneakers or something. You don't earn the nickname "Sky-walker" unless there's a *really* good reason. I just wish someone had told this to Kenny Walker.

The defining Thompson story: During the same afternoon as Havlicek's final game, Thompson was battling Gervin for the 1978 scoring title.[57] Back then, the Boston Garden's PA announcer rattled off NBA scores during time-outs (remember, we didn't have T-shirt cannons and JumboTrons back then), so after giving the Nuggets-Pistons halftime score, he added, "David Thompson has 53 points," and everyone gasped in disbelief. I remember thinking, "He's gonna break 100! He's gonna beat Wilt!" He ended up with 73 points, but the fact remains, Thompson was so explosive that an eight-year-old NBA fan honestly believed he *could* score 100-plus points in a game.[58] So what happened to him? He developed a monster coke problem like so many other rich celebs in the late seventies, battled a variety of injuries and eventually blew out his knee after falling down a Studio 54 stairwell.[59] When Jordan arrived in November 1984,

56. Growing up in Carolina, Thompson shot hoops on a dirt surface in his backyard. Some wonder if this led to his freakish jumping ability, especially since MJ grew up playing on a dirt court. If my son shows any promise at all with hoops, I'm building a clay basketball court in my backyard.

57. That was one of the great random sports days: Havlicek's final game, Thompson exploding for 73 (a record for noncenters for 28 years), Gervin responding with 63 and Gary Player coming back from seven strokes to win the '78 Masters. If ESPN Classic had ever started a show called *The Greatest* SportsCenters *We Ever Could Have Had,* April 9, 1978, would rank right up there.

58. Another weird fact about April 9, 1978: Thompson broke Wilt's record for most points in a quarter (32) and held it for five hours until Gervin broke it (33). Also, Thompson made 20 of his first 21 shots in the game. Strangely, everyone agrees that he wasn't forcing shots or gunning for the title. He just had it going.

59. The Studio 54 incident happened in 1984, well after the likes of Andy Warhol and Liza Minnelli had stopped hanging out there. Had Thompson's career ended in '79 because he got flung down a Studio 54 stairwell by Bianca Jagger's boyfriend or something, now *that* would have been cool.

Thompson was already gone. And maybe it's impossible to capture the magnitude of Thompson's premature demise, but screw it, let's try.

David Thompson was . . .

1. The most underrated superstar of the past thirty-five years
2. The single biggest NBA tragedy other than Lenny Bias

Two strong statements, right? Since you bought my book, I feel obligated to back them up. During the first two postmerger seasons ('77 and '78), Thompson averaged a 27–5–4, shot 52 percent and made consecutive first-team All-NBAs during one of the richest talent stretches in league history.[60] How old was Thompson when he finished third in the MVP voting and nearly brought the Nuggets to the 1978 Finals? *Twenty-three.* Check out his numbers from ages twenty-two to twenty-four compared to other famous two-guards for that same age span:

PLAYER	YEAR	AGE	G	PPG	RPG	APG	FG%	FTA[61]	ALL-NBA
Thompson	1977	22	82	25.9	4.1	4.1	50.7	7.6	first team
Thompson	1978	23	80	27.2	4.9	4.5	52.1	8.4	first team
Thompson	1979	24	76	24.0	3.6	3.0	51.2	7.7	none
M. Jordan	1985	22	82	28.2	6.5	5.9	51.5	9.1	second team
M. Jordan	1986	23	18	22.7	3.6	2.9	45.7	6.9	broke foot
M. Jordan	1987	24	80	37.1	5.2	4.6	48.2	10.9	first team
K. Bryant	1999	22	50	19.9	5.3	3.8	46.5	5.6	none
K. Bryant	2000	23	66	22.5	6.3	4.9	46.8	6.1	second team
K. Bryant	2001	24	68	28.5	5.9	5.0	46.4	7.0	first team
A. Iverson	1999	23	48	26.8	4.9	4.6	41.2	7.4	first team
A. Iverson	2000	24	70	28.4	3.8	4.7	42.1	8.9	second team

60. In '77, Thompson bumped fellow ABA stars Doc and Gervin to second-team All-NBA. In '78, he bumped Westphal, Maravich and Walter Davis.

61. I included FT attempts per game because it gives you a good idea for how someone was attacking the rim. Average 8 or more and you're attacking the rim. I love making blanket statements.

PLAYER	YEAR	AGE	G	PPG	RPG	APG	FG%	FTA	ALL-NBA
A. Iverson	2001	25	71	31.1	3.8	4.6	42.0	10.1	first team (MVP)
McGrady	2001	22	77	26.8	7.5	4.6	45.1	7.9	second team
McGrady	2002	23	76	25.6	7.9	5.3	45.1	7.5	first team
McGrady	2003	24	75	32.1	6.5	5.5	45.7	9.6	first team
D. Wade	2004	22	61	16.2	4.0	4.5	46.5	5.2	none
D. Wade	2005	23	77	24.1	5.2	6.8	47.8	9.9	second team
D. Wade	2006	24	75	27.2	5.7	6.7	49.5	10.3	second team

So MJ, Kobe, Iverson,[62] T-Mac and Wade made the leap from twenty-three to twenty-four, but Thompson took a step backward. Why? Two words: nose candy. I can't explain why twenty-four becomes such a pivotal age for athletic shooting guards,[63] but that's the year things apparently fall into place from a physical and mental standpoint, and drugs robbed Thompson of reaching his true potential. Since he couldn't have possibly peaked at age twenty-three—that would defy everything that's ever happened historically—if you include his hypothetical leap year at age twenty-four, here are Thompson's first five seasons with drug-free projections:

YEAR	AGE	G	PPG	RPG	APG	FG%	FTA	ALL-NBA/ABA
1976	21	83	26.0	6.3	3.7	51.5	7.9	second team
1977	22	82	25.9	4.1	4.1	50.7	7.6	first team
1978	23	80	27.2	4.9	4.5	52.1	8.4	first team
1979	24	82	33.4	5.3	4.1	52.7	9.8	first team
1980	25	80	32.8	5.0	4.8	51.5	9.7	first team

62. Iverson peaked at 25 and not 24. I made the executive decision to bump Iverson's age down a year because he spent five months in jail and missed his senior year of high school. You know when a boxer gets described as a "young 35," it's really code for "he spent 8 years in the joint"? Iverson may have been 25 during the '01 season, but it was a "young 25." So there.

63. Spree and Penny made first-team NBAs for the first time at 24; Vince made second-team for the only time at 24. If you're drafting a fantasy team this year, look out for those 24-year-olds!

Based on those numbers, we're talking about a "top-three shooting guards ever" ceiling, which makes it so painful that the wheels came off. Imagine if Jordan had started doing loads of blow after the '87 season, blew out his knee during a Mars Blackmon shoot and was washed up at twenty-eight? That's basically what happened to Thompson. I'm using the word "basically" because it's unclear if Thompson had the same fiery competitive streak as Jordan; it's also unclear if he was victimized by the cocaine era and/or too weak to handle fame and success. So let's figure that out once and for all.

1973. Thompson popularizes the alley-oop and leads the Wolfpack to an undefeated record; they're ineligible to play in the NCAA Tournament.[64]

1974. The Wolfpack outlast Maryland in triple OT to earn the ACC's only NCAA bid (one of the most famous college games ever); shock Bill Walton's UCLA in the semis, with Thompson hitting the game-winner in double overtime (another of the most famous college games ever); and thrash Marquette for the title, with Thompson winning the '74 tourney MVP. That's one of the greatest seasons ever by a college player, right up there with Princeton's Bill Bradley (1965), Houston's Elvin Hayes (1969), Kansas' Danny Manning (1988) and Holy Cross' Steve "Air Hermo" Herman (1990).[65]

---

64. ACC teams were notorious for overpaying players in the '70s. The famous Thompson recruiting story (possibly apocryphal): he grew up in Carolina dreaming of playing for UNC, only NC State offered his family boatloads of cash, leading to Dad saying "Yes!" and a devastated Thompson sobbing through the ensuing press conference.

65. Hermo walked onto the Saders in 1990 like Mark Wahlberg in *Invincible*, only if the ending never happened and Wahlberg had Brian Scalabrine's game and looked like a beefier Kurt Nimphius. (By the way, these are all compliments. I loved Hermo. Anyone who could go from intramurals to Division I without cutting down his keg party appearances was right in my wheelhouse.) His biggest mistake was missing the Internet by 15 years; I would have absolutely started a www.airhermo.com blog and probably gotten kicked out of school. I guarantee he'll bring this book into a New York City bar within 2 weeks of its release and show 75 complete strangers this footnote, followed by everyone doing a series of shots. Please have one on me, Hermo.

1975. Wins every conceivable Player of the Year award but can't carry the depleted Wolfpack past North Carolina for the lone ACC bid. Great story from this season: In one of the dumbest ideas in the history of mankind, dunking was outlawed in many college conferences thanks to the idiotic Lew Alcindor Rule. In Thompson's last home game, he broke the rule with a thunderous second-half dunk, leading to the obligatory technical as well as near euphoria in the stands. By all accounts, this was one of the most randomly exciting moments in sports history. How much did Kareem suck? He even inadvertently caused a no-dunking ban.

1976. Wins ABA Rookie of the Year, gives Doc a worthy challenge in the watershed Dunk Contest, carries Denver to the Finals and makes Denver's franchise enough of an asset that they get picked over Kentucky as one of the four merger teams.

1977. With everyone expecting Doc to take the postmerger NBA by storm, Thompson makes a bigger splash, beating Doc statistically and leading Denver to a league-high 50 wins before falling to Portland (the eventual champs) in the first round.

1978. After 48 wins and Thompson missing his first scoring title by a fraction of a point, Denver becomes the first ABA team to win a playoff series before falling to Seattle in the Conference Finals. That summer, Thompson signs the biggest contract in the history of professional sports: five years, $4 million. A shitload of money in 1978.

(Hold on . . .)
(Cue up the ominous *Behind the Music* music . . .)
And that's when everything turned.
You can guess how the next few years turned out. I failed to find anything from 1973 to 1978 that made me think Thompson was anything other than Jordan before Jordan (a winner with a flair for the moment). He also understood something that Kobe and Jordan didn't know right away: namely, that his team would win more if he sacrificed some of his numbers to make everyone better. In NBA TV's Thompson documentary,

Skywalker, Issel made the following testimonial: "All of his teammates loved him because he helped you win games, and he was the type of player that made everyone on the court better, not a player who subtracted from everyone else on the team to get his stats."[66] The biggest difference between Thompson and Jordan: Thompson's vice (drugs) was infinitely worse for basketball than Jordan's vice (gambling). Had Thompson skipped coke and gambled away millions on golf every summer, we'd be looking at a top-twenty guy historically, someone who would have altered the Western landscape and broken through with shoe commercials, mainstream marketing and everything else. Do Magic's Lakers win five titles with Jordan before Jordan thriving in Denver and Walton's feet holding up in Portland? I'm going out on a limb and saying no. What a shame.

69. DENNIS RODMAN[67]

Resume: 14 years, 10 quality, 2 All-Stars . . . top 15 ('92, '95) . . . leader: rebounds (7 straight times), FG% (1x) . . . All-Defense (8x, six 1st) . . . Defensive Player of the Year ('90, '91) . . . 4-year peak: 7–18–2 . . . 2-year Playoffs peak: 8–14 (32 G) . . . played for 5 champs, started for three ('96, '97, '98 Bulls) . . . career: 13.2 RPG (13th)

Statistically, he's one of the three greatest rebounders ever (along with Russell and Chamberlain) because he grabbed such a significant percentage of his team's boards.[68] As the years pass, nobody will remember that those numbers in San Antonio and Detroit spiked partly because Rodman never

---

66. In that same documentary, Issel blamed the pressure of being the "$800,000 Man" for expediting Thompson's demise: "I think David changed when he got his big contract." This part was only missing a "Push It to the Limit" montage of Thompson taking friends to the bank, marrying someone while wearing a white tuxedo (à la Tony Montana), then bringing the wedding party over to look at a tiger.

67. I had Rodman ranked at no. 69 for two months before realizing the unintentional significance.

68. The '92 Pistons averaged 44.3 rebounds a game; Rodman grabbed 42% of them. Russell's highest percentage for one season was 35%; Wilt's highest was 37%.

strayed from the basket and cared more about rebounding than anything else, even if that meant not helping a teammate who had just been
beaten off the dribble. I'd rather have the Rodman from '87 to '91 (when
he was such a destructive rebounder/defender off the bench) and '96 to
'98 (when he cared about defense again and played Karl Malone so effectively in back-to-back Finals). Still, nobody will remember his considerable
talents since Rodman's legacy centers around abject insanity, colored hairdos, piercings and tattoos, an affair with Madonna, his *Bad as I Wanna Be*
book, the time he kicked a cameraman, the indefensible way he screwed
up the '95 Spurs in the Conference Finals[69] and the fact that he's probably
going to be found dead in a seedy Vegas hotel room within the next
five years. Could the '96 Bulls have won 72 games with Robert Horry instead of Rodman? No way. And doesn't he deserve credit for fitting in so
seamlessly with two pathologically competitive, historically unique teams
(Isiah's bad-boy Pistons and MJ's postbaseball Bulls)? That's why I have
Rodman ranked fifteen spots higher than Horry. Four other notes aug-
ment Rodman's case beyond five rings and jaw-dropping rebounding
numbers.

1. He played for ten conference finalists in three cities, ten 50-win teams
   and five 60-win teams, and he missed the playoffs once in his career (a
   40-win Pistons team in '93). From his rookie season in Detroit
   through his final Bulls season in '98, Rodman's teams finished 574–298
   in the regular season and 118–54 in the playoffs. Wow.[P29]
2. He guarded Larry Bird better than anyone. Nobody else came close.
   Other than Kevin McHale, nobody could defend so many different

69. Rodman acted up throughout the playoffs, got suspended for a game and removed
his sneakers during crunch time in one big moment in the Rockets series. He wasn't
a distraction as much as a dirty bomb. Let's just say that Madonna (his flame at the
time) was a bad influence on him. Also, I think they created four new forms of VD together.
P29. Rodman's regular-season winning percentage was .658. Other notables (not ac-
counting for stray missed games and using '97 L.A. for Horry, '08 Suns for Shaq and '65
Philly for Wilt) courtesy of our friends at ESPN Stats & Info: Magic .717; Bird .709; Russell .705; Duncan .695; Horry .687, Robinson .681; Kareem .681; Shaq .664; Kobe .658;
Jordan .650 (the Wiz stretch killed him); Wilt .644; West .610. That's another exclusive
club for Bird, Magic and Russell: The 700 Club.

types of players effectively: Magic, Bird, Malone, Kemp, Barkley, Worthy, Jordan . . .

3. When the '89 Pistons won their first title, Rodman averaged 24 minutes and 10.0 rebounds in 17 playoff games and doubled as the best defensive player in the league. On those two Pistons title teams, he was their third most indispensable guy behind Dumars and Isiah.

4. During his last good season on the '98 Bulls—at age thirty-six, when he was partying incessantly, to the point that MJ and Jackson had an intervention with him—Rodman played 80 regular-season games (15.0 RPG), then another 20 playoff games (11.8 RPG), logging nearly 3,600 minutes in all. The man was a physical freak. We'll see another fifty Horace Grants before we see another Dennis Rodman. And thank God. I think one was enough.

68. PETE MARAVICH

Resume: 10 years, 7 quality, 5 All-Stars . . . top 5 ('76, '77), top 10 ('73, '78) . . . 3-year peak: 28–5–6 . . . leader: scoring (1x) . . . never won a Playoffs in his prime

Any late-night-cable junkie has stumbled across a Steve Prefontaine movie and felt excited (because it's the one with Billy Crudup) or bummed out (because it's the one with Jared Leto). If I see Crudup or Jack Bauer's dad, I'm in. If I see the cockeyed blonde from *Melrose Place* or Leto wearing one of those awful wigs, I'm out. Either way, I always ask myself the same question: "Why did Hollywood feel the need to release competing biopics about a long-distance runner who finished fourth in the 1972 Olympics?" One would have been plenty, right? When competing Maravich biographies hit the bookstores in 2007, that seemed similarly strange because Pistol had died nineteen years before, never won anything other than some scoring titles and never played in the Final Four or past the second round of the NBA playoffs. We always hear that Bird and Magic saved the NBA from the depressing seventies. Doesn't that mean they saved it from players like Maravich?

Then you remember that two documentaries and a movie were made about him; that fans tell Pistol stories and trade Pistol tapes to this day; that his Topps cards command a higher price than those of any '70s player except Dr. J; that he seduced a whole new generation of fans on YouTube; that he may have been the greatest H-O-R-S-E player ever; that he destroyed an aging Frazier for 68 points in 1977 (and would have broken 70 if they hadn't whistled him for two cheap fouls in the final two minutes);[70] that he blew out his knee in '78 and was never the same; and that, out of all the pre-1980 stars, it was Pistol whose career would have been transformed most by a three-point line. That thing was *made* for him. Hell, he was shooting threes before they were threes.[71] Not only would the line have boosted his offensive stats, but opponents would have been forced to defend him 25 feet from the basket (inadvertently opening the floor for him). In every conceivable way, Pistol Pete was ahead of his time. Seeing him in person was like seeing twelve Globetrotters rolled into one: no pass was too far-fetched, no shot too far away. He'd glide across the court—all rubbery limbs, ball attached to his hand like a yo-yo, blank expression on his face—and you never knew what would happen next, just that the scoreboard never mattered as much as the show. Kids from that era remember his appearances on CBS's halftime H-O-R-S-E contests more fondly than any of his games. Even his basketball cards were cool, like the one from 1975, when he sported an extended goatee and looked like a count.

You can imagine my delight when Auerbach plucked an end-of-the-line Pistol off waivers during Bird's rookie season. *We picked up the Pistol for nothing?* I hadn't seen him in a while, though. Woefully gaunt and out of shape, limping on a bum knee and sporting a godawful perm that made him look like Arnold Horshack, Pistol struggled mightily to blend in with his first good NBA team. The Garden crowd adopted him anyway. Every time he jumped off the bench to enter a game, we roared.

---

70. One of the refs who helped eject Pistol that night? You guessed it—the guy who was serenaded by more "Bull-shit" chants than anyone ever, Mr. Dick Bavetta! Only Dick could help eject someone going for 75 points.
71. In the 68-point game, Maravich makes six or seven jumpers from three-point range like he's shooting free throws.

Every time he sank a jumper, we went bonkers. When he shared the court with Bird, Cowens, and Archibald—four of my top seventy—there was always a sense that something special could happen.[72] But like an abused dog from the pound, there was too much damage and too many bad habits picked up over the years. After Bill Fitch buried him in the '80 playoffs, Pistol retired the following fall and just missed playing for the '81 champs. I remember being particularly crushed by the whole thing, like I'd been given an expensive TV for free and it broke down after two months. I never knew that there was substantial evidence that he was a drunk and a loon, one of the first athletes pushed too far by an overbearing father,[73] someone who believed in UFOs and couldn't find peace until he retired and found Christianity in 1982. When he dropped dead at age forty, it was, fittingly, while playing a casual game of pickup hoops.

Even those who loved watching him have trouble putting his career in context. At dinner in Boston two years ago, my father was perplexed about the existence of two Maravich books until we spent the next few minutes remembering him and inadvertently making their case. Dad recalled that there was usually one nationally televised college game a week in the 1960s and "you tuned in every weekend praying LSU was on." When my wife asked which current player reminded us of Maravich, Dad's answer was simply, "There will *never* be another Maravich." We tried but couldn't express the experience of watching someone play on a completely different plane from everyone else. He made impossible shots look easy. He saw passing angles his teammates couldn't even imagine. He was the most entertaining player alive . . . and the most tortured one. You marveled at Pete Maravich, but you worried about him, too.

72. Seeing Maravich on the Celts reminded me of the *White Shadow* episode when street legend Bobby Magnum (played by former UCLA star Mike Warren, who later starred in *Hill Street Blues* and played Preacher in *Fast Break*—now that's an IMDb.com page!) joined Carver High and removed the team's ceiling for a few days before bookies from Oakland found him, then he tried to steal Coach Reeves' TV and everything went to shit. By the way, when I say "reminded me," I mean "reminded me even as it was happening when I was only ten." Even back then, I was making convoluted comparisons between sports and pop culture.
73. Press Maravich made Marv Marinovich, Richard Williams and J. D. McCoy's dad seem like Joey, Danny and Uncle Jesse by comparison. And you thought I was kidding about convoluted comparisons.

Stick Pistol in the modern era and he'd become the most polarizing figure in sports, someone who combined T.O.'s insanity, A-Rod's devotion to statistics and Nash's flair for delighting the crowds. Skip Bayless would blow a blood vessel on *First Take* screaming about Pistol's ball hogging. The *SportsCenter* guys would create cute catchphrases for his no-looks. Bloggers would chronicle his bizarre comments and ghastly hairdos. Fantasy owners would revere him as if he were LaDainian Tomlinson or Johan Santana. Nike would launch a line of Pistol shoes. He'd be the subject of countless homemade YouTube videos and have a trophy case filled with ESPYs. Yup, it's safe to say the Pistol was ahead of his time in every respect. And when Hollywood makes a big-budget movie about him someday, I hope they stop at one.

67. EARL MONROE

Resume: 13 years, 7 quality, 4 All-Stars . . . '68 Rookie of the Year . . . top 5 ('69) . . . 3-year peak: 24–4–5 . . . 2nd-best player on 1 runner-up ('71 Bullets), started for 1 champ ('73 Knicks) and 1 runner-up ('72 Knicks)

You could make a case for bumping Pearl down to a spot in the mid-eighties. He only made one All-NBA team and four All-Star teams. He got torched by Goodrich in the '72 Finals and averaged just a 16–3–3 over 16 games in the Playoffs for the '73 Knicks (his only ring). His knees and hips started going on him within his first few NBA years, transforming him from a gifted all-around player to a scorer and that's it. But can you blame Pearl that his career started late? After graduating from high school in South Philly and failing to get scholarship offers from any major colleges, Monroe worked as a shipping clerk for a year before making a "comeback" at Winston-Salem College, a tiny black college in North Carolina, spending the next four years ravaging his knees but delighting fans in nontelevised college games and soon-to-be-legendary summer playground games in Philly and New York. Like Maravich, the Pearl wasted two potential All-Star years in college because NBA teams were only allowed to draft four-year seniors. By the time he joined the Bullets, the Pearl was twenty-three years old and carrying God knows how much asphalt mileage on his knees.[74]

Doesn't matter. We're invoking the Walton Corollary here: even if a guy peaked for just two or three years as a truly great player, that's more appealing than someone who never peaked at all. You know someone was great when he had two playground nicknames (Black Jesus and Magic) *and* a mainstream nickname (Earl the Pearl); moved Woody Allen to write a *Sport* magazine profile about him; invented a specific signature move (the spin move);[75] became immortalized in *He Got Game* even though the movie was released twenty-five years after his prime; and owned such an unconventional offensive game based on spins and herky-jerky hesitation moves that nobody has replicated it since.[76] Ask any over-forty-five NBA junkie about Pearl and they practically have a John-Madden-raving-about-Brett-Favre-level orgasm about him, as well as the famous Pearl/Clyde duels that forced the Knicks to say, "Screw it, we can't stop this guy, let's trade for him." So maybe his career wasn't much different statistically from those of Hudson, Jo Jo, Jeff Malone, Rolando Blackmon, Calvin Murphy or Randy Smith. But none of those guys had their improvisational skills compared to a jazz musician's—the most frequent analogy used to describe Pearl's style—or inspired stories like the one David Halberstam captured in *Breaks* through the eyes of Maurice Lucas.

One day Earl Monroe, then at the peak of his fame as the star of the Baltimore Bullets (and before Julius Erving had replaced him, a special kind of hero to black fans and players since he could do what *no one else*

74. Another legend fitting this "lost years" criteria: Bird quit IU as a freshman, spent the next year playing pickup ball and being a garbageman and eventually came back for ISU. He entered the NBA a year later than he should have (maybe two) had he been happy at Indiana.

75. Grumpy Old Editor: "Monroe's spin move paved the way for misdirection dribbles of all kinds and arguably changed the way traveling was called, for better or worse." Um . . . I say this is a good thing!

76. Dave DeBusschere told William Goldman once that he watched everyone's eyes when he defended them, never buying any fakes until they actually looked at the basket . . . but Pearl was the one guy who never looked at the basket until right when he was releasing the ball, making him impossible to defend. Thought that was interesting.

could do), showed up. The word had been out for several days that Monroe would play and the crowd was much bigger than usual. When Monroe missed the start of play the disappointment among the other players and the crowd was tangible. Then, ten minutes into the game, a huge beautiful car, half the length of the street, had shown up—it was a Rolls, Luke had known instinctively—and out had come Earl Monroe. He was wearing the most ragged shorts imaginable, terrible ratty sneakers and an absolutely beautiful Panama hat. That, Luke knew immediately, was true style, the hat and the shorts and the Rolls. The crowd had begun to shout *Magic, Magic, Magic* (his playground nickname, different than his white media nickname which, given the nature of sportswriters who like things to rhyme, was the Pearl). Monroe had put on a show that day, dancing, whirling, faking, spinning, orchestrating his moves as he wished, never any move repeated twice, as if to repeat was somehow a betrayal of his people. Luke had watched him, taking his eyes off Monroe only long enough to watch the crowd watching him. The Black Jesus, he had thought, that's what he is—the Black Jesus.

(That's right, Daddy. Earl Monroe was pretty good.)

66. ADRIAN DANTLEY

Resume: 15 years, 12 quality, 6 All-Stars . . . 1977 Rookie of the Year . . . top 10 ('81, '84) . . . leader: scoring (2x), minutes (1x) . . . career: made FT (6th) . . . 30-plus PPG (4x) . . . 2-year Playoffs peak: 28–8–3 (21 G) . . . career: 54% FG (20th), 6,382 FT made (6th) . . . traded five times . . . 20K Point Club

65. ALEX ENGLISH

Resume: 15 years, 9 quality, 8 All-Stars . . . top 10 ('82, '83, '84) . . . 3-year peak: 29–5–4 . . . 2-year Playoffs peak: 29–8–3 (21 G) . . . leader:

scoring (1x), FG (3x) . . . 3 teams before prime[77] . . . won just 2 Playoffs in his prime . . . eight 2K-point seasons . . . 25K Point Club

There was common ground here beyond the whole "scoring forwards with androgynous first names" thing. Dantley and English entered the league in 1976, bounced around early in their careers, peaked on Western contenders that could never get over the hump, gave up almost as many points as they scored and can't be compared to any current players. Dantley was a six-foot-three low-post guy (number of guys fitting that description today: zero) who reached the free throw line so frequently, Bob Ryan decided after one particularly goofy Dantley game that any weird box score line should just be called a "Dantley."[78] Few were more efficient offensively, as evidenced by Dantley retiring with the highest field goal percentage (54 percent) of any noncenter. And English was a lanky forward who never seemed to get hot— he'd score 7–8 points per quarter and end up around 30 every game, only you barely noticed him except for the fact that he never seemed to miss. We'll probably see twenty more Englishes before we see another Dantley, only because Dantley's physical, unorthodox style isn't something taught at basketball camps and AAU scrimmages, where every quirk and idiosyncracy get banged out of every player by the time he turns fifteen.

What were the deciding factors for English getting the nod? Dantley was a pain in the bum, wearing out his welcome with five teams (all of which accepted 30 to 80 cents on the dollar to get rid of him).[79] Everyone loved English. That's the biggest reason. If you're looking for a dumb but karmic reason, neither guy played for a champion, but English filmed a hauntingly bad movie called *Amazing Grace and Chuck* in which his char-

77. Indiana signed English as a free agent and stupidly traded him for George McGinnis. That was one of my favorite makeup trades ever—the previous year, Denver had stupidly traded Bobby Jones for McGinnis. Poor McGinnis was like the shittiest gift in a Yankee swap; you never wanted to be the one who ended up with him at the end of the night.

78. These were the days when newspapers ran box scores with FGs made, FTs made, total points and that was it. Ryan's favorite "Dantley" ever: "9–28–46." When Kevin Durant went 24-for-26 from the line in a 46-point effort against the Clips in January '09, I immediately thought, "That's a great Dantley!"

79. The worst of the deals: L.A. gave him away for a washed-up Spencer Haywood right before Magic's rookie year, Dantley averaged 28 in Utah, L.A. won the title anyway, and Haywood didn't make an impact other than probably snorting the most lines at Jack Nicholson's house that season.

acter "starred" for the '86 Celtics.[80] For one "game" scene in that movie, English donned a Boston uniform and played 20 minutes with Bird, Parish, McHale and DJ in an exhibition game at the Garden. That's right, five of the top sixty-four guys on this list played in a legally sanctioned NBA contest together, and not just that, but English's cameo happened with one of the greatest teams ever. Top that one, Adrian Dantley. My favorite part of this story: the NBA allowing an All-Star player to play significant minutes for another team—kind of a big deal, when you think about it—just to accommodate one of the twenty worst sports movies ever made. Didn't anyone in Stern's office read the script? Or the scripts for *Celtic Pride, Eddie,* and *Like Mike,* for that matter? I always pictured Stern seeing *Chuck,* then immediately firing everyone involved in the English decision.

Anyway, there are two types of great players: guys we'll see again, and guys we'll never see again. Any rational fan would agree that Jordan was the greatest basketball player ever. (Crap, I just spoiled the ending to Chapter 10. Oh, well.) *But we've seen variations of Jordan already.* Jordan was an evolutionary version of Thompson (his hero, by the way); Kobe and Wade have re-created Jordan's game reasonably well. We'll see a few more superathletic, hypercompetitive shooting guards who are built like wide receivers, jump like kangaroos and possess the innate ability to control their bodies in midair. We won't see another Jordan, but we will see someone every ten years who brings many of his best qualities to the table. Okay, so when will we see another Dantley? Really, a six-foot-three post-up player[81] with a hundred different upfakes and herky-jerky moves who creates wiggle room in the paint with his abnormally gigantic ass? He was the J-Lo of NBA players. I'm seeing that again in my lifetime? There might be another Jordan, but there will never, ever, ever, ever, *ever* be another Dantley. In his honor, here's an All-Star team of players from the post-Russell era whose like will never be seen again, for genetic or physical reasons.

---

80. The plot for *Chuck:* An annoying Little League star (Chuck) stops pitching because he's concerned about the threat of nuclear war. Inspired by Chuck's noble stance, a few famous professional athletes (led by Amazing Grace, played by English) decide to stop playing as well until some antiweapon legislation is passed or something. By the end of the movie, you're actually rooting for a nuclear holocaust just so Chuck will die. It's that bad.
81. Dantley was listed at six foot five. No way. Dennis Johnson was two inches taller.

Starters: Kareem, Bird, Barkley, Magic, Gervin
Sixth man: McHale
Bench: Dantley, Maravich, Iverson/DJ,[82] Manute Bol, Spud Webb, Paul
   Mokeski
Injured List: Darko Milicic, Kurt Nimphius, Ken Bannister

Since the first ten players cracked the Pyramid and earned love in this
section, we'll concentrate on the last six guys and why they made it.

Manute. Let's just say there haven't been too many seven-foot-six, 200-
pound Sudanese centers from the University of Bridgeport with tribal
scars on their foreheads. Manute happened to be an underrated backup,
getting decent minutes for five different playoff teams, averaging 5 blocks
as a rookie, cracking 300 blocks three times and contributing significantly
(20 minutes a game, 5.8 rebounds, 4.3 blocks) for the TMC Warriors that
made the second round of the '89 playoffs. More importantly, of all the
players I watched walk by me in the Boston Garden tunnel, only four
stood out: Michael Jordan (because he was so overwhelmingly famous),
David Robinson (we'll get to why later), Larry Bird (ditto) and Manute.
He was breathtaking because of his surreal height and skin so dark that it
made him seem purple.[83] When Manute emerged from the tunnel, we'd
stop talking and gawk with our mouths agape, like everyone watching the
aliens emerge from the *Close Encounters* UFO. It was incredible. I would
have bought a ticket just to watch Manute Bol stroll by me.

Spud. We've seen effective tiny/pesky/speedy point guards before, but
Spud was the only one with game-changing ups. If he made an above-the-
rim play at home, his crowd would get more charged up than a red-hot
craps table. Know what else? For a change-of-pace backup with a
puncher's chance of completely screwing up the other team for a few minutes, you're not finding anyone better than the Spudster: playing for quality Atlanta teams in '86 and '88, Spud averaged 19 minutes, 10 points, 6

82. I couldn't pick between them. Sorry. So yes, it's actually a thirteen-player team with
a three-man injured list, impossible under the current roster rules. Sue me.
83. Our country is so uptight that this point might be considered racist. Here's my defense: Manute Bol was fucking purple. I don't know what else to tell you.

assists and at least one "Holy shit!" play in over 21 games in the playoffs. I always thought he was a genuine asset.[84]

Mokeski. I wrote about the "power of Mokeski" so many times for ESPN.com that I'm now prominently featured on his Wikipedia page. A backup center who somehow lasted for twelve seasons, poor Mokeski was extraordinarily unathletic and ran like he had two prosthetic legs; if that weren't enough, he tried to bring back the curly-perm/wispy-mustache combo that should have died in the early eighties. Throw in male pattern baldness and a disappearing chin and Mokeski looked like a Jersey cop who should have been standing in a donut line. So you can only imagine how bizarre it was that he had a semieffective game—physical defender, decent banger, reliable 18-footer, never did anything he couldn't do—and averaged 20 minutes for a 59-win Bucks team in 1985. I loved Mokeski to the degree that I spent three solid years searching for his game-worn jersey on eBay before finally giving up.

Darko. A seven-foot Serbian teenager with the upside of a cross between Derrick Coleman and David Robinson gets drafted too high by the wrong team, faces impossible expectations,[85] folds from the pressure, starts looking more pale/depressed/overwhelmed/bitter than a postpuberty Macaulay Culkin, then self-combusts to the point that he's completely and hopelessly useless before even turning old enough to legally rent a car? This will never happen again. I am almost positive.

Nimphius. Imagine Jon Bon Jovi's middle part from the Slippery When Wet world tour merged with George Clooney's extended mullet from *The Facts of Life*, with a dash of late-eighties Tommy Byron thrown in for good

---

84. Crazy Spud facts: Did you know he played for 14 seasons? Or that he started for six years—two in Atlanta, four in Sacramento?

85. Darko should sue Chad Ford for raising everyone's expectations too high, most famously with a 2002 column (look it up for comedy's sake) when he printed the following quote from Pistons scout Will Robinson: "That kid's going to be a star. He's a 7-footer that plays like a point guard. That kid's something special." Also from Robinson: "He's going to own the game. Own the game. We're going to have to build a new arena. The only thing that could destroy a kid like that is a woman." And a lack of talent and confidence. That, too.

measure. Then make him a seven-foot twelfth man and put him in tight blue eighties warm-ups on Detroit. There you go.

Bannister. I'm not sure how Bannister, a forward with the Knicks in the mid-eighties, got the nickname "the Animal." But I think I have a few ideas. Every time Kenny Bannister walked through the Garden tunnel, everyone went quiet, like something awful was happening.[86] He's the captain of the Thank God They Didn't Have HD Back Then All-Stars, which include Dennis Rodman, Greg "Cadillac" Anderson, Gheorge Muresan, Brook Steppe,[87] Tyrone Hill, the Cummings brothers (Terry and Pat), Mokeski, Anthony Mason, David Wesley, Ervin "No Magic" Johnson, the '87 Celtics, the '02 Kings, and the immortal Popeye Jones, about whom I once wrote, "Much like the Grand Canyon and the Sistine Chapel, you really have to see Popeye in person."

64. JERRY LUCAS

Resume: 11 years, 9 quality, 7 All-Stars . . . top 5 ('65, '66, '68), top 10 ('64, '67) . . . 4-year peak: 21–19–3 . . . leader: FG% (1x) . . . played for 1 champ ('73 Knicks), started for 1 runner-up ('72 Knicks, averaged a 19–11 in 16 Playoffs G) . . . traded twice in prime

What do we make of this guy? His teams never won in his prime. He was traded twice in his prime: once for Jim King and Billy Turner (after Lucas had averaged an 18–18 for the season, no less), once straight up for Cazzie Russell. He was infamous—repeat: *infamous*—for chasing down end-of-the-quarter heaves and ripping down uncontested free throw misses to pad his rebounding stats. Of the NBA 50 at 50 guys, he's one of the few who never generate feedback like "Man, you should have seen Lucas play"

86. That only happened for three people: Bannister, Cadillac and Popeye. They were the Bird, Magic, and MJ of ugly.
87. Here's how ugly Steppe was: in high school, I used to sneak one of those Zander Hollander NBA yearbooks (the ones with all the profiles and pictures) into math class, then pull out the page with Steppe's picture intermittently during math class to crack up my buddy Bish in the back row. Always worked, too.

or "You know who was something? That Jerry Lucas!" In today's era of su-
perskilled power forwards who can run the floor and play above the rim,
it's hard to imagine Jerry averaging an 18–10 in 2008, much less a 20–20.
For instance, let's say we grabbed Tyler Hansbrough before his rookie season and planted a chip in his brain that gave him Lucas' rebounding instincts. Where do you see his career going? Does he average a 20–12 every
game? I honestly don't know. So that's the question with Lucas—were
those numbers accomplished because of the style of play (run-and-gun,
lots of possessions) and lack of athletic forwards? Partially, yes. Still, those
numbers were mildly mind-blowing: Lucas nearly averaged a 20-20 for
four straight years, giving Oscar a running mate when the Royals extended Boston to two deciding games. During a five-year stretch in a
loaded league (1964–68), he made three first-team All-NBAs and two second teams. He also had a deadly one-handed push shot from 20-plus feet,
so if you're projecting him historically, it has to be mentioned that Lucas
would have been more valuable with a three-point line. We'll remember
him for his photographic memory,[88] a storied college and Olympics career and an NBA career in which he was basically Truck Robinson[89] with
a better career peak. If we're picking power forwards from that era, I'd
rather have Dave DeBusschere.

63. REGGIE MILLER

Resume: 15 years, 11 quality, 5 All-Stars . . . top 15 ('95, '96, '98) . . .
3-year peak: 22–3–3 . . . 2-year playoffs peak: 24–3–2, 89 threes, 42%
3FG (33 G) . . . leader: FT% (5x), threes (2x) . . . Playoffs: 20.6 points,
89% FT (144 G) . . . 80-plus games (10x) . . . career: threes (1st), Playoffs
threes (1st), 88.8% FT (9th)

---

88. Strange Lucas fact: his photographic memory was so remarkable that he ended up
writing a couple of memory books. There's a chance he's memorizing this page right now.
89. During a supercompetitive '77–'78 season, Truck averaged an astonishing 23–16 for
the Jazz and made first-team All-NBA with Doc, Walton, Thompson and Gervin. Since
he bounced around so much (four teams in his first five seasons) and got traded in '79
while averaging a 22–14, it's possible Truck got his nickname by threatening to run over
his coach in a truck or doing truckloads of blow.

If you're from Indiana, take a deep breath before we proceed. Then take another one. And another. Think happy thoughts. Get yourself into a good place. I'll wait for you.

(Twiddling my thumbs.)

(Humming happily to myself.)

You ready? Try not to take the following few paragraphs personally; I have no interest in feuding with Indiana, the same place that gave us Hickory High, David Letterman, Larry Legend and my hypothetical Pyramid. I want you to like this book. Every decision, comment and argument has been carefully made and thought out in an unbiased way (even with regards to that ninny Kareem). Please know that I have nothing against Reggie Miller other than his refusal to sell Marv Albert's jokes on TNT. Nothing during his career annoyed me other than the way he flopped to get calls (hey, he wasn't the only one). Even his pansy dance after draining a game-winner against Chicago in the '98 Eastern Finals didn't bother me. I liked watching Reggie play. I really did. Which makes what you're about to read so painful. I'll even put it in italics to soften the blow a little.

Reggie Miller was the most overrated "superstar" of the past thirty years.

(Exhale, people from Indiana. Work with me. We're gonna get through this. Did I mention that *Breaking Away* is one of my favorite sports movies?)

Here are the facts. Reggie played for sixteen seasons (1988–2005), his prime coinciding with the weakest stretch of talent since the merger (1994–98). Twenty-one superstars or near-superstars crossed paths with Reggie, all mortal locks for the All-Star team at their peaks, all of whom could be recognized by one name: Jordan, Bird, Barkley, Magic, Isiah, Hakeem, Robinson, Mailman, Moses, Shaq, Kobe, Garnett, Iverson, Payton, Nash, Nowitzki, Stockton, Pippen, Ewing, Duncan and 'Nique. For Reggie to earn the title "superstar," his career should have been just as successful and substantial as those of everyone else on that list, right? So why did Reggie end up with the lowest number of All-Star Game appearances of anyone on that list (five; nobody else had fewer than seven)? Also, Reggie was the only one who didn't make at least three combined appearances on first-second-team All-NBAs. Oh, wait . . . he didn't have any.

Here's what that means: At *no point* was Reggie considered one of the NBA's top ten players for a single season. Nine of his contemporaries at shooting guard made All-NBA (first or second): Jordan, Drexler, Dumars, Latrell Sprewell, Mitch Richmond, Kobe, T-Mac, Iverson and Ray Allen. Reggie only made third-team All-NBA three times ('95, '96 and '98). That's it. And his reputation as a "great" playoffs player has been slightly overblown. The Pacers were bounced from the first round in his first four trips to the Playoffs.[90] During their extended '94 playoffs run, everyone remembers Miller's trash-talking duel with Spike Lee (25 points in the fourth quarter of Game 5 at MSG, as immortalized in Dan Klores' "30 for 30" documentary *Winning Time*), but nobody mentions Game 7, when he went 2-for-10 in the second half, *air-balled* what would have been the game-winning 20-footer with 5 seconds remaining, then accidentally committed a flagrant foul on John Starks and killed their last chance.[91] During the '95 playoffs, Reggie came up big in Game 1 (8 points in 8.9 seconds for an improbable Pacers comeback) and Game 7 of the Knicks series (29 points) but no-showed in Game 7 when Orlando won by 21 points. During the '99 Eastern Finals, New York's Allan Houston torched Reggie and the heavily favored Pacers in a deciding Game 6. Like always with beloved athletes, we tend to forget bad memories and remember the good ones. Let the record show that Indiana was 9–15 in elimination games and 3–5 in deciding Game 5's or Game 7's during Reggie's career. I'm just saying. That's why Miller headlines an extensive group of Guys Who Had Great Careers but Weren't Quite Franchise Players. On the flip side, Reggie's flair for The Moment stood out over everyone else from his era except Jordan. We'll remember him as an accomplished clutch player, as well as a historically good three-point bomber and free throw shooter, someone capable of being the crunch-time scorer on a top-five team (which Indiana was in '94, '95, '98 and '00). If Indiana was protecting a lead in the final minute, you couldn't foul Reggie because he was a world-class cooler and a mortal lock to drain both free throws. And nobody—

90. Two of those exits came at the hands of Reggie Lewis and Boston. In the summer of '93, Lewis died and MJ went to play baseball; suddenly Miller had gotten rid of his toughest foes in the East. Miller couldn't have guarded Lewis unless he was allowed to hand-check him with a taser.

91. A shady call and more evidence that the NBA was determined to get New York in the '94 Finals. Let's just say that from 1993 to 2006, the NBA may have dabbled in pro wrestling tactics a little. I tried to sweep it under the rug in this book because that's what people do when they're in love with someone: they lie for them. And I love the NBA.

repeat: nobody—received more ridiculous calls than Reggie over the last
twelve years, so either the officials enjoyed watching him or David Stern
made the desperate order after Jordan's baseball sabbatical: "We need
more superstars—from now on, Reggie Miller gets every call!"[92]

Here's the problem: superstars affect games even when they're missing
shots, but Reggie was a mediocre defensive player who couldn't rebound
or create shots for teammates, someone who needed an offense constructed in a specific way so he could succeed. Since he couldn't consistently beat good defenders off the dribble, the Pacers sprinted him around
a series of picks—almost like a mouse going through a maze—to spring
him for open looks, which meant their big men needed to keep setting
picks, their point guard needed to kill time waiting for him to get
open . . . basically, everyone else tailored their games to his game. Can you
win a title that way? Obviously not. And if you want to get stat-dorky, seriously, how difficult could it be to play 36 minutes and C-plus defense
and finish with a 21–3–3 every night? That's what Reggie averaged from
1990 to 2001. You can win a title with your second-best guy giving you
those stats, but not your best guy. In fairness to Reggie, Indiana always
asked him to do too much—at the end of close games, you always knew
the ball was going to him, something he embraced and enjoyed, but still.
Unlike Stockton, McHale, Worthy, Drexler, DJ and Pippen, Reggie never
played with anyone better than him (the biggest reason Indiana never
won a title).[93] He wins points for excelling over an exceptionally long period of time, and since he was a unique player, it felt like his historical impact was bigger than it was. Nobody had bigger stones in big moments, a
crucial quality that unquestionably lifted his teammates. He made enough
game-winners that NBA TV ran a Reggie mini-marathon during the 2005
season. And he pretty much saved professional basketball in Indiana,
which is why everyone loves him so much there.

Still, how does what's described in the previous paragraph make him a
superstar? During his best playoff run in 1995, Reggie averaged 25.5

92. Don't rule this out.
93. Then again, Ray Allen would have given his left nut to play with the likes of Rik Smits
and Jermaine O'Neal.

points over 17 games as the Pacers fell one game short of the Finals.[94] In
the 2000 playoffs, he averaged 24 points over 22 games as the Pacers lost
to the Lakers in six. He was what he was: a streaky shooting guard who
scared opponents when it mattered but didn't do much else. On a very
good team, he could be the difference between 45 wins and a first-round
and 55 wins and a third-round, which doesn't differentiate him from fifteen other guys of his era. Reggie was really a poor man's Sam Jones: a
genuine asset on a good team, a crunch-time killer and someone who
couldn't win a title unless he played with someone better than him. Does
that make him a superstar? I say no. Of course, you might disagree, like
my old friend Eric "Toast" Marshall did: "I think it depends on your definition of the word 'superstar.' He's been the marquee player for a good
team for seventeen years. He has been a devastating player, one whom the
entire other team always has to be conscious of. Someone should do a
study on the shooting percentage of the guy guarding Reggie in playoff
games. I'll bet it's like 37 percent. That kind of work away from the ball is
as valuable as being a great passer or great rebounder because it creates
shots for everyone (think Rip Hamilton). Also, the Indiana offense benefited greatly by his movement without the ball. Many mediocre players
were successful playing with Reggie. Name one significant player on the
team who got better after leaving the Pacers (Best, Davis, Rose, etc.). You
can't."

   All great points. Unfortunately, it's my book. I say that Reggie wasn't a
superstar. On the other hand, he was memorable enough to earn nearly
1,400 words and become our cutoff guy for Level 1 in the next hardcover . . . until this next guy blew him for the paperback.

---

94. Not a footnote as much as an asterisk—that year they stupidly shortened the three-
point line. Check out YouTube to see where Reggie fired those back-to-back threes (they
were 21-footers at best). That might have been the NBA's most memorable "we didn't
think this through" panic rule other than the "can't leave the bench even if your star just
got hit by a tire iron right in front of you" rule.

62. RAY ALLEN

Resume: 14 years, 12 quality, 9 All-Stars . . . top 10 ('05), top 15 ('01) . . . 3-year peak: 22–5–4, 43% 3FG, 88% FT . . . '01 Playoffs: 25–6–4, 48% 3FG (18 G) . . . '05 Playoffs: 27–4–4 (11 G) . . . '08 Finals: 20–5–4, record 22 threes . . . career: 21–4–4, 40% 3FG, 89.4% FT . . . career leader: threes (2nd) . . . Playoffs: 253 threes (5th), 40.2% . . . starter, 1 champ ('08 Celts), 1 runner-up ('10 Celts)

A rejuvenated Ray-Ray thrived in the 2009 season (18–4–3, 49% FG, 41% 3FG, 95% FT) and especially in the playoffs; in the first round against Chicago, he sank a game-winning three and two game-tying threes, scored 51 points in Game 6 and earned some long overdue "Wow, Ray Allen is really good!" national chatter. One season later, Allen helped the aging Celtics sneak into the 2010 Finals, broke the single-game record for threes (eight in Game 2) and defended Kobe well enough that he wore down on the other end. Even though he missed 24 of 28 threes in the final five Finals games, took an 0-for-13 collar in Game 4 and staggered to a Starksian 3-for-14 in Game 7, Allen's poor shooting reaffirmed his greatness because every Boston fan (including me) watched those misses thinking, "All right, *this* one is going in." We never wanted him to stop shooting. The defining moment: Allen suffered a charley horse just 135 seconds into Game 3, missed his first *twelve* shots, then found himself in the corner with a wide-open three—down 4 points, 54 seconds to play—that he launched without hesitation. Even though Allen was two misses away from tying Dennis Johnson's dubious 0-for-14 Finals record, guess what? Everyone in the building believed that thirteenth shot was going in. Everyone. Including me. Sadly, tragically, regretfully, Allen missed it by a half inch. My friend Lewis (die-hard Lakers fan) emailed me later, "I can't believe Allen missed that shot, I almost shit my pants." He was 0 for 12!!!!!!!! Now that's a great shooter.

So how long can Allen keep going? Remember, an aging Miller thrived as a home run threat, cooler[95] and occasional clutch scorer without having

---

95. That's my nickname for elite FT shooters who ice games at the line; they're almost like closers in baseball with how they protect leads. You can't win a title without a cooler. As Rick Adelman's Blazers teams will tell you.

Allen's modern advantages in dieting, conditioning, sleep study, video study and sports medicine. I'd compare the modern advantage for older NBA stars to Sandra Bullock continuing to carry chick flicks and heartwarming Disney-esque movies at age forty-six. In Bullock's era, female stars have remained more ageless than ever because of teeth whitening, better hairstyling, better dieting, weight training, yoga, Pilates, liposuction, Botox, implants and everything else. Bullock's shelf life outlasted Meg Ryan's shelf life for the same reason Allen's shelf life will probably last longer than Miller's shelf life: nowadays, you can remain more ageless than ever. (And yes, if Allen was Bullock and Miller was Ryan, then Andrew Toney was definitely Goldie Hawn.) Don't bet against Ray pulling a Bullock on us.

For his nine-year prime (1999–2007), Ray-Ray was remarkably efficient (23–5–4, 45% FG, 40% 3FG, 90% FT), had the prettiest jumper of any star player and rarely attempted anything he couldn't do. If he were a baseball player, he would have been Wade Boggs—not a franchise guy, but someone with a few elite skills (milking pitch counts, getting on base, stroking singles and rarely missing a game, in Boggs' case) that made him a genuine asset as long as you surrounded him with other quality players. Allen played on only two contenders in his prime (the '01 Bucks and '05 Sonics), which makes me wonder how we'd remember him if he'd thrived on Miller's Indiana teams from 1994 to 2004 . . . or, conversely, how we'd remember Reggie had he spent his prime relying on low-post scoring, shot blocking, and rebounding from Ervin Johnson, Jerome James, Predrag Drobniak, Armon Gilliam, Tractor Traylor, Scott Williams, Reggie Evans, Jason Caffey, Danny Fortson, Vitaly Potapenko, Nick Collison, Johan Petro, Robert Swift and a washed-up Anthony Mason.[96] You can't blame Allen for never sniffing the Finals until 2008, especially when the NBA rigged the 2001 Eastern Finals so Iverson could advance to the next round. But that's for the next book.[P30]

---

96. That's the complete list of relevant centers and power forwards who played on Allen's team from 1999 through 2007. Ray Allen will now light himself on fire.

P30. If crooked NBA playoff series were heavyweight boxers, then '02 Lakers-Kings was George Foreman and '01 Bucks-Sixers was Earnie Shavers. In other words, people only remember George, but Earnie was almost as memorable. Philly won in 7 by finishing ahead 186–120 in FT's, 12–3 in techs and 5–0 in flagrants. Games 1 and 4 swung on a controversial lane violation and two incredible no-calls. Milwaukee's Glenn Robinson didn't attempt a FT until Game 5. Karl and Allen were fined a combined $85,000 for claiming *during* the series that it was rigged. Anyway, Allen averaged 27.1 PPG (including a record 9 threes in Game 6) and outplayed Iverson that series.

One more thing: big props to Ray-Ray for giving a startlingly capable performance as Jesus Shuttlesworth in *He Got Game*. His acting chops were solid and he carried off a threesome with real-life porn stars Chasey Lain and Jill Kelly, as well as one of the better sequences in any recent sports movie: Allen's climactic one-on-one game with Denzel Washington (playing his father) that wasn't scripted by Spike Lee, leading to an incredible turn of events where Denzel scored the first four points of the game off an increasingly-pissed-off-in-real-life Allen, who quickly scored the next ten and saved himself from getting mocked by the camera crew for the rest of the shoot. Do you think Pearl or Maravich could have pulled off Jesus Shuttlesworth? That's just enough to sneak him into the low sixties in the Pyramid. While we're here, allow me three more thoughts on Ray/Jesus:

1. You know how NBA teams use movie clips to get fans fired up during games? For years, I've had a running joke about which clip would be the worst possible choice, finally deciding it would be the scene from *The Shining* when Jack Nicholson comes flying out of nowhere and buries an ax into Scatman Crothers' chest. I always thought that would lead to forty-five seconds of horrified silence. But imagine a big Allen three-pointer, followed by a visitor's time-out and the crowd going bonkers, abruptly followed by the JumboTron playing Ray's threesome from *He Got Game* . . . actually, what am I saying? That would lead to even more cheering! Nothing will ever top the Jack/Scatman scene.[97]

2. With Denzel in the house, L.A. missed a chance to screw with Allen before Game 5 of the 2008 Finals: they should have shown Denzel scoring those four *He Got Game* baskets on the JumboTron, then cut to a grinning Denzel sitting courtside. They even could have had him dressed like Papa Shuttlesworth just to mess with Ray's head—he could have worn a fake afro, the red and black Nike outfit and an electronic tracking bracelet on his right sneaker, then sat between Lain and

---

97. Three other things I want to see during an NBA game: the wave going in opposite directions (would it cause an earthquake or something?), the arena going dead silent before a key FT attempt from an opponent (would totally psych out the other team), and the crowd rattling an opposing FT shooter by screaming, "The power of Christ compels you! The power of Christ compels you! THE POWER OF CHRIST COMPELS YOU!"

Kelly. You can't tell me Allen wouldn't have been freaked out. Why don't teams think of this stuff?

3. My theory about why *Game* turned out to be disappointing: In the spring of '98, Spike delivered a 136-minute cut of *Game* to four Touchstone studio executives. All of them liked the movie. All of them thought it was about thirty-five to forty minutes too long and needed to be chopped down. All of them agreed that the subplot with Denzel and the hooker was depressing and should be jettisoned. They also asked Lee to reshoot the ending, since the original (Denzel getting double-crossed and going back to jail) made them want to inhale a garageful of carbon monoxide. And they wanted Spike to stop kidding around and use a real soundtrack, because the movie was dying for hip-hop and droning jazz made about as much sense as Garth Brooks. So Spike agreed to everything. Begrudgingly. The Touchstone execs promised to stay in touch, then flew back to Los Angeles . . . only their plane was struck by a meteor and they were never seen again. Meanwhile, Spike still had a movie to release. Someone else from Touchstone called to check in, leading to this exchange:

EXEC: How's the movie coming?

SPIKE: Good, good. Just finished the final cut.

EXEC: Great! You incorporated the notes from the meteor guys, right?

SPIKE (*smiling*): Ummmmm . . . yeah. Fixed everything.

EXEC: Fantastic! Can't wait to see it!

And that's how we ended up with the all-time "that should have been better" sports movie. Potential can be a dangerous thing. And yet I digress.[98]

___

98. Three scenes make *Game* kinda-sorta worth it for me: Denzel waxing poetically about Pearl, the Denzel-Jesus game, and the aftermath when a winded Denzel hands the letter of intent to Jesus, who drops it in disgust. The next few seconds were more in Denzel's wheelhouse than Tim Wakefield trying to sneak a fastball past Albert Pujols. He shakes his head, just a beaten man headed back to prison who needs to get one final message across, finally keeping eye contact with Allen and telling him, "You get that hatred out of your heart, or you're just gonna end up another nigger . . . [pause] . . . like your father." Now *that,* my friends, is a chill scene.

EIGHT

THE PYRAMID: LEVEL 2

61. BOB MCADOO

Resume: 14 years, 7 quality, 5 All-Stars . . . '75 MVP . . . MVP runner-up:
'74, '76 . . . '73 Rookie of the Year . . . Top 5 ('75), top 10 ('74) . . . 3-year
peak: 32–14–3 . . . 3-year Playoffs peak: 32–14 (22 G) . . . leader: scoring (3x), minutes (1x), FG% (1x), FT (1x) . . . bench player for two
champs ('82, '85 Lakers) . . . traded 3 times in prime

60. NATE ARCHIBALD

Resume: 13 years, 7 quality, 6 All-Stars . . . top 5 ('73, '75, '76), top 10
('72, '81) . . . 2-year peak: 31–3–10 . . . leader: points (1x), assists (1x),

minutes (1x) . . . only player to lead NBA in points and assists (34.0, 11.4) . . . started for 1 champ ('81 Celts)

Remember when everyone called Ben Wallace underrated for so long that he became *overrated,* leading to the Bulls killing their franchise by giving away Tyson Chandler so they could sign Wallace to an unconscionable $60 million deal? The same thing happened to McAdoo from a historical standpoint. When the NBA left Mac off its 50 at 50 list and outraged every NBA junkie, the subsequent backlash turned out to be the best possible thing for McAdoo's legacy. Now he's a little overrated, if that makes sense.

The case for McAdoo: For a three-year stretch in Buffalo, he was the best NBA player not named Kareem, averaging a 32–14 as an undersized center and scoring on anyone and everyone . . . because of his body (six foot nine, 210 pounds) and offensive game (unstoppable facing the basket, better with a fast pace), he had the misfortune of peaking in the wrong era (the slow-down seventies) . . . in fact, if you could pick any player to play center for the Nash/D'Antoni Phoenix teams, you'd pick McAdoo . . . you can't blame him for getting traded to a series of awful teams (first the Knicks, then Boston, then Detroit, then New Jersey) . . . after Jersey traded him to the Lakers,[1] Mac became a game-changing bench player for two title teams, submitting one of the single greatest sixth-man seasons in 1982: averaging a 15–5 in 21 minutes a game, then a 17–7 with 56 percent shooting in just 26 playoff minutes per game . . . and if you're talking aesthetics, nobody in this Pyramid had a more fun name, few were cooler to watch (Mac played with a particularly detached, effortless, cooler-than-cool style), and few had a more distinct calling card (a beautiful and unblockable jumper released from the top of his head)[2] . . . again, he was a victim of his era more than anything—not just the style of play and his bad luck finding a good team, but that he peaked in the "it's okay to get a huge contract, stop caring, and dabble in coke" era . . . it's also worth mentioning that Dr. Jack Ramsay, a notoriously tough

1. Trading for an NBA player with baggage is like dating a girl with baggage: you might be happy for a few months, but 19 out of 20 times, it will end badly. (And I mean *badly,* as in, "Why does it hurt when I pee?" or "I wonder who left 59 hang-ups on my answering machine?") The McAdoo/Lakers trade was the 20th time.
2. We've all played hoops with someone who had McAdoo's jumper and we envied the guy for it. For me, it was my buddy House. When you have McAdoo's jumper, it's like being the one kid in high school who has a donkey dick. Everyone will remember you.

person to win over, coached Mac on those Buffalo teams, loved him, swore by him, and even told *Sports Illustrated* in 1976, "The thing to remember about Mac is that he is going to get much, much better. In every aspect of his game . . . He works hard. He takes care of his body so he'll be around for a long time. He goes almost 48 minutes a night, always learning. Mostly, he wants to be the best who ever lived. He wants that very badly." Or . . . not.

The case against McAdoo: He thrived during the weakest three NBA seasons of the past fifty years (that '74–'76 stretch we keep bringing up) and Buffalo never made it past the second round . . . after the merger, his numbers dipped significantly and he developed such a selfish reputation that four teams dumped him in a five-year span . . . when Boston owner John Y. Brown dealt three first-round picks for Mac, Red Auerbach was so distraught that he nearly quit that spring to take over the Knicks (an honorable-mention what-if candidate) . . . Mac played for one .500 team in the next five years ('77–'81) before getting released by the Pistons[3] . . . if you're really feeling cynical, you could call Mac the poster boy of a decade that nearly destroyed the league, the most renowned of the Talented/Overpaid/Selfish/Passionless Stars That Fans Disliked and Wondered During Games if They Gave a Shit and/or Were on Drugs.[4]

I would argue that McAdoo was overrated *and* underrated. Maybe the merger exposed him, but he also peaked in the worst possible era for his personality and game. Give him credit for being a pioneer of sorts because, before McAdoo, nobody imagined that an NBA offense could revolve around a jump-shooting big man.[5] Throw him in a time machine, stick him in the 2002 draft, give him to Chicago as its number two pick,

3. Pistons GM Jack McCloskey explained the release like this: "He could have given us 10 to 12 minutes a game. He said that he didn't want to play part-time because it would drive the value of his next contract down. Prior to that, I might have been the only guy in Detroit who thought Bob McAdoo was really injured, but after he said that, I lost all respect."

4. The complete list: McAdoo, Haywood, Thompson, John Lucas, Sidney Wicks, Pete Maravich, Robert Parish (G-State version), George McGinnis, Truck Robinson, Terry Furlow, Marvin Barnes, John Drew, Bernard King, Micheal Ray Richardson and yes . . . Kareem.

5. Another pioneer move by Doo: after his NBA career ended in '86, he starred in Italy, playing another 7 years and averaging a 27–9 over there. When my friend Wildes recently moved from Manhattan (the NBA of hooking up) to West Hartford (the Italian League), I predicted he'd put up inflated numbers and started calling him Euro McAdoo. Then he quickly found a girlfriend. I think I put too much pressure on him.

put him under a rookie contract for five years and Mac would have evolved into a more unstoppable version of Dirk Nowitzki, especially if he'd found a coach like D'Antoni or Nellie along the way. And what if he learned to shoot threes? Yikes.

As for Archibald, you could call him Tiny McAdoo because they had such similar careers, right down to being relative pioneers, peaking early as superstars, bouncing around in relative obscurity and finding the Juvenation Machine (in Tiny's case, on a few 60-win teams in Boston). After making a name for himself on the New York playgrounds, Tiny became a hero to every local point guard who followed him (Kenny Anderson, Stephon Marbury and Bassy Telfair, to name three). His career is remembered unfairly because everyone mentions the "only guy to lead the league in points and assists in the same year" first, which is like remembering Bruce Springsteen's career by praising him for selling so many *Born in the USA* albums. The thing that stood out about Tiny—and remains relevant now, even if you're watching the '81 All-Star Game or a Sixers-Celtics battle—was the complete control he wielded over every game. If playing point guard is like mastering Grand Theft Auto, then the final mission should include the following things: your handle is so superior that opponents would never think of pressuring you full-court; you can dribble to any spot on the floor at any time of the game, and if you need to do it, you can always get to the rim and/or draw a foul if your team needs a hoop; no teammate would dare bring it upcourt if you're on the floor; every teammate who grabs a defensive rebound immediately looks for you; and defenders play four feet off you at all times because they don't want to have their ankles broken, which means you're starting the offense between the foul line and the top of the key on every possession. Of all the point guards I've watched in person in my lifetime, only seven completed that final mission: Tiny, Isiah, Kevin Johnson, Steve Nash, sober John Lucas, young Tim Hardaway and Chris Paul. You never forgot any of those guys were on the court, not for a second.

One other thing about Tiny: when he separated his shoulder during Game 3 of the Eastern Finals in '82, it robbed us of a fascinating Lakers-Celtics Finals. Boston had an 18-game winning streak that season and loved experimenting with a truly batty lineup: Parish, McHale, Tiny, Cedric Maxwell . . . and Larry Bird playing two-guard. (The Legend was surprisingly quick back then, as evidenced by his three straight All-Defenses from '82 to '84, and besides, the league wasn't stacked with athletic two-guards yet.) Meanwhile, the Lakers were running teams off the floor. Kareem and Wilkes still had their fastball, McAdoo had evolved into a supersub, Magic was playing three positions, and they had two elite ball-handlers (Magic and Nixon) and a deadly 1–3–1 press that wreaked havoc. So Tiny's injury prevented the highest-scoring Finals of all time, and beyond that, Bird and Magic could have been playing two-guard and defending each other in crunch time. Now *that*, my friends, is a great injury what-if.

59. ROBERT PARISH

Resume: 21 years, 14 quality, 9 All-Stars . . . top 10 ('82), top 15 ('89) . . . started for 3 champs ('81, '84, '86 Celtics) and 2 runner-ups ('85, '87) . . . 3-year peak: 19–11–3 . . . career leader: games (1st), rebounds (8th) . . . averaged a 15–9 or better 12 times

One of the tougher Pyramid calls. His longevity and durability were simply astounding; he played 14 seasons in Boston alone, missing just 42 games *total* and never playing fewer than 74 games during the Bird era. In five seasons from '84 through '88, Chief churned out 494 games (including playoffs) and limped around on a badly sprained ankle in the '87 playoffs. His consistency was uncanny—he never seemed to have good streaks or bad streaks, rarely exploded for the occasional 35–20, never yelled at officials, never got into fights or barked at teammates—to the point that he almost seemed like a cyborg. Hell, Parish even *looked* the same for his whole career.[6] Except for his first Boston season when he grew a mustache, he never gained weight, changed his hair, grew weird facial hair or anything. I can see any eighties Celtics highlight and know the season immediately just from Larry Bird's hair and mustache, just like how I could tell

6. He's a charter member of the Tony La Russa All-Stars for Guys Who Have Looked the Same for So Long That It's Almost Creepy.

any *Miami Vice* season based on Don Johnson's hair and weight.[7] But Parish? From 1982 to 1993, there's no way to tell. It's impossible. He always kept himself in shape, alternately loping like a gazelle and limping around during dead balls like a creaky old man. Chief always kept you on your toes.

So what's the problem? Parish was really, really good . . . but never great. His elite skills were big-game rebounding (you could always count on Chief for 15–20 boards in a Game 7), intelligent defense, a reliable turnaround jumper, a sneaky baseline spin move that worked like a Jedi mind trick (guys knew it was coming yet kept falling for it), fantastic picks (he was one of the first centers to thrive on high screens), high percentage shooting (54 percent or higher in every Boston season) and an unparalleled ability to outsprint other centers for easy layups and dunks. He didn't mind being a complementary player (like Sam Jones, he never wanted the pressure of carrying a team every night), didn't care about shots and willingly did the dirty work for everyone else. Within a few years, Boston fans learned to appreciate him and started chanting "Cheeeeeeeeeeeeeeeeeef" every time he made a good play. If Robert Parish was your *fourth*-best guy, you were in fantastic shape. At the same time, he couldn't have fallen into a cushier situation—a talented team that had elite low-post players (Maxwell, then McHale), one of the best offensive players ever (Bird), intelligent guards (Archibald, DJ, Henderson, Ainge) and above-average backup centers in every year but 1987 (Rick Robey, McHale, and Bill Walton, to name three), as well as a rabid fan base and media corps that would have ripped him if he'd coasted like he did with Golden State.[8] We always hear about stars like Maravich who never found the right team; here's a case where someone found the perfect team.

So I guess it depends on what you want from your big guy. From a talent standpoint, fourteen centers had better Pyramid resumes (we'll get to

---

7. FYI: if you're flicking channels, come across *Vice*, and see a skinny Johnson with short hair, you're in for a classic episode.

8. Parish played there from 1977 to 1980 and had a reputation for mailing it in and being a pothead; that's how he became available in the McHale/Parish–for–Joe Barry Carroll hijacking. Also, Chief was arrested during the '91 season for having a giant package of pot FedExed to his house. Did this affect his Pyramid ranking? Absolutely. I moved him up a few spots.

them). During his prime, Boston fans were always hoping he neutralized better guys or played them to a relative standstill . . . and with the exception of the '85 Finals, he usually did or came close. That made him more valuable than you might think. For instance, let's say Bill Gates developed a computer program that allowed us to effectively simulate games with players from different eras (using not just statistics but intangibles) and we started a twelve-team sim league of all-time greats, with the draft going in snake fashion (last pick of the first round gets the first pick of the second round). I'd grab an elite scorer, a rebounder/low-post player, a point guard and a perimeter shooter with my first four picks (in some order), wait for everyone else to snap up the top twelve centers, then grab Parish with my sixth-round pick, knowing he'd thrive as a complementary player. So if I was picking fifth, I'd grab Bird in Round 1; Pettit, Malone or Barkley in Round 2 (unless Havlicek somehow fell to me); Isiah or Stockton in Round 3 (unless Kobe somehow fell to me); McHale in Round 4 (unless I needed a point guard, in which case I'd take Frazier or Nash); the best two-guard available in Round 5 (Drexler, Greer or someone like Sam Jones if he slid), then Chief with my sixth pick. In a dream scenario, I'm ending up with Bird, Malone, Isiah, McHale, Jones and Parish as my top six picks, then I'm gunning for a long-range shooter (Reggie Miller) and a hybrid guard (Joe Dumars?) from there. That's a nice top eight: I have size, shooting, speed, low-post guys, defense, clutch scoring . . . everything you'd want from a team. And the key would be Parish holding his own at center and not caring that we stuck him with doing all the dirty work. Not many Hall of Famers would accept that role, but he would, and that's what made him so valuable.

One last Parish story: His defining moment happened after Bill Laimbeer clotheslined Bird, causing a brawl and getting the Legend tossed from Game 4 of the '87 Eastern Finals. Game 5 shifted to the Garden and you could *feel* the collective hatred for Laimbeer. We wanted blood.[9] Laimbeer loved tormenting Parish and seeing how far he could push such a fundamentally serene guy, so the ensuing altercation was almost preor-

9. Only twice have I been part of a crowd that loathed an opponent to that degree—this game and Game 6 of the '86 Finals, right after Ralph Sampson picked a fight with Jerry Sichting, when we caused his backbone to crumble as the game went along—and it's an experience unlike anything else in sports. To be honest, it's a little scary. Like being at a Jerry Springer taping with fifteen thousand people.

dained. Late in the second quarter, Parish took a Laimbeer elbow to the ribs, and something snapped—it was like the *Naked Gun* scene when Reggie Jackson decides that he has to kill the queen, only there wasn't a beeping signal triggering Chief, just fifteen thousand fans pining for vengeance. They ran down to Boston's side for a fast break. Laimbeer had position on Parish for a rebound, only his left arm accidentally poked Parish in the chest. And the Chief—for the one and only time in his career—*completely and totally lost his shit,* doling out a one-two sucker punch from behind and belting Laimbeer to the floor as everyone else stood in shock.[10] What did we do? We gasped . . . then we cheered. We kept cheering. We willed the Chief to do it. We brainwashed him. I will believe that until the day I die.

(Follow-up note: Laimbeer was broadcasting a 2002 playoff game in Boston when they started showing '87 highlights on the scoreboard. From our seats, my father and I could see Laimbeer trying *not* to watch and inevitably getting sucked in. He watched the Bird clothesline/fight with an evil smirk on his face. He barely flinched when they showed Parish clocking him. When they showed Bird's famous steal, he shook his head slightly and glanced away. He finally looked away for good as they showed the Celtics celebrating Game 7. You could tell the series still killed him fifteen years later. "That was great," my normally unvindictive father said when it was over. "God, I hate that guy." The lesson, as always: Bill Laimbeer was an asshole.)[P31]

58. BERNARD KING

Resume: 14 years, 10 quality, 4 All-Stars . . . '84 MVP runner-up . . . top 5 ('84, '85), top 10 ('82) . . . 2-year peak: 29–6–3, 55% FG . . . leader: scoring (1x) . . . '84 playoffs: 35–6–3, 57% FG (12 G) . . . missed 374 G and 60-plus G three times

10. This includes referee Jack Madden, who stood under the basket watching the whole thing and never called a foul. Maybe the most astounding no-call in NBA history.
P31. There's an 93.4 percent chance that Joakim Noah is going to become this generation's Laimbeer. Love him if he's on your team, hate him with every fiber of your being if he's not.

I love Bernard too much to write a coherent take on him, so let's describe him in unrelated, semihysterical, fawning clumps:

- If you named a sandwich after Bernard, it would be a corned beef sandwich with Russian dressing, Swiss cheese, cole slaw and a dash of spicy mustard. Why? Because that's the single greatest sandwich that nobody ever talks about, just like Bernard is the best basketball player that nobody ever talks about.[11] He's the player we hope Carmelo Anthony becomes someday, an inside/outside small forward with an unstoppable array of moves. Bernard's first step was unparalleled. Nobody could block his turnaround jumper, and if they overplayed him on it, Bernard would show them the turnaround and spin the other way for an uncontested leaner (so you were screwed either way). His stop-and-pop jumper was exquisite, maybe the best of its kind. He single-handedly brought back the art of the running two-handed slam (especially on follow-up rebounds). And he was absolutely devastating in transition, which made it such a shame that he was stuck on Hubie's plodding Knicks teams for those peak years.[12]
- If we're judging guys simply by how great they were at their apex, then Bernard has to be considered one of the five unstoppable scorers of the post-Russell era along with MJ, Kobe, Gervin and Shaq. From the fall of 1983 to the spring of 1985, *nobody* could guard him. Check out Game 4 of the Knicks-Celts series in '84 on ESPN Classic sometime, when Bernard was triple-teamed by a soon-to-be champion and finished with 46. Awe-inspiring stuff.[13] That series went seven even though Boston had Bird, McHale, Parish, DJ, Maxwell, Ainge, Scott Wedman, Gerald Henderson and M. L. Carr; Bernard was flanked by Bill Cartwright, Truck Robinson, Darrell Walker,

---

11. If you have a friend who *wouldn't* enjoy both halves of the Bernard King sandwich, dump him from your life now because he can't be trusted. My Mount Rushmore for sandwiches looks like this: the French dip, the turkey BLT, the Bernard King and homemade meatloaf on French bread with ketchup and spicy mustard.

12. GOE still blames Hubie for running Bernard ragged on a shitty team in a last-ditch effort to save his job, eventually causing him to break down. Had Bernard played on the Showtime Lakers, it would have been all over.

13. From the bible (aka *Drive*): "During that playoffs, Bernard was automatic—the best scoring machine I have ever seen. His release was amazing. You'd always come within a fraction of getting a piece of his shot, but he wouldn't allow it. He always had you off-balance."

Trent Tucker, Rory Sparrow, Louis Orr, Ernie Grunfeld and a six-foot-seven homeless guy that they found on 34th Street right before the series. How many players could have carried a lousy supporting cast to seven games against a loaded Celtics team? Other than Jordan and LeBron, I can't think of another postmerger player who does it.

- The new MSG opened twenty-five months before the "And here comes Willis!" game in February 1968. Bernard broke the building's scoring record on Christmas Day 1984, dropping 60 in a CBS loss to the Nets, each point coming in the flow of the game. The mark outlasted MJ, 'Nique, Wade, Shaq, Robinson, Bird, you name it. Knicks fans became attached to it. This would be the one way Bernard lived on. Well, until February 2009, when Kobe exploded for 61 against a run-and-gun Knicks team that didn't have a conventional two-guard on its roster, breaking the MSG record in garbage time of a blowout Lakers victory. I watched the second half rooting against it; something seemed unsettling about Bernard's record falling only because Kobe was having a field day against the likes of Wilson Chandler and Jared Jeffries. I wasn't alone. The real Knicks fans were furious at New York's sloppy defensive performance and lack of gumption to protect Bernard's 60, as well as all the loud Laker fans who somehow snuck into the building and chanted "MVP!" Goldman emailed me, "It was the worst night of maybe my life at the Garden," and he's owned season tickets since the Walt Bellamy days. One Knicks buddy emailed me the next day, "I literally didn't sleep last night." With the Boston Garden and Chicago Stadium gone, can you think of any other player/building combinations that would have endured like that in the NBA? Me neither.

- Bernard was a notable semicasualty of a tumultuous era, battling substance abuse issues in the late seventies and early eighties, getting traded twice (once for Wayne Cooper and a second-round pick) before turning his career around after signing with the Knicks, then tragically blowing out his knee in 1985[14] while averaging 35 points a

14. That '85 Knicks team ranked among the ugliest ever with Ken Bannister, Pat Cummings, Orr, Williams, Grunfeld and head coach Hubie Brown. When they played the Celtics that year, people passed out in the stands like the crowds that saw *The Exorcist* in 1973. I always pictured Bernard sneaking out after games to meet women so that none of his teammates would join him.

game. Had King came along twenty years later during the "just say no" and Dr. James Andrews eras, he would have become one of the thirty greatest players ever. It's not even up for discussion.[15]

- With the possible exception of Muhammad Ali and Howard Cosell, no athlete and announcer were matched more perfectly than King and Marv Albert. Even the way Marv said his name was perfect: "Here's King from the left side . . . *yesssss!* Forty . . . *five* points for . . . Bah-nard King!" His game resonated with New Yorkers to the degree that it's impossible to imagine a better Bernard home base than MSG. Going to school in Connecticut during that stretch, I went out of my way to watch Bernard even though I hated the Knicks. He was that good.

- If you were a kid in the early eighties, you had a Nerf hoop in your room, you loved basketball and you *didn't* pretend to be Bernard on those running two-handed slams . . . well, I say you're lying. That was one of the two identifiable traits that were unique to him—his fingerprint, if you will—along with the peculiar way he jogged upcourt with his chest puffed out. And yes, everyone tried to imitate that barrel-chested gait as well.

- You know how certain uniforms just look right on some guys? As good as Bernard looked in New York's blue road uniform, I gotta say, remember the '82–'83 season when the Knicks wore those wacky jerseys with the player's number sitting on *top* of the team's name? For whatever reason, that uniform gave Bernard superpowers; it was like how Dr. J could jump a foot higher when he had his 'fro. Hell, I would have bought that throwback by now if it didn't say "New York" on it.

- If that's not enough, Bernard starred in one of my favorite movies, *Fast Break,*[16] the only sports flick that can't be remade because it's so

15. Bernard averaged 28.4 a game for the '91 Bullets when he was 34. If only he and Dr. Andrews had crossed paths in time.

16. Quick rehash of the plot: The great Gabe Kaplan plays a New York basketball junkie who gets a coaching job at tiny Cadwallader State College in Nevada, where they pay him $50 for every win. His wife refuses to go—remember, this was the Wet Blanket Girlfriend era of sports movies—so Gabe ditches her and brings four local stars who couldn't get into college: Hustler, D. C. Dacey (on the lam from the law, as well as an early prototype for Derrick Coleman's game), Preacher (a reverend point guard fleeing from the mob) and Swish (a top female player playing in drag). They turn Cadwallader State College around and Hustler wins a ton of money from the Nevada State coach in billiards, agreeing to forgo the money if the two teams play a game. You can guess what happens next.

unbelievably inappropriate: there's gay-bashing, a car ride where the players eat a pound of marijuana, a coach who encourages a white player to drop an *n*-bomb so it would trigger a bench-clearing brawl, a transvestite shooting guard, the glorification of players who have no business going to college and everything else. It's one of those movies where you see the players toking up and *know* they used real grass for the scene. King plays Hustler, a pot-smoking pool shark[17] who carries Cadwallader College to an undefeated season, and I mention this only because it's the most entertaining performance by an NBA player in a movie—better than Doc in *The Fish That Saved Pittsburgh*, better than Malik Sealy and Rick Fox in *Eddie*, better than Kareem in *Airplane*, even better than Ray Allen as Jesus. I will never figure out two things about Bernard's career: why the NBA left him off 50 at 50, and why he didn't win a Best Supporting Actor Oscar in 1979 over the little schmuck from *Kramer vs. Kramer*.

The good news? Bernard gets to live on in this book. And ESPN Classic. And my office, where I have not one but two framed posters of *Fast Break*.

57. TOMMY HEINSOHN

Resume: 9 years, 8 quality, 6 All-Stars . . . '57 Rookie of the Year . . . top 10 ('61, '62, '63, '64) . . . 4-year peak: 22–10–2 . . . '63 Playoffs: 25–9 (11 G) . . . started for 8 champs ('50s, '60s Celtics) . . . Playoffs: 20–10, 40% FG (104 G)

56. PAUL ARIZIN

Resume: 10 years, 10 quality, 10 All-Stars . . . '56 MVP runner-up . . . top 5 ('52, '56, '57), top 10 ('59) . . . 4-year peak: 24–8–2 . . . best player on 1 champ ('56 Warriors), averaged a 28–9 (12 G) . . . season leader: scoring (2x), minutes (2x), FG% (1x) . . . missed 2 years (war service)

17. In retrospect, not a lot of acting here—Bernard landed in rehab a year later. Kaplan told me once that they shot the movie in 60 days and Bernard gave them 58 good ones. He didn't elaborate.

Did you know Arizin was the first NBA player to employ something called the jump shot? That he was the best player and crunch-time guy for the last pre-Russell champion (the '56 Warriors)? That he became the first player to average 20-plus points in nine straight seasons? That they called him "Pitching Paul"? That he struggled with a chronic sinus problem that left him wheezing and grunting as he ran up and down the court? That he made first-team All-NBA in his second season ('52) and missed the next two seasons because the Marines pulled him away for the Korean War? That he returned in '54 without missing a beat and tossed up a 21–9? That he retired from the NBA after averaging a 23–7 in 12 playoff games for a Philly squad that nearly beat the '62 Celtics, then played another three years in the Eastern Basketball League and averaged a 25–7 for Camden?[18] Give him back those two Korean War years, pad his career totals by keeping him in the NBA through 1965, and suddenly we're talking about one of the best careers by any forward.

If Arizin's prime was cut short by his time in Korea, then Heinsohn's prime was cut short by the countries of Nicotinea and Boozea. If you wanted to party with someone from the Russell era, really, it *had* to be either Heinsohn or Johnny "Red" Kerr. Heinsohn's regular-season stats weren't that overwhelming, although he was probably the best all-around forward other than Pettit and Baylor from '57 to '64, someone who defended bigger guys and provided a little muscle during a hockey-like era where everyone threw down. He also served a crucial chemistry role for those early Russell teams, not just because he was such a fun-loving jokester and prankster,[19] but also because he served as a lightning rod for the press (who criticized him for shooting too much and called

18. Arizin left treadmarks fleeing from Wilt for a high-paying job at IBM, moonlighting in the Eastern League for his basketball fix. Isn't it amazing that, as late as the mid-'60s, NBA stars left the league because they could make more money elsewhere?
19. The old Heinsohn stories are funny—you have to love an era when exploding cigars and sliced shoelaces were hysterically funny acts. Tommy sounds like the kind of guy who'd sneak into your hotel room, take a horrendous dump, not flush it and let it fester in there for 10 hours until you came back to your room and passed out. Needless to say, he would have been a fun person to have on your college hall. And where did he go to college? That's right . . . Holy Cross!

him "Tommy Gun") and Auerbach (who yelled at him constantly as a way to take out his frustrations about the entire team) and inadvertently directed negative attention away from everyone else.[20] What really stood out was Tommy's playoffs record. For one thing, he played for nine years and won eight titles as either the third- or fourth-best player on those teams. (Find me a better title-per-seasons-played ratio. You won't.) His playoffs stats (20–9) were slightly better than his regular-season stats (19–9), and he carried the Celtics offensively in Cousy's final playoff run with a sparkling effort (25–9, 46 percent shooting). During Game 7 of the '57 Finals against St. Louis, as Cousy and Sharman stumbled to a combined 5-for-40 from the field, Heinsohn played one of the greatest games by a rookie: battling Pettit, he notched a startling 37 points and 23 rebounds as the Celtics prevailed in double OT. In 1980, Magic played a similarly memorable Finals clincher and everyone placed the game on a pedestal. Tommy? People only remember him sobbing into a towel after fouling out.

So why give Arizin the nod over Heinsohn? Because the NBA convened a panel in 1971 to figure out its Silver Anniversary Team, and here are the players they picked:[21] Bob Cousy, Bill Sharman, Bob Davies, Sam Jones (guards); Bill Russell, George Mikan (centers); Bob Pettit, Joe Fulks, Dolph Schayes, Paul Arizin (forwards). Since Arizin made the cut over Heinsohn, obviously, he should make the cut over Heinsohn in the Pyramid, right?

(Note: I can't believe I'm boning over a Holy Cross grad like this. Let's just move on.)[22]

---

20. Russell in *Second Wind:* "Tommy was so gifted and so smart that if he had made up his mind that he was going to play every night, the only forward who would have been any competition for him was Baylor. Not even Pettit could have come close to him."

21. Only retired players were eligible for selection and had to have one All-NBA first team on their resume.

22. Back in the late '90s, my old college roomie JackO and I ran into Tommy at the Four's. Tommy had a cigarette in one hand and a Scotch in the other—just like we'd always imagined if the moment ever happened—so we quickly approached him, played the H.C. card and talked to him for 20 minutes. It's my all-time "interaction with a famous person" moment. I'm not kidding. We were so happy afterward that we didn't know what to do with ourselves.

55. DOMINIQUE WILKINS

Resume: 15 years, 11 quality seasons, 9 All-Stars . . . '86 MVP runner-up . . . top 5 ('86), top 10 ('87, '88, '91, '93) . . . leader: scoring (1x) . . . 3-year peak: 30–7–3 . . . 3-year Playoffs peak: 29–7–3 (30 G) . . . eight 2K-point seasons . . . career: points (10th)

If you made a Slipped Through the Cracks of History All-Star Team, 'Nique makes the starting five along with Westphal, Moses, Kemp, Gus Williams and sixth man Andrew Toney. Nobody ever mentions these guys anymore. It's mystifying. Just remember these eight things about our man 'Nique.

1. His best teammates were Doc Rivers, Kevin Willis, Antoine Carr, John Battle, Spud Webb, a not-quite-there-yet Mookie Blaylock and a just-about-washed-up Moses. During 'Nique's prime ('85 to '94), only one teammate cracked an All-NBA team (Kevin Willis, a third-teamer in '92) and just four made an All-Star team (Rivers in '88, Moses in '89, Willis in '92 and Mookie in '94). Of everyone in my top sixty with one exception (Bernard), 'Nique had the least help. It's just a fact.

2. The Hawks won 50 games or more for three straight years ('86 through '88) during the league's strongest period, when there were only twenty-three teams, the Bird/Magic/Moses/Isiah generation was still thriving *and* the MJ/Hakeem/Malone generation was coming into its own. During that time, 'Nique averaged 30.0 points per game and doubled as his team's only bona fide All-Star during a time when most contenders had two, three or even four All-Star-caliber guys. Quite a feat.

3. 'Nique averaged somewhere between 26 and 31 points for a solid decade ('85 through '94). The list of noncenters who can say that: Jordan, Iverson, West, 'Nique . . . and that's the list.

4. MJ was better at controlling his body in the air and creating impossible shots, but 'Nique was the best in-game dunker of his generation. Nobody dunked on people as consistently and violently; he made it an art form and sought out victims. His single most identifiable dunk was

the one where he jumped in traffic off two feet, brought the ball up like he was going to dunk it right away, brought it down again to buy himself an extra split second as the defender fell back to earth, then ripped it through the hoop. He did this over and over and over. Nobody blocked a 'Nique dunk. It just didn't happen.[23]

5. Along those same lines, nobody fired up a home crowd more than 'Nique . . . and that lame Atlanta crowd in the eighties and nineties certainly needed the help. As former Hawks president Stan Kasten said once, "Dominique is a showman. People denigrate that, but it's important. In the old ABA, coaches used to call a time-out whenever the Doc dunked. Don't let the crowd get fired up. Coaches do the same thing against 'Nique." There's something to be said for that: only a few players could send their crowd into a near-frenzy, and 'Nique was one.

6. I know this has nothing to do with anything, but if you're discussing his competitive spirit, it has to be mentioned that 'Nique gave MJ everything he could handle in the '87 and '88 Slam Dunk Contests and was absolutely *robbed* (that's right, italics) in '87 for reasons that remain unclear. That was the Dunk Contest equivalent of the '06 Finals.[24]

7. 'Nique had the single hippest poster of the entire 1980s: one where he casually finished off a reverse dunk in a just-about-empty Meadowlands arena with empty seats cluttering the background behind him. It's hard to properly explain how mesmerizing this was, so I'll only say this: My basement was littered with every sports poster you can imagine. I practically had a sports poster fetish. Name any good one from the eighties and I guarantee it was hanging somewhere in that basement. The 'Nique poster was given the coveted spot right between the Ping-Pong table and pool table on the wall directly over my stereo. And that's where it remained for the entire decade. Everyone who ever went down there loved it, commented on it and stared at it. In retrospect, the poster

23. During the '87 season, Larry Legend made the mistake of challenging 'Nique on a fast break and got dunked on so violently that the momentum sent him sprawling into the basket support like he had been struck by a car. This nearly caused a bigger Atlanta riot than the bomb that spoiled the '96 Olympics. People went berserk. They almost charged the court.

24. 'Nique was ten times more bummed out than he should have been afterward. If you asked him whether he would have rather won the '87 Dunk Contest or the '88 duel against Bird, I'd bet he'd say Bird, but I'd also bet that he would pause for a split second.

personified that era from '81 to '84 perfectly—the league was becoming cool, only the fans hadn't caught on yet. [25]

8. Of the 600-plus NBA games I have attended, 'Nique made the single most spectacular play I've ever seen: during the '88 playoffs, he bricked a jumper from the top of the key, jumped from one step in front of the foul line and rammed home the rebound over Boston's entire front line. I can't even properly describe it; everyone in the Garden made this low-pitched "oooooooh" noise when it happened, almost like a "swoooooosh." We didn't know what to do. He pulled a Bob Beamon. It seemed like he jumped 30 feet. This was a superhuman act and I will never forget it for as long as I live.

So why didn't Wilkins get selected for the NBA's 50 at 50? He never played in a Conference Finals, which hurt his cause unless you remember that his prime coincided with three Eastern juggernauts (the mid-eighties Celtics, late-eighties Pistons and early-nineties Bulls). He battled the stigma of being a "me first" guy throughout his career, someone who cared about getting his numbers, dunking on a few guys and that's it.[26] Doc Rivers once joked that you could stand in the huddle with Wilkins during the final 30 seconds of a one-point playoff game and ask him, "'Nique, how many points do you have?" and Wilkins would respond without missing a beat, "Thirty-seven, and I'd have 39 if they called that foul back in the second quarter." Doesn't sound like someone with a firm grasp of The Secret. He never displayed the all-around brilliance of many contemporaries, always making for a better foil than anything. And he was a self-absorbed scorer who rarely moved without the ball and always seemed to be holding his right hand up in the "I'm open!" stance. I hated playing with those guys. But to claim that Wilkins wasn't one of the best fifty NBA players ever in 1996 . . . that's just absurd.

25. I will never forgive my mother for throwing out all my hockey cards in the late-'70s or for throwing out my posters in the mid-'90s. What would I have done with them? I don't know; they'd probably be in my attic gathering dust. It's the principle, that's all.
26. 'Nique's porous defense was the turd in the punch bowl of the famous Bird-'Nique shootout in '88. He was Ominique Wilkins that night.

54. DENNIS JOHNSON

Resume: 14 years, 10 quality, 5 All-Stars . . . '79 Finals MVP (23–6–6) . . . top 5 ('81), top 10 ('80) . . . All-Defense (9x, six 1st) . . . started for 3 champs ('79 Sonics, '84, '86 Celts) and 3 runner-ups ('78, '85, '87) . . . 3-year peak: 19–4–5 . . . '87 Playoffs: 19–4–9, 41.9 MPG (23 G) . . . never played fewer than 72 games, missed 48 games total

Yet another reason why we need to blow up the Hall of Fame: Poor DJ passed away in 2007 before Springfield found a place for him, leading to a 2010 ceremony when he made it posthumously and his peers paid tribute with a series of "It's just too bad DJ couldn't have been here to see this" comments. I hate when that happens. Either you're a Hall of Famer or you're not. This isn't the Oscars or Emmys, where only a certain number of nominees can win each year. You shouldn't have to "wait your turn."

Here's what we know for sure:

1. Johnson was the greatest defensive guard of his era, making nine straight All-Defensive appearances from 1979 to 1987 (first or second team) and becoming one of the only players ever described as "destructive" on that end. The Celtics traded for him before the '84 season[27] because Andrew Toney had been torturing them every spring. The Sixers never beat them again. And every Celtics fan remembers how the '84 Finals turned when DJ demanded to guard Magic before Game 4,[28] as well as DJ's singular obliteration of Robert Reid in the '86 Finals. An All-Defensive team for the past thirty years can only include four guys—DJ, Payton, Pippen and Hakeem—as well as a juicy argument between Garnett, Rodman and Ben Wallace for the power forward spot.

27. Seattle traded him for Westphal in 1980 and finished 22 games worse the following season; Phoenix traded him for Rick Robey in 1983 and finished 12 games worse. Nobody ever seemed to appreciate DJ until he was gone.
28. Really, KC Jones needed to watch three Finals games before realizing, "Maybe I should have the best defensive guard alive checking the key to L.A.'s offense?"

2. For the short list of best big-game guards, it's Frazier, West, Miller, Jordan, Sam Jones, DJ and maybe Isiah (depending on how much you want to blame him for Bird's steal). DJ played in six Finals and two other conference Finals, going down as the best all-around guard for 11 straight seasons on teams that won 47, 52, 56, 57, 46, 53, 62, 63, 67, 59 and 57 games. He averaged 17.3 points, 5.6 assists, and 4.3 rebounds for his playoff career, including an astonishing 23-game run for a banged-up '87 Celtics team on which he averaged a 19–9 and 42 minutes per game guarding the likes of John Lucas, Sidney Moncrief, Isiah Thomas, Vinnie Johnson and Magic.

3. Larry Bird called him the greatest he ever played with, which seems relevant since the Legend played with McHale, Parish, Walton, Archibald, Cowens and Maravich (all Hall of Famers). Although I do feel like he was sticking it to McHale a little. More on this in a few pages.

4. In fourteen seasons, DJ played in 1,100 of a possible 1,148 regular-season games, missed more than 5 games just once (missing 10 in the '89 season, near the tail end of his career) and played in another 180 playoff games (eleventh on the all-time list). The guy was built like an Albanian oak.

5. He made the all-time "We'll never see anyone like this specific guy again" team. There's never been a guard like DJ before or since.[29]

The last paragraph should have clinched his Hall of Fame spot years ago. Could you compare Dennis Johnson to anyone else on the planet? He splashed onto the scene as a high-flying, physical two-guard for the Sonics, evolved into a scorer for Phoenix, reincarnated himself as a heady point guard in Boston and peaked as the ringleader of a loaded '86 team that scored 114 points a game. He could defend anyone shorter than six foot nine and lock them down. He was such an intelligent player that Bird

---

29. And then there's this: apparently the guy was hung like a tripod. I knew someone who knew someone who worked in Boston's clubhouse during the Bird era. (I know, one of those friend-of-a-friend stories, but in this case, the story is too bizarre and nobody could have made it up.) A former Celtic was visiting the locker room, saw DJ naked, was impressed by DJs, um, equipment, and said something like, "Damn, DJ, how the hell did you get that thing?" And as the story went, DJ responded, "I dip it in beans . . . human beans!" Then everyone cracked up. After hearing that story, I immediately named my fantasy hoops team "Human Beans." How could a story that wacky be made up?

and DJ had a secret ESP play for six straight years, in which Bird would linger near the basket like he was waiting for someone to set him a pick, then DJ would whip a pass by the defender's ears and Bird would catch it at the last possible second for a layup (and the only way that play happened was if they locked eyes). He was one of those classic only-when-it-counts shooters who could be riding a 3-for-14 game into the final minute, then nail a wide-open 20-footer to win the game. Every Celtic loved playing with him because of his competitiveness and the way he carried himself in big games with a noticeable swagger. I can't remember following anyone who enjoyed the actual process of *winning* more than him. There's a great scene in the '87 team video when the Celts are boarding the bus after a Game 6 shellacking in the Pistons series. Still sulking about Dennis Rodman's antics, DJ sarcastically waves his hand over his head and says something like, "Yeah, okay, we'll see what happens on Sunday." Sure enough, the Celts pulled out an absolute slugfest of a seventh game, with DJ following Rodman around in the final seconds and sarcastically mimicking Rodman's high-stepped gait while waving his hand over his head. The lesson, as always: don't mess with Dennis Johnson.[30]

I loved so many things about watching him play: the way he'd suddenly strip an unsuspecting guard at midcourt (you *never* see that anymore) like a pickpocket swiping a wallet; the ESP plays with Bird; the supernatural way he rose to the occasion in big moments (like the game-winner in Game 4 of the '85 Finals); his unsurpassed knack for grabbing big rebounds in traffic; the way he always made one huge play in a must-win game (my personal favorite was in Game 7 against the '87 Bucks, when he went flying full speed out of bounds to save a loose ball in the final 90 seconds, then somehow whipped it off Sikma as he careened into the entire Bucks bench). Every time I get sucked into an old Celtics game from the eighties on ESPN Classic or NBA TV, there's always a point in the game

---

30. Wait, I'm not done talking about dicks. My buddy Gus worked for an Orlando TV station in the early-'90s and had the "guy who holds the boom mike for TV interviews right after games" job. He saw nearly every player naked and eventually made an All-Dick Team, the funniest list ever rattled off by any of my friends. You're not gonna believe this, but there were no white guys. I don't remember every starter, but I do remember Gus making Vinnie Johnson the sixth man. That killed me. His MVP? Orlando swingman Jerry "Ice" Reynolds—literally, he was a swingman—who dwarfed everyone else to the degree that Ice's teammates discussed his icicle in reverential tones. I'm still disappointed we never got a *SportsCentury* about this.

where I find myself saying, "Holy crap, I forgot how good Dennis Johnson was."

Few remember his defining moment: the waning seconds of Game 5 in the '87 Eastern finals, when Bird picked off Isiah's pass and found DJ for the winning layup. Right after Bird snatched the ball from Laimbeer's grimy hands, as everyone else was still processing what had happened, DJ started cutting toward the basket with his hands up. From the mid-seventies to right now, I can only pinpoint a handful of players who would have instinctively known to cut toward the basket there: MJ, Magic, Frazier, Stockton, Reggie, Mullin, Barry, Isiah (ironically, the one who threw the pass), Horry, Wade, Kidd, Iverson, Nash, Kobe and that's about it. Nobody else starts moving for a full second after that steal happens. If DJ had never made that cut, Bird would have been forced to launch a fall-away 10-footer over the backboard to win the game . . . which he probably would have made, but that's beside the point. Don't forget that DJ was chugging full speed as he caught the pass from his left, with Dumars charging from the right, meaning he had to shield the ball from Dumars, turn his body and make an extremely difficult reverse layup that came within a hair of missing (believe me, I was there). Of course, few people remember this, just as few remember how great a basketball player Dennis Johnson was. As my father said on the phone when DJ died, "He was the best guard on the best team I ever watched in my entire life."

Agreed. DJ should have made the trip to Springfield when he was still alive. At least he lives on in this book.

53. BILL SHARMAN

Resume: 12 years, 8 quality, 8 All-Stars . . . top 5 ('56, '57, '58, '59), top 10 ('53, 55, '60) . . . started for 4 champs in Boston ('57, '59, '60, '61) . . . leader: FT% (7x) . . . 3-year peak: 21–3–4 . . . best Playoffs FT shooter, 75+ games (91.1%)

The NBA's best two-guard until Jerry West showed up; the first shooter to regularly crack 40 percent from the field and shoot 90 percent from the line; half of the most successful backcourt in the history of the league.

Factoring in team success, individual careers, statistics and total games played together, we haven't seen anything approaching Cousy and Sharman. (Lemme know when we'll see two guards from the same team make first-team All-NBA for four straight years again.)[31] When Sharman retired in 1961, only twenty-two noncenters had played 500 games or more at that time. Of those twenty-two players, Sharman ranked first in free throw percentage (88 percent) and second in shooting percentage (42.6 percent, just behind Bob Pettit); he was the only guard to crack 40 percent from the field. So Sharman was *significantly* better than any other two-guard from his era; the numbers, awards and titles back this up, as does the fact that Sharman held off Sam Jones for four solid years. Sharman even moonlighted as a third baseman in Brooklyn's farm system from 1950 to 1955, getting called up at the end of the '51 season and being thrown out of a game for yelling at an umpire, becoming the only player in major league history to get ejected from a game without ever actually appearing in one. Bizarre. But that gives you an idea of his athletic pedigree. He was also famous for being the first player to (a) study opponents' tendencies and keep notes on them and (b) create a daily routine of stretching, exercising, and shooting and make a concerted effort to stick to that routine.[32]

What doesn't live on historically was Sharman's defense. By all accounts, he was that decade's best lockdown defender and a feisty competitor who had more fights than Jake LaMotta. Jerry West once remembered being a rookie and making seven straight shots against an aging Sharman, then Sharman preventing an eighth shot simply by taking a swing at him. As West told the *L.A. Times* years later, "I'll tell you this, you did not drive by him. He got into more fights than Mike Tyson. You respected him as a player." Sounds like my kind of guy. I'd tell you more, but Sharman retired when my mother was twelve.

31. A more interesting debate: what are the next five "greatest backcourt of all time" combos using that same criteria? I'd go with Isiah and Dumars, Chauncey Billups and Rip Hamilton, Frazier and Monroe, and Ginobili and Parker for the next five, with honorable mention going to Mo Cheeks and Andrew Toney, and Rondo and Ray Allen, and DJ and Gus Williams.
32. I love the thought of Sharman shooting extra free throws and doing jumping jacks after practice while Heinsohn sipped a beer, smoked a Marlboro and heckled him from the sidelines. You know this happened.

52. DOLPH SCHAYES

Resume: 15 years, 11 quality, 12 All-Stars . . . '58 MVP runner-up . . . top
5 ('52, '53, '54, '55, '57, '58), top 10 ('50, '51, '56, '59, '60, '61) . . . leader: rebounds (1x), FT% (3x), minutes (2x) . . . career FT: 85% . . . 5-year peak:
23–13–3 . . . best player on champ ('55 Nats)

You have to love the days when NBA superstars had names like Dolph.
Schayes excelled in two different eras (pre-shot-clock, post-shot-clock),
won an Imaginary Playoffs MVP and a ring for the '55 Nats, stuck around
for an abnormally long time (fifteen years, which was like twenty-five
years back then), exhibited a startling degree of durability (missing three
games total in his first twelve seasons) and finished as the second most
successful forward of the pre-Elgin era. Still, we have to penalize him for
excelling as a set-shooting, slow-as-molasses power forward during a time
when black players were few and far between. When Russell entered the
league, Syracuse and Schayes won only two playoffs in the next seven
years. What would happen if he played now? Whom would he defend?
How would he score? Would he have been better than Danny Ferry? I also
couldn't shake his shooting stats—Schayes only shot 40 percent in a season twice and finished at a deadly 38 percent for his career, well behind
contemporaries such as Hagan (45 percent), Twyman (45 percent), Ed
Macauley (44 percent), Pettit (44 percent), George Yardley (42 percent)
and Arizin (42 percent). Maybe Cousy's shooting stats were equally brutal, but his playmaking skills would have translated nicely to today's game.
In short, I'm just not seeing the Dolphster. But you can't argue with five
top fives and six top tens, so he had to crack the top fifty. Barely.[33]

33. I'd be lying if I said Danny Schayes didn't affect this ranking. Dolph's genes produced
one of the all-time stiffs of the '80s.[P32]
P32. Dolph sent me a long, handwritten complaint about that footnote. I felt terrible.
Researched Danny's career and found out he played 18 years, peaked with an 11–7
stretch from '88 to '91 and averaged a 16–7 in the '88 playoffs (11 games). Certainly no
stiff. Dolph was right. Speaking of Dolph, he played most of the '52 season with a broken right arm. How? By doing everything left-handed. Amazing. And yes, that was a year
after Mikan played with a broken leg. You could do these things in professional basketball when there were no black guys.

51. ELVIN HAYES

Resume: 16 years, 12 quality, 12 All-Stars . . . top 5 ('75, '77, '79), top 10 ('73, '74, '76) . . . best player on 1 champ ('78 Bullets) and 2 runner-ups ('75, '79) . . . missed 9 games in his entire career . . . traded once in his prime . . . '75 playoffs: 26–11 (17 G) . . . '78, '79 playoffs: 22–14 (40 G) . . . 3-year peak: 28–17 . . . 25K-15K Club

The Big E played 50,000 minutes exactly. (Yes, it was intentional.) He missed 9 games in a sixteen-year career and never played fewer than 80 games in a season. He scored over 27,000 points and grabbed over 16,000 rebounds. And in the last three minutes of a huge game, you wouldn't have wanted him on the floor. We'll remember Hayes as his generation's Karl Malone, a gifted power forward with terrific numbers who played differently when the bread needed to be buttered . . . although Malone carried a little more weight with his peers and weaseled his way into two MVP awards, whereas Hayes never cracked the top two in the balloting. It's worth mentioning that the Big E played his first four years for the Rockets,[34] averaged a 27–16 and doubled as their franchise player when they moved to Houston (the same city where he memorably starred in college), only things deteriorated so badly that they gave him away before the '72–'73 season for Jack Marin and cash considerations.[35] Jack Marin and cash considerations? That was the whole trade? Other than eye-opening numbers and a memorable no-show in the '75 Finals, Hayes stands out for five reasons:

1. My favorite basketball writer growing up, Bob Ryan, openly detested Elvin's game and took shots at the Big E any time he could. Any time someone choked in the clutch or shrank from a big moment, regard-

34. *SI* from February 1974: "During his four years with the Rockets, Hayes was variously considered a ball hog, a rotten apple, a dumbbell and a guaranteed loser." Well, then.
35. Marin was best known for a disorienting red birthmark that took up much of his right arm. I remember being patently terrified of him as a little kid. These days, he would have just cluttered that arm up with tattoos and we wouldn't have noticed it. GOE adds, "He was also part of a great Bullets team that you're overlooking with Unseld, Monroe, Kevin Loughery and Gus Johnson. A classic second-best team that is now forgotten." That might be his grumpiest and oldest interruption yet.

less of the sport, you could count on Ryan to compare that player to Hayes. Since Ryan is one of the more rational writers around, as well as the best hoops writer of my lifetime, I'm trusting his judgment here.

2. You know the annoying "Emm Vee Pee!" chants that get serenaded on every top-twenty player in the league? All empirical evidence suggests that Elvin Hayes and Bullets fans are to blame. Down the stretch of the '79 season, when there were three favorites to win the award (Malone, Gervin and Hayes), Washington fans started chanting "Emm Vee Pee!" every time he made a good play. Now we get to hear that chant when the likes of Joe Johnson makes a three. Awesome. By the way, with players voting for MVP for the majority of Elvin's career, the Big E cracked the top six only three times—fifth in '74, third in '75, third in '79—which makes me wonder if the other guys respected him that much. I'm guessing no.

3. He certainly didn't distinguish himself in the '78 Finals, scoring 133 points in the first six games but only 19 in the fourth quarters, earning derisive comments in Curry Kirkpatrick's *SI* Finals feature like "Individualism overcame Elvin in yet another big contest," "Hayes once more disappeared in the moments of crisis," "In between his hiding and complaining to everybody about the officials," and "[It's] imperative for the Bullets that their only real 'name' player and 10-year All-Star justify his status by not dissolving at the end of the seventh game." What happened? Elvin scored 12 points in Game 7 and fouled out with 10 minutes to play in a close game. They won the title on the road without him. I find this interesting.[36]

4. According to Filip Bondy in *Tip Off,* before Hayes' final season with the Rockets in '84, he made a big deal about mentoring prized rookie Ralph Sampson, causing Houston coach Bill Fitch to pull Sampson aside and tell him, "You stay away from that no-good fucking prick." Elvin Hayes, everybody!

5. Hayes' signature shot? The fall-away/turnaround. My theory on the fall-away: it's a passive-aggressive shot that says more about a player

---

36. During the postgame celebration, Hayes responded to a few needling questions about his Game 7 no-show by saying, "They can say whatever they want. But they gotta say one thing: E's a world champion. He wears the ring." The Sports Guy enjoyed E's use of the third-person nickname tense on that one.

than you think. For instance, Jordan, McHale and Hakeem all had tremendous fall-aways—in fact, MJ developed the shot to save his body from undue punishment driving to the basket—but it was one piece of their offensive arsenal, a weapon used to complement the other weapons already in place.[P33] Well, five basketball stars in the past sixty years have been famous for either failing miserably in the clutch or lacking the ability to rise to the occasion: Wilt, Hayes, Malone, Ewing and Garnett. All five were famous for their fall-away/turnaround jumpers and took heat because their fall-aways pulled them out of rebounding position. If it missed, almost always it was a one-shot possession. On top of that, it never leads to free throws—either the shot falls or the other team gets it. Could you make the case that the fall-away, fundamentally, is a loser's shot? For a big man, it's the dumbest shot you can take—only one good thing can happen and that's it—as well as a symbol of a larger problem, namely, that a team's best big man would rather move away from the basket than toward it. Of the handful of differences that led Tim Duncan to become more successful than Garnett, the biggest was their mind-set in close games. Duncan made a concerted effort to plant his ass down low, post up and take high-percentage shots (either jump hooks, drop-step layups, mini-fall-aways or "I'm putting my shoulder into you and getting to the rim" layups) that might also lead to fouls, tip-ins, or putback layups, whereas Garnett mostly settled for 18-footers and fall-aways.

So here's my take: the fall-away says, "I'd rather stay out here." It says, "I'm afraid to fail." It says, "I want to win this game, but only on my terms." In a related story, Elvin Hayes attempted more fall-aways than anyone who ever played in the NBA. Draw your own conclusions.

50. JAMES WORTHY

Resume: 12 years, 8 quality, 7 All-Stars . . . '88 Finals MVP . . . top 15 ('90, '91) . . . 2nd- or 3rd-best player for 3 champs ('85, '87, '88 Lakers)

P33. Not so coincidentally, Kobe mastered that same fall-away during the 2009–10 seasons to save undue mileage.

and 3 runner-ups ('84, '89, '91) . . . 2-year peak: 21–5–4, 55% FG . . . playoffs (143 G): 21–5–2, 54% FG (5th-best ever, 100+ games)

If you made an All-Star team of Guys Who Made a Jump Historically Because They Were Fortunate Enough to Play on Some Really Good Teams, here's your starting five: Parish, Worthy, Scottie Pippen, Walt Frazier and K. C. Jones (who snuck into the Hall of Fame even though he couldn't shoot). At the same time, each player had skill sets and personalities that lent themselves to semicomplementary roles on winning teams (we covered the benefits in Parish's section), so it's tough to penalize them for being that way. You can win titles with guys like Pippen, Frazier and Worthy. You know, as long as they aren't the best guy on your team.[P34]

Worthy stood out for his athleticism (off the charts), transition finishes (as good as anyone), and signature freeze-the-ball-high-above, swooping one-handed slam (one of the five memorable signature dunks of the eighties, along with Doc's tomahawk dunk, Bernard's running two-hander, 'Nique's windmill and MJ's tilt-the-body one-hander). I already made this joke, but let's tweak it: anyone who had a Nerf hoop in the eighties and claims he didn't attempt Worthy's swooping dunk or Bernard's two-hander at least five hundred times is lying. Worthy had an unstoppable first step and absolutely abused slower defenders. Defensively, he played Bird better than any quality offensive player and helped swing the '87 Finals that way. He wasn't the greatest rebounder but had a knack for grabbing big ones in big moments. And you can't forget Game 7 of the '88 Finals, when he carried the Lakers with a 36–16–10 against a superior defensive team and rightfully earned the nickname "Big Game

P34. I asked ESPN's J. A. Adande (a childhood Lakers fanatic) to describe Big Game James in one word. Here's what he wrote: "The word was 'unfair.' Magic, Kareem . . . and Worthy, too? As if opponents didn't have their hands full dealing with two all-time greats, now they had to contend with a Hall of Famer? Unfair. Worthy could spin around defenders, dribble past them or shoot over them from up to 20 feet. A third scoring option who had three ways to beat you? Unfair. It's also unfair that Worthy doesn't get enough credit for liberating big men. Coming out of Carolina, everyone assumed he was a power forward and never imagined he'd evolve into such a devastating small forward. Instead of just rebounding and defending, the 6'9" Magic led fast breaks and the 6'9" Worthy finished them. Before Worthy, 6'9" meant Bill Russell or Maurice Lucas. After Worthy, 6'9" could be Shareef Abdur-Rahim, Andrei Kirilenko or Kevin Durant . . . even if putting those guys in Worthy's class would be unfair, too."

James."[37] Had he developed a three-point shot—and it's unclear why he didn't[38]—Worthy would have been unstoppable. We also can't forget that he spent three years at Carolina and another seven playing for Pat Riley, a notorious practice Nazi, which explains why Worthy's legs went so quickly after just ten quality NBA seasons. You can't penalize him for a lack of longevity.

You also can't discuss Worthy without mentioning the Wilkins/Worthy what-if (page 175) and Worthy's thank-God-it-never-happened Clippers career, which would be neat to simulate *Sliding Doors*–style if we had the ability to do so. One thing's for sure: had Worthy gone second in the '82 draft, he wouldn't have cracked the top fifty of the Pyramid. You need some luck with this stuff and he had it. While we're here, I'd like to honor him for two other things: being a starting forward on the All-Time Bearded All-Stars,[39] and being the subject of Peter Vecsey's funniest joke ever, after Worthy was arrested for soliciting two prostitutes and arranging for them to meet him in a Houston hotel room (Vecsey cracked in his *New York Post* column, "James always did have trouble scoring against double teams"). High comedy for 1991, I'm telling you.

49. BILLY CUNNINGHAM

Resume: 11 years, 8 quality, 5 All-Stars (1 ABA) . . . '73 ABA MVP . . . '69 BS MVP . . . top 5 ('69, '70, '71), top 10 ('72), top 5 ABA ('73) . . . 5-year peak: 24–12–4 . . . '73 ABA: 24–12–6 . . . '73 Playoffs: 24–12–5 (12 G) . . . career: 21.2 PPG, 10.4 RPG (both top 40) . . . Playoffs: 20–10–4 (54 G)

37. It's hard to take that nickname seriously when he sucked in the '84 Finals and basically blew the series with his backcourt lob that Gerald Henderson picked off in Game 2. Whatever, it rhymes. I like nicknames that rhyme—even "Never Nervous Pervis" made Ellison seem like 50 percent less of a bust.

38. In his first five seasons, Worthy missed 42 of 43 threes. In the next two seasons, he "improved" to 4-for-39. So for his first seven seasons, Worthy took 82 threes and missed 77 of them. That has to be some sort of record, right?

39. The starting five: Bill Walton, Worthy, Jamaal Wilkes, Baron Davis and Walt Frazier, with Brian Winters as sixth man and Mike Newlin, Phil Jackson, Mike Gminski and World B. Free coming off the bench. I'm excluding Kareem out of sheer spite.

Billy was the starting small forward on the Guys I Would Have Loved if I Had Seen Them Play Team: a lefty small forward who played bigger than his size and had a game best described as a cross between Manu Ginobili's and Shawn Marion's, only with the superintelligent hoops IQ of a kid weaned in the New York schoolyards. Like Bernard's, his career was derailed by a major knee injury. Unlike Bernard, he never really recovered. But Cunningham was the sixth man for one of the greatest teams ever (the '67 Sixers) and the NBA's best small forward for a five-year stretch ('68 to '72) before winning the ABA MVP . . . and then he got hurt and that was that. Billy C.'s calling card was his Manu-like drives. He grew up in Brooklyn and played on an outdoor court where it was so windy that everyone was afraid to take 20-footers, so everyone adjusted by taking the biscuit to the basket in any way possible. (After researching this book, I'm convinced that the guy who surpasses MJ will be a poor kid with two parents and two older brothers who grew up playing on a clay court where it was too windy to shoot 20-footers. Mark my words, he will break every record in the book.) Billy also may have been MVP of the White Guys Who Played Like Black Guys team (we made it!), a massively important topic for Jabaal Abdul-Simmons. You can't really define what it takes to make this hallowed team; it's more of a "you know it when you see it" thing, although here are three good rules of thumb: Could the player in question have pulled a C. Thomas Howell in *Soul Man* and just pretended he was black without anyone noticing? Had the player actually been black instead of white, would his career (and the way we enjoyed it) have made more sense? In other words, did it almost seem like a mistake that he was white? And could the player do Billy Hoyle's routine on an inner-city playground court and immediately win the respect of everyone there? Here are the Billy Hoyle All-Stars:

Starters. Dave Cowens, Chambers, Cunningham, Westphal and Jason Williams,[40] or as I like to call them, the Honorary Brothers. You know what's appealing about this group other than a complete lack of White Man's Disease? They would have made a fantastic starting five! What would have been more fun than watching White Chocolate running the

---

40. Not to be confused with Jay "I Shouldn't Have Bought a Motorcycle" Williams or Jayson "I Didn't Kill My Chauffeur" Williams.

fast break with Cunningham and Chambers on the wings, or Westphal and Cowens running high screens in crunch time?

Sixth Man. Bobby Jones, among the confusing players in NBA history— a skinny, unassuming diabetic who played above the rim as much as any player black or white. Other than Big Shot Rob, no forward mastered the "run-the-floor, defend-the-rim, shut-down-a-hot-scorer, crash-the-boards, don't-take-anything-off-the-table" role better than Jones. Even his name made him sound black.

Bench. Dan Majerle, Brent Barry, Bobby Sura, David Lee, Andrei Kirilenko and Chris Andersen. This would have been an entertaining nucleus for a modern team even if they would have given up 125 points a game.[41]

Coach. Doug Collins, who would have edged out Westphal for a starting spot had he stayed healthy as an NBA player. He'll have to settle for coaching the Billy Hoyle All-Stars and serving as Mike Fratello's assistant (along with Dick Versace and Jimmy Rogers) on the What the Fuck Did He Do to His Hair? All-Stars.[42]

48. HAL GREER

Resume: 15 years, 11 quality seasons, 10 All-Stars . . . top 10 ('63, '64, '65, '66, '67, '68, '69) . . . 5-year peak: 25–5–4 . . . 2nd-best player for one champ ('67 Sixers) . . . '67 Playoffs: 28–6–5 (15 G) . . . Playoffs: 20–6–4 (92 G) . . . 20K Point Club

During three summers spent researching this book, I loved learning about forgotten greats who played before my time—guys with whom I had no history whatsoever—and how after-the-fact portraits of them were col-

41. Sura played so black that House (who fancied himself a black person, and still does) bought a game-worn Sura jersey on eBay and wore it in pickup games for a few years. They were like kindred spirits.
42. The starting five for that team: Jack Sikma, Rick Barry, Jason Kidd, Scottie Pippen and Anthony Mason, with Moochie Norris, Steve Nash, Chris Andersen, Darnell Hillman and Chris Kaman coming off the bench.

ored by a collection of anecdotes and stories that always skewed one of six possible ways from players, coaches, and reporters who were there.

1. **Gushing overcompensation.** Everyone from Star X's era feels like Star X doesn't get his proper due, so their stories include hard-to-believe anecdotes like "One time, we were trailing the Hawks by two in a Game 7. They got a fast break and Russell sprinted full-court to block the game-winning layup, only he was going so fast that he landed in the twenty-seventh row of the stands—I swear to God, Sam Jones and I counted the rows after the game!" and impossible-to-prove statements that ignore all contrary evidence to the fact, like, "Look, if Oscar played now, he'd still be the best guard in the league, I can guarantee you that one."[43] You'll also see this happen with druggies like Micheal Ray Richardson, Roy Tarpley and Marvin Barnes—yeah, we know those guys would have been good, but as the years pass, the ceiling was lifted for them, so now you'll hear "as good as Magic" (for Micheal Ray), "as good as Barkley" (for Tarp) and "coulda been the greatest forward ever" (for Barnes). Pop a Quaalude and settle down.

2. **Backhanded compliments.** Everyone praises everyone else from their era (that's just the way it works), but sometimes you find sneaky digs strewn in. Bird would always say things about McHale like, "If Kevin wanted to, he could be the top defender in the league" and "He's so awesome on some nights, then other nights he's just average. He makes it look so easy." Translation: *I wish he gave more of a shit.* Or ex-teammates would describe a mercurial guy by saying something like, "Hey, what can I tell you, Wilt was Wilt." Anytime you say someone's name twice as a way to describe him, that means he was either annoying, unpredictable, a complete asshole, a blowhard, as dumb as a rock, or some combination of those five things.

3. **Outright potshots.** Only reserved for renowned cheap-shot artists (like Laimbeer or Clyde Lovelette), selfish gunners (like Mark Aguirre), holier-than-thou pricks (like Rick Barry), moody enigmas (like Adrian Dantley) and, of course, Wilt Chamberlain.

43. This category always seems to have over-the-top affirmations like "I swear to God," "I can promise you," and "I don't have a doubt in my mind."

4. **Totally biased evaluations of a teammate or former player.** My favorite: Pat Riley deciding upon James Worthy's retirement that Worthy was "the greatest small forward ever." Had he said something like, "If you came up with twenty-five qualities for the perfect small forward, James would have had the highest number of them of anyone ever" or even "When God came up with the idea of a small forward, He was thinking of a guy like James Worthy," I'd accept that. But you can't tell me that James Worthy was better than Larry Bird, Rick Barry or Scottie Pippen and expect me to take you seriously after that. You just can't. Same for Bird repeatedly claiming that DJ was the best player he ever played with. Um, you played with McHale at his zenith. You're not topping that one, Larry. Sorry.[44]

5. **Enlightening evaluations.** Sadly, this never happens enough. Here's an example of a wonderful critique of Marvin "Bad News" Barnes by Steve Jones, a former teammate of News in St. Louis, for *Loose Balls*:

> Marvin just attacked the ball on the glass. If he was on the right side of the rim and the ball went to the left, he didn't just stand there like most guys and figure he had no shot at it, he went across the lane and got the ball. When he was in the mood, he could get a rebound, throw an outlet pass to a guard, then race down the court and catch a return pass for a dunk as well as any big man in basketball. He had an 18-foot range on his jumper and a good power game inside. He had every physical ingredient you'd want in a big man and he had the killer spirit to go with it. He didn't just want to beat you, he wanted to embarrass you. But so much of what Marvin did was counter productive to his career. He disdained practice. He stayed up all night. He didn't listen to anyone about anything, but then he'd come out and play a great game. You'd see that and know that the gods had touched this man and made him a great player, only he had no idea what he had. And he kept pushing things and pushing things, like a little kid trying to see what he could get away with. He was the star and he knew it. Also, management gave

---

44. I just ducked a lightning bolt.

him carte blanche to do what he wanted, and what he wanted to do was run amok.

You can't do better than that. Steve Jones just summed up every memorable/tantalizing/tragic quality of Marvin's career in exactly 248 words.[45] The only way Jones could have done better is if he said, "Look, when you come into the NBA with the nickname 'Bad News,' you're probably headed for a disappointing career."[46] Then again, that was the perfect storm of subject and speaker—Barnes messed up in the least forgivable way possible, which meant Jones could be candid about him, and Jones was an eloquent guy who worked as a broadcaster for thirty years (and counting). If our ninety-six Pyramid guys had Jones wrapping up their careers in 248 words, this book would have been much easier to write.

6. **I-can't-think-of-anything-memorable-to-say Cliché Bukkake.** And now we've come full circle to Mr. Greer. By all accounts, he was either the second- or third-best guard of the sixties (depending on your feelings about Sam Jones), playing in ten straight All-Star Games, making seven second-team All-NBAs, serving as a prototype for modern two-guards, hitting a high percentage of outside shots (career: 45 percent), rebounding a little (career: 5.0), scoring 23–25 a night in his prime, draining 80 percent of his free throws, playing good defense and taking as little off the table as possible. Greer retired in 1974 as the all-time leader in games played (1,122) and averaged a sterling 28–6–5 in the '67 playoffs for the Sixers. So it's not like he lacked a top-fifty resume or anything. But check out these quotes from his "Top 50" profile page on NBA.com (the first three) and *Tall Tales* (the fourth one).

Greer: "Consistency. For me, that was the thing. I would like to be remembered as a great, consistent player."

---

45. Steve Jones' nickname? "Snapper." He *refuses* to reveal why they called him "Snapper." He's even ducked the question in NBA.com chats other than to say that two ABA teammates in New Orleans gave it to him and that there's a story behind it. My guess involves a French Quarter hooker, a whip and hot beignets.
46. Earning the nickname "Bad News" as a professional athlete is like earning the nickname "One-Night Stand" as a sorority girl—really, there's no getting around the implicit message.

Dolph Schayes: "Hal Greer always came to play. He came to practice the same way, to every team function the same way. Every bus and plane and train, he was on time. Hal Greer punched the clock. Hal Greer brought the lunch pail."

Herald-Tribune: "If there were an award given for a player who is most respected by basketball insiders, while getting the minimum public appreciation, Greer could win hands down."

Al Bianchi: "We called Greer 'Bulldog' because he had that kind of expression on his face and it never changed."

Did you enjoy that round of Cliché Bukkake? I'd throw in this quote: "There's never been an exciting guy named Hal ever, not in the history of mankind." I could only unearth one interesting tidbit about Greer: everyone from that era raves about his gorgeous jumper.[47] In *Tall Tales,* Alex Hannum calls it "the best medium-range jump shot ever" (hyperbole alert) and Bianchi gushes, "No one could ever stop and take a jumper faster than Greer." In fact, Greer's jumper was so reliable that he's the only player who shot his jumper for free throws; remarkably, he finished his career shooting 80 percent from the line. See, I knew I could dig up something interesting about Hal Greer.

47. PAUL PIERCE

Resume: 12 years, 10 quality, 8 All-Stars . . . Finals MVP ('08) . . . top 10 ('09), top 15 ('02, '03, '08) . . . 3-year peak: 26–7–4 . . . 2-year Playoffs peak: 26–9–5 (26 G) . . . '08 Playoffs: 20–5–5 (26 G) . . . leader: FT (1x) . . . career: 23–6–4, 80% FT, 37% 3FG . . . Playoffs: 21–7–4, 82% FT (101 G) . . . 2nd-best player, 1 champ ('08 Celts) and 1 runner-up ('10 Celts)

---

47. If I could have anybody's jump shot, I'd take Mike Miller's. It's perfect. It's like seeing Halle Berry go topless in *Swordfish* for the first time—you don't even know what to say while you're watching it. Words can't do it justice. Ray Allen's jumper ranks second. Eric Gordon's jumper ranks third. And Shawn Marion's jumper ranks last.

The resume for Pierce: Outdueled LeBron in Game 7 of the 2008 Eastern Finals, then outplayed Kobe in the '08 Finals (major points there) . . . finished the Double Zeros as the best small forward not named Le-Bron . . . repeatedly raised his level of play in big games (dating back to the '02 playoffs), even steamrolling Orlando in the 2010 Eastern Finals (24.3 PPG, 8.3 RPG, 52% FG) when he was a little past his prime[P35] . . . exhibited remarkable durability, missing an extended stretch of games only once (when the Celtics shelved him while tanking for Oden or Durant in '07) . . . a memorably tough competitor who in 2000 didn't miss a single preseason game after getting nearly stabbed to death by a gangbanger two weeks earlier[48] . . . deemed Celtics' best natural scorer ever by no less than Bob Ryan . . . thrived despite having some of the worst facial hair in NBA history (he's the only athlete whose mustache/beard made fans think of aging aunts and grandmothers) . . . and considering he's only thirty-three and just signed a four-year, $61 million extension to remain a Celtic, we still have a ways to go.

Maybe I'm a little too close to it—after all, I probably watched 80 percent of his games, attended most of the home games for his first four years and spent an inordinate amount of time wondering about dopey things like, "Shit, why do I have a terrible feeling he was smoking dope with Ricky Davis until 5:45 a.m. this morning?" But after watching Pierce evolve from "guy with franchise potential" to "guy who led a championship team," I realized his career was a microcosm of the modern NBA fan experience. After some early stumbles during the discouraging Pitino era,[49] Pierce emerged as a potential stud, signed a six-year extension for

---

P35. Has to be mentioned: Artest manhandled him in the 2010 Finals.

48. Pierce cracked 4 teeth against the '04 Suns, slipped in a mouthpiece and returned to win the game. The next day, he underwent seven hours of dental surgery. The next day, he played against Charlotte and made the game-winning shot. Tough dude.[P36]

P36. Laker fans loathe Pierce for getting wheeled off with a possible knee injury during the '08 Finals (Game 1), then "miraculously" returning minutes later (and beating them). That earned him "Wheelchair!" taunts at every ensuing home Lakers game. In the 2010 Finals, Boston fans retaliated by chanting "No means no!" at Kobe and "Ug-ly sister!" at Lamar Odom (married to Khloe Kardashian). Give Boston fans a light smack and we retaliate by hitting you over the head with a two-by-four.

49. Pitino changed the roster so much that by Christmas '99, my dad and I were joking what it would be like if Pitino were Santa Claus: "We hated to give up Prancer, but when you have a chance to pick up a new sled and two elves, you have to do it."

$71 million, then led the Celtics to the 2002 Eastern Finals and submitted a heroic performance in Game 3 (a comeback win from 25 down) before Boston ultimately fell short. After that happened, he probably thought, "All right, I'm here. I made it. I knew this would happen. I'm one of the greats!" Then he started acting like a complete ass.[50] He played on the '02 World Championships team that disgraced itself, then returned with a petulant attitude (the scowling, chest-pounding, whining, and ref-baiting were insufferable), acting like a prima donna behind the scenes and partying way too much for anyone's liking. And this just kept going on and going on, without anyone truly calling him on it—you know, because this was the post-Y2K NBA and guys could act like jerks with few or no repercussions—until everything crested in the '05 playoffs when Pierce committed a boneheaded foul that got him ejected and nearly blew the Indiana series.

Boston fans found themselves in an all-too-frequent position for NBA diehards in the past two decades: we were tired of Pierce's act, thought he needed a fresh start somewhere else and wondered if he was a lost cause, but we knew our team couldn't possibly get equal value. So what do you do? Keep crossing your fingers and hoping that a talented star who's already made more money than he'll ever need will suddenly realize, "You know, I'm wasting my potential, maybe I should straighten myself out"? Or admit he's a falling stock and cash out? There's no right answer. Teams that owned Baron Davis, Charles Barkley, T-Mac, Allen and C-Webber cashed out and eventually regretted it. Teams that owned Kenny Anderson, Stephon Marbury, Derrick Coleman, Larry Johnson and Kemp cashed out and never regretted it. And then there's Boston and Indiana, who found themselves in similar predicaments with underachieving franchise guys— Pierce and Jermaine O'Neal—only both teams rode it out over trading them for 60–70 cents on the dollar, a decision that worked out spectacularly for Boston and unbearably for Indiana. You never know with this stuff. You really don't.

The thing is, the Celtics *wanted* to cash out. That summer, they agreed to a tentative trade with Portland for Nick Van Exel's expiring contract

---

50. My take: Pierce came back too soon and never dealt with that near-death experience. Eventually, he just got angry and started playing that way. Throw in the pressures of a big contract and his conduct was explainable. Maybe it wasn't likable, but it was explainable.

and the number three pick (planning to take Chris Paul)[51] before Pierce squashed the deal by playing the "I'll make everyone in Portland miserable" card. Maybe that was the turning point. Maybe he matured in his late twenties like so many of us do.[52] Maybe enough time had passed since the stabbing and he'd stopped being bitter. Maybe he caught an old Celtics game from the Bird era on ESPN Classic, noticed the Garden swaying and thought to himself, "It used to mean something to be a Celtic; I can do something about this." Maybe he'd been partying too much and calmed down.[53] Whatever happened, he became everything we ever wanted in the 2005–6 season, carrying a young Celtics team, outplaying opposing stars, lifting them in crunch time and doing everything with a smile. Remember when Angelina Jolie broke up with Billy Bob Thornton, stopped wearing a vial of his blood around her neck, stopped dressing like a goth harlot, started adopting third-world babies and fighting AIDS, turned Brad Pitt into Mike Brady and basically became Mother Teresa, only the transformation from "bad" to "good" was so seamless that there was something creepy about it? That was Pierce.[54] By December, with rumors flying of a blockbuster trade to launch our umpteenth rebuilding effort, I started getting emails from season-ticket holders telling me, "I don't care that we're blowing close games, it's been worth the money just to watch Pierce every night, we better not trade him."

What usually happens when an NBA star finds himself stuck in a hopeless situation? He pouts and starts looking for his own stats. He wonders aloud if his team is truly "committed to winning." He misses twelve games with a

51. As much as I enjoyed the '08 title season, would I trade it for 15 years of CP3? No. But I *did* think about it.

52. In my twenties, I drank too much, smoked too much pot and showed horrible taste in women, and that's when I was broke. What if I were making $14 million a year, living in a mansion with buddies and sampling hot groupies every night? It would have been a disaster. I would *not* have handled it well. Also, this book would have been dedicated to my four illegitimate kids: Billy junior, Billy the second, DaBill and LeBill.

53. My money is on this "maybe." Ricky could corrupt anybody. This should be a game show: *Ricky Davis Can Corrupt Anybody.* "This week, Ricky teaches a high school basketball team in Utah how to wash Patrón tequila down with Courvoisier!"

54. My thoughts from January 2006: "Pierce's career season has been simply astounding to watch on a day-to-day basis—like having a brooding, underachieving teenage son who suddenly starts shaking everyone's hand, taking out the garbage, cleaning up his room and bringing home A's. You hope for these things, you keep your fingers crossed, you keep the faith, but you never actually expect it to happen."

five-game hamstring injury. After a tough loss, he saunters off the court with an expression that says, *Hey, it wasn't my fault. I didn't ask to play with these shitheads.* Eventually, he pushes to play somewhere else, only because he wants to be paid like a franchise player without the responsibility of actually carrying a franchise. But that was the beautiful thing about Pierce before the Allen/Garnett trades: He *wanted* to be a Celtic. He *wanted* to be there when things turned around. Everyone will remember his '08 season, but Pierce's greatest season had already happened, the year he accepted the responsibility of a franchise player and killed himself every night. The groundwork for everything that happened afterward was laid then and there. Where did it come from? I couldn't tell you. But it's the reason a team like Denver ended up keeping 'Melo for two extra years (and being vindicated), because you never want a great player "getting it" as soon as he's playing for someone else.

By the 2008 playoffs, Pierce was right where we wanted him to be. Defensively, he pushed himself to heights unseen by giving LeBron everything he could handle in the second round, demolishing Tayshaun Prince in the Eastern Finals and taking over Kobe duty during the 24-point comeback in Game 4. Offensively, he evolved into a game manager of sorts, picking his spots, keeping teammates involved and showing a knack for taking over at the right times. Spiritually, he became the heart of the team, the only one who seemed utterly convinced that they would win the championship. With ten minutes to go in Game 6 and Boston locked into the title, the Lakers called time-out and Pierce turned to face the crowd behind the Celtics' bench, watching fans dance to the arena sound system music and nodding happily. You could see him soaking in the moment. He wasn't even doing it for the cameras; it was one of those times when you could study someone from a distance and read every single thing he was thinking. He was thinking about the past ten years, and all the bad things that had happened, and all the times he'd given up hope, and now he was reminding himself to enjoy the moment. You could see it. All of it.

I wrote a postgame passage that could have been written about twenty coulda-gone-either-way stars had the best-case scenario of their careers been realized:

> We watched that guy grow up. We watched him become a man. We believed in him, we gave up on him, and we believed in him again. I don't mean

to sound like the old man in *Pretty Woman*,[55] but part of me wanted to walk onto the court Tuesday night and just tell Pierce, "It's hard for me to say this without sounding condescending, but I'm proud of you." We spend so much time complaining about sports and being disappointed that our favorite players never end up being who we wanted them to be, but in Pierce's case, he became *everything* we wanted him to be. When he held up the Finals MVP trophy after the game and screamed to the crowd in delight, I don't think I've ever been happier for a Boston athlete. How many guys stick with a crummy franchise for 10 solid years, then get a chance to lead that same team to a championship? Does that *ever* happen in sports anymore?

46. DAVE DEBUSSCHERE

Resume: 12 years, 10 quality, 8 All-Stars . . . top 10 ('69) . . . All-Defense (6x) . . . 4-year peak: 17–12–3 . . . Playoffs peak: 16–13–3 (41 G) . . . 3rd-best player for 2 champs ('69, '73 Knicks) and 1 runner-up ('72 Knicks) . . . player-coach ('64, '65 Pistons)

Two changes would have transformed Dave's career historically. First, they didn't create the All-Defense team until the '68–'69 season. (From that point on, Dave made the first team every year until he retired.) Second, they didn't create the three-point line until the '79–'80 season. (Dave had been retired for six years, having spent his career shooting threes that counted as twos.) Add those tweaks and we're looking at twelve All-Defenses, a career average of 20–11 and a well-earned reputation as the

---

55. I'll defend this reference even though it's a chick flick: Julia Roberts' performance was the movie version of Doc Gooden's '85 season, where you would have believed any outcome for her career after it was over (10 Cy Youngs, 10 Oscars, anything). When you can pull off the "sleazy Hollywood hooker becomes a trophy girlfriend for a zillionaire in 48 hours" premise, you've done something special. Remember when Richard Gere confided to George Costanza that Julia was a hooker, how you thought, "My God, how could you do that?" even though she *was* a hooker? That they pulled off such a convoluted, manipulative premise and made it entertaining has to be considered one of the 10 greatest achievements in the history of modern film. So there.

best three-point-shooting forward of his era. Even so, he left a borderline top-fifty resume, transformed the Knicks defensively, sparked countless "Dee-fense! Dee-fense!" chants at MSG, banged bigger bodies, controlled the boards, made clutch shots and never cared about stats. Everyone remembers Willis sinking those first two jumpers in Game 7 of the '70 Finals, or Frazier finishing with a magnificent 36–7–19, but nobody remembers DeBusschere finishing with 18 points and 17 rebounds and refusing to let Elgin breathe.[56] I was always fascinated that he retired on the heels of his best all-around statistical season (18 points, 11 rebounds, 3.4 assists and 76 percent FT shooting), at the tender age of thirty-three, after the Knicks were smoked by Boston in the '74 Eastern Finals. Maybe Dave thought he was slipping defensively. Maybe he wanted to go out on top when he was still good. I don't know.

Sadly, every NBA fan under forty remembers DeBusschere for one thing and one thing only: when he was running the Knicks in the mid-eighties and practically passed out with joy during the Ewing lottery. That shouldn't be the first thing we remember about one of the great winners of his era, one of the few guys you absolutely would have wanted in your NBA foxhole. And since he resonated with so many New Yorkers, I asked one of the most famous Knick fans to explain why DeBusschere mattered so much. Here's William Goldman[57] remembering his favorite Knick:

> I thought it was a dumb trade, even for the Knicks. We get rid of our center, Walt Bellamy, who one season averaged 30 points a game and our rugged point guard, Howie Komives.
>
> And for what? This guy from Detroit.
>
> That's all he was to those of us who lived in Magic Town back then.

---

56. Grumpy Old Editor's favorite "nobody tried more than DeBusschere" memory: "Dave scored on a jumper to put the Knicks ahead in Game 3 of the 1970 Finals. When West hit the 65-footer to tie it, Dave was somehow already under that basket—and dropped to the ground in shock like Michael Cooper."

57. I feel funny even mentioning Goldman's credentials: he's the greatest living screenwriter, an Oscar winner, and the author or coauthor of three of my favorite books (*Wait Till Next Year, Adventures in the Screen Trade*, and *Which Lie Did I Tell?: More Adventures in the Screen Trade*). He's also been a Knicks season ticket holder for over 40 years. He is overqualified to discuss DeBusschere.

Oh, sure, we knew some stuff—none of it thrilling. Like he was the youngest coach in NBA history, and a total wipeout until he quit. And a major league pitcher. For a couple of years. No Koufax. There was no one, not one Knick nut in the city who predicted that our lives were going to shine till he retired six years later.

What we didn't realize was that the greatest defensive forward in history had come to save us.

I don't think there's much doubt that Michael Jordan was the greatest player ever. Not just the championships or the stats, it's this: We have TV. We can see him play. Plus he is still with us, young enough to spark rumors that maybe, just maybe, he might come back for one more year.

Not a lot of footage on Dave. Retired in '74. Died six years ago, at an unfair sixty-two.

If you are reading this, obviously you have your all-time team. No one would attack you if your guys are West and Oscar, Magic and Elgin and Russ.

Here's mine:

Michael and Clyde.[58]

Wilt.

Bird.

And Dave.

I was at his funeral and of course a lot of famous NBA people were there. You expected that. What was so shocking was how devastated they were. Not just the tears. It was the look of blind disbelief on their faces.

Because they knew this: Dave was the toughest of them all. And he would attend all their funerals.

None of them were meant to come to his. . . .

45. NATE THURMOND

Resume: 14 years, 9 quality, 7 All-Stars . . . '67 MVP runner-up . . . All-Defense (5x) . . . started for two runner-ups ('64, '67 Warriors) . . . '67

---

58. He means Frazier, not Drexler. There's only one Clyde in New York.

Playoffs: 16–23–3 . . . 4-year peak: 21–20–4 . . . recorded the first-ever quadruple double (22–14–13–12)[59]

Congratulations, Nate! You're the winner of the "Wow, I had no idea how good this guy was until I started busting my butt on this book!" award. Let the record show that:

1. You were the third-best center of the late sixties and early seventies, only you never made an All-NBA team because you had the misfortune of going against the Wilt/Russell combo, then Willis/Wilt and Kareem/Wilt. You averaged *exactly* 15.0 points and 15.0 rebounds for your career (kind of amazing).

2. You were a proven warrior whose career was altered historically by two decisions that had nothing to do with you: Rick Barry jumping to the ABA (crippling a Warriors team that would have contended for the next six or seven years), and Golden State trading you for Clifford Ray in a money-saving deal right before Barry peaked and they won the '75 title. You landed in Chicago and lost an agonizing 7-game series in the West Finals to (wait for it) G-State. Not fair.[60]

3. The Warriors traded Wilt in his prime partly because they wanted to make you their center. And partly because Wilt was a selfish head case who made too much money. But still.

4. Wilt and Kareem called you their toughest defender in the early seventies. You averaged 2.9 blocks during the first year they kept track, when you were just about washed up, so who knows how many you were getting in your prime. God forbid we kept track of blocks until 1974. What were stat guys doing back then? Do you think Maurice Podoloff suggested blocks in the early sixties and the NBA's lead statistician angrily responded, "Look, we're fucking overworked as it is—we have to keep track of points, rebounds *and* assists! Get off our backs"?

59. This happened in '75 after they started keeping track of blocks/steals. Odds are, Russell and Wilt would have had a few in their day. And by "a few," I mean "a few dozen."
60. The series ended with Norm Van Lier sprawled on his knees, his head hanging, unable to stand for Barry's clinching FTs because he was so distraught. Bob Ryan says Chicago's Van Lier/Jerry Sloan backcourt was the "physically and mentally" toughest backcourt that he's ever seen. Chicago averaged 52 W's from '71 to '75 and got swallowed up by Kareem's Bucks and West's Lakers in the West.

5. You had the greatest bald-head/full-beard combo of anyone in the history of professional sports with the possible exception of Granville Waiters. So there's that. We penalized you a few spots only because of your curiously terrible shooting: 42 percent for your career (other than Chris Dudley, the worst percentage by any center who played 750 games or more); 38 percent in the '69, '71, '73, and '75 playoffs combined (35 games); 37 percent in the '75 playoffs (13 games).[61] So you were like Dikembe Mutombo but better. Who wants to sex Nate Thurmond?[62]

44. CLYDE DREXLER

Resume: 15 years, 14 quality, 10 All-Stars . . . '92 MVP runner-up . . . top 5 ('92), top 10 ('88, '91), top 15 ('90, '95) . . . 4-year peak: 25–7–6 . . . 3-year Playoffs peak: 23–8–7 (58 G) . . . 2nd-best player on one champ ('95 Rockets), best player on two runner-ups ('90, '92 Blazers) . . . Playoffs: 20–7–6 (145 G) . . . '90 Finals: 26–8–6 . . . '95 Playoffs: 21–7–5 (22 G) . . . career: 22K–6K–6K . . . member of '92 Dream Team

Gets the nod over Greer for one reason: during the most competitive stretch in league history (1990–93), Portland made the Finals twice with Drexler as its lone blue-chipper. We'll remember him as the only basketball player other than Michael J. Fox who succeeded at a memorably high level even though he dribbled on fast breaks with his head down. We'll remember him as the poor man's 'Nique in the "ignite the home crowd with a fast-break dunk" department. We'll remember him for battling male pattern baldness but refusing to shave his head like so many others. We'll remember him for one of the truly great nicknames: "Clyde the Glide." And we'll remember him for being the fragile, too-unselfish-for-his-own-good leader of a memorably unpredictable Blazers juggernaut that consistently

61. Of the 36 centers who played 75+ playoff games, Thurmond had the second-lowest FG% (41.6%), trailing only Jason Collins (37%). Russell was fourth-lowest (43%), Dave Cowens was seventh-lowest (45%) and Mark West was first (56.6%), so you can't read *too* much into it. But still.

62. Sorry, I couldn't resist. "Who wants to sex Mutombo?" is my favorite NBA urban legend other than "Are you ready for Maggette?"

shot itself in the foot at the worst possible moments. Poor Clyde never seemed to make smart decisions at pivotal times, never seemed to understand when a game was slipping away and his team needed him to assert his will, and never grasped the basic premise of "Look, I'm good at a lot of things, and I'm not so good at other things, so maybe I should just do what I'm good at."[63]

For instance, of any player who attempted at least two 3-pointers per playoff game, guess who has the worst percentage? That's right—Clyde at 28 percent. Twenty-eight percent! That didn't stop him from clanging 133 of 178 threes (23 percent) in Portland's 58-game playoffs run from 1990 to 1992. During the '92 playoffs, Clyde was 19-for-81 on three-pointers (23.5 percent) and 179-for-344 (53 percent) on two-pointers. If you were a Portland fan, what made you happier that spring, Clyde launching a three or Clyde either driving to the basket or pulling up for a 15-footer? He just didn't get it. Ideally, Clyde should have been the second-best guy on a great team—like a McHale, Worthy or Pippen—an unselfish sidekick who wasn't quite great enough to carry someone to a title. This finally happened when Houston reunited Clyde and Hakeem, leading to a rare "gunning for a ring late in his career" success story when the Rockets swept Orlando in the '95 Finals. Because of that, I have Clyde ranked forty-fourth . . . and yet I feel terrible for him because his career was swallowed up by Jordan. The MJ shadows are everywhere. This goes beyond Clyde being the poor man's Jordan, a rival shooting guard who filled the stat sheet 85 percent as well but wasn't the same suck-the-soul-out-of-you competitive killer (and that's an understatement). Consider three things:

• Clyde showed enough promise that when Portland landed the number two pick in the '84 draft, the Blazers decided, "We're all set in the Exciting Perimeter Scorer department, so let's pick a center with surgically repaired tibias."[64] Besides being the single greatest NBA what-

63. The greatest example: In Game 1 of the '92 Finals, after MJ's fifth three-pointer, Clyde came back down and forced a three to "respond." Air ball. So awkward when it happened. Nobody had less of a sense of the moment than Drexler.
64. I'm being generous with the "showed enough promise" compliment here; Clyde averaged 18 minutes and an 8–3–2. Not exactly MJ territory. On the other hand, anytime you have a chance to take a five-year senior who missed two years because of stress fractures, you gotta do it.

if, did you know Portland allegedly offered that pick plus Drexler for Ralph Sampson? What if Houston had said yes? Can you imagine? How many titles would the Hakeem/Clyde/MJ combo have won? Would we remember Jordan's career differently? And if Sampson had played in Portland and never injured his back in that freak fall in Boston, would we remember him as a top-thirty guy? The biggest loser of that near-trade was probably Clyde: he could have played with a Pantheon center for his entire prime. You know, instead of going to battle with Sam Bowie and Kevin Duckworth.

• Clyde peaked as the '92 Blazers blew through the playoffs (25–7–7, MVP runner-up, a slew of "Drexler has arrived!" features), with the defending champion Bulls waiting for a Finals that many believed was a toss-up. As the argument went, Drexler and Jordan could potentially cancel each other out—I know, heresy in retrospect—and Drexler's supporting cast was deeper, giving Portland a legitimate chance as long as MJ didn't destroy Clyde. That led to a few days of "Jordan or Drexler?" hype, which in retrospect, given everything we know about Jordan's homicidal competitiveness, was like covering a screaming child in teriyaki sauce and waving it in front of a pissed-off Rottweiler. In Game 1, Jordan nailed six threes in the first half—the famous Shrug Game—obliterating the MJ-Clyde argument once and for all. As the series kept going, Drexler was pounded by a disappointed national media for "not taking over" and "not asserting himself" and "not standing up to MJ," with Peter Vecsey angrily leading the way.[65] The series stretched to a sixth game in Chicago with the Blazers taking a commanding 15-point lead in the fourth quarter, then giving much of it away with Drexler on the floor and Jordan resting on the bench. Chicago finished them off, Jordan easily won the Finals MVP and nobody ever mentioned "Jordan or Drexler?" again.

• One month later, Drexler and Jordan were both on the Dream Team, only MJ hadn't fully resolved "Jordan or Drexler?" to his liking. He attacked Drexler in scrimmages with particular relish and

65. Vecsey's take: "Enough of the gentlemanly behavior. Later for his nice-guy image. You can't think about beating Jordan by being permissive or overly respectful." Translation: "Grow some balls, Clyde!"

kept talking trash about the Finals; as the story goes, Magic pulled him aside and asked him to ease up before Clyde's confidence was ruined for the Olympics.[P37] And apparently Jordan did ease up. But between that and the '92 Finals, the psychological damage was done. Clyde slumped for the next two years, with his stats dipping to 19–6–5 in 112 combined games, his shooting percentage free-falling (49 percent from '85 to '92, 43 percent from '93 to '94) and the Blazers subsequently floundering (consecutive first-round exits). Was Jordan responsible for Drexler's funk? It's hard to figure a thirty-year-old suddenly dropping from the top five to barely an All-Star unless it was the late seventies and he was plowing through booger sugar. Anyway, it's tough to remember one star affecting another star's career in so many different and distinct ways. Even when Drexler finally climbed the mountain and won a title in Houston, it happened when Jordan had just returned from his wink-wink baseball sabbatical and couldn't get past Orlando. Had that Bulls team somehow made the Finals and gotten thrashed by Houston, Clyde would have gotten his sweet revenge. Didn't happen. Years later, many would discount those two Houston championships because they happened during Jordan's baseball years. Shit, even Clyde Drexler's ring has Jordan's shadow looming over it.

43. JASON KIDD

Resume: 16 years, 13 quality, 10 All-Stars . . . MVP runner-up ('02) . . . '95 Rookie of the Year . . . top 5 ('99, '00, '01, '02, '04), top 10 ('03) . . . All-Defense (9x, four 1st) . . . 4-year peak: 16–7–10 . . . leader: assists (5x), minutes (1x) . . . best player on 2 runner-ups ('02–'03 Nets), 20–8–9 (40 G) . . . top 4 assists (12x) . . . traded 3x (once in prime) . . . Playoffs: 15–7–9, 39.5% FG (121 G) . . . career: assists (2nd), steals (4th)

P37. Clyde showed up for one Dream Team practice with two left sneakers, then was so worried about getting teased that he *played* in them. When MJ found out what happened, he snickered for days. It's the defining "MJ was in Clyde's head" story.

My buddy J-Bug fittingly summed up J-Kidd's destiny three years into his career. We were attending a Suns-Celtics game and Kidd bricked a three that never had a chance even as it was leaving his hand. After the shot clunked off the rim and nearly took Antoine Walker's head off, a second passed and the Bug decided, "Every time I watch Jason Kidd play, initially it's like seeing a girl walk into a bar who's just drop-dead gorgeous, but then when he throws up one of those bricks, it's like the gorgeous girl taking off her jacket and you see she has tiny mosquito bites for tits."

Hey, I didn't say it. But that was one of Bug's better moments, right up there with the time he convinced someone at Sully's Pub that he was a Formula One driver. Maybe Kidd was a smoking-hot girl in nearly every respect—fantastic defender, great rebounder for his size, impeccably smart on fast breaks, completely unselfish, someone who lived to make everyone else better—but if shooting ability were a bra size, he would have been wearing a 32A for his entire career. For his career (through 2008), Kidd shot just 40 percent from the field,[66] which would have been fine in the fifties if he were battling Cousy and McGuire every night. Of the post-1976 guards who played at least 600 games (through '08), Kidd has the fourth-lowest shooting percentage. His playoff percentages are even bleaker: of the post-1976 guards who played 80-plus postseason games, Kidd currently ranks sixth from the bottom (39.5 percent, ahead of bricklayers Lindsay Hunter, Greg Anthony, Nate McMillan, Howard Eisley and Bruce Bowen),[67] and just ahead of Drexler with the second-lowest three-point percentage of anyone who attempted at least two per game (30 percent). Much as Greg Maddux notched 355 wins without a heater, every other aspect of Kidd's game had to be perfect to compensate for its one shortcoming. And for eight or nine years, that was pretty much the case.

Until joining Dirk Nowitzki in Dallas, Kidd had always been the best player on his team—not his fault, but still, if your best guy is a 40 percent shooter, you're not winning a title. And as much as teammates loved play-

66. FG percentages of the best modern PGs: Tiny (47%), GP (47%), KJ (49%), Stockton (52%), Isiah (45%), Nash (49%), Mo Cheeks (52%), Mark Price (47%), Gus Williams (46%), Tim Hardaway (43%).
67. When they finally turn Poe's "Cask of Amontillado" into a movie, I want Hunter to play Montresor.

ing with him, Kidd was a handful behind the scenes, quietly wearing out his welcome with three different teams—Dallas, Phoenix and New Jersey, all of whom were anxious to dump him—feuding with Jimmy Jackson and Jamal Mashburn in Dallas, curiously bleaching his hair white-blond for the '00 playoffs, battling domestic violence charges in 2001, pushing Byron Scott out as Nets coach in 2004, plodding through an ugly (and public) divorce in 2007 and pushing for a 2008 trade (and getting it) in the messiest way possible. We never mention Kidd in any discussion of head cases of the last twenty years, even though all evidence points to him being moody, enigmatic and unpredictable.

Did we confuse Kidd's unselfishness with him being a good guy? Probably a little. Much of Kidd's "struggles" were semiexplainable except for that bleached afro, which remains unexplainable and gets funnier over time. (It looked like Wesley Snipes' hair in *Demolition Man* crossed with Jules' afro in *Pulp Fiction*, minus the muttonchops.) The Dallas situation imploded for three reasons: three young stars were given too much money too soon; two feuded over singer Toni Braxton (who can rank splitting up the mid-nineties Mavs right up there with her six Grammy awards);[68] and new Mavs coach Jim Cleamons decided to adopt Chicago's "triangle" even though he had the most gifted open-court point guard since Magic Johnson. (I remember almost crying the first time I went to a game and saw Kidd completely shackled in that triangle. It was like paying for a Sharon Stone movie back then where she didn't get naked.)[69] The Phoenix situation deteriorated because of the aforementioned incident with his wife. The Jersey situation fell apart because Kidd couldn't stand playing with Vince anymore, and really, can you blame him? Speaking of Vince, Kidd's unfortunate luck with teammates was remarkable. Mashburn and Jackson were top-six lottery picks who didn't pan out until after they were traded. Kidd played with a variety of name guys in Phoenix—Antonio McDyess, Danny Manning, Penny Hardaway, Rex Chapman, Kevin John-

68. This scandal led to roughly 200,000 Brandon-Kelly-Dylan jokes at the time.
69. Dallas *did* get Sam Cassell and Michael Finley back. Of course, Dallas f'ed up a year later with an eight-player deal that basically landed them Shawn Bradley and Robert Pack for Cassell, Jimmy Jackson and Chris Gatling. That same season, they dealt Mashburn for Sasha Danilovic and Kurt Thomas. So not only did Braxton implode the Kidd-Mashburn-Jackson nucleus, she eventually turned them into Finley and a load of crap. Thank you, Toni.

son, Robert Horry, Cedric Ceballos, Clifford Robinson, Shawn Marion, Tom Gugliotta—but caught each at the wrong point of his career. Even during a successful run in Jersey, he turned chicken shit into chicken salad in his first two years, carrying a team with Keith Van Horn, Kerry Kittles, Kenyon Martin, Todd McCulloch, Lucious Harris and rookie Richard Jefferson to the Finals, then bringing the same group back a year later with an aging Dikembe Mutombo replacing Van Horn/McCulloch.

Which brings us to the strongest case for Kidd in the top forty-five of the Pyramid. Look at the teammates in the previous paragraph, then look at these records: 32–23, 56–26, 27–23, 53–29, 51–31, 52–30, 49–33, 47–35. The first five belong to Phoenix from '97 to '01; the last three belong to Jersey from '02 to '04. For those eight seasons, Kidd finished 137 games over .500, made five first-team All-NBAs (and one second-team All-NBA) and made the Finals twice playing with *one* All-Star during that entire stretch (K-Mart in '04). We always hear that KG never had a great supporting cast in Minnesota, but Christ, what about Jason Kidd? He also stands out for making every All-Star Game 20–25 percent more watchable;[70] for averaging an Oscar-like 20–9–8 and melting the Celtics in the '02 Eastern Finals; for his Magic-like talent for grabbing a rebound, turning on the jets, going coast to coast and getting to the rim; for subjecting us to forty thousand camera shots of his wife and young son during the '02 and '03 playoffs;[71] for perfecting the "jump in front of someone and take a charge on a fast break layup" move that led to them putting a circle under the basket; and for having the "J-Kidd" moniker that (along with "C-Webb") was responsible for the ensuing sports acronym craze that spiraled out of control and eventually led to Linda Cohn calling Pudge Rodriguez "I-Rod." Looking back, I enjoyed the J-Kidd era as much as I enjoyed the Michelle Pfeiffer era—yeah, maybe they weren't curvy, but they made up for it in other ways.

70. Kidd and Stockton should have been grandfathered into every All-Star Game until each turned fifty. Seriously, I'd rather watch a 50-year-old Stockton run an All-Star offense than Tyreke Evans.

71. Comedian Guy Torry made fun of Kidd's son at a Shaq roast, joking about his oversized head and little-kid mustache, comparing him to the Great Gazoo of *The Flintstones* and basically crossing every comedy line. When they showed Shaq sprawled over the dais laughing his ass off, supposedly Kidd was bitter and it's been awkward with them ever since. I feel like you need to know these things.

42. WES UNSELD

Resume: 13 years, 12 quality, 5 All-Stars . . . '78 Finals MVP . . . '69 MVP . . . '69 Rookie of the Year . . . Top 5 ('69) . . . leader: rebounds (1x), FG% (1x) . . . 4-year peak: 15–17–3 . . . 3rd-best playoff rebounder (14.9 RPG) . . . 2nd-best player on 1 champ ('78 Bullets) and 3 runner-ups ('71, '74, '79) . . . '71 Playoffs: 13–19–4 (18 G)

Big Wes submitted the weirdest resume of anyone in the top seventy-five. His peers got carried away and voted him MVP as a rookie, then he didn't make the All-Star team the following season (or another All-NBA team ever). He wrecked his knee during the '74 season and dropped off the offensive map, averaging just 8 points per game for his last eight seasons. He was indisputably the worst shot blocker of any great center, someone who couldn't have jumped over a picture of that Sunday's *Washington Post*. He gained enough weight during the latter half of his career that his screens worked partly because defenders spent two full seconds making their way around this mammoth man.[72] It's hard to imagine him being nearly as successful today. A six-foot-six center who couldn't score, run the floor, or protect the rim? How would that work? Even when Wes and the '78 Bullets won their sole title, they stumbled into the trophy only because Bill Walton's broken foot opened the door for every pseudo-contender.[73]

Then you delve into Wesley's resume a little deeper. He injured his left knee during his second season and blew it out for good in Season 6, still averaging a 14–17–4 during his first five years. He played on four different Bullets teams that made the Finals in a nine-year span—a really good '71 team that lost Gus Johnson before the Finals, a heavily favored '75 team that the Warriors swept, and the experienced '78 and '79 teams that split

72. My all-time team for Guys You Wouldn't Have Wanted to Follow in a Bathroom Had They Been in There for a Half Hour or More": Unseld (C), Hot Plate Williams (PF), Charles Barkley (SF), Micheal Ray Richardson (SG), John Bagley (PG). I picked Micheal Ray because he may have been too coked up to remember to flush.

73. The '78 Bullets were easily the worst post-Russell champs, finishing 44–38 with a point differential of 0.9. During the regular season, their opponents finished better than them in FG%, FT%, steals, assists and blocks and averaged 2.5 fewer turnovers a game. Of their 38 losses, 14 of them came by double digits.

with the Sonics—even though they didn't have a traditional superstar (unless you want to count Hayes, and I don't). Everyone remembers him as *the* enforcer of that era along with Willis Reed and Bob Lanier, the one guy you didn't want to cross in any way, as well as the best locker room guy other than Paul Silas. He cared only about making everyone else better and his team's success reflects that: not just four Finals appearances, but Washington finishing 176 games over .500 and making the playoffs for every one of Unseld's first eleven years. His outlet passes were the single biggest strength of his game, only we didn't have a way of measuring their impact—if he threw a crisp fifty-foot outlet pass to Monroe, leading to a two-on-one break and a layup for Kevin Loughery, only Loughery and Monroe were accounted for statistically, right?[74]

That brings up a larger point: our collective failure to come up with meaningful, easy-to-understand statistics to measure NBA players. I first complained about this on my old website a few years before the statistical revolution in baseball inevitably trickled over to the NBA and NFL. Back in 2001, I openly pined for the following stats:

Clutch FG and FT percentage. We have this now in various forms; 82games.com even tweaked it into "clutch" (last 5 minutes, three-point lead or less) and "super-clutch" (last 2 minutes, three-point lead or less). Manu Ginobili's '08 stats were absolutely mind-blowing: 61.9% FG super-clutch and 57.4% FG clutch. Why didn't we have this when Karl Malone was in his prime? Damn it all.

Plus/minus. A hockey staple that the basketball community ignored until 82games.com launched it for the 2002–3 season, eventually leading to Eddy Curry setting the unofficial record for worst plus-minus for anyone who played at least 1,500 minutes in a season. During the '07–'08 season, Eddy played 1,529 minutes and finished with a plus/minus of -10.1. In

---

74. In Ken Shouler's book, Bob Ryan raves, "No man in history ever began more fast breaks with 50-foot outlet passes than Wes Unseld did," and Auerbach adds, "Wes was the greatest outlet passer of them all, the only one I'd rate better than Russell."

other words, Eddy made the team ten points worse just by stepping onto the court.[75]

Nitty-gritties. I created this one to cover any time someone (a) takes a charge, (b) comes up with a loose ball in a crowd of two or more people, (c) saves a loose ball heading out of bounds by whipping it off an opposing player, or (d) tips a rebound to a teammate. Shane Battier would have led the last decade in nitty-gritties, James Posey would have finished second, and Tim Thomas would have been last.

Wide-open FG percentage. Tracks every wide-open jumper launched by a player from 15 feet and beyond. Not only do we have this stat now, but NBA teams separate shots into zones and rely on this information to help them target specific role players (usually point guards who sink a surprising number of open 18-footers from the top of the key or swingmen who drain threes from the corner with startling accuracy).[P38] One of the reasons I loved Cleveland's 2008 trade for Mo Williams was because he had finished second in open FG percentage (51 percent) the previous season.

Dunks. Another underground stat that went mainstream over the past few years, although I'd break it down even further into subcategories like "Rebound Dunks," "Dunks on Somebody's Head," "Alley-Oop Dunks," "Dunks That Got the Home Crowd So Fired Up That the Opponents Needed a Time-out," and "Dunks That Caused Every Black Player or Fan

75. That was the first Double Whopper Double: Eddy hit double figures in negative plus-minus and body fat. Eddy was recently hit with a gay sexual harassment suit by his chauffeur, who made a far-fetched claim that Eddy swung his dick at him and said, "You know you want to touch it, Dave." Then Malik Rose defended Eddy by saying, "I know for a fact Eddy's not gay," spawning a few days of "How exactly do you know this, Malik?" chatter. Then we learned that Eddy had six kids by two different women . . . and those are the kids we know about. So maybe that's how Malik knew. Or maybe he said, "Hey Eddy, in the mood for some gay sex tonight?" and Eddy turned him down. Or maybe they had a threesome together. Or maybe Eddy tried to boink Malik's girlfriend. Did House and I spend fifteen minutes on the phone trying to figure this out? Of course we did.

P38. Now we have www.hoopdata.com breaking this information down for fans. A godsend for no-lifers like me who want to know things like "What's Paul Pierce's FG percentage from 16–23 feet?"

in the Building to Stand Up in Disbelief and Make the Face Where It Looks Like They Smelled a Life-Altering Fart."

Ref bitching. Every time a player complains to a referee, that's one RB. I was joking about this one at the time; back then I wrote, "We're creating this just so Antoine Walker would finally get to hold his own record." Now I'm wondering if this stat wouldn't be wildly fun to monitor. Kobe would lead the league every season. There's no question.

Unforced turnovers. In tennis, this covers every time a player messes up without any provocation. In basketball, that would cover every time someone screws up an easy fast break with a bad decision; commits a dribbling or palming violation; gets whistled for an offensive charge or a three-second violation; blows an uncontested layup or dunk; accidentally throws the ball out of bounds, commits an offensive goaltending, lane violation, or flagrant foul; or loses track of the shot clock and fails to get a shot off before the 24 seconds expires. That's a wide range of inexcusable fuck-ups we're covering there. You're telling me that wouldn't be valuable?

Defensive stops. When a defender single-handedly prevents his opponent from scoring on an isolation play, a low-post play or a perimeter drive, that's a stop. Cause a turnover or an unforced turnover in the process, that's a superstop. By the way, I threw this idea at Houston's Daryl Morey last year and his response was, "Why do you think we have Chuck Hayes?"[76]

Russells. Any blocked shot that immediately triggers a fast-break layup or dunk. We always hear about how many times Russell blocked a shot, kept it in play and launched a fast break. Why couldn't we measure that? And conversely, wouldn't this measure all the times Dwight Howard stu-

76. Morey became the league's first statistically savvy GM when Houston hired him in 2007. We became friends when he worked for the Celtics. He runs the Sloan Sports Analytical Conference every year (which I nicknamed Dorkapalooza), and when he invited me in 2009, once I saw him swarmed by MIT grads the way the paparazzi swarm Britney, I nicknamed him "Dork Elvis." He admitted this was funny. Begrudgingly.

pidly swats the ball out of bounds (and maybe convince him to stop do-ing it)?[77]

Mega-assists. Would cover any pass that directly leads to an easy layup, an easy dunk, an alley-oop dunk or a teammate being fouled as the only re-course from stopping him from making an easy layup or dunk (and each free throw made, which counts as a half-mega-assist). The last part is cru-cial because, incredibly, we don't credit playmakers for making great passes that led to "I had to hack him or else he would have scored" fouls. Larry Bird was the mega-assist master—by my unofficial calculations, he finished with 373 mega-assists in Game 6 of the '86 Finals, which has to be a record—but Steve Nash would have given him a run for his money dur-ing the Seven Seconds or Less era. It's bizarre that we haven't figured out a better way to value assists. Imagine if baseball only kept track of hits and didn't differentiate between singles, doubles, triples and homers, and if every official scorer counted hits differently. That's how idiotic the NBA's current assist system is.

Unselds. Let's name it after Big Wes! Think of it like a hockey assist—any outlet pass past the opposing three-point line that creates an instant fast break (and ultimately a layup or dunk) counts as an Unseld. We'll use Kevin Love as our test case over the next few years; if you're a T-Wolves fan who watches every game, please, keep track of this for us. How many Un-selds can Love come up with?[78]

---

77. I initially called this *Swing Blocks* before realizing it sounded like a gay porn movie. Couldn't you see an early-nineties VCR tape of *Swing Blocks* with all the NBA's Duke grads on the cover dressed like construction workers?[P39]

P39. At Dorkapalooza 2010 (aka MIT's Sloan Conference, in which statheads convene to debate stat stuff . . . and yes, I go every year), John Huizinga presented a study playing off my "Russells" concept that definitively proved Howard's blocks were overrated. Howard had the NBA's least valuable block percentage (24% of his "blocks" were goal-tends) and did a poor job of saving/creating points with blocks (in '08, Howard's 232 blocks saved/created 149 points, while Duncan's 149 blocks generated 167 points). I love Dorkapalooza.

78. I thought about creating another stat for successful screens and picks, but that seems too arbitrary. Sorry, Wes.

This all sounds great, right? One problem: our statistical community is more obsessed with comparing players, chasing impossible-to-prove-objectively stats like "adjusted plus-minus" and pushing marketable formulas like PER or wages of wins. That mind-set works in baseball, an individual sport in which your teammates don't matter unless they can help you get PEDs. (Sorry, I had to.) Every conceivable diamond talent can be measured objectively. I thought Derek Jeter was a great shortstop until the defensive stats told me otherwise. I thought Wade Boggs was wrong for a leadoff hitter; turns out that an OBP machine who drags pitch counts along is just what you want. But basketball isn't baseball. When John Hollinger's PER metric decides that Marreese Speights is the 30th most efficient offensive player in basketball while Shane Battier is 284th, obviously I'm dubious.[79] So while the statistical community is trying to clone cows, NBA front offices are only worried about gourmet cheeseburgers. They spend millions figuring out hyperintelligent stats to measure defensive stops, shooting percentages from various offensive zones, Russells, Unselds and everything else, then hoard that information for themselves like it's the Cold War or something. Fans like you and me *could* have a better idea of what we're watching . . . only we don't.

In my opinion, there's no ironclad way to assign statistical value to every player when so much of an individual's success (as well as his numbers) hinges on situations and team success, as well as his willingness to put the team ahead of himself. Look at the four-year effect Unseld had on Kevin Loughery, a starting guard in his late twenties when Wes joined the Bullets:

PLAYER	YEAR	MPG	PPG	APG	FG%	FGA
Loughery	1967–68	31.9	17.0	3.5	40.2	15.9
Loughery	1969–70	38.1	22.3	5.0	43.9	20.2

79. Hollinger is a great guy and we've had good-natured arguments about this. He admits his formula is a work in progress—it values "per-48-minute" production, rebounds, and FG% too much. But he still believes in it. If this were *Lost,* I'd be Locke and he'd be Jack. Neither one of us is right or wrong; that's the great thing. Okay, that's not true—I'm right. But the man does make me think.

As Loughery told Elliott Kalb, "When Wes came to the Bullets, my scoring average jumped from 14 to 22, all because of him[80] . . . He could grab a rebound and throw it all the way downcourt before it hit the ground. All of a sudden, I became Paul Warfield—a wide receiver catching passes ahead of the field." Couldn't we measure that impact in a tangible way? Instead of unearthing complicated formulas to evaluate seasons or careers, we should spend our energies making hyperspecific stats better (the gourmet cheeseburger analogy), then using that enhanced information and combining it with team success, our own educated opinions, and thoughts from players and coaches to piece together a complete picture. Basketball is an objective sport *and* a subjective sport, dammit. That's what makes it so much fun to follow. So on the surface, yeah, it seems peculiar that Unseld cracked the top forty-five, or even that he took home the '78 Finals MVP by averaging a piddling 9–12–4. But as teammate Mitch Kupchak explained to Ken Shouler, "Unseld was the consummate team basketball player; his only objective was to win. Statistics were never important to him. You can't begin to imagine what he did to make his teammates better—set picks, made outlet passes, guarded the bigger center. He was the MVP of the ['79 Finals]." Wes Unseld earned this spot. But if I could have pointed to stats like "led the league in Unselds for 10 straight years" or "career leader in Unselds," this section would have been a helluva lot easier to write.[81]

41. GARY PAYTON

Resume: 17 years, 10 quality, 9 All-Stars . . . top 5 ('98, '00), top 10 ('95, '96, '97, '99, '02), top 15 ('94, '01) . . . All-Defense (9x 1st team) . . . Defensive

---

80. Actually, it jumped from 15.9 to 22. What's a little Wes talk without a dab of gushing exaggeration?

81. You would *not* have wanted him as your GM. I emailed House, a long-suffering Bullets fan, and asked him for his four favorite abominable Unseld moves. His return email via BlackBerry: "Traded Ben Wallace for Isaac Austin; [Mitch] Richmond for C-Webb; number one for washed-up Mark Price; acquisition/gross-overpay of Kevin Duckworth; $25 million for Jahidi White; traded our number one three straight years for *shit;* failed to lock up Juwan [Howard] the summer before his contract year, lowballed after Juwan put up big numbers, then paid $30–40 million more than the contract would have cost the previous summer after Stern voided free-agent signing by Miami. Sure there's more but I'm doing this off top of my head—playing golf right now. I love Wes but HE SUCKED!"

Player of the Year ('96) . . . leader: steals (1x), threes (1x) . . . 3-year peak: 23–5–9 . . . best player on runner-up ('96 Sonics), 21–5–7 (21 G) . . . five top-6 MVP finishes . . . career: assists (7th), steals (3rd) . . . 20K Point Club

During the 2008 Finals, I wrote that Rajon Rondo brought a ton of stuff to the table and took a good share of stuff off it; in other words, he was bringing forks and plates and removing the knives and spoons, but you could still eat a decent meal with him because you had forks and plates. Well, Gary Payton was the all-time table test guy. He brought you sterling-silver forks and knives from Hoagland's, with some gorgeous plates to match, only you didn't have spoons for dessert and you had to drink wine out of paper cups because he broke all the glasses. Could you have a memorable meal with him? Absolutely. But you also left the meal saying, "Man, I wish we'd had spoons and wineglasses." Here's everything he brought to the table and took away from it:

Forks/knives/plates. The best all-around point guard of the nineties . . . top player on a 64-win Seattle team that grabbed two Finals wins from the '96 Bulls . . . one of the legendary trash-talkers of all time . . . one of the five best defensive guards ever . . . his 1999–2000 season (24–7–9, 153 steals, 45 percent FG, 82 games, 3,425 minutes) ranks in the pantheon of Greatest Point Guard Seasons Ever . . . helped make the shaved-head thing popular in the early nineties, then stuck with it through thick and thin . . . probably should have been nominated for an Oscar for his turn in *Eddie* as an unnamed street player who battled the late Malik Sealy[82] . . . other than Oscar and Magic, the only superstar guard who developed a killer low-post game and punished smaller guards . . . defended MJ as well as anyone ever, holding him to 23.7 points in the last half of the '96 Finals and a 5-for-19 performance in Game 6[83] . . . GP and John

82. Payton was listed as playing "Rumeal Smith" in the closing credits, even though they never mentioned his character's name in the movie. Really, they couldn't have called him "Gary Dayton" or "Gary Parton"? How did they come up with Rumeal Smith? This has been bothering me for 13 years.
83. George Karl murdered Seattle by not switching GP onto MJ until Game 4, an unforgivable brainfart that disqualifies him from any "one of the best coaches of his generation" discussion.

Malkovich would have been been my all-time favorite cross-ethnic look-alikes if not for Britney Spears/Pedro Martinez and Harry Carson/Glenn Close . . . if Shawn Kemp hadn't self-destructed, GP would have won at least one title . . . on a personal note, I watched Kidd, Stockton and GP in their absolute primes and thought GP was the most talented all-around player of the three (he just had no holes) . . . and you have to love anyone with an ego large enough to name his sons Gary Payton Jr. and Gary Payton II.

Missing spoons/glasses. Only played at a high level for ten years, a curiously low number for a modern superstar . . . traded by Seattle in 2002, strange because franchises normally don't trade signature guys, right? . . . his last few seasons for the Lakers, Celtics and Heat were shamefully bad; I even suggested changing the name of "jumping the shark" to "pulling a GP" after the '04 Finals . . . developed a well-earned reputation as a coach-killer and locker room lawyer, someone who fought or nearly came to blows with multiple teammates and had a knack for selling teammates out in times of crisis[84] . . . played with a volatile, trash-talking swagger that seemed to derail the Sonics almost as much as it helped them . . . definitely described by a few teammates like this: "What can I say? Gary is Gary" . . . nobody in the top fifty vacillated more times between "totally untradeable" and "we are definitely receptive to a trade."

So yeah, GP was more talented than Stockton, as we witnessed in the '96 Conference Finals when Payton did everything but stick a red ball in Stockton's mouth, duct-tape him to a chair and introduce him to the Gimp. But ask anyone from that era whom they'd rather have as a teammate and nearly all would pick Stockton, simply because they wouldn't

84. At halftime of Game 1 of the '94 Nuggets series, before the Sonics infamously blew a 2–0 lead to an eighth seed, Payton and Ricky Pierce had an altercation that led to both guys threatening to get their guns before things calmed down. It was just like the fight Rick Reilly and I had at the 2008 ESPYs.[P40]

P40. In December '09, Gilbert Arenas took that footnote twenty steps farther by bringing four guns into Washington's locker room and urging teammate Jarvaris Crittendon to "pick one." (Arenas was suspended without pay for the season, convicted of a felony and given the title of "Most Untradeable Contract Ever.") What started the Gilbert/Jarvaris bad blood? An airplane card game gone awry. See? All NBA feuds start over cards or women! I keep telling you!

have wanted to deal with Payton's bullshit. Can you win a championship when your point guard has a gigantic ego and cares more about making himself look good than his teammates? Apparently not—Payton never won anything. Switch Payton and Stockton in '92 and it's hard to imagine Karl Malone having the same type of career; the first time he folded in a playoff game, Payton would have ripped him to shreds publicly and privately. As the years pass, nobody will remember this delightful trait: they'll see his offensive numbers and defensive honors and assume Payton was his generation's best two-way guard. And in a way, that was true. But Stockton gave his team a better chance to win, taking care of everyone, never rocking the boat, coming through in the clutch and always putting the team above himself. So I'd pick him. It's not even close, actually. On the other hand, I remember betting the Phoenix money line for their first-round series against the heavily favored '97 Sonics, nearly pulling off an upset, then losing simply because Payton played out of his freaking mind. I specifically remember making up a "Never bet against GP" rule right then and there. Stockton was good, but he was never *that* good.

One subplot with Payton's career needs to be mentioned: after he landed in Miami, his mini-renaissance as a role player was riveting because he figured out that he *wasn't* good anymore and adjusted accordingly. In Boston, a washed-up Payton was still trying to beat guys off the dribble, posting up, demanding to cover top scorers and sulking when he didn't get the ball. It was like watching Jason Alexander order people around on the set of some crappy sitcom ("Don't you realize who I am? I'm Jason Alexander!") and failing to realize his time had come and gone. In Miami, Payton willingly took a backseat to Wade—with the exception of one "Don't you do that to me, I'm Gary Payton!" blowup in the Chicago series where he flipped out on Wade on national TV—treating us to roughly 900 plays that started with a resigned GP flipping the ball to Wade in crunch time, then trudging up the court to stand in his spot near the corner, like a Wimbledon ball boy getting back into position between serves. When they needed his experience in the Finals, he dusted off the cobwebs and delivered two of the biggest plays of the series: an off-balance jumper that beat the shot clock and won Game 3, and an old-school lefty banker in the final 30 seconds of overtime in Game 5. The second one was funny because GP reacted to the chest bumps and high fives afterward with one of those "See, you guys forgot, I used to be pretty good!" looks on his face. Like he belted out the retro swagger.

Still, there was something distressing about Payton's reincarnation as a middling supporting player, someone who could barely handle the likes of Jason Terry. Should we *really* have been surprised when *Gary Payton* made a clutch play? This was one of the ten best point guards of all time! Things had fallen to that level?[85] Maybe we couldn't blame GP for hanging on for a few more paychecks or being unable to realize when it was over; after all, it's his career and not ours, and most overcompetitive people have trouble determining the right time to call it quits. That's part of what makes them overcompetitive in the first place. And since Payton earned crunch-time minutes for a championship team and contributed to its title, you couldn't compare him to the '89 version of Kareem or anything. But when I remember GP getting that ring that season, I don't remember the pair of clutch shots as much as being surprised when he made them. Was a championship ring worth sinking to that level of expectations? Only Gary Payton knows.

40. PATRICK EWING

Resume: 17 years, 11 quality, 12 All-Stars . . . '86 Rookie of the Year . . . top 5 ('90), top 10 ('88, '89, '91, '92, '93, '97) . . . best player on 1 runner-up ('94 Knicks) . . . 2-year peak: 28–11, 3.6 BPG, 53% FG . . . '90 Playoffs: 29–11 (10 G) . . . '94, '95 playoffs: 20–11, 2.8 BPG, 45% FG (36 G) . . . member of '92 Dream Team . . . 20K-10K Club

Knicks fans did their damnedest to talk themselves into the Patrick Ewing era.[86] Everyone believed Ewing was the Evolutionary Russell, a destructive

---

85. What would be the equivalent in other walks of life? Springsteen getting a standing O at the Meadowlands after a rocking solo in his new gig as the harmonica player for Kings of Leon?

86. I have multiple New York friends who swear that Knicks fans were subconsciously predisposed to root against Ewing because so many Knicks fans love St. John's and that was the height of the Johnnies-Hoyas Big East rivalry back then.

defensive force who would own the league someday. Only it didn't happen . . . and it didn't happen . . . and then it seemed like it was happening, only it turned out to be a dick tease . . . and it didn't happen . . . and at some point everyone except for the delusional Knicks fans realized that it was never going to happen. You know those movie scenes where a male character dies in a hospital bed and his wife stands over him talking like he didn't die, and everyone else in the room feels awkward, and then finally someone comes over and says, "Honey, he's gone" and tries to pull her away, so she starts screaming, "Nooooooo! Nooooo, he's fine! He's gonna wake up!" and then she collapses and has a crying seizure? That was every Knicks fan from 1995 to 1999. When Hakeem turned Ewing into ground beef in the '94 Finals, Ewing dropped dead in a "This guy's carrying us to a title someday" sense. But the Knicks fans kept standing there over the hospital bed waiting for him to wake up.

Eventually they decided that Ewing's career was either "frustrating" (the glass-half-full take) or "phenomenally disappointing" (the glass-half-empty take). He peaked during the '90 season, averaging a 29–11 with 4 blocks and 55 percent shooting for a 45-win Knicks team, saving the Knicks with a 44–13 in a must-win Game 4 against Boston, then leading them to a shocking upset in the decisive fifth game (31 points). Sitting in the Garden as Ewing took over and swished an improbable backbreaking three, I remember thinking, "Shit, he's putting it all together; we're in serious trouble." But Detroit easily dispatched them in the second round and Ewing was never that good again. Why? Because of his knees. College Ewing prowled the paint like a tiger, jumped around like House of Pain and contested every shot within fifteen feet of the rim. NBA veteran Ewing picked his spots, jogged with huge strides and crouched before every jump. Never a great rebounder[87] or passer, never someone with a treasure chest of low-post moves, that subtle erosion of athleticism turned him into an elite center who did everything well and nothing great. Actually, it was a little sad. Poor Ewing perfected his "intense" game face, bellowed at the MSG crowd, pounded his chest after big plays, played up the whole "I'm a warrior!" angle in interviews and even made a clumsy effort

---

87. Ewing never cracked the top three in rebounding and currently has the 54th-highest career rebounding average, just ahead of Sikma (56th), Laimbeer (57th) and Rony Seikaly (64th).

to become an intimidating enforcer. All of it kind of worked . . . but not really. The sophisticated Knicks fans saw right through him, endlessly debating his virtues and repeatedly coming back to the same conclusion: *As long as this is our best guy, we probably can't win the title.*

That's when Pat Riley nearly salvaged Ewing's superstardom, remaking the Knicks into Bad Boys II and adopting thugball tactics to exact as much as he could from his secretly limited center (nearly ruining basketball in the process). They lost back-to-back slugfests to Chicago before catching a break with Jordan's "baseball sabbatical," reaching the Finals behind a monster effort from Ewing in Game 7 (22–20–7 with 5 blocks and the winning tip against Indiana) before squandering a disheartening Finals. The following year, Reggie Miller ripped out their hearts in the Eastern Semis, with Ewing missing a series-deciding 6-foot bunny. Just like that the Ewing window had closed, although it took a few more years for everyone to realize it.[88] Before the 2001 season, the Knicks finally cut the cord (and inadvertently destroyed their future) by turning Ewing's expiring deal into a slew of horrendous contracts; then we watched Ewing slog through the "fifteen-year-old poodle with cataracts who starts going to the bathroom in the house and needs to be put to sleep" stage. Did we ever figure out why centers age in dog years once they hit their late thirties? They always have one final season where they gain 20 pounds, lose all hand-eye coordination, run in slow motion, and jump like their shoes are loaded with razor blades; all they have left is their turnaround jumper. It's like an automobile being completely stripped except for the radio. That's the turnaround jumper. For Ewing, that season happened twice, in Seattle and Orlando. And then he was done.

He hasn't endured for a few reasons. Ewing lacked charisma and may have been the most uncomfortable postmerger interview other than Moses Malone.[89] He had some legitimate weaknesses—horrendous

---

88. Notice how I avoided any mention of the excruciating Knicks-Heat playoff battles? I always wanted a Bizarro ESPN Classic channel that featured programming like *NBA's Greatest Games: Miami 65, New York 56, SportsCentury and Beyond: Rusty Hilger, The Very Best of the Magic Hour, Games That Ended Prematurely Because Somebody Died, Actors Who Threw Like Women* (hosted by Tim Robbins), *Best Magic Johnson Comebacks, Inside Schwartz, NHL Instant Classic: Columbus at Minnesota* and *Nancy Lieberman's 500 Most Awkward Sideline Interviews.*

89. When Ewing became head of the Players Association, it was like finding out that Flavor Flav had been named the president of Viacom.

hands, shaky at crunch time, dubious rebounder, awful passer out of double-teams, couldn't make his teammates better—and he lacked a fan-friendly game that wouldn't exactly be remembered fondly. Even Ewing's shining moment (the '94 Finals) turned into a train wreck: Ewing averaged 18.9 points and shot 36 percent, while Hakeem averaged a 27–9 with 3.9 blocks and 50 percent shooting. And it wasn't even THAT close. Ewing ranks this highly because you could build a contender around him in his prime, and because he absolutely could have won the '94 championship playing with Richmond, Rice, Miller, or really any good two-guard other than John Starks. Much like fellow Dream Team players Drexler, Robinson and Malone, we'll remember Ewing as a second banana masquerading as a first banana, even if Knicks fans never wanted to admit it at the time. Now they do.[90]

One last Ewing thought: When I was writing for my old website, a reader named Dave Cirilli sent in his elaborate Ewing Theory, which centered around the inexplicable phenomenon that both the Hoyas and Knicks seemed to play better every time Ewing was sitting on the bench. After tinkering with it and finding various examples,[91] Dave emailed me and we honed the language over the next few weeks, eventually deciding that two crucial elements were needed for any situation to qualify for Ewing status: a star athlete receives an inordinate amount of media attention and fan interest, yet his teams never win anything substantial with him; and that same athlete leaves his team (either by injury, trade, graduation, free agency or retirement) and both the media and fans immediately write off the team for the near future (for either the rest of the season or the following season). I wrote about the theory and had some fun with it.[92] A few months later, Ewing tore an Achilles tendon during Game 2 of the '99 Eastern Finals. The heavily favored Pacers seemed like a mortal

90. My favorite Ewing moment: When an Atlanta strip joint (Gold Club) was busted for drugs and prostitution, a number of celebs were revealed as pay-for-play customers in the ensuing trial, including Ewing, who made the following testimony: "The girls danced, started fondling me, I got aroused, they performed oral sex. I hung around a little bit and talked to them, then I left." As Marv Albert would say, *yes!*

91. His original examples: Donyell Marshall ('95 UConn), Peyton Manning ('98 Tennessee), Keith Van Horn ('98 Utah), Don Mattingly ('96 Yankees), Bret Hart ('97 WWF).

92. Some enjoyable pop culture examples: Shannen Doherty (*90210*), David Lee Roth (Van Halen), Shelley Long (*Cheers*), David Caruso (*NYPD Blue*), Sonny Corleone (the Corleones), Craig Kilborn (*Daily Show*).

lock . . . only with Ewing himself involved, suddenly this had become the *ultimate* test of the Ewing Theory. Heading into Game 3, Dave was oozing with confidence and predicting in no uncertain terms, "Ewing's injury is the best thing that ever could have happened to the Knicks; they're definitely making the Finals now." Incredibly, the Knicks won three of the next four and advanced to the Finals *as I was playing up Dave's Ewing theory prediction on my website!* My three thousand readers at the time couldn't have been more impressed. From there, Ewing Theory instances kept happening—Mo Vaughn ('99 Red Sox), Barry Sanders ('99 Lions), Trent Green ('99 Rams), Griffey and A-Rod ('00 and '01 Mariners), Dan Marino ('00 Dolphins)—and I finally unveiled Dave's Ewing Theory to a national audience on ESPN.com in 2001, predicting that Drew Bledsoe was the single most logical Ewing Theory candidate for the future. Only a few months later, Bledsoe went down, the '02 Patriots won their first Super Bowl without him and I looked like Nostrasimbo. You have to admit, that was amazing. Since then, we've had some other classics (Nomar and the '04 Red Sox and Tiki and the '07 Giants being the best), but none could have happened without the great Patrick Ewing.

Here's my point: if your prime inspired a sports theory that hypothesized why your teams played better without you, you probably shouldn't crack the top thirty-five of a Hall of Fame Pyramid.

39. DIRK NOWITZKI

Resume: 12 years, 10 quality, 9 All-Stars . . . '07 MVP, 25–9–3, 50% FG, 42% 3FG, 90% FT . . . top 5 ('05, '06, '07, '09), top 10 ('02, '03, '10), top 15 ('04, '08) . . . 3-year peak: 26–9–4 (51%–89%–41%) . . . best player on runner-up ('06 Mavs), 27–12–3 (23 G) . . . 10 straight 22–8 seasons . . . Playoffs: 26–11, 46% FG, 88% FT (103 G)

The NBA's alpha dog almost ended up being German. Yup, we came *that* close in the 2006 playoffs—if not for the heroics of Wade, Salvatore, Payton and others, Germany would have made its biggest advancement on American culture since David Hasselhoff infiltrated the horny brains of teenage guys with *Baywatch*. Personally, I was terrified—this was the same country that started two world wars and deliberately injured Pele in *Victory.* Had Nowitzki grabbed the conch that spring, maybe Germany would have gotten its swagger back, maybe the bad blood would have gotten going again and maybe our lives would have eventually been in danger. Instead the Mavs fell apart in the Finals and so did Dirk, who secured his spot on the "Crap, It's Just Not in Me" All-Stars along with Karl Malone, Drexler, KJ, Ewing and Sampson. How close did we come? Hop into the NBA Time Machine with me; we're heading back to 2006. Dirk had just completed his finest regular season and made a run at becoming the toughest NBA player in the history of Europe.[93] (Note: Dirk developed such a nasty streak that even when Ashton Kutcher punk'd him, it seemed like Dirk wanted to kick Ashton's ass for a few seconds, which would have been the greatest and most random fight ever—but that's a whole other story.) Although we liked following a cocky, snarling 7-foot German with a 25-foot range during a sublimely efficient offensive season, questions lingered about his crunch-time prowess and Dallas' title prospects when its best player seemed soft and couldn't guard anyone.[94]After all, nobody ever won a title with an all-offense, no-defense guy leading the way. Then Dirk broke through with the following moments:

- **Game 7, San Antonio series (Round 2).** Playing on the road against the champs, trailing by three in the final 20 seconds and still reeling from a gut-wrenching three by Ginobili on the previous possession, Dallas calls the season-deciding play for Dirk. He gets the ball and backs Bruce Bowen into the paint with a herky-jerky, grind-you-backward move developed the previous summer. With Bowen overplaying him, Dirk weasels past him and somehow avoids getting tripped, kicked, or punched in the balls. Then he barrels toward the basket, absorbs the contact from Ginobili,[95] finishes a twisting layup,

93. That's like driving the nicest-smelling New York City cab.
94. The "soft" tag started in '03 when Dirk refused to limp around with an injured knee in the '03 Conference Finals. Strangely, nobody remembers this decision now.
95. Ginobili's dumb foul takes its rightful place alongside Rasheed leaving Big Shot Rob in the '05 Finals, Pau Gasol not helping Ray Allen on the game-clinching drive (Game 4, '08 Finals) and no Kings fouling Shaq on the offensive rebound right before Big Shot Brob's game-winning shot (Game 4, Kings-Lakers series) as one of the four dumbest defensive plays of the last decade.

draws the foul *and* buries the free throw. Tie game! Remember, the Mavs were 20 seconds away from blowing a three-games-to-one series lead and a 20-point lead in Game 7; they never would have been the same after that. Considering the circumstances, shouldn't that play rank with Magic's sky hook against the '87 Celtics, Bird's steal-and-pass against the '87 Pistons, MJ's basket-steal-basket sequence to end the '98 Finals, Jerry West's half-court bomb to extend Game 3 of the '70 Finals and every other "I need to come up big *Right Now*" clutch play in NBA history? And since they ended up winning in OT and eventually made the Finals, another question has to be asked: how many superstars single-handedly altered the course of the playoffs with one play? At this specific point in time, it sure seemed like Dirk was making a leap from franchise guy to potential Pantheon guy.[96]

- **Game 5, Phoenix Series (Western Finals).** Dirk torches Phoenix with one of the best performances of the decade: 50 points, 12 rebounds and an unforgettable "there's no effing way we're losing" explosion in the second half (scoring 24 of 34 Dallas points to ice it). Could anyone guard him? Opponents couldn't use taller Duncan/Garnett types because Dirk was beating those guys off the dribble or, even worse, pulling them 25 feet away and shooting threes over them. The gritty Bowen/Raja types had no chance because of his creative high-post game (fueled by his deadly fall-away). Who was left? Lankier forwards like Shawn Marion had the best chance on paper because they could stay in front of him, make him work for his points and force him to settle for 16-footers,[97] but Dirk learned to adjust when his shot wasn't falling, adopting Larry Bird's ploy of crashing the offensive boards and getting his points on putbacks and foul shots. At this specific point in time, with his confidence swelling, there wasn't a way to fully shut him down. Here's what I wrote: "Dirk is playing at a higher level than any forward since Bird. . . . He's been a killer all

96. In a seven-game stretch from Game 3 of the Spurs series through Game 3 of the Suns series, Dirk averaged a 29–15. Yikes.
97. That's how Stephen Jackson throttled him in the '07 playoffs, although we didn't know about that yet because we're still in the NBA time machine, remember?

spring, a true assassin, and I certainly never imagined writing that about Dirk Nowitzki."

To bang my point home that Nowitzki was better than anyone realized, I created something in that same column called the 42 Club: I added up the point, rebound and assist averages for franchise guys during the playoffs, and if the number topped 42, that meant we were probably talking about a potential Level 4 (or higher) guy.[98] To figure out the members, I allowed only guys who played 13 or more playoff games in one postseason, since that's a legitimate sampling (more than a month of basketball at the highest level). Here were the 42 Club members from 1977 to 2010 (so we can include LeBron):

Michael Jordan (6x): 49.4 ('89); 50.7 ('90); 45.9 ('91); 46.5 ('92); 47.8 ('93); 43.8 ('97)

Shaquille O'Neal (4x): 43.6 ('98); 49.2 ('00); 49.0 ('01); 43.9 ('02)

Larry Bird (4x): 42.0 ('81); 44.4 ('84); 43.4 ('86); 44.2 ('87)[99]

LeBron James (3x): 44.7 ('06), 43.6 ('08), 51.7 ('09)

Moses Malone (2x): 43.0 ('81), 43.3 ('83)

Magic Johnson (2x): 43.8 ('86), 42.5 ('91)

Karl Malone (2x): 43.0 ('92), 42.9 ('94)

Hakeem Olajuwon (2x): 44.2 ('94), 47.8 ('95)

Tim Duncan (2x): 42.7 ('01), 45.4 ('03)

Kareem Abdul-Jabbar (1x): 47.1 ('80)

Charles Barkley (1x): 44.5 ('93)

Kobe Bryant (1x): 42.8 ('01)

Allen Iverson (1x): 43.7 ('01)

Kevin Garnett (1x): 44.0 ('04)

Dirk Nowitzki (1x): 45.1 ('06 pre-finals)

98. I also liked the idea of a 42 Club because it reminded me of the Five-Timer Club on *SNL* for five-time hosts, only there was no way to have a weak link like Elliott Gould. Everyone was Tom Hanks and Steve Martin.

99. If we made a Platinum wing in the 42 Club for any member who also topped 50% FG shooting and 80% FT shooting that same playoffs, our Platinum members would be Jordan (4x), Bird (2x) and that's it. Also, please tell Patrick Ewing that the Platinum wing of the 42 Club isn't a place for him to get blown.

There wasn't a single fraud on that list with the possible exception of . . . well, I'm trying to be nice, but fuck it—Karl Malone! Every other memorable spring from 1977 to 2010 is represented except for Walton in '77 (didn't score enough points), Bernard in '84 (only played 12 games), Magic in '87 and '88 (barely missed), and Wade in '06 (didn't heat up until the last two rounds). Just like in real life, the best playoff seasons of Ewing, Robinson, and Drexler fell a tad short. Career-year/MVP seasons for KG, Barkley, and Iverson all qualified, as did Kobe's ridiculous '01 season when he quietly peaked as an all-around player. I also like that our most dominant player (MJ) leads with six appearances, and his precocious next-generation challenger (LeBron) cracked the 42 Club at the tender age of twenty-one. Everything about the concept checks out; there are no flukes, no aberrations, no injustices. It just works. I had never imagined that Dirk could potentially crack a list of elite playoff performers; just two summers before, I'd skewered Dallas for refusing to part with Nowitzki in a Shaq trade. The 50-point game altered my opinion. As I wrote the next day, "He's the most unstoppable player in basketball, a true franchise guy, and I think he's headed for his first championship in about two weeks."

So what happened? Dallas won the first two Finals games, carried a 13-point lead into the final six minutes of Game 3 in Miami . . . and collapsed faster than a Corey Haim acting comeback. Wade took over, the refs took over and the Mavs lost their composure. Even after Miami's big comeback, Nowitzki (a 90.1 percent FT shooter that season) had a chance to tie the game with two freebies in the final three seconds. He clanked the first one. Ballgame. So much for making the leap. Dallas pulled a bigger no-show in Game 4 than Corey Haim in *Fever Lake*, then rallied in Game 5 before getting screwed by more dubulent[100] officiating, although they did commit a number of brain farts down the stretch and Josh Howard missed two key free throws in overtime. By Game 6, they were more rattled than Corey Haim watching the coke scenes in *Scarface*. In retrospect, Miami deserved to win for being a tougher, more experienced team. Dallas got tight down the stretch; Miami stayed cool. Dallas complained for two straight weeks;

---

100. I made up that word: "dubulent" is a cross between "dubious" and "fraudulent." If Webster's ever picks it up, they should just show Wade's free throw numbers in the '06 Finals as its definition.

Miami didn't complain about anything. Avery Johnson looked tighter than a whipped husband afraid to get a lap dance at someone else's bachelor party; Pat Riley always looked like he was getting ready for a postgame bottle of chardonnay on his boat. Even the body language of the two stars was different: Wade was cooler than cool, but Nowitzki was constantly frowning, yanking his mouthpiece out and acting more bitchy than Corey Haim when he was banned from the *Lost Boys 2* shoot.[101] Let the record show that Dirk sucked in all four of those losses while his teammates imploded around him. And in an amazing wrinkle for 42 Club purposes, Dirk finished the '06 playoffs with . . .

(Drumroll, please . . .)

A 41.6!

See? The formula never fails. The following season, Dirk stumbled into an MVP Award that was invalidated by the great Golden State Collapse of '07. Now he's hitting the latter half of his career and we can safely say that Dirk Nowitzki missed the boat as an alpha dog. Sure, he's one of the best forty players ever. But he was never the dominant guy for an entire season, and as far as I'm concerned, America is safe.

---

101. I just felt like breaking the "most Corey Haim references ever made in one paragraph in a sports book" record. I was feeling it.[P41]

P41. Did Corey Haim die a few months after *TBOB* was released? Of course he did. Our running tally of *TBOB* damage: Oden as the next Bowie, Oden's knee, Pryzbilla's knee, Corey Haim, Gilbert Arenas' career.

NINE

THE PYRAMID: LEVEL 3

DAVID ROBINSON

SPURS — CENTER

38. GEORGE MIKAN

Resume: 9 years, 7 quality, 4 All-Stars . . . Top 5 ('50, '51, '52, '53, '54) . . . leader: scoring (3x), rebounds (2x) . . . best player for 7 straight champs (including NBL and BAA) . . . 3-year peak: 28–14–3, 42% FG . . . playoffs: 23–14 (60 g's)

Give yourself a high five because you just reached the dumbest moment of the book. I mean, where would *you* rank the best player of the pre-shot-clock era? Calling someone the greatest pre-shot-clock force is like calling One on One: Dr. J vs. Larry Bird the greatest computer sports game of the early eighties.[1] In other words, you're not saying much. The six-foot-ten Mikan peaked with a tiny three-second lane, no shot clock, no seven-footers, no goaltending rules and barely any black players . . . and it's not like he was throwing up Wilt-like numbers. Look how he compared to his peers during his last four quality years (1951–54).[2]

PLAYER	GAMES	PPG	RPG	FG%	FGA
George Mikan	274	22.6	14.1	40.0	19.7
Ed Macualey	272	19.7	8.6	44.8	13.9
Dolph Schayes	272	16.5	13.4	36.8	13.4
Bob Cousy	278	19.1	6.3	36.5	18.4
Neil Johnston	206	18.0	10.3	45.3	13.3
Paul Arizin	131	21.3	10.6	43.1	15.9
Alex Groza	66	21.7	10.7	47.0	15.8

So Mikan led everyone in scoring and rebounding (but not in a staggering way) while attempting the most shots (by far) in a sport tailored to his specific attributes and talents (size and toughness). Make no mistake: Big George was *not* dynamic to watch. Here's how Leonard Koppett described him: "The Lakers would bring the ball up slowly, waiting for the lumbering Mikan to get into position in the pivot. Then they would concentrate on getting the ball in to Big George, whose huge left elbow would open a swath as he turned into the basket. . . . Mikan was simply too big in bulk to be blocked out. He couldn't jump very high, but he didn't have to. He couldn't run, but he didn't have to." No wonder the league nearly went under. The sport started moving against Mikan before the 1951–52 season, when they expanded the three-second lane to 12 feet so Big George couldn't plant himself next to the basket anymore. In the three

1. I spent roughly 10,000 hours playing Doc vs. Larry in 1984. If I'd had NBA Live 2011 at the time, Doc vs. Larry wouldn't have come out of the box. You could say the same about Mikan in 1951. If Dwight Howard had been playing back then, Mikan wouldn't have come out of the box.
2. They didn't even keep rebounding stats until '51. What the hell was going on back then? It's amazing they even kept track of points.

seasons preceding that rule change ('49 to '51), he averaged 28 points on 42 percent shooting. For the next three years ('52 to '54), he averaged 21 points on 39 percent shooting. Given how Mikan struggled to adjust to the three-second rule and the post-shot-clock era, you can only imagine how his career would have suffered when they changed the goaltending rules and allowed more black players. Every piece of evidence points to Mikan having better timing than anything: he entered and departed the league at the quintessential times. Unfortunately, we can't stick him lower than Level 3 because I can't risk offending my nursing home demographic.

Two fun things about George: First, he's the only player in NBA history to successfully carry off the "thick glasses and dorky kneepads" combination. Every Mikan picture or clip makes him look like the starting center for Lambda Lambda Lambda's intramural hoops team.[3] Second, he may have been the toughest player of that era, breaking ten different bones and taking 160 stitches during his nine-year career. He helped Minny win the 1950 title playing with a broken wrist. During the 1951 playoffs, he played with a fractured leg when Minny fell to Rochester in the Western Finals. As Mikan told *Newsday* years later, "The doctors taped a plate on it for the playoffs. I played all right, scored in the 20s. I couldn't run, sort of hopped down the court." He was like the Bizarro Vince Carter. Of course, he just inadvertently proved the point of the previous few paragraphs—that Mikan excelled during an era when centers could score 20 a game in the playoffs while hopping around with a plate taped to their broken leg.

37. ALLEN IVERSON

Resume: 14 years, 12 quality, 9 All-Stars . . . '01 MVP . . . '97 Rookie of the Year . . . Top 5 ('99, '01, '05), Top 10 ('00, '02, '03), Top-15 ('06) . . . 3-year peak: 31–4–7 . . . best player on runner-up ('01 Sixers), 33–5–6 (22 G) . . . leader: scoring (4x), steals (3x), TO's (2x), minutes (1x) . . . 30-plus PPG (5x) . . . Playoffs: 30–6–4, 40% FG (67 g's) . . . 20K Point Club

---

3. I spent about 20 minutes trying to figure out what current celebrity Mikan looked like. The answer? A giant, bespectacled Jason Biggs. I'm glad I'm here.

As the years and decades pass, both Iverson and no. 21 on the Pyramid will be picked apart by an army of statisticians looking for various ways to undermine their careers. And that's fine. Just know that Iverson passed the Season Ticket Test every year this decade (starting with his '01 MVP season): when season tickets arrive in the mail, the recipient invariably checks the schedule, marks certain can't-miss games and writes those dates down on a calendar. The importance of those games is measured by rivalries, superstars, incoming rookies and the "I need to see that guy" factor. That's it. From 1997 to 2007, Iverson always made my list. Always. So I don't give a crap about Iverson's win shares, his ranking among top-fifty scorers with the lowest shooting percentage or whatever.[4] Every post-Y2K ticket to an Iverson game guaranteed a professional, first-class performance (no different from reservations at a particularly good restaurant or hotel), and for whatever reason, he was always more breathtaking in person. He's listed at six feet but couldn't be taller than five-foot-ten, so every time he attacked the basket, it was like watching an undersized running back ram into the line of scrimmage for five yards a pop (think Emmitt Smith). He took implausible angles on his drives (angles that couldn't be seen as they unfolded, even if you'd been watching him for ten years) and drained an obscene number of layups and floaters in traffic. He had a knack for going 9-for-24 but somehow making the two biggest shots of the game. And he played with an eff-you intensity that only KG and Kobe matched (although MJ remains the king of this category). For years and years, the most intimidating player in the league wasn't taller than Rebecca Romijn. I always thought it was interesting that Iverson averaged 28 minutes of playing time in his eight All-Star Games and played crunch time in every close one; even his temporary coaches didn't want to risk pissing him off.

Iverson's career personifies how the media can negatively sway everyone's perception of a particular athlete. There was a generational twinge to the anti-Iverson sentiment, fueled by media folks in their forties, fifties and

---

4. The case against Iverson: he's a ball hog (averaged 23-plus shots in 7 straight seasons); he's a horrible three-point shooter (31% career, three straight sub-30% years from '02 to '04); he turned the ball over too much (3.8 career per game, four seasons of 4.4 or higher); and he was a 2-guard in a point guard's body (so you had to match him with a tall point guard to keep Iverson from defending bigger 2-guards). The only defensible gripe was his three-point shooting—nobody who sucks that much from deep should attempt nearly 3,300 threes in 12 seasons.

sixties who couldn't understand him and didn't seem interested in trying. Nearly all of them played up his infamous aversion to practice (overrated over the years) and atypical appearance (the cornrows/tattoos combination) over describing the incredible thrill of watching him play in person. They weren't interested in figuring out how an alleged coach-killer who allegedly monopolized the ball, allegedly hated to practice and allegedly couldn't sublimate his game to make his teammates better doubled as one of the most revered players by his peers.[5] They glossed over the fact that he was saddled with an incompetent front office, a subpar supporting cast and a revolving door of coaches in Philly.[6] They didn't care that he was one of the most influential African American athletes ever, a trendsetter who shoved the NBA into the hip-hop era (whether the league was ready or not) and resonated with blacks in a way that even Jordan couldn't duplicate. They weren't so interested in one of the most fascinating, complex athletes of my lifetime: a legendary partier and devoted family man; a loyal teammate who shot too much; a featherweight who carried himself like a heavyweight; an intimidating competitor who was always the smallest guy on the court; an ex-con with a shady entourage who also ranked among the most intuitive, self-aware, articulate superstars in any sport. If I could pick any modern athlete to spend a week with in his prime for a magazine feature, I would pick Allen Iverson. In a heartbeat.

And yeah, his field goal percentage wasn't that good and he took too many shots. Whatever. Fifty years from now, I hope people realize that Iverson had better balance than everyone else, that he was faster and more coordinated than everyone else, that he took a superhuman pounding and kept getting up, that he was one of the all-time athletic superfreaks. We already know that he was the best high school football player in Virginia history, but he also would have been a world-class soccer player, boxer or center fielder, someone

5. Right before Philly dealt Iverson to Denver in 2006, the ex-players on *NBA Coast to Coast* (Greg Anthony, Tim Legler and Jon Barry) traded Iverson war stories like they were talking about a Mayan warrior.

6. Iverson only played with two All-Stars in Philly: Theo Ratliff and a becoming-decrepit Dikembe Mutombo. His prime was saddled with overpaid role players (Eric Snow, Aaron McKie, Kyle Korver, Kenny Thomas, Marc Jackson, Brian Skinner, Greg Buckner, Tyrone Hill, George Lynch, Corliss Williamson), overpaid underachievers (Derrick Coleman, Keith Van Horn, Sam Dalembert, Joe Smith), overpaid and washed-up veterans (Todd MacCulloch, Toni Kukoc, Chris Webber, Glenn Robinson, Matt Geiger, Billy Owens) and underachieving lottery picks (Jerry Stackhouse, Tim Thomas, Larry Hughes).

who could have picked his sport in track and competed for an Olympic spot, and while we're here, I can't *fathom* how much ground he could have covered on a tennis court. (Tangent that's too important for a footnote: Every time the World Cup rolls around, I always find myself thinking about which NBA players could have excelled at soccer. Iverson would have been the best soccer player ever. I think this is indisputable, actually. Deron Williams would have been a great stopper. Josh Smith could have been unstoppable soaring above the pack to head corner kicks. And can you imagine a better goalie than LeBron? It would be like having a six-foot-nine human octopus in the net. How could anyone score on him? Couldn't we teach Bron the rudimentary aspects of playing goal, then throw him in a couple of Columbus' MLS games? Like you would turn the channel if this happened?) Iverson wrecked his body on and off the court and somehow kept his fastball, which shouldn't be counted as an achievement but remains amazing nonetheless.[7] And he deserves loads of credit for dragging a mediocre Sixers team to the '01 Finals when so many other scoring machines had failed before him. Unlike Gervin, McAdoo and Dominique, Iverson played with a swagger that pushed a decent team to a whole other level. He believed they could win, he killed himself to that end, and everyone else eventually followed. Watching Game 7 of the Bullets-Spurs series from '79 and Game 7 of the Bucks-Sixers from '01, the biggest difference between Gervin and Iverson—two spectacular offensive players—was the way they carried themselves. Gervin never gave the sense that the game was life or death, whereas Iverson went into foxhole mode, with his ferocity lifting his teammates and energizing the crowd.[8]

That ferocity separated Iverson from everyone else after Jordan retired; for most of his twenties, he was the Association's single most menacing player. He had a darker edge that belonged to nobody else, a switch that instantly transformed him into a character from *The Wire*. I remember at-

---

7. You could fill an entire chapter with secondhand Iverson stories of the "I heard he slept with ten women in one night" and "I heard he was out drinking all night, then played a day game in Boston and scored 49" variety. By all accounts, the guy doesn't sleep. He's a vampire. Might explain why his career came to a screeching halt in 2009.

8. When his teammates couldn't match that ferocity, that's when things fell apart. Just ask Keith Van Horn, who might still be in therapy from playing with the Answer. There were times when Iverson looked so pissed off at KVH for letting him down, the possibility of a postgame shower rape was in play.

tending a Boston-Philly game when Iverson was whistled for a technical, yelped in disbelief, then followed the referee toward the scorer's table before finally screaming "Fuck you!" at the top of his lungs. The official whirled around and pulled his whistle toward his mouth for a second technical. They were maybe 25 feet away from me, so I could see everything up close. And I swear on my daughter's life, the following moment happened: As the ref started to blow the whistle, Iverson's eyes widened and he moved angrily toward him, almost like someone getting written up for a parking ticket who decides it would be easier just to punch out the meter maid. For a split second, there was real violence in the air. The rattled official lowered his whistle and never called the second technical. By sheer force of personality, Iverson kept himself in the game.

Look, I'm not condoning what happened. It was a frightening moment. I specifically remember thinking, "I am frightened." But I haven't seen a basketball player bully a referee like that before or since; it was like playing an intramural hoops game against the football team and watching the biggest offensive lineman intimidate a 130-pound freshman ref. And that goes back to the seeing-him-in-person thing. At his peak, Iverson played with a compelling, hostile, bloodthirsty energy that nobody else had. He was relentless in every sense of the word, a warrior, an alpha dog, a tornado. He was so quick and coordinated that it genuinely defies description. He was enough of a lunatic that officials occasionally cowered in his presence. And none of this makes total sense unless you watched him live. Could you win a title if Iverson was your best player and you didn't have a franchise big man? Of course not. Could you win a title with Iverson as the second-best player and crunch-time scorer? Yeah, possibly. Would you pay to see him in his prime? In the words of Mr. Big, absah-fuckin'-lutely.[9] I will remember him.

9. That's right, I quoted from *Sex and the City*. To this day, I will defend Season One for being funny, well written and original. I cannot defend the next few years, obviously. But Season One was solid. You can add this footnote to my "Gay List" (of tidbits that would make one of my friends say, "He's definitely not gay, but . . ."), along with the fact that I enjoyed the first season of *Friends,* I loved Bronski Beat's "Smalltown Boy" video, I own every Smiths and Cure album as well as *And the Band Played On* on DVD; two of my favorite shows ever were *90210* and *Melrose Place* and I went to a Coldplay concert and would go again.[P42]

P42. Gay list add: In my Boston hotel room during the 2010 Finals, I went to MTV.com and watched that week's episode of *The Hills* on my laptop.

36. STEVE NASH

Resume: 14 years, 10 quality, 7 All-Stars . . . MVP: '05, '06 . . . '07 MVP
runner-up . . . BS MVP ('07) . . . top 5 ('05, '06, '07), top 10 ('08, '10), top 15
('02, '03) . . . leader: assists (4x), FT% (2x) . . . 4-year peak: 17–4–11, 51%
FG, 45% 3FG, 90% FT . . . 3-year Playoffs peak: 21–4–11, 49% FG, 40%
3FG, 90% FT (46 G) . . . career: 90.3 FT% (2nd), 43.1% 3FG (5th), assists
(8th)

The case for Nash cracking the top-40: won back-to-back MVPs, a sentence that looks so unbelievable in print, my eyeballs just popped out of my head Allan Ray–style (only Bird, Magic, MJ, Russell, Wilt, Duncan, Moses, Kareem and Nash did it) . . . along with Bird and Nowitzki, one of three 50–40–90 Club members to make an All-NBA team (and he did it twice)[10] . . . exceptionally fun to watch on the offensive end . . . willed himself into becoming a Stockton-like crunch-time assassin . . . you could call him the Evolutionary Cousy (or, Cousy with a jumpshot) . . . helped bring back three dying art forms: passing, fast breaks and crappy hair . . . five-time winner of the Guy Everyone in the League Would Have Killed to Play With Award ('05, '06, '07, '08, '10) . . . replaced Wayne Gretzky as Canada's most popular athlete after the Janet Jones gambling scandal . . . improved the careers of Shawn Marion and Amar'e Stoudemire by at least 35 percent . . . the only player this decade who inspired Tim Thomas to give a shit[11] . . . drew a handful of "that's one bad-ass white boy" compliments from Charles Barkley over the past few years . . . probably would have starred in a Finals if (a) Phoenix's owner wasn't such a cheapskate, (b) Joe Johnson didn't break his face early in the '04 playoffs, (c) Tim Donaghy

10. The 50-40-90 Club covers anyone who topped 50% FG, 40% 3FG and 90% FT shooting in one season. Not easy.

11. No small feat. Here's how I described Thomas in 2008: "Is there an NBA forward alive who couldn't average 31 minutes, 12 points, five rebounds and three assists, miss 70 percent of his 3-pointers and allow his guy to score at will? If baseball has VORP (value over replacement player), then basketball should have VOTT (value over Tim Thomas). He's such a dog that PETA might protest this paragraph." Ten months later, *Basketball Prospectus* unveiled a WARP stat that revealed Thomas scored *exactly at replacement level* for the '08 and '09 seasons. Stu Scott, give me a boo yeah!

reffing Game 3 and the Amar'e/Diaw leaving-the-bench suspensions[12] never happened in '07, (d) Tim Duncan didn't hit that crazy three in Game 1 of the '08 Spurs series, and/or (e) Jason Richardson had boxed out Ron Artest in Game 5 of the '10 Lakers series . . . the more Nash plays with his teammates, the better he gets (like Gretzky during his Edmonton days) . . . and he's the one modern NBA superstar who lived up to the words "franchise player" through thick and thin.

(When Nash re-signed for three more years in 2009, I remember thinking, "Why the hell would he stay in Phoenix?" In America, we're accustomed to superstars who find themselves stuck on a sinking ship, then bolt for greener pastures or selfishly demand a trade without considering the ramifications of that request. Once you say, "You guys aren't good enough to play with me, I need a better team," the situation becomes irreparable. Nash always understood that. He's Canadian. He's loyal. He's the leader. Franchise players are supposed to lead. So he stayed knowing that his Finals window had probably closed. Now here's why you have to love sports: in his finest season given his age, Nash banged out a 17–11 with 51–43–94 percentages—unprecedented numbers for a thirty-six-year-old point guard—while brewing the league's best chemistry, performing open-heart surgery on Amar'e Stoudemire [who reinvented himself to the degree that New York stupidly gave him $100 million], leading unproven youngsters like Jared Dudley, Robin Lopez and Gordan Dragic,[P43] finally beating San Antonio in a series [and sobbing in the locker room afterwards], and somehow dragging a fringe playoff team within two wins of the 2010 Finals.[P44]

---

12. We can't use seatbelts, and we can't put a rope around the bench because a player could go flying into the rope during play and get practically decapitated . . . but what about an electric-fence-type device where they'd get shocked if they ventured onto the court, like what people use with their dogs in the backyard? Wouldn't that be worth it just to see Eddy Curry zone out, stand up to stretch and accidentally electroshock himself?

P43. We invited Nash and Dudley to an ESPN dinner at the 2010 Sundance Festival. Nash said there were three reasons he wasn't aging: a no-sugar diet, a sleep journal and a steady supply of undetectable PEDs. (Fine, I made the last one up.) He said the no-sugar diet made him recover faster after games; half the 2010 Suns followed suit and cut their sugar intake, including Dudley, who lost 20 pounds and became an elite bench player. I wouldn't have believed it until we watched Jared read his menu aloud and ask Nash, "Can I have this? What about this?" Not only does Nash make his teammates better, he orders for them!

P44. Nash added to an unfortunate record that spring: 118 career postseason games without making an NBA Finals. Nobody else is in triple digits.

Now we're looking at a *career*. Ten straight elite years, nine 50-win teams, two MVPs, seven All-Stars, multiple All-NBAs, the best shooting percentages in point guard history, and pole position for the "guard everyone in his generation would have loved playing with most" contest over Kidd. That's why I moved him from Level 4 to Level 3 for the paperback.)

The case against Nash cracking the top forty: Struggled with a bad back during his first four seasons, missing 64 games in all (and rendering the first third of his career moot) . . . an ineffective defensive player who doesn't get steals and can't be hidden against elite point guards . . . looks like a cross between Jackie Earle Haley and James Blunt . . . the validity of his consecutive MVP trophies can be easily picked apart, although he should have won in '07 . . . of all players who benefited from the rule changes before the '05 season, Nash was number one on the list . . . creamed offensively in the playoffs by Mike Bibby ('02, '04) and Tony Parker ('07, '08), a huge reason for his team's exits in those years . . . you have to wonder about the top-forty credentials of anyone who was offered a perfectly reasonable six-year, $60 million free agent offer by Phoenix in his prime, asked Mark Cuban to match that offer, and had Cuban basically say to him, "Sorry, that's a little rich for my blood; we'd rather spend that money on Erick Dampier." I mean, when Cuban wonders about the fiscal sanity of a contract, THAT is saying something.

So why stick Nash this high? For three reasons that went beyond everything we just mentioned. First, he played for a series of all-offense/no-defense teams in Dallas and Phoenix and never landed on a quality defensive team that protected him the way the Lakers protected Magic. His deficiencies were *constantly* exposed on that end, so we were always thinking about them. That's not totally fair. If you think Nash sucked on defense, you should have seen Magic pretending to be a bullfighter in the late eighties and early nineties. *Olé! Olé!* But Magic's teammates could protect him. When Nash's opponents beat him off the dribble, they scored because he never had smart team defenders or a shot blocker behind him. It's like Kate Hudson's performance in *Almost Famous*—she's a semi-abysmal actress, but give her a fantastic script and a great part and suddenly she's getting an Oscar nomination. Had Nash switched places with Tony Parker (another lousy defender) for the past four years and gotten protected by Popovich and Duncan, we wouldn't have complained about his defense as much. It's all about situations.

Second, former teammate Paul Shirley argued Nash's MVP credentials with me once by emailing me an excellent point about how valuable Nash really was to Phoenix, saying that Nash's style was contagious to the rest of the Suns as soon as he showed up from Dallas. Within a few weeks, everyone started playing unselfishly and getting each other easy baskets, like his magnanimity had seeped into everyone else by osmosis . . . and when you think about it, that's the single most important way you can affect a basketball team. In my lifetime, only Bird, Magic, Kidd and Walton affected their teams to that same degree. And Isaiah Rider, if this were Bizarro World.

Third, Nash's magnificent performance during the '07 season— ironically, the season when he *didn't* win the MVP—pushed him up a level for me. He never had a killer instinct until that year; even when he dropped 48 in an '05 playoff game because the Spurs were blanketing his teammates and daring Nash to score, he seemed sheepish about it afterward. But falling short in '05 and '06 hardened him; maybe he didn't go to the dark side like Danny LaRusso during the Terry Silver era, but he developed a nasty edge that nobody remembered seeing before. My guess: Nash spent the summer mulling over his career and everything that had happened, ultimately realizing that he couldn't do anything more other than win his first title. Then he thought long and hard about how to do it, ultimately cutting off his hair (feel the symbolism, baby!) and getting in superb shape so he wouldn't wear down in the playoffs again. When he showed up for training camp and realized the Marion-Stoudemire soap opera would be an ongoing problem,[13] Boris Diaw was out of shape, and new free agent Marcus Banks couldn't help, something snapped inside him. Exit, nice Steve Nash. Enter, icy Steve Nash. Suddenly he was tripping guys on picks, barking at officials and getting testy with his own teammates, eventually righting the ship and leading the Suns to the highest level of offensive basketball we've witnessed in twenty years. Really, it was a virtuoso season for him as an offensive player and a leader; borrowing the same tactic that once worked so well for Magic, Isiah and Stockton,

13. They had an alpha dog battle that revolved around important stuff like "Why did he get the best seat on the charter last night?" and "Why is his locker in a better spot than mine?" Also, they fought over a chew toy once. Whoops, I'm thinking of my dogs. Sorry.

Nash used the first 40 minutes to get everyone else going, then took over in crunch time if the Suns needed it. Sometimes he'd even unleash the "Look, there's no way we're effing losing this game!" glare on his face, an absolute staple for any MVP candidate.

Somewhere along the line, he won me over. Once one of the harsher critics of the voting for his back-to-back MVPs, I ended up writing the following about Nash during the '07 playoffs: "Regardless of what happens in San Antonio, I love what happened to Nash this season; his competitive spirit, toughness and leadership reminds me of Bird, Magic, MJ and Isiah back in the day. That's the highest praise I can give. At the very least, you know the Suns won't get blown out—they'll be in the game and fighting until the very end. You can count on that from them. He's the reason." You could go to war with Steve Nash, and really, that's all that matters.

35. KEVIN MCHALE

Resume: 13 years, 10 quality, 7 All-Stars . . . Top 5 ('87) . . . All-Defense (6x, three 1st) . . . season leader: FG% (2x) . . . 2nd-best player on one champ ('86 Celts) and 2 runner-ups ('85, '87); 6th man for 2 other champs ('81, '84) . . . 2-year peak: 24–9–3, 60% FG . . . 3-year Playoffs peak: 24–9, 59% FG . . . 3rd-best Playoff FG ever, 100+ games (56.6%) . . . career: 55% FG (12th), 80% FT

The starting power forward on the Players I Miss Most from the Old Days team. Watch an old Celtics game on ESPN Classic and think of Tim Duncan while you study McHale: long arms, quick feet, tortuous low-post moves, an unblockable sky hook, underrated passing, an uncanny ability to block shots and keep the ball in play. It's all there. Duncan ran the floor better; McHale had a wider arsenal of low-post moves. Other than that, they're basically the same. Duncan was a little faster and a little more athletic; McHale was better at handling double-teams (and sometimes even triple-teams). Of course, we'll see ten Duncans before we see another McHale. John Salley once described the experience of guarding McHale down low as "being in the man's *chamber*." Nobody could score more ways down low; not even Hakeem. McHale feasted on defenders with the following three moves: the jump hook (he could do it with either hand, although he never missed the righty one and could shoot it from a variety of angles), the turnaround fall-away (he could do it from both sides and from either direction; completely unblockable), and the step-back jumper from 12–15 feet (which always went in, forcing defenders to play up on him).[14]

Since he could convert those three shots at any point of any game, and the defender *knew* this, that set up the following alternative moves: up-and-under no. 1 (faked a turnaround, drew the guy in the air, pivoted, and did an ugly scoop shot), up-and-under no. 2 (faked a jump hook, drew the guy in the air, ducked under him, and did an ugly scoop shot),[15] the hesitation turnaround (showed the turnaround, waited for the defender to jump, drew the contact, then did a modified turnaround anyway), the double jump hook (showed the jump hook, drew the guy in the air, turned into him, drew contact and finished the jump hook), the running jump hook (started off on the left side, faked the jumper, drew the guy in the air, put the ball on the ground and unleashed an ugly running jump hook), and the drop-step (started off on the left side with the defender overplaying for the righty hook, then did a quick drop-step toward the baseline and laid the ball in). Then there were the combination moves, which nobody has been able to execute except Hakeem (who mastered the first one): combo no. 1 (faked the turnaround, pivoted, faked the righty jump hook, twisted the guy around and did the up-and-under), combo no. 2 (faked the righty jump hook, faked the full turnaround, twisted the guy around and did the modifed turnaround), and combo no. 3 (faked the righty jump hook, faked the up-and-under, caused the guy to freeze, then shot the step-back jumper).[16]

For those of you scoring at home, that's *twelve* different low-post

14. McHale told Jack McCallum in 1990, "The footwork is important, but my success begins with the premise that I can shoot the ball. That's where so many big guys get off track right away. Everything is predicated on my defensive guy thinking, 'If McHale shoots the ball, he's going to make it.' . . . The one thing I know right away is when I'm going to take a jump shot. When the entry pass is in the air, and I feel my guy with just one hand on me, playing off me, there's no way I am not going to shoot. And there's no way he's going to block it."

15. I incorporated this move into my own game. Unstoppable. House and I played like a thousand hours of one-on-one and two-on-two in college and he always fell for it. I had the double jump hook as well.

16. During an ESPN shoot, I got Paul Pierce to fall for this move at the EA headquarters in Vancouver. He claims he wasn't trying, but there's video and everything. I sank combo no. 3 right in the mug of a guy who'd win Finals MVP ten months later. Come on, how many people can say that?

moves. Twelve! McHale had more combinations on his menu than Panda Express. If you were wondering how any forward could top 60 percent shooting for two straight years in his prime . . . well, that's how. Did you know certain high school and college coaches show McHale tapes to their big men? And don't forget, during the first half of the eighties, McHale was the NBA's top defensive player, someone who protected the rim and defended any low-post scorer or perimeter player: Toney, Julius, Hakeem, Worthy, Moses, Kareem, you name him. He was THE stopper in the NBA. Some other fun facts about my favorite underrated Celtic:

Fact No. 1. McHale played the entire '86–'87 postseason on a broken left foot. It wasn't sprained or bruised—the thing was *broken*. That didn't stop McHale from posting the following numbers in 21 playoff games: 21–9, 58% FG, 39.4 minutes. He risked his career—literally—to help the Celtics try to repeat as champions. Remember him limping up and down the court like a wounded animal? Remember Rick Mahorn purposely stepping on the broken foot during the Detroit series? Remember how he dragged the foot around for a whopping 53 minutes in a double-OT win in Game 4 of the Milwaukee series that year? He never thought about saying "Get me my ring, boys," sucked it up and kept playing . . . and was never the same. Ever. Which reminds me . . .

Fact No. 2. When McHale injured his foot near the end of that season, he had been playing the best basketball of his life (26–10–3, 2.2 blocks, 60.4% FG, 84% FT). Even Bird admits that McHale could have taken the 1987 MVP. So how good would McHale have been without suffering that foot injury? If Len Bias hadn't passed away, McHale could have rested until the Conference Finals. Instead, he played in pain and broke the same foot in the first round. (And if Bias had been around, maybe McHale wouldn't have averaged nearly 40 minutes a game in the first place.)[17] All we know is that he never had the same lateral movement or the same spring in his feet again. (What's interesting is that McHale has no regrets; if he had to do it over again, he would.) But the foot problems invariably led to ankle

---

17. Didn't help that KC Jones coached every game like it was Game 7 of the Finals. I was rereading *48 Minutes* (the book about a specific '87 Cavs-Celtics game by Terry Pluto and Bob Ryan) and laughed when I came to the box score at the end: KC played McHale and Bird 51 and 49 minutes respectively in an OT game against a bad team in January. This shit happened all the time. No wonder those guys broke down.

problems in both feet; McHale badly sprained his left ankle in Seattle during the '90–'91 season, an injury that effectively ended his career two years later. I swear, if McHale hadn't injured that damned foot, he would have thrived into his early forties on that Panda Express menu.

Fact No. 3. McHale was the funniest Celtic of all time. (For further evidence, trek down to your local library and get a copy of Jack McCallum's *Unfinished Business*, or better yet, just buy it online. Come on, you already splurged for this book. Go crazy!) One of the true tragedies in sports history was that McHale decided to run the Timberwolves into the ground instead of heading right into sports broadcasting, where he would have become the John Madden of basketball. Remember, this was the guy who actually stole scenes from Woody on an episode of *Cheers*.[P45]

Fact No. 4. His uneasy alliance with Larry Legend remains the most intriguing subplot of the Bird era. People always assumed they were friends—you know, the whole "two big goofy-looking white guys" factor—but they rarely mingled and McHale was the only teammate Bird always avoided praising, partly because of their friendly rivalry, partly because Larry resented the fact that basketball didn't consume McHale like it consumed him.[18] Even after their careers were over, Bird bemoaned the fact that McHale never drove himself to become the best player in the league, saying that his teammate could have become an MVP had he "really wanted it." Larry almost seemed disappointed that McHale never pushed himself harder because, in turn, Bird would have had to push *himself* an extra notch to keep his place as the alpha dog on

P45. NBA TV hired McHale for the 2009–10 season: good as a studio guy, solid as a color guy, but definitely no John Madden. And yet I still think it would have happened had he gone right from playing to TV. You can't prove me wrong, because it's a hypothetical, so we'll never know. Hah!

18. McHale never imagined going pro until his senior year. Here's what he told McCallum: "I was at a party with some football players and somebody brought in the *Sporting News* that had me rated as the top forward and second-best center in basketball. 'Hey, you're going to be a top-five pick,' someone told me, and I said, 'Really?' . . . I played in all those postseason All-Star games basically for the travel. I had no thoughts of improving myself in the draft or getting more money or anything like that. I remember I picked up the paper and read that Darrell Griffith wasn't going to play in the All-Star game in Hawaii because he didn't want to take the chance at getting hurt. And I thought, 'What's with this guy? Miss a free trip to Hawaii?' I went over there, drank piña coladas and beer, and won the MVP." How could you not like this guy?

the team. Still, nobody should ever question McHale's desire after the '87 playoffs. Not even the Basketball Jesus. To his credit, McHale always took the high road with Bird—dutiful teammate, perfect second banana, never daring to challenge him publicly, always willing to fade into the background. One of my favorite McHale quotes came after the legendary Dominique/Larry duel, when McHale said, "Sometimes after Larry plays a game like this it makes me think ahead . . . I'll be retired in Minnesota and Larry will be retired in Indiana, and we probably won't see each other much. But a lot of nights I'll just lie there and remember games like this, and what it was like to play with him." Somebody turn the heat on, because I just got the chills.

Fact No. 5. Nobody had a weirder body; it was almost like someone gave him Freddy Krueger's arms and put them on backward. Bill Fitch said McHale had "an incomplete body . . . he's waiting for the rest of the parts to come by mail." McCallum described McHale's body as "Frankensteinesque . . . deep bags under the eyes, unusually long arms, shoulders that appear to be coming off the hinges." Of his awkward running style, poet Donald Hall wrote that McHale "lopes down the floor like an Irish setter, his hair flopping like ears." Danny Ainge once quipped that McHale on a fast break looked like a "baby deer on ice." But until Hakeem came along, no big man had quicker feet; nobody was better at the "miss a short jumper and jump up again quickly to tap the ball in" play (McHale hopped like a kangaroo). And McHale's turnaround could be touched only by Hakeem's turnaround in the Turnaround Pantheon (the toughest shot in basketball, bar none). So McHale *was* a great athlete. He just didn't look like one.

Make no mistake, he had some great moments: coming up with some huge blocks against Philly in Game 7 of the '81 playoffs; pouring in 56 points against Detroit; eating Ralph Sampson alive in the '86 Finals; playing on the broken foot during that double-OT game in Milwaukee; his forgotten 33-point performance in the Bird-Dominique game; even his retro farewell in Game 2 of the Charlotte series in '93, when he had the Garden rocking one last time with a 33-point flashback performance. Over any single game, one image is embedded in my brain: every crucial road victory from the Bird era ended the same way, with the Celtics prancing happily out of the arena and McHale crammed in the middle of it all, holding both arms in the air with his fists clenched. Name the game, you'll see it: Game 4 in Houston ('86), Game 4 in Los Angeles ('84, '85), Game 6 in Philly ('81, '82), Game 4 in Milwaukee ('87), Game 6 in Atlanta ('88) . . . it doesn't matter. He did it *every* time. In a funny way, it became McHale's legacy along with the post-up moves. He may have looked ridiculous as hell—giant arms craning up in the air, armpit hair flying everywhere, a goofy smile on his face—but McHale's sweaty armpits doubled as our disgusting victory cigar. He was amazing to watch, unstoppable at times, laugh-out-loud funny, inventive, ahead of his time, the ideal teammate . . . and the one NBA legend who felt obligated to rub his armpits in the collective faces of 18,000 fans. I miss those days, and I miss those armpits.

34. GEORGE GERVIN

Resume: 14 years, 11 quality, 12 All-Stars . . . '78 and '79 MVP runner-up . . . Top 5 ('78, '79, '80, '81, '82), Top 10 ABA ('75, '76), Top 10 NBA ('77, '83) . . . leader: scoring (4x) . . . record: points in one quarter (33) . . . 5th-leading Playoffs scorer (27.0 PPG, 59 G) . . . 3-year peak: 30–5–3, 54% FG, 85% FT . . . career: 25–3–3, 50% FG, 84% FT . . . '75 Playoffs: 34–14 (6 G) . . . '79 Playoffs: 29–6–3, 54% FG (14 G) . . . 3 straight scoring titles (1 of 6 players ever)

33. SAM JONES

Resume: 12 years, 8 quality, 5 All-Stars . . . Top 10 ('65, '66, '67) . . . 3-year peak: 24–5–3 . . . 5-year Playoffs peak: 25–3–5, 47% FG . . . played for 10 champs ('59–'66, '68–69 Celts), 2nd-best player (3x), 3rd-best player (3x) . . . 3rd-best player on one runner-up ('67 Celts) . . . career: 46% FG, 80% FT

The Ice/Sam debate doubles as the enduring point of this book. When measuring the impact of a player's career, it's easy to get swayed by individual triggers (scoring/rebounding stats, All-Star appearances, All-NBA nods) and situational triggers (either a lack of playoff success or an inordinate amount of playoff success), as well as things that have nothing to do with anything (like a cool nickname or distinctive shot). Upon first glance, you'd assume Ice was a better player than Sam and that's that. So let's break it down Dr. Jack–style:

Originality. Sam provided the DNA model for nearly every great shooting guard from the past forty years, a six-foot-four athlete with long arms, an explosive first step, a killer bank shot and no discernible holes in his game. Ice was a six-foot-eight string bean who weighed about an Olsen Twin and a half at his peak, looked like a dead ringer for a black John Holmes[19] and could have been knocked over by one of Billy Paultz's farts. We'll never see anyone like him again. I am sure of this. *Slight Edge: Ice.*

Calling Card. Sam owned the most accurate bank shot of his era, making them from 22-degree angles, 64-degree angles . . . it didn't matter. Meanwhile, Ice owned the most accurate bank shot of *his* era and it wasn't even his signature shot: He could routinely sink his world-famous finger roll from as far as 12–15 feet, like he was trying to win a stuffed animal at a carnival. I can't pick between these two shots because I love them both to the point that I'm writing this with a boner right now. What's tragic is that we probably won't see either shot again—at least to that degree of success and frequency—because of the basketball camp mentality that infected today's game. Everyone shoots the same and plays the same, like they're coming off an assembly line or something. That's why we rarely see finger rolls or bankers anymore, and hell will probably freeze over before we see another old-school hook shot. *Slight Edge: Ice.*

19. I forgot to include Ice and Holmes in my pantheon of Cross-Racial Lookalikes: they even had the same facial hair and body types. The Ice/Holmes parallels are eerie: they both started in 1972, had primes from '77 to '83, set a few records, had cool nicknames ("Ice" and "Johnny Wadd"), battled whispers about personal problems, flamed out remarkably fast and were gone by 1986. You could even make a parallel between Ice's depressing final season on Chicago and Holmes playing a gay sultan. And yes, I know this is the third Holmes-related footnote in the book. Just know the over/under was 4.5.

Nickname. Gervin had one of the best NBA nicknames ever, "the Ice-man";[20] Sam never had a nickname, fitting because he received less attention and fanfare than anyone in the top forty. We're deducting points here only because Val Kilmer went by "Iceman" in *Top Gun* and had such disturbing homoerotic tension with Maverick. *Edge: Ice.*

Best What-if. Sam played behind the great Bill Sharman for four full seasons in an eight-team league—with no hope of stealing Sharman's job because of the black/white thing—until he finally landed crunch-time minutes in the '61 playoffs (25.8 MPG, 13.1 PPG) and the starting spot after a banged-up Sharman retired that summer.[21] Throw in four years of college and two years of military service and Sam didn't start until he was twenty-eight, making the rest of his career even more astounding. (Note: Jones and Russell were the first greats to maintain a high level of play into their mid-thirties.) Then again, "What if Sam hadn't lost much of his twenties?" can't compare with Gervin getting drafted by the '72 Virginia Squires and teamed up with a young Julius Erving for one year before the cash-poor Squires sold Doc to the Nets. What if Ice and Doc had played their whole careers together? Can you imagine a late seventies NBA team trying to match up with them? Would that have been the coolest team for the rest of eternity? And who thought it would be a good idea to stick a professional basketball team in Virginia? *Edge: Ice.*

Scoring Ability. Ice was the number two all-time shooting guard from an "I'm getting my 30–35 tonight in the flow of the game and you're not stopping me" efficiency standpoint, nestled comfortably between MJ (number one)[22] and Kobe (number three). Sam's scoring had an on/off switch; Ice just scored and scored and rarely had those "Uh-oh, look out, he's starting to catch fire!" streaks, peaking in 1978–80 with these *Money-ball* numbers: 30 points per game, 54 percent shooting, 85 percent free

20. Virginia teammate Fatty Taylor gave Gervin his nickname during Ice's rookie year, marveling at how Ice could score all game without sweating.
21. Sam's per-36-minute numbers in '59, '60 and '61? 20–9–3, 45% FG. For '62 and '63? 22–7–4, 47% FG.
22. They played together on the '86 Bulls when Ice was three levels beyond washed up.

throw shooting. During the '78 season, he had a game in Chicago where he scored 37 points on *17-for-18 shooting*. As one Spurs teammate joked in 1982, "The only way to stop Ice is to hold practice." Sam wasn't in that class, but he was remarkably steady in big games (we're getting to that); it should also be mentioned that Sam had 25-foot range and would have been helped by a three-point line, whereas the three-point line didn't help Ice at all. Poor Sam came along twenty years too soon in every respect. *Edge: Ice.*

Head Case Potential. Gervin endured constant criticism for his priorities (did he care more about scoring titles or winning titles?); his defense (outstandingly crappy); his squawking about being underpaid (constant); his dedication (he skipped practice so frequently that *SI* casually mentioned in 1982, "Gervin is habitually late for workouts and sometimes doesn't show up at all," like they were talking about an asthma condition or something); his effort issues (when the Spurs gave him a six-year, $3.9 million extension before the '81 season, they included a $14,000 bonus for every win between 36 and 56 games);[23] and his personal life, which was endlessly rumored about.[24] Here's how Ice summed up his relative lack of popularity in 1978: "Whereas I never went fly like some of the boys.[25] I'm conservative. I got the short hair, the pencil 'stache, the simple clothes. Plus I'm 6'8", 183—no, make that 185—and when you look at me all you see is bone. Otherwise in Detroit I'm known as Twig according to my physique. I just do my thing and stay consistent. I figure the people be recognizing the Iceman pretty soon now. Whereas I be up there in a minute."[26] It would

23. The NBA Players Association would flip if this happened now. Every Spur was given the same bonus, although the $$$ changed depending on the player. According to *SI*, the Spurs won on opening night and a teammate yelled, "One down, eighty-one to go!" Gervin corrected him: "No, one down, thirty-five to go."

24. I'm not sure why anyone speculated about Gervin: he weighed less than any Charlie's Angel, coasted through certain games, referred to himself in the third person, made way too much money, skipped practices all the time with no explanation, was washed up at thirty-three even though he never suffered a major injury and answered to the nickname "Ice." I don't see any red flags.

25. This quote inexplicably started with "Whereas," like Ice was answering a question even though he wasn't. Since he said "Whereas" two other times, I think that was just his vocal tic. Whereas, I don't know why I'm telling you this.

26. This came from Curry Kirkpatrick's *SI* feature about Ice. Curry's talents obscured a meanspirited tendency to make certain NBA players sound like Buckwheat. Like how he included this Bob McAdoo quote in the first paragraph of a '76 Mac profile: "It be hard not to get buckets in this league. If I be doin' any less, people think I be doggin' it."

have been fun following him and covering him, but you might not have enjoyed coaching him or playing with him. As for Sam, he was a head case only in one respect: He never liked the pressure of being "the guy" and preferred to be a complementary star. According to Russell's *Second Wind*, Sam carried the team enough times that Russ finally asked him why it didn't happen more often; Sam responded, "No, I don't want to do that. I don't want the responsibility of having to play like that every night." Russell respected that choice, pointing out how so many players wanted to be paid like stars without actually carrying the star's load every night, so Sam's acceptance of his own limitations was admirable in a way, even as it frustrated the hell out of Russell that Sam was satisfied with being an afterthought some nights. Then again, Sam turned into Jimmy Chitwood with games on the line. Here's how Russell described it:

> I never could guess what Sam was going to do or say, with one major exception: I knew exactly how he would react in our huddle during the final seconds of a crucial game. I'm talking about a situation where we'd be one point behind, with five seconds to go in a game that meant not just first place or pride but a whole season, when everything was on the line. . . . Red would be looking around at faces, trying to decide which play to call. It's a moment when even the better players in the NBA will start coughing, tying their shoelaces and looking the other way. At such moments I knew what Sam would do as well as I know my own name. "Give me the ball," he'd say. "I'll make it."[27] And all of us would look at him, and we'd know by looking that he meant what he said. Not only that, but you knew that he'd make it.

Defensive Prowess. The old joke about Sam: the best part of his defense was Russell. But he wasn't better or worse than most of the guys back then—great athlete, well conditioned, long arms, knew where to go and what to do—while Ice was the worst defensive player of anyone in the top thirty-five. Part of this wasn't Ice's fault: the Spurs didn't care about de-

---

27. Did Jimmy Chitwood steal this line from Sam Jones, or did Sam steal it from Jimmy, because Hickory High's championship hypothetically happened before Jones played for the Celtics? My head hurts.

fense, only that he outscored whomever was guarding him. Which he usually did. Still, defense wins championships . . . and when your franchise
guy is a futile defensive player, that doesn't bode well for your title hopes.
The Spurs made a conscious decision, "We're revolving everything around
Ice's offense, running and gunning, scoring a ton of points and hoping
our snazzy black uniforms catch on with inner-city gangs," which was
probably the right move. With Ice leading the way from 1974 to 1983
(ABA + NBA), the Spurs won 45, 51, 50, 44, 52, 48, 41, 52, 48 and 53
games—not a bad run by any means. But it didn't translate to success in
the playoffs. They lost ten of eighteen playoff series and made the Conference Finals three times ('79, '82 and '83). Ice averaged a 27–7–3 over that
stretch, but these were the relevant numbers: 31–41 (overall playoff
record), 0–4 (Game 7's), zero (Finals appearances).

Gervin's best chance happened in '79, the second year of a peculiar
two-spring vacuum with no dominant NBA team, when the Spurs
jumped out to a three-games-to-one lead in the Eastern Finals over the
aging Bullets. Ice scored 71 points combined in Games 3 and 4 at home,
telling *SI* afterward, "The Bullets know they can't stop Ice. Ice knows he's
got them on the run."[28] But the Bullets staved off elimination in Game 5
and shockingly stole Game 6 in Texas, with Ice scoring just 20 points and
getting hounded by Grevey and Bobby Dandridge all game.[29]

When Washington went bigger in the second half, Kirkpatrick explained later, "What this personnel switch did was force [San Antonio
coach Doug] Moe to decide where to hide Gervin's lazy, idling defense.
On the tricky scorer, Dandridge, or on the power rebounder, [Greg] Ballard?" Does that sound like someone you'd want to go to war with? Moe
picked Ballard, who finished with a 19–12 and combined with Bobby D
for 17 of the last 19 Bullets points. Ice went scoreless in the first quarter
of Game 7, headed into halftime with eight, then exploded for 34 in the
second half . . . but the Spurs blew a six-point lead in the final three
minutes, gave up the winning jumper to Dandridge and became the

28. Ice paved the way for Rickey Henderson and every other star from future generations
who constantly referred to himself in the third person. Bill Simmons loves Ice for this.
29. Grevey explained later, "If Gervin doesn't get the ball for a while, he goes into a lull.
He stops running and working for it. I was in his chest." That was the rap on Ice—if you
beat him up, knocked him around and hounded him, eventually he'd stop trying as
hard.

third team ever to blow a 3–1 lead in a playoff series. Ice completely disappeared in the final three minutes: no points, one brick off the backboard.

Looking back, that was the seminal moment of Ice's career: his biggest test, his chance to make the Finals and put himself on the map, and his team *made history failing*. He'd never get that close again. Can we blame his supporting cast? To some degree, yes. During that 1974–83 stretch, his best teammates were Silas (a stud until he blew out his knee in the '76 playoffs), Larry Kenon (a starter on the seventies Head Case All-Stars[30] and All-Time All-Afro teams);[31] Artis Gilmore (on his last legs), Johnny Moore and Mike Mitchell. Not exactly a murderer's row. Like Jason Kidd, Gervin turned chicken shit into chicken salad to some degree. (By the way, San Antonio's front office wasn't helping matters: from 1977 to 1982, San Antonio traded away three first-rounders and took Frankie Sanders, Reggie Johnson and Wiley Peck with the other three.) On the other hand, five memorable all-offense/no-defense superstars from the past four decades—Gervin, McAdoo, Maravich, Vince and Dominique—never became the best guy for a Finals team. This can't be a coincidence. It just can't. *Edge: Sam.*

Winnability. We hinted around this word in the Parish/Worthy sections, so screw it: I'm just creating it. Couldn't you argue that "winnability" is a specific trait? In other words, does a player's overall package of skills and intangibles (personality, efficiency, sense of the moment, leadership, teamwork, lack of glaring weaknesses) inadvertently lend itself to a winning situation? It's hard to imagine Gervin playing for a championship team unless it happened later in his career—a little like McAdoo with the '82 Lakers, with a contender bringing him off the bench as instant offense[32]—or as the second-best player on a team with a franchise big guy

30. Kenon sulked after S.A. fans voted Gervin Most Popular Spur in '77, telling reporters, "This town has Gervinitis. They don't recognize me enough. I'm the best player in the game." There's a reason he wasn't in Chapter 1.

31. Starters: Gilmore, Kenon, Doc, Darnell Hillman, Moochie Norris. Sixth man: Ben Wallace. Yes, I had to play Doc at 2 to get everyone in. Sue me.

32. With Ice on his last legs and the Spurs in a free fall, it's a shame no '84 contender traded for him. Imagine the '84 Finals with Ice instead of Mike McGee. Even would have been a fair trade: McGee averaged 17 MPG and 10 PPG and shot 56% for the '84 and '85 Lakers.

like Hakeem, Kareem or Duncan. And even then, I'm not totally sure it would work. Would the '95 Rockets have cruised to the title if you switched '82 Gervin with '95 Drexler? Could they have covered up for his defense? Probably not.[33] On the flip side, you'd have to admit that Sam Jones winning ten rings in twelve seasons ranks absurdly high on the Winnability Scale. He could play either guard spot, didn't care about stats and made monster plays when it mattered. I'm not sure what's left. Sam Jones definitely knew The Secret. *Big Edge: Sam.*

Clutchness. We just covered Gervin's clutchness issues. (Lack of clutchness? Anti-clutchness? A-Rodability? A-Rodianism?) Even when Ice battled Pete Maravich in CBS's legendary H-O-R-S-E tournament, he blew the clinching shot and Pistol finished him off with two of his patented moves: the sitting-in-the-floor layup and jumping-from-out-of-bounds reverse layup. Meanwhile, Sam's teams finished 9–0 in Game 7's and 13–2 in elimination games, with Sam scoring a combined 37 off the bench in Game 7's against Syracuse and St. Louis, then averaging 30.1 points in eight other Game 7's or deciding Game 5's as a starter. You know what's amazing? Sam had so many playoff heroics that I couldn't even scrape together a complete list. Here are the ones we know for sure: '62 Philly, Game 7 (27 points, game-winning jumper with two seconds left) . . . '62 Lakers, do-or-die Game 6 (35 points in L.A.) . . . '62 Lakers, Game 7 (27 points, 5 in OT) . . . '63 Cincy, Game 7 (outscored Oscar, 47–43)[34] . . . '65 Philly, Game 7 (37 points in the "Havlicek steals the ball!" game) . . . '66 Cincy, Game 5 (34 points in deciding game) . . . '66 Lakers, Game 7 (22 points) . . . '68 Sixers, Game 7 (22 points) . . . '69 Lakers, must-win Game 4 (down by one, Sam hits the game-winning jumper at the buzzer) . . . '69 Lakers, Game 7 (24 points in L.A.).[35]

---

33. During the first season when his contract included win bonuses, Ice dropped 42 on G-State and said afterward, "Yeah, I told you I'd get 40. Only points don't make me no money. Only W's. Nothing but W's. From now on when I get my 40's I'm gonna make sure that we win, too."

34. God forbid there was tape of this one. Oscar and Sam guarding each other in a do-or-die playoff game and combining for 90 points?

35. I could only find one "Sam choked" game: Game 4 of the '63 Finals, with Sam inbounding the ball in a tie game and three seconds remaining, Jerry West picked off his pass for a buzzer-beating, game-winning layup. Auerbach complained about the timekeeper afterward, but I saw the clip and it seemed legit. That's the only buzzer-beating steal/layup in Finals history as far as I can tell.

Sam and Jerry West were known as the Association's first two clutch scorers for a reason. *Big Edge: Sam.*

Defining quote. I'd narrow it down to these two:

> *Sam on scoring 2,000 points (1965): "That doesn't mean a thing. Every guy on this team has the ability to score 2,000 points if that's what he's asked to do. There's a lot of unselfishness by others in those 2,000 points I scored."*
>
> *Gervin on his legacy (1980): "I'm perfectly happy being known as George Gervin, scoring machine, because in this game the person who puts the ball in the hole is the person that usually gets ahead."*

Which guy would you have wanted as a teammate? Which guy would you have wanted in your NBA foxhole with you? Which guy would you trust with your life on the line in a big game? Which guy was predisposed to thriving with great teammates? Please. *Edge: Sam.*

We'll give the last word to Russell (from *Second Wind*):

> Whenever the pressure was greatest, Sam was eager for the ball. To me, that's one sign of a champion. Even with all the talent, the mental sharpness, the fun, the confidence and your focus honed down to winning, there'll be a level of competition where it all evens out. Then the pressure builds, and for a champion it is a test of heart. . . . Heart in champions has to do with the depth of your motivation, and how well your mind and body react to pressure. It's concentration—that is, being able to do what you do best under maximum pain and stress.[36] Sam Jones has a champion's heart. On the court he always had something in reserve. You could think he'd been squeezed out of his last drop of strength and cunning, but if you looked closely, you'd see him coming with something else he'd tucked away out of sight. Though sometimes he'd do things that made me want to break him in two, his presence gave me great comfort in key games. In Los Angeles, Jerry West was called "Mr. Clutch," and he was, but in the seventh game of a championship series, I'll take Sam over any player who's ever walked on a court.

36. Just like Karl Malone, only the exact opposite.

Now I ask you: Would you rather go to war with George Gervin or Sam Jones?

(I thought so.)

32. WALT FRAZIER

Resume: 13 years, 9 quality, 7 All-Stars . . . Top 5 ('70, '72, '74, '75), Top 10 ('71, '73) . . . All-Defense (7 1st teams) . . . Playoffs: 20–6–7 (93 G) . . . 6-year peak: 22–7–7 . . . best or 2nd-best player on 2 champs ('70, and '73 Knicks) and one runner-up ('72)

If you're measuring guys by extremes and italicizing "the" to hammer the point home, Frazier's resume includes three extremes: one of *the* best big-game guards ever; one of *the* best defensive guards ever; and one of *the* single greatest performances ever (Game 7 of the '70 Finals, when he notched 36 points, 19 assists, 7 rebounds and 5 steals and outclutched the actual Mr. Clutch). Beyond his pickpocketing skills (terrifying), rebounding (underrated), playmaking (top-notch) and demeanor (always in control), what stood out was Frazier's Oscar-like ability to get the precise shots he wanted in tight games. You know how McHale had a killer low-post game? Clyde had a killer high-post game.[37] He started 25 feet from the basket, backed his defender down, shaked and baked a few times, settled on his preferred spot near the top of the key, then turned slightly and launched that moonshot jumper right in the guy's face . . . *swish.*[38] That's what made him so memorable on the road—not just how he always rose to the occasion, but the demoralizing effect those jumpers had on crowds. They knew the jumper was coming ("oh, shit"), they knew it

37. I always loved Clyde for carrying off another first name as his nickname. When does that ever happen? For instance, if I was Bill "Rufus" Simmons, that would be weird. But Walt "Clyde" Frazier sounded perfect. Maybe it's a black/white thing. All right, it's definitely a black/white thing.
38. In Game 7 of the NYK-Boston series in '73, when New York became the first team to win a Game 7 in Boston, Frazier kills Jo Jo White down the stretch with 19-footers. Couldn't be stopped. It's demoralizing to watch even thirty-five years later.

("shit"), they knew it ("send a double"), they knew it (*"shit"*) . . . and then it went in (dead silence).

Quick tangent: I am too young to remember watching Clyde live, but in my basketball-watching lifetime, only seven guys were crowd-killers: Jordan, Bird, Kobe, Bernard, Isiah, Andrew Toney, and strangely enough, Vinnie Johnson.[P46] When those guys got going, you could see the future unfold before it started manifesting itself. We knew it was in the works, our guys knew it, our coaches knew it, everyone knew it . . . and then the points came in bunches and sucked all forms of life out of the building. It was like frolicking in the ocean, seeing a giant wave coming from fifteen seconds away, then remaining in place and getting crushed by it. Jordan and Bird were the all-time crowd-killers; they loved playing on the road, loved shutting everyone up and considered it the best possible challenge. When Fernando Medina took the famous photo of Jordan's final shot of the '98 Finals, that was the definitive crowd-killing moment: an entire section of Utah fans sitting behind the basket, screaming in horror and bracing for the inevitable as the ball drifted toward the basket. My favorite crowd-killing moment happened after Bird had been fouled in the last few seconds with the Celtics trailing by one, only he wasn't satisfied with the noise level of the pathetic Clippers crowd, *so he stepped away from the line and waved his arms.* That's right, the Legend was imploring the crowd to pump up the volume. I mean, who does that? Do I even need to tell you that he swished the free throws? Probably not.

Frazier was the most infamous crowd-killer of his generation and, taking it in a slightly different direction, the master of the impact play—whether it was stripping someone at midcourt when the Knicks needed a hoop, dramatically setting up and draining a high-post jumper or whatever. You always hear about guys like Gervin or English who finished with a "quiet" 39; Clyde routinely finished with a loud 25 and four deafening steals. His relationship with the MSG faithful ranked among the most unique in sports; they appreciated him to the fullest, understood exactly what he brought to the table and connected to him spiritually in an atyp-

P46. There's a 99.12% chance we'll be adding Durant to this list soon.

ical way. When the Knicks struggled after Reed and DeBusschere retired, those same fans took out their frustrations by turning on Frazier as if he were to blame. Eventually they gave him away as compensation for signing free agent Jim Cleamons in 1977, an ignominious end to a particularly dignified career. Clyde was a lightning rod in every respect: he carried himself with particular style during a fairly bland era, became an iconic Manhattan personality because of his muttonchop sideburns, mink coats, Rolls-Royces, swank apartments, stamp-of-approval party appearances and enviable bachelor life,[39] and on top of that, he stood out for the way he connected with those MSG crowds. So maybe it made sense that his career ended in such a messy, ugly fashion; if you connect with a crowd positively when things are going well, maybe you connect negatively when everything is falling apart. Fans are fickle and that's just the way it is.

Two lingering questions about Frazier. First, his career ended so abruptly that it's hard to make sense of it. He played nine good years and then was cooked without a drug problem or major injury to blame. Bizarre. And second, he peaked during the best possible era for his specific gifts—no three-point line, no slash-and-kick, no complex defensive strategies, mostly physical guards imposing their will and playing that high-post game. Not until the merger did NBA teams start differentiating between point guards and shooting guards. Before that? You were just a guard. Nobody cared who brought the ball up. Was it a coincidence that Frazier lost his fastball immediately after the merger, when the sport became faster and speedy point guards such as John Lucas, Norm Nixon, Gus Williams, Kevin Porter and Johnny Davis became all the rage?[40] Hard to say. Had Frazier come along ten years later, maybe he would have been a hybrid guard like Dennis Johnson . . . and maybe he wouldn't have been

---

39. I'd love to know who banged more high-caliber ladies from 1969 to 1975, Frazier or Joe Namath. Had they kept score, it's a better battle than Federer and Nadal in the '08 Wimbledon Finals. I'd make Namath a slight favorite.

40. Tiny Archibald was the one ahead-of-his-time point guard playing in that 1970–1975 stretch, and that's when he peaked statistically and had the famous lead-the-league-in-points/assists season. Makes you wonder what would have happened had there been more Tinys.

as effective. Again, we don't know.[41] But we do know that an inordinate number of fans from Frazier's generation—including a few that influenced me over the years—have Clyde ranked among the greatest ever. For instance, I always found it interesting that my father, a lifelong basketball fan and thirty-seven-year NBA season ticket holder who remembers everyone from Cousy to LeBron, ranks Jordan and Frazier as his all-time backcourt. So maybe I'm not old enough to remember seeing Frazier kill a crowd, but I grew up with my father telling me, "Frazier *killed* us. He was an assassin. You didn't want any part of him in a big game—he was always the best guy on the court. I've never been happier to see anyone retire." And that's good enough for me.

31. DAVE COWENS

Resume: 11 years, 8 quality, 7 All-Stars . . . '73 MVP . . . '75 MVP runner-up . . . '71 Rookie of the Year . . . Top 10 ('73, '75, '76) . . . All-Defense (2x) . . . Playoffs: 14.4 RPG (5th all-time) . . . 4-year peak: 20–16–4, 46% FG . . . 4-year Playoffs peak: 21–16–4 (50 g's) . . . best or 2nd-best player on 2 champs ('74, '76 Celts), 21–15–4 (36 g's) . . . starter for 68-win team ('73)

When Dad bought our second season ticket in 1977, our new section hugged one side of the player's tunnel and the wives' section hugged the other side.[42] Hondo's wife (or, as Brent Musburger called her, "John Havlicek's lovely wife, Beth") and kids sat in the parallel row to our right during that first season. I remember checking out Hondo's daughter from ten feet away and thinking, "Someday I'll marry her and I can spend Christmas with the Hondos!" Then Hondo retired and the wives' section

41. Frazier's attempt to shatter the Unintentional Comedy Scale as a Knicks announcer for the past two-plus decades did not factor into this ranking.

42. This was back when the players actually had wives. By the mid-nineties, this became the "girlfriends, hos, bimbos and the-bitch-claims-she's-pregnant-but-the-paternity-test-hasn't-come-back-yet" section.

was in constant flux, a little like how the cast of *Law and Order* changes every year. When Scott Wedman joined the team in 1982, we also picked up his beautiful spouse, Kim, who easily could have passed for the hottest daughter on *Eight Is Enough*. After we traded for Bill Walton, his wife and kids crammed into that three-seat row next to the railing—like seeing five people stack into the backseat of a Volkswagen or something—only every kid had Walton's gigantic head crammed onto a tiny body.[43] You get the idea. The wives/girlfriends/families invariably filled in the blanks with each player. Danny Ainge's wife couldn't have been more cute and wholesome. Bird's wife was unsurprisingly normal and down to earth (like the Patty Scialfa of the NBA). Reggie Lewis's wife was brash and loud; she clearly wore the pants in the family. Dino Radja married a leggy European who carried herself like Brigitte Nielsen in *Rocky IV;* you could picture them chain-smoking after games while Dino complained about Todd Day. Sherman Douglas' wife showed up in saggy jogging pants and ate like a Shetland pony for three hours. Dee Brown had one of those "Shit, I didn't realize I was going to be famous when I married her" wives as a rookie, won the Dunk Contest and soon traded up for the best-looking wife of that decade.

Nobody stood out more than Robert Parish's not-so-better half, a Gina Gershon look-alike who carried on like a profane bunshee, to the degree that she'd scream at officials as everyone else wondered, "Hey, do you think the Chief is just afraid to break up with her because he doesn't want to wake up with his house on fire?" An aspiring singer who sang the national anthem before a few Celtics games,[44] Mrs. Chief detested referee Jake O'Donnell so much that she vaulted over two other girlfriends at halftime of one game, leaned over the railing, showered him with obscenities and actually had to be held back like a hockey player. For a second, we thought she might break free, hurtle off the railing and deliver a flying

---

43. It seemed inconceivable then that any Walton kid would make the NBA. When Luke broke out at Arizona, I remember asking my dad, "Wasn't that the little Walton kid who looked like Rocky Dennis?" Now he's something of a ladies' man: I even had a reader compare him to Jennifer Love Hewitt in that guys love JLH (and it makes girls furious) and girls love Luke (and it makes guys furious).

44. When that happened, Dad and I debated whether a kookier person had ever sung that song in front of more than 15,000 people, ultimately deciding no.

elbow like Macho Man Savage . . . and if it happened, none of us would have been even remotely surprised. She missed her true calling by about fifteen years: reality TV. Too bad.[45]

What does this have to do with Dave Cowens? Near the end of his career we noticed a new lady started sitting in the wives' section: She looked a little like Linda Blair, only with frizzy reddish brown hair and a sane smile. She couldn't have been more pleasant to everyone who approached her. You could have easily imagined her baking cookies every afternoon. We couldn't figure out which player she was dating for the first few games, finally putting two and two together when Cowens was heading out to the court after halftime and stopped to talk to her with a shit-eating smile on his face. I remember thinking the same thing as everyone else: "Good God, Dave Cowens has a girlfriend!" How was this possible? The guy had a competitiveness disorder, playing every game in fifth gear, berating officials like they were busboys, bellowing out instructions to teammates, diving for loose balls, crashing over three guys for rebounds, battling bigger centers game after game and getting into fights at least once a month. Whenever Cowens fouled out, he stood in disbelief with his hands stuck on his hips, staring the offending official down and hoping the guy might change his mind. *Don't you realize what you just did? This means I can't play anymore! Don't you realize what you just fucking did?* The Newlin/flopping story doubled as the ultimate Cowens moment: after eight years of dealing with lousy referees and opponents who didn't respect the sport, he finally snapped and took the law in his own hands. Even after all these years, he remains my father's favorite Celtic—the guy who never took a night off, the guy who cared just a little bit more than everyone else.[46]

And now he had a girlfriend? I was totally confused. *Does this mean*

45. Once they mercifully separated and Mrs. Chief accused Chief of hitting her during an allegedly wild brawl, we read her allegations at my father's house—my dad, my stepmother and me—and agreed within seconds that either (a) the Chief was innocent, or (b) if he laid his hands on her in an inappropriate way, it was only because he feared for his own life. We all wanted to testify at the divorce trial in his defense. And my stepmother is a raging feminist and successful doctor who went to Smith College. That's how crazy Mrs. Chief was.

46. Grumpy Old Editor: "Mine too, and I hate the Celtics." He's a delight.

they hold hands and go on dates? Do they sleep in the same bed together? I kept picturing her forgetting to buy milk and Cowens flipping out the same way he freaked after an especially terrible call. That's what separated Cowens from everyone else: he played with such unbridled ferocity that little kids couldn't *conceive* of him having a girlfriend. Imagine Jason from *Friday the 13th* heading home from a weekend of killing camp counselors, showering, changing into clean clothes, then taking his lady to Outback Steakhouse. That was Cowens with a girlfriend. I remember being even more dumbfounded when they got married. *There's a Mrs. Dave Cowens?* Of course, marriage ended up domesticating him like Adrian Balboa softened Rocky. Within two years of getting betrothed, a calmer Cowens had walked away from a huge paycheck on a potential championship team (the '81 Celtics, who *did* win the title), blaming ravaged ankles, tired knees and a fire that was no longer burning inside him. And there wasn't a Clubber Lang out there to insult his wife, kill Red Auerbach and lure him back into uniform. Too bad.

We'll remember him for everything I already covered in the prologue, as well as his '73 MVP award (dubious, but whatever), two titles, a clutch 28–14 in Game 7 of the '74 Finals and the quirkiest career of anyone in the Pyramid. He enrolled in mechanics school, covered the '76 Olympics as a newspaper reporter, rode the subway to home games, bought a 30-acre Christmas tree farm in Kentucky and moonlighted as a taxi driver.[47] He capped off a night of celebrating the '74 championship by sleeping on a park bench in Boston Common. When the Celtics lowballed Paul Silas and dealt him to Denver after the '76 title season, then replaced him with anti-Celtics Curtis Rowe and Sidney Wicks, a distraught Cowens took an unpaid leave of absence for 32 games and accepted a PR job at Suffolk Downs racetrack to experience a traditional nine-to-five job. When Bob Ryan skewered him for the Newlin bullrush, Cowens wrote a rebuttal in the *Boston Globe* and railed against the evils of flopping. He became the league's last player-coach during the '79 season. He even refused to hang on as a much-needed bench player after the Parish/McHale trade, walking

---

47. Imagine being drunk in your mid-twenties, stumbling out of a bar, hailing a taxi and getting picked up by Cowens. That's reason no. 736 why I wish I had been single in Boston in 1976 instead of 1996.

away from a giant paycheck and writing a goodbye column in the *Boston Herald* explaining his motives. By contrast, his postplaying career has been unfathomably mundane—a few coaching gigs, that's about it—and part of me wishes he'd flamed out in dramatic style, crashing a motorcycle into a polar bear in Alaska at 130 miles an hour or something. It's just tough for the Newlin story to have the same lasting impact when you saw Cowens unassumingly holding a clipboard and looking like he just finished your taxes. Oh, well.

One last Cowens thought: Unlike most stars from the sixties and seventies, Cowens would be just as effective today because of his durability and athleticism.[48] For the "Wine Cellar" chapter that's coming up, I gave him strong consideration for a bench spot because of his versatility and intensity—seriously, can you think of a better guy to change the pace of a game off the bench than '74 Dave Cowens doing his "bull in a china shop" routine?—ultimately leaving him off because of his up-and-down shooting (career: 44 percent), impeccable timing (he never faced Wilt or Shaq in their primes, both of whom would have bulldozed him) and neverending struggles with foul trouble. You can't watch a memorable Celtics game from the seventies without an announcer saying, "That's the sixth on Cowens!" or "One more and he's gone!" He couldn't help himself. The man cared just a little *too* much. Here's how he explained his leave of absence to *SI* in 1976: "I'd been thinking about it for three months. I even thought seriously about quitting before the season started, but I figured, aw, I'd try it and see how it was. And then I just didn't have it. Nothing. When somebody drives right by you and you shrug your shoulders and say, 'Aw, what the hell,' when you go down and make a basket like a robot, when you win or lose a ballgame and it doesn't matter either way, when you can't even get mad at the refs, then something's wrong. I couldn't do anything about it. When there's nothing left, there's no use making believe there is. I don't want to spoil the Celtics and I don't want to take their money if I'm not earning it."

48. I could totally see Cowens playing center on some of Nash's Suns teams, or anchoring the '07 Warriors team that ended up beating Dallas. Really, he could have fit in with any modern NBA team as long as he didn't play with Vince, T-Mac or Rasheed, any of whom he would have strangled within five weeks.

In other words, Dave Cowens was turning into everyone else in the NBA. And he didn't like it. Now that's a guy I want in my NBA Foxhole.

30. WILLIS REED

Resume: 10 years, 7 quality, 7 All-Stars . . . Finals MVP: '70, '73 . . . '70 MVP . . . '65 Rookie of the Year . . . Top 5 ('70), Top 10 ('67, '68, '69, '71) . . . 5-year peak: 21–14–2 . . . 2-year Playoffs peak: 25–14, 50% FG (28 G) . . . best or second-best player on 2 champs ('70, '73 Knicks)

Hey, it's another undersized lefty center, inspirational leader and world-class hombre who protected his teammates! Both Reed and Cowens won an MVP trophy, a Rookie of the Year trophy and two rings. They played in seven All-Star Games apiece and each took home an All-Star MVP. They played for exactly ten years and couldn't stay healthy for the last few (although Cowens lasted better than Reed did). Their home crowds connected with them in a "Springsteen playing the Meadowlands" kind of way. They finished with nearly identical career scoring/rebounding numbers (18–14 for Cowens, 19–13 for Reed). And neither of them became a good coach for the same reason: namely, that an overcompetitive legend couldn't possibly coach modern NBA players without going on a three-state killing spree.

So why not honor them with a Dr. Jack breakdown? Because Reed was better defensively and had a higher ceiling offensively, that's why.[49] Willis played 28 playoff games against Unseld (twice), Russell, Kareem and Wilt and averaged a 25–14 with 50 percent shooting as the Knicks prevailed in four of their five playoff series in '69 and '70, a more impressive stretch than anything Cowens ever offered.[50] Willis peaked with a terrific '70 Knicks team that surpassed any Boston edition from that decade. Cowens had a defining "tough guy" story (the Newlin incident), but Reed's "tough guy"

49. See, I told you this book would be free of Boston biases! And you were worried after I put Sam ahead of the Iceman. Just wait until we get to the top five.
50. From March 24, 1970, through Game 4 of the '70 Finals, Willis played seven games vs. Unseld, five vs. Kareem, and four vs. Wilt and averaged 29.6 points and 17.5 rebounds a game.

story was more impressive (the '67 Lakers massacre where he decked three Lakers and sent their bench scurrying). Cowens' greatest game (Game 7, '74 Finals) can't hold a candle to Reed's greatest game (Game 7, '70 Finals), and Cowens' defining moment (skidding across the floor after pickpocketing Oscar) can't come close to matching Reed's defining moment ("And here comes Willis!"). Considering Willis wasted two years playing forward to accommodate the likes of Walt Bellamy, the distance between Cowens and Reed should have been bigger than it was.[51] And you can't gloss over Reed's reputation as the premier enforcer of a much rougher era.

His remarkable Game 7 comeback shouldn't matter for Pyramid purposes, but it's hard not to give Willis credit for single-handedly swaying the '70 Finals and providing one of the most famous sports moments of the twentieth century. Of all the NBA players who gritted through a debilitating injury, Willis stood out because he was literally *dragging* his right leg underneath him, like when your foot falls asleep and you can't put any weight on it for a few seconds (only that was his right leg for a solid hour). That's what made it so remarkable when he drained the first two jumpers and nearly broke Madison Square Garden's roof. We can all agree Willis' injury *seemed* worse than any other injury. Was it as gruesome as it looked? We know that Reed tore his right quadricep muscle, specifically a part called the rector femoris, which controls movement between hip and thigh. According to my favorite injury expert, *Baseball Prospectus* writer Will Carroll, you can feel that muscle by standing up, pushing your fingers into the center of your right thigh right inside the hip, then raising your right knee like you're shooting a layup.

(Come on, just stand up and do it. I don't ask for much.)

(Come on, just freaking do it! You're pissing me off.)

(Thank you.)

Okay, once you raised that right knee, did you feel that specific part of the muscle tightening? That's what Willis ripped in Game 5 of the '70 Finals. All control had been severed between his hip and right leg, and as Carroll points out, "Willis' right leg was a lot bigger than ours." As for

---

51. The Knicks relived this fuckup 20 years later, playing Ewing and Bill Cartwright together for three frustrating years. You know a franchise is historically inept when they start repeating old mistakes like Dubya did with Iraq.

quantifying the level of pain, Carroll believes that it hinges on the impossible-to-determine combination of painkiller injections,[52] adrenaline (running high for a Game 7, especially after the crowd went ballistic) and Willis' pain threshold (obviously high). Was Willis draining two uncontested shots on a dead leg more impressive than Kirk Gibson limping off the bench, timing baseball's top reliever and pushing off a ravaged knee for his Roy Hobbs–like game-winning home run in the '88 World Series? Was Reed's Game 7 cameo more courageous than Larry Bird spending the night in traction with a wrecked back, showing up for Game 5 of the Pacers-Celtics series the next morning, playing with a cumbersome back brace, banging his head in the first half and breaking a bone near his eye, then returning midway through the third quarter and beating Indiana with a vintage Larry Legend performance? There's no way to know, no Pain Scale that measures it.

But here's what we *do* know: of all the legendary playing-in-pain performances, Willis Reed had the only one that swung the deciding game of an entire season. Top that, Dave Cowens.

29. DAVID ROBINSON

Resume: 14 years, 10 quality, 10 All-Stars . . . '95 MVP . . . runner-up: '94, '96 . . . '90 Rookie of the Year . . . Top 5 ('91, '92, '95, '96), Top 10 ('94, '98), Top 15 ('90, '93, '00, '01) . . . All-Defense (8x) . . . Defensive Player of the Year ('92) . . . leader: scoring (1x), rebounds (1x), blocks (1x) . . . 3-year peak: 28–11–3 . . . 2-year Playoffs peak: 24–11–3 (25 G) . . . 2nd-best player on 1 champ ('99 Spurs), starter for 1 champ ('03 Spurs) . . . scored 71 points (one game) . . . one quadruple double (34–10–10–10) . . . member of '92 Dream Team . . . 20K-10K Club

I mentioned seeing every relevant NBA player from 1976 to 1995 strolling through the Nancy Parish Memorial Tunnel and how only four stood out. Not including Ken Bannister or Popeye Jones, of course.

52. According to the *New York Times*, Willis was injected with 250 milligrams of an anesthetic called carbocaine. If I told you that a famous person used something called carbocaine in 1970, would you have guessed Willis Reed or Keith Richards?

One was Manute. Already covered him.

The second was Bird. Nearly everyone in our section had watched the Legend walking by us dozens and dozens of times, but that didn't stop us from staring at him the next time. This was the single most famous person who kept popping up in any of our lives. You worked, you slept, you ate, you went to the bathroom, you studied, you dated, you worked out, you did whatever normal people do . . . and then you went to the Boston Garden for a basketball game, and suddenly one of the greatest players ever was ambling by you again. When does that stop becoming surreal?[53]

The third one was Jordan. He reached a high enough level of fame by the mid-nineties that every entrance was accompanied by a barrage of flashbulbs, shrieks of "Michael!" and fans screaming hysterically for no real reason, like we were attending an all-girls private school and the Jonas Brothers had just walked in. What fascinated me was the way Jordan carried himself—keep moving, keep looking down, keep a small smile on your face—never breaking character even as strange palms bounced off his shoulders, even if someone was screaming "*Myyyyyyy-kallllllllllll!!!!!!!*" from three feet away and blowing out his eardrum. He just kept plowing forward with a tiny grin. When he reached the floor and started preparing for the game, knowing the whole time that everyone was taking pictures, staring and waiting for him to pick his nose and scratch his nuts or something . . . I mean, there was just something dignified about the way he *existed*. Famous people are famous for a reason.

The fourth one? David Robinson. During his rookie year in 1990, I buzzed down from college to catch his first game at the Garden. That seemed like a worthy trip at the time; everyone had been waiting for him to join the NBA for two years and the "Russell 2.0" tag didn't seem far-fetched yet. Everyone attending this game already knew what he looked like. So when Robinson emerged from that tunnel, nothing should have happened other than everyone thinking, "Cool, there he is." Instead, we made this sound: "Whoa." Is that a sound or a murmur? I don't know.

---

53. One pretty lady in my section swooned every time Bird walked by and studied him to the point that she noticed there was a barely perceptible quarter-sized stain on the left front leg of his shorts. It drove her crazy. "Would it be out of line if I offered to wash his shorts?" she asked once. These are the questions that get asked when you're sitting that close to NBA players.

But it was breathtaking to watch him glide by for the first time, like standing a few feet away from a prize thoroughbred or a brand-new Ferrari Testarossa. To this day, I have never seen anyone that close who looked more like a basketball player than David Robinson: The man was taller and more regal than we expected, but so absurdly chiseled that he looked like a touched-up model in a Soloflex ad. He walked proudly with his chest puffed out, his head held high, and a friendly smile on his face. He was strikingly handsome and even the most devout heterosexual males would have admitted it. Really, he was just a specimen. That's the best way I can describe it. He was a freaking specimen. My dad said later that it was the only time he'd ever heard the "Whoa" sound in all his years sitting in that tunnel. We all made it. None of us could believe what we were seeing. Some guys are just destined to play basketball for a living.[54]

At that specific point in time, I would have wagered anything that Robinson would become one of the ten greatest players ever. Never happened. He failed to dominate the NBA despite having every conceivable tool you'd want for a center: Russell's defensive instincts, Wilt's strength and agility, Gilmore's height, Parish's ability to run the floor, Hakeem's footwork and hand-eye coordination . . . and if that weren't enough, the guy was *left-handed*. If we ever start cloning basketball players someday, Jordan, LeBron and Robinson will be one-two-three in some order.[55] On paper, you couldn't ask for a better center. In *The Golden Boys*, Cameron Stauth reveals that a twenty-five-year-old Robinson was the committee's number four choice for the team—behind Bird/Magic/Jordan and ahead of everyone else—and there were always rumors that Chicago held internal discussions about offering Jordan straight up for Robinson before the '92 and '93 seasons. That's how good everyone thought Robinson would be. The guy had everything.[56]

---

54. Please add this entire paragraph to my Gay List. Thank you. By the way, Young Wilt was supposedly the king of the "Whoa!" category.

55. Paul Mokeski would be last.

56. The Robinson hype machine peaked in 1991 when Pat Riley said, "David is the spitting image of Russell, only David is a better athlete" and Cotton Fitzsimmons argued that he'd already surpassed Bird, MJ and Magic, saying, "They're all MVPs—this guy is more. He's the greatest impact player the league has seen since Kareem."

Well, almost everything. The same qualities that made him a special person also limited his basketball ceiling. Robinson might have been his generation's most intelligent player, the guy scoring 1310 on his SATs, playing the piano, and dabbling in naval science in his spare time.[57] Do book smarts matter on a basketball court? Not really. If anything, those extra brain cells wounded Robinson. Every early Robinson story centered around him "overthinking" things and needing to let "the game come to him." He routinely sucked in crunch time, maybe because he was thinking about big-picture things like "I need to come through or else my legacy will be questioned someday." A peaceful Christian who tried to find good in everyone, he lacked the requisite leadership skills—much less MJ's "keep this up and I'm bringing you into the locker room, locking the door and beating the living crap out of you" quality, for that matter—to handle Dennis Rodman as Rodman spiraled out of control and undermined San Antonio's '95 playoff run. He never developed the same cutthroat attitude that defined Hakeem in his prime. It just wasn't in him. When Jordan went on his "baseball sabbatical" and left a gaping opening for Robinson to become The Guy, Hakeem bulldozed him out of the way and won consecutive titles. Everything crested in the '95 playoffs—Robinson's MVP season, by the way—when Hakeem delivered such a one-sided asswhupping in the '95 Western Finals that it eventually found a home on YouTube in a clip appropriately titled "Olajuwon Dominates Robinson." Hakeem slapped up a 35–13–5 with 4 blocks per game, made the game-winning assist in Game 1, outscored Robinson 81–41 in the deciding two games and abused him with one particularly evil "Dream Shake" in Game 2 that became the defining moment of the series. So much for the Hakeem-Robinson debate.[58]

---

57. I took my SATs around the same time and scored a 1330. That's one of my enduring highlights from high school—narrowly beating David Robinson on the SATs. *Yeah, 1330 to 1310! I fucked that guy up!*

58. Best moment of the series: Robinson getting presented with the MVP before Game 2, then a pissed-off Hakeem destroying him in San Antonio with a Hall of Fame eff-you performance. By Game 5, Robinson was a shell of himself. Here's how Leigh Montville described it in *SI*: "Robinson was tentative, off-balance, hitting only six of 17 shots for 19 points, grabbing but 10 boards, missing important foul shots. Lost. David Robinson was lost. 'I've never felt this way before,' he said afterward. 'For the first time in my life, I felt I let my teammates down.' "

When Robinson finally became a champion in '99, it happened only because Tim Duncan assumed alpha dog duties and allowed Robinson to settle into his destiny as a complementary guy . . . although, of course, that title doesn't count because the '99 season never happened. Even if his personality prevented him from reaching his full potential as a player (and by the way, no. 29 in the Pyramid isn't too shabby), those same generous, thoughtful, unselfish qualities made him the greatest *person* out of anyone from his generation of stars. You know when you read about some people and feel embarrassed because you never touched people's lives in the same way? That's how Robinson made people feel; he's the guy who once spent $9 million of his own money to build a school in San Antonio. My favorite Robinson memory was the way he reacted during the Steve Kerr Game, when Kerr shook off the cobwebs and caught fire in Game 6 of the '03 Mavs-Spurs series. Since Kerr was popular with teammates and his barrage of threes was completely unexpected (he was their twelfth man that year), San Antonio's bench was reacting like a fifteenth-seed pulling off a March Madness upset. Right in the middle of everything was Robinson. He couldn't have been more overjoyed. You can actually see him jumping up and down like a little kid at one point. I guarantee he remembers that game as one of the highlights of his career. And in the big scheme of things, you know what? That counts for something. Nobody in the Pyramid was a better teammate or person than David Robinson. On the other hand, that's not a great sign for Robinson's legacy: my favorite Robinson moment was him cheering a teammate from the Spurs bench.

He only played fourteen seasons and struggled with back/knee issues for the last two—with nobody fully recognizing how much he had slipped because he *looked* exactly the same[59]—before rallying in the 2003 Finals to help the Spurs clinch a second title. His career was hindered slightly by a late start (thanks to four college years and a two-year navy stint), too many coaches (five in his first six years), and a crummy supporting cast (before Duncan, his only teammate to make an All-Star team was Sean Elliott). He wasn't a twenty-four-year-old rookie because he bounced

---

59. Robinson belonged to the Tony LaRussa All-Stars, maybe my favorite example other than Coach K or LaRussa himself. By the way, Robinson averaged a 6–6 in the Mavs/Lakers series (12 games) before rallying a little in the Finals (11–7).

around Juco schools, spent time in prison, or repeated his senior year of high school three times; the guy served our country and fulfilled his responsibilities, so he deserves historical extra credit there. If there's a what-if with Robinson other than losing two years with the navy stint, it's that the Spurs botched the number three pick in '89 by drafting Elliott ahead of Glen Rice, an indefensible decision[60] that became worse as the years passed and Rice evolved into a crunch-time killer and murderous three-point shooter for Charlotte and Miami. Had Rice been taking the big Spurs shots in the mid-nineties, the Spurs would have snuck into the Finals during Robinson's prime and he might have cracked Level 4. Instead I'll remember him for one sound: "Whoa."[61]

28. DWYANE WADE

Resume: 7 years, 6 quality, 6 All-Stars . . . '06 Finals MVP . . . top 5 ('09, '10), top 10 ('05, '06), top 15 ('07) . . . All-Defense (3x) . . . leader: scoring (1x) . . . '06 Finals: 37–8–4 . . . '09 season: 30–8–5, 2.2 steals, 49% FG . . . All-Star MVP ('10) . . . Playoffs: 26–5–6, 48% FG (66 G) . . . best player, 1 champ ('06 Heat) . . . career PPG: 25.4 (10th)

Of all the memorable subplots from the summer of 2010—two of the generation's best players possibly switching teams; Cleveland's collective psyche hanging by a thread; the Knicks spending two years gutting their team, then being unable to sign anyone other than Amar'e Stoudemire; the Bulls potentially owning the decade (and falling short); Atlanta giving Joe Johnson $120 million right after he led them to a second-round sweep in which they lost by 25 points per game; "Worldwide Wes" becoming a

60. Elliott averaged a 22–7 and shot 43% from three as a senior at Arizona; Rice averaged a 26–6, shot 52% from three and led Michigan to the '89 title. At no point in his life was Elliott a better small forward than Rice. Also, Rice averaged 20-plus points in six different NBA seasons and peaked in '97 for Charlotte: 27 points a game and a surreal 47% from three (taking 440 of them).
61. That's not totally true. I'll also remember him for being the Michael Spinks to Hakeem's Mike Tyson.

household name; Wade and Bosh hiring documentary crews to follow them; New Jersey's new owner Mikhail Prokhorov (or as I affectionately nicknamed the six-foot-eight billionaire, "Mutant Russian Mark Cuban") recruiting free agents with rap superstar Jay-Z (a minority owner who owns 1 percent more of the Nets than you do); a clumsy race to break news in the Twitter era that nearly set back sports reporting twenty-five years; owners spending the previous twelve months telling us that we needed to change the sport's economic structure or there would be a 2011 lockout, then spending a combined $114 million on Drew Gooden, Amir Johnson, Channing Frye and Darko Milicic within twenty-four hours of the start of free agency; and the incredible parallels between LeBron's Miami signing and Hulk Hogan's heel turn at 1996's Bash on the Beach[P47]—the strangest subplot had to be LeBron (no championships) generating the lion's share of attention while Wade (one championship) became a summer afterthought.

I could understand that happening two seasons earlier, when Wade was recovering from various injuries and battling a faint whiff of "Let's hope he isn't the next Penny Hardaway/Grant Hill" concerns.[62] But he reclaimed superstar status during the 2008 Olympics, where he played better than anyone, then kept momentum going with the best all-around statistical season by a shooting guard since Jordan. The following year, he carried a rotten Miami team to 47 wins and submitted a significantly better playoff showing against Boston (33–6–7, 56.4% FG) than Kobe did three rounds later (29–8–4, 40.5% FG). I can't remember a shooting guard with a better blend of skills: Wade creates for himself and others, defends at a high level, never mails in games or quarters, rises to the occasion when it matters and, most important, straddles the "making everyone else better" and "it's time for me to take over" lines better than anyone. The Bulls never enjoyed playing with Jordan until 1991. The Lak-

P47. That was the pay-per-view when Hogan turned on Macho Man Randy Savage, joined the evil Outsiders (Kevin Nash and Scott Hall) and formed the New World Order as announcers Dusty Rhodes and Bobby Heenan screamed, "He's the third man! What the hell is going on here??? Hulk Hogan has betrayed WCW!" With Cleveland being WCW, of course.

62. In 2006 I wrote, "[Wade] takes an Iversonian punishment every game, only he's not a freak of nature like Iverson was/is. If Wade doesn't start picking his spots, he'll go Earl Campbell on us and be gone from the league by 2011."

ers never enjoyed playing with Kobe from 2003 to 2008. Wade's team-mates always enjoyed playing with him. That quality sets him apart, as do the uncanny parallels between Wade and Jack Bauer: not just their fear-lessness and respective abilities to carry their own shows, but their career peaks and valleys from 2002–3 (Wade's breakout at Marquette and Jack's first two seasons of *24*) to 2006 (the year they both peaked) to 2007–08 (when things fell apart and their shows nearly got canceled) to 2009 (re-demption as franchise guys for both).[P48]

So why weren't Knicks fans or Bulls fans clamoring for Wade like they clamored for LeBron? Because few fans realize how terrific he's been. Hell, just compare his career to Kobe's career . . .

> Wade: 25–5–7, 48.2% FG, 77% FT (451 games); 26–5–6, 48% FG, 79% FT (66 playoff games)
> Kobe: 25–5–5, 45.5% FG, 84% FT (1021 games); 26–5–5, 45% FG, 82% FT (198 playoff games)

. . . and look how they compare during the two seasons in their prime when neither of them had any help:

> Wade ('09 & '10): 28–5–7, 48% FG, 20.8 FGA, 9.4 FTA, 90–72 record, 4–8 playoffs
> Kobe ('06 & '07): 33–6–5, 46% FG, 25.0 FGA, 10.1 FTA, 87–75 record, 4–8 playoffs

Could Wade have taken back-to-back titles with Pau Gasol, Andrew Bynum, Lamar Odom, Ron Artest/Trevor Ariza, Derek Fisher and Phil Jackson instead of the likes of Michael Beasley, Mario Chalmers, Quentin Richardson and Jermaine O'Neal's decrepit body that made police ca-daver dogs howl every time they caught a whiff of him?[P49] Um . . . yeah.

P48. In 2010, 24 careened to an end with a fairly unwatchable final season just a few weeks after Miami got wiped out by Boston in the first round. I was excited for the Bauer/Wade parallels to conclude with Bauer leaving TV and Wade leaving Miami, but Wade stayed. Why? Because rich athletes don't willingly leave South Beach unless some-one's holding a gun to their head.

P49. One week after I wrote this, O'Neal signed with my beloved Celtics for two years. Of course he did.

We already witnessed Wade's ceiling during Miami's four 2006 Finals victories, when he averaged 39.3 points and 8.3 rebounds and inspired me to write, "Sometime during the past four weeks, Wade matured into the single best player in the league, someone who instinctively balanced the line between deferring to teammates and taking over games (kinda like what we always *wanted* Kobe to be, only it never happened)." Put in simpler terms, it's the single best Jordan impersonation ever done. In a 2008 feature about the 50 Greatest Finals performances since 1977, John Hollinger ranked Wade's thrashing of Dallas first[63]—partly because he finished with the highest PER rating, partly because Wade's numbers were achieved during a slower-paced series and partly because he may have wagered with someone who dared him to write the single nuttiest column in ESPN.com history—and wrote, "While it seems strange to have somebody besides Jordan in the top spot, the truth is Jordan never dominated a Finals to this extent. At the time, many called Wade's performance Jordanesque. It turns out they might have been selling him short."[64]

Sure. If they had a head injury. Forget about the obvious advantages in Wade's era (no hand-checking, no hard fouls); that series goes down as the biggest travesty in NBA officiating history. It was a damned disgrace. It turned people off on the league. After Game 5 played out like a WWE match, I probably received two thousand emails in twelve hours from frustrated fans, many of whom were ready to give up on the league because they felt like the results were preordained. The reality? The NBA was fighting through a fundamental crisis with its style of play that went beyond the whole "let's change the hand-check rules and speed up play to get more scoring" issue. Some teams embraced the new rules, attacked the basket, pushed the ball and thought outside the box; others stuck to what worked from 1994 to 2005, slowing the pace, killing themselves on defense and revolving offensively around one creator. Miami and Dallas represented the old-school and new-school ways of thinking, so after Game 5 of the Finals—when Wade took 25 free throws (as many as Dallas' entire

---

63. I originally had "Wade's assassination of Dallas" here for like 3 months before realizing the macabre double meaning. See, I'm a relatively thoughtful person! Right?

64. I am either going to autograph a copy of this book for Hollinger or I'm going to beat him unconscious with it. I haven't decided yet.

team) and made the winning ones after a reckless drive because Bennett Salvatore bailed him out from 30 feet away—I wrote things like, "That's not basketball, it's a star system," "Seeing an individual triumph over a team *yet again* would erase every positive outcome from the 2005–6 season," and "I'm starting to feel like the future of the NBA is at stake."[65] Nothing against Wade or Miami, but nobody wanted to watch predictable offense anymore. We didn't want to watch one guy create every shot in crunch time while everyone stood around, and we certainly didn't want officials deciding games based on their interpretations of the "superstar barrelling into the paint and trying to draw contact" conundrum.

None of this was Wade's fault; after Miami prevailed in six games, you couldn't blame him for attempting 97 free throws (a startling number). It's not like he was calling his own fouls. But combined with Tim Donaghy's scandalous firing one year later, the 2006 Finals made fans, media members and league executives finally start saying the words "officiating crisis."[P50] And in the process, Wade received something of a historical shaft. When people remember that Finals, they remember the referees more than Wade's brilliant performance. Even in the *TBOB* hardcover, where Wade finished 55th in the Pyramid (too low in retrospect), I mistakenly discounted his defining moment—when he threw on that MJ cape and single-handedly willed Miami to a title—because I couldn't think of that series without grimacing at the calls. That wasn't fair to Wade. Nor was the way everyone overlooked him during the summer of 2010, when he was regarded as something of a consolation prize, the second-cutest girl in the bar for the dudes who didn't get to sleep with LeBron. He could have exacted revenge by signing with Chicago (a budding

---

65. That game provoked one of my angriest columns ever. After it led ESPN.com, a frustrated Mark Cuban posted a link on his blog with the headline "BILL SIMMONS IS MY HERO" and the note, "I never have to say a word again. Bill Simmons, as one of the 19 die hard [sic] says it all. It is so nice to know there are people who pay attention. Thank you bill." This was my favorite Cuban moment ever other than the time I watched him greet seedy Knicks owner James Dolan at the 2008 NBA Technology Summit by screaming, "Jim-mayyyyyyyy!" and giving him a big hug, like they hadn't seen each other outside of a Champagne Room in like five years.

P50. Of course, rectifying that crisis has been about as easy as keeping a *Bachelor* couple together. That's for the next book—the book that gets me blown up like DeNiro at the beginning of *Casino*.

powerhouse with Derrick Rose, Joakim Noah and tons of cap space), where he would have made the Finals multiple times and had everyone saying, "Wow, I can't believe we didn't think it was a bigger deal when Dwyane Wade was a free agent." Instead, he stayed in South Beach, swayed Bosh, then convinced LeBron to give up money (and the love of Cleveland fans, and good standing with sports fans everywhere) to blindside the Cavaliers on a nationally televised special and join Wade in *Wade's* city.

Was it disappointing that Wade didn't want to vanquish his biggest rival, or was it brilliant that he brought LeBron to his level and turned them into co-stars of a Hollywood blockbuster? I'm leaning toward the latter. Like always, we underestimated Dwyane Wade. No matter how many rings Wade and LeBron win together in Miami, Wade will always have one more.[P51] Could he leapfrog LeBron in the Pyramid potentially? I keep coming back to Game 4 against the 2010 Celtics, when Wade avoided a sweep with a virtuoso evisceration: 46 points and only eight missed shots, without any help, playing against swarming double and triple teams designed to stop him and him alone. It was like watching a high-risk figure-skating routine. Wade knew he had to nail his triple axels, his double toe loops, everything . . . anything less than a 9.9 on the degree-of-difficulty scale and Miami gets swept. So that's what he did. He nailed the routine. After Boston finished Miami off in Game 5, I wrote, "We know Wade is great. We just don't know *how* great. He owes it to himself to find out." We're about to find out. And if LeBron hijacks Wade's franchise from him, or if their mega-alliance with Bosh ends up bombing worse than the Planet Hollywood chains . . . I guess we'll always have the 2006 Finals.

P51. LeBron's one-hour ESPN show (and subsequent gutting of Cleveland) drew so much attention that Wade's summer indiscretions were overlooked. Multiple teams believed Wade used his free agent meetings to gain intelligence on them for Miami president Pat Riley. He also hired his own documentary crew, leading to a transparent moment when he asked for a second Chicago meeting—clearly the move of some producer or director who told him, "Let's leak information that you want to meet them a second time, and that you want to be closer to your kids post-divorce (in Illinois), then we'll meet them again, and then after that, we'll shoot a scene of you walking along Lake Michigan deep in thought like you're deciding what to do. Just trust me. It will be great TV." You can't sneak this crap by me. I've logged too much reality TV over the years. It's one of my vices, along with gambling, Sour Patch kids, Sly Stallone movies and unprotected sex in hotel saunas. (Just kidding on the last one.) I know fake reality, dammit!

27. BILL WALTON

Resume: 10 years, 4 quality, 2 All-Stars . . . '77 Finals MVP . . . '78 MVP, '77 runner-up . . . Top 5 ('78), Top 10 ('77) . . . All-Defense (2x) . . . leader: rebounds (1x), blocks (1x) . . . best player on 1 champ ('77 Blazers), 6th man on 1 champ ('86 Celts) . . . '77 Playoffs: 18.2 PPG, 15.5 RPG, 5.5 APG, 3.4 BPG

Imagine you became GM of your favorite team and were given the power to pull any NBA center from a time machine, then stick that player on your team—only his career would unfold exactly like it did when he played. Under these rules, would you rather have fourteen quality years of Robinson or two and a half transcendent years from Walton (one and a half as a starter, one as a sixth man)? I take Walton, and here's why: for that one transcendent year when we catch lightning in a bottle with him, I am *guaranteed* a title as long as I flank him with a good rebounder, a decent shooter and quick guards. How many players guaranteed you an NBA title? Jordan, Bird, Magic, Russell, Kareem, Hakeem, Duncan, Shaq, Moses, Wilt (if his head was on straight), Mikan (as long as it was the early fifties) . . . really, that's the whole list. Walton cracked that group for one magical year, prevailing with the worst supporting cast of any post-merger champion: Mo Lucas, Lionel Hollins, Bobby Gross, Johnny Davis, Dave Twardzik, Lloyd Neal and that's about it. For eleven months from March 29, 1977, to March 1, 1978, including the '77 playoffs, Portland finished 70–15 during an especially competitive era.[66] And everything—*everything*—ran through Walton. Maybe some centers were better in specific areas, but none was the best passer, rebounder, shot blocker, outlet passer, defensive anchor, crunch-time scorer, emotional leader and undisputed "guy we revolve our offense around" for their team at the same time. If you made a checklist of what you want from a center, he's the only player who gets check marks in every category.[67] And if you tin-

66. Of those 15 losses, three were by double digits and five were by three points or less.
67. And that includes size. Walton was listed at six-foot-eleven but he was easily seven-foot-two or seven-foot-three. When he played in Boston, he was at least 2 inches taller than Parish and McHale. He never wanted to be thought of as a seven-footer.

kered with his game to make it "better," really, what would you do? Maybe give him Kareem's sky hook or a few McHale low-post moves? We're picking nits at that point, right?

The big redhead peaked on the ultimate stage: the '77 Finals, when he averaged a 19–19–5 with 4 blocks and slapped up an ungodly 20–23–8 with seven blocks in the deciding game, then ripped off his jersey and celebrated shirtless with the delirious Portland fans. It's on the short list of most dominating individual performances that actually meant something, right up there with Russell's Game 7 of the '62 Finals, Wilt's Game 5 against Boston in '67, Pettit's Game 6 of the '57 Finals, Jordan's Game 6 of the '98 Finals, Frazier's Game 7 of the '70 Finals, Kareem's Game 5 of the '80 Finals, Magic's Game 6 of the '80 Finals, Duncan's Game 6 of the '03 Finals, Hakeem's Game 5 in the '95 Spurs series and Bird's Game 6 of the '86 Finals. Fortunately, NBA TV and ESPN Classic run an inordinate number of '77 Blazers games; it's one thing to read about Walton, and it's another thing to marvel at his Unseld-like outlets, Bird-like passing and deadly bank shots, as well as the way he constantly lifted his teammates and made them better. He controlled the basket on both ends. That's the best way to describe it. We haven't seen anything like it since.[68]

Quick tangent: during that star-crossed '78 season when Walton's body broke down right as the Blazers were decimating everyone, they played in Boston right before my Christmas break. I had just turned eight. For me to remember a random Celtics game from December '77 means that it left a significant imprint on me. And here's what I remember: Portland showed up in Boston and absolutely kicked the small intestines out of us. It's not like we were good anymore; that was the year Hondo retired, Heinsohn got fired and everything fell apart. They caught us at the perfect time. With that said, the Blazers reached a level that I hadn't seen in person before. They turned the game into a layup line for four quarters. Every time we missed, Walton grabbed the rebound and started another fast break. There was no conceivable way to beat them. We missed, they

---

68. My favorite Walton trait other than the exquisite passing: he always kept the ball over his head after every rebound on either end and was always in position to make a play. Walton tapes should be shown to fledgling high school centers for the rest of eternity.

scored. We missed, they scored. They were a machine. I remember leaving the Garden with my father and feeling like we had both been beaten up or something. By the time I turned twenty-five, I remembered the score being 151–72; actually, the final score was 113–81. But you get the point. Other than the '86 Celtics and '96 Bulls, that's the best team I've ever seen in person. And all because of Walton.

You can't overstate how damaging those lost Walton years were for anyone who truly cared about basketball. From a comedy standpoint, it would be like Eddie Murphy releasing *48 Hours* and *Trading Places*, disappearing for the next eight years, coming back and releasing *Beverly Hills Cop,* then disappearing for good. From a musical standpoint, it was like Cobain killing himself right as Nirvana was recording the follow-up to *Nevermind.* Of course, the perfect pop culture comparison would be Tupac Shakur—funny because you can't find a blacker guy than 'Pac or a whiter guy than Walton—because their careers started out stormy (Walton's injuries and political activism, 'Pac's jail time and brash lyrics) and had an ominous, this-could-end-at-any-time feel (thanks to Walton's feet and 'Pac's death wish), only they returned at full strength and blew everyone away for a solid year (Walton's 70–15 stretch, Tupac's *All Eyez on Me* album)[69] before getting pulled away for good (Walton because of his feet, 'Pac because he was murdered). Then they lingered for the next decade or so, with Walton's comebacks repeatedly getting cut short and Death Row Records repeatedly releasing lost songs and re-dubs that weren't as good as the stuff 'Pac made when he was alive. The big difference was that Walton found redemption on the '86 Celtics; Tupac won't find redemption unless he returns from the dead. (And don't rule it out.) I do wonder if Walton and Tupac were helped historically by their brief apexes; we romanticize them years later and wonder what could have been, only Tupac loved the thug life too much and Walton's misshapen feet were

69. That double album included "Life Goes On," "All About the U," "Picture Me Rollin'," "California Love," "I Ain't Mad at Chu" and "How Do U Want It" . . . and the B-side of the "How Do U Want It" single was "Hit 'Em Up," the one where he declared war on Biggie Smalls. I keep waiting for Shaq to remake "Hit 'Em Up" about Kobe, although technically, "Tell Me How My Ass Tastes" could have qualified.

never meant to handle the NBA. They each had a fatal flaw and that was that.

But you know what? They were original prototypes. One of a kind. Give me Walton for two and a half years over fourteen years of Robinson, and give me four years of 'Pac over a full career of any other rapper. My favorite Tupac song is "Picture Me Rollin'," an uplifting effort right after his release from prison, when he's cruising around in his 500 Benz, relishing his freedom and telling everyone who kept him down over the years (I'm translating into honky-speak), "Now that I'm out on the streets and being me again, I sincerely hope you take a few moments to think about me happily driving around in my expensive car as a free man. By the way, go fuck yourself." That's really the whole point of the song. At one point he taunts, "Can you see me now? Heheheh. Move to the side a little bit so you can get a *clear* picture. Can you see it? Hahah. Picture me rollin'." Fantastic. And it's one of his catchier tunes, the kind of song that makes you want to ride around in a convertible and pretend you're black. (Wait, you don't do that? Um . . . me neither.) Anyway, the song ends with Tupac taunting everyone from Clinton Correctional Facility, his old stomping grounds:

> Any time y'all wanna see me again
> Rewind this track right here,
> Close your eyes and picture me rollin'.

I feel that way about Walton and the Blazers. They didn't roll for long, but they *rolled*. And I don't even need to rewind the tapes to picture it.[70]

26. RICK BARRY

Resume: 14 years, 10 quality, 12 All-Stars . . . '75 Finals MVP . . . BS MVP ('75) . . . Top 5 NBA ('66, '67, '74, '75, '76), Top 5 ABA ('69, '70, '71, '72), Top 10 ('73) . . . '67 All-Star MVP (38 points) . . . season leader:

70. My apologies to Walton for not coming up with the perfect Grateful Dead song here.

points (1x), FT% (9x), steals (1x) . . . best player on champ ('75 Warriors) and runner-up ('67 Warriors) . . . '67 Playoffs: 35–8–4 (15 G); '75 Playoffs: 28–6–6, 44% FG, 92% FT (17 G) . . . 3-Year ABA Playoffs peak: 34–8–4, 49% FG (31 G) . . . 3-year NBA Playoffs peak: 27–7–6, 45% FG, 91% FT (40 G) . . . career: 24.8 PPG (13th), 89.3 FT (3rd), 5.1 APG . . . 25K Point Club

We already nailed an inordinate number of Barryisms throughout the book: his various hairstyles, his controversial leap to the ABA, his announcing foibles, his autobiography with the worst cover ever, the year they robbed him of the MVP and the reasons why. Say what you want about the guy, but he was definitely interesting. Especially if you were his hair stylist. We'll remember him as the most notorious asshole in NBA history, a perfectionist who held inferior teammates in disdain, had an almost pathological need to rub everyone the wrong way, and earned a reputation (fair or unfair) for not being able to click with black teammates. Remember when Jeff Beebe flips out during the near-plane crash in *Almost Famous*, berates Russell Hammond and finally screams, "You act like you're above us! You always have!" as their bassist chimes in, "Finally the truth." That was Rick Barry. He acted like he was above everyone else. Five former teammates or coworkers threw him under the bus in the same 1983 *SI* feature: Robert Parish ("He had a bad attitude. He was always looking down at you."), Phil Smith ("He was the same on TV. He was so critical of everyone. Like he was Mr. Perfect."), Mike Dunleavy ("He lacks diplomacy. If they sent him to the U.N. he'd end up starting World War III"),[71] Billy Paultz ("Around the league they thought of him as the most arrogant guy ever. I couldn't believe it. Half the players disliked Rick. The other half hated him"), and then-Warriors executive VP Ken Macker ("You'll never find a bunch of players sitting around talking about the good old days with Rick. His teammates and his opponents generally and thor-

---

71. After watching Dunleavy destroy the Clippers and make no friends in the process, this quote kills me. Dunleavy wouldn't start World War III—he'd just keep you in the war for twenty-five years as casualties mounted and he blamed everyone else.

oughly detested him"). Poor Barry was the Daniel LaRusso of the NBA—
there was just something about him that rubbed people the wrong way.

The quintessential Barry story: when he threw away Game 7 of the '76
Western Finals because his teammates never defended him in the Ricky
Sobers fight.[72] Barry probably watched the highlights at halftime and
confirmed his own suspicions that his teammates sold him out; the second half started and Barry simply stopped shooting. During the last few
minutes, coach Al Attles probably threatened him because Barry suddenly became Barry again; even with a late surge, the defending champs
ended up falling at home to an inferior team. You won't find a more indefensible playoff defeat in a deciding game. When I was working for
Jimmy Kimmel's show, we used Barry for a comedy bit and I couldn't resist asking him what happened in that series. He quickly replied, "We
should have won Game 7. We were rallying and I had a pick-and-roll
with Clifford Ray, but he couldn't catch the damned pass." Then he shook
his head in disgust and let out one of those "I wish Cliff were here right
now so I could shoot him a nasty look" groans. Twenty-seven years later,
Rick Barry—Hall of Famer, NBA champ, one of the eight best forwards
of all time—couldn't let that play go. It was weird. Sure enough, I watched
the tape a few weeks later: the Warriors were roaring back, Ray set a pick
and rolled to the basket, and Barry delivered the ball right off Ray's hands
and out of bounds. The cameras caught Barry frozen in disbelief. It's the
defining Barry moment in the defining "Rick Barry was a prick" game.

Poor Barry was his own worst enemy. He fled from a perfect situation
in 1967—the top scorer on a Finals team that had a young Hall of Fame
center (Nate Thurmond) and a quality second scoring option (Jeff
Mullins)—and jumped to the ABA's Oakland Oaks. Why? Because his
father-in-law (Bruce Hale) had been named their coach, even though the
move meant sitting out an entire season and playing in an inferior league
that could have gone belly up at any time. Has there ever been a dumber
career move by an NBA superstar that didn't involve the words "Birming-

---

72. Which they didn't. If anything, they were either silently cheering Sobers or figuring
out how to jump in, pretend to break it up and "accidentally" sock Barry a couple of
times. Again, Barry spends the next minute postfight repeatedly touching his wig to
make sure it didn't get messed up. I wish Sobers had pulled it off and waved it to the
crowd like they do in wrestling.

ham Barons"? You can't even say Barry did it for the money; San Fran matched Oakland's offer and he still left. How could he forget to put in his contract, "If the team moves or Bruce Hale gets fired, I can opt out immediately"? He sat out a year and injured his knee the following season. Then he watched in horror as the Oaks moved to Washington (Barry couldn't extricate himself from his ABA contract) and Virginia (Barry finally forced a trade by insulting Virginians in a 1970 *SI* feature, saying that he didn't want his son "to come home from school saying, 'Hi y'all, Daad' ") before dragging the Nets to the '72 ABA Finals and returning to Golden State the next season. So the best forward of that generation wasted *five full years of his prime* in a second-rate league because he wanted to play for his father-in-law? Two years later, Barry nearly dumped the Warriors again to become CBS' lead color guy, changing his mind at the last minute.[73] After the '77 season, he pissed on Warriors fans a third time by signing with the Rockets as a free agent (killing his relationship with Golden State owner Franklin Mieuli forever). Just like Roger Clemens at the end, Barry retired belonging to nobody: no farewell tour, no retirement ceremony, nothing.

How could we possibly rank him this high? Barry was the second-best passing forward ever, a beautiful creator who made everyone better as long as they didn't cross him. He could score with anyone when he was younger, averaging 35.6 points in his second NBA season (trailing only Wilt, Baylor and Jordan as the highest average ever) and 34.7 points in the '67 playoffs.[74] He was one of those born-before-his-time shooters who thrived with a three-point line, draining 40 of 97 threes (41.2 percent) in 31 ABA playoff games. He wasn't a great defensive player but crafty enough that he led the league in steals once (2.8 per game). He's one of the

73. Barry's ego was so huge that he nearly chose TV over the NBA in his prime. It's amazing the guy didn't release a sex tape. Did I mention he wore a wig for the entire '76 season? I mentioned that, right?

74. Devil's advocate point: He averaged a ton of shots that year—29 during the season and 33+ in the playoffs. In Game 3 of the Finals, he scored 55 on 48 shots. As for Game 4, here's how Frank Deford described it: "[Barry] handled the ball 59 times. Twice he lost it, three times he was fouled before shooting, 43 times he shot and only 11 times did he pass off. On occasion, it looked as if his teammates were trying to steer the ball away from him, and in the fifth game Coach Bill Sharman risked censure by sitting Barry down for a long period." The lesson, as always: don't trust stats.

best free throw shooters of all time, probably the greatest end-of-the-game cooler ever.[75] He slapped together one of the single best seasons in basketball history in 1975, doing every single thing that needed to be done and pulling off one of the bigger Finals upsets ever. And he actually would have been fun to play basketball with . . . as long as you didn't disappoint him or make a dumb mistake. Had they formed a Dream Team for the '76 Olympics, Barry would have become the team's alpha dog and everything would have revolved around his passing and creating. That counts for something in the big scheme of things.[76]

We'll remember him as an inordinately talented player and inordinately screwed-up person, and over everything else, that's why it didn't seem right to make him a Level 4 guy. Other than the '75 Finals, his defining moment happened two years after WatermelonGate, when a freelancer named Tony Kornheiser profiled Barry for one of the most memorable features in *SI*'s history, "A Voice Crying in the Wilderness." Kornheiser tried to figure out how such a great player could be forgotten so quickly, cleverly arguing that Barry's biggest problem was "face discrimination" and comparing him to the annoying, know-it-all actor that Dustin Hoffman played in *Tootsie* who rubbed everyone the wrong way. The piece starts like this:

75. And he shot them underhanded! Did we ever figure out why underhanded free throws faded away when Barry was nailing 90 percent of them? Oh, wait, I know—because it made the players look like pansies. I forgot.

76. Here's who I *think* they pick for the 1976 Dream Team: Barry, Kareem, Doc, Hondo, and Tiny (starters); Cowens, Thompson, Maravich, Walton, Westphal, McAdoo, college's John Lucas (bench). Westphal makes it over Jo Jo with the "crap, we need more white guys" rule. Here's 1980: Kareem, Bird, Doc, Gervin, Magic (starters); Moses, Gus Williams, DJ, Westphal, Sikma, Bobby Jones, college's Kevin McHale (bench). Jones beats out Marques Johnson with the "crap, we need more white guys" rule. (Please don't think I agree with this—that was just the thinking back then.) Here's 1984: Kareem, Bird, Doc, Magic, Moncrief (starters); Moses, King, Isiah, McHale, Jim Paxson, and college's MJ and Ewing (bench). I'm furious about Paxson making it over Andrew Toney because of the white/black thing even though it's my own hypothetical. Put Toney on there, and mother of schnikes! What a team! Here's 1988: Ewing, Bird, Barkley, Magic, MJ (starters); Isiah, Drexler, K. Malone, Stockton, Mullin, and college's David Robinson and Danny Manning. With 'Nique and Worthy in disbelief that both were bumped for Stockton. Anyway, I like '84 the most if that Toney/Paxson switch is made. Loaded team, everyone would have gotten along, Bird and Magic leading the way, King and Bird in crunch time, Isiah, MJ, Moses, Toney, and McHale off the bench, Young Ewing wreaking havoc defensively . . . holy mother of God.

Rick Barry has a problem. He would like people to regard him with love and affection, as they do Jerry West and John Havlicek. They do not.

"The way I looked alienated a lot of people," Barry says. "I've seen films of myself and seen the faces I made. I looked terrible." He closes his eyes to the memory and shakes his head. "I acted like a jerk. Did a lot of stupid things. Opened my big mouth and said a lot of things that upset and hurt people. I was an easy person to hate. And I can understand that. I tell kids, "There's nothing wrong with playing the way Rick Barry played, but don't act the way Rick Barry acted." I tell my own kids, "Do as I say, not as I did."

What bothers him isn't that he's not beloved.

"It bothers me," Barry says, "that I'm not even liked."

And he wasn't. But I can't drop him below no. 26. He brought too much to the table. If Barry's career was relived as a twelve-person dinner party with Barry hosting, then the following things would definitely happen: Dinner would start late because one of Barry's chefs quit that afternoon; everyone would comment on the table looking absolutely fantastic; two guests would storm out during the appetizers after Barry makes an inappropriate joke about one of their kids; another couple would leave before dessert because Barry keeps arguing politics with the husband and won't shut up; there would be multiple awkward interactions with Barry second-guessing one of the waiters (highlighted by one accidentally inappropriate racial joke); and the rest of the guests would ultimately decide to ignore his bullshit and savor the wonderful wine, first-rate filet mignon and an unbelievable round of soufflés and ports. Sure, they would bitch about him the entire way home . . . but a great meal is a great meal.

25. JOHN STOCKTON

Resume: 19 years, 10 quality, 10 All-Stars . . . Top 5 ('94, '95), Top 10 ('88, '89, '90, '92, '93, '96), Top 15 ('91, '97, '99) . . . Playoffs record: most assists (24) . . . 5-year peak: 16–3–14 . . . leader: assists (9x), steals (2x) . . . '88 Playoffs: 19–4–15 (11 G) . . . 2nd-best player on 2 runner-ups

('97, '98 Jazz) . . . Playoffs: 13–10.4, 80% FT (182 G) . . . missed 22 games total, played 82 games in 17 of 19 seasons . . . career: assists (1st), games (3rd), steals (1st)

For Jazz fans, watching Stockton was like being trapped in the missionary position for two decades. Yeah, you were having regular sex (or in this case, winning games), but you weren't exactly bragging to your friends or anything. He was very, very, very, very good but never great, personified by all those second-team and third-team All-NBA appearances and the fact that he never cracked the top six of the MVP voting. He bored everyone to death with those predictable high screens with Malone, the blank expression on his face[77] and a sweeping lack of flair. He made the Dream Team only because Isiah had burned so many bridges that Stockton was a much safer choice.[78] I always thought he was more fun *not* to like. He didn't have a nickname and modeled his haircut after the LEGO Man. He deserves partial responsibility for Utah's appallingly methodical style of play in the nineties. He pulled enough dirty stunts over the years to make Bruce Bowen blush, routinely tripping opponents as they curled off screens, setting moving picks by sticking his knee out at the last second, "mistakenly" punching in the nuts anyone who blind-picked him . . . and yet nobody ever called him out on this shit because he looked like he could have replaced Brenda and Brandon's dad on *90210*.[79]

You can't pick a point when Stockton's career peaked because it never happened. From 1988 to 1995, he averaged between 14.7 and 17.2 points and 12.3 and 14.5 assists during the "assists are suddenly easier to get" era. His shooting numbers were outstanding (51.5 percent career FG, 38.4

77. Stockton's face looked like that of a recovering alcoholic who stopped drinking and couldn't remember how to be fun anymore. Like you'd be trapped making small talk with him at a Christmas party for 20 minutes and thinking about intentionally choking on a crab cake just to get away.

78. A bitter Thomas torched Stockton for 44 points the next season. In their next encounter, Malone sought revenge and nailed Thomas with a vicious elbow, opening up a 40-stitch cut over his eye. Too bad for Isiah that this didn't happen in the playoffs— Malone would have missed the elbow.

79. Can't you see Stockton whirling around in the opening credits like James Eckhouse did, with that "That's right, I'm Mr. Effing Walsh" grin on his face? Come on, really? You can't see it?

percent career threes, 82.6 percent FT); he shot 53 percent or better seven times and reached 57.4 percent in 1988. Curiously, those numbers dipped in the playoffs (47.3 percent in 182 postseason games); from '92 to '96, Stockton shot just 44 percent and missed 107 of 153 threes (30 percent). After submitting a monster performance in the '88 playoffs (20–4–15, including a 24-assist game against L.A.), Stockton wasn't exactly Big Shot John for the rest of his postseason prime. The '89 Jazz got swept by seventh-seed G-State (starting Winston Garland at point guard, no less). Kevin Johnson and the '90 Suns stole a deciding Game 5 in Utah. The Blazers eliminated them in the '91 and '92 playoffs, with Stockton going 6-for-25 in the last two '92 losses and getting outplayed by Terry Porter (a 26–8 for the series). The '93 Jazz blew a 2–1 lead and lost to Seattle in the first round, with Stockton shooting 4-for-14 in a potential Game 4 clincher at home. The '94 Jazz lost in the Western Finals to Houston; Stockton missed 38 of 65 shots and averaged just 9.4 assists in the series. The '95 Jazz blew a deciding Game 5 at home to Houston, with Stockton contributing just 5 assists and 12 points on 4-for-14 shooting. And when the '96 Jazz lost Game 7 of the Western Finals to Seattle, the point guard matchup brought back memories of Olajuwon-Robinson the previous year: 20.8 points, 6.4 assists and 56 percent shooting for GP; 10.1 points, 7.6 assists and 39 percent shooting for Stockton.

By the time Payton had finished whipping him like a dominatrix, Stockton was thirty-four and heading toward the twilight of his career. Then fate intervened. Magic and Isiah were gone. KJ and Price were fading away. Penny was a blown-out knee waiting to happen. Tim Hardaway tore an ACL and became much easier to defend. Kidd and Marbury weren't ready. Kenny Anderson and Damon Stoudamire would never be ready. Rod Strickland and Nick Van Exel were crazy. Mark Jackson and Mookie Blaylock weren't in his class. Really, who was left?[80] And the pace of NBA games had slowed so much that fast breaks were obsolete and every team milked possessions for 18–20 seconds at a time, a godsend of a development for a point guard in his mid-thirties. By dumb luck and

80. Call it the Great Point Guard Drought of 1997. Fortunately, Chauncey Billups, Steve Nash, Mike Bibby, Andre Miller and others showed up in the next three drafts.

sheer attrition, Stockton remained the league's second-best point guard. When the '97 Jazz won 64 games and made the Finals, Stockton enjoyed his best playoff numbers in five years (16–4–0, 52 percent FG) against Darrick Martin (first round), Van Exel (second round), Matt Maloney (Western Finals), and Steve Kerr (Finals). When they returned to the Finals in '98, Stockton made a bunch of memorable crunch-time plays against Maloney (first round), Avery Johnson (second round), Van Exel (Western Finals), and Kerr (Finals).[81] So much for the glory days of battling Magic, GP and KJ.

I would argue that Stockton enjoyed the luckiest career of any top-forty guy. He lasted long enough that we forget his playoffs resume from '89 to '96 and remember only his big moments in '97 and '98 . . . you know, when he was lighting up Maloney.[82] We marvel at his gaudy assist numbers, forgetting that they came during an era when the criteria for assists inexplicably softened. And we gloss over his good fortune of playing with one of the best coaches ever (Jerry Sloan) and best power forwards ever (Malone, who complemented him perfectly in every respect). Look, *I was there.* He wasn't better than Isiah, Magic, Payton or even Hardaway and KJ at their peaks. He couldn't guard anyone for the last half of his career. He didn't have an extra playoff gear like so many other greats. Had he arrived at a different time, landed on the wrong team or blown out a knee, Stockton just as easily could have been Mark Price. So why the high ranking? Because he wore me down. Even after turning forty, he kept playing at a fairly high level and putting on a "how to run a basketball team" clinic. There was a crunch-time moment in the 2002 playoffs with Utah trailing by six and desperately needing a hoop to silence a raucous Sacramento crowd. As Stockton was tearing down the court, I was sitting there thinking, "Pull-up three, he's going for the pull-up three," only because I'd seen it so many times. Mike Bibby didn't know him as well. Thinking Stockton intended to take it coast-to-coast, Bibby started backpedaling at the three-

---

81. The most memorable Stockton play: his series-winning three in the '97 Western Finals that was highlighted by Karl Malone's couldn't-have-been-more-illegal moving pick/bear hug on Barkley, as well as Stockton deliriously jumping up and down in one of those "Wait, that guy isn't a robot?" moments.
82. Stockton drove Maloney out of the league. He just owned him. There's a 45 percent chance Maloney is working as Stockton's full-time dog walker right now.

point line ... and as soon as Bibby's momentum started to lean backward, Stockton pulled up and launched one of his trademark "my momentum is taking me forward, but somehow I stopped my body long
enough to launch this baby" threes right in Bibby's mug.

Swish.

Three-point game.

Mike Bibby's head shaking in disgust.

And I remember thinking, "That's why I'm gonna miss John Stockton."
Even after seventeen years and counting, you knew him inside and out,
knew every one of his moves, knew what he was doing before he even did
it and he was still pulling that crap off. Unbelievable. Watching Stockton
in his waning years reminded me of a family member or longtime friend
who gets you with the same two moves every time, like my uncle Bob, who
lived off the same pull-up jumper going to his right for about forty-five
years. There's something to be said for that. Isiah was better at his peak,
but would you rather have an A-plus point guard for ten quality years or
an A-minus for seventeen years pulling off the same exact shit in 2003 that
he pulled in 1987? Interesting debate. I'd still take Isiah, but I had to think
about it. As late as 1996? I wouldn't have thought about it. Stockton wasn't
flashy like Magic or as naturally gifted as Nash. He stood out only because
of his short shorts[83] and a vague resemblance to David Duchovny.[P52] Only
Utah fans and basketball nerds truly appreciated him; Stockton's final few
months barely registered a thump against Jordan's third and final farewell
in 2003. Too bad. He should have gotten more credit for being the most
fundamentally sound point guard ever, for playing the position selflessly
and thoughtfully for an extraordinary length of time. Most points play at
a high level for nine to twelve years; Stockton did it for eighteen and didn't
miss a single game in seventeen of them. Only Nash was better at running
high screens. Only Magic was better at going coast-to-coast in big mo-

83. Kudos to Stockton for making a valiant attempt to keep the whole Tight Shorts thing
going in the mid-'90s despite mounting opposition.

P52. Duchovny came on my podcast in 2010; he was outraged by the Stockton comparison and twice as outraged that I mistakenly left his wife (Tea Leoni) off my Diane Lane
All-Stars for over-40 celebs who remain smoking hot (Jennifer Aniston, Monica Bel-
lucci, Heather Graham, Halle Berry, Salma Hayek, etc.). An indefensible oversight. Although it was weird to tell someone, "You're so right, your wife is totally hot!"

ments. And nobody owned the "we're up by one, we're on the road, the crowd's going bonkers, there's a minute left, the other team just got a fast break dunk, they have all the momentum, and that's why I'm bringing it down and dropping a 25-footer on them" sequence quite like Stockton did. He was one of a kind. Boring as hell . . . but one of a kind.

(One last thought: here's where you have to love the Level 3/Level 4 debate. Stockton was the defining Level 3 guy for me, but you could easily make the case that his longevity and assist numbers sneak him up a level. See, the Pyramid works! It works, dammit!)

TEN

THE PYRAMID: LEVEL 4

JOHN HAVLICEK   FORWARD

24. SCOTTIE PIPPEN

Resume: 17 years, 12 quality, 7 All-Stars . . . Top 5 ('94, '95, '96), Top 10 ('92, '97), top 15 ('93, '98) . . . All-Defense (10x, eight 1st) . . . leader: steals (1x) . . . 4-year peak: 20–8–6, 49% FG . . . 4-year Playoffs peak: 21–8–6 (61 g's) . . . 2nd-best player on six champs ('91–'93, '96–'98 Bulls) . . . '91 Playoffs: 22–9–6 (17 G) . . . member of '92 Dream Team . . . All-Star MVP (1994: 29–11–12, 4 steals)

Some scattered thoughts that will eventually resemble an explanation . . .

1. The first five Dream Team choices were Jordan/Magic/Bird, then Robinson and Pippen in that order. Those were the five "no-brainers,"

according to the committee. From there, they spent the next few weeks choosing a roster that eventually included Barkley, Malone, Stockton, Drexler, Mullin and Ewing (and not Isiah). I don't know, this seems relevant. Eighteen years later, when I wrote the upcoming "Wine Cellar" chapter, my first five choices were Bird, Magic, Jordan, Pippen and McHale. I could not have a Wine Cellar team without those five. From there, I spent the next few days figuring out the other seven spots, changing my mind at least five hundred times.

2. Of anyone I've ever seen in person, Pippen was the best defender. We always hear how Bird and Magic played "free safety," a nice way of saying that they always guarded the other team's weakest offensive player, then used that advantage to roam around, sneak behind low-post guys and jump passing lanes. Extending that analogy, Scottie was a *strong* safety out of the Ronnie Lott mold, a consistently destructive presence who became nearly as enjoyable to watch defensively as Jordan was offensively. Nobody covered more ground or moved faster from point A to point B. It was like watching a cheetah in a wildlife special—one second Scottie would be minding his own business, the next second he would be pouncing. Everyone remembers Kerr's jumper to win the '97 Finals, but nobody remembers Pippen tipping Utah's ensuing inbounds pass, then chasing it down and flipping it to Toni Kukoc to clinch the game. No other player except for Jordan, LeBron and *maybe* Kobe had the physical gifts and instincts to make that play.

3. Only Jordan was a better all-around player in the nineties . . . and that was debatable.[1] From '91 to '95, Pippen averaged a 20–8–6 with 2.4 steals, shot 50 percent and doubled as the league's top defensive player. In the playoffs from '91 to '98, he averaged 17–23 points, 7–9 boards and 4–7 assists every spring and consistently defended the other team's best scorer. During MJ's "sabbatical," Scottie (20.8 PPG, 8.7 RPG, 5.6 APG, 49% FG) dragged the Bulls to within one fecally pungent call of the Eastern Finals[2] and should have been our '94 MVP runner-up be-

1. Ron Harper told *SI* in '99, "Everybody talks about MJ first, but Pip had a more all-around game. Defense, offensive rebounds and defensive boards: Pip made the game easier for us to play."

2. Hue Hollins whistled a touch foul on a last-second Hubie Davis jumper in Game 5, pretty much gift-wrapping the series for the Knicks. Even Vince McMahon was embarrassed by that call.

hind Hakeem. The following year, he became one of four postmerger players (along with Cowens in '78, Kevin Garnett in '03, and LeBron in '09) to lead his team in total points, rebounds, assists, steals and blocks in the same season. And he redefined the "point forward" concept during the nineties, allowing the Bulls to play any combination of guards without suffering in the ballhandling/defense departments.[3] Chuck Daly created a great term to describe Scottie: a "fill in the blanks" guy. If a teammate was getting killed defensively, Scottie had his back. If you needed rebounding, Scottie went down low and grabbed some boards. If you needed scoring, Scottie could create a shot or attack the rim. If you needed a turnover, Scottie had a better chance of getting it than anyone. If you needed ballhandling, he could do it. And if you needed to shut someone down, he did it. Like the Wolf in *Pulp Fiction*, Scottie specialized in cleaning up everyone else's mess. When Magic was running amok in the '91 Finals, Scottie put the clamps on him. When the Knicks were shoving an MJ-less Chicago team around in the '94 playoffs, Scottie dunked on Ewing and stood over him defiantly. During the Charles Smith game the year before, Pippen and Horace Grant were the ones stuffing Smith and saving the series. When the '98 Pacers nearly snuffed out the MJ era, Jordan and Pippen crashed the boards in Game 7 and willed themselves to the line again and again, two smaller guys dominating the paint against a bigger team. They just wanted it more.[4]

4. During the Dream Team practices, Daly called Scottie his second-best player and told David Halberstam, "You never really know how good a player is until you coach him, but Pippen was a great surprise in Barcelona—the confidence with which he played and the absolutely complete nature of his game, both on offense and defense. No one else really expected it." According to Halberstam, MJ returned to Chicago after the Olympics and told Phil Jackson, "Scottie came in as just one

---

3. Another NBA tragedy: watching Scottie toiling away for one season in a stilted, slow-it-down "Hey, Scottie, dump it into Hakeem or Barkley, go to the corner and stand there" offense. Almost as bad as Kidd in the triangle.

4. Scottie in '93: "I hope [MJ] leads the league in scoring for the rest of his career. And when it's all over, I'll be able to say, 'I helped him do it. And I played with the greatest player ever.' " Now that's a second banana!

of the other players, and none of the others knew how good he was, but then he kept playing, and by the end of the week it was clear that he was the top guard there—over Clyde and Magic and Stockton. It was great for people to see him in that setting and see how good he really was." For those of you scoring at home, that's sixteen combined rings paying homage.[5]

5. Irrefutable fact: Jordan never would have retired in '99 unless he knew for sure that Scottie was leaving. You think Crockett was trying to win a seventh title without Tubbs? No way. I always liked the *Miami Vice* analogy for them: Crockett got most of the attention and deservedly so . . . but he still wasn't taking Calderone down without Tubbs.[6] You could also rely on Tubbs/Pippen to carry their own episodes every now and then, although Tubbs never could have carried a whole season of *Vice* like Pippen carried that '94 Bulls team. His detractors conveniently forget that season, just like they ignore Older Scottie leading Portland to within one self-destructive quarter of the 2000 Finals, or how he jeopardized his impending free agency in the '98 playoffs by gutting it out with a herniated disc, even limping around in Game 6 of the Finals just because the Bulls needed his presence. If you're poking holes, you can easily dismiss him as Jordan's sidekick or mention his infamous migraine before Game 7 of the '90 Pistons series (which happened only a few days after his father passed away, but whatever). Hey, if all else fails and you want to discredit Pippen, just bring up the quitter thing.

And so where you stand on Scottie depends on one question: do you give up on anyone who ever made a stupid mistake?

We all remember that fateful '94 Knicks series, when Scottie refused to finish Game 3 because Phil Jackson called the final play for Kukoc (who

5. Jackson told *SI* in '99, "[Scottie] was probably the player most liked by the others. He mingled. He could bring out the best in the players and communicate the best. Leadership, real leadership, is one of his strengths. Everybody would say Michael is a great leader. He leads by example, by rebuke, by harsh words. Scottie's leadership was equally dominant, but it's a leadership of patting the back, support."

6. Don't forget, Tubbs had to bang Calderon's ugly daughter just to get to Calderon. Much bigger sacrifice than Scottie passing up some shots. She looked like Andy Pettitte with a crewcut.

swished the game-winner with Pippen sulking on the bench). A betrayed Bill Cartwright screamed at Pippen afterward with tears rolling down his face, later calling it the biggest disappointment of his career.[7] And maybe it was. Of course, Scottie carried a Jordan-less Bulls squad to 55 wins by himself. It had become *his* team, and when it's *your* team, a mind-set takes hold: everything rests on your shoulders, everyone is gunning for you and you can't take a night off. You become the pumped-up star of your own action movie. Unless you think like a superhero, you won't survive. Scottie wasn't wired that way, so he had to play the role of the alpha dog . . . and Game 3 was his Chitwood moment. He'd earned the right to say, "Coach, I'll make it." Jackson took the moment away and gave it to Kukoc, a slap in the face if you understood Scottie's back story. He hailed from a dirt-poor town in Arkansas, one of twelve siblings with an ailing father who couldn't work anymore. After an improbable growth spurt propelled him to NAIA Division I stardom, Scottie's stock skyrocketed right before the '87 draft,[8] with Chicago landing him in the lottery and locking him up with a six-year bargain of a deal (and eventually tacking on a five-year extension that became a bigger bargain).[9] When the Bulls courted Kukoc for most of Scottie's career, Scottie never forgave them for it. Or Kukoc, for that matter. So that's what led to the regrettable decision in the Kukoc game: a Molotov cocktail of money, jealousy, insecurity, ego and competitiveness exploded at the worst possible time. Scottie apologized, his team forgave him, he took the heat and that was that. Shit happens. The Bulls won three more rings with him. Everyone forgets that part. If you think one selfish moment should overshadow a totally unselfish career, maybe you should climb off your high horse before you get hurt.

Scottie finally escaped Jordan's shadow in Portland, where he led a dysfunctional Blazers team to the precipice of the 2000 Finals—15-point

7. It narrowly edged the time Cartwright realized that he couldn't grow a full goatee.
8. NBA draft code words "upside," "length" and "wingspan" were pretty much invented during the Pippen draft.
9. Had Scottie played out that rookie contract and become a free agent in '93, right as Jordan was retiring, his value would have soared. For the first *eleven years* of his career, Scottie Pippen was woefully underpaid. He was the 122nd-highest-paid player in the NBA in 1998.

lead, 10 minutes to play—before everything fell apart in a quagmire of improbable threes, shaky calls and bad coaching. Critics pointed to that game as more evidence that Scottie couldn't be the best guy on a championship team. Good, that puts him with these guys: Cousy, Malone, LeBron, Barkley, Garnett, McHale, Gervin, Oscar, Kobe, Robinson, Ewing and Baylor. I hope history remembers him as an exceptional athlete who redefined his position, routinely played hurt, allowed Jordan to blossom into "best player ever" status and ended up with enough rings for two hands. Every time I tried to talk myself out of putting Pippen in the top twenty-five, I kept thinking about the time Chicago's soon-to-be-legendary '96 team cruised through Boston right before Christmas. They were 19–2, working on a 10-game winning streak and generating the first wave of "greatest team ever" buzz, a complete affront to everyone who loved the '86 Celtics in Boston. Come on, they couldn't be *that* good, right? Then Jordan and Pippen came out and whupped our crummy team for two-plus hours.[10] This was like watching Andre the Giant in his prime, when he'd come out smiling for a battle royal as the crowd went bonkers, then disdainfully tossed jabronies out of the ring for the next twenty minutes. By the fourth quarter, two-thirds of the crowd was rooting for Chicago under the rarely seen and entirely defensible "not only is our team reprehensible, but we used to root for a great team, we know greatness, we understand greatness and *this* is greatness" corollary. Jordan and Pippen finished with 37 points apiece. Scottie chipped in 12 assists and 9 rebounds for good measure. Then they flew to the next city and kicked the shit out of somebody else. Don't tell me that Scottie Pippen wasn't great.[11]

10. Our three best guys that year: Dana Barros, Todd Day and Dino Radja. Little known fact: Dino was the last 19–10 guy (in '96) who also smoked butts before and after games. In a related story, we went 33–49.

11. You know I feel passionate about something when I spring a double negative on you.

23. ISIAH THOMAS

Resume: 13 years, 12 quality, 12 All-Stars . . . '90 Finals MVP . . . Top 5
('84, '85, '86), Top 10 ('83, '87) . . . two All-Star MVPs . . . leader: assists
(1x), minutes (1x) . . . 4-year peak: 21–4–11, 47% FG . . . career: assists
(5th), steals (15th) . . . Playoffs: 20–5–9 (111 G) . . . '90 Finals: 28–5–7,
11-for-16 threes . . . best player on 2 champs ('88, '89 Pistons) and one
runner-up ('88)

An unusually lengthy Pro/Con list for the only Pyramid Guy who ever
threatened me with bodily harm:

Pro: Holds the title of Best Pure Point Guard Ever as well as the guy who
nailed the most categories on a "here's what I want from my dream point
guard" checklist: scoring, crunch-time scoring, passing, penetration,
quickness, leadership, competitiveness, toughness, defense, ability to run
a fast break and willingness to sacrifice his own numbers to get everyone
else involved. Really, he had everything you'd want except a three-point
shot. There's a reason he became the best player on a team that won two
titles in a row (and should have won three). If you doubt his leadership,
watch what happens after the Pistons clinch the '90 title on a last-second
miss—everyone runs right toward Isiah and lifts him to the sky.

Con: His poor career field goal percentage hurts him historically. My
dumb explanation: Isiah averaged 105 threes during his first thirteen seasons and made a ghastly 29 percent (398-for-1,373), although you can't
totally blame him because of the league's poor three-point shooting from
'81 to '86 (see page 140).[12] He was deadly from 18–20 feet; anything beyond was sketchy. Remove those threes from his resume (45.2 percent career FG) and he made 6,796 of 14,577 two-pointers (46.8 percent). You
could say Isiah was born after his time: had he arrived 10–15 years earlier,

12. Remember, Isiah made 28% of his threes in '83 and somehow finished second in the
league. If he'd come along ten years later, it'd have been a bigger part of his arsenal.

he wouldn't have been seduced by those dumb threes, and had he arrived six years later, he would have made a higher percentage. He's the anti-Maravich in this respect.

Pro: Routinely unstoppable in big games and big moments. Remember when he dropped 16 points in the last 91 seconds of regulation to keep Detroit alive in the '84 Knicks series? Or the 25-point third quarter in Game 6 of the '88 Finals? That's what I loved about Isiah—he only brought out the heavy artillery when his team needed it.

Con: Somehow got off the hook historically for the single biggest NBA crunch-time brain fart since the merger: setting up Larry Bird's series-altering steal in the '87 Eastern Finals. Actually, it was a two-part brainfart—he should have called time out, and he never should have thrown a lazy pass toward his own basket. Indefensible.[13]

Pro: His overcompetitive/nasty/tenacious side made him a cross between a point guard and a pit bull and provided the spine for a series of especially tough Pistons teams. You have to admire any six-footer who threw the first punch in fights with Laimbeer and Cartwright, as well as anyone who would choke his own trainer during a game.[14]

Con: That same overcompetitive/nasty/tenacious streak made him one of the poorest sports in any league. Isiah disgraced the Pistons after two play-off exits (the "if Bird was white, he'd just be another good player" non-sense in '87, and the orchestrated walkout during Chicago's sweep in the '91 Eastern Finals), organized the freeze-out of Jordan during the '85 All-Star Game, stabbed Adrian Dantley in the back with the Dantley/Aguirre

13. On the other hand, this was one of the ten greatest moments of my life . . . so thank you, Isiah!

14. One of my favorite clips: Isiah getting busted open by Malone's elbow, flipping out and briefly strangling his trainer as the guy was trying to stop the bleeding. That was the only inexplicable strangulation in NBA history. Even the Spree/Carlesimo incident was semiexplicable.

trade, burned so many bridges that they decided to leave him off the Dream Team (more on this in a second) and may have even been responsible for the Simpson/Goldman murders in 1994.[15]

Pro: Mastered the "I'm giving up my own numbers to get everyone else involved, then I'll take over the last three minutes if they need me" point guard conundrum faster than anyone ever. He also eked the best possible basketball out of one-dimensional scorers (Dantley, Tripucka, Mark Aguirre), guys who couldn't create their own shots (John Salley, Rick Mahorn, Rodman, Laimbeer), streaky shooters (Vinnie Johnson, James Edwards), and even reluctant shooters (Dumars). If the '07 Suns were like operating a Formula One race car for Nash, then running those Detroit teams was like operating a high-risk/high-reward hedge fund—you had to know when to ride a hot hand, juggle the egos of various investors, trust your gut over conventional wisdom and command an extraordinarily high amount of trust with everyone involved.

Con: For some reason, that rare talent didn't translate to any other walk of life: poor Isiah goes down as one of the worst coaches, worst GMs, worst TV guys and worst commissioners of the past thirty years. If you think what he did to the Knicks was bad, read up on what happened with the CBA; he could have invited all the players and executives into one penthouse suite, then rained bullets on them from a helicopter *The Godfather: Part III*–style and not done as much damage.

Pro: If you're penalizing Isiah for retiring after just thirteen seasons, don't forget that he tore an Achilles during the '94 season and felt like his skills had eroded just enough that he couldn't have survived the nine-month rehab process and kept playing at a high level. I always appreciated him for that. How many great athletes walk away exactly when they should walk away?

15. What, you don't believe me? Isiah retired on May 24, 1994, and suddenly had a ton of time on his hands; the murders happened two weeks later. You don't think that's a coincidence? Prove me wrong!

Con: Inexplicably kissed Magic before every game of the '87 and '88 Finals. We've never heard a good explanation. Ever.[16]

You can't discuss Isiah's career without delving into his incredible omission from the Dream Team. The reasons were simple: supposedly Jordan wouldn't play if Isiah was involved, and enough of the other players despised him that the committee decided, "Screw it, Isiah isn't worth the trouble." Understood. But they picked that team after the summer of '91, with Isiah coming off three Finals appearances and two Conference Finals appearances as one of the five most important players of that generation (along with Moses, Bird, Jordan and Magic). Leaving him off the Dream Team was like leaving Billy Joel out of the "We Are the World" video.[17] You just couldn't do it. His stats don't totally reflect his impact during the first ten years of his career—although three straight first-team All-NBAs, Finals MVP and back-to-back titles certainly help—and the Dream Team would have cemented his legacy. So he was robbed. And then some.

One last thought: say what you want about All-Star Games, but they're an accurate snapshot of who mattered in every given year. It's like being a dad and getting the biggest leg of the chicken. In All-Star Games, the daddies get the biggest legs (or in this case, minutes). So that got me thinking . . . who were the chicken leg guys in All-Star history, the ones who simply had to play big minutes because they were who they were? Leaving out centers (it's too easy for two great centers to split minutes in an All-Star Game), here's how the career minute totals of forwards and guards broke down (minimum: six All-Stars except for LeBron/Wade) . . .

---

16. And if you're nitpicking, I want to know why it was okay to show Magic and Isiah kissing on network TV, but when Matt the Gay Guy made a move on Billy's best man before Billy's wedding five years later on *Melrose Place,* Fox didn't have the balls to show their kiss.

17. I mulled this analogy long and hard: At the time, Joel was the fourth-most-famous person in that video behind Michael Jackson (MJ), Bruce Springsteen (Bird), and Stevie Wonder (Magic) and just ahead of Bob Dylan (who had lost his fastball). Finishing the analogy: Michael McDonald (Barkley), Huey Lewis (David Robinson), Tina Turner (Ewing), Lionel Ritchie (Mullin), Kenny Rogers (Malone), Tom Petty (Stockton), Quincy Jones (Chuck Daly) and George Michael (Christian Laettner). Sadly, there's no basketball equivalent to Dan Aykroyd singing in the chorus.

Averaged 28-plus minutes: Jordan (13 games, 382 minutes); Oscar (12/380); Cousy (12/368); Pettit (11/360); West (12/341); Magic (11/338); Elgin (11/321); Isiah (11/318); Doc (11/316); Bird (10/287); LeBron (6/183)

Averaged 23–27 minutes: Havlicek (13/303); Kobe (11/298); Duncan (12/276); Shaq (12/275); Garnett (12/273); Moses (11/271); Iverson (9/239); Gervin (9/215); Barkley (9/209); Lucas (8/183); Frazier (7/183); Pippen (7/173); McGrady (7/172); Archibald (6/162); Wade (6/159)

Averaged 18–22 minutes: Hayes (12/264); Malone (12/244); Greer (10/207); Stockton (10/197); Wilkens (9/182); R. Allen (9/182); Nowitzki (9/174); Drexler (9/166); 'Nique (8/159); English (8/158); Worthy (7/142); Nash (6/125)

Holy shit! Other than the random appearance from Lucas, the chicken leg breakdown went exactly like you'd think it would go, right? The Stockton/Malone numbers were low because they never cared about playing in their later years; Kobe's numbers were skewed because he only played 3 minutes in the '08 game; and the Garnett/Duncan numbers were low because they cost each other minutes splitting time. Other than that, it's a surprisingly accurate reflection of which noncenters mattered most over the last fifty-plus years. And that's the thing: Isiah *mattered*. He deserved to be on the original Dream Team. It's true.[18]

22. KEVIN GARNETT

Resume: 15 years, 12 quality, 13 All-Stars . . . '04 MVP . . . '00 runner-up . . . top 5 ('00, '03, '04, '08), top 10 ('01, '02, '05), top 15 ('98, '07) . . . All-Defense (10x, right 1st) . . . Defensive Player of the Year ('08) . . . '03 All-Star MVP . . . leader: rebounds (4x) . . . 3-year peak: 23–14–6, 50% FG . . . '04 Playoffs: 24–15–5, 43.4 MPG (18 G) . . . '08 Playoffs: 20–11–3, 50% FG, 81% FT (26 G) . . . missed playoffs 3 straight years . . . Best player on champ ('08 Celtics), starter on runner-up ('10 Celts) . . . 20K-10K Club

18. I say we make it up to him by letting him pick the 2012 Dream Team. "And starting at center, weighing more than Angola's entire team . . . Eddy Curry!"

Right after graduating from college, I became hooked on Watergate and spent a few weeks reading the Woodward/Bernstein books, watching and rewatching *All the President's Men* and wasting too much time figuring out Deep Throat's identity. That was right up there with "Who killed JFK?" for me. Who was Deep Throat? I had to know. Every time I watched the movie on cable from 1992 to 2005—and since it resides in my permanent "I can't pass this up even though I just watched it three weeks ago" rotation, that was often—my favorite scenes were those hushed conversations in the dark parking garage with Bob Redford (playing Woodward) and Hal Holbrook (playing Throat). They always nailed the lighting just right; you could kinda see Holbrook, but not totally; and he was always sucking on a cigarette, acting furtively, talking in a raspy voice and doing everything you ever thought Deep Throat would do. When we finally learned in 2005 that Throat was a former FBI and CIA executive named Mark Felt, I was crushed. It was more fun *not* knowing. Turns out Deep Throat was a failing grandfather who wanted to make his family some cash before he croaked, so he outed himself for a quickie book. I found the whole thing wildly disappointing. Things were much more fun when Hal Holbrook was Deep Throat, you know? And if you're an NBA fan, maybe it was more fun when Kevin Garnett toiled away in Minnesota as we wondered, "Exactly how great is this guy?"

We didn't know the answer and were fine with this. We like arguing about this stuff. Here was one of the greatest forwards ever, one of the fiercest competitors in any sport, someone with a chance to finish with historic scoring and rebounding numbers, one of the killer defensive players of his era . . . and we had no clue how good he really was. He played with seven quality players in his first twelve seasons: Joe Smith, Tom Gugliotta, Stephon Marbury, Terrell Brandon, Sam Cassell, Sprewell and Wally Szczerbiak. He never played for a decent coach and certainly didn't have a cagey front office pulling strings for him.[19] His NBA clock

19. I'd make a GM joke about McHale here, but he handed Boston the '08 title so I can't be an ingrate. By the way, KG faded after '08 with a mysterious knee problem loosely described as "I spent 13 solid years playing 1,100-plus games and 40 minutes a night at an intensity normally reserved for mothers trying to rescue their children who are trapped under a truck" but with an "-itis" at the end. He missed the last four months of the '09 season, went under the knife that summer, limped through the '10 season, then had a

was ticking and he knew it; he had become an attractive single woman in her late thirties with rumbling ovaries. Garnett's famed intensity slowly morphed into something else: frustration and despair, with a touch of "I might kill everyone on my team tonight" thrown in. Still, he couldn't ask out. He just couldn't do it to everyone in 'Sota. To keep the domestic analogies going, he was like an unhappy husband who couldn't stomach the thought of divorce because he didn't want to hurt the kids.

There wasn't a more tragic figure in the league. Heading into that 2006–7 season, Minnesota released Paul Shirley, who sent me a gushing email about KG's everyday brilliance and declared that if KG had played on a contender his entire career, "people would speak of him as a candidate for best player ever." Would that become KG's legacy: the coulda-shoulda-woulda star who ended up being the Ernie Banks or Barry Sanders of basketball? Every time I watched him play in person, I always admired his command of the room, how he seemed larger than life at all times, how it was nearly impossible to stop glancing at him. The guy just *seemed* famous. He stood out. Applying my world-renowned Foreigner Test, if you brought an exchange student to his first NBA game and the guy had no idea what anyone looked like, then you asked him to watch everyone warming up and pick the guy who seemed like he should be the best guy, Garnett would have been the one he picked.

That charisma never translated to playoff success: The T-Wolves got knocked out of the first round in Garnett's first seven playoffs appearances. In nine elimination games over that stretch (Minny won two of them), Garnett averaged an 18–11–6 and shot 40 percent.[20] Things turned during his MVP season in 2004, when Garnett had a certified monster Game 7 (a 32–21 against the Kings) before Cassell got injured and they fell to the Lakers. Then the Spree/Cassell dynamic imploded, Minnesota made all the wrong moves to replace them (Ricky Davis and Marko Jaric,

---

roller-coaster playoffs in which he looked washed up, then he didn't, then he did, then he didn't . . . it was like seeing Cameron Diaz on a fifty-foot movie screen and having the "Is she hot? Is she ugly? Is she hot? Is she ugly?" inner dialogue, but for ten weeks instead of two hours. In a tight Game 7 of the Finals, Gasol and Kobe grabbed 33 rebounds combined . . . and KG grabbed 3. It's probably over. Or close to being over.

20. In his only Game 5 ('98 against Seattle), KG practically crapped himself with 7 points, 4 rebounds and 10 TOs.

anyone?) and Garnett became the only top forty Pyramid guy to miss the playoffs for *three* straight years.[P53] Wasn't it his job to carry a subpar team? Wasn't that what Barkley did in the late eighties and early nineties in Philly? And how much did his personality have to do with it? Every time I watched a Wolves-Clippers game during that stretch, I always pictured Garnett snapping afterward and killing everyone in the locker room except for Ricky Davis, who would have calmly watched the whole thing unfold while sipping from a malt 40. Poor Garnett had become the Tiffani-Amber Thiessen of the NBA, someone with all the tools who should have been more successful than he was. It just didn't make sense.[21]

By now, the Garnett vs. Duncan argument was in full swing and centered around a hypothetical, impossible-to-prove argument: "If Duncan had Garnett's teammates from 1998 to 2007 and vice versa, wouldn't KG be the guy with four rings?" I thought that was bullshit—what set Duncan apart was his ability to raise his game to another level in big moments. Just as selfless and competitive as Garnett, Duncan channeled his intensity and saved peak performances for when they mattered most. He knew there was a crucial difference between a ho-hum January game in Atlanta and a must-win playoff game in L.A. He developed reliable mental alerts like "Unless I grab 20 rebounds tonight, we're going to lose" or "If I don't take over this game right now and score every time down the floor, we're cooked." Meanwhile, Garnett never wavered from how he played—ever— even if it meant passing the game-winning shot because some untalented doofus like Troy Hudson had a better look.[22] Once Pierce and Allen were

---

P53. One fun tidbit during this stretch: we learned KG keeps in shape by running on the beaches of Malibu every summer. The sheer comedy of a seven-foot black guy sprinting along the sands of the whitest, most uptight place on the planet can't be calculated. Some of his neighbors probably hadn't seen a black person in twenty years. Imagine them glancing up from their morning coffee on the deck and seeing Garnett sprinting toward their beach house.

21. Every red-blooded male born between 1965 and 1980 dug T.A.T. for the Kelly Kapowski/Valerie Malone resume, only it never translated to a movie career or a leading sitcom role. She couldn't have had Christina Applegate's career?

22. KG fans defend his unclutchness because he never got clutch reps in his formative years (whereas Duncan did). Decent point. Think of KG's career like a video game: spend a ton of time playing Grand Theft Auto and you're more likely to complete a mission than someone who doesn't own a PlayStation, right? To borrow a Gladwell phrase, Duncan was a playoff outlier.

flanking him in Boston, that freed him to do Garnett things (protect the rim, make high-percentage decisions, control the boards, draw centers away from the hoop with his killer 18-footer, throw up a 20–12 every night and raise everyone else's play with his unparalleled intensity) without dealing with the pressure of making big shots. After 25 up-and-down playoff games fueled the "Is KG clutch?" debate yet again,[23] Garnett stood near Boston's bench before Game 6 of the 2008 Finals, muttered a few things to psyche himself up and head-butted the basket support as hard as he could. Watching from about fifty feet away, my dad and I raced to make the "Uh-oh, I think we're getting killer KG" comment. The signature moment: a three-point play when KG got knocked down and flung a line drive that banked in, then lay on the floor with his arms raised, screaming at the ceiling as the crowd went bonkers. We were like 18,000 people pouring Red Bull down his throat that night. He finished with a 26–14, played his usual terrific defense and found his swagger: a level of passion and intensity unique to him and only him. Let the record show that KG played one of his better games to clinch a championship. It's something Elvin Hayes can't say, or Karl Malone, or Patrick Ewing, or Chris Webber, or anyone else from the not-so-clutch group that Garnett escaped.

What Garnett did for the '08 Celtics can't be measured by statistics; it would belittle what happened. He transformed the culture of a perennial doormat. He taught teammates to care about defense, practice, professionalism, and leaving everything they had on the court. He taught them to stop caring about stats and start caring about wins. He single-handedly transformed the careers of three youngsters (Rajon Rondo, Leon Powe and Kendrick Perkins), one veteran (Pierce), and one embattled coach (Doc Rivers). He played every exhibition game like it was the seventh game of the Finals. During blowouts, he cheered on teammates like it was a tight game; because of that, the bench guys did the same and turned into a bunch of giddy March Madness scrubs. I have never watched a more contagious, selfless, team-oriented player on a daily basis. By Thanksgiving, the entire team followed his lead. Every time a young player went for

23. After Game 3, I wrote a column that included the question "Is Garnett on pace to pass Hayes, Chamberlain and Malone as the biggest choke artist in the history of the NBA Finals?" Sadly, it had to be asked—he had missed 36 of his last 50 shots with the likes of Pau Gasol and Ronny Turiaf guarding him.

his own stats or snapped at the coach, KG set him straight. Every time one of his teammates was intimidated, KG had his back. Every time one of his teammates got knocked down, KG rushed over to pick him up; eventually, four teammates were rushing over to help that fifth guy up. Every time an opponent kept going for a shot after a whistle, KG defiantly blocked the shot just out of principle.[24] Eventually, everyone started doing it. No shots after the whistle against the Celtics. That was the rule.

So it was a series of little things, baby steps if you will, but they added up to something much bigger and built the backbone of an eventual championship. A wonderful all-around player, ultimately Kevin Garnett was only as good as his teammates. And I'm fine with that. We'll remember him like Jimmy Page or Keith Richards, a gifted guitarist who needed an equally gifted band to make a memorable album ... and any solo album would ultimately be forgettable.[25] That was our answer. Unlike with Deep Throat, I'm glad we know the truth.

21. BOB COUSY

Resume: 13 years, 13 quality, 13 All-Stars . . . '57 MVP . . . Top 5 ('52, '53, '54, '55, '56, '57, '58, '59, '60, '61), Top 10 ('62, '63) . . . two All-Star MVPs . . . records: most assists in one half (19), most playoff FTs made (30) . . . leader: assists (8x) . . . 2nd-best player on 6 champs (Boston) . . . 3-year Playoffs peak: 20–6–9 (32 G) . . . career: 18–8–5, 38% FG, 80% FT

The Cooz should start fading historically soon—if it hasn't happened already—which is one of the reasons I wanted to write this book. We can't let that happen to a beloved Holy Cross grad. Future generations will point to his field goal shooting and say, "By any statistical calculation,

24. This was fun during the regular season and not as much fun in the playoffs, as Boston struggled vs. Atlanta and KG was blocking shots after whistles but refusing to post up Solomon Jones. I think I screamed, "Come on, KG, take this goddamned stiff to the hoop!" at least 250 times that spring.
25. Extending this analogy, Duncan was like Eric Clapton—great in a band and really good by himself, although there's no way Duncan ever would have done something as sleazy as stealing George Harrison's wife.

Nash and Stockton were decidedly better." Fortunately, I'm here. Allow me to make the case for Cooz in four parts:

1. His poor shooting (37.5 percent for his career) was deceivingly abysmal because he peaked in the fifties, an unglorious decade for field goal percentages and scoring. Of the 66 players who played at least 300 games from 1951 to 1960, Ken Sears led everyone (45 percent), Freddie Scolari brought up the bottom (33 percent) and Cousy ranked forty-second (37 percent). Stretch that to a 500-game minimum and twenty-two players qualify: Neil Johnston leads the way (44 percent), Jack McMahon brings up the rear (34 percent) and Cousy ranks fifteenth (just three spots behind alleged deadeye Dolph Schayes). Comparing him to his point guard rivals from 1951 to 1963 (400-game minimum), Gene Shue shot 39.9 percent, Dick McGuire shot 39.6 percent, Bobby Wanzer shot 39.2 percent, Cousy shot 37 percent, Andy Phillip shot 36.8 percent, Slater Martin shot 36.5 percent . . . and Cousy's teams consistently averaged more shots and points than anyone else.[26] Fast-forward to the high-scoring eighties: of the 124 players who played 500 games or more from 1981 to 1990, Artis Gilmore led the way at 63 percent, Elston Turner brought up the back at 43 percent and Isiah Thomas ranked 105th (46 percent). If you narrow the list to point guards (twenty-three in all), Mo Cheeks ranks first (53 percent), Darnell Valentine ranks last (43 percent) and Isiah ranks fifteenth. In other words, Isiah was actually a *worse* shooter for his era than Cousy. J-Kidd sucked more than both of them combined, the seventh-worst shooter from 1995 to 2008 of anyone who played 500 games or more (40 percent). While we're on the subject, Baron Davis (41 percent career), Kenny Anderson (42 percent), Iverson (42.6 percent) and Tim Hardaway (43 percent) were poorer shooters for their respective eras. So you can't penalize the Cooz for peaking during a quantity-over-quality era of shot selection.

26. Cooz had a phenomenal French/New York accent. He couldn't pronounce *R*, but that didn't stop him from announcing Celtics games for two solid decades, leading to him calling Rodney Rogers "Wodd-ney" in 2002. When they acquired Bryant Stith in the mid-nineties, we just assumed Cooz would grunt his name like a deaf-mute. He settled on "Bwwwy-unn."

2. You know how everyone makes a fuss about that stupid Tiny Archibald record? Cousy finished second in points and first in assists in '54 and '55; unlike Tiny's Royals, the Celtics made the playoffs both times. He cracked the top four in scoring four straight times ('52–'55), finished in the top ten in scoring four other times, never finished lower than third in assists in thirteen seasons and won eight straight assist titles. Let's say we assigned points for every top ten finish in scoring or assists per game—10 points for first place, 9 for second and so on, with 0 points for anything outside the top ten—then tallied up the combined points for each player's career.[27] Here's how the top point guards of all-time finish with that scoring system: Oscar, 181; Cousy, 164; Stockton, 139; West, 102;[28] Kidd, 96; Magic, 94; Wilkens, 89; Tiny, 87; Isiah, 64; Payton, 51. Just for kicks, a second list with the same scoring system, only first-team All-NBAs are worth 10 and second-team All-NBAs worth 5: Oscar, 281; Cousy, 274; West, 212; Magic, 189; Stockton, 189; Kidd, 151; Tiny, 127; Isiah, 104; Payton, 96; Wilkens, 89.

I hate the phrase "devil's advocate" because it makes me think of that excruciating Keanu Reeves/Al Pacino movie that couldn't even get the Charlize Theron nude scene right, but screw it: can you think of a valid reason why West (one title) and Oscar (one title) have endured historically as all-timers, but everyone has been so anxious to dump Cousy (six titles)? You can't play the "he couldn't have hacked it once the game sped up" card (like we used with Mikan earlier) because Cooz and Bob Pettit were the only NBA superstars who thrived pre-Russell and post-Russell. (If anything, Cooz was better off in a run-and-gun era—he led the league in assists as late as 1959 and 1960 and made second-team All-NBA in the final two years of his career.) You can't play the "he couldn't shoot" card because that's untrue. You can't play the "Russell made his career" card because he was better statistically pre-Russell and made just as many All-NBA teams without him. As recently as 1980, Cousy made the NBA's 35th Anniversary twelve-man team. So what happened?

27. To clarify, when Cousy finished first in assists and second in scoring in '55, he'd get 10 points for assists and 9 points for scoring for a total of 19.
28. I know, I know . . . West wasn't a true point guard. But he handled the ball for L.A. during the second half of his career and even led the NBA in assists in '72. So there.

3. Cousy got screwed historically by his first four years (the pre-shot-clock era, when nobody scored more than 75–85 points a game) and the last five years (when they started counting assists differently). Cousy averaged 8.9 assists for a '59 Celtics team that averaged 116.4 points per game; John Stockton averaged 12.4 assists for a '94 Jazz team that averaged 101.9 points per game. How am I supposed to make sense of that?[29] How do we know Cousy wasn't averaging 15–16 assists per game if we applied the current criteria? By all accounts, nobody ran a better fast break and the stats reflect it: eight straight titles and four times where he finished with at least 30 percent more dimes than the number two guy. Cousy finished his career in 1963 with 6,945 assists; the next-highest guy (Dick McGuire) had 4,205. So it's not like he was a little bit better than his peers, or a tad better, or even just better. He was *significantly* better.

4. Like fellow pioneers Erving, Russell and Baylor, Cousy deserves credit for pushing basketball in a more entertaining, fan-friendly direction. Here's how *SI*'s Herbert Warren Wind[30] described his impact in January '56:

Cousy is regarded by most experts as nothing less than the greatest all-round player in the 64-year history of basketball. . . . In recent years, when the game was coming very close to developing into a race-horse shooting match between men who had developed unstoppable shots and who could do very little else, Bob Cousy, above and beyond anyone else, has blazed the trail back to good basketball. Cousy has, in truth, gone much further: he has opened the road to better basketball. Perhaps no player or coach in the game's history has understood the true breath of basketball as well as he. He has shown, in what has amounted to an enlightened revolution, that basketball offers a hundred and one possibilities of maneuvers no one ever dreamed of before. Reversing your dribble or passing behind your back and so on—those stunts had been done for

29. Tommy Heinsohn claimed in Elliott Kalb's book that assists only counted in the fifties if you passed to someone without dribbling. In other words, none of Cousy's fast-break passes counted as assists. Could this be true? Again, it's hard to trust someone who once compared Leon Powe to Moses Malone.

30. You had to like the fifties, when sportswriters had names like "Herbert Warren Wind." I wonder if I would have been "William John Simmons" back then. Kinda catchy.

years, but if you combine those moves with a sense of basketball, then you are going some place. Increase your repertoire of moves, and the man playing you, by guarding against one, gives you the opening you need to move into another. It is not unlike learning to speak a new language. The larger your vocabulary, the better you will speak it, as long as you are building on a sound foundation.

To repeat: Cousy opened the door for Magic, Nash, the ABA guys and everyone else. Until he started doing his thing in college and professionally, white players hadn't even considered the notion "Wait, while we're trying to win the game, what if we tried to entertain the fans as well?" And it's not like Cousy was playing like some reckless "and-1" tour scrub; every move had a purpose, every decision stayed true to the player he was. Watch Nash running the show now and that's what Cousy was like back then, only better. There's a reason he became the NBA's first iconic guard, the league's answer to Unitas, Mays and Mantle. People loved watching him. People loved playing with him. His teams usually won. What more do you want?[31] As then Knicks coach Joe Lapchick extolled, "I've seen Johnny Beckman, Nat Holman, that wonderful player Hank Luisetti, Bob Davies, George Mikan, the best of the big men—to name just a few. Bob Cousy, though, is the best I've ever seen. He does so many things. He's regularly one of the league's top five scorers. [He's] been a top leader in assists for the last five seasons. He's become a very capable defensive player, a tremendous pass stealer. He always shows you something new, something you've never seen before. Any mistake against him and you pay the full price. One step and he's past the defense. He's quick, he's smart, he's tireless, he has spirit, and he is probably the best finisher in sports today."

That just about covers it. And if you're worried about his ability in the clutch, check out those six rings, or his famous 50-point playoff game against Syracuse (25-for-25 from the line). The Cooz did everything. Beyond the statistics and testimonials, Cousy deserves credit for forming the Players Association and empathizing with blacks during an era when few

31. Grumpy Old Editor wholeheartedly disagrees: "Granted, Cousy is a good guy and an innovator for an all-white league. But unlike Russell and even Sharman, his game does not survive beyond the sixties. And the idea of him as a pioneer when *Black Magic* screams otherwise is a joke. If he played in New York, you would have buried him." I am firing him soon.

whites stuck up for them. My second-favorite Cousy moment happened when he broke down during Bill Russell's *SportsCentury* documentary, despondent that he didn't fully realize how much Russell was suffering at the time. It was the most emotional moment in ESPN history that didn't involve Jim Valvano or Chris Connelly, and if you don't think it gets a little dusty in the Sports Guy Mansion every time it comes on, you're crazy. Of course, that doesn't top the all-time greatest Cousy moment: when he filmed the free throw shooting scene in *Blue Chips* with Nick Nolte and made twenty-one in a row for the take they ended up using . . . even though he was sixty-five at the time.[32] Now that, my friends, is a Level Four guy. Let's see John Stockton top that feat with a 75-person movie crew silently watching in 2025.

20. LEBRON JAMES

Resume: 7 years, 7 quality, 6 All-Stars . . . '09 MVP, '10 MVP . . . '04 Rookie of the Year . . . All-Star MVP ('06, '08) . . . top 5 ('06, '08, '09, '10), top 10 ('05, '07) . . . All-Defense (2x) . . . 3-year peak: 29–8–8, 49% FG . . . '09 Playoffs: 35–9–7, 51% FG (14 G) . . . leader: scoring (1x), minutes (2x), FT (1x) . . . best player on runner-up ('07 Cavs) . . . youngest to reach 10,000 points (age 23) . . . career: 27.8 PPG (3rd), 7.0 APG (26th) . . . Playoffs: 29–8–7 (71 G)

Game 5, 2010 playoffs, Celtics-Cavaliers. Or as it's better known, the Night Professional Basketball Was Assassinated in Cleveland. No specific moment stands out, just the image of an uncharacteristically subdued LeBron drifting through a 25-point blowout, looking like his face had been injected with Karl Malone Big Game Botox. More than any specific play, I remember what Charles Barkley said in TNT's postgame show. Former great players *want* new guys to be great. It's like an exclusive club: you can't let just anyone in, and they might have to fight their way past the bouncer, but once they get there, the legends are delighted to see them.

---

32. Cooz played an athletic director named Vic. I hate to nitpick here, but couldn't they have gone with Bob Kiley or Bill Corsey there? How did they settle on "Vic"? Do you think Vic ever tried to recruit Rumeal Smith? That was an inside joke for the three people who have been reading every footnote so far.

Congratulations. Have a seat. Would you like one of MJ's cigars? Can Russell mix you a drink? We're glad you're made it. LeBron seemed like a lock for the Legends Club. Right until he coasted through Game 5. Barkley's face captured the moment better than any highlight: he looked crestfallen. Like he just found out someone died.

"I gotta tell you something," he said to Ernie Johnson. "As a fan—and I've said all year that LeBron James was the best basketball player in the world—but I'm 100 percent disappointed. Not the fact that he didn't have a good game, he clearly didn't have a good game. But his mentality . . . I go back, I played against a Michael Jordan, a Karl Malone, a Patrick Ewing, listen, their gun was gonna be empty by the end of the game. And I did not see that tonight. . . . This was clearly the biggest game of the season. I did not see the aggression that I needed from an MVP at home."

Exactly. It was . . . dumbfounding. And so we found ourselves frantically rewriting the Book of LBJ yet again. During his rookie season in 2004, I predicted LeBron would average a triple-double for the season "comfortably" and projected a "33–12–13 every night." Trapped on his second straight lousy team in 2005 (LeBron led them to the playoffs, anyway), I compared his situation to an early Tom Hanks movie, where you spend most of the time feeling sorry that he's not in something better.[33] I did some nitpicking in 2006 and 2007, worrying about LeBron's self-proclaimed desire to become a "global icon" and writing that "the erosion of LeBron's passing skills is the biggest tragedy of the past few years other than Lindsay Lohan losing her boobs." He won me and everyone else back during the 2007 playoffs, getting swept in the Finals, but not before sub-

---

33. I like the Hanks analogy for LeBron. *Bosom Buddies* was high school. *Splash* and *Bachelor Party* were LeBron's rookie season (when he put himself on the map). Hanks' 1985–88 stage (*The Money Pit, Volunteers, Nothing in Common,* etc.) was LeBron's "I feel bad he's not in something better" stage. *Big* was definitely Game 5 vs. the 2007 Pistons: the official arrival of a major talent. *Punchline* was the '07 Finals sweep. *The 'burbs* was a good performance in a forgettable movie/'08 season. *Turner and Hooch* was his '09 MVP season (statistically incredible, no help). *The Bonfire of the Vanities* was the '09 playoff flameout (when LeBron fell victim to a bad matchup). *A League of Their Own* was his '10 MVP season (another virtuoso performance, a little more help), and *Sleepless in Seattle* was the '10 playoff mail-in/flameout (the one that made us wonder, "Wait a second, he could be the defining star of his generation, is he going to fucking blow this and just make chick flicks?"). So will Miami yield a *Philadelphia/Forrest Gump/Apollo 13/Toy Story* run? Or did I just severely overthink this? (Thinking.) You're right. . . . I severely overthought it. Sorry.

mitting an ESPN Classic performance in Game 5 at Detroit: scoring twenty-nine of Cleveland's last thirty points, overpowering the Pistons and hushing their fans like nobody since Jordan. Along with so many other sports junkies, I watch thousands of hours of games every year hoping something special will happen, whether it's a sixty-point game, a no-hitter, a seven-run comeback, a back-and-forth NFL game, a boxing pay-per-view or whatever else. Occasionally, it pays off. Maybe there are degrees of the word, but still, every time we click on a game or attend one, deep down, we're hoping something special happens. That night was special. Watching King James finally earn his nickname made me feel like my basketball life was being irrevocably altered. *Hold onto your seats, everybody. . . . It's happening! LeBron James is making the leap!*[34]

By the 2008 All-Star Game, LeBron had evolved into a surreal cross between ABA Doc (his transition game), '92 Pippen (his dominant athleticism on both ends) and Bo Jackson (his ability to overpower opponents), with a dash of Jordan's competitiveness and Magic's unselfishness thrown in . . . only if that Molotov NBA Superstar cocktail was mixed together in Karl Malone's 275-pound body. Only twenty-three years old, he didn't have a reliable twenty-footer or post-up game—and still threw up thirty a night, easy. Had you told me, "Starting next season, this man-child will win back-to-back MVP trophies so convincingly that you'll write his 2010 MVP campaign was the most dominating since Shaq in 2000" (which happened), I would have believed it. I would have believed anything. Especially LeBron becoming the league's first you-gotta-see-him-live-once ticket since Jordan. Fans arrived early at every road game (as they had for MJ once upon a time), just to watch LeBron prance around, soar for alley-oops over incredulous teammates, lob one-handed half-court shots, jump playfully on Shaq's back, giggle at everyone's jokes and carry on like some supercoordinated, mutant four-year-old dealing with a severe sugar rush.[35]

---

34. In retrospect, that game may have been the worst thing that ever happened to LeBron. It made everyone believe that he was the next Jordan when, really, he may have been more of a Magic-Pippen-Doc hybrid and that one scoring explosion was a total aberration.

35. During his annual Clippers visit in 2010, I asked a longtime season ticket holder named Lenny if he was getting MJ flashbacks from all the flashing lightbulbs and screaming. "Oh, definitely," he said. "That was the only other guy who caused . . . *this.*"

He always gave them at least two highlights: usually his Nitrous Cannister Coast-to-Coast Dunk (as patented by Doctor J, in which LeBron swipes a pass, flicks his nitrous switch, kicks into fifth gear, needs just four strides to go from midcourt to the rim and rips home a dunk, and as he's doing it, the court briefly shrinks in size) and his Smoke Monster Block (when he comes flying out of nowhere for a hellacious weak side block, causing the opponent to briefly react like they just got attacked by the Smoke Monster in *Lost*). He always left them feeling like they had gotten their money's worth, like they could tell someone some day, "Yeah, I saw Le-Bron James play."

My friend Hirschy[36] believed that LeBron's greatest highlight hadn't happened yet—like a follow-up dunk that he grabbed from behind the backboard or something—and once we saw it, our lives would be altered irrevocably. These are the things you imagine when seeing a six-foot-nine, 280-pound behemoth who might have been created in a laboratory by scientists during the Reagan administration. The Greatest Highlight Ever was always in play. You never left for food or drinks unless LeBron took a breather. Of course, it was about more than highlights. Night after night after night, LeBron cranked out thirty points, eight rebounds and seven assists, made half of his shots, made 80 percent of his free throws and played superior defense, all while carrying glorified role players and an overmatched coaching staff that couldn't offer much more than "Hey, guys, get out of his way." He vacillated between MJ Mode and Magic Mode effortlessly, as if swinging from "Okay, they're guarding me with one guy, I'll score at will" to "Okay, they're doubling me, I'll create good shots for everyone else" was a simple flick of a switch. And he was the most galvanizing superstar teammate since Magic. His last two Cleveland teams orchestrated goofy pregame intros, traded countless chest bumps, farted on one another on the bench, hung out on road trips and supported each other in every way. LeBron's

---

36. That was Paul Hirschheimer, longtime NBA Entertainment honcho and die-hard Knicks fan, as well as someone who took a sincere interest in this book, hooked me up with countless game tapes and demanded that Bernard crack the top-60 as his only payment. Done and done. Although Bernard would have made it anyway (I love 'Nard), and G.O.E. points out that he would have "destroyed the manuscript" if I didn't. So there's that, too.

in-traffic dunks (and he unleashed them more frequently than anyone since Dominique) always resonated more whenever he joyously sought out his bench for feedback. Few players in history had more fun playing basketball than LeBron James during that 2009–10 season. That February, I worried that everything came too easy to him, that for true greatness to manifest itself "you need to lose a few times, need to lick your wounds and taste your own blood, need to sit in silence in the locker room of another lost season wondering what went wrong, and then you need to say, 'Never again, not ever, I am *not* letting this happen again.' Given how easy basketball comes to him right now, given how many people probably kiss his rear end on a day-to-day basis, given how much he enjoys playing and being part of a team, I just don't think LeBron James has hit that point yet."

Fast-forward to the last two games of the Boston series, when LeBron hit that aforementioned point like the iceberg struck the *Titanic*.[37] Suddenly the Jordan comparisons seemed silly. Jordan never would have coasted through Game 5 or allowed his team to quit in the final 90 seconds of Game 6. Winning meant so much to Jordan (and Bird, and Magic, and Russell) that his teammates didn't have a choice; they either followed his lead or else. LeBron apparently wasn't wired like that. Which made me wonder if—after seven seasons, 548 regular-season games and 71 playoff games—LeBron had finally reached his unreachable ceiling. Maybe he was just a gregarious, larger-than-life, supremely gifted basketball player who was better at making us say *"Wow!"* than anything else. If his genetic makeup included that cutthroat Jordan chromosome, or Magic's leadership chromosome, it would have surfaced by 2010. What if he was just Evolutionary Doctor J?[38] By the time Philly blew the 1982 Finals, before Moses showed up and propelled Philly to a title, the consensus on Doc was this: phenomenal player, loved by all, basketball ambassador, one of the best ever . . . doesn't quite have *it*. Even when Philly won the 1983 title, everyone considered that to

37. I tweeted that night, "The 'Kobe is better than LeBron' demo reacted to Game 5 like Don Shula's house after the Tyree Catch."
38. FYI: That's not a bad thing—we haven't even reached Doc on the Pyramid yet.

be Moses' team. Will we feel that way about Wade's Miami teams in 2011 or 2012 if they win? Was LeBron better than just being Doc 2.0 all along, only we never fully appreciated how bad his Cleveland teams were?[39] Or was there something else going on here?

Between Games 5 and 6 of the 2010 Boston series, an Austin, Texas, reader named Chris Rider sent me a fascinating hypothesis: He thought you could define what was most important to every basketball star in one word. For Jordan, Chris believed it was winning. ("Hands down, all he wanted to do was win. And that's overused for a lot of athletes, but not him.")[40] For Kobe, it was "greatness." ("Yes, he's going to win some, but only because he wants to be considered great and that will be a by-product at times. But you'd also see him shoot his team out of a game; jack 3s when he should press the issue and get to the paint. He didn't mind losing a few games if people came away saying, 'Kobe is great; look what happens when he doesn't shoot.' ") And for LeBron, it was "amaze." ("I think he just really wants to amaze people. Which is why he spends ten minutes before the game throwing underhand half-court shots. Why he celebrates amazing dunks and blocks, but isn't working just as hard to win. I know the Cavs aren't great without him, but he's got *plenty* on that team to win rings with.") Was that totally fair? Probably not. But for fun, let's extend Chris' game.

Russell, Magic and Bird: Championships
Duncan, West and Havlicek: Winning
Walton: Teamwork
Wilt: Numbers
Oscar and Barry: Perfection
Shaq: Fame
Kareem and Elgin: Pride
Malone and Garnett: Work
Barkley: Fun

39. Don't rule this out. LeBron never played with a true All-Star, only a peculiar blend of specialized role players, discount guys, unpolished young guys, washed-up veterans, misguided free agent signings and bargain pickups from teams cutting payroll. His best teammates from 2004–2010: Mo Williams, Larry Hughes, Ricky Davis, Antwan Jamison, Anderson Varejao and a washed-up Shaq. He emulated Jordan's first seven years without a Pippen or a Grant.
40. I actually disagree with this. The word for Jordan was "vanquish."

Cousy, Stockton, Isiah, Pippen and Nash: Team
Doc and LeBron: Amaze

Chris was right: in Cleveland, LeBron wanted to amaze over anything else. Once he finally tired of carrying lesser players and sought help, he announced his decision during a callously hateful free agency special on ESPN, just two days after his Twitter account opened, a few days before his website and management company launched, and a few weeks before he started filming his first sports movie.[41] You could say The Decision amazed, that's for sure.[42] Throughout the summer, its stench lingered like a decomposing body trapped in a hot attic. In the span of sixty minutes, LeBron blindsided Cleveland as viciously as any athlete ever did; turned the country against him without doing drugs, saying something offensive, committing a crime or doing something sexually inappropriate; came off like a giant pussy for wanting to join forces with Wade over wanting to beat him (something Jordan never, ever, *ever* would have done); angered everyone in the Legends Club (none of whom could believe Wade and Jordan wanted to be each other's Robin over being Batman on their own teams); created a phrase that quickly became a euphemism for leaving a job, jerking off or taking a dump ("I'm taking my talents to South Beach"); dejuvenated Jim Gray's career (which wasn't even juvenated to begin with); nearly blew up the Internet and sports radio; and sparked two months of intense psychoanalysis in which writers wondered if Le-Bron played it so stupidly because (a) he was a child star who had too much success too soon (like Britney Spears), (b) he lacked a father figure (or any wise person in his life who would have said, "Wait, you can't do it this way"), (c) he wanted to re-create what he had in high school (when he and four close buddies picked the same prep school and thrived to-gether), (d) he lacked killer instinct (and knew he needed Wade, or some-one like him), (e) he fled because former teammate Delonte West had an

41. LeBron spent much of the previous summer promoting a documentary *(More Than a Game)* and a related book *(Shooting Stars)* about his high school team. Both forget-table.
42. Six biggest NBA moments that didn't happen during a game: (1) Magic/HIV; (2) Bias; (3) '64 All-Stars refusing to play without a labor agreement; (4) The Decision; (5) MJ announcing "I'm back"; and (6) Kathryn Faber settling with Kobe over going to trial. Although if the next footnote is true . . . that cracks the top-5.

affair with his mother (a nasty Internet rumor that gained legs as the summer went along)[43], and/or (f) he wanted to avoid state taxes, hang out with pals, live in South Beach and cavort with models.

Of course, Kobe spent the summer of 2010 like he always did: killing himself in workouts and figuring out ways to stave off Father Time. LeBron? Heading into his first Miami season, he still lacks a fallaway jumper, spin move or effective jump hook (a shame because his passing would make him a beast from the low post). It's not that his priorities were out of whack, just that he had too many . . . or maybe that he wasn't cut out for this in the first place. After his final Cleveland game, I wrote that LeBron faced one of the greatest sports decisions ever: "winning (Chicago), loyalty (Cleveland) or a chance at immortality (New York)." I never thought he would pick "Help!!!!!!" There's a chance LeBron was miscast all along, that God intended him to be Magic 2.0—an unselfish facilitator, the ultimate teammate, a walking triple double every night, someone capable of playing four positions and filling in any blank, someone just as happy setting up the game-winning shot as making it—and those seven Cleveland seasons pushed him in a direction that he never wanted. There's a chance The Decision was really about embracing The Secret: someone sacrificing individual glory because Miami gave him the best chance to win, and because nobody knows how to push that button better than Pat Riley. There's a chance I will feel differently about this five years from now.

But today? August 2010? I feel like LeBron James copped out. In pickup basketball, there's an unwritten rule to keep teams relatively equal to max-

---

43. Whether the West rumor is true or untrue (and I know a number of connected NBA people who believe it's true), the way Cleveland unraveled in Round 2 gave it extra life. As the story goes, LeBron found out after Game 3—in which the Cavs blew out Boston by 29—and blamed his teammates for not alerting him sooner. Delonte played 87 minutes in the first three games (10 for 17 FG); then 20 minutes in Game 4 (0 for 7 FG), 9 minutes in Game 5 (2 points) and 14 minutes in Game 6 (0 for 2 FG), all Cleveland losses. So after Game 3, Delonte fell apart and *something* happened to LeBron. My take: either the rumor was true, or the rumor was untrue but still submarined the team just with its potency (and everyone scurrying around trying to squash it). Just don't tell me *nothing* happened. For an extraordinarily close team that such made a big deal about being an extraordinarily close team for two years, you didn't find it strange that LeBron avoided mentioning a single teammate during The Decision or afterward? It was like he couldn't wait to get away from them.

imize competitiveness of the games. If two players are noticeably better than the rest and have any pride at all—especially if they play similar positions—then beating each other trumps any other scenario. *They want that test.* Otherwise, what's the point? If two alpha dogs land on the same team by coincidence—like Kareem and Magic, or Shaq and Kobe—that's one thing. That's sports. Shit happens. But two perimeter players willingly deciding that it would be easier to join forces than compete against each other? There's no "secret" to that. When I handed in my hardcover manuscript, I thought LeBron might surpass Jordan and Russell for the top pyramid spot some day. He took himself out of the running within twelve months. Then again, we're the ones who wanted it for him. Maybe *he* never wanted it. The most telling moment was the decision itself, when LeBron said, "I've decided to take my talents to South Beach." Not the Miami Heat, or even Miami itself. South Beach. A place that, as far as I can tell, doesn't have a basketball arena. A place where stars can act like stars, where life is easy, where the sun is always shining, where appearance matters more than anything else, where gorgeous women practically get churned off an assembly line.[44] It's beautiful there, and easy. If you're looking for Bizarro Cleveland, look no further than South Beach.

That was the choice LeBron James made in the end: not Miami, not the Heat, but South Beach. That's what he said. As someone who was twenty-five once, I can't blame him. As someone who loves basketball, I can't forgive him.[45]

44. One day after The Decision, a Detroit reader named Justin e-mailed me, "The generational shift in the NBA: Jordan = John McClane. Kobe = Maximus. LBJ = Vincent Chase."

45. LeBron's hardcover ranking (no. 20) didn't budge despite him winning a second MVP and having his best all-around regular season. (As House put it, "It's the only sensible treatment for a superstar who voluntarily accepted a ceiling on his greatness.") If LeBron averages a triple double and leads Miami to 70+ wins and a title? It's budging. He'd leapfrog the next four guys. At least.

19. CHARLES BARKLEY

Resume: 16 years, 12 quality, 11 All-Stars . . . '93 MVP . . . '90 runner-up . . . Top 5 ('88, '89, '90, '91, '93), Top 10 ('86, '87, '92, '94, '95), Top 15 ('96) . . . season leader: rebounds (1x) . . . 3-year peak: 26–13–4 . . . best player on runner-up ('93 Suns), 27–14–4 (24 G) . . . '90 Playoffs: 25–16–4 (10 G) . . . '94 Playoffs: 28–13–5 (10 G) . . . member of '92 Dream Team . . . career: 22.1 PPG, 11.7 RPG, 54% FG . . . Playoffs: 23.0 PPG, 12.9 RPG, 51.3 FG (123 G) . . . 20K–10K Club

18. KARL MALONE

Resume: 19 years, 17 quality, 14 All-Stars . . . MVP: '97, '99 . . . '98 runner-up . . . Top 5 ('89, '90, '91, '92, '93, '94, '95, '96, '97, '98, '99), Top 10 ('88, '00), Top 15 ('01) . . . All-Defense (3x) . . . 2 All-Star MVP's . . . 3-year peak: 30–11–2 . . . career: 25–10, 52% FG, 74% FT . . . Playoffs: 25–10, 46% FG (193 G) . . . best player on 2 runner-ups ('97, '98 Jazz) . . . member of '92 Dream Team . . . career: FTs and FTAs (1st); points (2nd); rebounds (6th); games (4th); minutes (2nd), 25.0 PPG (10th), 10.1 RPG, 52% FG . . . 35K–14K Club (one of two members)

Put it this way: You'd think less of me if I *didn't* do a Dr. Jack Breakdown of Barkley and Malone, right? We can't have that. Without further ado . . .

Nickname. Charles went by "The Round Mound of Rebound," "Sir Charles," "Chuck Wagon" . . . he had nearly as many nicknames as Apollo Creed. None of them stuck. For some reason, it feels like "Chuck" (the name everyone endearingly calls him now) counts as a nickname, but that's really just a proper name. Meanwhile, Malone had "the Mailman," a clever alias that took on a second life in the '97 and '98 playoffs when shit-stirring columnists like myself started calling him "Mail Fraud." *Edge: Malone.*

Durability. Barkley missed 121 games from '91 to '99 and only played six 79-plus game seasons. Malone had ten 82-game seasons and seven 90-

plus game seasons (including playoffs) and missed 10 games total in his eighteen Utah seasons. Guess which guy was the workout fanatic and which guy consumed fried foods, drank tons of beer and bled gravy. *Edge: Malone.*

Bad luck. Barkley made the Eastern Finals as a rookie before Toney's feet crumbled, Doc started fading and Moses' rear end expanded. Still, Philly didn't have to completely panic—they screwed Chuck by trading the number one pick in the '86 draft for Roy Hinson and $750,000 (why not just take Brad Daugherty?), then dealing Moses for Jeff Ruland and Clifford Robinson in one of the five worst trades of the eighties that didn't involve Ted Stepien. That meant poor Chuck had to carry a series of uninspiring Philly teams before cannibalizing them and forcing the Phoenix trade. Barkley had good teammates for the remainder of his career, but he was thirty by that time and his cholesterol level was already at 522. As for Malone, his buddy Stockton took care of him for nearly two full decades and gave him a wingman for roughly 700,000 high screens. Something tells me Barkley would love to go back in time to 1984 and switch places with him.[46] *Edge: Barkley.*

Draft-day outfit. Barkley wore a double-breasted maroonish purple sportscoat with a matching tie that made him look like an eighties movie usher or a security guard at a casino that's going out of business. Malone wore a silver-blue sports coat with a blue shirt, cream-colored pants and a pink tie that only went down to his navel. I'll put it this way: Barkley's outfit was funny, but Malone's outfit makes me laugh out loud even twenty-six years later. No contest. *Edge: Malone.*[47]

Ability to finish in transition. Everyone was afraid to take a charge from Malone, a brilliant finisher who was built like a defensive end and always

46. On second thought, Barkley and Salt Lake would have been like Kurt Cobain and Courtney Love: just a deadly, horrifying match in every respect.
47. The NBA should throw a charity dinner where every NBA star has to show up wearing the same outfit that they wore on draft day. They could make tickets ten grand and I'd be willing to pay twenty just to be in the room. "Hakeem, I love your 1984 prom tuxedo! Looks terrific!"

led with his right knee (with the message being "This is going right into your nuts if you stand in front of me"). But you know what? He couldn't top Barkley in those early Philly years, when Chuck was a frightening blend of power and finesse and even *he* couldn't harness it. He ate up Bird's best teams because they lacked athletes who could handle him in transition, especially when he grabbed a rebound and took off on one of those rollicking full-court forays that usually ended up with him throwing a two-handed tomahawk in DJ's mug as the Spectrum erupted. That's his legacy, at least for me. Wake me up when we see someone under six-foot-five do a better impression of a runaway train. Nobody ever caused more players to cower for their lives than Barkley; if they kept stats for something this dumb, I'd bet anything that nobody tried to take a charge from Chuck from 1984 through 1991. It never happened. *Edge: Barkley.*

Most distinct strength. Moses was the best offensive rebounder of my lifetime; Barkley was second.[48] From '87 through '90, Chuck averaged nearly *five* offensive rebounds a game. He grabbed 510 offensive rebounds in 123 playoff games. He holds the NBA record for most offensive rebounds in a half (13) and quarter (11). Did I mention that the guy was six-foot-four-and-a-half? When will we ever see anything like that again? As for Malone, he mastered the screener's role in the high screen better than anyone ever. How much of that success hinged on the familiarity of playing with Stockton? A shitload. But that became one of the deadlier plays in NBA history . . . you know, as long as it wasn't happening with 2 minutes left in a huge game. *Edge: Malone.*

Defining game. For Barkley, it has to be the 56-point ass-kicking against G-State in the '94 playoffs right after C-Webb's shoe commercial came out and included a clip of Webber dunking on Barkley. That's one of my ten favorite "Hardwood Classics" games and a virtuoso evisceration of epic proportions. For Malone, unfortunately, it's Game 1 of the '97

48. In '86, Chuck and Moses finished 2nd and 3rd in offensive rebounds. After getting split up, Chuck finished 1st and Moses 4th in '87; they finished 1–2 in '88 and '89; then Moses 1st and Barkley 2nd in '90. Why did Philly break up a historic rebounding combo? Because an abnormal number of NBA executives are fucking idiots! I keep telling you.

Finals—right after he had been handed the MVP Award, when he choked on two go-ahead free throws in the last 20 seconds and Jordan drained the game-winner. We never took the Mailman seriously as an MVP again. At least I didn't. *Edge: Barkley.*

Defining record. Either "15 field goals in one playoff half" or "most points scored within 90 minutes of finishing off 100 chicken wings at the Ground Round" for Barkley. I can't decide. For Malone, it's definitely his "most 2,000-point seasons (twelve)" record, which LeBron will be breaking in 2017. *Edge: Malone.*

Defining tough-guy story. Malone avenged Isiah's 44-point killing of Stockton with a vicious elbow that busted open Isiah's eyebrow and would have earned a thirty-five-game suspension had it happened today.[49] Barkley didn't just start a fight with Shaq (not a misprint), he fought the '90 Pistons in a brawl that spilled into the first two rows of the stands in Detroit and became the spiritual godfather of the Artest melee (with Chuck even taking a swing at a fan). If you got into a brawl, you wanted either guy on your side . . . but Chuck had a higher upside. *Edge: Barkley.*

Unintentional comedy. For whatever reason, both guys were wildly fun to imitate. My old boss Kimmel could spend fifteen solid minutes talking like Malone; all you do is deepen your voice, refer to yourself in the third person, talk in abrupt sentences in the present tense, add a slight southern accent and use a lot of double negatives.[50] For Barkley, just make him sound like Muhammad Ali circa 1973 after about four drinks, then have him repeat himself over and over again and start sentences with prepositions like "First of all . . ." and "Number one . . ." Frankly, I can't decide. So I left it up to Kimmel. His take? "Karl Malone love making up jokes. Karl

---

49. Malone and Stockton ranked right behind Laimbeer and Mahorn and just ahead of Ainge on the Top Five Dirtiest Guys of the MJ Era list. It's true. I know there's an eight-year-old Mormon kid crying right now and screaming, "Noooo! Noooooooooo!" But it's true. Scratch Salt Lake City off any book-signing tour for me.

50. For example: "Karl Malone don't like no HIV. Karl Malone don't want to worry about no blood hitting Karl Malone in the eye."

Malone always say, 'laughter is the best Mexican.' " Couldn't have said it better myself. *Edge: Malone.*

Defensive prowess. Malone got better as the years passed and started making All-Defense teams *after* the midway point of his career, even reinventing himself as a grizzled defense/picks/rebounding guy for the '04 Lakers: he did a fabulous job defending Tim Duncan in Round 2, holding him to just 17.5 points and 38 percent shooting in the last four games (all Laker wins). Then he injured a knee in the Minnesota series and crushed L.A.'s hopes for a title. Too bad. As for the shorter Barkley, his low-post defense ranged from consistently bad to legitimately atrocious, although he tallied a decent share of steals, blocks and momentum-swinging fast-break blocks. Barkley's kryptonite was any tall power forward with a polished low-post game (the McHale/Duncan types). That's when he moved into "crap, I'm just going to have to outscore you" mode. *Big edge: Malone.*

Acuity for handling male pattern baldness. Barkley shrewdly shaved his head; Malone kept going with the Ed Harris look, finally shaving his head during the late nineties (but not before doing some Rogaine ads first). *Edge: Barkley.*

Peak year. We're using that MVP season for Malone even though I've been pissing on it throughout the book: 64 wins, 27.4 points, 9.9 rebounds, 4.5 assists, 55% shooting and first-team All-D is nothing to sneeze at (even in a diluted league). For Barkley, we're going with that secretly incredible '90 season (page 256) when he tossed up a 25–12–4 on an uninspiring Philly team and dragged them to a division title,[51] shooting an ungodly 60 percent from the field even though he stupidly hoisted up 92 threes (making 20 of them). Do you realize that Barkley made 686 of 1,085 two-pointers that year? That's 64 percent! During one of the most competitive seasons in the history of the league no less. *Edge: Barkley.*

---

51. Would KG have won 53 games and a division title playing with Johnny Dawkins, Hersey Hawkins, Ron Anderson, a fairly washed-up Mike Gminski and a just-about-washed-up Rick Mahorn in an extremely competitive season? No way.

Crunch-time abilities. They both had fatal flaws: Malone routinely and famously shrank from the moment; Barkley thought he was better than he was. Always better off playing Tony Almeida than Jack Bauer, Chuck measured himself by Jordan and wanted to dominate close games like MJ did . . . and that's what usually ended up killing his teams in the end. Even if those 56-point Golden State explosions rarely happened, Chuck carried himself in crunch time like he had dozens of them bursting out of his pockets. Watch some of those playoff contests from '93 to '95: had Chuck shared the ball in crunch time instead of firing up dumb threes, trying to run fast breaks and doing the "I'm getting the ball, backing in and stopping our offense for 6 seconds while I decide what to do" routine, the Suns would have captured the title at least once. But he couldn't do it. He always wanted to be The Man even though he wasn't totally that player. And that's why he doesn't have a ring. I actually think you'd have a better chance of winning a hypothetical ring with Malone than Barkley—like Garnett, Malone always secretly knew his place. Barkley didn't.[52] *Edge: even.*

Fatal flaw. The deer-in-the-headlights routine in big games for Malone. Time and time again, he came up short when it mattered (Game 1 of the '97 Finals and Game 6 of the '98 Finals were the best examples), and it's impossible to forget NBC's Bill Walton just ripping him apart during that '97 Finals and repeatedly asking in a cracking voice, "What has happened to Karl Maloooooooone?" But you know what? I can forgive that. Plenty of great players didn't totally have "it" inside them. Here's what can't be forgiven: Barkley's refusal to stop partying or get into reasonable shape; his career should have been 15 percent better than it was.[53] When Pip-

---

52. The definitive Barkley stat: in 44 playoff games from '93 to '95, he hoisted up 124 threes and made just 33 (27 percent). That's an embarrassment. I would have fined him ten grand per three.

53. There's a famous story about Barkley hitting Manhattan the night before a Sunday afternoon game at MSG, subsequently stinking out the joint, then Danny Ainge waving his ring afterward and screaming, "That's why you'll never have one of these!" Only when Barkley's personal life began to fall apart recently (a $400,000 debt to a Vegas casino plus a DUI arrest) did the media start mentioning Barkley's drinking. Everyone loved him too much. Including me. I spent two days with him for a 2002 column and buried three phenomenal Barkley stories. I just liked the guy.

pen lobbed shots at Barkley's lack of conditioning after their unhappy '99 marriage, Ron Harper defended Scottie by saying, "Everybody knows Charles is a great guy, but every year he's talking about winning a championship, and then he comes to training camp out of shape. That shows what kind of guy he is. Pip wants to win. If you aren't doing what you should be doing, he's going to let you know." Ouch. Barkley got himself in shape for those first two Phoenix seasons and that's it.[54] Malone stayed in superb shape for two solid decades. *Major edge: Malone.*

Personality/charisma. Barkley wins over Malone and everyone else in league history. Who would have been a more fun teammate than Charles Barkley? He loved gambling, drinking, eating, and busting on everyone's balls. (Wait, that sounds like me!) As for Malone, he was fun to hang out with if you wanted to herd some cattle or needed a workout partner at 7:00 a.m. Um, I'll take Chuck. And you wonder why he never reached his potential. *Major edge: Barkley.*

Head to head. They only met twice in the playoffs: 1997 and 1998 (with Utah winning both times), but Barkley was injured in '98 and only played 4 games (87 minutes in all), while the tight '97 series was swung by the obscenely lopsided Stockton-Maloney matchup. In '97, Malone averaged 22 points and 11.5 rebounds and shot 45 percent (56 for 125); Barkley went for 17.2 points and 11.0 rebounds and shot 42 percent (27 for 63). Not exactly Hagler-Hearns. When they were playing for quality teams in their primes ('93 and '94), they met in the regular season seven times: the Suns won five, with Barkley averaging 23.4 points, 11.4 rebounds and 4.3 assists and Malone averaging 21.8 points, 8 rebounds and 3.4 assists. Edge to Barkley. And then there's this one: Heading into

54. Biggest help: spending the summer playing on the Dream Team and getting pushed by MJ. This also drove LeBron to new heights—working out with Kobe and Wade during the '08 Olympics and getting those "Shit, I still need to get better" juices flowing. Like the effect Stephon Marbury had on Carmelo Anthony in Athens, only the exact opposite.

the '92 Olympics, many thought the Dream Team would be Malone's breakthrough. Jack McCallum even wrote, "Many observers think that [Malone and Pippen] will benefit the most from the worldwide exposure, since both are extremely photogenic athletes who, as Malone puts it, 'haven't exactly been plastered all over everything.' " So what happened? Barkley emerged as the Dream Team's second-best player, number one power forward and breakout star. That has to count for *something*, right? Chuck blended in with great teammates better than Malone did, led the team in scoring and became its dominant personality. It's just a fact. By the end of the Olympics, *SI* was describing him as the "talk of the Olympic games," with McCallum gushing, "His astonishing range of abilities—outrebounding much taller players, running the floor like a guard and getting his shot off with either hand while bouncing off bodies around the basket—seem more pronounced when performed within the Dream Team galaxy."[55]

What happened to Malone? He sank into the shadows as a supporting player (like one of those *SNL* cast members who appears in the opening credits after the main cast with one of those "and featuring Karl Malone . . ." graphics), getting press only after he raised a fuss about competing against an HIV-positive Magic before the '93 season.[56] Then Barkley carried Phoenix to 62 wins and gave the Bulls everything they could handle in the '93 Finals. After the '93 season, the Barkley-Malone argument was dead; Barkley had won. After the '94 season? Still dead. Then Malone kept chugging along and chugging along, Barkley let himself go and things began to shift. Barkley's apex was definitely better, but not *so* much better that it outweighed Malone's longevity and consistency. Malone maximized the potential of his career; Barkley can't say the same. It's true. *Final edge: Malone (barely).*

55. This should have given Chuck the winnability edge over Malone, but his penchant for carousing and keeping teammates out for all hours made it a draw. MJ would have loved playing with Barkley, but he would have been more productive with Malone.

56. Are we sure Malone wasn't a giant a-hole? What about when Kobe accused him of hitting on his wife? Actually, that made me like the Mailman more. Go Karl! I never thought Karl allegedly telling Mrs. Kobe that he was "hunting little Mexican girls" got its just comedic due.

17. BOB PETTIT

Resume: 11 years, 10 quality, 11 All-Stars . . . MVP: '56, '59 . . . Runner-up: '57, '61 . . . Top 5 ('55–'64), Top 10 ('65) . . . '55 Rookie of the Year . . . 4 All-Star MVPs . . . 3-year peak: 28–18–3 . . . leader: scoring (2x), rebounds (1x) . . . career: 26.4 PPG (6th), 16.2 RPG (3rd) . . . Play-offs: 26–15–3 (88 G) . . . best player on one champ ('58 Hawks) and 3 runners-up ('57, '60, '61) . . . first member of 20K–10K Club

I'm asking for a little leap of faith, like when you watched *The Hangover* and never questioned how the boys could have done so many different things in Vegas during one ten-hour blackout.[57] Could Pettit hang with guys like Duncan and Bosh today? Probably not. Offensively, I think he'd be okay—a less athletic cross between Carlos Boozer and Paul Pierce. (Pettit had three go-to moves: a don't-leave-me-alone 18-footer, a leaning jumper coming off screens and a reliable turnaround that Bob Ryan once called "monotonous." He couldn't dunk unless a donut and coffee were involved. Tom Heinsohn once described Pettit's cagey offensive game by calling him "the master of the half-inch." Mrs. Pettit had no comment.) Defensively, you wouldn't be able to hide him. But everyone from that era describes Pettit the same way: *Relentless. Banger. Warrior. Hard-nosed.* Remember Boston's more physical playoff games when Bird couldn't get his outside shot going, so he'd switch gears and start banging bodies down low (eventually pulling down 18 boards and getting to the line 12 times)? That was Pettit. In 64 playoff games in his prime ('57 to '63), he averaged 28 points, 16 rebounds and a whopping 11.7 free throw attempts.[58] He also exhibited remarkable durability, playing 746 of a possible 754 games (including playoffs) without the help of chartered planes, arthroscopic surgeons, stretching routines and strength/conditioning coaches. And you can't play the "Pettit only

57. Grumpy Old Editor refused to make the leap: "Ranking Pettit this high is a joke. He'd be like every oversized white guy with post moves and cement feet who gets trampled in his first pro season. Think Kent Benson or Big Country Reeves." Yeah, but still.
58. If not for Hack-a-Shaq, Pettit would have averaged more FTs per game than anyone with 50-plus career playoff games (10.4). That's reason no. 345 to hate Hack-a-Shaq.

thrived because the black guys weren't around yet" card because nine of
Pettit's eleven seasons coincided with Russell, seven with Elgin, six with
Wilt, and five with Oscar and West, even capturing the '62 All-Star MVP
by scoring 25 points and notching a game-high 27 rebounds. Check out
these numbers from '59 to '64.

PLAYER	Gs	PPG	RPG	FG%	TEAM RECORD 1959–64
Pettit (Hawks)	457	28.4	17.4	44.7	269-197 (.577)
Wilt (Warriors)	391	33.2	25.2	50.6	223-171 (.566)
Russell (Celtics)	454	15.3	23.8	44.5	345-121 (.740)
Baylor (Lakers)	419	30.8	15.8	43.0	243-223 (.521)
Oscar (Royals)	309	30.2	10.7	48.7	173-146 (.542)
J. West (Lakers)	281	25.8	7.2	45.3	185-134 (.580)

Beyond that, Pettit and Wilt were the only two alpha dogs to topple
Russell's Celtics. Pettit avoided a Game 7 in Boston with a then-record
50 points, including 18 of St. Louis's last 21, as well as a jumper and a
clinching tip in the final 20 seconds to seal the 1958 title. So what if Russell was limping around in a cast and only played 20 minutes? That's still
one of the better performances in Finals history.[59] Pettit hasn't endured
historically partly because no tape exists of that game, and partly because he didn't have that one "thing" that kept him relevant along the
lines of Oscar averaging a triple double, Russell winning eleven titles in
thirteen years or even West becoming the NBA's logo. He just missed the
television era, didn't play in a big market and lacked an identifiably
transcendent skill like Bird's passing or Baylor's hang time. If you want
to dig deeper, his southern roots (as well as the damaging Cleo Hill incident) probably linger for many of the great black players from that era,
none of whom seem that interested in singing his praises these days.
(Russell battled Pettit in four separate NBA Finals and only mentioned

59. Did you know that the '58 Hawks were the last all-white team to win a title? I'm going
out on a limb and predicting that's holding true 100, 200, and 500 years from now.

him once in *Second Wind,* with a little dig about how Pettit traveled every time he made an offensive move and the refs never called.) But you know what really killed Pettit historically? His hair. He made Locke on *Lost* look like Michael Landon. You can't penalize him for that. You also can't penalize him for Russell's injury in the '58 Finals; only one year earlier, Boston needed a double-OT Game 7 in the Finals to defeat the Hawks. If he played today, Pettit would shave his head, grow a Fu Manchu, get a prominent tattoo, wax his body, and look like a fucking bad-ass. Back then, it was perfectly fine for the league's best power forward to look like he should be teaching eleventh-grade shop. You can't judge.

16. JULIUS ERVING

Resume: 16 years, 14 quality, 16 All-Stars (5 ABA) . . . '74, '75, '76 ABA MVP, '74, '76 Playoffs MVP . . . '81 NBA MVP . . . '80 runner-up . . . Top 5 NBA ('78, '80–'83), Top 10 NBA ('77, '84), Top 5 ABA ('73–'76), Top 10 ABA ('72) . . . two All-Star MVP's . . . ABA leader: scoring (3x) . . . 3-year NBA peak: 25–7–4 . . . best player on 2 ABA champs ('74, '76 Nets) and 3 runner-ups ('77, '80, '82 Sixers), 3rd-best player on NBA champ ('83 Sixers) . . . '76 Playoffs: 35–13–5 (13 G) . . . '80 Playoffs: 25–8–4 (18 G) . . . career ABA: 28.7 PPG (1st), 12.1 RPG (3rd) . . . career: points (5th), steals (13th) . . . 30K-10K Club

The case against Doc being ranked this high: Couldn't shoot a 15-footer . . . surprisingly subpar defender . . . too passive offensively . . . too nice a guy, not enough of a killer . . . more style than substance . . . unwittingly overrated by the national media because he was so gracious and well-spoken . . . put up his peak numbers in a ramshackle league where nobody played defense, then never approached those numbers after the merger . . . lost five straight playoff series in his NBA prime in which he barely outplayed Bob Gross (1977), got outplayed by Bob Dandridge ('78), played Larry Kenon to a draw ('79), played Jamaal Wilkes to a draw ('80) and got severely outplayed by Larry Bird ('81) . . . struggled enough with sore knees in the late seventies that *SI* ran a March '79 feature called "Hey, What's Up with the Doc?"[60] . . . never won an NBA ring until Moses saved him.

The case for Doc being ranked this high: One of the most ground-breaking, important and influential players ever . . . one of the most exciting players ever . . . ushered in the Wait a Second, This Dunking Thing Is Really Fun! Era, which eventually turned basketball into a billion-dollar business . . . single-handedly carried the failing ABA for three extra years . . . excelled at finishing fast breaks like nobody except for Barkley and LeBron . . . filled a crucial void in the seventies as "the only beloved black basketball player during a time when fans were turning against basketball because it was considered to be 'too black' " . . . probably the captain of the Articulate and Classy All-Time NBA team . . . along with Cousy, Russell, Wilt, Bird, Magic, Elgin, Mikan and Jordan, one of the nine most *important* NBA players ever . . . did I mention that he carried *The Fish That Saved Pittsburgh*?

(Quick tangent: *Fish* was the goofier bastard cousin of *Fast Break*. Doc played Moses Guthrie, the star of the Pittsburgh Pisces, who have their season turned around by a young waterboy and a wacky astrologist. Highlight no. 1: Doc's acting made Keanu Reeves look like Philip Seymour Hoffman. Highlight no. 2: Doc awkwardly takes a date to a playground at night, then does dunks for her with bad seventies music playing. Somehow this brings them closer together. Highlight no. 3: The basketball scenes are so poorly edited that in one scene, one of Doc's teammates (Driftwood) takes a jumper, then they cut to him standing under the basket as it goes in. Highlight no. 4: They play Kareem's Lakers in the climactic scene and *everyone* has a glazed "Instead of paying us in cash, can't they

---

60. If you were a seventies magazine editor and *didn't* use a "What's up, Doc?"–type headline for Doc, you lost your job. I'm almost positive. Here's Doc's former ABA coach Al Bianchi (from the same story): "Julie used to take off and really soar. And that's the sad part of seeing him now. The Doc can't fly no more." An unnamed NBA coach added, "I don't know if it's the big contract, plain disgust, concern about his longevity or just that he's burnt out and can't do it nightly anymore, but Dr. J is not the player we once knew. The electricity isn't there. The truth is that—except for a few playoff games in '77 and the all-star games—the guy has been on vacation for three years. Somebody else has been masquerading as no. 6. On a consistent basis Julius has played to about 40 percent, tops, of the ability he showed in the ABA."

pay us in coke?" look. Highlight no. 5: Kareem disappears for the entire fourth quarter for reasons that remain unclear. It's never mentioned or addressed. Phenomenal. I love this movie.)[P54]

Back to the "nine most important players ever" point: What happens to professional basketball without Julius Winfield Erving? Elgin and Russell turned a horizontal game into a vertical one, but Doc grabbed the torch, explored the limits of gravity and individual expression, ignited the playgrounds, delighted fans, inspired the likes of Thompson and Jordan and stamped his creative imprint on everything we're watching today. He's like Cousy in this respect; Cousy showed that you could entertain NBA fans while you tried to win and so did Doc. They just did it in different ways. Cousy modernized professional basketball; Doc colorized it, repossessed it, turned it into a black man's game. If he'd never showed up, would it have happened anyway? Yeah, probably. But it's like Apple with home computers, Bill James with baseball statistics, Lorne Michaels with sketch comedy . . . maybe the seeds for the revolution were in place, but somebody had to have the foresight to water those seeds and see what would happen. For basketball, that person ended up being Doc.

His glory years happened in the ABA, with little record of what happened because those teams could barely get fans to show up (much less land a local TV contract). Doc's eye-popping statistics overshadow the meat of the story: few professional athletes were ever described in such glowing, you-had-to-be-there-to-understand terms. It's like hearing William Goldman try to describe watching Brando in his prime on Broadway and ultimately failing, but in the process of failing, he was so passionate about it that the point was still made. Everyone in the ABA revered Doc. There was an implicit understanding that he was the league's meal ticket, the one player who could never be undercut, clotheslined, elbowed, or injured.[61] His open-court dunks had such a galvanizing effect

P54. I've heard two explanations: either filming ran late and Kareem had to leave, or Kareem thought he was getting paid more and walked off the set. I like the latter explanation because it's more ninny evidence for Kareem.

61. I'm dubious of Doc's ABA stats. This was already a league where nobody played D, only ABA opponents were about as physical with Doc as President Obama's cronies are with the prez during a White House basketball game. Could that help explain why he never found quite the same success in the NBA? I think so.

on crowds—not just home crowds, but away crowds—that Hubie Brown created a "no dunks for Doc" rule for Kentucky home games because any exciting Doc dunk turned the crowd against the Colonels. (Now that's a magical player—when you can sway opposing crowds to your side, you know you've accomplished something.) His foul line slam in the '76 Slam Dunk Contest remains one of the single most thrilling basketball moments that ever happened. It almost caused a fucking riot. And if you're wondering about Doc's ceiling as a basketball player, his five-game stretch in the '76 Finals ranks among the greatest ever submitted at any level: 45–12, 48–14, 31–10, 34–15, 31–19 with none other than Bobby Jones defending him.

So why didn't he reach similar heights in the NBA? Because the league was so much more talented and tumultuous—that postmerger stretch from '77 to '79 was a mess of transactions, drugs and contrasting styles.[62] Because coaching and defensive plans became more elaborate, with every quality team making Doc shoot 20-footers and fouling him on any potential dunk. Because Doc played the NBA's most stacked position (small forward) and dealt with a steady stream of Walter Davis, Bernard King, Dantley, Dandridge, Havlicek, Barry, Wilkes, Kenon, Bobby Jones, Bird, Dominique (note: this list keeps going and going) every night for the next decade. Because his knees were slightly shot from riding coach and playing on bad floors for five grueling ABA years. Because more and more players started doing the same superathletic things. It's not like he was a bust or anything—he led the Sixers to four Finals and a title, averaged a 30–7–5 in the '77 Finals, averaged a 26–7–5 in the '80 Finals, won the '81 MVP (debunked in the MVP chapter, but still), made five first-team All-NBAs, remained the league's biggest draw and submitted four iconic plays (the "Rock-a-baby" dunk over Michael Cooper in 1983, the tomahawk dunk over Walton in the '77 Finals, a vicious slam over Kareem in the '77 All-Star Game, and the swooping

62. Poor Doc played for one of the most selfish/overpaid teams ever assembled (the postmerger 76ers), shared the ball with me-first guys like McGinnis and Free and never played with a table-setter until Mo Cheeks in 1980. Doc was too nice to fight for shots. If he had a drawback, it was a legendary weakness for the ladies—he even knocked up a beat writer who covered Philly in the late seventies (fathering future tennis player Alexandra Stevenson with her). When they said Doc was the greatest interview in the league, they weren't kidding.

behind-the-basket finger roll over Kareem in the '80 Finals). Just the
NBA portion of his career easily propels him into the Hall of Fame. For
all-time purposes, the length of Doc's career also sets him apart: sixteen
seasons, all good/excellent/superior to varying degrees with remarkable
durability,[63] and even when he faded a little near the end, he never disgraced himself like so many others.

How do we translate Doc to modern times when his old-school style
couldn't totally succeed now? He couldn't post anyone up unless it was a
guard. He couldn't consistently drain 18-foot jumpers, much less threes.
During the '81 playoffs, Boston's Bill Fitch threw bigger forwards on him
(usually McHale or Maxwell), had them play five feet off, then angled him
toward the shot blockers in the middle (keeping him away from the baseline). For the most part, it worked. That was Doc's fatal flaw: he couldn't
totally make teams pay for playing off him. (When Jordan entered the
league, Doc's good friend Peter Vecsey was touting MJ's praises to an
unimpressed Erving and finally yelped, "Julius, you don't understand, he's
you with a jump shot!") As the years pass, I'm sure people will pick Doc's
resume apart with everything mentioned in the first paragraph, his star
will fade, and that will be that. All I can tell you is this: I was young, but I
was there. And Julius Erving remains one of the most gripping, terrifying,
and unforgettable players I have ever seen in person. If he was filling the
lane on a break, your blood raced. If he was charging toward a center and
cocking the ball above his head, your heart pounded. Over everything
else, I will remember his hands—his gigantic, freak-show, Freddy Krueger
fingers—and how he palmed basketballs like softballs. One signature Doc
play never got enough acclaim: the Sixers would clear out for him on the
left side, with Doc's defender playing five feet off and forcing him to the
middle as always, only every once in a while, Doc would take the bait,
dribble into the paint like he was setting up a baby hook or something . . . and then, before you could blink, he'd explode toward the rim,

63. In Doc's first 14 seasons, he played 1,277 of a possible 1,349 games (including *seven*
seasons of 95 games or more) without suffering a major injury. That's an average of 91.2
games per year! Considering his style of play—acrobatic, up-and-down, above the
rim—that's incredible, no? Or do we credit the Obama treatment for at least some of
that durability? Much like no pitcher wanted to be the dick who broke Cal Ripken's hand
and ended his streak, nobody wanted to be the dick who broke Doc's leg with a hard
foul. Let's agree that he was superdurable and superrespected.

grow Plastic Man arms and spin the ball (again, which he was holding like a softball) off the backboard and in with some absurd angle. He did it easily and beautifully, like a sudden gust of 110 mph wind, like nothing you have ever seen. His opponents would shake their heads in disbelief. The fans would make one of those incredulous moans, followed by five seconds of "Did you just see that?" murmurs. And Doc would jog back up the court like nothing ever happened, classy as always, just another two points for him. One of a kind.

15. ELGIN BAYLOR

Resume: 14 years, 10 quality, 11 All-Stars . . . '63 MVP runner-up . . . '59 Rookie of the Year . . . Top 5 ('59, '60, '61, '62, '63, '64, '65, '67, '68, '69) . . . All-Star MVP ('59) . . . 3-year peak: 35–17–5 . . . best or 2nd-best player on 8 runner-ups ('60s Lakers) . . . 4-year Playoffs peak: 35–15–4, 46% FG (47 G) . . . Playoffs: 27–13–4 (134 G) . . . career: 27.4 PPG (4th), 13.5 RPG (10th) . . . 20K-10K Club

Jesse Owens. Jackie Robinson. Bill Russell. Jim Brown. Elgin Baylor. Oscar Robertson. Muhammad Ali.

Elgin doesn't belong on the list. That's what you're thinking. Not the guy who wore goofy sweaters to the lottery every year. Not the unofficial caretaker for the worst franchise in professional sports. You might accept him on the Worst GM list, or even the Celebs Who Looked Most Like Nipsey Russell list. But not the list above. Not with Jesse and Jackie and Russell and Brown and Oscar and Ali. That's a stretch. That's what you're thinking.

So come back with me to 1958, the year Elgin graduated from the University of Seattle and joined the Lakers. If you don't think the city is teeming with black people now, you should have seen Minneapolis in 1958. America hadn't started changing yet. Blacks were referred to as "Negroes" and "coloreds." They drank from different water fountains, stood in their own lines for movies and were discriminated against in nearly every walk of life. When Elgin entered the NBA, the unwritten rule was that every team could only employ two black players. Nobody challenged it except the Celtics. Elgin strolled into a league where nobody played above the rim except Russell, nobody dunked, and everyone played the same way: rebound, run the floor, get a quick shot. Quantity over quality. That's what worked. Or so they thought. Because Elgin changed everything. He did things that nobody had ever seen. He defied gravity. Elgin would drive from the left side, take off with the basketball, elevate, hang in the air, hang in the air, then release the ball after everyone else was already back on the ground. You could call him the godfather of hang time. You could call him the godfather of the "wow" play. You could point to his entrance into the league as the precise moment when basketball changed for the better. Along with Russell, Elgin turned a horizontal game into a vertical one. He averaged a 25–15 and carried the Lakers to the Finals as a rookie. He scored 71 in New York in his second season.[64] He averaged 34.8 points and 19.8 rebounds in his third season—as a six-foot-five forward, no less—and topped himself the following year by somehow averaging that incredible 38–19–5 on military leave (page 233). When he carried the '62 Lakers to the cusp of a championship, he came within an errant Frank Selvy 10-footer of winning Game 7 in Boston.[65] He would never come closer to a ring. Elgin wrecked his knee during the '64 season and was never the same, although he still made ten first-team All-NBAs and played in seven Finals. During the first two weeks of the '72 season, Elgin believed he was holding back a potential champ and retired after nine games. The Lakers quickly rolled off a 33-game streak and cruised to a title. How many stars have the dignity to walk away when it's time? How many would have walked away from a guaranteed ring? When does that ever happen?

Elgin lived through some things that we like to forget happened now. Lord knows how many racial slurs bounced off him, how many N-bombs were lobbed from the stands, how much daily prejudice he en-

---

64. Wilt quickly broke that mark by scoring 73 at the old MSG. They played a triple-OT game against each other in December '61 where Wilt finished with 78 and Elgin had 63. This absolutely would have led *SportsCenter* in 1961.

65. Elgin exploded for 61 in Game 5, causing Cousy to say later, "[When] we held Elgin to 61, I remember going up to Satch Sanders and telling him sincerely that he'd done a helluva job defensively. And he had. He made Elgin work for every basket. But that's how good Elgin was." Cooz always called him "Elgin" because the word "Baylor" was simply unattainable for him.

dured as the league's signature black forward.[66] Russell bottled everything up and used it as fuel for the next game, he wouldn't suffer, but his opponents would suffer. Oscar morphed into the angriest dude in the league, a great player playing with an even greater chip on his shoulder. Elgin didn't have the same mean streak. He loved to joke with teammates. He never stopped talking. He loved life and loved playing basketball. He couldn't hide it. And so his body soaked up every ugly slight like a sponge. Only a few of those stories live on (like the West Virginia exhibition game on page 242). If you read about black stars from the fifties and sixties, everything comes back to the same point: the respect they earned from peers and fans was disproportionate to the way they were treated in their everyday lives. When Russell bought a house in a white Massachusetts suburb, his neighbors broke in, trashed the house and defecated on his bed. When Elgin was serving our country in 1961 and potentially sacrificing his livelihood, there were dozens of towns and cities strewn across America who wouldn't serve him a meal. Black stars felt like two people at once, revered in one circle and discriminated against in another. Just because America changed over the last four decades doesn't mean those guys stopped remembering the way it used to be. Throw in today's nine-figure contracts and the babying/deifying/celebritizing of today's basketball stars and you can see why they might be bitter.

Do modern players realize that someone like Elgin paved the way for their eight-car garages with the 1964 All-Star Game in Boston, or how the mood in the locker room turned defiant only when Lakers owner Bob Short tried to order Elgin and West around like two busboys? The story never developed legs historically, although we hear about Curt Flood and Marvin Miller all the time. That just goes with the territory with Elgin. Only die-hard fans realize that, by any calculation, Elgin was the third best forward ever. From a historical standpoint, it definitely hinders him that he never won a title or that there just isn't enough "I can't believe how

---

66. In *Wilt, 1962,* Gary M. Pomerantz writes that Don Barksdale was frozen out by teammates on the '53 Baltimore Bullets (they didn't pass to him for an entire quarter) and broke into tears on the bench. They finished 16–54 that season and folded a year later. Karma.

good he was" videotape of him.[67] He lacked that signature "thing" to carry him through eternity, nothing with the legs of Oscar's triple double or Russell's eleven rings. You rarely hear Elgin mentioned with the big boys anymore. Unless you're talking to an NBA fan over the age of fifty. Then they defend Elgin and berate you for not realizing how unbelievable he was.

My theory? Everything that happened after Elgin's playing career obscured the career itself. The Clippers hired Elgin to run them in 1986, and really, he's been something of a punch line ever since. After purchasing Clips tickets in 2004, I wrote about him:

> Blessed with a kind face and a happy smile, almost like the grandfather in a UPN sitcom, he's the Hall of Famer who sits with the other embarrassed GMs during the lottery every spring. I have made many jokes about Elgin over the years.[68] He's an easy target. This is a man once described by TNT's Reggie Theus as "a veteran of the lottery process"—and he meant it as a compliment. I wrote after last June's draft, "Having Elgin run your team must be like getting in the car with my mom at night, when she's careening off curbs and saying things like, 'I can't believe how bad my eyes have gotten' and 'We shouldn't have ordered that bottle of wine.' Just constant fear." Well, Elgin wasn't too happy about that one. Much to my surprise, he reads more Clippers-related articles and columns than one would think. When he found out I was coming for lunch, he wasn't pleased. Coincidentally, he ended up in the Staples cafeteria at the same time; one of my lunch partners asked Elgin at the salad bar if he wanted to join us. Elgin glanced over at our table, noticed me sitting there and growled, "That guy's an [expletive]." Only he used a seven-

---

67. I've seen some of the early Elgin tapes and can't emphasize this strongly enough—watching Elgin dismantle his "peers" is like watching the *Back to the Future* scene when Marty McFly cranks his electric guitar solo as everyone else stares at him in disbelief. Imagine a 2009 player dunking routinely from the three-point line. That's what Elgin looked like compared to everyone else.

68. In fairness to Elgin, he had bad luck with two potential franchise guys (Danny Manning and Livingston suffered crippling knee injuries), lost Derek Smith and Ron Harper to torn ACLs and never bottomed out in the right draft. His biggest mistakes were trading down from no. 2 in '95 (McDyess went 2nd, Sheed went 4th, KG went 5th) and botching no. 1 in '98 (misfiring with Michael Olowokandi over Pierce, Nowitzki, Vince, and others). Okay, maybe he was a bad GM.

letter expletive, placing most of his emphasis on the first three letters. For instance, let's pretend the word was *bassbowl*. Elgin would have said it, "That guy's a *BASS*-bowl."

People loved that story. Of everything I ever wrote for ESPN.com, it's easily one of the most popular anecdotes I ever passed along. *You bass-bowl!* I heard that ten times a year at Clippers games. It took me two years to win Elgin over, but by his final season we were getting along really well. When I filmed an ESPN piece about shooting a half-court shot at a Clippers game, their organization had been splintered into various camps. I knew there was a festering power struggle when Dunleavy and I had a good-natured shooting contest for $100 and I ended up winning. We were on camera and I forgot to collect. Dunleavy disappeared.[69] Elgin quickly limped over looking like he had just seen an old lady get mugged.

"He never paid you, did he?" Elgin whispered.

I shook my head. Elgin made a face.

"That's typical," he hissed.

When Elgin gets mad, he stammers a little. So the next few words came out like this: "And you-you-you know what else? He went first, but after you made your shot, he-he-he made it seem like he had the last shot. Did you catch that?"

"I caught it," I said. "I thought it was funny that he cheated."

Elgin made another face.

"I'm glad you caught that," he said. "I didn't think you caught it."

We ended up rapping for the next twenty-five minutes while the camera guys packed up their stuff. Every time I ever question my choice in life for a profession, I always come back to moments like this: talking hoops with someone like Elg, someone who will live on long after we're both gone. The Dunleavy thing just killed him. You could see it. Even though Elgin was the most beloved figure in the Clippers office—and that's an understatement—Dunleavy knew how to play the political game and Elgin was too freaking old to bother. Times were changing with the Clip-

---

69. He never paid me. Bad coach, bad GM and a welcher to boot. I got him back by sponsoring his basketball-reference.com page and thanking him for all the wasted years of my season ticket money. No, really. Best $10 I ever spent.

pers. Elg could see the writing on the wall. I could see it in his face that day, and I could see it for the rest of that season. Worried that the 2008–9 campaign would be his last, I called a mutual friend to schedule lunch with Elgin in August. I wanted to write a column about him. At seventy-four years old, he was the oldest high-ranking NBA employee by far, the last link to the days of Russell and Cousy, when black players ate at a Greyhound bus station because nobody else would serve them, when you wrecked your knee and were never the same, when you played twenty-seven exhibition games in twenty days because your owner made you. One time I asked Elg how he felt about chartered planes and he flew off the handle.

"Sheeeeeeeeeet," he said. "When I played, we flew coach and carried our own bags! We landed two, three, four times! You ever hear about the time we crashed in a cornfield?"

I heard. It's the closest an American professional sports team ever came to perishing in a plane crash. For Elgin Baylor, it was just another thing that happened to him. That's why I thought it would make for a great column—just lunch with Elgin, him ranting and raving about stuff like that. To make sure Elg would show up, I mentioned to our mutual friend, "Make sure you tell him that he should have tipped in the Selvy shot. I saw the tape."

A few hours later, my phone rang.

"Elg is going nuts," our friend said. "He says you don't know what you're talking about. He says Sam Jones pushed him, that's why he didn't tip it in. He says Sam even admitted it to him afterward."[70]

"I don't know," I said. "That's not what the tape shows."

"Well, you picked the right button to push. He'll be there for lunch. Just be ready to hear about this for an hour."

We scheduled a date and planned to see each other then. A week later, they postponed. We planned on rescheduling, then fate intervened: the power struggle escalated and the Clippers kept yanking Elgin around, fi-

---

70. Add Elgin to the list of people over 35 who had a memory destroyed by YouTube. For me, it was finding out that Jimmy Snuka's famous steel cage leap at MSG vs. Bob Backlund—which seemed like 25 feet at the time—was actually closer to 10. I still haven't totally gotten over it.

nally canning him and handing his GM responsibilities to Dunleavy.[71] The team's employees were told that Elgin resigned, only the terse PR release that followed never mentioned anything about a resignation, nor Elgin's fifty-year association with the NBA and all the hits he took along the way.[72] We elected our first black president six weeks later, something that wouldn't have happened without the strength of people like Elgin once upon a time. You are probably younger than forty, so when you think of him, you probably remember Elg wearing one of those Bill Cosby sweaters and wincing because the Clippers' lottery number came too soon. That's the wrong memory. Think about him creating hang time from scratch. Think of him putting up a 38–19 in his spare time. Think of him dropping 71 on the Knicks. Think of his eyes narrowing as they passed along his owner's condescending message during that snowy night in Boston. Think of him retiring with dignity because he didn't want to hang on for a ring. Think of him telling Rod Hundley that he couldn't play that exhibition game in West Virginia, not because he was trying to prove a point, but because it would have made him feel like less of a human being.

Elgin left the Clippers on the same day that Barack Obama took part in his second presidential debate. The two events weren't related at all. Or so it seemed. On his final night in the NBA, his Clippers friends called and emailed to say goodbye. None of them heard back from him. Elgin Baylor was gone and didn't want to be found. Fifty years, gone in a flash. For the most underappreciated superstar in NBA history, it couldn't have ended any other way.

71. The Clips replacing Elg with Dunleavy—who had already bombed as Bucks GM— was like a bumbling CEO on Wall Street firing his loyal, longtime chauffeur who covered up 15 different potential crimes and 25 affairs over the years, then replacing him with the CEO's loser nephew who just got released from jail for his third DUI. Dunleavy got fired within 18 months.

72. Elgin got revenge by suing the Clips for age/racial discrimination two months later, claiming that he had been unfairly compensated for the previous 20 years. The suit is still pending.

14. JOHN HAVLICEK

Resume: 16 seasons, 13 quality, 13 All-Stars . . . '74 Finals MVP . . . Top 5 ('71, '72, '73, '74), Top 10 ('64, '66, '68, '69, '70, '75, '76) . . . All-Defense (8x, five 1st) . . . 3-year peak: 27–9–8 . . . 4-year Playoffs peak: 27–9–6 (57 G) . . . leader: minutes (2x) . . . most career assists for a nonguard (6,114) . . . best or 2nd-best player on 4 champs ('68, '69, '74, '76), played for 8 champs in all (8–0 in the Finals) . . . Playoffs: 22–7–5 (172 G) . . . career: minutes (10th), points (14th) . . . 25K Point Club

Here's the enduring Havlicek question for me: would it have been better for him historically if he were black?

That question admittedly seems strange. If the Association nearly went under because it was too black, then why would Havlicek's color be a negative? Because color never stops being the elephant in the room for white guys, that's why. Remember when Bird clinched "best forward ever" status coming off three straight MVPs and his best statistical season? He had just finished off the '87 Pistons in the most memorable way possible, with Magic-Bird IV looming in the next round . . . and you know what became a national story? Those moronic "he'd be just another good guy if he were black" claims from Rodman and Isiah. The pinnacle of the career of one of the five greatest players ever and people were still talking about color. This time, unfairly. But it always seems to come up. It's a black man's game. It just is. Shit, one of my first choices for a title was *The Book of Basketball: A White Man's Thoughts on a Black Man's Game.* My publishing company talked me out of it. Can't play the race card in the title. Or something. Everyone's sphincters tighten whenever a white guy discusses race and sports. Malcolm Gladwell made one request for this book: an extended footnote where I compared the all-time teams for Whites, Blacks, Biracials and Foreigners and figured out who'd win a hypothetical tournament. He's biracial. He loves talking about race. And I do too . . . but when you're white, the degree of difficulty skyrockets. You can't screw up. You have to say everything perfectly. You have no leeway. So I'm giving Gladwell that footnote—look, here it is[73]—but had to write a two-hundred-word preamble so it didn't come out of nowhere.

Back to white guys. When we evaluate them, they fall into six categories. Either "undeniably and stereotypically white" (think Mark Madsen), "white but effective" (think Matt Bonner or Steve Kerr), "deceivingly white" (the Billy Hoyle All-Stars), "nonissue white" (guys who excelled to the point that you stopped thinking about their color, like Bird or West), "totally overrated white" (guys whose stock became inflated specifically because of their color: think Danny Ferry or Adam Morrison), and "totally underrated white," which I will define as "someone who was unfairly evaluated in the past tense because he was white." We have one example for that last category and only one: John Havlicek. Read this next paragraph like you don't know any better, then tell me what color you would have guessed.

So there's this three-sport high school star who plays basketball exclusively at Ohio State, even though Woody Hayes lobbies every summer to play him at receiver as well. After getting drafted as a receiver by the Cleveland Browns,[74] he lands on the Celtics as their number one pick and becomes an effective swingman for them, playing three different positions, guarding all types of players and even taking over in crunch time. What

---

73. The biracial team was too tough to figure after I couldn't get hold of Dave Chappelle. Here are the ten-man rotations for the other teams weighted toward post-1976 guys. *Whites:* Walton, Bird, Barry, West, Stockton (starters); Havlicek (6th man), Cowens, McHale, Maravich, Cousy (bench). *Blacks:* Russell, Moses, Doc, Jordan, Magic (starters); LeBron (6th man), Kareem, Oscar, Kobe, Barkley (bench). *Foreigners:* Hakeem, Duncan, Nowitzki, Nash, Petrovic (starters), Ginobili (6th man), Gasol, Rik Smits, Detlef Schrempf, Tony Parker (bench). Obviously the foreigners would get wiped out. The blacks might be *too* loaded; I can't imagine Kobe-Oscar-Kareem coming off the bench. Plus, Barkley and MJ definitely would be involved in one off-court, casino-related incident during the 7-game series. Check out the Whites again. Barry is the only prick on the team. Their passing skills would have been off the charts. They could run the 2nd team's offense through McHale and play him at crunch time with Bird and Walton. Defensively, they'd get exploited at PG and they're undersized, but it's a flexible team that would enjoy playing together. For a 7-game series, the blacks would be a -400 favorite because of the hypercompetitive Russell-Jordan-Magic trio. But you know what? I'd bet on the whites at +350 if only because of the odds. You don't know how much this kills Jabaal Abdul-Simmons.

74. Hondo was Cleveland's last cut of the '62 preseason even though he ran a 4.6 40 and caught everything; he couldn't master blocking and everyone ran the ball back then. He's your answer for the trivia question "Who's the only person to play professionally with Bill Russell and Jim Brown?"

sets him apart is the way he runs and never stops running; he has the endurance of a Kenyan marathoner. Nobody can keep up. He runs and runs and runs. He fills the lane on every fast break. He sprints back and forth along the sideline trying to get open. He's such a remarkable athlete that Boston sportswriters openly wonder if he should pitch for the Red Sox in his spare time. As his team ages and the scoring burden shifts to him, he never changes his balls-to-the-wall style even as he's averaging 45–46 minutes a game. His teams finish 8–0 in the Finals; he leads them in scoring four of those times. He wins titles thirteen years apart with two totally different rosters. He wins the '74 Finals MVP after playing 289 of 291 possible minutes, prompting *Sports Illustrated* to point out a few months later, "A case could have been made that [he] was more like Most Valuable in the Game Today. Or the Best Athlete the NBA has ever had—which would rank him right up there universally because few other sports demand anywhere near as much of an athlete as pro basketball." He makes seven second-team All-NBAs (including two thirteen years apart) and four straight first-team NBAs. He makes five All-Defense teams; that number would have doubled if they'd had those teams during his first six years. He retires in 1978, but not before cracking the top five in nearly every relevant category except assists and rebounds. His peers remember him as one of the clutch players of his era, as well as one of the most athletic and versatile, with Bill Russell saying simply in 1974, "He is the best all-around player I ever saw." He goes down for eternity as a physical specimen and elite basketball player of the highest order. The end.

Would you have said black or white? Admit it . . . you would have said black. And that's the problem with Havlicek historically: he had a blue-collar last name, a wife who looked like a classy news anchor, two of the whitest looks ever (a crew cut in the mid-sixties, curly hair and bushy sideburns in the seventies) and one of those generic, aw-shucks personalities that was impossible to define. Good guy. Simple guy. White guy. That's all we remember.[75] Give him darker skin, Doc's ABA afro, a snazzy Fu Manchu, and a name like Johnny Harmon and you know what hap-

75. *SI* never wrote a Havlicek feature until October '74 (one of those "the old man is still doing it" features). During his overly sentimental farewell tour, an amused Cowens remarked, "John's never had a definite profile like Russell or Cousy. He's played all these games without being recognized, and now everybody is apologizing for it."

pens? Havlicek becomes properly rated. I am convinced. (You were surprised to see him at no. 13 weren't you?)[76] Other than LeBron, no perimeter player fulfilled more functions on a basketball court than Hondo. Other than Malone and Kareem, nobody played at a higher level for a longer and more durable time. Other than Russell and Sam Jones, nobody won more titles. Other than Jordan and Bird, nobody had more *memorable* clutch moments. Other than Magic and West, nobody did a better job of reinventing his game as the years passed. Behind Bird, Magic, Russell and Duncan, he might rank fifth on the Winnability Scale. Only Russell and Jordan came through more times for championship teams.

And then there's this: Only Russell and Kareem spread postseason heroics over a longer time frame. Hondo's series-saving steal against the '65 Sixers became one of the five most famous plays ever. He played all 48 minutes in the clincher of the '66 Finals, with L.A. coach Fred Schaus saying afterward, "No one in the league his size is even close to Havlicek in quickness. He is entirely responsible for the trend to small, quick forwards." He made the winning jumper of the '68 Finals and averaged a 26–9–8 in 19 playoff games—serving as Russell's unofficial lead assistant in his spare time (Russell handled the defense and subs, Hondo handled the offense)—with *SI*'s Frank Deford noting afterward, "Because Havlicek can play the whole game at top speed and because he can move about the lineup so nimbly, he makes it possible for Russell always to replace whoever is tired or cold with the best man on his bench, regardless of position." He averaged a 25–10–6 on the '69 championship team, playing an inconceivable 850 minutes in 18 games (47.2 per game, a playoff record for 15-plus games), making the game-winning shot of the Knicks series and carrying Boston's offense in the Finals. He led the '73 Celtics to a team record 68 wins, separated his shooting shoulder in the Eastern Finals and played left-handed in Games 5 through 7 (with Boston falling short). He pulled off the epic 289/291 in the '74 Finals and made a super-clutch banker to extend the famous double-OT game. He gutted through constant pain from an injured right foot in the '76 playoffs, made the sin-

76. Grumpy Old Editor wasn't as surprised: "As someone who would have given Jabaal a run for his money in the 'I wanna be black' contest, and who hated the Celtics almost as a religious requirement, I never doubted how good Havlicek was. Choose-up game? After Jordan, he might be my first choice."

gle biggest shot of the Finals (the running banker in the triple-OT game) and played 58 minutes in Game 5 when doctors had ordered him to play no more than 25.

Havlicek was the ultimate winner. You would have wanted him in your NBA foxhole. You wouldn't have blinked when *SI* wrote things like "It is altogether unlikely that you will ever see another Havlicek. The dimension Havlicek has brought to basketball is entirely and uniquely his own, and it will probably go with him once he finally winds down," or when peers like Jerry West raved, "Superstar is a bad word. In our league people look at players, watch them dribble between their legs, watch them make spectacular plays, and they say, 'There's a superstar.' Well, John Havlicek *is* a superstar, and most of the others are figments of writers' imaginations," or even when Rick Barry admitted during Hondo's final season, "Havlicek is the only true superstar." And if you have any doubt about his resume, remember that Havlicek was so consistently cool under pressure that everyone started calling him "Hondo." That's right, John Wayne's nickname. The guy was named after John fucking Wayne! The point is, we reached a point with Havlicek where everyone agreed, "This is one of the greatest NBA players ever." It wasn't a debate. Now it is. And it's only because he was white.[77]

---

77. One of the toughest calls in the book: Hondo for Level 4 or Level 5. I decided on L4 for two reasons. First, every Pantheon guy qualifies for "If you surrounded him with a good team, you were winning a title or coming damned close" status and Hondo wasn't quite there. Second, he never won MVP (finishing top five just twice) and made just four first-team All-NBAs (getting squeezed out from '66 to '70). Even with the playoff heroics and superhuman minutes, I just couldn't justify it. So our four cutoff guys were Miller (Level 1), Nowitzki (Level 2), Stockton (Level 3), and Hondo (Level 4). I like it.

ELEVEN

THE PYRAMID: PANTHEON

13. MOSES MALONE

Resume: 19 years, 13 quality, 12 All-Stars . . . '83 Finals MVP . . . MVP: '79,
'82, '83 . . . Top 5 ('79, '82, '83, '85), Top 10 ('80, '81, '84, '87) . . . 5-year peak:
26–15, 52% FG . . . leader: rebounds (6x), minutes (1x) . . . best player on
1 champ ('83 Sixers) and 1 runner-up ('81 Rockets) . . . '81 Playoffs: 27–15,
45.5 MPG (21 G) . . . '84 Playoffs: 26–16 (13 G) . . . Playoffs: 22–14
(100 G) . . . career: points (6th), rebounds (3rd), games (5th), minutes
(4th) . . . 25K-15K Club

I just spent the last two hours trying to figure out the top twelve modern
celebrities who extracted the most success (financial and careerwise) from
one gimmick. Important note: this doesn't necessarily mean that they *only*

had one gimmick, just that they had one ploy that brought them inordinate success. Call it the Buffer List. Here's the top twelve:

1. Michael Buffer
2. Simon Cowell
3. Tyler Perry
4. Moses Malone
5. the Bee Gees
6. Jeff Foxworthy
7. Vanna White
8. Robert Wuhl
9. Oprah's friend Gayle
10. Phil Niekro
11. Jared from Subway
12. Monica Lewinsky[1]

Why Buffer over Simon? Because Buffer's gimmick worked so well that he spawned a career for his brother, Bruce, who became the Frank Stallone of ringside announcing for the UFC. I don't know if that's more of an insult to Bruce or Frank.

Back to Moses and his one gimmick: he crashed the boards. He crashed the living hell out of them. He annihilated them. He left them for dead. And it wasn't just about numbers—Moses finished as the greatest offensive rebounder ever by any calculation, grabbing a higher percentage of

1. Honorable mention suggestions from my friends: Kim Kardashian, Verne Troyer, Miss Elizabeth, Fluff the Caddy, Kevin Federline, Stuttering John, Gallagher, Michael Myers, Gary Coleman, Dirk Diggler, Buddy Ryan, Carrot Top, J. J. Redick, Spencer and Heidi, Steven Seagal, Red from *Shawshank*, Shannon Elizabeth, Trig and Bristol Palin, Shannon Whirry, Jon Hein, Bruce Buffer, Adrienne Barbeau, Willard Scott, Morganna, Andrew Dice Clay, John "Motor Mouth" Moschitta, Little Oral Annie, Vanilla Ice, Jerome from *The Time*, Bruce Vilanch, Cytherea, Kobayashi, Hurley from *Lost* and Jeffrey Ross, who arguably could have made the top-12 for dominating celebrity roasts MJ-style in the 2000s. Unfortunately, it didn't translate into financial success or even a sitcom deal. Although he altered my life in a small way by saying about Penny Marshall, "I wouldn't fuck her with Bea Arthur's dick" . . . with Bea Arthur sitting right there. Third most underrated moment of the new millenium in my opinion, just behind pilot Sully landing on the Hudson River and President Dubya throwing a strike with a bulletproof vest right before Game 3 of the '01 World Series. By the way, Paris Hilton missed the Buffer List because she didn't even have a single gimmick. Although maybe that *was* her gimmick—not having a gimmick. Crap, I need to think about this some more.

his team's total rebounds in '79 (38.4 percent) than Russell or Wilt ever did in one season—but about the relentless way he attacked the boards. The best way to describe it: Imagine a quality prison basketball game in the playground where players had to maim someone to draw a foul. Imagine the game included one inordinately good rebounder: perfect instincts, light on his feet, supertough, superphysical, uncanny rejumpability (© Jay Bilas). Imagine this guy had all kinds of positioning tricks and always seemed to know where the ricochets were going (to the point that it always seemed unfair). Imagine this guy loved crashing the boards, lived for it, couldn't get enough of it. Then imagine the warden told him before an organized playground game against inmates from another prison, "We're playing four 10-minute quarters. I made a bet with the other warden that you couldn't grab 40 rebounds in 40 minutes. If you can do it, I'm paroling you. You have my word."

Now, imagine watching that guy rebound. That was Moses from 1978 to 1983.

Rodman's rebounding barrage made us feel like he was doing it partly for numbers and attention. Moses did it out of pure love. That's just the way he played. He protected the glass with such ferocity that his Houston teammates incorporated a "play" loosely called "If Moses has position, just throw up a shot and he'll tip it in if it misses." Remember the first Clubber-Rocky fight in *Rocky III* when Rocky returns to his corner after the second round and says in a terrified mumble, "I can't keep him off me"? Every center who battled Moses had that same look by the fourth quarter. He particularly loved sticking it to Kareem, a finesse center who wanted no part of banging with him. When Houston stunned the '81 Lakers in their three-game series, Moses finished with 94 points and 53 rebounds, doing everything short of actually marinating Kareem, grilling him and eating him. When Philly swept the '83 Lakers, Moses averaged a 26–18 and outrebounded Kareem by a 70–30 margin.[2] Nobody from Moses' peak could handle him. What I always found interesting: the same blue-collar themes appeared in every Bird article or feature, but Moses

---

2. In *Giant Steps*, aka "The Revisionist History of My Career," Kareem *never* mentioned Moses. Not once. If Moses-Kareem was a *Good Will Hunting* scene, Moses was Will and Kareem was the ponytailed Harvard douche. *Hey, Kareem, do you like apples?*

worked equally hard and exacted just as much from a similarly challenged body. His hands were so tiny that he could barely palm a basketball. Listed at six-foot-ten (a stretch) with short arms, Moses was such a string bean during his early years that Houston played him at power forward.[3] He wasn't a good passer, didn't have any post-up moves, couldn't shoot from more than 8 feet. None of it mattered. Like Bird, he grew up dirt-poor, fell in love with basketball, succeeded early, kept plugging away and developed a tunnel vision for the sport. Like Bird, he busted his ass and concentrated only on the things he could do. Like Bird, he was blessed with one supernatural quality that set him apart: quick feet for Moses, hand-eye coordination for Bird. And like Bird (with his contagious passing), Moses had one unforgettable trick that transformed his career and hasn't been duplicated since.

See, Moses figured out a loophole in the rebounding system. Let's say you're a big guy and you have a pretty good idea that a shot might be going up soon. And let's say your guy is positioned right between you and the basket. You have two choices: either try to sneak around him (even though he knows you're coming) or come at him from behind and shove him off balance without the officials noticing. Moses eschewed both options. He lurked along the baseline on either side of the basket, biding his time, biding his time, letting everyone else get position for a rebound . . . and then, when he felt like a shot was coming up, he'd slyly sneak under the backboard, start backing up, slam his butt into his opponent to create the extra foot of space he needed, then jump right to where the rebound was headed. There was no way to stop it. Again, you could have position under the basket and he would still get the rebound. Watch Moses on Classic or NBA TV sometime—I guarantee he pulls the Ass Attack trick fifteen or twenty times. Moses Malone attacked people with his ass. That's what he did. Of the hundreds and hundreds of games I watched while researching this book, nothing startled me as much as the Moses Ass Attack. Once you notice it, you can't stop looking for it.[4]

And over everything else, that's how Moses pilfered three MVPs and

3. Watching young Moses is like seeing Vince Vaughn in *Swingers*—he's so much skinnier that it's completely disconcerting and you can't stop thinking about it.
4. Why doesn't anyone else use this trick? I don't know. Maybe he was an Ass Attack savant.

appeared in two Finals.[5] So why not rank him higher? His dominant stretch didn't last long enough for reasons that remain unclear: Moses peaked from '79 to '83, signed the biggest contract in NBA history, won a Finals MVP, and never approached those heights again. (Philly even dumped him in 1986 for Jeff Ruland and Clifford Robinson when Moses was only thirty.) He might be the only player to average a 20–10 with four different teams, but isn't it strange that three teams gave up on him? And he hasn't endured like other seventies/eighties legends for a relatively unfair reason: his unpolished personality worked against him. Moses might hold the all-time NBA records for most mumbled answers and uncomfortable interactions. It was all little stuff, like how he dealt with the same Houston beat reporters for years and refused to call them anything more than *Post* and *Chronicle* . . . but at the same time, your legend can't grow unless media members are talking and writing about you, or teammates and peers are gushing with mythical stories about you. There has to be *something* there to capture. When *SI* assigned the great Frank Deford to profile Malone's rise in 1979, even Deford struggled and announced early in the piece, "Malone is not particularly articulate about all this. Indeed, in his heavy bass voice, speaking in the argot of his impoverished Southern subculture, he sometimes seems obtuse." Translation: Don't expect any illuminating moments in this feature, folks!

And that's how it went for Moses Malone. He stayed out of trouble, showed up on time, cashed his paychecks and always gave a crap.[6] Why spend eight thousand words describing him when you could just remember all those backboards he demolished, or all those opposing centers who made Rocky's "I can't keep him off me" face. He kicks off the Pantheon for

---

5. In 1982, Houston GM Ray Patterson said, "There have been only four dominant players: Wilt, Russell, Abdul-Jabbar, and Mo." (I would have thrown in Walter Dukes for his legendary B.O., but whatever.) And Patterson said that *after* he traded him; the Rockets didn't have a choice because Philly had signed Moses to a $13.2 million offer sheet.

6. Another thing in his favor: he had one of the best athlete names ever. If you were writing a movie about the first player to jump from high school to the pros, wouldn't you give him a name like Moses Malone? Everything crested when Nike released their "Moses" poster with Malone dressed like the religious Moses, only with NBA shorts and a basketball. It's proudly framed in my office. As is Nike's "Supreme Court" poster with eleven early-eighties NBA stars dressed like Supreme Court justices (including Artis Gilmore standing defiantly in the middle). I keep telling you: the eighties were fantastic.

one reason and one reason only: at his peak, Moses guaranteed you a title as long as you surrounded him with a solid supporting cast. There's something to be said for that.

12. SHAQUILLE O'NEAL

Resume: 18 years, 14 quality, 15 All-Stars . . . Finals MVP: '00, '01, '02 . . . '00 MVP . . . Runner-up: '95, '05 . . . Simmons MVP: '05 . . . six top-5 MVP finishes . . . '93 Rookie of the Year . . . All-Star MVP ('00, '04, '09) . . . top 5 ('98, '00, '01, '02, '03, '04, '05, '06), top 10 ('95, '99), top 15 ('94, '96, '97, '09) . . . league leader: scoring (2x), FG% (9x) . . . 2-year peak: 29–14–4 . . . 3-year Playoffs peak: 30–14–3, 55% FG (58 G) . . . '00 Finals: 38–17 . . . '01 Finals: 33–16–5 . . . '02 Finals: 36-12-4 . . . swept in Playoffs 6 different times . . . 25K-10K Club . . . best or 2nd-best player on 4 champs ('00, '01, '02 Lakers, '06 Heat) and 2 runner-ups ('95 Magic, '04 Lakers) . . . career: 58.1% FG (2nd), 24.1 PPG (19th), 11.0 RPG (29th), blocks (8th), minutes (20th)

After I wrote a column about Shaq's initial quest to enter the Pantheon (May 2000), a reader identified only as Plixx2 emailed to say, "I enjoyed the Pantheon and agree that Shaq is close, but not close enough. I think in 10–15 years people will look at Shaq's career like they look back at Peter North's career . . . dominant, but not the best."[7]

Solid analogy at the time, even better now. Dominant, but not the best. Memorable, but not the best. Unstoppable, but not the best. Shaq won three Finals MVP's in overpowering fashion, but he only took home one regular season MVP. He won four rings and could have won a fifth if Dwyane Wade hadn't gotten hurt in 2005 . . . but he somehow got swept out of the playoffs *six* other times. He became such a singular fantasy advantage that my league forced teams to pay a Shaq Tax for two straight

---

7. The best part of this analogy: North was the master of the money shot; Shaq was the master of the monster "don't try to block this or I will put your arms through the hoop with the ball" dunk. Both moves left their opponents wincing, recoiling backward in fear and then needing two or three seconds to recover. And possibly a towel.

years (pick him and lose a sixth-round pick)[8] . . . but his free throw struggles made him such a liability that he was pulled late from a few close
playoff battles.[9] He only took basketball seriously for one entire season
(1999–2000) and intermittently for the other eighteen . . . and yet, his
playoff performances from 2000 to 2002 rank among the all-time greatest.
He played for five teams in all (nobody else in the top fifteen played for
more than two except Moses) . . . but made the first three better when he
arrived and significantly worse when he left. We have written him off multiple times during his career (either as a potential superstar, a superstar, a
super-duper star, a fading superstar or a viable starting center) . . . but
each time, he made everyone eat their words.

On the other hand, Shaq left everyone with superstar blue balls. He became rich and famous before accomplishing anything worthy of those
words; midway through his rookie year in Orlando, he'd already signed a
seven-year, $40 million contract, starred in *Blue Chips*, recorded a rap
album and become a household name. There were "the next Wilt" flashes
for the next three years but never anything too lasting, with resentment
building that Shaq personified the dangerous Too Much Too Fast Too
Soon era. Orlando shocked Jordan's Bulls and made the Finals. (Here
comes Shaq!) Then Houston swept them as Hakeem administered young
Shaq a first-class spanking. (There goes Shaq!) He ditched Orlando for the
Lakers and gave them post-Magic relevancy again. (Here comes Shaq!)
They did nothing for three years other than get juicy title odds in Vegas
and choke every spring. (There goes Shaq!) He matured into a dominant
force, won an MVP and rolled to his first title. (Here comes Shaq!) He suffered through four alternately satisfying and frustrating Laker years, feuding with Kobe, battling weight issues, mailing in regular seasons and
ultimately kicking ass in the playoffs for two more rings. (Here/there
comes/goes Shaq!) Once he moved to Miami and transformed the Heat,

8. We also made him a "6th man" for 2 other years where nobody was allowed to draft
him as a center. Any time fantasy leagues change their rules for someone, you know that
person is good.
9. The crazy thing about Shaq's FT shooting: he shoots them like line drives. Imagine
you're trying to throw a rolled-up piece of paper into a garbage can—instinctively,
would you throw it with a Nowitzki-like arc, or would you whip it in a straight line at the
can? You'd throw it with the arc. So why would Shaq whip straight line drives at the rim
for fourteen consecutive years? Have we ever definitively answered this question? And
while we're here, was it my imagination or did Shaq become cross-eyed in close games?

we appreciated him a little more fully—his locker room presence, his passing ability, how teammates had a knack for peaking when they played with him, how he quietly had the most engaging personality of anyone— and I wrote during that season, "Shaq is like DeNiro in the seventies and eighties—everyone in the cast looks a little better when he's involved." His fourth title in Miami gave his career some extra weight; his recent resurgence in Phoenix opened the door that he might break some records or come close; then his injury-plagued overweight campaign for the 2009–10 Cavaliers made us think he was washed up again. Who can predict anything with Shaquille O'Neal? I will never count him out, and I will never count him in. Four things epitomize the Shaq era over everything else:

1. His per-game averages for the 2000 Finals: 45 minutes, 38 points, 17 rebounds . . . 38 percent from the line.[10] That's Apex Shaq in a nutshell.

2. Bill Russell's teams finished 716–299 in the regular season for an absurd .705 winning percentage. That's the standard. From 1994 (his second season) to 2006 (his fourteenth), Shaq's teams finished 654–298 (.687) and never won fewer than 50. But because of his dreadful free throw shooting, Shaq was yanked in and out of the lineup in close playoff games more than any other Pantheon guy. This can't be forgotten—it was the turd in the punch bowl of Shaq's career. Kinda like how Pacino was secretly five foot six and they could only cast shorter costars for him. No, really.

3. In my annual "Who has the highest trade value?" column for 2002, I picked Shaq first with the following explanation: "Seems a little dubious that he's ranked this high, right? After all, he turned thirty years old this season, he's always threatening to retire and he was responsible for *Kazaam*.[11] But here's the thing . . . If the Lakers ever traded him, Shaq

10. Shaq's scoring/rebounding averages in the Finals: 28–12 ('95), 38–17 ('00), 33–16 ('01), 36–12 ('02), 27–11 ('04). In his first 19 NBA Finals games, he averaged 34.2 PPG. He also averaged a 38–15 in the last 2 games of the '02 Western Finals (both must-wins) and a 25–18 in the last 2 games of the '95 Bulls series.

11. In the '90s. Shaq mistakenly thought he could act and rap. This led to him playing a magical genie in a movie called *Kazaam*. It wasn't even awful in a fun way; it was just awful. With that said, I absolutely think he should take over the lead role of *CSI* when he retires.

is vindictive enough that he would postpone his eventual retirement plans, then devote the next decade of his life to winning championships, haunting the Lakers and making them rue the day. And the Lakers *know* this. When motivated and hungry, he's the most dominant player in the league. Nobody can stop him. Nobody. Not even Duncan. And that's why the Lakers would never, ever, ever, ever, ever, ever, *ever* trade Shaq, not under any circumstances . . . which makes him the undisputed number one player on this list." Of course, they traded him two years later. And he *did* come back to haunt them. You couldn't make this stuff up.

4. His first three times upon leaving a team (1996, 2004, 2008), Shaq shrewdly created a controversy to deflect that he was leaving because it was time to go. He blamed Penny Hardaway's budding hubris for splitting Orlando; really, Shaq just wanted to live in California and play for the Lakers. When they dumped him because of his poor conditioning and because he made it clear that he'd go on cruise control without a mammoth extension, he deflected local blame by declaring war on Kobe (one of his smartest political moves and another reason why Shaq should run for office someday). When Miami dumped him because he looked washed-up and out of shape, he went right after Pat Riley and played the "I'm totally betrayed" card. Much like preelection Obama was a savvier politician than people realized, Shaq was a savvier athlete than people realized. Nobody made more money playing basketball. Ever.[12] And no NBA player resonated on so many levels: with teammates, opponents, fans, media members, critics, little kids, you name it. Even as we kept hearing stories that Shaq was polarizing behind the scenes—someone who frustrated teammates by being out of shape, bristled when others got more attention, put himself above the team, undermined coaches, partied too much in Miami, played selfishly in his second Phoenix season, and (most indefensibly) griped about his playoff minutes when he was washed up in Cleveland—we mostly looked the other way. Shaq played us

12. Through 2010, Shaq had earned over $290 million just in salary. That doesn't include endorsements or business opportunities. And he did it despite frequently turning off the button in his brain that told him, "You should be lively and interesting during this interview, and you definitely shouldn't mumble your words."

perfectly. He made us laugh more than any other superstar except Barkley, coming up with clever nicknames (like "Shaqapulco," his Miami estate) and analogies (like when he compared his three most famous teammates to Corleones, with Wade being Michael, Kobe being Sonny and Penny being Fredo).[13] The league was just more entertaining with him in it.

One last thought: of any two old-school/new-school players, Shaq and Wilt resemble each other most. Switch situations for '59 Wilt and '92 Shaq and Shaq matches Wilt's numbers (and possibly exceeds them), while Wilt wouldn't have topped Shaq's best work. So why rank Wilt higher? *Because Shaq left something on the table.* He was given too much too soon: wealth, attention, accolades, everything. He never had a rival center like Russell to push him in his prime. He never had to worry about his next paycheck. He could coast on physical skills and that's mostly what he did. Shaq turned out to be the least competitive superstar of his era, someone who enjoyed winning but wasn't destroyed by losing, someone who kept everything in its proper perspective. Chuck Klosterman pointed this out on my podcast once: for whatever reason, we react to every after-the-fact story about Michael Jordan's "legendary" competitiveness like it's the coolest thing ever. *He pistol-whipped Brad Sellers in the shower once? Awesome! He slipped a roofie into Barkley's martini before Game 5 of the '93 Finals? Cunning!*[14] But really, Jordan's competitiveness was pathological. He obsessed over winning to the point that it was creepy. He challenged teammates to the point that it became detrimental. Only during his last three Chicago years did he find an acceptable, Russell-like balance as a competitor, teammate and person. But Shaq had that balance all along. He always knew what he was.[15]

13. My single favorite Shaqism. The analogy worked and became eerie when you consider the potential parallels between Sonny's tollbooth execution and Kobe's brush with moral death after being accused of rape. Whoops, we're not supposed to discuss this. My bad.

14. By the way, MJ didn't do these things.

15. You can't play the "Wait, why didn't you give Wilt the same leeway here?" card for this reason: Wilt never knew what the hell he wanted. He was constantly changing his mind, his game, his goals, everything. He talked himself into whatever reality suited him the most at the time (or even after he was finished playing). Shaq never did that.

My theory: basketball was never as much fun for Shaq as everything else happening in his life. Officials allowed opponents to defend him differently, shove him out of position and pull his shoulders on dunks. Teams fouled him in key moments and flashed a giant spotlight on his one weakness. The loathsome Hack-a-Shaq tactics were insulting and maybe even a little humiliating. Even when he kicked everyone's asses (like from 2000 to 2002), he received a decent amount of credit[16] . . . but not really. The guy couldn't win. And so Shaq could have earned a top-five Pyramid spot and multiple MVPs, but he happily settled for no. 12, some top-five records, three Finals MVPs and a fantastically fun ride. It reminds me of a life decision I made in college: instead of killing myself gunning for a 3.5 or higher, I worked for our newspaper and radio station, wrote a weekly sports column, then spent an inordinate amount of time hanging with my friends, partying, procrastinating and creating memories. I graduated with a 3.04 and wouldn't change a thing. Neither would Shaq, who probably finished with a 3.68 in this analogy. If there's a difference, it's that Shaq convinced himself that his 3.68 was really a 4.0. And it wasn't.

(Important note: Okay, I lied a little. It wasn't a life decision. I just spent a lot of time procrastinating, hated studying and could always be talked into things like "Want to go outside and play stickball for twelve hours?" or "What if we drunkenly whip a golf ball against the metal door in our hall, then jump out of the way as it comes flying back at us, and the only way you can win is by not getting hit?"[17] It's actually a miracle that I lived through college, much less graduated with a 3.04. I'm done comparing myself to Pyramid guys.)

11. HAKEEM OLAJUWON

Resume: 18 years, 14 quality, 12 All-Stars . . . Finals MVP: '94, '95 . . . '94 MVP . . . '93 runner-up . . . Top 5 ('87, '88, '89, '93, '94, '97), Top 10 ('86,

---

16. One series never earned him enough credit: his demolition of Philly's Dikembe Mutombo in the '01 Finals. Dikembe was considered the best defensive center of his generation and Shaq rolled through him for 44–20, 28–20, 30–12, 34–14 and 29–13 (despite missing 36 FTs).

17. We called this game "Jai Alai." You could only lose; you couldn't win.

'90, '96), Top 15 ('91, '95, '99) . . . All-Defense (9x, five 1st) . . . Defensive Player of the Year ('93, '94) . . . 4-year peak: 27–13–2 . . . Playoff record: most blocks (10) . . . record: career blocks . . . season leader: rebounds (2x), blocks (3x) . . . best player on 2 champs ('94, '95 Rockets), one runner-up ('86) . . . '86 plus '94–'95 Playoffs: 29–11–4 (65 G) . . . '95 Playoffs: 33–10–4.5, 62 blocks (beat Malone, Barkley, Robinson, and Shaq) . . . Playoffs (145 G): 25.9 PPG (6th), 11.2 RPG . . . 25K–10K Club

Here's a new game show for you: *See If You Can Replicate Hakeem Olajuwon's Career!*

We have the blueprint. Just go out and find one of the best young athletes in a country that's obsessed with soccer. (The country doesn't matter—could be South American, could be European, could be African, whatever.) Has to be someone who spent his childhood dreaming of a professional soccer career and developed world-class balance and footwork at a precocious age. (I'm talking thirteen, fourteen or fifteen, or as those years are sometimes called, "the dawn of masturbating.") We need to make sure he never considers basketball, not even in passing. (Unofficial odds of this happening now that basketball has gone global: 100 to 1.) We need to hope the kid starts growing, only the growth spurt doesn't affect his world-class balance and footwork. (Unofficial odds of this happening: 50 to 1 . . . so just between the last two variables, we are now talking about 50,000-to-1 odds.) We need to make sure an authority figure says, "Wow, this kid was put on earth to play basketball" and pushes him in that direction, then the kid takes to the sport naturally, as if he's been playing hoops his whole life. (Not as likely as you'd think.) We need to make sure the kid voyages to America, finds the right college, makes all the necessary cultural adjustments, figures out the sport and its nuances on the fly, welcomes the attention and pressure and somehow keeps his "little man trapped in a big man's body" athletic skills. (Okay odds, not great.) We need to make sure this college resides near an NBA team that features one of the six best centers ever during his zenith, and not just that, but we need to hope this guy is nice enough to play pickup with our kid every summer, take the kid under his wing and teach him every conceivable trick. (Hakeem's mentor? That's right, Moses Malone. Are you kidding me?)[18] We need to hope our kid emerges as the best young center in basketball and doesn't handle his chance in America like Borat did. (Definitely unlikely.) We need to make sure the right professional team drafts him and his body slowly fills out without costing him that world-class athleticism. (Unlikely, but not improbable.) We need to hope he develops the best collection of unstoppable low-post moves by anyone not named Kevin McHale. (Now we're talking lightning in a bottle multiplied by three.) And finally, we need to hope that he has the necessary competitive chops, truly gives a shit, measures himself by his peers and takes great pleasure in destroying them. (Since only fifteen or twenty basketball players have been wired like that over the past seventy-five years, you do the math.)

Add everything up and here are your odds that we'll see another Hakeem Olajuwon: a kajillionpilliongazillionfrazillionfriggallionmillion to one. You will see fifty reasonably close replicas of Jordan (and we've already seen two: Kobe and Wade) before you see another Dream. So go on YouTube, watch his highlights and congratulate yourself for seeing the only Hall of Famer who would have made it had he been anywhere from five foot eleven to six foot ten (his actual height). We knew something special could happen when he was whipping through Kareem and the '86 Lakers like an Oklahoma twister. Strangely, the soon-to-be-ousted champs couldn't stop heaping praise on him. Maurice Lucas simply said, "The rebirth of a bigger Moses Malone."[19] Magic decided, "In terms of raw athletic ability, Akeem is the best I've ever seen." Mitch Kupchak summed it up best: "I can compare him to, maybe, Alvin Robertson in terms of being able to do everything. That tells you something, since Robertson is a guard. I've never seen anyone that strong, that quick, that relentless and who also happens to be seven feet tall."

Thank you, Mitch! You just did my job for me. Hakeem finished his

---

18. Of all the Pyramid guys, Hakeem was the best example of Gladwell's *Outliers* theory—someone who succeeded for reasons that went well beyond pure talent. Hakeem spending the summers learning from Moses was like Bill Gates and Paul Allen going to a high school that just happened to have the most advanced computer programming in the country.

19. Grumpy Old Editor: "That's a sentence worthy of Moses Malone." And it is.

coming-out party by averaging a 25–12–3 (blocks) in the '86 Finals and holding his own against the greatest slew of big men in NBA history. During a must-win Game 5 where tag-team partner Ralph Sampson was ejected for starting a brawl, an inspired Hakeem exploded for 32 points, 14 rebounds and 8 assists. If I did my "Who has the highest trade value?" column that summer, Hakeem would have finished first even after Jordan's 63-point game in Boston. But a promising Rockets juggernaut quickly self-combusted in a haze of drugs and bad luck, with Sampson getting shipped to Golden State for lemons Sleepy Floyd and Joe Barry Carroll (cleverly nicknamed "Joe Barely Cares" by Peter Vecsey).[20] Poor Hakeem wasted his youth toiling away on undermanned teams while submitting dazzling across-the-board numbers and at least three "Holy mother of God!" displays of athleticism per game. We always hear about the lack of support for superstars like KG or Oscar, but jeez, the Rockets baked Hakeem a shit soufflé of teammates for six solid years (1987–1993). He complained for much of that time, explaining to *Sports Illustrated* in 1991 that it was nothing personal, but "all I was saying was, you don't build with these guys. I wasn't criticizing my teammates. I was only saying that it's O.K. to have one or two guys [like that], but not a whole team of them. After all, my career's on the line."[21]

By this point, Dream's reputation as a head case was gaining steam. During his first few seasons, he spelled his name "Akeem" and played with a trigger-happy fury, starting multiple fights and near-fights, constantly blowing up at officials, and pacing around like some menacing hothead at a bar.[22] He eventually rededicated himself to Islam, found inner peace, started fasting during Ramadan (even though it chewed up a month of

---

20. This one ranks high on the list of trades that were a major news story at the time but seem positively pedestrian now. At the time, it was one of the five biggest NBA trades ever. Nobody thought it was a red flag that Houston was getting guys nicknamed "Sleepy" and "Barely Cares."

21. I'm almost positive this qualifies as criticizing your teammates. In his defense, Dream's best teammates from 1988 to 1992 were Sleepy, Carroll, Otis Thorpe, Buck Johnson, Vernon Maxwell, Kenny Smith and Mike Woodson. Hakeem played with one All-Star from '87 through '95 (Thorpe in '92).

22. Dream had such little control over his temper that Kupchak goaded him into a wild fight in Game 5 of the '86 West Finals (Sampson won it at the buzzer). Shades of the dorky *Fast Break* backup getting Nevada State's best player to punch him by dropping an N-bomb. Okay, not really. I just hadn't referenced *Fast Break* in a while.

every regular season), changed the spelling to "Hakeem" and channeled his hostilities into his play (still superb) . . . only when he started bitching about his supporting cast, it became difficult to discern whether everything was screwed on correctly. After he battled a mysterious heart ailment during the '91 season, his stock dropped to the degree that I distinctly remember driving around once and hearing Boston radio host Glenn Ordway—a blowhard whose basketball opinion I had always respected—pooh-pooh a caller's idea of a Reggie Lewis/Hakeem swap, saying the Celtics would never do it. I loved Reggie as much as anyone, but this was Hakeem Olajuwon! You only had to see him in person once to think, "I will probably not see fifteen better basketball players while I am alive." When his supporting cast improved for the 1992–93 season—which doubled as a career year for him, not so coincidentally—he broke through during Jordan's "baseball sabbatical," winning the 1994 MVP, winning back-to-back Finals MVPs and pillaging Shaq, Robinson and Ewing in the process. At no other point in NBA history has one superstar specifically and undeniably thrashed his three biggest rivals in the span of thirteen months. It remains Hakeem's greatest feat. He would remain relevant for another five seasons, making All-NBA teams fourteen years apart (second team in '86, third team in '99). Now he's one of the twelve greatest players ever by any calculation. And to think, it all started on a soccer field in Nigeria with somebody saying, "Man, I bet that kid would be good at basketball."

My one historical nitpick: you could argue that Hakeem's prime (1992–95) worked so well because he *didn't* play with another transcendent guy. Hakeem was something of a ball stopper: he caught the entry pass, thought about it, checked the defense, thought about it some more, made sure he wasn't getting double-teamed, tried to get a feel for which way his defender was leaning, then picked an In-N-Out Burger move to exploit the situation.[23] As weird as this sounds, he was better off playing with a band of three-point

---

23. If McHale had the Panda Express menu, then Hakeem was In-N-Out—only a few options, but all were otherworldly. The complete list: the up-and-under, the double clutch jump hook, the deadly fall-away, the deadly over-the-backboard fall-away; the fake fall-away, fake up and under, the step-back jumper; and the Dream Shake (which can't be described—it's the equivalent of the Animal Burger). My Mount Rushmore of fast-food options: Chick-fil-A, Subway, Astro Burger and Arby's. In-N-Out would have made it if their fries didn't suck.

shooters and quality role players; he didn't need help from a second scorer like Dominique or Kobe, nor did he need an elite point guard to keep hooking him up the way Stockton helped Malone. He just needed some dudes to spread the floor and one other rebounder. For a salary cap era that hadn't even really kicked in yet, Hakeem became the ideal franchise player: a guaranteed 44–49 wins even when flanked by mediocrity, and if you upgraded his supporting cast from crap to decent, you could beat anyone in a playoff series as long as Dream was inspired.[24] So he was like Schwarzenegger or Stallone at their peaks—you were having a big opening weekend with Dream regardless of the script or the rest of the cast—and if you had to pick any franchise center to carry a crappy team for a few years, you would have picked Dream over anyone but Kareem. That quality separated him from every nineties contemporary except Jordan; he really *was* a franchise player. On the other hand, I'm not convinced Dream could have tailored his game to an up-tempo team like the Showtime Lakers, or even a brilliant half-court passing team like the '86 Celtics. Playing with the likes of Kenny Smith, Sam Cassell, Robert Horry, Mario Elie, Otis Thorpe and an aging Clyde Drexler worked perfectly, even if it didn't totally make sense why. Throw in Jordan's "sabbatical" and an unlucky career turned into a fairly lucky one, and that's before we get to the kajillionpilliongazillionfrazillionfriggallionmillion-to-one odds that he made it in the first place.

Now that we have that settled, let's quickly delve into something that I normally hate: numbers. You always hear about stats with Wilt, Oscar, Bird, Magic and LeBron, but Hakeem never comes up even though he's the all-time "holy shit" stat guy other than Wilt. He averaged a 20–11 as a rookie and never dipped below a 21–12 for the next twelve years, seemingly peaking in '89 and '90 (averaging a 25–14–3 with 2.3 steals and 4.1 blocks), then peaking again from '92 to '95 (a 27–11–4 with 3.9 blocks). If we created a stat called "stocks" (just steals plus blocks), Hakeem topped 300-plus stocks with at least 100 blocks/steals in twelve different seasons (nearly double anyone else),[25] notched 550 in 1990 (the only time anyone's ever topped 500) and finished

24. In Game 6 of the '87 playoffs (when Houston got knocked out by Seattle) Hakeem nearly beat Seattle by himself by slapping up a 49–25. A 49–25! *What?*
25. The complete list since '74 (2x minimum): Hakeem (12x), Robinson (7x), Ben Wallace (4x), Julius Erving (7x), Kareem (3x), Ewing (3x), Bobby Jones (3x), Jordan (2x), Josh Smith (2x), Andrei Kirilenko (2x), Elvin Hayes (2x), Terry Tyler (2x). MJ is the only guard on the list.

with 1,045 combined in '89 and '90 (the only time anyone ever topped 1,000 combined in two years). During his peak, Dream caused *five turnovers* per game along with countless other layups and runners he probably affected from game to game. (Note: I like "stocks" because it gives you an accurate reflection of his athletic ability and the havoc he wreaked on both ends. No modern center was better offensively *and* defensively than Dream. I should have come up with "stocks" four hundred pages ago. Crap.) He finished with 5,992 career stocks in 1,238 games (and another 717 stocks in 145 playoff games), coming within 8 stocks of becoming the only living member of the 6,000 Stock Club. As it is, he'll have to settle for being the only living member of the 5,900 Stock Club. And the 5,500 Stock Club. And the 5,000 Stock Club. And the 4,500 Stock Club. Robinson, Ewing, Kareem, Mutombo, Jordan, and every other post-1974 guy couldn't come within 70 percent of that 5,992.

And then there's this: During the slow-it-down, overcoached, way-too-physical mid-nineties, he played 197 games in '94 and '95 (over 8,000 minutes in twenty months as his team's only all-around threat) and averaged a 31–10–4 with 53 percent shooting and 218 stocks in 45 playoffs games against eight opponents with win totals ranging from 47 to 62.[26] With the league battling image/style/likability problems during Jordan's "sabbatical," that stretch of brilliance never resonated like it should have. Neither did Hakeem's longevity: he averaged a 21–12 as a rookie, with a 21–13 and 20 stocks in the '85 playoffs (5 games); fifteen years later, he averaged a 19–10 (regular season) and a 20–11 with 21 stocks in the '99 playoffs (5 games). He made the playoffs every year for his first fifteen except '92, never winning fewer than 42 games or more than 58, yet he only played with four All-Stars during his career (Sampson, Thorpe, Drexler and Barkley). He led the Rockets to the '86 Finals and came within a break or two of leading them there eleven years later;[27] except for Kareem, no center stayed *that* good for *that* long. Fifteen years? Even *ER* didn't last as long as Hakeem. When you remember that

26. The '95 Rockets won the title despite never having home-court advantage and winning two deciding games on the road (Utah and Phoenix). During those two title seasons, they won *eight* do-or-die games (four on the road) with Hakeem averaging a 32–11–6.

27. A bigger deal than you realize. Only Russell and Kareem were the best players on Finals teams at least 12 years apart. As for the worst players, the unofficial record holder is Will Perdue (played for Finals champs nine years apart).

Hakeem never would have made it without a series of miracles and mini-miracles that could never be replicated, I'm going out on a limb and saying that nobody will ever end up winning the *See If You Can Replicate Hakeem's Career!* game show. Not even if they change cloning laws in this country.[28]

10. OSCAR ROBERTSON

Resume: 14 years, 13 quality, 12 All-Stars . . . '64 MVP . . . '61 Rookie of the Year . . . Top 5 ('61, '62, '63, '64, '65, '67, '68, '69), Top 10 ('70, '71) . . . 3 All-Star MVPs . . . 5-year peak: 30–10–11 (first 5 seasons) . . . 2-year Playoffs peak: 31–11–9, 47.2 MPG (22 g's) . . . leader: assists (6x), FT% (2x) . . . career: 25.5 PPG (8th), 9.5 APG (3rd), 7.5 RPG, FT's (3rd), assists (4th), points (10th) . . . 2nd-best player on champ ('71 Bucks), starter on runner-up ('74 Bucks) . . . 25K Point Club

Back in February 2008, I was killing time in an airline club waiting for my delayed flight to board. Sitting only twenty feet away? NBA legend Oscar Robertson. Did I jump at the chance to make small talk with one of the ten greatest players who ever lived? Did I say to myself, "This is a gift from God, I can introduce myself to Oscar, tell him about my book, maybe even have him help me figure some Pyramid stuff out"? Did I even say, "Screw it, I gotta shake his hand"?

Nope. I never approached him.

Had I heard too many stories about Oscar being a miserable crank? Was I still scarred from finishing his 2003 autobiography, *The Big O: My Life, My Times, My Game,* maybe the angriest, most self-congratulatory basketball book ever written by anyone not named "Wilt"?[29] Did I feel bad because Oscar was a profoundly bitter product of everything that hap-

---

28. And if they do, I hope they start with Paul Mokeski.

29. Oscar wrote this bizarre book himself. He spends 331 pages railing against everyone, spinning stories his way and writing I-was-so-great things like "I ended the night with 43 points, including 21 of 22 free throws. No other Royal had more than 20." (His way of explaining Cincy's Game 7 loss to the '63 Celtics.) I finished the book and thought, "Now there's someone who didn't totally get The Secret." Even his defense of his excruciating announcing career is self-serving—apparently it was CBS' fault for not working with him, Brent Musburger's fault for not making him better and the NBA's fault for not wanting a black announcer to succeed. The Big O's book explained a lot. Let's put it that way.

pened to him? I don't know. But he may as well have been wearing a BE-
WARE OF OSCAR sign. And so we killed time just twenty feet apart for the
next three hours. I never said a word to him.

There are few happy Oscar stories. Teammates lived in perpetual fear of
letting him down. Coaches struggled to reach him and ultimately left him
alone. Referees dreaded calling his games, knowing they couldn't toss the
league's best all-around player even as he was serenading them with
F-bombs. Fans struggled to connect with a prodigy who had little interest
in connecting with them. After he finished in the top five for assists and
points for nine straight years, made nine straight first-team All-NBA appearances, averaged a triple double for the first five years of his career,
won the '64 MVP with Russell and Wilt in their primes and transformed
the role of guards in professional basketball, his team still decided, "We
need to get rid of him." Even his hometown paper (the *Cincinnati En-
quirer*) piled on by writing in February 1970, "For years, Oscar has privately scorned the Royals management; he has ridiculed Cincinnati and
its fans; he has knocked other players, both on his team and others; and he
has never been willing to pay a compliment. He is, has been and probably
will grow old a bitter man, convinced that it was all a plot." Of course,
Oscar included this excerpt in his book thirty years later as proof that the
notoriously right-wing newspaper was bigoted. Maybe both sides were
right.

Oscar grew up like Bizarro Jimmy Chitwood in *Bizarro Hoosiers,* the
never-released movie where a black basketball team prevailed . . . but not
before facing profound prejudice and hostility along the way.[30] When
Oscar's Crispus Attucks High School became the first all-black champion
in state history in 1955, Indianapolis rerouted its annual championship
parade toward the ghetto, with the implication being, *We don't trust the
blacks to behave themselves, so let's keep this self-contained.* Oscar never got
over it. Nor did he get over Indiana University's coach, Branch Mc-
Cracken, for recruiting him by saying, "I hope you're not the kind of kid
who wants money to go to school." (Note: If you don't think Oscar didn't
immediately stand up and walk out of the room, then you don't know

30. Crap, I just gave Disney a crappy idea for a formulaic sports movie. "Think *Remember the Titans* crossed with *Glory Road* crossed with *Mississippi Burning.* If we can get Jon
Hamm as the Crispus Attucks coach, we just need a director and we're good to go!"

Oscar well enough. Yes, that was a triple negative. I was due.) He chose the University of Cincinnati and had experiences that defy imagination six decades later. *This stuff actually happened?* His teachers belittled him in class and went out of their way to make him feel dumb. In Dallas, fans greeted him by tossing a black cat into his locker room.[31] In Houston, he couldn't check into his hotel because of a NO BLACKS ALLOWED sign . . . only his team stayed there anyway, with poor Oscar stuck sleeping in a Texas Southern dorm room. In North Carolina, someone delivered him a pregame letter from the Grand Wizard of the Ku Klux Klan that simply read, "Don't ever come to the South." In St. Louis, he and a black team-mate strolled into a restaurant and were greeted by stony silence, followed by every other customer clearing out within a minute or two. Even in downtown Cincinnati, they had "colored" water fountains and a cinema that wouldn't allow blacks as patrons . . . a theater that stood only half a block from where he starred for the Bearcats. Night after night, Oscar was filling a gym with fans and couldn't even walk down the street to catch a movie.

At some point, the Big O snapped, shut himself off and settled for tak-ing his frustrations out on everyone else. I don't blame him one iota— even in photos of Oscar from high school to the NBA, you can actually *see* the grim transformation in his face. Young Oscar is wide-eyed, innocent, grinning happily in every photo. Older Oscar looks like he's smoldering, like he's barely happy enough to fake a smile for the photographer. Had Magic or Jordan dealt with everything Oscar dealt with, they would not rank higher than him in this book. There's no way. So in a Pyramid that hinges on five dynamics—individual brilliance, respect from peers, the statistical fruits/spoils of whatever era, team success and an intangible

---

31. How much of a closed-minded asshole did you have to be to say the words "Oscar Robertson's playing against us tonight—let's rattle him by sticking a black cat in his locker room"? I mean, the losers who spend an hour making lame signs to hold up dur-ing games are bad enough, but imagine making a plan that includes questions like, "When do you want to stop by the pound and pick up the black cat?" and "Should we throw it in there before the game or at halftime? On the short list of the Worst Sports Fans of All Time, the black cat culprits rank up there with the ASU students who chanted "PLO" after Steve Kerr's father was assassinated in Lebanon. Other candidates: White Sox fans on Disco Demolition Night; everyone who was mean to Jackie Robinson or Larry Doby; William Ligue Sr. and Jr.; and the dude who threw beer at Ron Artest in Detroit.

connection with teammates—Oscar's career remains the toughest to project. Yes, he was brilliant. Yes, his opponents and teammates revered him. Yes, he took advantage of some undeniable gifts from his particular era. No, his teams didn't succeed as much as you'd think. No, his teammates didn't love playing with him (as much as they respected him). His statistics were remarkable, sure, but didn't we just spend a book that's now the size of *War and Peace* proving that basketball is more than just numbers? Shouldn't it matter that Oscar never made the Finals until his eleventh season, well after his prime, when he rode Kareem's gangly body to his first title?[32] Or that Oscar thrived statistically but missed four postseasons and only won two playoffs *total*? Or that three former teammates went on the record with the following quotes (from *Tall Tales*)?

> Jerry Lucas: "Oscar was a perfectionist and he'd yell at you if you messed up. Then you saw that he yelled at everyone, so you learned not to take it personally."

> Zelmo Beaty: "He was such a perfectionist that I never could have lived up to his expectations. The way he'd scream at Wayne Embry: 'You dummy, catch the ball . . . I put the ball right in your hands, how could you drop that one?' I felt sorry for Wayne."

> Wayne Embry: "Oscar was so far ahead of us humans that you could never come up to his level. But because of his greatness and what he meant to the franchise, you hated to fail him. Oscar's greatness sometimes overwhelmed Adrian Smith. [He'd] tell Oscar, 'Please, O, you know I'm trying, I really am. You gotta believe me, O.' "

Oscar's demanding personality overwhelmed everyone around him. After his playing career ended and CBS jettisoned him in 1975, nobody hired him as a coach, general manager, broadcaster, or adviser for the next thirty-four years (and counting). He resurfaced occasionally as the

---

32. Bill Bradley's take on Oscar: "Perhaps he doesn't give lesser players a large enough margin of error, but when they listen to him he makes All-Stars of meager talents. He controls events on the court with aplomb and the authoritarian hand of a symphony conductor." Sounds like a delight!

Grumpy Old Superstar in any story comparing the good old days to whatever was happening in the current era.[33] You could always rely on one churlish Oscar quote about how today's players make too much money; how he never could have palmed the ball so blatantly back in his day; how he would have loved to have played in an era of charter planes, personal trainers and low expectations; how today's triple doubles didn't matter because you could get an assist for anything nowadays. Every Oscar quote makes it sound like Dana Carvey should be playing him with Robert Downey Jr.'s *Tropic Thunder* makeup. *Back in my day, I used to get triple doubles playing in bad sneakers with nails sticking out of the floor and fans throwing stuff at me and I loved it!* There's just enough evidence that Oscar was an insufferable curmudgeon that he vacillated as high as no. 6 and as low as no. 12 for my Pantheon over a three-month span, ultimately settling here.

We know this much: every teammate and opponent revered his talents; the consensus seems to be "Jordan before Jordan"; and even West admits that it took him three or four years just to catch up to Oscar's level. But since every laudatory Oscar story centers around his uncanny consistency and not quotes like "nobody was better when it mattered" and "this guy could turn chicken shit into chicken salad," how can we reconcile his phenomenal individual success with his undeniable lack of team success? His supporting cast was serviceable from 1961 to 1966 (Lucas, Twyman, Embry, and '66 All-Star MVP Adrian Smith were his four best teammates); you could argue his teams slightly overachieved by finishing 60 games over .500, going 55–25 in '64 and dragging two Russell teams to a deciding playoff game. On the flip side, he played with quality players from '67 to '70—not just Lucas and Smith, but youngsters who went on to bigger and better things, like Jon McGlocklin, Bob Love, Happy Hairston, and Tom Van Arsdale—and never dominated an increasingly diluted league. Considering Jordan's supporting cast was equally uninspired and his league

---

33. I only found one Oscar story that made him seem semilikable: In *Tall Tales,* it's revealed Oscar called rebounds "ballboards." The book has a story in which Oscar's excited about playing with some young teammate, scrimmages with the guy, gets disappointed, and finally screams at him, "Man, get out of here—you can't grab me no ballboards!" And even that story was angry. Do you think it's a coincidence that one of the Sesame Street muppets was named *Oscar the Grouch*?

was tougher, it's hard to fathom why Jordan's teams kept improving while Oscar's teams wilted over time. Both were famously brutal with teammates, only Jordan's competitiveness boosted his team's collective confidence while Oscar chipped away at it. Can you succeed when you're petrified of letting your best guy down? Beyond that, can you succeed when your best scorer also happens to be the guy running your team? Obviously not. The Royals never won anything . . . and really, never did anyone else who fit that category.[34]

The bigger problem is that Oscar's top-ten resume rests mostly on one thing: his dominance from 1961 to 1965, when he *averaged* a triple double and unleashed holy hell from the guard position.[35] Those numbers make more sense than you'd think. Much like Wilt, Oscar was four or five years ahead of his time from a physical standpoint. There were only four "modern" guards during Oscar's rookie season; since the other three (Sam Jones, Greer, and West) were shooting guards, Oscar physically overpowered defenders the same way that Wilt boned up on the Darrell Imhoffs and Walt Bellamys. Imagine if 2009 Dwyane Wade played against a steady stream of Jason Terrys and Steve Blakes every night for 70 games, and for the other 12 he had to play against Kobe and Pierce. Then imagine every power forward was six foot six and under, and imagine there were only seven elite centers in a thirty-team league. Next, imagine he played in a run-and-gun era where there were 80 rebounds and 120 field goal attempts available *every game*. Would Wade average a 35–10–10 for the season? Of course he would. How is that different from Oscar's situation as a rookie? There were eight teams and eighty-eight players total, along with an unwritten "don't have more than two black guys on your roster" rule. So in a peculiar twist, some of Oscar's early success happened *because* of racism. Unleashing Oscar on a mostly white NBA in 1960 was like un-

34. When the guy running your offense averages 1,700 FG attempts and 900 FT attempts for nine solid years, and his team finishes 2–6 in playoff series over that stretch, haven't we reestablished the premise that you can't seriously contend if your PG doubles as your top scoring option? It's no accident that Oscar finished with the following totals on the '71 Bucks: 19–6–8, 1193 FGA, 385 FTA (regular season); 18–5–9, 210 FGA, 59 FTA (14 playoff games).

35. Borrowing a premise from Elliott Kalb, Oscar's PT/REB/ASS averages from his first 5 seasons (30.3, 10.4, 10.6) surpass the best possible one-of-the-first-5-years in each category from Bird ('84: 24.2, 10.1, 6.6); Magic ('82: 18.6, 9.6, 9.5); LeBron ('08: 30.0, 7.9, 7.2); Bryant ('01: 28.5, 5.9, 5.0); and nearly West ('62: 30.8, 7.9, 5.4).

leashing a horny Madonna on a nightclub filled with good-looking twenty-year-old Hispanic dancers. Check out the cream of the crop for Oscar's first season.

> *1961 All-Stars (guards): Oscar and Greer (black); West, Cousy, Tom Gola, Gene Shue, Larry Costello, Hot Rod Hundley, Richie Guerin (white)*
>
> *1961 assist leaders (guards in top twenty): Oscar, Guy Rodgers (black); West, Cousy, Gola, Shue, Costello, Hundley, Guerin, Johnny McCarthy, Bucky Bockhorn,[36] Chuck Noble (white)[37]*

KC Jones, Al Attles and West were Oscar's only opponents who could dream of handling him physically. Oscar used his size with scorching results, backing smaller players down, finding his favorite spots 15 feet from the hoop, then turning around and shooting over whomever. The Big O mastered a deadly high-post game that hadn't even been invented yet— like watching a Wild West duel where one guy pulls out a revolver and the other guy pulls out an Uzi. Within five years, the color of the league changed, the pace of the games slowed and Oscar lost that Uzi/revolver advantage to some degree.

> *1966 All-Stars (guards): Oscar, Greer, Rodgers, Sam Jones, Eddie Miles (black); West, Ohl, Adrian Smith (white)*
>
> *1966 assist leaders (guards in top twenty): Oscar, Rodgers, Wilkens, Greer, Mahdi Abdul-Rahman, Dick Barnett, Wali Jones, Sam Jones (black); West, Guerin, Ohl, Adrian Smith, Kevin Loughery, Howard Komives, Johnny Egan (white)*

---

36. I nominate Bucky Bockhorn as the whitest name in the history of professional sports. I picture a flattopped Bucky Bockhorn chain-smoking during halftime while drinking a glass of whole milk.

37. Since the league grew from 17 percent black to 75 percent black from 1960 to 1977, and that percentage stayed consistent ever since, only a fool would argue that a "modern" black player didn't have an enormous advantage. Even Walt Bellamy kicked ass for a couple of seasons. Ask yourself what would happen to the NBA in 2009 if 55 percent of the league suddenly transformed from black to white. A question that Adam Morrison and J. J. Redick ask themselves often. And I mean *often*.

Is that why Oscar's stats dropped slightly (28–6–10 from '66–'70) when he should have been peaking like West?[38] The Royals never won a playoff series after 1965; from 1968 to 1970, they missed the postseason completely as Oscar gained weight and said things like "My primary purpose is to get the team moving, establish community out there and make some money." There was no magic in his game, just a quality that Frank Deford described in 1968 as "eerily consistent," adding, "In eight years as a pro he has never averaged less than 28.3 points a game or more than 31.4, and in six of the eight years his average varied less than a point. In assists and free throws he has maintained the same level of consistency. He is like a .333 hitter who arrived at that figure by going 1 for 3 with one walk in every game of the season." [39] Instead of Mr. Clutch, Oscar was Mr. Groundhog Day. That went for his personality, too. He grumbled about being underpaid and marginalized so relentlessly that the Royals swapped him for Gus Johnson, only Oscar pushed for a $700K extension from Baltimore before vetoing the trade. (Before you excuse his behavior by saying, "The guy was frustrated, he just wanted to win," consider Magic Johnson's plight late in his career. He was saddled with Kareem's corpse in '89, a Mychal Thompson/Vlade Divac center combo in '90, then a Divac/Sam Perkins combo in '91. His best teammate was Worthy, an excellent player who couldn't crack my top forty-five. His second-best teammate was Byron Scott, never an All-Star and a textbook "right time, right place guy." In a loaded league, did Magic give up, point fingers or demand a trade? Nope. He averaged 59 wins per year and dragged the Lakers to two Finals.)[40] When the Royals shipped Oscar to Milwaukee, I know it's romantic to think, "They just wanted to give him a chance at a ring." Here's the reality: Cousy decided Oscar wasn't worth big money anymore and sent him packing for 40 cents on the dollar, then tabbed Tiny Archibald to re-

---

38. West peaked statistically in year ten with a 31–5–8 and 50% FG, then 31–4–8 in 18 playoff games.

39. Grumpy Old Editor: "So true—watching any single game was doubly frustrating. He never raised his game to the spectacular moment, ever, and yet at the end of the game, there were those maddening stats in the box score."

40. This analogy works better than you think: '89 Magic was the same age as '68 Oscar, although his sex life was infinitely more exciting.

place him.[41] The following players would never have been traded unless they demanded out: Bird, Magic, Jordan, West, Duncan, Shaq, Hakeem or Russell. In Oscar's case, the Royals moved in a different direction. Big difference.

Clearly, something was a little *off* with the Big O. You never heard the word "happy" with him, except for that transcendent '71 season when the Bucks destroyed everyone in their path. He ended up leaving Milwaukee just as unhappily as he'd left Cincinnati, furious that the team lowballed him (in Oscar's mind) before the '75 season. Sam Goldpaper's subsequent *New York Times* story started, "Pro basketball has lost what once was its greatest and most complete player. Oscar Robertson, after 14 seasons and many contract disputes, announced his retirement last night." You couldn't get through the second sentence of Oscar's basketball obituary without finding something negative. Twenty-eight years later, Jack Mc-Callum's *SI* feature wondering why Oscar had effectively disappeared from basketball started, "The Big O is known in basketball circles for being the Big Grind, a hoops curmudgeon who protests that in his day the players were better, the coaches smarter, the ball rounder. The reputation is not entirely undeserved. But today—40 years after a season in which he averaged a triple-double in points, rebounds and assists—Oscar Robertson wants you to know that he does not spend his hours stewing in a kettle of his own bile. Well, wants you to know is a little strong because, frankly, he doesn't much care what you think."

Again, complimentary . . . but negative. Nobody sifted through Oscar's never-ending acrimony well enough to figure him out. Even when he heroically donated a kidney to his ailing daughter in 1997 (saving her life), the moment came and went; you probably didn't remember until I reminded you. His biggest legacy had nothing to do with talent: Oscar's ballsy performance as president of the Players Association led to skyrocketing contracts, the ABA/NBA merger, an overhaul of free agency and

---

41. This fascinates me. Cousy played on six champs and understood The Secret as well as everyone, but he decided it made sense to trade Oscar for Flynn Robinson and Charlie Paulk after the Knicks and Lakers turned down every overture. Said Cousy after the trade, "Two superstars don't always mesh. The onus is on Oscar. If he decides to adjust to Alcindor, he could be terrific." Even though Oscar adjusted, doesn't it worry you that Cousy wondered if he could? By the way, Paulk lasted two years. There's a reason Cousy became an announcer.

every eight-figure deal we see today, only he never gets credit because the struggles of NBA players haven't been romanticized by writers or documentarians. Even stranger, of all the NBA legends who ever lived, only Oscar doesn't belong to a current franchise because the Royals moved to Kansas City in 1973 (and then Sacramento in 1985). He can't go back home like Russell/Bird in Boston, or Magic/West/Kareem in Los Angeles, or even Willis/Clyde/Ewing in New York, simply because home doesn't exist. He's a historical nomad. He belongs to nobody. And maybe it's better that way. To this day, Oscar remains damaged goods—a victim of his vile racial climate, someone who battled a rare form of post-traumatic stress disorder that can't be defined. As his teammate during Oscar's prime, you would have respected the hell out of him, you would have felt sorry for him, you would have marveled at him . . . but ultimately, I'm not sure you would have enjoyed playing with him that much. This was a man who decided during the epilogue of his book, "Once I heard someone say that in order to write love songs, you have to have been through some bad times. To write a love song, you had to have your heart broken. If that's the case, I can state right here and now that I could write the greatest songs in the world."

Of all the injuries that determined the ninety-six spots of my Pyramid, I can tell you this much: Oscar Robertson's broken heart resonates the most.[P55]

P55. Jason Whitlock thought my Oscar take was too harsh. I asked him to wait a couple of weeks and reread it, then write this footnote. Here's what he sent: "I devoured TBOB in 2.5 days. It was a joyful ride until the 10-page evisceration of the Big O. TBOB's cold and surgical analysis of the damage 1950s/1960s-style racism did to Robertson's personality and play left me outraged. The dissection seemed to lack the proper amount of sympathy. Robertson, like Russell, was cursed by intelligence the equal of his talent. Unlike Russell, Robertson never played for Red Auerbach, a courageous visionary willing to construct an environment that catered to a black superstar's identity. I wanted TBOB to feel sorry for Robertson, and excuse the human warts brought on by abuse. When I reread the passage 3 weeks later before writing this footnote, something different caught my attention: the nuanced empathy. TBOB captured Robertson's situation perfectly; that's all you can ask from a book that aspires to be the NBA's bible. Authentic history is filled with context and devoid of pity."

9. JERRY WEST

Resume: 14 years, 12 quality, 14 All-Stars . . . '69 Finals MVP . . . Simmons MVP ('70) . . . MVP runner-up: '66, '70, '71, '72 . . . Top 5 ('62, '63, '64, '65, '66, '67, '70, '71, '72, '73), Top 10 ('68, '69) . . . All-Defense (4x) . . . records: FTs, season (840); points, Playoff series (46.3) . . . leader: scoring (1x), assists (1x) . . . career: 27.0 PPG (5th), 27–7–6, 47% FG, 81% FT . . . 4-year peak: 30–6–6 . . . Playoffs (153 G): 29.3 PPG (3rd) . . . Finals: 30.5 PPG (55 G) . . . best player on one champ ('72 Lakers), best or 2nd-best player on 8 runner-ups ('62, '63, '65, '66, '68, '69, '70, '73 Lakers) . . . averaged a 26–5–10 during L.A.'s 33-game winning streak ('72) . . . 25K Point Club

"Ahead of Oscar?" you're saying. "Really? *Ahead of Oscar?*"

My defense in four parts:

1. They made the signature West move (going right, leaning forward, ready to make one last high dribble for a pull-up jumper) the league's logo. It remains the league's logo to this day. This seems relevant. If the Academy decided that the Oscar trophy should look like Laurence Olivier instead of Marlon Brando fifty years ago, wouldn't that have meant something?[42]

2. The Royals traded Oscar and the Lakers *never* would have traded West. (During the '70 season, the Royals floated a West-Oscar or Wilt-Oscar trade out there and the Lakers quickly said no.) Oscar's first four years were unquestionably better than Jerry's first four years; during the '65 season, *SI* wrote, "[West] is, above all else, an exceptional basketball player of a cut and magnetism comparable (some even say superior) to Oscar Robertson,"[43] with Warriors coach Alex Hannum adding, "Oscar does the right thing more often, but in some phases I now believe West is superior to Robertson. He creates many problems for a defense, and he is more exciting because of the increased range of his

---

42. Jabaal Abdul-Simmons counters, "Of course the NBA modeled the Logo after *a white man!*"

43. Jabaal counters, "Of course *SI* said the white man was just as good!"

long shot." So let's call it dead even for that year and the next two (West might even get a slight edge). West was undeniably superior for the next five seasons, with *SI* deciding in 1972, "There has been a groundswell for West the last few seasons, so that now he is often accepted as the equal, or the superior, of Oscar Robertson as the finest guard of all time."[44] As Oscar broke down over the '72 and '73 seasons, West submitted two more spectacular years (making first-team All-NBA both times and making two Finals). Why take Oscar over West when the last two-thirds of West's career was significantly better?

3. Any player from their generation would have rather dealt with West than Oscar as a teammate and if they say otherwise, they're lying. As early as 1965, *SI* wrote, "There is one intangible that nobody talks much about because it is hard to judge accurately, or even to judge at all. West seems to have a more settling influence on his team; he is not, like Robertson, a complainer. He does not bait officials." Even opponents loved the Logo. When the Lakers held Jerry West Night in March 1971, Bill Russell paid his own way to be there and said during the ceremony, "Jerry, I once wrote that success is a journey, and that the greatest honor a man can have is the respect and friendship of his peers. You have that more than any man I know. Jerry, you are, in every sense of the word, truly a champion. If I could have one wish granted, it would be that you would always be happy." Don't these stories count in the big scheme of things?[45]

4. As I keep mentioning, I'm somewhat of an evolutionary snob. To re-borrow the car analogy from much earlier, you'd rather race a 2010 BMW than a 1964 BMW; you'd rather drive cross-country in a 2010 BMW; you'd rather bet your life on getting 250,000 miles out of a 2010 BMW. You just would. It's the safe pick. They make finer auto-

---

44. Interesting note that may or may not have been racially motivated: West earned two laudatory *SI* megafeatures during his career (one in March '65, the other in February '72). They never wrote *one* about Oscar. Maybe that's because they thought he was a prick. But isn't it weird that "Jordan before Jordan" couldn't earn a single *SI* feature during his apex when West, Russell, Cousy and Wilt earned at least two each?

45. I like the days when the NBA held "(Fill in the Star) Night," gave them gifts and brought in peers to pay tribute to those guys, only the star was still playing. Can you imagine if a team like San Antonio held Tim Duncan Night if he wasn't retired? How mortified would Duncan be on a scale of 1 to 10? 15? 22? 27?

mobiles now—better torque, better engines, better shocks, better balance, better acceleration, better engineering, better everything. With that said, they *did* make a couple of transcendent cars in the sixties. And you know who was like the '64 Beemer? The Logo. Moses was the perfect self-made center, Bird the perfect self-made forward, and West the perfect self-made shooting guard—a little undersized (only six foot three, but with an 81-inch wingspan),[46] a good athlete (but not great), never dominating (but routinely unstoppable), and someone who willed himself to be better than he should have been. Watching him forty-plus years later is like watching a human basketball camp. Technically, he's perfect. His jumper is perfect. His defensive technique is perfect. His dribbling is right out of an infomercial. He runs in the most economical way possible. He could go right or left, attack the rim, pull up on a dime, post you up—the man had no holes other than a genetic inability to play above the rim. I watched him enough on tape to make the following proclamation: throw 1966 West in a time machine, insert him into the 2010–11 season and he'd make the All-Star team easy. He had a "modern" game, for lack of a better word. If anything, he may have been born too soon; much like Maravich and DeBusschere, the three-point line would have been an enormous advantage for him.

The same way Oscar was helped by a triple-double infatuation historically—West's legacy was wounded by the lack of a three-point line, the lack of All-Defense teams (didn't start until 1969) and that they didn't keep track of steals until 1973–74.[47]

As much as I hate trusting numbers to paint an overall picture, this 13-month stretch that started with the '65 playoffs and went through the '66 playoffs does a decent job of describing why the Logo mattered so much:

46. An 81-inch wingspan? Jay Bilas just hosed himself down.
47. Lenny Wilkens in *Tall Tales*: "I wish they had kept track of steals when Jerry and I played because we would have been the league leaders. He had hands that were as quick as a snake's tongue." West only played two months of the '74 season before blowing out his knee (ending his career), but in those 31 games, he had 81 steals. And that was at the tail end of his basketball life! Imagine West's resume if he was averaging 3 steals a game, made 3 three's a game, shot 40-plus from three and made 13 first-team All-Defenses.

'66 regular season: 79 games, 3,218 minutes (40.7 MPG) . . . 31.3 PPG,
    7.1 RPG, 6.1 APG . . . made 818 of 1,731 FGs (47.3%) . . . made 840
    of 977 FTs (86%) . . . record: 45–35
'65 and '66 Playoffs: 25 games, 1,089 minutes (43.6 MG) . . . 37.0 PPG,
    6.1 RPG, 5.4 APG . . . made 340 of 708 FGs (48%) . . . made 246 of
    279 FTs (88%) . . . record: 12–13 (lost twice in Finals)

Some things to keep in mind: First, Elgin blew out his knee in the '65
playoffs and limped through the '66 season (even missing 31 games).
Considering the Lakers squandered consecutive Finals to Boston teams
that featured five Hall of Famers and three top thirty-five Pyramid guys
(and nearly stole Game 7 in '66 to boot), that's pretty impressive for a
team with one great player. (So maybe that player was a little greater than
we thought?) Second, those 840 made free throws in '66? An all-time
record. It's never been topped. Not even by the Dipper. Including those 25
playoff games, imagine the sheer will of a six-foot-three guard getting to
the line nearly 1,300 times in 104 games—one-fourth of which were
games of the highest possible pressure—during a time when basketball
resembled hockey and players were routinely creamed on drives. Along
with Mikan, Russell, Kobe and Jordan, he's one of the five toughest NBA
superstars ever. Third, West finished the '66 regular season with the following rankings: second in points, fourth in assists, second in field goals
made and attempted, tenth in field goal percentage, first in free throws
made and attempted, fourth in free throw percentage and seventh in minutes, and if they'd kept track of steals, he would have cracked the top three
there. (To put those numbers in perspective, not even Michael Jordan ever
finished in the top ten in nine major categories.) Fourth, West set the
record for most points per game in a playoffs (five games or more), averaging 40.6 points during a remarkable '65 playoffs that included one of
the more heroic performances you never knew about: without Elgin, West
carried the Lakers by averaging a jaw-dropping 46.3 points in the first
round (squeezing them past Baltimore in six). Both of those records (40.6
and 46.3) still stand.

You won't find a better stretch of all-around basketball. And that was a
common theme of West's career: he always delivered whatever his team

needed. They needed him to shut a hot shooter down and he did it.[48] They needed him to make a big shot and he did it. They needed him to score points for most of the sixties, so that's what he did. During the last stage of his career (1969–1973), the Lakers needed West to be more of a ballhandler, so that's what he did (even cracking the top three in assists in '71 and '72). Because of his reckless style, he suffered so many injuries (and played through all of them) that people stopped keeping track: broken noses, busted thumbs, pulled hamstrings, sprained ankles, concussions, you name it. He raised his game so consistently that it earned his "Mr. Clutch" moniker, delivering a few iconic moments along the way—like his steal and buzzer-beating layup to win Game 3 of the '62 Finals, or his game-saving 60-footer in Game 3 of the '70 Finals, or a 53-point, 10-assist explosion in Game 1 of the '69 Finals that Russell himself blessed as "the greatest clutch performance ever against the Celtics."

If there was a telling moment from West's career, it was the way Russell's Celtics grew to revere him as the years passed. During the '69 Finals, Larry Siegfried was talking to Deford about the good fortune of West's hamstring injury—West had scored 197 points in the first five games before pulling his hamstring late in Game 5—and explained, "[West] is the master. They can talk about the others, build them up, but he is the one. He is the only guard . . . . His tribute is what the players think of him. We've played at about the same time but, if we hadn't, the one player I'd most like to see win a championship is Jerry West." After the soul-crushing Game 7 defeat, John Havlicek told Terry Pluto, "The guy I felt terrible for in those playoffs was Jerry West. He was so great, and he was absolutely devastated. As we came off the court, I went up to Jerry and told him, 'I love you and I just hope you get a championship. You deserve it as much as anyone who has ever played this game.' He was too emotionally spent to say anything, but you could feel his absolute and total dejection over losing."

And that's what stands out about West's career more than anything: he

---

48. Red Auerbach in *Tall Tales*: "What people don't realize is that Jerry West is one of the greatest defensive guards ever." He failed to add, "My only regret is that I never had a chance to coach him!" That was a Red staple for every retired number ceremony from 1980 to 2007; it was more reliable than Michael Buffer screaming, "Let's get ready to rummmmm-mble!" That's right, *two* Buffer footnotes in the Pantheon. And you know what? We might go for three. Don't put it past me.

had *horrible* luck. What happens if Selvy's shot falls? What happens if Elgin's body doesn't break down? What happens if the Lakers don't stupidly waive Don Nelson, who played such a crucial role for Boston in the '68 and '69 Finals? What happens if West doesn't pull his hamstring at the end of Game 5 in the '69 Finals, or if Wilt doesn't milk an injury and enrage his coach during the last five minutes of Game 7? What happens if Wilt and Baylor don't get hurt during the '70 regular season, or if Willis never limps onto the court for Game 7 of the Finals and drives the crowd into a frenzy? When everything finally and belatedly fell into place during the '72 season—a record 69 wins, a 33-game winning streak and his first title—West may have shattered the record for Most Fans with No Discernible Rooting Interest Who Just Felt Overwhelmingly Happy for a Winning Player.[49]

And so I'm forced to use the If My Life Depended on It Test here. From everything we just covered about West and Oscar, if your life depended on it and you could only pick one franchise player from 1960 to 1974, but you *had* to win at least three titles during that span, how could you not pick West? Even at his peak, teammates lived in fear of letting Oscar down. They walked on eggshells with him. They struggled to connect with him the same way a group of musicians would struggle to connect with someone who resides on a higher plane and blames them for being inferior. On the flip side, we have copious amounts of evidence to suggest that West elevated his teams—he didn't just make them better, they *wanted* to win for him, and not just that, he connected with them in the right way. Jerry West had a better handle on The Secret than Oscar Robertson, and that's why West was better. By a hair, but still.

8. KOBE BRYANT

Resume: 14 years, 13 quality, 12 All-Stars . . . Finals MVP: '09 . . . MVP: '08 . . . BS MVP: '06 . . . top 5 ('02, '03, '04, '06, '07, '08, '09, '10), top 10 ('00,

---

49. Even his postplaying career helps the West vs. Oscar argument—nobody wanted to hire Oscar, but West built eight title teams in two distinctly different eras (Shaq/Kobe and Magic/Kareem). He's the only top 20 Pyramid guy who thrived in basketball after his career ended. Does this mean he was a shrewder player than everyone realized, or was his success running the Lakers just a complete coincidence? I go with the former.

'01), top 15 ('99, '05) . . . All-Star MVP ('02, '07, '09) . . . All-Defense (10x, eight 1st) . . . scoring leader (2x) . . . 2nd-most points, one game (81) . . . 1st or 2nd best player on 5 champs ('00, '01, '02, '09, '10 Lakers) and 2 runner-ups ('04, '08) . . . 2-year peak: 33–6–5 . . . '01 Playoffs: 29–7–6, 47% FG (16 G) . . . '08–'10 Playoffs: 30-6-6, 46% FG (68 G) . . . 25K Point Club . . . career: 25.3 PPG (11th)

Question: What movie best captured the secret of basketball?

You answered *Hoosiers* without blinking. Don't lie. I know you did. And sure, that movie taught us about teamwork, fundamentals and the human spirit, as well as underrated lessons like "Don't tell the ref that the drunk guy who just wandered onto the court is one of your assistants"; "Women are fickle and evil, especially when they haven't boinked anyone in a while and they live with their mom"; "The basket is ten feet high even in a giant stadium"; "Whites will always beat blacks in basketball because they care more and they are smarter" (just kidding; that joke was for Spike Lee, who thought *Hoosiers* was secretly racist and might be right); "If the coach kicks someone off the team and then allows him back a few weeks later, this guy can just randomly show up in the movie again and it never has to be addressed"; and "If the best player on your team has scored 85 percent of your points in a championship game, and you have the ball with a chance to win, don't get fancy—clear the floor and run a freaking play for him." But *Hoosiers* was the wrong answer. Sorry.

The right answer? That's right . . . *Teen Wolf.*

Most people mistakenly think it's a werewolf comedy. Nope. It's a thinking man's basketball movie. You missed the signs because you were too busy wondering how Michael J. Fox[50] nearly notched a triple double in the climactic game even though he was five-foot-four and dribbled with his head down . . . why Mick was allowed to stand under the basket to psych Fox out for the last two free throws . . . why they never ran more

---

50. Undeniable symbolism given Kobe's love for MJ: an actor with the initials MJ played the Wolf (the character who represented Kobe's struggles the most). Also, my friend Christian once argued that Fox picked number 42 as an homage to Jackie Robinson because he was the first werewolf to play organized, competitive basketball. Lots to think about with *Teen Wolf.*

plays for Fat Boy when his hook shot was sublime . . . why the Wolf's high school wasn't deluged with reporters and camera crews from around the country . . . why Coach Finstock never gets more credit in the Greatest Sports Movie Characters Ever discussion[51] . . . even where "Win in the End" ranks against "You're the Best" and "No Easy Way Out" in the pantheon of Greatest Cheesy Eighties Sports Movie Montages. I don't blame you for getting sidetracked; you just missed the movie's enduring lesson.

After Fox first transforms into the wolf—the most amazing sports movie game to attend, narrowly edging the Allies/Nazi game from *Victory*, and only because you can't top a sparsely attended high school hoops contest in which a player turns into a monster and starts dunking on everyone—once the shock wears off and the Wolf starts kicking ass, his teammates turn into props. At one point later in the season, a teammate is dribbling up the court and the Wolf swipes the ball from him, zigzags through traffic and gets a layup. The success goes right to his head. He starts banging the hottest chick in school. His buddy Stiles starts marketing "Wolf" T-shirts. He's the big wolf on campus. But even with the team winning and making a late run at the playoffs, his teammates can't help resenting the Wolf and wishing they played for someone else. He's getting all the credit. He's taking all the shots. They have no stake in the team's performance anymore. So they stop working as hard and openly grumble about Fox/Wolf. With his personal life falling apart as well, he makes a stunning decision to play the regional championship game as himself. You know the rest. The team meshes together and everyone plays a key role (especially number 45, who turns into Bill Russell); Fox explodes for an 18–8 with three steals[52] and sinks the winning free throws (after recovering from a flagrant foul on a give-and-go that

51. His enduring advice: "There are three rules that I live by: never get less than twelve hours sleep; never play cards with a guy who has the same first name as a city; and never get involved with a woman with a tattoo of a dagger on her body. Now you stick to that, and everything else is cream cheese." This was also good: "It doesn't matter how you play the game, it's whether you win or lose. And even that doesn't make all that much difference."

52. From what we saw, Fox notched 14 points (5-for-6 FG, 4-for-4 FT), 6 assists, and 2 steals. Number 45 (young Bill Russell) chipped in with 10 points and 3 blocks. Fat Boy had 5 and number 33 had 6. We saw 35 of the 47 points after Fox's return; I projected his stats for the 12 we missed and ignored looped footage (no sports movie had worse editing).

took eight seconds to complete even with four seconds left on the clock); the fans happily pour onto the court as Fox plants a smooch on his homely friend Boof; and we learn that you can still derive individual glory from winning. The end.

What does this have to do with Kobe? He spent his career vacillating between a Fox and a Wolf. The Fox persona dominated his first five NBA seasons, peaking in Year Five with his unparalled uber-sidekick performance in the '01 playoffs. He battled an identity crisis during Los Angeles' third title season—half-man, half-wolf—before morphing into the Wolf over the following two seasons, lowlighted by a sexual assault charge, the ugly deterioration of his relationship with Shaq,[53] and his meltdown during his team's stunning collapse in the 2004 Finals (in the four Detroit victories, Kobe missed fifty-seven of eighty-six shots). After the Lakers chose Kobe over Shaq that summer, the Wolf assumed command for a surreal three-year stretch that we'll remember for these three things:

1. Phil Jackson stepping down after Shaq's departure for Miami, then releasing a devastating book, *The Last Season,* in which he repeatedly skewered Bryant for being immature ("Ask Shaq to do something and he'll say: 'No, I don't want to do that.' But after a little pouting, he will do it. Ask Kobe and he'll say, 'Okay,' and then he will do whatever he wants.") and selfish ("Kobe is missing out by not finding a way to become part of a system that involves giving something larger than himself. He could have been heir apparent to MJ and maybe won as many championships. He may still win a championship or two, but the boyish hero image has been replaced by that of a callous gunslinger."). The most damning passage, by far: " 'You're not gonna believe this,' [Mitch

53. When Colorado police interrogated Kobe about sexual assault, Kobe inexplicably mentioned that Shaq dealt with stuff like this (apparently meaning a hookup gone wrong) all the time. FYI: This is why Shaq hated Kobe! Also, there's a legendary tale—probably apocryphal—about David Stern's team having an emergency meeting to discuss Kobe's charges, with someone theorizing that Kobe's mistake was not realizing this innocent Colorado girl wasn't as experienced as NBA groupies, so when he tried for "the trinity," it didn't go over too well. A confused Stern apparently asked someone to explain the trinity. There was an awkward silence, followed by someone hesitantly explaining a popular sexual act in NBA circles that I am afraid to even print. Apparently the look on Stern's face was beyond priceless and hasn't been approached before or since. Also, House and I had a coin flip to see who got to use "The Trinity" for their next fantasy team name. House won.

Kupchak] said, telling me about Kobe and the rape allegations in Colorado. Was I surprised? Yes, but not entirely. Kobe can be consumed with surprising anger, which he's displayed toward me and his teammates." Yeeesh. You weren't entirely surprised that your best player was accused of rape??? How did those two ever join forces again after that book?[P56]

2. Kobe's 81-point game defined his pre-Gasol legacy for better *and* worse. He was bitterly selfish that season—irritated by his brutal supporting cast, Shaq's success in Miami and the thought of his prime wasting away—to the degree that I joked, "The best part about playing craps with Kobe must be watching him eventually drift over to the 'Don't Pass' line."[54] But 81 points??? No perimeter player can hit that mark without a disarming amount of ballhogging. I watched with my father: we found ourselves fascinated by Kobe's icy demeanor, the lack of enthusiasm from L.A.'s bench, even the dysfunctional way his teammates killed themselves going for rebounds and steals to get him more shots.[55] When an exhausted Kobe reached eighty-one and Jackson (who had returned that season) subbed for him, his teammates greeted him with halfhearted hugs and high-fives. The best reaction belonged to Jackson, who seemed amused, supportive and somewhat mortified, like how Halle Berry's husband probably looked after sitting

P56. Jackson's *The Last Season* featured the greatest random NBA anecdote ever: "I did hear of one (players-only) meeting that made quite an impression on players. During a West Coast trip, Jack McMahon, who coached the Cincinnati Royals in the 1960s, called a meeting in his hotel to restore order. The players dreaded it, but according to my former Knicks teammate, Jerry Lucas, they were greeted with two cases of beer, four quarts of whiskey and three hookers. 'Guys, you figure this out,' McMahon said before leaving the room. The Royals figured it out, all right, going on a long winning streak." The sixties, everybody! Can't they work that story into a *Mad Men* episode?

54. That wasn't even the best craps joke of my career—when I was bartending, a friend of mine dated a girl who couldn't have orgasms (she had like a mental block), and when he was complaining about it I joked, "I want to play craps with her just to see if she keeps betting on the 'Don't Come' line." I am the king of hacky craps jokes.

55. It's always riveting to watch a basketball player score copious amounts of points, even if he's freezing out teammates in the process. At halftime in a Pitino-era Celtics game, they had a Special Olympics scrimmage, and one kid seemed a little too, um, competent to be playing in it. Not only did he drop like 20 points in 4 minutes, I'm convinced to this day that he was the impetus for *The Ringer*. In fact, this kid was so good that everyone in my section feared Pitino would sign him to a $30 million deal. But guess what? Even though it didn't seem quite fair that the kid was playing, it was still a moment. Everyone was riveted. Everyone was cheering. Of course, I was drunk at the time, so this might not have happened the way I remember it. The important thing is that *I* believe it happened.

through his first screening of *Monster's Ball*. Only later would we appreciate the significance of the second-highest scoring outburst ever ... as well as the comedy of Kobe finishing with just two assists. Never has an NBA star wolfed it up quite like that.

3. The 2006 Lakers blew a 3–1 series lead to Phoenix, with Kobe's teammates blowing Game 7 so badly that Kobe came out after halftime and spitefully took just two shots over the next fourteen minutes of game action (as Phoenix's lead ballooned to 25, no less). I'd blame him more if he hadn't been playing with the likes of Kwame Brown and Smush Parker, but still. Not his finest hour. One year later (after Phoenix carved the Lakers up in Round One), Kobe petulantly demanded out and nearly landed in Chicago twice before ultimately staying put.[P57] Of the best fifteen players ever, he's the only non-center nearly traded in his prime. Even more damning, nobody was saying back then, "Wow, they're really gonna trade someone as great as Kobe?" But Jackson and Derek Fisher slowly pulled him back into the fold, with Kobe embracing his inner Fox shortly before the hideously one-sided Gasol trade. Three Finals appearances and two titles later, the consensus seems to be that Kobe "gets it," although every time the Wolf creeps out—like during Game 7 of the 2010 Finals, when Boston swarmed him with double-teams and dared him to hoist low-percentage shots (and for three quarters, he obliged)—we're reminded that Kobe never totally figured this thing out. He always wants to win, but he always wants to be the hero. And sometimes, you can't be both.

Looking back, Kobe never seemed totally comfortable in his own skin—dating back to his ill-fated decision to shave his tiny head MJ-style in the late nineties, or his unintentionally hilarious rap duet with Tyra Banks during All-Star Weekend in 2000—with the Fox/Wolf internal struggle symbolizing everything. He spent the past five years systematically rehabbing his image as a player and public figure, starting with a number change (from 8 to 24), then a self-provided nickname ("Black

P57. The first time, Chicago refused to include Luol Deng in the deal. (That one fact pretty much ends any "Kobe was better than MJ" argument.) A few weeks later, the Bulls included Deng in their offer (along with two of Ty Thomas, Joakim Noah and Ben Gordon, plus draft picks), but Kobe vetoed it because he thought they were gutting their team.

Mamba")[P58], then an identity change (he's evolved into a devoted family man and marvelous teammate with a wonderful sense of humor, or so we're expected to believe), then a "coolness" change (Nike fake-leaked a video of Kobe apparently jumping a speeding car), then a stylistic change (smartly shifting to an efficient offensive game centered around an improved outside shot, a deadly fallaway and multiple low-post moves), eventually finding himself as the defensive specialist and crunch-time stud of our 2008 Olympic team.[56] When Spain whittled America's lead to two late in the Gold Medal game, we called time-out as I thought to myself, "This was my biggest fear: a tight game with the crowd going crazy and multiple U.S. guys saying, 'I got it!' " Instead, everyone deferred to Kobe and he came through. Never has the best-player-alive argument been resolved so organically. The next two years were fascinating: many fans vaulting Kobe to Jordan's level without Kobe totally earning it. His crunch-time numbers paled in comparison to LeBron's numbers in 2009 and 2010, only everyone believed Kobe was the league's premiere assassin.[P59] He played eighteen Finals games from 2008–10 and didn't submit one ESPN Classic performance, only nobody could consider that stretch a failure since the Lakers won two titles. He was great, but how great? We argued his merits until our faces turned purple on television shows, radio shows, columns, blogs, message boards and Twitter. People defended him passionately and ripped him just as passionately. Still, nobody could deny the girth of his resume after they were fitting him for a fifth ring.

P58. Kobe's explanation: "The black mamba can strike with 99 percent accuracy at maximum speed, in rapid succession. That's the kind of basketball precision I want to have. Not being able to train the last two summers, I was in a gunfight with a rusty butter knife. I did my share of killing, but I was just fighting to survive." It's funny when wrestlers change gimmicks, it's funny when Diddy changes nicknames, and it's downright hysterical when an NBA star once accused of sexual assault decides it would be a fantastic idea to embrace the identity of a thirteen-foot serpent.

56. That stretch led to more pop culture/sports analogies than any athlete I can remember. My unofficial count from columns includes Tony Montana, Sonny Corleone, Michael Corleone, Fox/Wolf, Hollywood Hulk Hogan, Crockett/Tubbs (along with Shaq), Eddie Murphy, A-Rod, a porn actress named Houston and my personal favorite, Marlo Stanfield. *"My name is my name!"* Couldn't you see Kobe screaming that?

P59. According to 82games.com, LeBron's '09 crunch-time stats (56% FG, 31.2 FGA, 20.8 FTA, 55.9 PPG and 12.6 APG per 48 minutes) were superior to Kobe's numbers (46% FG, 39.1 FGA, 18.2 FTA, 56.7 PPG, 5.7 APG). The '10 season was much more one-sided: LeBron's 49% FG, 41.0 FGA, 26.1 FTA, 66.1 PPG and 8.3 APG easily trumped Kobe's 44% FG, 36.0 FGA, 18.9 FTA, 51.2 PPG and 3.6 APG.

By any calculation, Kobe had passed Oscar and Jerry as the third-best guard ever.

Did Oscar and Jerry have a fair chance to hold him off? When Gladwell and I exchanged emails for an ESPN.com feature in 2009, I mentioned how Kobe's era enabled a career that wasn't possible forty years ago. There are so many ways to extend a basketball star's prime today—training techniques, medical advancements, video breakdowns, better equipment—that he's been a kid in a candy store these past few years. It went beyond heeding Jordan's "every summer, I need to add one thing to my game" lesson (like Kobe learning low-post moves from Olajuwon after winning the '09 title), or Malone's "take care of your body and your body will take care of you" lesson. A defining Kobe story: when Michael Lewis wrote about Shane Battier studying hours of video to help himself defend Kobe's moves, Kobe had someone create a similar video breakdown, broke down his own moves, then added a few wrinkles to keep Battier on his toes (almost like they were playing chess). Another defining Kobe story: when I visited Nike's development building (in which they customize sneakers for specific athletes), their department head confessed that Kobe was their favorite client. Why? Because he kept pushing them to make perfect shoes for him, repeatedly putting himself through grueling workouts with sensors all over his body. After the 2009 playoffs, Kobe pressed them to create a low-top sneaker that would prevent him from rolling his ankles—which seems incongruous on paper—yet Nike believed they pulled it off. And only because he kept challenging them. Back in the days of Oscar and Jerry? He's wearing crummy Chuck Taylors and rolling his ankles.

Gladwell thought I was describing a capitalization rate, "which refers to how efficiently any group makes use of its talent. Sub-Saharan Africa is radically undercapitalized when it comes to, say, physics: There are a large number of people who live there who have the ability to be physicists but never get the chance to develop that talent. Canada, by contrast, is highly capitalized when it comes to hockey players: If you can play hockey in Canada, trust me, we will find you. One of my favorite psychologists, James Flynn, looked at capitalization rates in the United States for various occupations: For example, what percentage of American men who are intellectually capable of holding the top tier of managerial/professional jobs actually end up getting a job like that. The number is surprisingly low, like

60 percent or so. That suggests we have a lot of room for improvement. What you're saying with the NBA is that over the past decade, it has become more and more highly capitalized: There isn't more talent than before, but there is—for a variety of reasons—a more efficient use of talent."[P60]

Which is why Kobe never scratched Jordan's ceiling as a player, but his career—the totality of it—might end up being greater. Heading into the 2010–11 season, he's only thirty-two years old, with a staggering fourteen seasons and 1,219 games on his odometer (regular season plus play-offs).[P61] Let's say he plays four more quality years and averages 24 points, makes two more Finals (winning one), locks down one first-team All-NBA and three second-teams, and avoids a debilitating injury. (Conceivable.) Here's his hypothetical resume after the 2013–14 season: six rings and nine Finals appearances; 60,000 minutes (regular season and playoffs combined); 34,000 points (third all-time); 1,300 regular season games (the record is 1,611, held by Robert Parish); 6,500 playoff points (easily a record); nine first-team All-NBAs, five seconds and two thirds. Again, that's a *reasonable* scenario (health permitting). Throw in three hanging-around seasons and he's suddenly the Kareem of non-centers, either the third- or fourth-best player in history. The sheer volume of numbers will add up: rings, All-NBAs, All-Star appearances, points scored, games played, playoff games, total minutes. At the very least, "Jordan vs. Kobe" will be a debate. And I will get angry and tell you to shut up, and that we need to stop comparing people to Jordan, but still, it's a debate. Someone could ask, "If you were starting a team and could grab one guy for his entire career, would you rather take 1984–2003 MJ (with five full years of missed seasons) or 1997–2016 Kobe (with 0 missed seasons)?" And someone else will have trouble answering. Not me. But someone.

P60. Piggybacking this point: We have an unusual number of older stars (Nash, Dirk, Duncan, Pierce, Kobe, etc.) extending their peaks; an unusual number of under-twenty-five stars (Durant, Howard, Paul, Rose, Rondo, etc.) coming through; and an unusual number of franchise players (LeBron, Melo, Howard, Bosh, Wade, etc.) seizing their primes and almost-primes. Why? Because potential stars rarely get sidetracked by drugs, money or injury anymore. They have a significantly higher chance of succeeding now. And for longer.

P61. Of the straight-from-high-school stars from 1989–2000 (T-Mac, KG, Kobe, Kemp, Al Harrington, Jermaine O'Neal, Jonathan Bender, Rashard Lewis and Darius Miles), only Kobe and Lewis avoided major knee problems . . . and Kobe's played two more seasons and 14,000 more minutes than Lewis.

So those are the stakes for Kobe, someone who remade his career thanks to a fortuitous trade and a breathtaking amount of hard work. He only cares about getting better and keeping what he already earned. He learned to trust his teammates—not totally, but enough. He earned begrudging appreciation from even die-hard Kobe bashers like myself, and if there was a silver lining in the LeBron/Wade alliance last summer, it was the thought of Kobe watching The Decision, shaking his head, calling them "pussies" under his breath, then heading out for a late-night workout. Say what you want about Kobe Bean Bryant, but he never took the easy way out. Still, we'll always wonder if his ego squandered his prime to some degree. During the 2004 playoffs, Phil Jackson said about him, "Sometimes his needs to overwhelm the rest of the ballclub's necessity . . . as we get into the playoffs, that'll dissipate, because he knows that he's got to put his ego aside and conform to what we have to do if we're going to go anywhere in the playoffs. Any player that takes it on himself to do that [play for himself] knows that he's going against the basic principles of basketball. That's a selfish approach to the game. You know when you're breaking down the team or you're breaking down and doing things individualistic, you're going to have, you know, some unhappy teammates . . . and he knows these things . . . Intuitively, I have to trust the fact that he's going to come back to that spot and know that the timing's right. The season's over, things have been accomplished, records have been stuck in the books, statistics are all jelled in, now let's go ahead and play basketball as we're supposed to play it."

Exactly. Kobe knew the right way to play, but for many years, playing that way wasn't his first choice. He's the only great player who knew The Secret and didn't take care of it. Following him back then, at least for me, was like having a friend purchase a beautiful $10 million mansion—like one of those ones in New Orleans where they film bad Brad Pitt movies—then paint it a weird color, refuse to hire a housekeeper, decorate it with goofy modern furniture and basically ruin the house. *Buddy, what the fuck are you doing? Don't you realize what you have here?* For years and years, Kobe never did. He played basketball with a singular mentality, trusting his own exploits would lift teammates but only intermittently bothering to make them better in a conventional way. Even on the biggest night of his career (Game 7 of the 2010 Finals), his demons bubbled to the surface:

three quarters of Kobe wolfing it up before a timely switch back to Fox mode averted disaster. Detractors villfied him for a dreadful performance (six of twenty-four shooting, appalling shot selection); defenders cele-brated his defense, free throw shooting (eight of nine in the last quarter) and rebounding (fifteen in all). Did Kobe Bryant play well enough in that game, or did Boston's ragged performance allow him to dodge the biggest bullet of his career? There was no right answer.[P62] We argued about it all summer. We will continue to argue about it. For the most polarizing NBA superstar since Wilt, it was just another polarizing night at the office.

7. TIM DUNCAN

Resume: 13 years, 13 quality, 12 All-Stars . . . Finals MVP: '99, '03, '06 . . . MVP: '02, '03 . . . Runner-up: '01, '04 . . . '97 Rookie of the Year . . . top 5 ('98, '99, '00, '01, '02, '03, '04, '05, '07), top 10 ('06, '08, '09), top 15 ('10) . . . All-Star MVP ('00) . . . All-Defense (13x, 8 first) . . . leader: FG (1x), re-bounds (1x) . . . best player on 4 champs ('99, '03, '05, '07 Spurs) . . . '03 Playoffs: 25–15–5, 3.3 blocks, 53% FG (24 G) . . . 2-year peak: 24–13–4, 51% FG . . . Playoffs: 23–12–4 (170 G) . . . career: 21.1 PPG (36th), 11.6 RPG (20th), 2.3 BPG (17th), 50.8% FG

I once asked my father, "Would you read a column about how underrated Tim Duncan is?"

Dad made a face. He played with his hair. He seemed confused. "A whole column on Tim Duncan?"

"You wouldn't read it?"

"I don't think so. I'd see the headline, skim the first two paragraphs, and flip to the next article."

P62. Actually, there was: Kobe *sucked* in that game. When they removed him with 4:00 remaining in the third quarter—trailing by 9, with Kobe having bricked 15 of 19 shots—the vibe in the stands was like nothing I've ever felt before. Their Lakers weren't just blowing the title; their idol was scorching his own legacy. He never would have lived that game down. Then Boston started throwing up bricks, got outworked on the boards and let them off the hook. For the series, Kobe shot 28 percent in the 7 fourth quarters . . . but considering he had a broken finger and sore knees from playing 304 games in 32 months (plus extra duty in the '08 Olympics), you had to cut him some slack. As much as it killed me. Although it doesn't stop me from making "6 for 24" jokes all summer.

"Seriously? He's the best player of the past ten years!"

"Nahhhhhhh," Dad maintained. "Nobody wants to read about Tim Duncan. He's not that interesting."

At least that's what Dad keeps telling himself. Duncan's prowess had been a sore subject with him (and me) since the 1997 lottery, when the Celtics had a 36 percent chance of landing the first pick and San Antonio plucked it away.[57] Our lost savior carried the Spurs to four titles over the next decade, a number that could have stretched to six if not for Fisher's miracle shot in 2004 and Nowitzki's heroic three-point play in 2006. What did we miss besides a slew of 58-win seasons and a few titles? For starters, the chance to follow the most consistent superstar in NBA history: just year after year of 23–12's, 25–13's and 21–11's with 50% shooting. He kicked things off by submitting one of the best postmerger debut seasons: 21–12, 271 stocks, 56 wins, first-team All-NBA and Rookie of the Year. He captured a title in his second season, succeeding McHale and Hakeem as the Dude with the Most Low-Post Moves Who Should Be Double-Teamed at All Times. And it went from there. His placid demeanor never wavered, nor did his trademark shot (an old-school banker off the glass). Still chugging along as a top-five player after 1,000-plus regular-season and playoffs games, he made up for the natural erosion in physical skills with an ever-expanding hoops IQ; he's been the league's smartest player for nearly his entire career.[58] If there's a major difference between Young Duncan and Older Duncan, it's how he kept improving as a help defender and overall communicator. Whenever I watch the Spurs in person, that's the first thing I always notice: how well they talk on defense. It's a friendly, competitive chatter, like five buddies maintaining a running dialogue at a blackjack table as they figure out ways to bust the dealer. Duncan remains the hub of it all, the oversize big brother looking

57. Blame me for this. I broke plans to watch the lottery with Dad, choosing to monitor the proceedings at the Cape Cod house of a girlfriend my friends referred to only as "the Lunatic." Needless to say, we didn't make it too long. But even as the trip was unfolding, I thought to myself, "This is the wrong move. I'm selling Dad down the river. I don't even like this girl that much." But I couldn't stop myself. The C's ended up with the third and sixth picks. I set the franchise back five years. Again, I blame me.

58. Beyond the usual "smartest player" instincts, Duncan had a knack for picking his spots and sensing exactly when his team needed him to take over. If they needed a 34–22 from TD in a must-win playoff game, he did it. If they needed an 18-point fourth quarter from TD, he did it. If they only needed him to do dirty work, protect the rim, draw double teams for other guys and make everyone else better, he did it. He could adapt to any game and any situation. That's what separated him from KG.

out for everyone else, the one always throwing an arm around a teammate's shoulder. He's their defensive anchor, smartest player, emotional leader, crunch-time scorer and most competitive gamer, one of those rare superstars who can't be measured by statistics alone. Fifty years from now, some stat geek will crunch numbers from Duncan's era and come to the conclusion that Duncan wasn't better than Karl Malone. And he'll be wrong.

Now, I'm not a fan of the whole overrated/underrated thing. With so many TV and radio shows, columnists, bloggers and educated sports fans around, it's nearly impossible for anything to be rated improperly anymore. But I say Tim Duncan is underrated. You know what else? I say he's *wildly* underrated. Four rings, two MVPs, three Finals MVPs and nine first-team All-NBA nods . . . and he's still chugging along. Do you realize his best teammates were Robinson (turned thirty-three in Duncan's rookie year), Ginobili (never a top-fifteen player) and Tony Parker (ditto)? Or that he never played for a dominant team because the Spurs were always trapped atop the standings, relying on failed lottery picks, foreign rookies, journeymen, aging vets and head cases with baggage for "new" blood? Maybe that's one reason we failed to appreciate him: he never starred for a potential 70-win juggernaut that generated a slew of regular season hype. Another reason: he always had a little too much Pete Sampras in him. He lacked Shaq's sense of humor, Kobe's singular intensity, KG's menacing demeanor, Iverson's swagger, LeBron's jaw-dropping athleticism, Wade's knack for self-promotion, Nash's fan-friendly skills or even Dirk's villainous fist pump. The defining Duncan quality? The way he bulged his eyes in disbelief after every dubious call, a grating habit that became old within a few years. His other "problem" was steadfast consistency. If you keep banging out first-class seasons with none standing out more than any other, who's going to notice after a while?

There's a Hollywood precedent: once upon a time, Harrison Ford pumped out monster hits for fifteen solid years before everyone suddenly noticed, "Wait a second—Harrison Ford is unquestionably the biggest movie star of his generation!" From 1977 to 1992, Ford starred in three *Star Wars* movies, three *Indiana Jones* movies, *Blade Runner, Working Girl, Witness, Presumed Innocent* and *Patriot Games,* but it wasn't until he carried *The Fugitive* that everyone realized he was consistently more bankable than Stallone, Reynolds, Eastwood, Cruise, Costner, Schwarzenegger and every other peer. As with Duncan, we knew little about Ford outside of his work.[59] As with Duncan, there wasn't anything inherently compelling about him. Ford only worried about delivering the goods, and we eventually appreciated him for it.

Will the same happen for Duncan someday? It's not like he lacks numbers or credentials. He closed out a '99 Lakers sweep against Shaq with a 37–14–4 and a 33–14–4 in Games 3 and 4, averaged a 27–14 in the '99 Finals, and became the second-youngest player to win Finals MVP. He carried a truly underwhelming supporting cast[60] to a high 2002 playoff seed by topping 3,200 minutes, 2,000 points, 1,000 boards, 300 assists, and 200 blocks by season's end. In the '02 playoffs, battling the two-time defending champs with a crappy team and Robinson missing the first two games, Duncan averaged a 29–17–5 in a five-game loss to eventual champ L.A. (superior to Shaq's 21–12–3). During one seven-game stretch against the Lakers and Mavericks in the '03 playoffs, he averaged a 31–17–6 (and closed out Shaq's team with a 37–16–4).[61] He cruised to a 2003 Finals MVP by throttling Jersey with a 24–17–5, closing the Nets out with a near quadruple double (a should-have-been-legendary 21–20–10–8) and getting little help from an aging Robinson (playoffs: 7.8 PPG, 6.6 RPG) or anyone else (Parker, Ginobili and Stephen Jackson combined for less than 37 PPG and shot 40 percent combined). After a discouraging summer in 2004 (Fisher's shocker and a crushing Olympics defeat),[62] a visibly worn Duncan adopted Pedro Serrano's bald/goatee look, fought through nagging injuries and led the Spurs over Detroit in a choppy Finals, winning Fi-

59. It struck me as I'm writing this—I don't even know if Duncan has a wife and kids. Or anything about him. He's one of those guys who could pop up in *Us Weekly* dating someone like Eva Mendes and you'd be thoroughly confused, only you wouldn't be able to figure out why.

60. Bruce Bowen, Antonio Daniels, rookie Tony Parker, Malik Rose, Danny Ferry, Charles Smith, a past-his-prime David Robinson, a pretty-much-past-his-prime Steve Smith and a past-his-being-past-his-prime Terry Porter. And everyone claimed KG didn't have help?

61. That Lakers series was tied at 2–2 when Duncan put up a 64–30 in the next two wins (16 for 25 in the 29-point blowout that clinched it). Shaq had a 51–22 in those games. Also, Duncan's '03 postseason had the highest win share rating ever: 5.98. I'd be more excited if I knew what this means.

62. Duncan never received enough credit here: after playing 275 of a possible 289 games the previous three years, he sucked it up and represented his country while KG passed. Why? Because KG was tired from making it past the second round for the first time. But KG is the "warrior"? Really? Wait, why do I keep ripping a Celtic?

nals MVP by default despite Ben Wallace and Rasheed Wallace tag-teaming him for seven games. (Phoenix's Mike D'Antoni summed it up best: "[Duncan] is the ultimate winner, and that's why they're so good. . . . I hate saying it, but he's the best player in the game." Translation: *Duncan is so good, I just threw my 2005 MVP under the bus.*) When he captured a fourth title with his best Spurs team (2007), he officially grabbed the "greatest power forward ever" belt. For his first twelve years of his career, Duncan was never *not* one of the league's top three most untradeable players.[63]

And yet . . . you're not totally sold. You remember Shaq bulldozing everyone for three straight Finals. You remember Hakeem grabbing the center torch in '94 and '95. You remember Moses carrying Philly in the "Fo Fo Fo" season, beating up Kareem and putting up that crazy 51–32 game in 1981. You don't really remember Duncan going Keyser Söze on anyone. That's what bothers you. To be ranked this high, you had to kick a little ass, right? (Here's my counter: Look at his 2003 season again. He left a trail of asses. It's true.) But really, that's what made him more special than anything—like Bird, Russell and Magic, he always saved his A-game for when his team desperately needed it. The perfect Duncan game? Twenty-two points, 13 rebounds, 3 blocks, get everyone else involved, anchor the defense, win by 10, everyone goes home. He didn't give a crap about stats. He really didn't. Remember when the media stupidly voted Parker the 2007 Finals MVP? Nobody was happier for him than Duncan. That's what makes Duncan great. If you want to play the "What unique trait will we remember about him?" card, go with this one: he could also play any style. During the deadly slow-it-down, grind-it-out, defense-beats-offense era (1999–2004), Duncan won two titles. During the transition period as everyone adjusted to the new rules (2005–6, when the NBA called hand checking and allowed moving picks), he won a third title. In the drive-and-dish/offense-beats-defense/smallball era, he won a fourth crown and excelled as one of the few big guys polished enough to punish players down low *and* talented enough to guard quicker players on the

---

63. In my annual "Who has the highest NBA trade value?" column gimmick that started on my old website in 2001 and continued at ESPN, Duncan finished no. 2, no. 2, no. 3, no. 1, no. 2, no. 1, no. 3, no. 3, and no. 4. From 1997 to 2008, San Antonio finished 615–265 with him during the regular season, 91–57 in the playoffs, won four titles and finished 4–0 in the Finals. Now that's consistency.

other end. For the purposes of this book, he made everyone else better and came through when it mattered. I don't know what's left.

You would have wanted to play with Tim Duncan. The man had no holes. Except for the fact that my dad probably skipped this section of the book and went right to Wilt.

6. WILT CHAMBERLAIN

Resume: 14 years, 13 quality, 13 All-Stars . . . MVP: '60, '66, 67, '68 . . . runner-up: '62, '64 . . . Finals MVP '('67, '72) . . . '60 Rookie of the Year . . . Top 5 ('60, '61, '62, '64, '66, '67, '68), Top-10 ('63, '65, '72) . . . first 3-year peak: 43–24–4 . . . second 2-year peak: 24–24–8 . . . 3-year Play-offs peak: 32–27–4 (35 G) . . . leader: scoring (7x), rebounds (11x), total assists (1x), FG% (9x), minutes (8x) . . . season records: 50.4 PPG, 27.2 RPG, 72.7% FG . . . career records: 30.1 PPG, 22.9 RPG, 50-plus games (118), most points (100), most rebounds (55); consecutive scoring titles (7) . . . career: rebounds (1st), points (4th), minutes (4th) . . . 30–22 for 10 straight seasons . . . best player on 1 champ ('67 Sixers) and 1 runner-up ('64 Warriors), 2nd-best player on one champ ('72 Lakers) and 3 runner-ups ('69, '70, '73 Lakers) . . . 30K-20K Club (only member)

We already said more than enough about the Dipper, although his '67 and '72 seasons remain a testament to the "Wilt could have been the greatest player ever if he knew what he wanted" argument. Two years ago I met a longtime Celtics fan named Paul Kelleher, one of those classic Boston Irish old guys with white hair and a kicking accent. He had been coming to the Garden since the fifties. Of course, I had to ask him about Russell and Chamberlain. His response: "Wilt was the most talented player I ever saw, but Russell just wanted it more." And I thought, "Great—I wasted a ten-thousand-word chapter explaining what this guy just summed up in one sentence." But that was a nice way to put it.[64]

---

64. Grumpy Old Editor's grizzled take: "No one coasted more, ever, not even Eddy Curry. Wilt coasted during so many seasons that he should have been named an honorary member of the gag pop group The Coasters. Putting Wilt in the Pantheon? I thought you were a radical."

Still, I couldn't let the book slip away without passing along one dissenting opinion about Wilt, so I enlisted my friend Chuck Klosterman[65] and gave him five hundred words. Here's what he wrote.

Nobody ever rooted for Goliath when he was alive, but I feel for him now that he's dead. How can you not? Wilt Chamberlain is the archetype of a tragic figure—a widely criticized, universally unappreciated, self-destructive coach-killer who happens to be the greatest tangible basketball player of all time. I can't think of any other athlete whose reputation is so vastly inferior to his actual achievements. Are there any other two-time NBA champions who are perceived as failures by virtually all basketball historians? I can't think of one. Is it reasonable for a man to average 50.4 points a game while finishing second in the MVP voting? It is not. But this is Wilt's legacy (and it always will be).

The problem, of course, is my use of the word "tangible." Anything described as "tangibly good" is inferred to mean "intangibly flawed." This is why Chamberlain always loses in any comparison with Bill Russell. Russell possessed intangible greatness, which means sportswriters can make him into whatever metaphor they desire. Russell was the central figure for a superior franchise, so history suggests he was the greater, more meaningful force. His wins validate everything. If you side with Chamberlain, it seems like you're siding with the absurdity of numbers. But consider this question: In an alternative universe (and with a different attitude), could Chamberlain have been Russell? Probably. Could Russell have been Wilt? Never. No chance. Chamberlain is the only human who could have ever been Chamberlain.

Basketball was a different game in the 1960s, so certain statistical anomalies are irrelevant. But get this: In 1961–62, Chamberlain scored 60 or more points in fifteen different games. Michael Jordan accomplished that five times *in his professional life*. Since his retirement in 1973, no player's single-season rebound average has equaled Chamberlain's clip

---

65. Please check out any of Chuck's books. He's the only sports atheist I know—loves sports, loves following sports, doesn't root for specific teams. Had we known each other in college, we either would have been best friends or fought to the death. Or maybe both.

for the totality of his 1,045-game career (22.9).[66] You can come up with these kinds of factoids all night; Wilt's numerical dominance is so profound that people have stopped thinking about it. And even when they do, it tends to work against him: when writers cite the year Chamberlain led the league in assists, it's generally used to show how Wilt was confused (he seemed to believe piling up assists proved he was unselfish, which is kind of like claiming you've slept with 20,000 women to prove you were interesting). He just didn't get it. He didn't understand team dynamics or the reality of perception. But how much does that matter now? If Chamberlain's personal statistics are moot, so are Russell's achievements within the context of his team. They're both historical footnotes. The real question is this: who was better *in a vacuum*? If we erase the social meaning of their careers—in other words, if we ignore the unsophisticated cliché that suggests the only thing valuable about sports is who wins the last game of the season—which of these two men was better at the game?

It's possible the answer is still Russell. But everything tangible points to Wilt.[67]

5. LARRY BIRD

Resume: 13 years, 10 quality, 12 All-Stars . . . Finals MVP: '84, '86 . . . MVP: '84, '85, '86 . . . BS MVP ('81) . . . runner-up: '81, '82, '83, '88 . . . '80 Rookie of the Year . . . Top 5 ('80, '81, '82, '83, '84, '85, '86, '87, '88), Top 10 ('90) . . . All-Defense (2x) . . . leader: threes (2x), FT% (4x) . . . 5-year peak: 28–10–7, 51% FG, 90% FT . . . 4-year Playoffs peak: 27–10–7, 50% FG, 90% FT (84 G) . . . '84 Finals: 27–14–3 . . . '86

66. Chuck's footnote: "Yes, yes—I realize rebounds were 'easier to come by' in the premodern era. Everybody concedes that. But it doesn't matter: If you divide Chamberlain's lifetime board numbers *in half*, the quotient (11.45) is still competitive with the full career averages for Barkley, Moses, and Shaq. Or think about it this way: If Chamberlain had never played during the second half of any game in his entire career, he would still have eight more career rebounds than Dennis Rodman."

67. Forgot to mention: I thought of Chuck for a dissenting Wilt opinion because he's the only other person I know who read Wilt's 1973 autobiography. I think we even exchanged "What about that stewardess blowing Wilt!" emails. Do they have lifetime achievement Pulitzers? I really think the committee needs to reexamine Wilt's body of work.

Finals: 24–10–10 . . . '87 Playoffs: 27–10–9, 43.9 MPG (23 G) . . . career: 24–10–6, 50% FG, 88.6% FT (9th) . . . highest career APG, forwards (6.1) . . . Playoffs: 24–10–6.5, 89% FT . . . best player on 3 champs ('81, '84, '86 Celts) and two runner-ups ('85, '87) . . . member of '92 Dream Team . . . 20K Point Club

And you worried this book would be biased? *Hah!* The Bird-Magic argument mirrors Oscar-West because we reached a definitive conclusion— Oscar was better than West (1965), Bird was better than Magic (1986)—that shifted improbably over the second half of their careers. Would you rather have nine transcendent seasons from Bird, followed by a four-year stretch where he wasn't remotely the same (and missed 60 percent of his games), or a twelve-year stretch of A-plus Magic seasons without a dip in impact? I'd rather have those three extra Magic years. And if I get struck by lightning or a telephone pole falls on me, so be it.[68]

We covered Bird's brilliance in the prologue but didn't delve into his numbers enough. Bird filled box scores to the degree that Boston reporters started a fantasy league modeled after Bird's all-around talents in 1984 or 1985; as far as I can discern, it was the first of its kind. They threw in money, drafted teams of players, added up their points, rebounds and assists (the 42 Club premise, basically), and the team with the highest total took the prize. Since Bird was the obvious number one pick, they called it the Larry Bird League. Larry even drew their draft order for the first few years—or so they claimed. When people are creating fantasy leagues and naming them after you, you're breaking new ground, no? So how do we measure that impact? I created a simple formula that's the bastard cousin of the 42 Club—add up a player's final placements in the NBA's yearly rankings for points, rebounds and assists per game. The lower the number,

---

68. Did you ever try to come up with the dumbest parallel for the Bird-Magic rivalry? I like this one: the two Shannons (Whirry and Tweed) were the Bird and Magic of Cinemax. From 1992 to 1995, Whirry starred in *Animal Instincts, Body of Influence, Lady in Waiting, Fatal Pursuit, Animal Instincts II, Private Obsession, Playback* and *Dangerous Prey*, while Tweed carried, from 1992 to 1996, *Night Eyes II, Night Eyes III, Indecent Behavior, The Naked Truth, Cold Sweat, Possessed by the Night, Indecent Behavior II, Night Fire, Hard Vice, Indecent Behavior III, Hotline, Body Chemistry 4, Electra, The Dark Dancer* and *Scorned* (probably her epic). What a stretch! And it happened right before Internet porn took off. Just like we'll never see another Bird and Magic, we will never see anything like the two Shannons.

the better. For instance, Bird ranked second in points, eighth in rebounds and nineteenth in assists in 1985. So . . . $2 + 8 + 19 = 29$.

That's a better score than you think. If we made 33 the cutoff point, limited the list to players who made the top twenty in all three categories, only counted post-Russell players[69] and called it the Legends Club, only eleven post-1969 seasons qualify: 1976 Kareem (18), 1972 Kareem (21), 2003 Garnett (24), 1986 Bird (25), 1974 Kareem (26), 1979 Kareem (26), 1985 Bird (29), 1984 Bird (30), 1970 Billy Cunningham (31), 1981 Bird (32), 1982 Bird (33). That's it. Magic didn't make it. Neither did Jordan or LeBron. Bird made it four times and nearly five (with 35 in 1987). He's also one of three players to crack the top fifty all-time in the three most relevant per-game career categories. As well as the top 75. And the top 100. And the top 125.

> Bird: 24.3 PPG (17th), 6.3 APG (42nd), 10.0 RPG (47th)
>
> Wilt: 30.1 PPG (2nd), 22.9 RPG (1st), 4.4 APG (129th)
>
> Oscar: 25.7 PPG (8th), 9.5 APG (4th), 7.5 RPG (135th)
>
> Elgin: 27.4 PPG (4th), 4.3 APG (135th), 13.5 RPG (10th)
>
> Cunningham: 21.2 PPG (37th), 4.3 APG (137th), 10.4 RPG (38th)
>
> Magic: 19.5 PPG (66th), 11.2 APG (1st), 7.2 RPG (151th)
>
> LeBron (ongoing): 27.83 PPG (3rd), 7.0 APG (26th), 7.0 RPG (155th)

And we didn't even mention that he's the ninth-best free throw shooter ever (89 percent), or that he came within a heartbeat of being the only member of the career 50–40–90 Percentage Club (finishing with 50% FG, 38% 3FG, and 89% FT). That's the crazy thing about Bird: his game was never about stats, but nobody put up numbers quite like his. So there you go. Allow me three lingering Bird-related what-ifs that don't include the name Len Bias, just for kicks.

No. 1: What if Bird's back had held up? Five Hall of Famers were fascinating from a "How long could they have kept going at a reasonably high level if they hadn't been sidetracked or retired prematurely?" standpoint. Stockton and Havlicek could have prospered as role players into their mid-

---

69. It was just too easy to crack the Legends Club preexpansion: Wilt put up a 7 and three 9's, Oscar/Elgin did it multiple times, and even the likes of Neil Johnston and Dolph Schayes made it.

forties; they were physical freaks along the lines of Jaclyn Smith still looking boinkable after she turned sixty. Magic would have reinvented himself
as a power forward had HIV not derailed him, and since he loved the limelight too much to walk away, his last few seasons could have been more depressing than Pacino/De Niro in *Righteous Kill*. McHale's Panda Express
menu could have worked forever had his legs held up; he could have gone
on low-post autopilot. And Bird would have happily evolved into an over-
seer/faciliator (his role on the '91 and '92 Celts when he wasn't in traction),
hanging out on the perimeter, launching threes, swinging the ball, feeding
big guys and soaking in the "Lar-ree!" chants. Like Matt Bonner on his
greatest day ever. This would have kept going until he turned forty-five or
became bored, whichever happened first. Ironically, Bird's skill set lent itself to an unusually long career even though his back believed otherwise.[70]

No. 2: What if Boston had traded Rick Robey sooner? The only NBA
player who routinely shut down Bird was teammate Rick Robey, a backup
center who doubled as Bird's drinking buddy and fellow troublemaker.
When the Celtics swapped Robey for Dennis Johnson before the '84 season, Bird immediately rolled off the best five-year stretch in the history of
the forward position. This wasn't a coincidence. As soon as we master
time machine technology, let's travel back in time and frame Robey for a
murder right before the '82 season. I just want to see what happens.

No. 3: What if Bird had come along ten or fifteen years later? The dirty little secret of Bird's success: fantastic timing. His heyday (1980–88) coincided
with the last generation of all-offense/no-defense forwards (Dantley, English, etc.),[71] and that's not counting all the fringe swingmen (Ernie Grunfeld,

70. Considering Bird and Magic became good friends, isn't it conceivable—repeat:
conceivable—that they'd become teammates once in their waning years? Imagine them
offering Orlando a package deal for 1994–95: *sign us for one year*. How fast does Orlando
say yes, 0.09 seconds? How weird would it have been to have Magic on the Magic, or Bird
wearing that goofy black Orlando uniform and throwing alley-oops for Shaq? And what
if MJ returned from his basketball sabbatical for the '95 playoffs? Bird, Magic, *and* MJ in
one series? Also, I'd be wearing a straitjacket right now.
71. The complete list of all-O/no-D small forwards from 1980–88: Dantley, English, Dominique, Aguirre, Kiki Vandeweghe, John Drew, Tripucka, Chambers, Walter Davis,
Scott Wedman, Bernard King, Albert King, Jay Vincent, Purvis Short, Jamaal Wilkes,
Thurl Bailey, Marques Johnson, Mike Mitchell, Orlando Woolridge, Dale Ellis, Eddie
Johnson . . . and yes, Doc post-1983. A surprisingly large group for a 21-team league.

Gene Banks, etc.) and clumsy power forwards (Kent Benson, Ben Poquette, etc.) torched by Bird on a routine basis. His toughest defenders were Michael Cooper, Paul Pressey and Robert Reid, lanky athletes who made him work for every shot; nowadays, nine out of ten opponents would do that. By the late eighties, the small forward spot was teeming with athletes like Scottie Pippen, Xavier McDaniel, Dennis Rodman, Detlef Schrempf, Jerome Kersey, Rodney McCray, Gerald Wilkins and James Worthy, while the big forward spot featured the likes of Karl Malone, John Salley, Sam Perkins, Horace Grant, Kevin Willis, Hot Rod Williams and Roy Tarpley. The salad days of Tripucka and Benson were *long* gone. When Bird floundered in the '88 Eastern Finals, we assumed he was worn out and ignored a much more logical reason: maybe Rodman just shut his country ass down. Regardless, nobody realized what happened to forwards until the 1989 draft, when Danny Ferry (number two) and Michael Smith (number thirteen) bombed more memorably than Vanilla Ice's follow-up album. And the thing is, they didn't do anything wrong! They were just test cases for a totally different league. Had Ferry and Smith entered the NBA in 1975, they might have made multiple All-Star teams in the Don and Dick era. Going against the likes of Pippen, Malone and Rodman every night? Not a chance.[72]

You know what the Smith Experience was like, actually? Watching the newspaper industry battle the Internet these past ten years. *Sorry, fellas, the old days are over. You're gonna lose. I wish I had better news for you.* So let's say Bird bridged the gap between newspapers and the Internet for the forward position. If he'd come along ten or fifteen years later, he would have been the *New York Times* or *Wall Street Journal*: still successful, still a must-read, but not quite as iconic. On the other hand, he would have adopted the three-point line much more quickly, and he would have developed all the modern conditioning/training/dieting habits, and shit, maybe something as simple as Pilates would have saved his back . . .

(Now I'm talking myself out of this. Let's just move on.)

---

72. When Smith struggled as a Celtics rookie, Boston fans quickly arrived at the same conclusion: "There's noooooooooo way this guy can make it." He did leave one legacy: He was the single greatest H-O-R-S-E player in the history of the Celtics. Not even Bird could beat him.

4. MAGIC JOHNSON

Resume: 13 years, 12 quality, 12 All-Stars . . . Finals MVP: '80, '82, '87 . . . MVP: '87, 89, '90 . . . runner-up: '85, '91 . . . Top 5 ('83, '84, '85, '86, '87, '88, '89, '90, '91), Top 10 ('82) . . . leader: assists (4x), steals (2x), FT% (1x) . . . 3-year peak: 22–7–12 . . . 2-year Playoff peaks: 19–7–15 (40 G) . . . '80 Finals: 22–11–9 . . . '87 Finals: 26–8–13, 2.1 TO's, 54% FG . . . career: 19.5–7–11.2 (1st), 85% FT, 52% FG . . . Playoffs: 20–8, 12.5 APG (1st all-time) . . . best or second-best player on 5 champs ('80, '82, '85, '87, '88 Lakers) and 4 runner-ups . . . holds 12 different Playoff records (including most assists) . . . member of '92 Dream Team . . . 10K Assist Club

My vote for the most fascinating basketball career of all time. He's one of the most famous college players *and* professional players ever. He had an iconic game (Game 6, 1980) and iconic moment (the baby sky hook). He played in ten championship finals over a thirteen-year span, taking home six titles in all. He cocaptained the single greatest basketball team ever assembled (the '92 Dream Team). He starred in the greatest Finals ever (1984). He had one of the best porn names ever but became so famous so fast that we never realized it.[73] He battled Erving, Bird, Moses, Isiah and Jordan in the Finals over the span of twelve years as the league evolved from tape delay to mainstream. He meshed with his city on and off the court like nobody in league history. He was called a savior, a winner, a coach-killer, a choke artist and a loser, and then a winner again . . . and his prime hadn't even happened yet. He became the first man to kiss another man in prime time. His game will never be re-created in your lifetime or mine. His first retirement announcement doubled as one of the ten biggest sports moments of all time, one of three JFK-assassination-level moments for Generation X (along with the *Challenger* exploding and the O.J. car chase) where everyone my age remembers where they heard the news. He became the focal point of the world's single biggest

---

73. The Best Porn Name All-Stars: Dick Pound, Pete LaCock, Ken Bone, Misty Hyman, Ben Gay, Magic Johnson, Rich Harden, Dick Trickle, Rusty Kuntz, Billy "the Whopper" Paultz, Butch Huskey, Randy "Big Unit" Johnson, Hot Rod Williams, Dick Pole and Wayne Chism, with Mo Cheeks and Dick Harter as coaches.

health crisis in seventy-five years. And all of these things somehow happened between March '79 and August '92.

You know how Microsoft keeps releasing Windows with 1.0, 2.0, 3.0, and so on? There have been seven incarnations of Earvin "Magic" Johnson in all. In order:

Magic 1.0. The skinny kid with the big smile and bad facial hair from Michigan State. We hear too much about his NCAA title win and not enough about Magic becoming the first underclassman to get picked first in the NBA draft,[74] or what he specifically meant as the second basketball star other than Doc to transcend color; nobody thought of him as black, just charming and genuine. Throw in his infectious smile, unselfish passing, built-in rivalry with Bird and once-in-a-lifetime game (six foot nine, all arms and legs, capable of playing five positions), and Magic's color never mattered. For a league battling dueling "too black" and "our guys don't care" syndromes, this was absolutely crucial.

(Postscript: How terrific was Magic in high school and college that he actually got away with the nickname "Magic"? That's like giving yourself the nickname Long Dong Silver—you better be able to back that up. I always respected Magic for this one.)[75]

Magic 2.0. He quickly added to his legend by rejuvenating the Lakers and winning the '80 Finals MVP with a surreal 42–15–7 in Kareem's place— and then all hell broke loose. He missed 45 games of his second season with a knee injury, returned one month before the playoffs, then complained that his teammates (specifically, Norm Nixon) were jealous during an eventual upset loss to the Rockets, saying, "I try to give everybody the ball, keep everyone happy, but I guess it's never enough. I never heard of this kind of situation on a *winning* team. Everybody can't get the pub."[76]

---

74. Magic ('79) and Isiah ('81) weren't just the first two men to kiss each other in prime time; they were the first underclassmen to get picked first in the NBA draft; from 1946 to 1992, only three others (Chris Washburn, Chris Jackson and Kenny Anderson) were picked in the top 5.
75. Kudos to me for using Magic and Long Dong Silver in an analogy that had nothing to do with sex. I continue to amaze myself.
76. Magic's performance in a deciding Game 3 was one of the worst ever by a Pyramid guy: he missed 12 of 14 shots, bricked two free throws in the final 30 seconds and airballed the series-deciding shot.

Hardened by fallout from his record $25 million contract and a nasty (but not undeserved) reputation as a coach-killer (page 146), Magic 2.0 peaked in year three when the Lakers rolled through the '82 playoffs. Now a devastating all-around player who played four positions and filled any void— a little like Will Ferrell on *Saturday Night Live* in that he could carry the show *and* serve as a valuable utility guy—Magic thrived defensively on L.A.'s deadly half-court trap and topped 200 steals. We've never seen anyone quite like '82 Magic and the stats back it up: no modern player came closer to averaging a triple double (18.6 PPG, 9.6 RPG, 9.5 APG). But the Lakers still didn't belong to him because he was splitting point guard duties with Nixon (something that seems incongruous in retrospect)[77] and his teammates still bristled about his salary and public image. Even Kareem's 1983 autobiography dismissed the long-believed assumption that Magic's enthusiasm rejuvenated his career, griped about the 1980 Finals MVP vote and proclaimed, "We didn't repeat as champs in 1981 because Earvin got injured, and when he came back he had forgotten what made us and him so successful." Ouch.

(Postscript: Magic didn't take those barbs personally because, again, Kareem was a ninny. But you'd think Kareem would have appreciated Magic more after not playing with a single All-Star from 1976 through 1979.)

Magic 3.0. Didn't emerge until the Lakers got swept in the '83 Finals, settled their alpha-dog/point-guard issue by swapping Nixon for the rights to Byron Scott (giving Magic the keys to Showtime), then got roughed up by a hungry Boston team that hijacked the '84 Finals. It was a double whammy for Magic—not only did Bird's team win, but Magic choked badly in crunch time of Game 2, Game 4 and Game 7. (I mean, *badly.* Like, everyone rehashed it all summer.) Magic rebounded by leading the Lakers

---

77. During the same time, the Doobie Brothers had a similar platoon going with Michael McDonald and Patrick Simmons as their lead vocalists. Like Nixon, Simmons had been there first . . . and like Magic, McDonald was clearly more talented and capable of pushing the band to another level. Mikey Mac left for a hugely successful solo career— twenty-five years later, he's still cranking out albums and spitting all over microphones. I should also mention that (a) the woman who broke his heart and caused "Minute by Minute," "What a Fool Believes" and "I Keep Forgetting" must have given him the greatest sex ever, and (b) my buddy Bish and I made a dunk video on a 9-foot rim in 1988 set to Mikey Mac's "Our Love" that will end my career if it ever lands on YouTube.

to the '85 title, winning the climactic Game 6 in Boston and exorcising a kajillion Laker demons. That's when Magic 3.0 peaked as a point guard extraordinare and the King of Showtime, but someone who still needed an alpha dog (in this case, Kareem) to carry the scoring load for him.

(Postscript: It's hard to overstate how badly Magic's reputation suffered after the '84 Finals, when he mistakenly dribbled out the clock at the end of regulation in Game 2, threw the ball away on another potential game-winning possession in Game 4, bricked two free throws with the score tied and 35 seconds remaining in Game 4, then made consecutive turnovers in the last 80 seconds to squander a winnable Game 7. That August, *SI*'s Alexander Wolff even wrote an essay titled "Johnson in the Clutch: Don't Call Him Magic, Just Call Him Unreliable."[78] Even after his ludicrously good performance in the '85 Finals, the consensus was, "Yeah, but he could never win without Kareem.")

Magic 4.0. Didn't emerge until a young Rockets team trounced the '86 Lakers and Kareem suddenly looked 200 years old. Hardened for a third time, Magic reinvented himself as a crunch-time scorer, pulling the Lakers past Boston with a Pantheonic Finals performance: A 26–8–13 with 54 percent shooting, one remarkably clutch shot (the do-or-die baby sky hook over McHale and Parish in Game 4) and just 13 turnovers. Amazing. Incredible. He captured MVP and Finals MVP, finally grabbing the conch from Bird as the league's alpha dog. From 1987 to 1991, Magic 4.0 tallied three MVPs and two rings, made the Finals four times, won 60-plus games per year and single-handedly kept the declining Lakers among the NBA's elite. Off the court, he emulated Jordan's marketing savvy and reinvented himself as a commercial pitchman and celebrity, even launching a Rat Pack of sorts with Eddie Murphy and Arsenio Hall.[79] Suddenly he was the face of Hollywood, the guy who bridged every genre, a legendary per-

---

78. An excerpt: "Calling on Magic [in the clutch] is like asking Busby Berkeley to step in and direct the climactic scene in an Ingmar Bergman movie." I was just thinking that! Nobody slammed out awkward pop culture references like *SI* in the seventies and eighties.

79. Eddie: Sinatra; Magic: Dean; Arsenio: Sammy. I always thought *The Black Pack* would be a great documentary: they were on top of the world for four years, then Magic got HIV, Eddie's career went in the tank and Arsenio had financial problems. And that's just the start of it. I'd say more, but my legal team just electroshocked me.

former and partier who knew everyone. You always hear the phrase "larger than life," but in Magic's case, he really was.[80]

Magic 5.0. And just like that, he became the face of HIV: November 7, 1991. I remember feeling like a family member had been diagnosed with terminal cancer. When my college girlfriend called me at our school's newspaper office to tell me the news, my knees actually went weak. *Magic is gonna die?* Even when he kept hanging around over the next twelve months—first the '92 All-Star Game, then the Dream Team, then a brief comeback that fell apart—an unspoken expiration date lingered over everything. Nobody expected him to survive long. Then again, nobody understood the difference between HIV and full-blown AIDS. We needed someone famous like Magic to teach us about it. Which he did.

Magic 6.0. My least favorite version. After riding high for fifteen years and getting the "magic" carpet pulled from under him, poor Earvin spent the next decade hanging around like Wooderson from *Dazed and Confused.*[81] And you know what? That stretch did more damage to the perception of his basketball career than anyone realizes. He wasted a curious amount of time squashing rumors about his sexuality, even releasing a 1993 autobiography colored with tales about his (*very hetero!*) escapades and shamelessly plowing through the talk show circuit as "the (*very hetero!*) stud who banged so many chicks that he ended up with HIV, which means this could happen to you as well!" (Important note: This relentless campaign inadvertently hampered the sex lives of all red-blooded American males between the ages of eighteen and forty for the next eight years. For the first four years, everyone was terrified to have unprotected sex unless they were shitfaced drunk. For the next four, the guys weren't terrified but the girls still were, although it's possible they were just out of shape and didn't

80. Something rarely mentioned here—the combination of Magic's HIV, Warren Beatty getting old and Eddie Murphy left a huge void for Hollywood Alpha Dogs getting laid by the elite of the elite. Then Leo DiCaprio and Ben Affleck showed up. Void filled!

81. One *GQ* writer believed that Magic and alter ego Earvin battled like Superman and Bizarro Superman. Earvin had a longtime girlfriend named Cookie; Magic cheated on her relentlessly. Earvin had an illegitimate son; Magic carried on like the boy didn't exist. Earvin was a shrewd investor who tripled his NBA income off the court; Magic behaved like a college kid on spring break. Post-HIV Earvin educated everyone about his virus; post-HIV Magic bragged about his earlier, wilder ways.

want us to see them naked. Then the Paris Hilton/Britney Spears era happened, women got in shape and started dressing more provocatively, we figured out that you had a better chance of winning the lottery than getting HIV from conventional sex and it became a sexual free-for-all. Of course, I was married by then. Awesome. Thanks for ruining my twenties, Magic.) Did we really need to know about his elevator trysts, threesomes and foursomes, or bizarre philosophy about cheating on longtime girlfriend Cookie?[82] Was Magic educating America's youth about HIV or affirming and reaffirming his heterosexuality? The lowest point: Magic appeared on Arsenio's show right after the HIV announcement and was asked about his sexuality. Magic said that he wanted to make it clear, "I am not gay." The crowd applauded liked this was fantastic news, and even worse, Magic reacted to their homophobia like there was nothing wrong with it. It wasn't his best hour.

When his post–Dream Team comeback imploded because of HIV insensitivities, Magic bombed miserably on NBC (page 121), left television to coach the '94 Lakers, and resigned after sixteen frustrating games because he couldn't reach younger players. He toured with an exhibition hoops team across Europe—like a washed-up Bono wasting a winter singing karaoke at Irish bars—before becoming a talk show staple, one of those "I was very, very, *very* available to come on" guests along the lines of Richard Lewis, Teri Garr, and Carrot Top. On the heels of Jordan's much-ballyhooed return to the Bulls, Magic announced his intentions for another NBA comeback and volunteered his services for the '96 Olympic team. Nobody cared. Undaunted, he returned after the '96 All-Star Break and reinvented himself as L.A.'s new power forward for 32 games. This was fun for a week before we realized an older, bulkier Magic couldn't possibly shed five solid years of basketball rust. Even if his opponents accepted him—an underrated milestone for the acceptance of HIV in this country, by the way—Earvin had turned into Chris Rock's joke about how "you never want to be the guy who's just a little too old to be in the club" before retiring again

---

82. The philosophy: If his one-night stand didn't share his bed all night, the event was somehow okay. I wish I had thought of this rule in college. Wait, why am I making fun of this? Can't the Supreme Court pass this as a law?

that summer.[83] He quickly created a syndicated late night show for himself, hoping to revive Arsenio's successful tactic of "friendly celebrity brings on other celebrities, makes them feel comfortable, kisses butt, and everyone has fun." The show would have worked if Magic had been remotely capable of hosting it. (Personally, I was devastated when they canceled it—to this day, it's the only late night show to shatter the Unintentional Comedy Scale. You know how Magic always does his "There will nev-ah, ev-ah, *ev-ah* be another Larry Bird" routine? Trust me . . . there will nev-ah, ev-ah, *ev-ah* be another TV event like *The Magic Hour.*)[84] Even after that latest public failure, you still couldn't watch a Lakers home game without NBC's obligatory Magic interview. He inserted himself into every Shaq-Kobe title celebration like Don King after a big fight. He boasted about beating HIV and claimed the virus had been wiped from his body. When the NBA launched a coed three-on-three celebrity game during 2002 All-Star Weekend, a heavier Magic unbelievably showed up as a teammate of Justin Timberlake and Lisa Leslie. As you watched him, you couldn't help thinking, "Larry never would have lowered himself to this game." I didn't like anything about Magic 6.0 other than his durability.

Magic 7.0. This version had a happier ending. At least so far. Magic stepped back from the spotlight, became a visionary businessman, made hundreds of millions and opened a chain of successful movie theaters across the West Coast. His on-air skills improved so dramatically that ABC lured him away from TNT. He still spends much of his spare time educating people around the world about AIDS and HIV. And the fact

83. The All-Depressing Comeback Starting Five: Cousy (re-activated himself as Cincy's player-coach for seven painful games in '68) and Jordan (Wizards version, 2001–3) at guard; Cowens (returned as a bench player for the '83 Bucks) and Magic ('96) at forward; Mikan (post-shot-clock, 1956) at center; Red Holzman ('77 Knicks) as coach; and Jerry West (Grizzlies, 2002–6) as GM.

84. The lowlight happened when Howard Stern appeared as a guest, farted the song "Wipe Out," and made every inappropriate Magic-related joke possible. Desperate to stem a ratings slide, an overmatched Magic had to smile thinly and absorb the abuse. I can't remember a time when another celebrity was humiliated that publicly, and for that long, without Tom Sizemore being involved. The show capsized within eight weeks, costing syndicators more than $10 million.

that he's still alive and healthy, far exceeding everyone's expectations, might be his greatest accomplishment of all.

From a historical sense, Magic 6.0 cluttered our minds and overshadowed his actual NBA resume. He clearly enjoyed a better playing career than Bird until the Wooderson era destroyed that relatively small gap; now we "remember" them as equals even though Magic's prime lasted three extra years. Just know that I spent both Reagan terms rooting against Magic, calling him a choker and arguing Bird's merits until my face was blue . . . and then Magic captured my eternal respect after the baby sky hook and his December buzzer-beater in the Garden that same year. It wasn't that Magic made those shots as much as my reaction as he was taking them; my heart sank even as the ball was drifting toward the basket. Not even the biggest Celtics fan on the planet could deny it any longer. Magic Johnson was just as exceptional as Larry Bird. Beyond that, he remains the most breathtaking player who ever ran a fast break— better than Cousy, better than Nash, better than anyone—because his height, huge hands, Gretzky-like vision and sneaky-long arms allowed him to reach the rim faster than opponents anticipated. (I grew up in a sports world that had seven certainties: you weren't stopping Kareem's sky hook, you weren't covering Rice with one guy, you weren't blocking LT with one guy, you couldn't let Gretzky hang behind the net on a power play, you weren't sacking Marino, you weren't getting Boggs to chase a bad pitch and you weren't stopping Magic on a three-on-one.) And he's the single best leader in the history of the sport. Nobody *extracted* more from teammates, whether it was an All-Star Game, a mundane affair in December or any playoff game.

Digging a little further, only two modern players (Bird and Magic) played with enough unselfishness and intuition that those qualities permeated to everyone else. They lifted their teammates offensively much the way Russell lifted his teammates defensively, a domino effect that can't be measured by any statistic or formula other than wins. Play with Bird or Magic long enough and you started seeing angles that you'd never ordinarily see . . . and that went for the fans, too. Jordan may have peaked as the greatest individual player ever, but he never brought everyone else to a different level like Bird and Magic did. If you loved basketball—if you truly *loved* it—you treasured them both and savored every season, every series, every game, every play, every moment. That's just the way it was. They brought the game to a better place. Ultimately, it didn't matter which one of them ranked higher on the Pyramid.

(Or so I keep telling myself.) *

3. KAREEM ABDUL-JABBAR

Resume: 20 years, 13 quality, 15 All-Stars . . . Finals MVP: '71, '85 . . . MVP: '71, '72, '74, '76, '77, '80 . . . Simmons MVP ('73) . . . '70 Rookie of the Year . . . Top 5 ('71, '72, '73, '74, '76, '77, '80, '81, '84, '86), Top 10 ('70, '78, '79, '83, '85) . . . All-Defense (11x, five 1st) . . . leader: scoring (2x), rebounds (2x), blocks (4x), FG% (1x), minutes (1x) . . . career: points (1st), minutes (1st), FGs (1st), 25–11, 55.9% FG (9th) . . . Playoffs: 24–11–3, 237 games (1st), most FGs . . . best player on 4 champs ('71 Bucks, '80 Lakers, '82 Lakers, '85 Lakers) and 3 runner-ups . . . '71, '74, '80 Playoffs: 30–15–4 (45 G) . . . member of 35K-15K Club.[85]

Nobody in NBA history can approach the next two lines:

Kareem, 1971: 27-19-3, 61% FG, Finals MVP
Kareem, 1985: 26-9-5, 61% FG, Finals MVP

Chew on that one for a second. Kareem took home Finals MVPs *fourteen* seasons apart—once during year three of the Nixon presidency, once during year five of the Reagan presidency.[86] Things that happened between those two trophies: *The Godfather* and *The Godfather Part II*; Watergate and Nixon's resignation; John Belushi's rise to stardom and subsequent overdose; the Cambodia bombings; Hulkmania and Wrestle-

---

85. Out of respect for the mission of this book, I will resist all urges to take potshots at my least favorite NBA player for the next 3,000 words. You have my word.

86. Longest runs of excellence: Kareem, Nicklaus, Meryl Streep, Ric Flair, *The Simpsons*, Don Rickles, Clint Eastwood, Shawn Michaels, Jim Murray, Colonel Sanders, Johnny Carson, Don King, Walter Cronkite, Nina Hartley, Annie Leibovitz, Siegfried & Roy, Marv Albert, M&M's, Martin Scorsese, Johnny Cash, Converse Chuck Taylors, Michael Buffer (three references in the Pantheon!), Vin Scully, Steven Spielberg, Harrison Ford, Peter North, Roger Angell, U2, composer John Williams, the Rolling Stones and the U.S. Constitution.

Mania I; the rise and fall of disco; *Battle of the Network Stars; The Deer Hunter* and *Coming Home*; John Lennon's assassination; the Munich Massacre; eleven seasons of *M*A*S*H*; the apex and descent of John Travolta, Chevy Chase, Farrah Fawcett and Burt Reynolds; Atari and Intellivision; PacMan and Ms. PacMan; Coach's real-life death on *Cheers*; Mark Spitz, Bruce Jenner, Nadia Comaneci, Sugar Ray Leonard, Mary Lou Retton and Carl Lewis; "Who shot J.R.?"; the Iran hostage crisis; season one of *Miami Vice*; Patty Hearst's abduction; *Saturday Night Fever*; the creation of home computers, Apple and Microsoft; three Ali-Frazier fights; the first three *Rocky* and *Jaws* movies; the birth of rap; U2 and Madonna; the birth of cable TV, ESPN and MTV. By 1985, Bill Cosby, Eddie Murphy, Michael Jackson and Bruce Springsteen were the four biggest stars on the planet, the Cold War was at an all-time fervor, and Kareem was still cranking out Finals MVP trophies.

Only Jack Nicklaus can claim such extended athletic superiority, winning the Masters twenty-three years apart (1963 and 1986)—but really, what's more impressive, peaking over fifteen years in basketball, or peaking over twenty-three years in a sport that can be played with love handles and a potbelly? Kareem made first-team All-NBAs fifteen seasons apart. From 1971 to 1980, he captured six MVP awards and should have won seven (page 236). For the first seven years of his career, he *averaged* a 30–16–5 with 54 percent shooting. For the first twelve years (1970–1981), he never averaged less than a 24–10. From 1970 to 1986 (an astonishing seventeen-year span), he averaged between 21.5 and 34.5 points and made between 51 percent and 60 percent of his shots. He's one of the most durable superstars in sports history, missing just 80 of 1,640 regular season games, cracking the 80-plus mark eleven times, playing 237 of a possible 238 playoff games and logging over *65,000 minutes* in all.[87] He played for six championship teams. He reached ten Finals and fourteen Conference Finals. His teams averaged 56 wins per season, dipped below .500 just twice and finished with a .600-plus winning percentage sixteen times. After his fortieth birthday, the '87 Lakers called

---

87. The secret to Kareem's success: stretching. Kareem did yoga before anyone even knew what the hell yoga was. I'd make the "yet another reason to hate yoga" joke here but promised you a potshot-free zone. See? I'm a man of my word.

consecutive "we must score or we will lose" plays for him in the last 45 seconds of their biggest game (Game 4 at Boston): a delayed screen/alley-oop that tied it, then a post play in which he drew a foul. In a do-or-die Game 6 of the '88 Finals, the Lakers called time with 27 seconds to play, trailing by one, and ran their biggest play of the season for their forty-one-year-old center; he drew a foul and nailed both free throws for the eventual victory.

They relied on him at that advanced age for one reason: Kareem Abdul-Jabbar was the surest two points in NBA history. Listed at 7-foot-2 but definitely two inches taller—at least[88]—his unstoppable sky hook remains the only basketball shot that couldn't be blocked, an artistic achievement because of its consistency and efficiency. Every sky hook looked the same: in one motion, Kareem blocked off the defender with his left arm, swung his right arm over his head, reached as high as he could and flicked the basketball with his right wrist. *Swish.* Since defenders couldn't dream of challenging the release, they settled on making him miserable, pounding him like a blocking sled—with tacit approval from the officials, of course[89]—turning every 9-footer into a 13-footer and living with the odds from there. What else could they do? Kareem never needed a plan B, making him the *Groundhog Day* of NBA superstars. Fans struggled for ways to connect with him and failed, incapable of being thrilled by someone so predictable and aloof. Maybe it didn't help that Kareem skipped the '68 Olympics in protest of America's racial climate,[90] or that he bristled at the public's uneasiness about his religion and resented everyone's impossibly high expectations. He handled every interview like he was disarming a hand grenade: too smart for dumb questions,

88. Two centers lied about their heights: Kareem and Walton, who claimed to be 6'11" when he was at least 7'2". It's always funny when NBA players lie about their height—it's not like we can't see, right?

89. Nobody was a bigger whiner than Kareem except Rick Barry, but I gotta defend him here: opponents were allowed to "bend" the rules to defend him. In *Giant Steps,* Kareem mentioned that referee Richie Powers allowed Dave Cowens to manhandle him and jump over his back for rebounds in the '74 Finals. Elliot Kalb looked it up: Powers officiated Games 1, 3, 5 and 7 of the series . . . all Milwaukee defeats. Hmmmmm.

90. Like Oscar, Kareem had one too many early brushes with racism and never really recovered. When his high school coach tried to motivate him by yelling that he was "playing like a nigger," Kareem entered what he would call later "my white-hating period." Can white guys have a white-hating period? I think I had one when I was little.

too serious for frivolous jokes, too reserved for any semblance of personal candor. Unlike Chamberlain, he didn't have a compulsive need to be loved; he just wanted to be left alone. And for the most part, that's what fans did. When he changed his name a few weeks after Milwaukee won the '71 title, the NBA's dominant player was suddenly an introverted, intermittently sullen Muslim who towered over every center except Wilt, abhorred the press, relied on a robotic hook shot and pushed away the general public. You wouldn't exactly throw in a "Good times!" to end the previous sentence.

(Note that's too important to be a footnote: I always liked the fact that the best two athletes to adopt Muslim names happened to pick tremendously cool names—Muhammad Ali and Kareem Abdul-Jabbar. According to the website for Muslim names that I just Googled twenty seconds ago, Kareem's name means "generous, noble, friendly, precious and distinguished." I will fight off the obligatory dig about the pomposity of that choice because I promised a potshot-free zone. But imagine if he'd picked "Khustar," which means "surrounded by happiness." Would Kareem have been as imposing with a name like Khustar Abdul-Jabbar? Probably not. What if he'd gone with Musharraf, which means "one who is honored or exalted"? Musharraf Abdul-Jabaar? I don't think so. Not to sound like Colonel James, but Kareem Abdul-Jabbar . . . that's a great fucking name! By the way, my favorite Muslim name on that website: Khasib means "fertile, productive, and profuse." Should I make the Shawn Kemp joke or do you want to do it? Go ahead. You take it. Let's move on.)

But that's how it went through the 1970s. We kept hoping someone would supplant him and nobody did. Kareem's public stature suffered for four unrelated reasons: the goofy combination of his afro, facial hair and goggles added to his detachment (it almost seemed like a Halloween mask); his trade demands (Milwaukee finally obliged in 1975) made him seem like just another petulant black athlete who wanted his way (the public perception, not the reality); 1977's sucker punch of Kent Benson went over like a fart in church; and his ongoing battle with migraines made fans wonder if he was looking for excuses *not* to play. So what if the goggles were a result of his eyes getting poked so many times that doctors worried about permanent damage, that Benson elbowed him first, that Milwaukee had a lousy supporting cast and no Muslim population, that his headaches left him unable to function? Kareem never received the benefit of the doubt—not from anyone, not once, not ever. People grumbled that he didn't give a crap, mailed in games, played on cruise control, failed to make teammates better and only cared about money. That perception faded once Magic turned the Lakers into the league's most entertaining team, breathing life into Kareem's career in the process. *Sports Illustrated* ran a January 1980 feature with the headline "A Different Drummer" and the subhead "After years of moody introspection, Kareem Abdul-Jabbar is coming out of his shell." He made a well-received cameo in a comedy called *Airplane* that blew everyone away, playing himself as a pilot with the alias "Roger Murdock." A young passenger recognizes him and "Roger" denies it, leading to this exchange.[91]

KID: I think you're the greatest, but my dad says you don't work hard enough on defense. And he says that lots of times, you don't even run down court. And that you don't really try . . . except during the playoffs.

KAREEM: The hell I don't. Listen, kid, I've been hearing that crap ever since I was at UCLA. I'm out there busting my buns every night. Tell your old man to drag Walton and Lanier up and down the court for 48 minutes![P63]

By his last scene, when Kareem was being lugged from the cockpit with his Laker uniform and goggles on, everyone had the same reaction. *Kareem has a sense of humor? What?* He would have cruised to 1980's Comeback Personality of the Year Award if his single greatest playing moment—when he sprained an ankle in Game 5 of the '80 Finals, limped back in with the Lakers trailing, finished off a 40-point performance on one leg and willed them to a crucial victory—hadn't happened on tape delay and been overshadowed by Magic's series-clinching 42–15–7 two days later.[92] Just like that, Kareem's likability window had closed. The

91. Kareem also appeared in a fight scene in Bruce Lee's last movie (*Game of Death*), as well as episodes of *Mannix, Emergency!, Man from Atlantis, Tales from the Dark Side, 21 Jump Street* and *Diff'rent Strokes* on the last of which he played Arnold's substitute teacher, Mr. Wilkes. Couldn't they have called him Mr. Kabbar?

P63. Random fact: Kareem was only offered his *Airplane* part after Bruce Jenner turned it down to star in *Can't Stop the Music*. Or as it's also known, "The Worst Career Move Ever."

92. Nobody remembers Kareem averaging a 33–14 with 23 blocks in 5 games, or that he stayed back in L.A. for treatment and didn't even get to celebrate Game 6 with his team. This might be the best Finals MVP argument ever: Do you reward Kareem for carrying L.A. to 3 wins, or Magic for playing a game that Bob Ryan later called the best he'd ever seen in person? I vote for Kareem because Game 6 wasn't a must-win—Philly still had to win Game 7 in L.A. Not likely.

struggling Association moved forward with Bird and Magic, hitting its stride in the mid-eighties as Kareem settled into a new role as the aging, "How the hell is he still doing it?" superstar. And here's where memories can be unfair: Kareem's last six seasons (1984–89) unfortunately doubled as his most-seen stretch because the league's TV ratings took off. Few remember him demolishing the '71 Bullets, sinking the season-saving sky hook in double OT of the '74 Finals or hobbling around to save the '80 Finals; everyone remembers when he couldn't rebound, couldn't keep Moses off the boards (Kareem was thirty-six at the time, by the way), couldn't protect the rim, slowed L.A.'s fast break, lost his hair and hung around for one awkward season too long. The thing that made him greater than Wilt—his staggering longevity—wounded the *perception* of his career after the fact. Wilt broke every record. Russell won eleven titles. Jordan dominated the nineties. Kareem? He's the moody guy who peaked during the NBA's darkest era and wouldn't leave when it was time. What's fun about celebrating that?

Since Kareem was measured against Wilt from the moment he started popping armpit hair, let's keep the tradition going here. We already debunked the myth about Wilt's "inferior" supporting cast on page 59, but for the record, Wilt played with seven Pyramid guys (Greer, Arizin, West, Baylor, Cunningham, Thurmond and Goodrich) and Kareem played with five (Dandridge, Oscar, Worthy, McAdoo and Magic). Wilt's supporting cast picked up for the last two-thirds of his career (1965–74); Kareem's only picked up in the last half (1980–89). And Wilt never dealt with *anything* approaching Kareem's shit sandwich in the 1970s, when his only elite teammates were Oscar ('71 and '72), Dandridge ('71 through '75) and Jamaal Wilkes ('78 and '79). From '73 through '79, Kareem didn't play with a single All-Star or elite point guard.[93] In twenty seasons, he only played with one power forward who averaged ten rebounds: the immortal Cornell Warner in 1975. When he dragged the '74 Bucks to the Finals, their fourth and fifth leading "scorers" were Ron Washington and Jon Mc-Glocklin. When the Lakers acquired him in the summer of '75, they had to give up their best young players (Brian Winters, David Meyers and Ju-

---

93. Lucius Allen "ran" Kareem's Bucks/Lakers teams from '75 thru '77; he was so mediocre that Kareem actually led the '75 Bucks in assists with a paltry 263.

nior Bridgeman) and left Kareem without a decent foundation. When he dragged the '77 Lakers to the Western Finals without Kermit Washington and Lucius Allen (both injured), his crunch-time teammates were four piddling swingmen (Cazzie Russell, Earl Tatum, Don Chaney and Don Ford, with no rebounder or point guard to be seen).[94] Um, why is Wilt the one remembered as being "saddled" with a poor supporting cast again? Even Kareem admitted in 1980 to *SI*, "It's the misunderstanding most people have about basketball that one man can make a team. One man can be a crucial ingredient on a team, but one man cannot make a team . . . [and] I have played on only three good teams."

As for Wilt's statistical "superiority," we already established that the Dipper arrived during an optimal time: a mostly white league, no "modern" centers other than Russell, modified offensive goaltending, more possessions, and a less physical game that allowed him to play 48 minutes without any real physical repercussions. Those factors inflated his numbers, whereas Kareem's only advantage from 1970 to 1976 was dilution/overexpansion. Compare Wilt's third season ('62, his best statistically) with Kareem's third season ('72, his best statistically) and Wilt's season looks significantly better on paper.[95]

PLAYER	G	MIN	PTS	REB	AST	FGA	FGM	FG%	FTA	FTM	FT%
Wilt	80	48.5	50.4	25.7	2.4	39.5	20.0	50.6	13.3	6.7	61.3
Kareem	82	44.2	34.8	16.6	4.9	24.9	14.3	57.4	9.0	6.2	68.9

Then you keep digging:

1962 starting centers: Russell (Hall of Famer); Walt Bellamy, Wayne Embry, Johnny Kerr (quality starters); Clyde Lovellette, Darrall Imhoff, Walter Dukes, Ray Felix (stiffs)

94. In Round 2, they beat a Warriors team that featured Rick Barry, Gus Williams, Jamaal Wilkes, Phil Smith and a center combo of Clifford Ray and rookie Robert Parish. Kareem averaged 37 points for the series and dropped a 36–26 in Game 7.

95. According to Elliott Kalb, Kareem outscored Wilt 201–70 in five regular season games in '72, then 202–67 in six playoffs games (although Wilt's team won the series). In Game 6, with Oscar only able to play 7 minutes with an abdominal strain, Kareem put up a 37–25–8 and Wilt countered with a 22–24. The year before, Wilt outplayed Kareem in the Western Finals even though the Lakers fell in five.

1972 starting centers: Chamberlain, Reed, Cowens, Thurmond, Unseld,
Lanier, Elvin Hayes, (Hall of Famers); Jim McDaniels, Bellamy, El-
more Smith, Tom Boerwinkle (quality starters); Neal Walk, Jim Fox,
Bob Rule, Walt Wesley, Dale Schuleter (stiffs)

Throw in a dearth of athletic power forwards in '62 and Wilt could run
amok like the killer bear from *The Edge.* Kareem's pivot opponents were
undeniably better, as were the new wave of forwards fighting him for rebounds (Paul Silas, Bill Bridges, Clyde Lee, Happy Hairston, Connie
Hawkins, Spencer Haywood, Sidney Wicks, Dave DeBusschere, Jerry
Lucas and so on). As for the stylistic changes from 1962 to 1972:

	G'S	FGA	FTA	REB	FG%	PPG	OPP PTS
'62 season	80	107.7	37.1	71.4	42.6	118.8	
'72 season	82	95.5	31.2	51.1	45.5	110.2	
'62 Warriors	80	112.4	40.0	74.2	43.9	125.4	122.7
'72 Bucks	82	93.3	29.3	52.1	49.8	114.6	103.5

Can you say "statistical inflation"? Look at their percentages of their
teams' averages in the following categories.

% OF TEAM AVERAGE

	PTS	REB	FGA	FTA
'62 Wilt	40.2	34.6	35.1	33.3
'72 Kareem	29.7	31.8	26.7	30.1

To recap: Wilt scored 40 percent of his team's points; Kareem scored 30
percent but did it more efficiently in a more physical era (57.4 percent
shooting compared to Wilt's 50.6 percent); Kareem grabbed just 2.8 percent less of his team's available rebounds. Throw in Wilt's era-specific advantages (covered earlier), all those extra Philly possessions (roughly
23–24 per game) and the difference in wins (63 for Milwaukee, 49 for
Philly) and Kareem's '72 season may have been *more* impressive than

Wilt's legendary '62 season. In fact, Kareem's 35–17 has only been approached four times since 1972: McAdoo (31–15 in '74, 34–14 in '75), Moses (31–15 in '82) and Shaq (30–14 in '00). And it's not like '72 was a fluke: Kareem averaged at least a 30–16 for three straight years and topped 27 points and 14.5-plus rebounds in the same season six different times. In 97 playoff games from 1970 to 1981, Kareem *averaged* 29.4 points and 15.2 rebounds.[96]

So yeah, Wilt's statistical resume pops your eyes out on paper. But Kareem's peak was nearly as impressive. He excelled for a longer period of time. His teams performed consistently better and won three times as many titles. He was more reliable in clutch moments and a much safer bet at the free throw line. He had an infinitely better grasp of The Secret. The gap between his first and last Finals MVPs lasted as long as Wilt's entire career. Even his movie career was more entertaining.[97] Kareem Abdul-Jabbar may have been fun to dislike—and believe me, I did—but his greatness cannot be denied. He's the third-best basketball player of all time. Better than Oscar. Better than Wilt. Better than Magic or Bird. And since we finally have that settled, I will now light myself on fire.

2. BILL RUSSELL

Resume: 13 years, 12 quality, 12 All-Stars . . . MVP: '58, '61, '62, '63, '65 . . . Simmons MVP ('59) . . . runner-up: '59, '60 . . . Top 5 ('59, '63, '65) . . . Top 10 ('58, '60, '61, '62, '64, '66, '67, '68) . . . 3-year peak: 18–24–4 . . . 3-year Playoffs peak: 21–27–5 . . . leader: rebounds (5x) . . . career: 15.1 PPG, 22.5 RPG (2nd all-time), 4.3 APG . . . Playoffs: 16.2 PPG, 24.9 RPG (1st), 4.7 APG . . . record: rebounds, one half (32); rebounds, Finals (40); RPG, Finals (29.5) . . . best player on 11 champs

96. Jerry West told *SI* in 1980, "Kareem is a *player*. A great, great, great basketball *player*. My goodness, he does more things than anyone who has ever played this game. Wilt was a force. He could totally dominate a game. Take it. Make it his. People have thought that Kareem should be able to do that too. No. That would not make him a *player* of this game." He's a player. *A player!*

97. Kareem had *Airplane* and *Game of Death*; Wilt had *Conan the Destroyer*, which should be the first DVD release if Criterion ever makes an Unintentional Comedy Collection. Wilt spends the entire movie riding around on a horse and trying to seem angry; even the horse was a better actor than Wilt. He never made another movie.

and 2 runner-ups ('50s, '60s Celtics) . . . 10–0 in Game 7's, 16–2 in do-or-die games . . . only player-coach to win a title (2x)

Bill Bradley summed up number 6's career nicely in *Life on the Run:* "Russell never got as much recognition as he deserved. Race was one reason. During the early sixties no black artist got adequate publicity. Then, too, perhaps pro basketball didn't have the national following sufficient to merit enormous press attention. Most probably, I think he was overlooked because his greatest accomplishments were in the game's subtleties and in seeking to guarantee team victory in a society which tends to focus attention on the individual achiever."

Imagine if I could have been that succinct with the Pyramid; you would have finished this book two weeks ago. But Bradley missed one crucial part of the Russell Experience: Russell was *obsessed* with winning. A handful of NBA players were wired with overcompetitive DNA,[98] but Russell and Jordan stand alone in their singular devotion to prevailing over and over again. The single greatest Russell statistic other than eleven rings? Russell's teams finished 10–0 in deciding Game 5's or Game 7's. The single greatest Jordan statistic? The Bulls lost their first three games of the 1990–91 season, but after that, they never lost three in a row again with Jordan wearing a Chicago uniform.[99] Anyone can win two or three titles. Russell and Jordan defended their turf again and again and again, and beyond that, they measured themselves by those defenses. They searched for every possible edge even if they went about it in different ways. Russell embraced his biggest foe, befriended him and allowed him to shine in meaningless moments, even as he was secretly ripping out the guy's heart without him realizing it. Jordan settled for tearing out hearts and holding them up like the dude from *Temple of Doom.* He wanted his rivals to know it was happening. That's what he loved most—not the winning as much as the vanquishing. Russell just loved winning.

The other difference between them: at no point in Russell's career did a teammate hiss, "I hate that asshole" or "He cares about himself more

98. I vote that we name this gene after them: "Jordruss Gene." It's a specific pattern of chromosomes unique to them.
99. Including playoff games and MJ's 34 postbaseball games in '95, that's a 632-game stretch over six-plus seasons. That's not unfathomable—that's *de*fathomable.

than the team." Russell's teammates treasured and revered him. They sing his praises to this day. They maintain that you cannot place a statistical value on what he accomplished on a daily basis. Code words like "sacrifice" and "teammate" and "unselfish" pop up every time he's remembered. He's the only player who realized every component of basketball as a team game—not just playing, but coming together as a group, respecting one another, and embracing common goals—from the first game of his career through the last. In George Plimpton's "Sportsman of the Year" piece about Russell in 1968, he passed along a fascinating anecdote from Boston trainer Joe DiLauri that explained Russell to a tee:

> The big concern he has is for the Celtics. Nothing else really matters. That's why he seems so cold often to the press and the fans. They're not Celtics. After we won the championship last year he kicked everyone who wasn't a Celtic out of the dressing room—press, photographers, hangers-on, and also this poor guy who was tending a television camera in the locker room who said he had to have permission to leave it untended, pleading to stay, said he was going to lose his job, and it took three or four minutes to get him out. The press was pounding on the door, furious about deadlines and all, and Russell turned around and looked at us and he asked [Bailey] Howell to lead the team in prayer. He knew Bailey was a religious man—it was also his first year on a championship team—and he knew Bailey would appreciate it. Russell's not a religious man himself. Sam Jones said, "You pray?" And Russell said, "Yeah, Sam."

You never hear Jordan's teammates and coaches discuss him that way. Not even now. The most compelling part of his storyline, for years and years, was the collective attempt to channel his competitiveness into the greater good of the team. He needed to "trust" his teammates and "make them better." We heard this again and again. Then his supporting cast improved and Chicago started winning titles, so we stopped hearing it . . . even though he was playing the same way he always did.[100] Only

---

100. Young MJ was definitely stat-obsessed. During the '89 season, Jordan became so infatuated with triple doubles that he kept asking the official scorer what he needed during games (two more assists, one more rebound, whatever). The NBA found out and told the scorer that he couldn't give the info out. Sounds a little Wilt-esque, no?

after his baseball sabbatical did Jordan fully embrace the team dynamic, whereas Russell's sense of team was ingrained. Which brings us to the best part of Russell's resume, as well as the point that potentially undermines it: his success in tight games. Of Russell's eleven titles, six hinged on games that could have easily swung against the Celtics.[101] Each went in their favor, with only one involving an opponent missing a season-deciding shot (Frank Selvy in 1962). On the face of it, you might say it was luck, something of an Anton Chigurh coin flip that fell his way every time. But with close-knit, unselfish teams and an alpha dog who lives to make everyone else better, how much of it is really luck? In a tight game of teams between equal talents with the pressure mounting, wouldn't you wager on the close-knit/unselfish team led by the best defensive player ever? Isn't that what basketball is all about?

Now you're saying, "Wait a second . . . so why isn't Russell no. 1?" Because it's so difficult to project Russell into today's game. Athletically, he could have survived. No question. But Russell wasn't taller or thicker than Kevin Durant. How would he have defended Kareem?[102] What about Yao Ming, Rik Smits or Artis Gilmore? What about Shaq in his prime or even young Dwight Howard? And wouldn't his mediocre shooting become a bigger liability in today's game? Would Russell be 70 percent as effective now? Eighty percent? Is the number higher or lower? How can we know? Like with Oscar, Pettit, Elgin and Wilt, Russell's era-specific advantages are hard to ignore. It was easier to block shots when nobody was attacking the rim except for Wilt, just like it was easier to grab rebounds when opposing forwards were six-four and six-three instead of six-eight and six-eleven. Russell also had more value in the sixties: everyone played run-and-gun and every basket only counted for two points, so a rebounder/shot blocker was the biggest commodity you could have. Now it's a slash-and-kick game driven by perimeter stars; by the '09 season,

---

101. The list: 1957 (Game 7, double OT); 1962 (Game 7, Philly plus Game 7, L.A.); 1963 (Game 7, Cincy); 1965 (Game 7, Philly); 1968 (Game 7, Philly); 1969 (Games 4 and 7, L.A.).

102. Russell retired four months before Kareem entered the NBA. From what we know about Russell's competitive fire, am I really supposed to believe that Russ didn't watch a few UCLA games in '68 and '69 and think, "I am getting old, it's time to get out of Dodge soon"? By the way, why did everyone want to leave Dodge so badly? What was Dodge? Did we ever figure this out? Did that saying start because someone laid a horrendous fart in a Dodge Dart in like 1965?

when only five players averaged more than 10.0 rebounds and 39 players shot better than 40 percent on threes, you were better off with a LeBron-like scorer who created quality shots for himself and his teammates. And with gigantic salaries, salary cap rules and luxury tax hindrances, it's nearly impossible to assemble an unselfish infrastructure of team-first players and keep it in place—last decade, only the Spurs were able to do it for more than four years—which means Russell would battle 1-in-30 odds just that he'd be landing on the perfect team for *him*. So let's split the difference and put him on a modern contender—we'll switch him with Howard and say Russell averages 17.3 rebounds, 12.7 points and a record-breaking 6.2 blocks a game for the 2011 Magic. Do you feel like we're guaranteed a title? I don't feel like we are. We have a good chance . . . but it's not a lock.

And that's what sets the next guy apart. Stick '92 MJ or '96 MJ in any era and he immediately becomes the alpha dog. From 1946 to 1965, it would have been unfair and scientists would have tested him in the mistaken belief that he was an alien. From 1965 to 1976, he would have dominated on a higher level than West did . . . and West won a title and reached six other Finals. From 1977 to 1983, he would have crushed it. You know everything that happened from 1984 on. Throw in Jordan's individual and team success, as well as his lack of any conceivable holes—seriously, when we will ever see the league's best offensive player also make nine All-Defensive teams?—and Bill Russell will have to settle for second place. For once.

1. MICHAEL JORDAN

Resume: 15 years, 12 quality, 16 All-Stars . . . MVP: '88, '91, '92, '96, '98 . . . Simmons MVP: '90, '93, '97 . . . runner-up: '87, '89, '97 . . . '85 Rookie of the Year . . . Finals MVP: '91, '92, '93, '96, '97, '98 . . . Top 5 ('87, '88, '89, '90, '91, '92, '93, '96, '97, '98), Top 10 ('85) . . . All-Defense (nine 1st) . . . Defensive Player of the Year ('88) . . . 30+ PPG 8 times, 34+ PPG in 7 different Playoffs . . . 4-year peak: 34–6–6, 3.0 SPG, 52% FG . . . career: 30–6–5, 49.7% FG, 83.5% FT . . . Playoffs: 33.4 PPG (1st), 6.4 RPG, 5.7 APG (179 G) . . . Finals: 34–6–6 (35 G's) . . . leader: scoring (10x), steals (3x) . . . records: most scoring titles (10); consecutive scoring titles (7); most Finals MVPs (6); highest points, Finals (41.0 in '93);

most Playoffs points, career; most points, one Playoffs game (63); most points in one half, Finals game (35) . . . career: points (3rd), steals (2nd) . . . best player on 6 champs ('91–'93, '96–'98 Bulls) . . . 30K Point Club

In my lifetime, only one superstar was routinely described like Hannibal Lecter. *Michael is a killer. Michael will rip your heart out. If you give Michael an opening, he will kill you. Michael smells blood. Michael is going for the jugular. Nobody goes for the kill like Michael Jordan. They're on life support and Michael is pulling the plug. Michael will eat your liver and cap it off with a glass of Chianti.* I made up only the last line; everything else was definitely muttered by an announcer between 1988 and 1998. Our society enabled the competitor that Michael Jordan became: we value athletes who treasure winning, maximize their own potential, stay in superior shape, pump their fists, slap asses and would rather maim themselves than lose a game. Ronnie Lott had part of his pinkie amputated in the off-season in order to keep playing in the NFL. We loved Ronnie Lott for this. Now that's a guy who cares! Tiger won the 2008 U.S. Open playing with a torn ACL. Now that's a champion! Pete Rose bowled over Ray Fosse to score the winning run in the 1970 All-Star Game, separating Fosse's shoulder and altering his career. Hey, you don't block home plate when it's Pete Rose! We will always love the guys who care just a little more than everyone else, just like we will always hate the ones who don't. Why? Because we like to think that we'd play that way if we were blessed with those same gifts. Or something.

That's why we never judged Michael Jordan for his competitive disorder.[P64] If anything, we deified it. The man could do anything and it was okay. From 1984 to 1991, by all accounts—magazines, newspapers, books, you name it—Jordan pulled all the same shit that Kobe did this decade, only in a more indefensible and debilitating way. When Sam Smith finally called him out in his turned-out-to-be-totally-accurate 1992 book, *The Jordan Rules*, everyone reacted like we would now if Perez Hilton started lobbing

P64. Well, until his off-the-cuff, uncomfortable, petty, biting, rambling, vindictive, score-settling Hall of Fame speech in 2009. And then? He was judged. Harshly. Although that speech reaffirmed everything I wrote for this section, that's for sure. You are who you are.

online grenades at Obama's daughters. Jordan couldn't be an asshole, and even if he was, we didn't want to know. By the time Kobe rose to prominence, our society had become much more cynical: we gravitated toward tearing people down over building them up, so that's what we did. Had Jordan come along fifteen years later, the same thing would have happened to him.

Of course, Kobe's diva routine happened out of weakness: he couldn't figure out his own identity and settled on a slightly creepy Jordan impression, pursuing that goal by trying to excel on both ends (did it), win a few rings (did it), score as many points as possible (did it), mimic Jordan's celebratory fist pump (did it) and lead his own team to the title (finally did it). Everything about Kobe's handling of the inevitable transition from "the Robin to Shaq's Batman" to "Batman" was clumsy.[103] Jordan always knew who he was. He *had* to win at everything. He studied up on opponents and searched for any signs of weakness, even pumping beat writers and broadcasters for insider information. He soaked teammates in poker on team flights so brutally that coaches warned rookies to stay away. He lost in Ping-Pong to teammate Rod Higgins once, bought a table and became the best Ping-Pong player on the team. He dunked on Utah's John Stockton once, heard Utah owner Larry Miller scream, "Why don't you pick on someone your own size?" then dunked on center Mel Turpin and hissed at Miller afterward, "He big enough for you?" He bribed airport baggage guys to put out his suitcase first once, then wagered teammates that his bag would be the first one on the conveyor belt. He stormed out of a Bulls scrimmage once like a little kid because he thought Doug Collins screwed up the score. When a team of college All-Stars outscored the Dream Team in a half-assed scrimmage and made the mistake of puffing their chests out, Jordan started out the next day's scrimmage by pointing at Allan Houston and simply saying, "I got him" . . . and Houston didn't touch the ball for two hours.[104]

103. The biggest piece Kobe was/is missing: he just wasn't that cool. Forget about being the coolest guy in the room; Kobe wasn't ever the coolest guy on his team. Like A-Rod, Kobe always seems to be playing the part . . . and you're either cool or you're not. This will make sense in a few more pages.

104. The most famous of the stories: The time LaBradford Smith lit him up, strutted too much, and got outscored 47–0 by MJ the next night. This one is slightly apocryphal: Smith outscored MJ 37 to 25 on March 19, 1993. The next night, a pissed-off MJ scored 36 by halftime and finished with a 47–8–8 . . . but Smith *did* score 15. Chicago won both games.

Jordan measured everything by the result and every teammate by his capacity to care about that result. He tested them constantly and weeded out the ones who folded: Dennis Hopson, Brad Sellers, Will Perdue, Stacey King . . . it's a longer list than you think. He punched teammates in practice to reassert his dominance. In the early years, he went too far and his bloodthirsty fire crippled a few of his teams. Craig Hodges told Michael Wilbon about a 1990 incident in which Pippen made the mistake of challenging Jordan in practice, when Michael "proceeded, literally, to score on Scottie at will. It was incredible. I mean, Scottie Pippen even then was one of the best players in the league and Michael just rained points on him. Scottie had to step back and say, 'Slow up, man.'" For years and years, Jordan couldn't rein himself in. He cared about winning, but only on his terms—he also wanted to win scoring titles, drop 50 whenever he pleased and treat his teammates like the biggest bully in a prison block—which led Phil Jackson to adopt the triangle offense in a last-ditch effort to prevent Jordan from hogging the ball (and, Jackson hoped, embolden his supporting cast). By the 1991 playoffs, when his teammates had advanced to an acceptable level, Jordan found a workable balance between involving them and taking over big moments. The rest was history.[105]

You know Jordan's "best ever" credentials: his playoff chops, individual records and all-around honors surpass those of anyone else who ever played. He owns more iconic moments than anyone: the 63-point game at the Garden, the '87 Slam Dunk Contest, "the shot" against the '89 Cavs, the "Ohhhhhh, a spec-*tack*-ular move!" layup in the '91 Finals, those 6 threes in the '92 Finals (along with the shrug—you can't forget the shrug), 41 points per game in the 1993 Finals, the 72-win team in '96, the Flu Game in '97 and The Last Shot in '98. He demoralized eight memorable teams in eight years—the Bad Boy Pistons, the Showtime Lakers, Riley's Knicks, Drexler's Blazers, Barkley's Suns, Shaq's Magic, Malone's Jazz and Miller's Pacers—and none was ever quite the same.[106] He accomplished

---

105. After getting swept by the '91 Bulls, Detroit assistant Brendan Suhr said, "I think [MJ] finally realized that one player can't win at this level, that the farther you get in the playoffs, teams can always stop one man. He finally sees that." Sure. But you can't "see it" if your teammates suck.

106. Jordan's averages in his six Finals: 31–7–11, 36–5–6, 41–9–6, 27–5–4, 32–7–6, 34–4–2. That's four 42 Club appearances, by the way.

everything with just two Pyramid teammates (Scottie Pippen and Dennis Rodman) and a bunch of role players and pseudo-scrubs. When he captured that last title in 1998, we all agreed: *This is the greatest basketball player we will ever see.* That didn't stop us from looking for the next him. We spent the next eleven years anointing false successors, hyping young stars who weren't ready and overrating imitators who weren't really him. We need to stop looking.

My personal belief: Nobody will surpass Jordan. Ever. And I have four reasons why . . .

Reason no. 1: the four peaks. Most basketball players peak once and that's it (a career year, as we call it). An elite few peak a second time: Hakeem in '90 and '94, Barkley in '90 and '93, West in '66 and '70, and Shaq in '95 and '00, to name four. In rare cases, an athlete peaks three different times: Bird ('84, '86 and '87), Magic ('82, '85, '87), Kareem ('72, '76, '80) and Wilt ('62, '67, '72) released a 3.0 version that exceeded the 1.0 and 2.0 versions in many respects. Only Jordan peaked four times, and arguably, Jordan 4.0 was better than the other three versions. Here are the models:

- **MJ 1.0 ('89–'90).** His fifth and sixth seasons, normally when a star makes the leap and scratches the ceiling of his talents. Jordan carries a lousy '89 Bulls team to 47 wins and an Eastern Finals cameo during an extremely competitive year, finishing with the best all-around statistical season since the merger: 32.5 PPG, 8.0 APG, 8.0 RPG, 2.9 SPG, 54% FG, 85% FT (regular season), 34.8 PPG, 7.0 RPG, 7.6 APG, 2.5 SPG, 51% FG (playoffs). The following spring, he enjoys the finest series of his career (43.0 points, 7.4 assists, 6.6 rebounds and 55 percent shooting against Philly) before falling to Detroit in seven. As a pure athlete and scorer, here's the stretch when Jordan peaked: matchless athletic ability, maximum speed and explosiveness, Larry/Magic-level respect from officials, extreme durability (played 99 of 99 games despite old-school rules that allowed teams like the Pistons to hammer him on drives) and multiple defenders required to stop him. Unleash '89 Jordan into the current NBA with no hand checking or hard fouls and it's all over. He'd score 45 a game.[107]

- **MJ 2.0 (spring '93).** He's mastered everything at this point. A rigorous workout routine sculpts his body and whips him into superior shape, enabling him to absorb hard fouls, stop tiring at the end of games and abuse smaller defenders on the low post. He's a savvier all-around player, with a better sense of how (to use his teammates) and when (is the right time to take over a game), even defending his teammates (which he did repeatedly against Riley's Knicks, personified by the memorable "And one!" layup where he stood over Xavier McDaniel and yelped angrily at him) instead of undermining them publicly and privately. Only one problem: the man suddenly has no peers. He's the only NBA super-duper star without a relative equal driving him to remain on top. That puts him in a no-win situation. Once the media pressure and public attention becomes too much, he makes one of the most curious decisions in NBA history: he walks away at his apex.[108]

- **MJ 3.0 (winter '96).** Jordan shakes off the baseball rust,[109] rebuilds his body for basketball and plays more physically on both ends—instead of Barry Sanders, he's Emmitt Smith, picking his spots, plugging away, moving the chains and punishing defenders for four quarters. MJ 3.0 features descriptions like "extremely resourceful" and "cerebral on the Bird-Magic level." His baseball foibles taught him to embrace his teammates, accept their faults and adapt his own considerable skills to complement theirs. He finally understands The Secret.

---

107. True MJ facts: Scored 40-plus thirty-seven times in the '87 season; first with back-to-back 50-point playoffs games ('88); by the end of the '91 season, he had the NBA's highest scoring average in the regular season, playoffs and All-Star Game (and still does); he scored 60-plus five times (once in the playoffs) and 50-plus another thirty-four times (seven in playoffs); holds the record for consecutive games scoring double figures (866); only player to score 20-plus points in every Finals game (minimum: ten).

108. Well, unless Stern suspended him and told him to play baseball for 18 months. I didn't want to spoil the story.

109. It can't be forgotten that Jordan left the NBA for 21 months and rebuilt his body for baseball—stronger legs, thicker physique—didn't play competitively at all, then hopped right back into the NBA schedule with five weeks to play in March '95, and within five games, he'd already made a game-winner in Atlanta and scored 55 at MSG.

- **MJ 4.0 (spring '98).** My favorite version. His hops are pretty much gone, yet he makes up for it with renewed intensity and resiliency. Rarely does Jordan exhibit emotion anymore; even game-winning jumpers are celebrated with a simple fist pump and a relieved smile. Like Ali in the mid-seventies, he relies on guile, experience, memory, and heart and knows every trick (like the Bryon Russell push to win the '98 Finals).[110] Jordan 4.0 demonstrates a (I hate to use this word, but screw it) *surreal* ability to take command in optimum moments. You could say he evolved from the greatest basketball player ever to the greatest closer ever, and his collection of performances against superior Pacers and Jazz teams—as he fought the effects of his third straight 100-game season, coaxed as much as he could from a thirty-six-year-old body, carried Scottie Pippen's slack (derailed by a bad back) in the final two games and *still* managed to carry the Bulls to a title—remains the most extraordinary athletic achievement of my lifetime. Watch Game 6 of the '98 Finals sometime. He wins it by himself. No help. Just him. He scores 41 of Chicago's first 83 points, biding his time even as he's manipulating the proceedings. Down by three with 40 seconds to go, he goes for the kill—explodes for a coast-to-coast layup, strips Karl Malone on the other end and drains the game-winner, all in one sequence—without a single teammate touching the ball, a fitting conclusion to the most brilliant basketball game ever played. I know LeBron James is fantastic right now, but if he's still winning championships by himself at thirty-six on the fourth version of himself, we can start talking about him and Jordan. And only then.

Reason no. 2: pathological competitiveness. I can't imagine a killer like Jordan happening again, and here's why: the NBA is too buddy-buddy now. These stars grow up together, befriend one another, hang out during summers, play Team USA together, text and email each other . . . it's a big

---

110. Here's how great Jordan was: for his single greatest moment, he blatantly cheated . . . and nobody gave a shit. If anything, we applauded him for his ingenuity. Imagine if Kobe won the NBA title with a shove like that. We'd be bitching about it all summer. By the way, I always thought it was poetic that MJ pushed off a guy named Russell to swish the shot that clinched his status as the best ever.

circle jerk. Watch Kobe greet Carmelo after an allegedly hard-fought game; they look like old roommates reconnecting at a college reunion. The greats from Jordan's era always maintained a respectful distance; even when Magic and Isiah smooched, there was a coldness to it.[111] When Jordan and Barkley became close, part of me always wondered if Jordan sniffed out Barkley as a potential rival—a little like Russell with Wilt, or even how Natasha Henstridge hunted for a mate in *Species*—then befriended him as a way to undermine him competitively. You know what moment killed Barkley's chance to be a Pantheon guy? Game 2 of the 1993 Finals in Phoenix. He played as well as he possibly could (a 42–13 with 16-for-26 shooting), but Jordan exceeded him by tallying a 42–12–9 and destroying Dan Majerle down the stretch. You could see it written on Barkley's face as he walked off the court: *I can't beat this guy.* And he couldn't.

That goes back to that aforementioned Russell-Jordan gene. Jordan lived to vanquish and fueled himself by overreacting to every slight (real or manufactured). Rick Pitino questioned the seriousness of his hamstring injury during the '89 Knicks-Bulls series; Jordan made them pay.[112] The Magic knocked an out-of-NBA-shape Jordan out of the '95 playoffs; Jordan made them pay. Malone lobbied for the 1997 MVP; Jordan made Utah pay. That's just how it went. When Bulls GM Jerry Krause—someone whom Jordan openly detested[113]—glowingly courted European star Toni Kukoc, Jordan and Pippen wrecked Kukoc in the '92 Olympics with particular fury. Before the 1989 draft, it bothered Jordan that Krause had become infatuated with Majerle's potential, so he torched Thunder Dan in the '93 Finals and screamed "Fuck you, Majerle!" as the Bulls celebrated right after Phoenix's final miss in Game 6. Did Majerle do anything to

111. There's an extended moment after the '88 Eastern Finals ended when we see McHale give inspired advice to Isiah, followed by Isiah thanking him and slapping his hand. I remember screaming at the TV, "What the hell? Don't talk to him! What are you doing?" That's just the way it worked back then.

112. Pitino angered Jordan with his comments after Game 3. MJ's next three games: 47–11–6, 38–8–10, 40–5–10. Pitino signed with the University of Kentucky a few weeks later. I'm sure it was a coincidence.

113. Jordan frequently razzed Krause for his slovenly looks and generally unattractive appearance, as well as Krause's penchant for taking too much credit for the success of the Jordan era. And really, MJ was right. Saying Jerry Krause built the six-time champion Chicago Bulls is like calling *Lord of the Rings* a Sean Astin flick.

him? Of course not. Jordan just convinced himself that he did. That's how the man thought.

The two defining "Jordan was secretly a hypercompetitive lunatic" stories:

Story no. 1: It's Game 1 of the 1992 NBA Finals and the painfully forced "Drexler or Jordan?" storyline (page 396) is in full swing, as well as Portland's "we're gonna make them beat us by shooting threes" plan that they were stupid enough to mention to the press. Clyde Drexler is about to get athletically sodomized by Jordan on national television. We just don't know it yet. Portland jumps out to a 17–9 lead with six minutes remaining. Chicago's crowd can't get into it. Portland is running the floor and gaining confidence. Here's the Cliff's Notes version of the next 17 minutes of game time: MJ 3 . . . MJ 2 + 1 . . . MJ 3 . . . MJ 3 . . . MJ 2 . . . MJ 2 (first quarter ends: 33–30, Blazers, Jordan has 18 and sits down for a breather) . . . MJ comes back in (45–44, Chicago) . . . MJ 2 . . . MJ 3 . . . MJ steal +2 . . . MJ 2 . . . MJ 3 . . . MJ follow-up dunk for 2 . . . awkward Drexler air ball 3 . . . MJ 3 + shrug[114] . . . third Portland time-out of quarter . . . Chicago 66, Portland 49. Jordan scored 33 points in 17 minutes, 35 for the half, outscored Drexler by 27, and broke the record for playoff threes in one half. This actually happened.

Story no. 2: Jordan's opponents learned to leave him alone by the midnineties, leading to a phenomenon unlike anything else we've witnessed before or since: Michael became basketball's version of a sleeping tiger. In a league full of smack-talkers, chest-thumpers and yappers, incredibly, he remained completely off-limits. Even during the summer of 2001, when Jordan was running the Wizards but reportedly mulling a comeback, a slew of NBA teams voyaged to Los Angeles to watch a few California prospects work out. Jordan was there. So was L.A. native Paul Pierce, who spent a little time with Jordan because of his friendship with Chicago native (and then-Pierce teammate) Antoine Walker. At some point, Pierce started talking smack to MJ. *You better not come back. This is our league now. We don't want to embarrass you.* That kind of stuff. Jordan nodded happily with one of those "Okay, okay, just wait" faces, finally saying, "When's our first game against you guys? I'm

114. I always thought Magic's presence at courtside as an NBC announcer (as well as Bird's inevitable retirement) played a big part in this game: For the first time, the league belonged to Jordan and Jordan alone. Drexler was in the way. He had to be wiped out. If Magic got to witness it from midcourt, even better.

gonna make it a point to drop 40 on you." You could almost imagine Jordan pulling out a piece of paper and adding Pierce's name to the list of Guys Whose Butts Need to Be Kicked. Of course, Pierce's coach at the time (Jim O'Brien) overheard the running exchange and quickly pulled Pierce away, imploring his star, "*Never* talk to him. You hear me? That's the one guy you don't talk smack to!" And this was when Jordan had been retired for three full years. Three! Even then, at thirty-nine years old, a current NBA coach considered him a viable threat and someone who shouldn't be angered under any circumstances. Wake me up when this happens again in my lifetime.

Reason no. 3: command of the room. As I mentioned in David Robinson's section (page 456): Manute, Bird, Robinson and Jordan were the Mount Rushmore of great entrances in the Nancy Parish Memorial Tunnel. Jordan was a walking E. F. Hutton commercial. Remember those dopey ads when somebody said, "My broker is E. F. Hutton and he says . . ." and everyone else in the room suddenly shut up and leaned in to hear? That was MJ. Seeing him unhinged people like they were Beatles fans in the mid-sixties. Jordan possessed what a Boston writer named George Frazier once dubbed *duende*: a charisma, an Eastwoodian swagger, a sense of self-importance that can't be defined. He swallowed up the room even if 16,000 people were in it. As soon as Jordan entered the building, nobody else mattered. The way people's expressions instantly changed, the sounds they made . . . those little moments leave an imprint even fifteen years later.

Those reactions didn't change when he stopped playing basketball. At a party during the 2006 All-Star Weekend in Houston, Celtics honcho Rich Gotham and I were smoking stogies on a not-so-crowded cigar patio and ensuring bad breath for the rest of the night. Out of nowhere, Charles Oakley sauntered through the doorway[115] followed by a human tornado with Jordan and his posse at the epicenter. Here's what happens when MJ

---

115. This was a bigger moment than it might seem. See, Oakley is the real-life Shaft. You know those bar fight scenes in *Road House* when Swayze stands there motionless, with just a thin smile on his face, as ten drunk guys are brawling a few feet away? That's Oakley. You could hire extras to play gang members at a party, then have them fire blanks at each other ten feet away from Oakley and I'm not sure he'd flinch. My favorite Oakley fact: he served as MJ's enforcer in Chicago, now they're both retired . . . and from what I can tell, he's *still* Jordan's enforcer. Could there be a better tribute in life to someone's kickassability than MJ himself deciding, "You know what? I need to make sure he's still .

enters a room: it immediately becomes an *Entourage* scene. No matter how you felt about the party leading up to the moment, the party jumps from _____ (fill in whatever grade) to a solid A+. Like MJ's presence validates the entire night. So Jordan ambled in, glanced around, puffed on a cigar for a few seconds, then traded a few barbs with Oak while pretending there weren't twenty-five people packed around him snapping cell phone pictures. Ninety seconds later, they'd had enough. Time for a new room. Just like that, they were gone and the patio was mellow again. As Rich said later, it was like a "gust of wind." MJ was the gust; everyone else was the twigs, leaves, and branches flying around.

When he played, you had a little more time to prepare for that gust. You looked around fifteen minutes before game time and realized that 75 percent of the fans had already arrived; it sounded like the crowd before a Springsteen concert waiting for the lights to turn off. Every male patron with good seats had a glazed, giddy, "I'm important because I'm attending this important game" glow. Every female patron looked like she'd spent an extra ten minutes getting ready. Every little kid looked ready to spontaneously self-combust. Wide-eyed teenagers stood in the first few rows, rocking back and forth, holding pens, pathetically desperate, praying against billion-to-one odds that MJ would inexplicably leave the layup line, vault the press table and glide into the stands to sign autographs. As soon as Jordan made his grand entrance, he stopped the place cold. Every eye shifted to him. Fans started making strange sounds. Squeals and cries mixed with appreciative applause, and then a slow-developing roar emerged, almost like a chain reaction: "hhh-hhrrrrrrHHHRRRAAAAAAAHHHHHH!!!!!" MJ was in the house. And it's not like the energy faded from there. When he met the officials before the game, they oversold his jokes and looked like waiters working a customer for a huge tip. When he dispensed advice to a teammate, the other guy nodded intently like some life-altering secret was being revealed. When

---

on my side. I don't care if we're in our forties." Personally, I think Oak should have become the next great action hero. He's got the looks, the size, the swagger . . . at the very least, he could mumble through his lines and become the black Steven Seagal. We know everyone in the NBA was afraid of him, personified by the famous story of Oak slapping Barkley hard across the face during a '99 lockout players-only meeting. I once asked a relatively famous current player, "What makes Oakley more intimidating than everyone else?" His answer: "There's a lotta tough guys in the league, but Oak don't give a fuck." Well, then.

he strolled toward the scorer's table for the opening tap, every conversation in the first few rows came to a screeching halt. When he stood on the free throw line for the first time, thousands of camera flashes clicked to capture the moment for posterity. *I saw Michael Jordan play. Here he is shooting free throws. People will be impressed by this someday.* That's how you felt.

The moment always seemed bigger than you or me, as did the ongoing thrill of witnessing a vintage MJ performance and appreciating all the little things that made him *him.* He never slacked and always gave a crap. Physically, he controlled himself with a grace that nobody else quite had. Technically, he was perfect in every way—perfect physique, perfect running style, perfect defensive technique, perfect footwork, perfect shooting form—which always made it seem wrong if he dribbled a ball off his foot or threw a pass out of bounds. Spiritually, his teammates reacted to him the same way sitcom kids react to Dad when he comes home from work: everyone killing themselves to please him and hanging on his every word. The little things stood out more than the dunks and the breathtaking drives. The last time Jordan played in Boston as a Bull (December 1997), they were wiping out a young Celtics team and MJ seemed bored by the whole thing. That was always the best time to watch Jordan in person, when he was searching for dumb challenges to keep from coasting. As soon as Jordan and Walker started talking trash, I remember nudging a buddy and telling him, "Watch this, something's gonna happen." We followed Jordan and Walker as they jogged back and forth and kept a running dialogue going. After a Boston foul, Walker and Jordan lined up next to each other on the right side of the free throw line. Walker had inside position; Jordan stood to his left and kept talking smack. Walker made the mistake of jawing back. Never a good idea. I remember telling my buddy, "Watch this—Jordan's telling 'Twan he's gonna beat him inside and get the rebound. Watch this. Just wait." Sure enough, as his teammate prepared to launch the second free throw, Jordan's arms started swaying with his mouth moving the entire time. Walker's body tensed. The ball went up and MJ somehow leapfrogged past Walker, grabbed the rebound and jumped back up for a layup in one motion.

Who fouled Jordan from behind to prevent the layup? Antoine Walker.

We watched Michael strut and giggle his way to the charity stripe, thoroughly pleased with himself, like he'd just found a $100 bill on the ground. We watched Walker's head hang like that of a little kid who'd just been scolded by a parent. We watched the JumboTron show a closeup of Jordan lining up his first foul shot, an enormous grin spread across his face. His night had been made. So had ours. But that's what makes me laugh whenever I hear guys like Wade, Kobe and LeBron compared to him. *Nobody* had moments like the one I just described. They might be close physically or athletically, but in the "command of the room" sense? Not even LeBron could approach him. Even during Jordan's injury-plagued comeback with Washington,[116] there was one moment during his first Boston appearance in 2001 when Jordan drained a crunch-time jumper and looked like he might be heating up. He spun around and hopped back to the other end of the court, running with that distinctive gait in which his elbows swung back and forth like someone using a NordicTrack. With the crowd roaring—we loved the Celtics, but really, even the slim possibility of witnessing an ESPN Classic throwback performance trumped everything—Jordan glanced over to everyone in my section at midcourt, his eyebrows raised, and unleashed a defiant grin. And he melted us. He fucking *melted* us. Imagine a busty senior cheerleader winking at a school bus filled with ninth-grade boys, triple the reaction, and that was us. We spent the next twenty seconds buzzing and nudging each other. I don't even remember who won the game. I really don't. All I remember was this: MJ was back, MJ was on his game, MJ was feeling it . . . and the possibilities were endless. Some people are just larger than life.

I will believe LeBron has reached MJ status as soon as he owns every set of eyes in a 17,000-seat arena for three straight hours, and as soon as he can liquidate an entire section with one smile. And not a moment before.

Reason no. 4: the Jordan mystique. I'm retelling this story in the present tense because, as far as I'm concerned, it still feels like it happened three hours ago. Come back with me to that same 2006 All-Star Weekend in

---

116. This comeback didn't turn out so well: Jordan overdid his preseason conditioning and battled a variety of nagging knee and ligament issues for two years. Even worse, he was still running the team and built it around his strengths and weaknesses, hiring a yes-man coach (Doug Collins), slowing them down stylistically and making a horrible trade (Rip Hamilton for Jerry Stackhouse). They missed the playoffs both years. Even the signature book written about the comeback sucked. I now pretend this comeback never happened, and frankly, so should you.

Houston. I am drinking Bloody Marys on a Saturday afternoon with my buddy Sully and his Boston crew. We're debating a second round when Oakley saunters into the bar—and that's the right word, because the dude *saunters*—with three lady friends, eventually settling at the table right next to us. Oakley orders a round of shots for his table and a martini for himself. We quickly order a second round for ourselves. I mean, where else can you drink five feet away from the real-life Shaft?[117]

Twenty minutes later, Jordan shows up with two friends and stops the room cold. At first, it seems like he's just saying hello; then we realize he's sitting down. His friends move him into the inside booth, then block him with chairs on both sides so nobody can bother him. (Like my "Chair Armada" strategy in strip joints, as mentioned on page 260.) Oakley orders more drinks; we order food and drinks for our table. For all we know, we're staying all afternoon and evening. People stream over to say hello, pay tribute to Jordan, kiss his ring . . . he's like the real-life Michael Corleone (with Oakley as Luca Brasi). At one point, agent David Falk sits about thirty feet away, patiently waiting for an invite, finally giving up and coming over to say hello. (Falk asks MJ, "How late did you stay out last night?" followed by MJ casually saying "Seven-thirty," as we nod admiringly.)[118] The drinks keep coming and coming. Occasionally Oakley stands up and saunters around just to stretch his legs and look cool while I make comments like, "I wish you could rent Oak for parties." At one point, Oak thinks about ordering food, stands up, looks over at all of us eating, notices our friend Rich's cheeseburger, asks if it's a cheeseburger, asks if it's good, keeps glancing at it, keeps glancing at it . . . and I swear, we're all waiting for Oak to say the words, "Oak wants your cheeseburger, and he wants it now." But he doesn't. He ends up ordering one himself. Too bad.[119]

117. Oak had two legendary NBA feuds: One with Tyrone Hill (who reportedly welched on a poker debt), the other with Jeff McInnis (origins unclear but it definitely involved a woman). I have heard various accounts of the resolutions of these feuds, but each involved Oak laying the smack down like Marcellus Wallace seeking revenge on Zed and the Gimp. By the way, any time you hear about two NBA players who have a long-standing beef, there is a 100 percent chance that the beef started because someone owed money from a card game or someone boinked someone else's girlfriend or steady hookup. With no exceptions.

118. This is an underrated part of the story—not the 7:30 part, but that Falk was afraid to come over and he was only Jordan's agent at the time.

119. I wanted my son to have the initials B.O.S. for obvious reasons. The O candidates were awful: Oliver, Oscar, Omaha and so on. Then I noticed Oakley and liked the sound

Two solid hours pass. Everyone at Jordan's table finishes eating. The cigars come out. And I'm sitting there whispering, "There's no way that the cards aren't coming out soon. It's impossible. MJ has never sat this long in one place without the cards coming out. The man has a competitive disorder. The cards will come out. The cards will *definitely* come out."

Almost on cue, the cards emerge. They start playing a game called Bid Wist, a form of spades that's popular among NBA players.[120] Oakley and MJ team up against two of their friends and Jordan comes alive. Of course he does. We witness his legendary competitive streak in action: he's trash-talking nonstop in a deep voice, snickering sarcastically, cackling with every good card, even badgering one opponent to the point that the guy seems like a threat to start crying like one of Joe Pesci's minions in *Goodfellas*. This isn't Corporate MJ, the one you and I know. This is Urban MJ, the one that comes out for the Black Super Bowl,[121] the one that made an entire league cower for most of the nineties. It finally makes sense.

And I'm sitting there dying. I know, I know . . . I love cards and have a gambling problem. But what would make for a greater story than Sully and me calling winners against Oak and MJ? (Even if there isn't a chance in hell, it's fun to imagine and I have about seventeen Bloody Marys in me at that point. Cut me some slack.) Meanwhile, the day keeps getting stranger and stranger. Around six, Shaquille O'Neal shows up with his posse, wearing a three-piece suit with a vest that causes MJ to joke, "I'm glad you're living up to the responsibility of the dress code." Everyone laughs a little too loudly, because that's what you do when Michael Jordan makes a joke: you laugh your fucking ass off. A little bit later, an NBA assistant coach shows up wearing a red sweatshirt with a giant Jordan logo on it. (Who else runs into a

---

of it (strong name) and the thought of my son sharing the name of the single coolest person alive. Will you grow up to be a pussy with a middle name like Oakley? No way. And since my wife had just pumped a nine-pound fetus out of her body, was doped up on pain meds and had stitches in a place where you definitely wouldn't want to have stitches, she readily agreed. Would we have come up with that middle name if this 2006 Four Seasons story hadn't happened? Probably not. See, everything happens for a reason.

120. I'm almost positive that it's illegal for white people to play Bid Wist.

121. That's a nickname for All-Star Weekend that I used as the headline for my 2006 All-Star Weekend column after my friend J. A. Adande emailed me, "Have fun at the Black Super Bowl." College basketball's Final Four is the Caucasian Super Bowl (just 80,000 middle-aged white guys wearing warmup suits), the women's Final Four is the Lesbian Super Bowl (they cater some of the events toward a gay audience now), the Daytona 500 is the White Trash Super Bowl, and the Super Bowl is the Super Bowl.

friend randomly wearing their clothing line?) MJ keeps getting louder and louder, and he and Oakley are cleaning up, and everyone in the bar is watching them while pretending not to watch, and then suddenly . . .

MJ's wife shows up.

Uh-oh.

Everyone makes room for her. She sits down right next to him. Poor MJ looks like somebody who took a no-hitter into the ninth, then gave up a triple off the left-field wall. The trash-talking stops. He slumps in his seat like a little kid. The cigar goes out. No more hangin' with the boys. Time to be a husband again.[122] Watching the whole thing unfold, I lean over to Sully and say, "Look at that, he's just like us."

And he is. Just your average guy getting derailed by his wife. For once in my life, I don't want to be like Mike.

That story happened more than three years ago and I can still remember where everyone was sitting. Which brings us back to the Jordan mystique. He's the only celebrity who pulls that story off from beginning to end. His force of personality was that great. So yeah, LeBron might approach him soon, and if not him, someone else. You will instinctively want to pass the torch to that person. That's just the way this stuff works. Again, we always want the Next One to be greater than the Last One, and it's impossible for the Last One to keep defending the title once memories start fading. Just remember that Superstar X can't pass Jordan solely by putting up triple doubles, breaking scoring records and winning multiple titles. They have to beat a force of personality that compares to presidents and tycoons. They have to surpass a competitiveness better suited for a dictator. They have to keep peaking well after we believed they could keep peaking. They have to remain the coolest person in the room long after there's any tangible reason for them to hold that title. And they have to pull off stories with endings like, "Look at that, he's just like us." Michael Jordan was the greatest basketball player of all time, as well as the most memorable, and maybe you need to be both.

---

122. But not for much longer—she filed for divorce a couple of months later. The good news is that Juanita Jordan will always live on for this story, as well as for one of the most awkward TV moments ever: when MJ was celebrating his first title in the locker room, they threw it to Bob Costas, who mistakenly introduced Juanita as Michael's mother, followed by Michael coldly saying, "That's my wife."

TWELVE

THE LEGEND OF KEYSER SÖZE

STAR '86

KEVIN McHALE
Forward - Boston Celtics

AFTER KEVIN GARNETT gave the most incoherent postgame interview in sports history following the 2008 Finals,[1] I never imagined leaning on his insights for my Pulitzer winner. But before Boston's title defense commenced in October, a writer named Chris Jones asked the Ticket how long he thought Celtics fans would remember that 2008 team. Would their memories have a shelf life? Would the team's magical season eventually fade away? Here's how Jones described Garnett's response:

> "Listen," Garnett interrupted, leaning in closer, eyes narrowing. "It's the one thing that connects me to this city and these guys forever. Ain't no one can take that away. It's like knowledge." He pointed to the side of his bald, shining head. "Once it's obtained, it's obtained."

---

1. "Anythang is possaaaaaaabulllllllllllllllllllllllllllllllllllllllllllllllll!!!!!!!"

Perfect. Who knew that someone who never attended college would provide one of the more illuminating quotes in the book? He's right. Every championship season matters. So let's figure out which one mattered most. Please don't confuse this chapter with the consistently botched "Who's the greatest NBA team of all time?" argument that ranks among the dumbest in sports, right up there with "Emmitt or Barry?" "Gretzky or Lemieux?" "Ali, Marciano, or Louis?" "Elway, Montana or Marino?" "Should there be a college playoff system?" "Will pro soccer ever make it in America?" "Should golf be considered a sport?" "Was the 1985 NBA Lottery rigged?" and "If you mated two current superstars in a deliberate attempt to create the greatest athlete of all time, which two would you pick?"[2] Some topics just don't need to be debated. Especially this one. Russell's Celtics captured eleven titles in thirteen years, including eight straight from 1959 to 1966, while winning at least two playoff series against every Pyramid guy from that era. No NBA team has won four in a row since. Of course, when the league convened its 35th Anniversary panel in 1980 they threw in an extra wrinkle: pick the greatest single-season team ever as well.

You know who they picked? The 1967 Philadelphia Sixers.

That's right, the one team from 1959 to 1969—an eleven-year stretch— that defeated the Celtics in a playoffs series.

Take a step back and consider how brainless that is. If *The Sopranos* won ten of eleven Best Drama Emmys from 1997 to 2007, and *Mad Men* won the other year, nobody would ever say, "*Mad Men* was the best show of all time." If Tom Hanks won ten of eleven Best Actor Oscars from 1991 to 2002, and Russell Crowe won the other year, nobody would ever say, "Russell Crowe was the best actor of all time." You'd go with *The Sopranos* and you'd go with Hanks. It wouldn't even be a question. So please, if only for my sanity, let's all agree that Bill Russell's Celtic teams earned "greatest basketball team of all time" honors. We will never see anything like eight straight or eleven of thirteen ever again.

And since that's the case, what if we twist the argument and switch "greatest team ever" for "most invincible season ever"? Now we have something! Remember in *The Usual Suspects* when Verbal Kint told his

2. The answers, which I won't bother to defend because I shouldn't have to waste more than the minimum words: Emmitt; Gretzky; Ali; Montana; yes; no; no; yes; LeBron and Serena Williams.

Keyser Söze story: how Söze sought revenge for his murdered family and ripped through an entire town like a tornado from hell, killing everybody, burning everything down and leaving nothing in his wake? We're looking for the ultimate Keyser Söze team. We want to find the team that, more than anyone else, shredded everyone in its path and left us saying afterward, "Wow, *nobody* was beating those guys." Those Russell-Auerbach teams were unbeatable, but they never submitted a defining Söze season in an unfavorable preexpansion climate (8–9 teams, 88–99 players, cream of the crop at all times) as they constantly battled the "been here, done that" syndrome.[3]

Check out Boston's regular season record as well as its total number of Hall of Famers and Pyramid guys, point differential, overall playoff record, and Finals record from 1959 to 1966.

YEAR	REC	HF	PG	PD	PLA	FINALS
1959	52–20	7	5	6.5	8–3	4–0 (LA)
1960	59–16	7	5	8.3	8–5	4–3 (STL)
1961	57–22	7	5	5.6	8–2	4–1 (STL)
1962	60–20	6	5	9.2	8–6	4–3 (LA)
1963	58–22	8	5	7.2	8–5	4–2 (LA)
1964	59–21	7	5	7.9	8–2	4–1 (SF)
1965	62–18	5	4	8.4	8–4	4–1 (LA)
1966	54–26	4	4	4.9	12–6	4–3 (LA)

Here's the one great Philly season from 1967:

YEAR	REC	HF	PG	PD	PLA	FINALS
1967	68–13	3	2	9.4	12–4	4–2 (SF)

Hmmmmmm. Pay special attention to the '65 Celts and '67 Sixers. Heading into '65 as the back-to-back-to-back-to-back-to-back-to-back

3. You probably remember the first time you had sex. Like, all the details. Do you remember everything about the sixth time? What about the eighth? Or the eleventh? Been there, done that, right? But that first time . . . I mean, even twenty-five years later, I still remember everything about that magical night at the Neverland Ranch.

champs, the Celtics had exhausted so many different motivational gimmicks that "We need to win for Tommy Heinsohn, it's his last year!" was
their only galvanizing force other than Russell's puking, Auerbach's hol-
lering and the promise of playoff money. Two years later, the Sixers were
driven by a chance to capture their first title and topple Boston's dynasty,
as well as Wilt's obsession with beating Russell and proving he could be a
team player; those powerful, once-in-a-career incentives propelled them
to 68 wins (six more than the '65 Celts), a 9.4 scoring differential (one
point higher than the '65 Celts) and a 12–4 playoff record (four wins better than the Celts, who only played two rounds). And that wasn't the most
talented Russell team: the '60, '61 and '62 groups were better.[4] Comparing
Russell's Celtics to Robert DeNiro's career, the '65 team would be *Heat*.
Great movie, iconic movie, astoundingly rewatchable movie, but not his
best work.

Now add this: The '67 season featured an expansion team (Chicago)
and a hopeless doormat (the 20-win Bullets); Philly went 16–2 against
those clowns but finished 4–5 against its only opponent with a winning
percentage over .550 (the 60-win Celtics).[5] The '65 Celtics had one whipping boy (the 17-win Warriors, who dropped nine of ten to them) and
three legitimate foes: the 49-win Lakers (West and Elgin), the 48-win Royals (Oscar at his apex) and a 40-win Philly team became competitive after
stealing Wilt from San Fran in mid-January. Boston went 15–5 against
Cincy and Los Angeles and 3–3 against Wilt's Sixers. So what's more impressive—the back-to-back-to-back-to-back-to-back-to-back champs
winning 62 games in a tighter and more competitive league, or Philly winning 68 in an easier league with loads of incentive?

Any "most invincible season ever" argument hinges on motivation and
timing. The '96 Bulls wanted to avenge a disheartening playoff defeat. The
'71 Bucks and '83 Sixers smelled first titles for Oscar and Doc/Moses. The

---

4. The '65 Celtics didn't have a true point guard other than an aging KC Jones, who was
a worse shot than Dick Cheney. In crunch time, Sam and Hondo handled the ball for
them. Could you win the 2009 title with Kobe and Pierce as your ball handlers? Seems a
little far-fetched, right?
5. Six of the ten '67 teams won between 30 and 39 games; Baltimore won 20; San Fran
went 5–13 vs. Boston/Philly and 39–24 against everyone else; and Boston/Philly finished
a combined 128–34. (Hold on, era-appropriate pop culture reference coming . . .) That
season was more top-heavy than Jayne Mansfield!

'86 Celtics were rejuvenated by Bill Walton and sought retribution for blowing the '85 Finals. The '87 Lakers wanted to prove they weren't finished. And the '67 Sixers were blessed with a secret weapon that any Celtics team from 1960 to 1966 was fundamentally disqualified from having: a burning desire to prove themselves and accomplish the great unknown. In retrospect, the biggest tragedy of Russell's career was Selvy missing the winning shot of the '62 Finals.[6] Imagine an absurdly loaded '63 Celtics team declaring war and finishing something like 72–8. They had Russell in his prime, Sam Jones emerging as a top-ten player, Cousy and Heinsohn still thriving, Satch and KC killing teams defensively, Ramsey and Havlicek coming off the bench ... and unfortunately, the '63 Celts lacked any incentive other than "We need to win for Cooz in his last year" and "We could use the playoff money for cigarettes and rent."

We also can't ignore the benefits—and really, that's the perfect word— of a respected contender nipping at the alpha dog's heels. That wrinkle pushed the '86 Celtics, '87 Lakers and '67 Sixers to heights they might not have reached otherwise. For instance, the '67 Celtics jumped to a 14–2 start before eventually falling behind a 26–2 Sixers team. As Philly extended its record to 46–4 in January, the Celtics were ripping off eleven straight and staying close enough that Philly never relaxed. What if Boston won 45 games instead of 60? Are the Sixers still driving to the finish line like Secretariat in the Belmont? Contrast that with ho-hum seasons for the '60 C's (who started off 30–4 and opened an eight-game lead before blowing six of their next eight) and the '65 C's (46–9 and leading the league by double digits before "stumbling" to 14–9 down the stretch). Why couldn't they keep it up? They got bored! Nobody cared about anything like "Whoa, they might win 70 games!" back then; the league hadn't been around long enough to place such an achievement in perspective. That changed during the '67 season. Everyone wanted Philly to topple Boston's dynasty and break the 70-win barrier (or come damned close); between that and Boston breathing down Philly's neck, suddenly the NBA

6. The cousin of this event: the undefeated '07 Patriots pulling out a sloppy Week 14 game in Baltimore. Had they blown it, that would have been the kick in the ass they needed. No way they lose Super Bowl XLIV. At least this is what I keep telling myself. Hold on, I have to fire my BB gun at the right leg of my Plax Burress bobblehead again. I'll be right back.

had never seen a hungrier regular season team.[7] Again, much of this "most invincible team ever" stuff is totally, completely, undeniably circumstantial. That's why the twenty best single-season teams (don't worry, we're getting there) fall into one of three categories.

LEVEL ONE: A TEAM CAPTURING ITS FIRST TITLE

Think of it like hiking a gigantic mountain: you don't know if you can do it, you nearly get derailed a hundred times, you dig deeper than you ever thought you could, you tap into a level of passion that you didn't know you had, you still don't totally trust that it will happen . . . and then it happens. For instance, let's say you're handsome, funny, well dressed, and wealthy—like me, only if I were single.[8] Let's say someone introduces you to Kate Bosworth at a cocktail party in Manhattan. And let's say you're thinking, "Holy shit, I'm talking to Kate Bosworth!" and assuming you don't have a chance in hell with her. Are you hopping in a cab with her later that night? No way. Now, let's say you dated Meadow Soprano for three months, hooked up with an Olsen, and fooled around with Minka Kelly when she was between Mayer and Jeter . . . and then someone introduced you to Bosworth. You've been there before with female celebs. You've broken that barrier down. You have an inner confidence that you might not have had otherwise. Even better, she knows about you and Minka Kelly, giving you a little celebrity cachet with her. She doesn't have to worry about you high-fiving yourself after an orgasm or waiting for her to fall asleep so you can film her with your cell phone.[9]

---

7. If you don't think this pushed mainstream interest in the NBA to new heights, you're crazy. Remember, the media didn't exist in its current form—we were confined to newspapers, local news shows, and *SI*. They covered sports instead of hyping them. By the late sixties, that was changing as we witnessed with the "Can Philly win 70?" stuff. Media members were searching for future angles instead of just digesting what had already happened. Now? We create angles that aren't there! We've come a long way.

8. This was a joke—I am not well dressed.

9. I came up with this analogy after hitting a BlackBerry party with my friend Willy, who did *extremely* well for himself in Boston but couldn't muster up the confidence to approach Bosworth in L.A., mainly because her legs were so breathtaking that we were staring at them like pit bulls looking at a prime rib. She's like Dwyane Wade and Dwight Howard—you can't properly appreciate her until you see her in person.

So who has a better chance of sealing the deal with Kate Bosworth: Great-on-Paper You or Great-on-Paper-with-Confidence You? The second guy. It's not a debate. Well, basketball works the same way. Great-Team-on-Paper will never be as good as Great-Team-on-Paper-with-Confidence.

LEVEL TWO: A CHAMPION DEFENDING ITS TITLE

Sure, they might get bored during the regular season, battle overconfidence problems, struggle against the Disease of More and fail to find the same passion that carried them the previous year . . . but they snap into "You have no chance, we're the champs" mode as soon as there's money or pride on the line. When Lloyd Neal hissed in the locker room, "That's why we're the fucking champs!" after the '78 Blazers annihilated Philly, that's the definitive Level Two story. MJ's parade of threes in Game 1 of the '92 Finals is the definitive "That's why we're the fucking champs" game. L.A.'s roll through the 2001 playoffs was the definitive "That's why we're the fucking champs" postseason.[10]

LEVEL THREE: A GREAT TEAM WITH THE EFF-YOU EDGE

Only one scenario applies, and it requires a run-on sentence: you need an elite former championship team with a transcendent star in his prime coming off a disappointing playoff exit who regrouped and made the necessary tweaks before locking themselves into Söze mode for eight months trying to climb back over the mountain and reclaim what's theirs while taking out their frustrations from a previous collapse along the way. Think '86 Celts or '96 Bulls.

You can't enter the Söze zone as a Level One team. A shred of doubt loiters over everything. *Are we that good? Can we actually win? We aren't gonna blow this, are we?* The '91 Bulls are the best example: on paper, they

---

10. When it goes wrong for the defending champs, it's like that same guy hooking up with Bosworth for a few weeks, having a threesome with LC and Lo from *The Hills*, then dressing and acting like a douche and proudly showing his buddies his BlackBerry contact list every time he goes drinking with them.

were one of the six or seven greatest teams of all time by any statistical calculation. But I was there. I can report with complete certainty that most
"experts" (including me)[11] thought the Lakers would beat them in the Finals. You know, the old "experience over youth" thing. When the Bulls
blew Game 1 at home, nobody thought Chicago would sweep the next
four games. Not even Michael Jordan. (I specifically remember the Lakers
being 5-to-2 favorites after Game 1.) And honestly? They didn't become
great until the last few minutes of Game 5, when Phil Jackson finally convinced Jordan to trust his teammates once and for all—the much-retold,
"Michael, who's open?" story—and the Bulls took care of business.

Level Two and Level Three? That's another story. These teams *know*
how to take care of business. They *know* what works. They *know* how to
win. They *know* what it feels like to climb the mountain and know how to
get back there. At this point, we're arguing degrees. So what's more impressive: a dethroned champion channeling its hostility into the following
season and wreaking havoc, or a defending champion welcoming all com-
ers, relishing every challenge, developing an air of invincibility/superiority
and sticking it to everyone for an entire "Show me what you got!" season?
Fortunately, we have the perfect case study (the '96 and '97 Bulls) and perfect person to answer the question (Steve Kerr, a crunch-timer on both
teams and one of the more thoughtful ex-players, someone who genuinely wonders about this stuff). On paper, the '96 and '97 Bulls were
closer than you probably remember.

1996 Bulls: 72–10 (reg. season), 15–3 (playoffs), 13.4 point differential
1997 Bulls: 69–13 (reg. season), 15–4 (playoffs), 12.0 point differential

Now throw these wrinkles in:

- Chicago's '96 playoff record was skewed because of the Eastern Finals, when a much-anticipated Orlando rematch was derailed in

---

11. Game 3 (Chicago over L.A. in OT) was one of my worst gambling losses ever; trust
me that I did *not* have to look up the line (L.A. by 3) or the score (Bulls 104, L.A. 96). My
buddy Geoff and I watched at his mom's house, sat in shock for another 20 minutes,
then debated sneaking into her office and forging a check. The lesson, as always: don't
gamble in college.

Game 1 after Horace Grant (Orlando's best rebounder) left with a series-ending left elbow injury. When Nick Anderson (a worthy foil for Jordan in '95) went down in Game 3, the Bulls ended up sweeping a Magic team that should have been a worthy opponent. Remember, Penny made first-team All-NBA that year; the Bulls had nobody to defend Shaq; and Orlando had already beaten them once.[12]

- The '97 Bulls signed Brian Williams[13] for the stretch run, giving them something they lacked in '96: a lefty who could score with his back to the basket. Williams grabbed all of Bill Wennington's minutes in the '97 playoffs. You've seen Bill Wennington play, right? That's a bigger upgrade than Ashton Kutcher going from Brittany Murphy to Demi Moore.

- The league was better in '97 and Utah provided a more experienced Finals opponent than the happy-to-be-there '96 Sonics. Going 15–4 in the '97 postseason was no less impressive than 15–3 in '96.

Before I asked Kerr the "Who was better?" question, I had been leaning toward the '97 Bulls. The last part of my email: "Considering that you weren't in 'Eff You' mode in '97 because you had already climbed the mountain, but you guys still went out and kicked everybody's ass to 98.9 percent of the same degree you did the year before, in my mind, that's a greater accomplishment than just winning the title in '96 when you had all the necessary incentives in place. Does that make sense?"

Kerr's response:

Very interesting. I guess the question is, do you reward a team for having less motivation, or do you take points away? I could make an argu-

12. What a shame we missed an Orlando-Chicago bloodbath. This was the great lost series of the nineties. Meanwhile, we were treated to 738 unwatchable Knicks-Heat games. Damn it all.

13. Just to clarify, this was the Arizona grad who battled gay rumors, changed his name to Bison Dele, retired prematurely, invested in a desalination complex in Lebanon and was apparently murdered by his brother (although there was no trial because the brother killed himself, but evidence pointed strongly to him) during an around-the-world boating trip . . . not the NBC news anchor. We should also mention that my 1999 and 2000 fantasy hoop teams were called "Bison's Deli."

ment that the '96 team was better *because* we were more motivated. The hunger factor was huge for us that year and that helped make us a great team. Two things come to mind when I compare those teams. First is the Brian Williams factor. We got him for (the final 17 games) and he was huge for us down the stretch. Having a legit post-up scorer and athletic shot blocker was something we didn't have before. Secondly, when you've won a title already, there's a sense of superiority and invincibility that wasn't there before. The great teams use that in a positive way, which is what we did. Instead of "eff you" mode like in '96, it's more like "You have no chance against us" mode. We were so confident from already having won a title that we *knew* we were going to crush everyone that year. That's a dangerous mentality to have, obviously, if you don't have a mature team. It would be easy to stop working hard. But with MJ and all of our vets, there was no way that was going to happen. Anyway, for what it's worth, I thought the '96 team was better because of the edge we had. The "eff you" is a powerful force. But the '97 team was better on paper.[14]

Perfect! Thank you, Steve Kerr. We couldn't have asked for a better guy to solve that problem. That's why I have the "eff you" mode ranked as Level Three and the "superiority/invincibility" mode ranked one level below: because Kerr lived through both seasons, he's wicked smaht (© Will Hunting's buddy) and we can trust him. So if we're figuring out the single most invincible basketball team ever, really, there are three choices and only three: the '86 Celtics, '87 Lakers or '96 Bulls . . . although we're covering the best ten, because God forbid I ever took a shortcut in this book. One Stanley Roberts–size disclaimer: For any "most invincible" argument, it can't be forgotten that the NBA peaked competitively from 1984 to 1993, a few years after the merger but before overexpansion, the

14. Kerr submitted the greatest two-year sample of three-point shooting ever in '95 (52.4%, 1st all-time) and '96 (51.5%, 5th all-time), finishing 45.4% on threes for his career (2nd all-time). He won five rings, made a Finals-winning shot ('97, Game 6) and had a defining ESPN Classic game (Game 6, Dallas-SA in '03). He played with MJ, Duncan, Shaq, Pippen, Robinson and the '02 Jail Blazers and was coached by Phil Jackson and Gregg Popovich. He got in a practice fight with MJ and held his own. He made over $16 million in 15 years. He worked with Marv Albert on TNT. He got hired as a GM by Phoenix, built his team around The Secret (inadvertently, but still) and made the 2010 West Finals. Now he's making a crucial cameo in the second greatest NBA book ever written, or at least the longest one. Now *that* is a career!

megasalary boom and underclassmen flooding the college draft. Check out the roster of the '84 Celtics, who won two seventh games to clinch a fifteenth banner, outlasted a seemingly unbeatable Lakers team, and were never considered for my top ten:

STARTERS: Larry Bird (first of his three MVP years), Cedric Maxwell ('81 Finals MVP), Robert Parish (top–fifty-five Pyramid guy), Dennis Johnson (top–fifty-five Pyramid Guy, '79 Finals MVP), Gerald Henderson (good enough to get swapped for Seattle's unconditional number one pick that summer)[15]

BENCH: Kevin McHale (top-forty Pyramid guy, best sixth man ever), Danny Ainge (one-time All-Star, fourteen-year veteran), M. L. Carr (one of the league's better bench players), Scott Wedman (two-time All-Star, best player on an '81 Kings team that came within one win of the Finals), Quinn Buckner (former top-ten pick, 10-year veteran).

See the benefits of a smaller league (just twenty-three teams) with incompetently run teams routinely screwing up drafts and giving away number one picks? Once the league began adding franchises and diluting its talent pool, it became nearly impossible to construct juggernauts like the ones from the Bird-Magic era. In the last fifteen years, we've only seen two competitive monsters: Jordan's post-baseball Chicago teams and the first two Shaq-Kobe teams. In a thirty-team league with nearly every front office knowing what it's doing,[16] with owners constantly fearing the salary cap and luxury tax, you cannot build a contender with a three-time MVP, three Finals MVPs, four Pyramid guys, McHale coming off the bench, Ainge as your third guard and Wedman as your eighth man. You can't get lucky enough times; the odds are too great.

Hence, for the purposes of this chapter, I'm ignoring the pre-1960 teams (not enough black players, defense or quality shooting), severely

---

15. That's the pick that became Lenny Bias. I will now wander out into rush hour traffic.
16. I had to write "nearly" because of Chris Mullin, Bryan Colangelo, Ernie Grunfeld and everyone else who would have earned an invitation to the Atrocious GM Summit 2 if we had convened it for this book. Maybe the next one.

penalizing the 1970–76 teams (because of the expansion/ABA double whammy) and pre-1970 teams (because I've seen the tapes and you can't tell me with a straight face that the '65 Celts or '67 Sixers wouldn't have gotten swept by the '01 Lakers by 25 points a game), and I'm discounting the post-MJ teams (because it's impossible to put together a ridiculously talented team in a thirty-team league with cap/tax constraints). The teams left standing will be judged by four factors and only four.

1. Invincibility at the time coupled with a willingness of everyone else to concede, "We had no chance against those guys." This is a clear-cut yes-or-no question. You can easily tell from the articles written during the season and after the Finals. If writers are raving about the team and struggling to put them in a historical context, and if their opponents are gushing about them, then something magical just happened.

2. Level of consistent/methodical/transcendent greatness from October to June. You can figure this out with regular-season/playoffs records, double-digit winning streaks, high point differentials, few playoffs losses and high margins in closeout games. The last one is my favorite: when invincible teams smell blood, they shift into "we aren't just winning this, we're going to hopefully ruin their confidence for the next five years and give our fans a lifelong memory" mode.

3. Their defense of that "greatest season" the following year. Sorry, if you just submitted a historic season that might be remembered for eternity, shouldn't that mean something to everyone who was involved? Show some pride. Protect your title. Make us feel like you'd rather die than lose your championship belt. What's the point of winning a title if you aren't going to defend it?

4. Hypothetical ability to transcend eras and succeed no matter the year. And yes, this is the single toughest ingredient to project; we're eliminating nearly everyone before 1980 for the reasons laid out in the "How the Hell" chapter. God bless Russell's Celtics teams, but they weren't beating MJ's Bulls with Hondo and Sam Jones handling the ball, and they definitely weren't beating Bird's Celtics with Tommy Heinsohn guarding Kevin McHale. As for the hypothetical stuff, you're just going to have to trust my expertise. You've come this far. In the

words of Bobby Knight, relax and enjoy it. Whoops, he was talking · about rape. Bad example. Um, just relax and enjoy it.[17]

In my humble opinion, only twenty NBA champions deserved special commendation for this chapter. I narrowed it down to ten honorable mentions and an elite ten.

HONORABLE MENTION

THE '61 CELTICS (57–22, 8–2 IN PLAYOFFS)

Russell's most dominant team considering he was hitting his prime (19–30–5 in the playoffs), eight Hall of Famers were aboard and they rolled through the playoffs . . . but that 57–22 record screams of "When are the playoffs starting?" In their defense, they were coming off back-to-back titles and God knows how many exhibition/regular season games—playing something like 240–250 games in a twenty-four-month span, traveling by bus or train (or even worse, flying coach with connections)—without modern advances in training, workout equipment, medical care, dieting and everything else. Again, watch the first two seasons of *Mad Men* sometime and imagine playing basketball back then. Give the '61 Celtics a chartered plane, Dr. James Andrews, a dietitian and nicotine patches and God knows what would have happened.

THE '65 CELTICS (60–22, 8–4, 16-GAME WINNING STREAK)

Personified the "it's all about timing" point. Had San Francisco waited until the summer to gift-wrap Wilt for Philly, the Celtics would have

---

17. I wish Knight had made this comment to Connie Chung now during the overly politically correct era. ESPN would have offered around-the-clock twenty-four-hour coverage hosted by Bob Ley as we decided whether to throw Knight in jail or deport him.

played a 48-win Royals team in the Eastern Finals (they finished 8–2 against Cincy that year) and an Elginless Lakers team in the Finals. Instead, they barely survived a seven-game bloodbath against Wilt's Sixers that everyone remembers for "Havlicek steals the ball!" No discussion about the greatest of the great should include the words "barely survived." Unless you're talking about Uruguayan rugby.[18]

THE '67 76ERS (68–13, 12–4)

Beyond the pre-1970 issue and a weak competitive season, they were overrated for the following reasons: First, they caught the Russell era at the perfect time, immediately after Auerbach retired, when Russell struggled in his first year as player-coach. Second, the "special" component to Philly's season was its 68–13 record . . . but really, the 68 happened because Boston stayed close for a while and the national media, for whatever reason, made a big deal about the quest for 70.[19] Third, they only featured three Pyramid guys (Wilt, Greer and Cunningham, only a rookie), and when you think about it, how could the so-called greatest team of the NBA's first thirty-five years have only three Pyramid guys? Fourth, Wilt's poor free throw shooting would quickly manifest itself in a fictional round-robin tournament with the other all-time powerhouses; he infamously avoided the ball in the final two minutes, leaving Greer or Cunningham to match baskets with Jordan, Kobe, Bird or whomever. And fifth, for an allegedly "great" team, they couldn't defend their title even once, blowing a 3–1 lead to the '68 Celtics (with Wilt demanding a trade that summer). So much for our number one Silver Anniversary choice.

18. Come on . . . too soon? It's been nearly thirty-nine years! Comedy = cannibalism + time.

19. Had this happened with any of the Boston teams from 1960 to 1963 (the heel-nipping and national attention), they may have turned it up a notch and gone for 70. And you know it. Concede my hypothetical that can't be proven!

THE '70 KNICKS (60–22, 12–7)

Had the following things in their favor: three top-45 Pyramid guys and first-team All-Defense guys (Reed, Frazier and DeBusschere), a 10-plus point differential in the regular season, truly phenomenal home crowds, an undeniable grasp of The Secret, an 18-game winning streak and some of the most beautiful ball movement and perimeter shooting we've ever seen. But their playoff performance was lacking,[20] and you can't discount their failed title defense (losing a Game 7 to Baltimore at MSG). Throw in Russell (retired), Wilt (played 6 regular season games), Oscar (self-destructing in Cincy), Kareem (just a rookie) and expansion (five new teams since '67) and the '70 Knicks didn't do nearly enough butt-whupping for my liking. On the bright side, 20,785 books have been written about them. So they have that going for them.

THE '82 L.A. LAKERS (57–25, 12–2)

Along with the '01 Lakers, my favorite "should have been greater" team that was sideswiped by the Disease of More. By the spring (once they changed coaches, quelled chemistry issues and got Magic going again), they had the following trump cards in place: two of the five greatest players ever, a soul-crushing half-court offense anchored by Kareem, a once-in-a-generation fast break with two point guards (Magic and Norm Nixon), and an ahead-of-its-time 1-3-1 smallball trap with McAdoo anchoring the back, Norm Nixon up front, and Jamaal Wilkes, Magic and Michael Cooper covering the middle. They cruised to the degree that "best team ever" buzz built throughout the playoffs—10–0 heading into Game 3 of the Finals—before Philly salvaged two wins, the Lakers clinched in six, and everyone forgot about them five seconds later because CBS tape-delayed most of the series. But if you created a 32-team Best of

---

20. They lost six of eight road games, their playoff point differential was just 3.9, and Baltimore took them to 7 games in the first round.

All Time single-elimination, March Madness–type tournament, the '82 Lakers would be my sleeper. Nightmare matchup for just about anyone.[21]

THE '85 L.A. LAKERS (62–20, 15–4)

Had to be included because of their impressive playoff numbers (127.1 points scored, 16.3 point differential per win, 54.3 percent FG shooting, 11 double-digit wins, closeout game margins of 16, 19, 44, and 9), although it's still unclear if the best team won the title. (Note: That was the spring when Bird injured his shooting hand in a bar fight and stank in the Finals.) The '85 Lakers were the first smallball champion: Kareem had stopped rebounding consistently, they didn't have an elite power forward and their best lineup was Kareem-Worthy-Cooper-Scott-Magic. Despite Bird's struggles and Cedric Maxwell's no-show that season,[22] it's hard to fathom how a team blessed with Bird, Parish and McHale in their primes didn't just pound the living crap out of the Lakers down low. (Even twenty-odd years later, McHale and Ainge still bitch that the Celtics blew a golden chance to repeat. Had the Lakers been a truly great team, their Finals opponents wouldn't have been kicking themselves years later and bemoaning lost chances. Same goes for the '84 Celtics, by the way.) Their big issue was rebounding—one year later, the '86 Rockets busted the Lakers by butchering them on the boards. Why didn't the '85 Celtics do this? I have no idea. But everything probably evened out: L.A. blew the '84 Finals, Boston blew the '85 Finals, and that's that.

---

21. One way to stop them: this was the height of the coke era and the '82 Lakers, in retrospect, had a few "suspects" in their nine-man rotation. If I were a GM back then, wherever the Lakers partied after a game, I'd have sent $10K worth of hookers and coke to that location.

22. Max stuck a stamp on the '85 season, taking too long to recover from a minor knee surgery that should have sidelined him for six weeks. Auerbach vengefully traded him for Walton; even two decades later, a still-pissed Red protested vehemently when Boston's new owners retired Max's number 31 under the always offensive "We just bought the team, wouldn't it be fun to retire someone's number?" logic. Only eleven Boston numbers should be retired: Russell, Bird, Hondo, Cousy, Sharman, Cowens, McHale, Heinsohn, Parish, Sam Jones and (someday) Pierce.

THE '92 CHICAGO BULLS (67–15, 15–7)

A potential all-timer that didn't quite get there because of something Kerr mentioned with his invincibility/superiority comments about Level Two teams: "That's a dangerous mentality to have, obviously, if you don't have a mature team." Bingo. This should have been Jordan's best team: MJ was at the peak of his physical powers, as was Pippen, and they were blessed with the best nine-man rotation of any Bulls team during the MJ era. They had an answer for everything. But the playoffs . . . arrrrrrrgh. You shouldn't need seven games to topple the '92 Knicks. You shouldn't need six games to topple the '92 Blazers. You shouldn't have to rally from 15 down at home to clinch your title.

The Disease of More wreaked havoc with these guys. Pippen was kicking himself after signing a shortsighted contract extension, then learning the Bulls offered more money to Toni Kukoc. Grant was ticked because he didn't get enough acclaim for doing all the dirty work. Young guns Stacey King, B. J. Armstrong and Cliff Levingston believed they were good enough to be starting. And all hell broke loose when Sam Smith released *The Jordan Rules* in January of '92, a behind-the-scenes account of Chicago's first title season. We learned about Jordan's overcompetitiveness, gigantic ego, "selfish" nature[23] and mean-spirited methods for motivating inferior teammates; everyone was flabbergasted because we only knew Jordan from his inventive Nike commercials and articulate interviews. Infuriated by the candid portrayal and incensed that insiders provided material for the book—among them, reportedly, Grant, Phil Jackson and Jerry Reinsdorf—Jordan retreated into an icy shell and wouldn't emerge until he started playing for the Birmingham Barons three years later. That's what led to Chicago's spotty performance in the '92 playoffs. Tragically, that Bulls team had the highest ceiling of anyone

---

23. I used quotes because Smith played up a premise that wasn't necessarily true. MJ did whatever it took for his team to win, and really, during those first few Chicago years, his supporting cast sucked. What did you want him to do, pass up game-winning shots to set up Brad Sellers or Kyle Macy? Early MJ was only guilty of disparaging teammates and killing their confidence in some cases. Is that selfish? I'd argue he was just a dick. Big difference.

other than the '82 Lakers, '86 Celtics and '01 Lakers; watch Game 1 of the Finals not just for Jordan's epic undressing of Clyde Drexler but for the way the Bulls demolished Portland defensively. Then they relaxed and blew Game 2. And so it went for the Bulls that season: tons of potential, much of it realized . . . but not all of it. As it turned out, the only guy who could stop the '92 Bulls was Sam Smith.[24]

THE '00 L.A. LAKERS (67–15, 15–8, 19-GAME STREAK)

It's a shame we can't combine their '00 regular season with their '01 play-offs (14–1) and make them a superteam. The smoking guns: they started the '00 playoffs 11–6 (yuck) before beating Indy in six; and Portland would have beaten them if not for the most horrific fourth-quarter collapse in the history of the Association. The Blazers missed a few shots, got tight, stopped getting calls and got screwed by some illogical coaching decisions. Even the 2000 Source Awards didn't melt down that fast. What a startling game to rewatch. Even more startling: Mike Dunleavy was hired to coach another team after what happened. When the poor Clippers had to spend ten hours spraying Dunleavy with a fire hose to get the blood of the 2000 Blazers off his body, maybe that should have been a sign to look at other candidates.

THE '07 SAN ANTONIO SPURS (58–24, 16–4)

THE '08 BOSTON CELTICS (66–16, 16–10)

The Spurs lacked regular season chops and the Celtics lacked postseason chops, but they relied on the same formula: three elite players (Duncan-Parker-Ginobili for SA, Garnett-Pierce-Allen for Boston), multiple

---

24. This would be much funnier if I showed you a picture of Sam Smith. He looks like the skinny brother of the "Time to make the donuts!" guy from the old Dunkin' Donuts ads.

crunch-time scorers, effective role players and stifling defense. Including advancements in game planning, scouting, conditioning, defensive IQ, statistical study, DVD/editing, equipment, medicine, physical care, Internet/ mobile devices, high school basketball camps and everything else, you could argue these past two title teams weren't as loaded as the squads from the Bird-Magic era, but they were more prepared and more defensively sound.[25] Back in 1984, a pivotal coaching adjustment was KC Jones finally realizing after three freaking games that Dennis Johnson should have been hounding Magic.[26] In 2008? Coaches and scouts broke things down so meticulously that they could tell you the exact benefits—right down to the percentage point—of forcing Lamar Odom right instead of letting him go left. Should hyperintelligence matter when we're comparing teams from different decades? Absolutely. It's an era-specific advantage, just like smoking, lowtop sneakers, lack of fitness and rudimentary VD medication were detriments during the Russell era. But it doesn't change the fact that Kendrick Perkins couldn't have stopped Kareem in a million years, that Magic would have eaten Boston's point guards alive, or that Jordan would have ripped up the '07 Spurs.

If you're still dubious that this decade's finest teams couldn't have handled the best of the Bird-Magic-Jordan era, beyond the preexpansion advantages of having two more quality guys in your top nine, consider this caveat: if the 1986 Celtics hopped in a time machine, turned into a 2010 expansion team and reconfigured under current salary-cap/luxury-tax rules (we'll say a $70 million cap), do you realize how much money they would lose?[27] Here's a conservative estimate of their projected cap figures as well as the total amount of each hypothetical contract:

25. Biggest difference in 2008: how effectively teams space the floor and use corner threes. It's an advantage that the best '80s players (save for Bird) just hadn't figured out—the most efficient shot on the floor and a must-defend at all times.

26. The over/under of unprovoked shots at KC Jones' coaching ability was 9.5. I think we obliterated it 150 pages ago. And yes, he was the perfect guy to coach that '86 Celts team—just roll the ball out and let them do their thing.

27. For every dollar spent that exceeds the tax threshold, the offending team has to match those dollars in tax fees paid to the league. If the tax line is $60 million and you spend $80 million, you're looking at a $20 million tax as well. Plus you miss out on splitting the tax profit pool that's filled by offending teams. The old double whammy.

Larry Bird: $20 million (6 years, $120 million)

Kevin McHale: $15.5 million (6 years, $93 million)

Robert Parish: $15 million (5 years, $75 million)

Dennis Johnson: $13 million (5 years, $65 million)

Danny Ainge: $9 million (5 years, $45 million)

Bill Walton: $7 million (3 years, $21 million)

Scott Wedman: $6.5 million (5 years, $27.5 million)

Jerry Sichting: $1.8 million (2 years, $3.6 million)

Sam Vincent: $1.7 million (4 years, $6.8 million)

Greg Kite: $1.7 million (4 years, $6.8 million)

David Thirdkill: $1.2 million (1 year, $1.2 million)

Rick Carlisle: $400K (3 years, $1.2 million)[28]

Cap total: $92.8 million

Keep in mind, that's only twelve players and every modern team carries fifteen, so we'd have to bump the total by another $1.5–$3 million; the Parish/McHale salaries assume that nobody cleared copious amounts of cap space (like Orlando with Rashard Lewis) to offer them $110–$120 million in free agency (which definitely could have happened); and Wedman's number might be low when you remember what similar shooters like Jason Kapono and Vlad Radmanovic earned in free agency (and Wedman was better than those guys). Anyway, my "realistic" look at their projected salaries twenty-four years later yields a projected payroll of $95 million. Ninety-five million! The '86 Celtics wouldn't just lose money in 2009; they'd lose *outrageous, life-altering amounts of money,* upwards of $30–$35 million once you include the luxury tax. In other words, there's no conceivable way their nucleus could have remained intact. Which means they would have been forced to deal Parish or McHale—just for the hell of it, let's say they traded McHale to Dallas for Sam Perkins, Derek Harper and a future number one—and instead of swapping Cedric

---

28. Actual '86 cap figures: Bird ($1.8M), McHale ($1.0M), Johnson ($782.5K), Parish ($700K), Ainge ($550K), Walton ($425K), Wedman ($400K), Kite ($150K), Sichting ($125K), Carlisle ($90K), Vincent ($87.5K), Thirdkill (unknown).

Maxwell and a future number one to the Clippers for Bill Walton, they would have been forced to deal Maxwell[29] along with that number one pick (and possibly a second number one) to anyone with cap space just to ditch Max from their cap.

So let's look at our revised, tax-friendly '86 Celtics roster under 2009 rules:

Larry Bird: $20 million (6 years, $120 million)
Robert Parish: $15 million (5 years, $75 million)
Dennis Johnson: $13 million (5 years, $65 million)
Danny Ainge: $9 million (5 years, $45 million)
Scott Wedman: $5.5 million (5 years, $27.5 million)
Sam Perkins: $4 million (4 years, $16 million)
Derek Harper: $3 million (4 years, $12 million)
Jerry Sichting: $1.8 million (2 years, $3.6 million)
Sam Vincent: $1.7 million (4 years, $6.8 million)
Greg Kite: $1.7 million (4 years, $6.8 million)
David Thirdkill: $1.2 million (1 year, $1.2 million)
Rick Carlisle: $400K (3 years, $1.2 million)
Cap total: $77.3 million

Translation: Even after the above moves, they'd be guaranteed a $12–$15 million loss unless they made the second round. If their owners were afraid of taking that hit, maybe they would pursue *another* cap-friendly trade of Wedman or Ainge for a cheaper player or expiring contract that would weaken the team even more. This is all an elaborate way of saying that if they had been playing under the 2010 rules, there's no way in hell I would be bouncing my grandkids on my lap someday and telling them about the 1986 Boston Celtics. And that's why we had to discount twenty-

---

29. Max became a free agent after his inspiring '84 Finals performance. In modern times, Boston couldn't have afforded him and an idiot GM would have overpaid him something like $58 million for five years (instead of the four years at approximately $800,000 per that Boston gave him). There's no possible modern scenario in which the '86 Celts could have acquired Walton, which seems relevant since he transformed them from "top ten ever" to "potentially greatest ever."

first-century teams in this chapter. The rules were and are stacked against them. Literally.[30]

Without further ado, the ten greatest teams of all time.

THE ELITE TEN

10. THE '91 BULLS

Regular season (61–21): 35–6 at home . . . 9.0 SD (110–101) . . . 51% FG, 76% FT, 36% 3FG . . . 9–12 vs. 50-win teams . . . 56–15 (last 71 games) . . . winning streaks: 11 + 9

Playoffs (15–2): 8–1 at home . . . 11.7 PD (103.9–92.2) . . . 51.4 FG (1st), 45.0 defensive FG (2nd), 9.5 steals. . . . 9 double-digit wins . . . 2 losses by 4 points total . . . closeout margins: 9 + 5 + 21 + 7 . . . following season: won title (beat Portland in 6)

Cast and crew: Michael Jordan (super-duper star), Scottie Pippen (super-duper-wingman), Horace Grant (wingman), Bill Cartwright, John Paxson, B. J. Armstrong, Stacey King, Cliff Levingston (role players), Phil Jackson (coach)

Gaining steam historically because their playoff record and point differentials were accomplished during an extremely competitive season and featured the following facts: they swept the back-to-back champs and murdered the Isiah era; they won the last four Finals games and helped kill Showtime;[31] and of their two playoff losses, one happened in overtime (Game 3 against Barkley and the Sixers) and the other happened on a last-second three by Sam Perkins (Finals, Game 1). Do you realize that Jordan missed wide-open jumpers to *win* both of those games? We always hear about Philly's "Fo-Fo-Fo" postseason, but it wasn't as impressive as what

30. The same exercise for the '87 Lakers: Kareem $20M; Magic $20M; Worthy $14M; Thompson $11M; Cooper $7.5M; Rambis $6.0M; Scott $5.5M; Green $1.8M; Matthews $1.2M. Nine guys for $96 million. And by the way, it would have been humanly impossible for them to add Mychal Thompson.

31. I know, I know: HIV killed Showtime. But the '91 Bulls greased the skids. Okay, wrong choice of words. I'm getting out now. Quickly.

the '91 Bulls accomplished. We're penalizing them for the aforementioned Level One reason: you can't be great when you don't know if you're great until the very end, and the '91 Bulls didn't know until the six-minute mark of their last game.[32]

9. THE '72 L.A. LAKERS

Regular season (69–13): peak of 67–12 . . . 37–5 at home . . . 12.3 SD (121.0–108.7) . . . led league in points, rebounds, and assists, 2nd in FG (49%) and defensive FG (43%) . . . 20–6 vs. 49-win teams . . . longest winning streak: 33 (all-time record).

Playoffs (12–3): 6–2 at home . . . 3.3 SD (106.6–103.4) . . . 6 double-digit wins . . . 3 double-digit losses . . . 42.9% FG, 75.0% FT . . . closeout game margins of 11, 4, and 14 . . . following season: runners-up (lost to Knicks in 5)

Cast and crew: Jerry West, Wilt Chamberlain (superstars), Gail Goodrich (super wingman), Jim McMillian, Leroy Ellis, Happy Hairston, Pat Riley (role players), Bill Sharman (coach)

If you kept the 2008 Celtics intact, removed every foreigner from the league, relocated twelve teams to a competing league, allowed them to wreak havoc in a diluted NBA and gave them a Finals opponent missing its center and captain (the 2008 equivalent of Willis Reed), would they have finished better than 81–16? Yes. The answer is yes. So you can't forget how incompetent that era was. In a three-season span, the '70 Knicks, '71 Bucks and '72 Lakers ripped off four of the seven longest winning streaks of all time (33, 20 and 18).[33] If you were even a *little* loaded, in a watered-down league struggling to replenish its young talent that made you super-duper-duper-duper loaded. With that said, their 33-game streak remains

32. *Jordan Rules* is riveting to read in retrospect. Through March, Chicago's chemistry was still a mess because MJ was so brutal on his teammates. Then they ripped off a win streak, Pippen came into his own and MJ backed off. The rest was history.

33. The '60 Celts held the record with 17; from '70 to '72, it was broken three straight years. The league was so watered down that they should have dumped West as its logo and used a picture of Carl Spackler.

dumbfounding, and they certainly took care of business in the regular season. The playoffs? Not so much. It's also hard for me to reconcile the fact that their best two players—West and Wilt—were at the tail end of their careers. Not even their primes . . . *their careers.* It's a little reminiscent of the Stockton-Malone era peaking late for reasons that had nothing to do with Stockton or Malone. Anyway, I would have bumped them to honorable mention if not for that inconceivable streak. When nobody can approach 70-percent of your record, that record probably isn't going anywhere.

8. THE '83 PHILADELPHIA 76ERS

Regular season (65–17): peak of 57–9 . . . 35–6 at home . . . 7.7 PD (112.1–104.4) . . . 13–7 vs. 50-win teams . . . winning streaks: 14 + 10

Playoffs (12–1): 7–0 at home . . . 5.9 SD (105.8–99.9) . . . 4 double-digit wins . . . closeout game margins of 3, 12 + 7 . . . following season: lost in round one (Philly in 5).

Cast and Crew: Moses (super-duper star); Julius Erving, Andrew Toney (super wingmen); Mo Cheeks (wingman); Bobby Jones (6th man); Clint Richardson, Clemon Johnson, Marc Iavaroni (role players);[34] Billy Cunningham (coach)

My vote for Most Overrated Great Team. You had the following things in play: The Celtics turned against acerbic coach Bill Fitch[35] . . . James Worthy broke his leg and missed the last four months of the Lakers sea-

34. Clint Richardson, Earl Cureton and Marc Iavaroni? That's a Hamburger Helper bench.

35. They got swept by an inferior Bucks team in the second round. One major problem besides Fitch: The '83 Celts had too many guys. How do you juggle minutes between Bird, Parish, Maxwell, Henderson, Tiny, McHale, Ainge, Wedman, Buckner, M. L. Carr and Rick Robey? Half were unhappy and all hated the coach. The following year, KC took over, Robey was swapped for DJ, Tiny retired, Carr became a towel-waver and they won the title. The lesson, as always: You only need 9 guys. I kept warning Daryl Morey (Houston's GM) about this in October '08 and he kept making fun of me. "Too many guys? How could that be a bad thing?" Four months later he was frantically trying to swing 4-for-1's at the deadline.

son[36] . . . Larry Brown killed a 49-win Nets team by bolting to Kansas with six games left in the season . . . the other three 49-plus win teams (Milwaukee, SA and Phoenix) weren't threats . . . cocaine had ravaged the league and sapped the talents of some key stars . . . and the Sixers were a textbook Level One team. I'm not arguing the season itself as much as its ceiling; when you consider that Philly had Moses in his prime, Doc and Bobby at the tail end, Toney emerging as an unstoppable offensive force, and Mo Cheeks doing Mo Cheeks things, as well as an overwhelming amount of motivation, *of course* they were going to look splendid that year. Especially when they were handed a gift-wrapped decimated Lakers opponent missing Worthy, Nixon *and* McAdoo by Game 4 of the Finals. You know, only three of their five best players.

How do we know for sure that the '83 Sixers were overrated? Look at their title "defense," when they returned everyone from their top eight and couldn't get out of the first round. And it's not like the '84 Celtics knocked them out. Nope, it was the '84 Nets with Mike Gminski, Albert King, Buck Williams and a sober-for-a-few-weeks Micheal Ray Richardson . . . and the Nets won a do-or-die Game 5 in the Spectrum. Part of being a great champion is defending that title, right? What's worse than bowing in the

Here's the question we need to ask: removing the Sixers from that season and matching them against other superteams, what would happen? They certainly weren't great defensively; only Cheeks and Jones were above average and Jones was almost cooked. (Don't ask me who would have defended McHale, Duncan, Jordan, Kobe or Bird on this team because I have no clue.) Moses may have been one of the best rebounders ever (averaging a sterling 26–16 in the playoffs), but any team with size (like the '86 Celts, for instance) would have toyed with Philly since they didn't have any other big guys. Their outside shooting was more than a little sketchy; only Cheeks and Toney could make anything beyond 15 feet, and nobody had three-point range. Not to belabor the point about their crummy supporting cast, but did we mention that the '83 Sixers started Marc Iavaroni, a homeless man's Kurt Rambis who wouldn't have sniffed a nine-man rotation on a contender even six years later?

How do we know for sure that the '83 Sixers were overrated? Look at their title "defense," when they returned everyone from their top eight and couldn't get out of the first round. And it's not like the '84 Celtics knocked them out. Nope, it was the '84 Nets with Mike Gminski, Albert King, Buck Williams and a sober-for-a-few-weeks Micheal Ray Richardson . . . and the Nets won a do-or-die Game 5 in the Spectrum. Part of being a great champion is defending that title, right? What's worse than bowing in the

36. A tough blow for the Lakers and an even tougher blow for Big Game James, who had an unwieldy cast and could only have sex with groupies in the "cowgirl" and "reverse cowgirl" positions.

first round to Sugar and the Nets when you're healthy? Was there a more appalling title defense in the past thirty-five years with the possible exception of the Iron Sheik losing the WWE title in five weeks?[37] And since the league was considerably stronger in '84—L.A. had Worthy back (and rookie Byron Scott), the Celtics were running on all cylinders again, Bernard and Sugar had rejuvenated the New York–area teams, younger athletic foes like Detroit, Dallas and Atlanta were starting to get frisky— the turd that Philly dropped in the '84 punch bowl has to count for the legacy of the '83 Sixers. They were the classic "right place, right time" team and you can't tell me differently.

7. THE '71 MILWAUKEE BUCKS

Regular season (66–16): peak of 64–11 . . . 34–2 at home . . . 12.2 SD (118.4–106.2) . . . led league in FG% (51%), defensive FG% (42%), points (9,710), assists (27.4) . . . 13–8 vs. 48-win teams[38] . . . longest winning streaks: 20 + 16

Playoffs (12–2): 8–0 at home . . . 14.5 SD (109.1–94.6) . . . 11 double-digit wins . . . 49.7% FG, 72.1% FT . . . closeout game margins of 50, 18, + 12 . . . following season: lost in Western Finals (Lakers in 6)

Cast and Crew: Kareem Abdul-Jabbar (super-duper star, 32–16–3); Oscar Robertson (super wingman); Bobby Dandridge (wingman); Jon McGlocklin, Greg Smith, Bob Boozer, Lucius Allen (supporting cast); Larry Costello (coach)

Start to finish, this was the greatest NBA season *on paper.* They had two of the ten best basketball players ever, one juuuuuust past his prime (Oscar),

---

37. Inevitable counter from the Philly fans: "We got old!" Sorry, the stats don't back this up. Moses slipped a little (25–15 in '83, 23–13 in '84), but Doc/Toney/Cheeks were slightly better statistically and they got similar bench production. They weren't good enough collectively to combat the Year-After Syndrome in a much-improved league. How else would you drop from 77–18 to 54–33 without a major injury?

38. That includes a 1–4 record against the Knicks. Damn the Knicks for not showing up for the Finals. Damn them! Damn them to hell!

the other nearing the height of his powers (Kareem). During the regular season, they led the league in every relevant category, finished with the third-highest point differential ever and ripped off two killer winning streaks; they easily could have gotten 70 if they hadn't clinched the top seed so early. They destroyed every playoff opponent and set a record for postseason point differential that still stands.[39] They swept the Finals and won every game by at least eight points. And they only blew two home games in Milwaukee all year, second only to the '86 Celtics. Now that's a resume! Nobody seriously challenged them for nine solid months. Of course, that stupid Silver Anniversary panel voted for the '67 Sixers over the '71 Bucks as Best Team of the First 25 Years because . . . umm . . . I couldn't possibly tell you why. That was a doubly indefensible pick in that Russell's Celtics were the only logical choice, but if you were dumb enough to look elsewhere, then you *had* to take the '71 Bucks.

So why not stick them higher? Because that diluted era from 1969 to 1976 rewarded any team with two great players (Kareem-Oscar, Wilt-Jerry, Cowens-Hondo, whomever). Because basketball just wasn't fast enough or athletic enough yet. Because they caught a few significant breaks that year: the Lakers lost Elgin *and* West for the playoffs, the Celtics weren't ready yet, the defending champs choked away the Eastern Finals at home and the 42–40 Bullets played in the Finals without an injured Gus Johnson. Add everything up and the team probably wasn't as great as it looks on paper. No matter. We can't stick them lower than seventh.

6. THE '97 CHICAGO BULLS

Regular season (69–13): peak of 68–10 . . . 39–2 at home . . . 10.8 SD (103.1–92.3) . . . 19–9 vs. 50-win teams . . . winning streaks: 12 + 9

---

39. Their two losses: Game 4 at San Fran in the first round (by 2), Game 3 at L.A. (by 12). The S.F. series was weird: Games 1 and 4 were in San Fran (thanks to a scheduling conflict with Milwaukee's arena), meaning the teams traveled for four of the five games. I love the days when the NBA had scheduling conflicts. "Sorry, guys, we can't accommodate Game 4—we have a tractor pull that weekend."

Playoffs (15–4): 10–1 at home . . . 5.5 SD (92.5–87.0) . . . 6 double-digit wins . . . 43.2% FG, 31.9% 3FG . . . closeout margins: 1, 15, 13, + 4 . . . following season: won title (beat Jazz in 6)

Cast and crew: Michael Jordan (super-duper star), Scottie Pippen (super wingman), Dennis Rodman (wingman), Toni Kukoc, Brian Williams, Luc Longley, Steve Kerr, Ron Harper (role players), Phil Jackson (coach)

Ineligible for the top five because of a "can't include teams from back-to-back years" rule that I just made up ten seconds ago. Although they *were* worn down by the Finals after playing 200 games (not counting exhibition) in twenty months. With an oversized bull's-eye on their backs. With every contender gunning for them. With a gargantuan media horde greeting them in every city. With sold-out arenas of fans around the country saying happily, "I'm going to see the Bulls tonight!" When you remember how colossal Jordan (and the team to a lesser extent) was compared to the other sports at the time—hockey was dying, baseball was still recovering from a damaging strike, college hoops was getting murdered by underclassmen leaving too soon, tennis had nobody, Tiger was just breaking onto the golf scene but wasn't Tiger Woods yet, and only football had real star power (Elway, Favre, Sanders, and others)—that '97 Bulls team meant more to the sports landscape than anyone remembers.[P65] If they were like rock stars (and they were in many respects), then that two-season stretch was like one of U2's twenty-month concert tours that spans two hundred cities and thirty-five countries. They were clearly wearing down by the end of the tour (or in this case, the '97 Finals). You can see it in every Jazz-Bulls replay on ESPN Classic or NBA TV. Look for this when you're not concentrating on how rattled Karl Malone was.

P65. I meant "wasn't one of the greatest golfers yet," not "wasn't the guy who won majors while banging a steady stream of strippers, porn stars and diner waitresses before everything fell apart and his wife asked for $100 million alimony yet."

5. THE '01 LAKERS

Regular season (56–26): 31–10 at home . . . 3.4 SD (100.6–97.2) . . . longest winning streak: 8

Playoffs (15–1): 12.8 SD (103.4–90.6) . . . 46.7% FG, 38.6% 3FG, 67.6% FT, 15.0 stocks . . . 9 double-digit wins . . . only loss: overtime (Game 1, Philly) . . . following season: won title (beat Nets in 4)

Cast and crew: Shaq (super-duper star), Kobe (superstar), Robert Horry, Derek Fisher, Rick Fox, Brian Shaw, Tyronn Lue, Ron Harper, Horace Grant (role players), Phil Jackson (coach)

An upside pick that defies two ground rules established just pages earlier. Sue me. The Lakers had their regular season derailed by the Disease of More, bad luck with injuries (Shaq and Kobe missed 22 games combined) and a so-predictable-that-nobody-even-bothered-to-take-credit-for-predicting-it alpha dog battle as Kobe delved into petulant ballhog territory for the first time.[40] With everyone healthy by March, Jackson mentally coerced/brainwashed Kobe back into the fold and the Lakers unleashed an all-time Keyser Söze run in April, winning 23 of their last 24 and coming within an OT loss in the Finals of sweeping the entire playoffs.[41] So if we're trying to find the most invincible team of all time, and there were legitimate reasons for why the Lakers took a few months to get going . . . I mean, would *you* have wanted to play these guys that spring? We haven't seen anything approaching Shaqobe in the 2001 playoffs;[42] it's the only time in NBA history that two top-twenty Pyramid guys joined

40. The prologue in Phil Jackson's book, *More than a Game*, tells about his '01 battles with Kobe after Kobe basically decided, "Sorry, guys, I don't really like the triangle anymore, I'm going to be breaking plays and going for my own points now." Shades of Dirk Diggler's "We'll shoot when I'm good and goddamned ready. I'm the biggest star here!" tantrum, only for an entire regular season.

41. The one loss: Game 1, when Iverson went bonkers (48 points) and nearly stomped Ty Lue's head.

42. I just made that term up. It's like "Bennifer" or "Brangelina." Right down to the inevitable breakup in the end. If only we had thought of it in 2002.

forces as an inside/outside combo with both either approaching their primes or enjoying their primes. Check out Shaqobe's regular season and playoff numbers.

RS	G	PPG	FG%	FGA	FT%	FTA	RPG	APG	42CLUB
Shaq	74	28.7	57.2	19.2	51.3	13.1	12.7	3.7	45.1 (yes)
Kobe	68	28.5	46.4	22.2	85.3	8.2	5.9	5.0	39.4 (no)

PLY	PPG	FG%	FGA	FT%	FTA	RPG	APG	42CLUB
Shaq	30.4	55.5	21.5	52.5	12.5	15.4	3.2	49.0 (yes)
Kobe	29.4	46.9	22.4	82.1	9.3	7.3	6.1	42.8 (yes)

Good God! Two 42 Clubbers on the same title team? That's the one and only time it's ever happened. Just for shits and giggles, let's compare their combined 42 Club average to every other memorable one-two championship punch since Chamberlain and Greer combined for a jaw-dropping 49.3 in the '67 playoffs. Nobody topped 37.5 other than these ten combinations:

PLAYOFF COMBOS	G	PPG	RPG	APG	FG%	FT%	42CLUB
Shaqobe ('01)	16	29.9	11.3	4.7	51.1	65.2	45.9 (yes)
Kareem + Magic ('80)	15.5	25.9	10.0	6.4	55.2	79.6	42.3 (yes)
Hondo + Russell ('68)	19	20.2	15.7	6.4	43.6	71.5	42.2 (yes)
Wilt + West ('69)	18	22.4	14.3	5.0	48.7	63.1	41.7 (no)
MJ + Pippen ('92)	22	27.0	7.5	6.2	48.8	81.4	40.7 (no)
Shaqobe ('02)	19	27.6	9.2	3.7	47.9	69.4	40.5 (no)
Hakeem + Clyde ('95)	22	26.8	8.6	4.8	51.3	72.9	40.4 (no)
MJ + Pippen ('93)	22	27.6	6.8	5.8	47.1	73.7	40.2 (no)
Kareem + Oscar ('71)	14	22.4	12.0	5.7	50.3	70.6	40.1 (no)
Bird + McHale ('86)	18	25.4	9.0	5.5	54.6	85.2	39.9 (no)

A good example of how ridiculous Shaqobe's '01 postseason was: in the second round, you might remember them sweeping a quality Kings team. They prevailed by three in Game 1, with Shaq notching 44 points (17 for 32 FG), 21 rebounds and 7 blocks. They won Game 2 by six, with Shaq springing for a 43–20–3. In Sacramento for Game 3, Kobe dropped 36 and Shaq added a quiet 21–18 in a twenty-two-point drubbing. They finished the sweep with a six-point win as Kobe played the best all-around game of his career: 48 points, 16 rebounds, 15-for-29 from the field and 17-for-19 from the line with no less than Doug Christie (one first-team All-Defense and three second teams from 2001–4) guarding him. Again, this was a *really* good Kings team with the best crowd in the league . . . and the Lakers blew them out of their own building like Fartman. In fact, the '01 Lakers swept a 50-win Blazers team (that nearly beat them the previous spring), a 55-win Kings team (that almost beat them 12 months later), and a 58-win Spurs team (that won three titles in the next six years),[43] then came within an overtime loss of sweeping the 56-win Sixers, making them one of two NBA champs (the other: '95 Rockets) to beat four straight 50-win playoff teams. How does that 15–1 sound now?

One more thing: If you were creating the perfect Shaqobe team, you'd surround them with elite role players like Horry, Fox, Fisher, Shaw and Grant; you'd give them Phil Jackson for the Zen/harmony stuff; you'd definitely want 2000 or 2001 Shaq; and you'd want 2001 Kobe (only twenty-two with a ring and valuable playoff experience, back when his ego hadn't erupted yet and he was closer to Young Pippen than Young MJ). The 2001 Kobe might have been the greatest second banana of all time; teaming him with a twenty-eight-year-old Shaq was criminal. Matching them up against the '96 Bulls:

Center: Shaq vs. Longley
Forwards: Horry + Harper vs. Rodman + Pippen
Guards: Kobe + Fisher vs. Jordan + Harper

43. This was a hellacious sweep: the Lakers didn't have home-court advantage and still won by 14, 7, 39 and 29 points. Ripping through the West during that era was no joke: from 2000 to 2005, the West had thirty-one 50-win teams and five 60-win teams; the East had twelve 50-win teams and one 60-win team.

Bench: Grant, Lue, Shaw + Fox vs. Kukoc, Kerr, Wennington + Buechler
Coach: Jackson vs. Jackson

Would you take the '01 Lakers in that series? I feel like I would—they were a better version of the '95 Magic team that topped the Bulls. But what about the '86 Celtics?

Center: Shaq vs. Parish
Forwards: Horry + Harper vs. Bird + McHale
Guards: Kobe + Fisher vs. Johnson + Ainge
Bench: Grant, Lue, Shaw + Fox vs. Walton, Wedman, Sichting + Kite
Coach: Jackson vs. KC Jones[44]

Don't you think the '86 Celtics swallow them up? They'd have two Hall of Fame centers to throw at Shaq, a Hall of Fame defensive guard to throw at Kobe, and a scoring mismatch with Bird/McHale against the Guy Who's Not Robert Horry. The '86 Celtics were vulnerable against speedy point guards and athletic small forwards and the '01 Lakers didn't have anyone fitting either of those categories. Either way, they were the best team of the last twelve years and in the top five of all time regardless of how late they got going. Shit, will we ever see two top-twenty Pyramid guys playing on the same team in their primes again in our lifetimes?[P66]

4. THE '89 DETROIT PISTONS

Regular season (63–19) . . . 37–4 at home . . . 5.8 PD (106.6–100.8) . . . 49.4% FG, 44.7 defensive FG . . . 16–12 vs. 50-win teams

---

44. I'm cringing. This is like a wet T-shirt contest with Scarlett Johansson taking on both Olsen twins.

P66. I couldn't resist keeping that rhetorical question intact from the hardcover just for comedy's sake. Remember the good old days when it seemed completely improbable that two of the league's top-3 players woud ever end up on the same team again?

Playoffs (15–2): 8–1 at home[45] . . . 6 double-digit wins . . . 9.5 PD (100.6–92.9) . . . closeout margins: 15, 2, 9, + 8 (all on road) . . . following season: won title (beat Portland in 5)

Cast and crew: Isiah (superstar); Joe Dumars, Dennis Rodman (wingmen); Vinnie Johnson (sixth man); Bill Laimbeer, John Salley, James Edwards, Rick Mahorn, Mark Aguirre (supporting cast); Chuck Daly (coach)

Not technically a Level One team since they were hardened by crushing losses in '87 (Boston) and '88 (Lakers). No NBA champ had more versatility and toughness: they were physical as hell; they could execute a fast break or half-court offense equally well; they played defense as well as anyone with the exception of the '08 Celtics and the '96–'97 Bulls; they controlled the boards; they could exploit any mismatch; and they always seemed to have two different hot players going offensively. Fans unfairly discounted Isiah's Pistons because they couldn't beat Boston or the Lakers at their peaks—even though they defeated Jordan's Bulls twice and won back-to-back titles—and because they lacked a dominant center or super-duper star, which confused everyone who didn't follow basketball obsessively. I hated these bastards but grew to respect their hard-nosed swagger; they never allowed layups or dunks, never gave an inch, never stopped fighting and didn't care if they maimed you as long as they won. Their relentless competitiveness brought out the worst in opponents; I always found it fascinating that, for a team that ended up in so many fights, the Pistons never threw the first punch or had the most enraged guy in the brawl. And if you remember, the '87 Celtics and '88 Lakers spent so much energy fending them off that they were never the same afterward.

So much of what the Pistons accomplished was based on intimidation and the understanding that they'd do whatever it took to win, even if it

45. They were out of the Silverdome by then. Two years earlier was the best Silverdome year: Wrestlemania III (Andre-Hulk plus the watershed Savage-Steamboat match), the Bird-Laimbeer/Rodman brawl (Game 4) and Pope John Paul II celebrating mass there. That's right, big moments from Andre, Hulk, Macho Man, the Pope and the Basketball Jesus in one year!

meant intentionally stepping on McHale's broken foot (which Mahorn did repeatedly in '87) or hammering Jordan and Pippen during their forays to the basket. If you were frustrated by their elbows and shoves, if you were afraid of getting clocked every time you drove to the basket, if you were obsessing over punching Laimbeer instead of just thinking about ways to beat him . . . then they had you. That's what they wanted. You could say they figured out a loophole in the system, and after Pat Riley exploited that loophole even further with his bullying Knicks teams, the NBA finally stepped in and instituted taunting/fighting penalties and a system for flagrant fouls.[46] If we're judging the '89 Pistons against other landmark teams, the question remains: would they have succeeded to that degree with 2009 rules in place? Probably not. But they were so intelligent/competitive/versatile/bloodthirsty that those particular qualities translate to any era.

One bummer for these guys: 1989–90 was a transition period with the Bird Era slowing down, the Kareem Era ending, the Jordan Era not totally rolling yet, the Stockton-Malone Era stalling, the Hakeem era floundering, the Ewing/Robinson/Barkley peaks still a few years away, and only the Bulls and Blazers rounding into legitimate contenders. The Pistons filled a void of sorts and became the Larry Holmes of NBA champs: unliked, resented and ultimately dismissed. We wanted them to go away and eventually, like Holmes, they did. But like Holmes, when you watch those old tapes you end up thinking, "Man, those guys were *really* good."[47]

3. THE '87 L.A. LAKERS

Regular season (65–17): peak of 65–15 . . . 37–4 at home . . . 9.3 SD (117.8–108.5) . . . 12–6 vs. 50-win teams . . . 51.6 FG%, 78.9% FT . . . winning streaks: 11 + 10

46. But not before exploiting Detroit's personality for the infamous *Bad Boys* video (1989) that featured more cheap shots than a season of *Jerry Springer* shows. All copies of this tape have apparently been destroyed; you can't find it anywhere. One of the all-time hypocritical moves by a sports league, just behind baseball looking the other way with _____ (name an enhancer) during the McGwire-Sosa era.

47. The thing I respected most about those '89 and '90 Pistons teams: they took care of business on the road, closing six of eight series on the road and finishing 5–0 in road Finals games.

Playoffs (15–3): 10–0 at home . . . 11.4 SD (120.6–109.2) . . . 10 double-digit wins . . . 52.2% FG, 78.5% FT, 36.1% 3FG, 28.2 APG, 14.4 stocks . . . closeout game margins of 37, 12, 31, + 13 . . . following season: won title (beat Detroit in 7)

Cast and crew: Magic (super-duper star); Kareem + Worthy (super wingmen); Michael Cooper (sixth man); Byron Scott, A. C. Green, Mychal Thompson, Kurt Rambis (supporting cast); Pat Riley (coach)

How do we know this was Magic's best Lakers team? He said so himself after the Finals: "There's no question this is the best team I've played on. It's fast, it can shoot and rebound, it has inside people, it has everything. I've never played on a team that had everything before."[48] He left out the biggest reason: Magic jumped a level and cruised to his first MVP, submitting his best statistical year (regular season: 24–6–12; playoffs: 22–8–12, 53% FG and an impossible 78–13 assist/turnover ratio in the Finals) and gently yanking control from a declining Kareem. Their humiliating Rockets defeat qualified them for Level Three status; it also helped that they got faster instead of bigger, dumping Maurice Lucas and Mitch Kupchak, handing their minutes to Green and Rambis and routinely going smallball with Magic-Scott-Coop-Worthy-Kareem. They mastered the art of juggling transition and half-court offense, running on every opportunity and waiting for Kareem to drag his ass up the court otherwise. From there, they had three devastating options: Kareem posting up, Magic posting up (a new wrinkle) or Worthy facing up and beating slower forwards off the dribble. And of their two glaring weaknesses (defending quick point guards or dominant low-post scorers), one was miraculously solved when San Antonio gift-wrapped Mychal Thompson and FedExed him to them for their stretch run.

The Thompson trade would have sparked an Internet riot if it happened today (take how everyone reacted to the Pau Gasol hijacking, then square it): the Spurs were 18–31 and considering a full-fledged tank job with the David Robinson sweepstakes looming, unwilling to pay $1.4 mil-

48. Shades of Rollergirl raving about Dirk Diggler in *Amber Waves'* documentary about him. Is there a basketball scenario that can't be tied to *Boogie Nights*? I say no. And I think we proved it over these last 4,500 pages.

lion combined for Thompson and a decomposing Artis Gilmore. Lakers GM Jerry West barraged them with Thompson offers for a solid month, finally landing him for a pu-pu platter deluxe offer of Frank Brickowski, Petur Gudmundsson, a 1987 first-round pick (destined to be last) and cash. Everyone went crazy, and rightly so: Thompson was a former number one overall pick and one of the league's better low-post defenders.[49] Within a week of the trade, Thompson played crunch time in a CBS game against Philly as everyone collectively said, "My God, what the hell just happened?" Thompson earned 22 minutes per game in the playoffs, rested Kareem for chunks of time, gave McHale fits and made the most underrated play of the Finals: when he jumped over Parish and McHale in Game 4 (foul! foul!) and caused Kareem's pivotal free throw to bounce off their hands, setting the stage for Magic's soul-wrenching baby hook.[50] The Lakers also benefited from Lenny Bias' sudden death, a rash of Boston injuries, Houston's untimely demise and the up-and-coming Mavericks (55 wins, 3–2 against the Lakers) unexpectedly choking in the first round 1 against Seattle.[51] Since the playoffs expanded to sixteen teams in 1977, no Finals team ever played three worse conference opponents than the '87 Lakers: in this case, the 37-win Nuggets (round 1), 42-win Warriors (round 2) and 39-win Sonics (round 3). Meanwhile, the banged-up Celtics faced MJ's 40-win Bulls and endured seven-game slugfests against a veteran 50-win Bucks team and the 52-win Pistons. Gee, who do you think was fresher for the Finals?

And that's what makes ranking the '87 Lakers so difficult. Yes, they were a great team led by one of the five best players ever at his zenith. Yes, they

---

49. This sucked doubly for Boston: Thompson went to college with McHale and knew all of his moves; he was the only player in the '80s who could defend McHale by himself. Also, this was the first salary cap loophole trade: when Kupchak retired, the Lakers were allowed to use half of his salary cap number ($1.15 million) toward another player. Fans were thoroughly confused at the time: "Cap number, exception, half the number . . . what?"

50. The Spurs are living proof that the Tanking Karma Gods don't exist: they did it in '87 (Robinson) and '97 (Duncan).

51. The Mavs took them to seven games one year later, then Roy Tarpley got hooked on coke and they were done. Part of me wonders if Riley and West just sent unmarked packages of cocaine to every '80s rival and hoped they would succumb. Tarpley, Bias, Lucas/Wiggins/Lloyd . . .

had one of the only coaches that mattered. Yes, this was the best Lakers team of the Magic era. Yes, they caught a series of breaks. Yes, they had some flaws. Ultimately, they have to be ranked third for two reasons:

- Defensively, they were somewhere between okay and good—sixth in opponent's FG percentage, twelfth in points allowed, fourteenth in forcing turnovers and *last* in defensive rebounds. Kareem and Magic were liabilities. Byron Scott was okay. Green and Worthy were good, not great. Only Cooper and Thompson were elite. They couldn't lock teams down or sweep the boards, and quicker point guards routinely lit them up like nothing we've seen since . . . oh, wait, we see it every night with whomever Jason Kidd and Steve Nash are guarding. But remember Sleepy Floyd decimating the '87 Lakers for one of the all-time memorable scoring explosions: 34 points in the final 11 minutes of Game 4, 13 for 14 from the field, no threes, no shots from more than 15 feet, eight shots from 3 feet or less (six in traffic)?[52] Or Stockton, Isiah, Dumars, KJ and Hardaway going bonkers against them in later years? As many matchup problems as Magic caused offensively, he caused nearly the same number defensively. Against bigger backcourts like the '87 Celtics or '87 Sonics, it didn't matter. Against elite penetrators/distributors? It mattered. Cooper and Scott couldn't guard those guys; neither could Magic. So what do you do? Take the hits on one end and outscore them on the other. And for the most part, that's what the Lakers did. But that's a pretty glaring weakness, no? And we haven't even acknowledged Kareem's vulnerability against those explosive Hakeem/Tarpley types (none of whom faced L.A. in the '87 playoffs). I know it's nitpicking, but we can't see the words "glaring weakness" in any capacity with the Greatest NBA Team Ever.
- Even with Larry Bird dragging the carcass of an eleven-man roster into the '87 Finals (five of the top seven were either injured or unable

---

52. I once wrote an entire 2004 column about this game. Sleepy actually turns into a fireball at one point.

to play),[53] Boston came within a late-game collapse, a terrible break on a rebound, two sketchy calls and Bird's desperation three missing by 1/55,000th of an inch of tying the series at 2–2. And yeah, you could argue that the Garden willed the Celtics to those two home victories in the Finals. But when you consider the physical condition of that Boston team—I mean, Darren Daye (Game 4, Milwaukee) and Greg Kite (Game 3, Finals) had *signature playoff moments* for the '87 Celtics—it's hard to understand why the Best Lakers Team of the Magic Era didn't sweep them or at least finish them in five. They soured critics just enough that Jack McCallum wrote after the Finals, "They may not be 'one of the greatest teams ever,' a phrase that was bandied about after they devastated the defending-champion Celtics in Games 1 and 2. But they are, assuredly, the league's best team this season." Damning praise. I actually think the '87 Lakers were better than that; nobody blended transition and half-court better, and Magic had become a cold-blooded killer of the highest order. But they wouldn't have beaten these next two teams.

2. The '96 Chicago Bulls

Regular season (72–10): peak of 71–9 . . . 39–2 at home . . . 12.3 SD (105.2–92.9) . . . 1st in points scored, 2nd in points allowed . . . 47.8 FG% (7th), 74.6 FT% (14th), 44.7 RPG (4th), 24.7 APG (7th) . . . 12–4 vs. 49-win teams . . . 2 double-digit losses (fewest ever) . . . best winning streaks: 18 + 13

Playoffs (15–3): 10–0 at home . . . 10.6 SD (97.4–86.8) . . . fourth in PPG, 1st in PPG allowed . . . 10 double-digit wins . . . 44.3% FG (8th), 73.8%

---

53. Bird played 1,015 grueling minutes in 23 playoff games (44.1 minutes per game). That's the third-highest average for 20-plus playoff games in one postseason behind Allen Iverson in '01 (22 games, 1,016 minutes) and Thunder Dan Majerle in '93 (24 games, 1,071 minutes). Bird's '87 playoffs also ranks 11th in points, 5th in FTs made, 22nd in assists (first forward) and 80th in rebounds. Of course, it doesn't rank in Hollinger's top 50 for PER even though he averaged a 27–10–9, saved the season with the greatest steal in NBA history, logged superhuman minutes and nearly won the Finals by himself. And you wonder why I have trouble trusting player efficiency ratings.

FT (7th), 30.4% 3FG (11th), 35.7 RPG, 22.7 APG, 13.7 stocks . . . closeout
wins: 21, 13, 5, + 12 . . . following season: won title (beat Utah in 6)

Cast and crew: Michael Jordan (super-duper star), Scottie Pippen
(super wingman), Dennis Rodman (wingman), Toni Kukoc, Luc Longley,
Steve Kerr, Ron Harper, Bill Wennington (role players), Phil Jackson
(coach)

"Number two?" you're saying. "Number two? A team that went 87–13?
Really? You're that much of a homer?" Are you really asking that after I
dropped Bird below Magic in my Pyramid? There are specific reasons for
dropping the Bulls to no. 2, including . . .

- They took full advantage of the We Overexpanded and Overpaid
  Everybody era (1994–99). Was it a coincidence that Chicago banged
  out 72 wins during the same season when (a) the Association expanded to Vancouver and Toronto and (b) six teams won 26
  games or fewer (compared to two in 1986)? How do you explain
  Utah averaging 52 wins from '91 to '93, then 61 wins from '96 to
  '98 . . . even though they had a worse team and their two stars were
  in their mid-thirties? You don't find this fishy? As Bird told *SI* in '97,
  "The league is a lot more watered down than when I played, so if you
  have a star like Michael Jordan today, you rule the league. Once he
  leaves, things will level out."
- Jordan turned thirty-three this season with over 800 games (including playoffs) already on his NBA odometer. Pippen turned thirty before this season and hit the 800-game mark during it. Rodman
  turned thirty-five that season. Ron Harper turned thirty-two. Of
  their top five guys, only Kukoc was in his prime. And that's why even
  die-hard Chicago fans would concede that the Sistine Chapel of the
  Jordan-Pippen era was reached during the '92 season, when a
  younger, deeper Bulls team played two relatively perfect games:
  Game 7 vs. New York (110–81 final, 42 for MJ, a 17–11–11 for Scottie, a 58%–38% FG disparity) and Game 1 vs. Portland (122–89 final,
  63 points and 21 assists for MJ/Pippen). The '96 Bulls had a few postseason blowouts; none resonated like those two. And it comes down

to the age thing: Pippen and Jordan were just *better* in '92. Nobody remembers any of their '96 playoff games because their competition was weak, but also because Jordan and Pippen weren't as breathtaking anymore (like Wilt and West in '72, actually). They were smarter about their games and bodies, better teammates and leaders, more efficient in myriad ways, demoralizing defensively . . . but Jordan peaked from '91 to '93 and Pippen peaked from '92 to '94. The stats back it up and so do the tapes.

- The Bulls didn't play particularly well (for them) in the playoffs, missing 70 percent of their threes and getting subpar offensive performances from Pippen (39% FG, 64% FT), Kukoc (39% FG, missed 55 of 68 threes) and Kerr (32% on threes).[54] Even Jordan submitted his worst career playoff numbers of any title season (31–5–4, 46% FG). I want my Greatest Team Ever to leave me thinking after the playoffs, "Not only could they *not* have played better, I will probably never see another team play better than that in my life." You did not feel that way about the Bulls after the '96 playoffs. If anything, you were wondering if the Sonics could have stretched it to seven had Gary Payton been defending Jordan all series.

- Can you really have a Greatest Team Ever that featured so many rejects, castoffs, role players, and past-their-primers? Their third scorer was Kukoc, a frustratingly soft forward with considerable gifts (terrific passer, streaky three-point shooter, post-up potential) who never totally delivered for them.[55] Their center combination? Longley and Wennington. (If you're telling me that the Greatest NBA Team Ever should have a center combo that averaged 12 points and 6 rebounds a game, provided no low-post threat and little shot blocking and floundered as NBA players before and after playing with Jordan/Pippen, then you have lower expectations for this stuff than I

---

54. Of their top seven guys only Rodman thrived: he averaged 14.9 rebounds in the Finals (41 of 88 offensive), battled a red-hot Shawn Kemp and was their best guy in two wins (Games 2 and 6). He arguably could have won MVP considering MJ's struggles (22 for 60) in the final three games—you know, if you were using the same indefensible reasoning that led to Parker's '07 MVP and Maxwell's '81 MVP.

55. Kukoc won the "sixth man" award this year but stank in the playoffs. Chicago handed the post-Pippen/MJ team over to him and finished 13–37. For all the hype over the years, Kukoc never made a single All-Star team.

do.) Kerr frequently played crunch time, which was fine because he stretched defenses and was a Hall of Fame cooler . . . but he's another one who struggled mightily in the before/after portions of his Pippen/Jordan experience.[56] Harper was a terrific defender who hobbled around on a bad knee (the players even jokingly called him "Peg Leg") and couldn't shoot threes or create his own shot. And their ninth and tenth men were Jud Buechler and Randy Brown. Enough said. So if you're scoring at home, 70 percent of their ten-man rotation never made an All-Star team, averaged 7 rebounds a game or played for fewer than four teams.[57]

- Operating under Bob Ryan's time-tested Martian Premise—that is, a team of highly skilled aliens land on earth and challenge us to a seven-game basketball series with the future of mankind at stake—are you really saying you'd go to war with Longley and Wennington as your centers?[58] The dirty little secret of Jordan's six title seasons (twenty-four series in all) was his astounding luck with opposing centers: Ewing (four times), Brad Daugherty (twice), Alonzo Mourning (twice), Greg Ostertag (twice), Vlade Divac (twice), Mike Gminski, Bill Laimbeer, Rony Seikaly, Kevin Duckworth, Kevin Willis, Mark West, Shaq, Sam Perkins, Gheorge Muresan, Dikembe Mutombo, Jayson Williams and Rik Smits. He never battled two of that decade's dominant big men (Hakeem and Robinson) and only faced the third one (Shaq) twice. Was it a coincidence that Chicago's four toughest series from 1991 to 1998 were against quality low-post centers: Ewing ('92 and '93), Shaq ('95, when they lost) and Smits ('98)? Shaq, Hakeem and Robinson played eight games against the '96 Bulls

56. I once created a Ringo Starr Theory for MJ's teammates: you can't judge role players properly when they're playing with a guy who makes everyone else better. Armstrong, Longley, Grant, Kerr and Williams looked better than they were during their Chicago stints (just ask the teams that overpaid them after). Same for Scott, Green, Rambis and Nixon with Magic, or Ainge, Maxwell, Robey and Henderson with Bird.

57. The good news: Chicago could throw out a frightening whitewash—the twin vanilla towers of Wennington and Longley, with Kukoc, Kerr and Jud Buechler flanking them and Jack Haley cheering them on from the bench in streetclothes. That was almost a blizzard.

58. I just pulled a Paul Maguire there: started an argument with you, then debunked your point even though you never said anything. "Watch how I made you look bad, watch how I did that, watch this . . . *bam*! Right there!"

(including playoffs) and averaged a 27–11 on 58 percent shooting. The 47-win Knicks played them surprisingly tough in the second round—losing by 7, 11, 3 and 13, and winning Game 3 in OT—with a sore-kneed Ewing averaging a 23–11. During Orlando's upset the previous spring, Shaq blistered them for a 23–22 and a 27–13 in the deciding contests, averaging a 24–14 and shooting 83 free throws in six games. Well, what if the Martians had someone like Shaq or Moses in their prime? Wouldn't 2001 Shaq have feasted on Longley/Wennington the same way he feasted on Todd MacCulloch, Vlade Divac and everyone else in that phylum? I say yes, and if you're incorporating the Martian Premise, you have to assume the Martians would be better than the 2001 Lakers. I can't get past the center issue. I just can't.

Add everything up and that 72–10 record doesn't make a ton of sense . . . until you remember that the '94 Rockets ushered in the We Overexpanded and Everyone's Overpaid Era. You needed good chemistry and the right coach, you needed to stay healthy, you needed to play defense at a high level, and over everything else, you needed the league's dominant player. That was good enough. And that's not to belittle what the Bulls did; their 41–3 start ranks among the all-time "holy shit" statistics in NBA history, and as we covered in Pippen's Pyramid section, it was truly an experience to watch them play in person. Their defensive prowess and collective confidence were almost unparalleled, and their ability to maintain their focus/hunger as they became part of the day-to-day pop culture whirlwind—no other NBA team dealt with such a high level of scrutiny, media exposure and hysterical admiration from opposing fans, to the point that Jordan was trapped in his hotel on road trips like one of the Beatles—remains their single most impressive quality.

If it wasn't for one undeniable truth—namely, that you would have had to shoot Jordan with an elephant gun to prevent him from winning the title that season—I probably would have slid the '96 Bulls down to fourth for the aforementioned reasons, as well as the sobering fact that they won only eight more games than the '96 Sonics. I like a starting five of Payton, Kemp, Hersey Hawkins, Detlef Schrempf and a fading Sam Perkins . . .

but 64–18 with no bench?[59] How is that possible? What about San Antonio winning fifty-nine games with Robinson, Elliott, Avery Johnson, Vinnie Del Negro, Will Perdue, a fading Chuck Person and a washed-up
Charles Smith? I can't shake this stuff. Just because the '96 Bulls had the
greatest season ever and the greatest player ever doesn't mean they had the
greatest team ever.

1. THE 1986 BOSTON CELTICS

Regular season (67–15): peak of 64–13 . . . 40–1 at home . . . 9.4 SD
(114.1–104.7) . . . 29.1 APG (2nd), 46.4 RPG (1st), 50.8 FG% (2nd), 35.1
3FG% (1st), 79.4% FT (2nd), 46.1 defensive FG% (1st) . . . 18–2 vs. 49-
win teams . . . 3 double-digit losses (2nd-fewest ever) . . . best winning
streaks: 14 + 13

Playoffs (15–3): 10–0 at home . . . 10.6 SD (114.4–104.1) . . . fourth in
PPG, first in PPG allowed . . . 11 double-digit wins . . . 50.7% FG (2nd),
79.4% FT (1st), 39.1% 3FG (2nd), 15.0 stocks, 45.1 RPG, 28.4 APG
(2nd) . . . closeout wins: 18, 33, 13, + 17 . . . following season: lost in Finals (L.A. in 6)

Cast and crew: Larry Bird (super-duper star, 26–10–7–2, 50–90–42%);
Kevin McHale (super wingman, 26–10, 60% FG); Robert Parish, Dennis
Johnson (wingmen); Bill Walton (super-duper sixth man); Danny Ainge,
Scott Wedman, Jerry Sichting (supporting cast); KC Jones (coach)

---

59. Seattle's '96 bench: Vince Askew, Nate McMillan, Frank Brickowski and Ervin "No
Magic" Johnson (one of my favorite nicknames ever). Ervin had a long, Shannon
Sharpe–like face that was perfect for the "Hey, Ervin, why the long face?" heckle. That reminds me, I spent a lot of time heckling during the M. L. Carr and Rick Pitino eras in
Boston (mostly out of drunken bitterness). This was before the "let's keep noise going
for three straight hours" NBA arena era, so if you were sitting within ten rows of a depressing game, you could hear every sneaker squeak, play conversation, and heckle. During one dead Miami game, I screamed, "You never won without Magic!" from 20 feet
away at Pat Riley for four solid quarters. (You heard me, Pat. I know you heard me.) As
for referee insults, I was always partial to "Hey ref, bend over and use your good eye!"
Never failed to bring the house down.

Let's run through the Greatest Team Ever Checklist that I just made up thirty-seven seconds ago . . .

Pyramid guys. The '86 Celts had five of the top sixty, with no. 5 and no. 34 peaking that spring: 50.8 PPG, 17.9 RPG, 10.9 APG, 54% FG, 45 steals and 53 blocks combined in 18 playoff games. Fellas, here are your Greatest Inside/Outside Combo lifetime championship belts. Seriously, how did you stop them? Bird threw world-class entry passes and doubled as a dead-eye shooter. McHale had world-class low-post moves and commanded doubles and triples at all times. What could you do? Teams begrudgingly settled on doubling McHale with a guard and keeping someone on Bird, which meant Johnson and Ainge got to shoot wide-open 15-footers all game. (Not wide-open threes . . . wide-open 15-footers.) Throw in the Parish/Walton center duo (24.9 PPG, 15.2 RPG, 3.1 APG, 42 blocks) and the Celtics were basically announcing, "Our front line is going to notch 75 points and 33 rebounds, protect the rim, shoot 50-plus from the field and hit wide-open shooters and cutters all night; you will be foolish to double-team any of them, and you will not get a break from them for four quarters . . . good luck."[60]

Quality of competition. The league was tougher in '86 than '96 (fewer teams, deeper teams, lower salaries), so considering the '86 Celts finished only five wins behind the '96 Bulls (87–13 vs. 82–18), can those five extra wins be attributed to playing in a watered-down league with someone who was *clearly* the best player (and pathologically competitive to boot)? Absolutely. Although the '86 Celts would have thrived in a high-caliber season; they finished 18–2 against 49-win teams (30–5 including playoffs) but slacked against easier competition.[61] Going against a steady stream of

---

60. Of the hundreds of tapes I watched, no postmerger player had an easier time scoring playoff points than '86 McHale: 39 MPG, 24.9 PPG, 58% FG, 79% FT, 16.1 FGA, 7.8 FTA. He barely broke a sweat. The Panda Express post-up menu was churning out orders like clockwork. "Who wants a no. 3? Can I interest you in a combo no. 2? Please, try an up-and-under egg roll, I insist!"

61. They went 15–0 vs. Milwaukee, Atlanta, L.A. and Houston and 3–2 vs. Philly (one loss by 6 points, the other by Doc's banked 3 at the buzzer) but lost ten games to sub-.500 teams, including 26-win Indy, 29-win Cleveland, 30-win (and MJ-less) Chicago and the 23-win Knicks. Peter May's *The Last Banner* has one recurring theme: the play-

'96 creampuffs, a bored Bird would have spent weeks at a time seeing how many 30-footers he could make or shooting only with his left hand.

Extended stretch of dominance. The C's didn't get rolling until January because of Bird's sore back. As soon as he rounded into shape, they ripped off a 39–5 stretch that included an 11–0 mark against the Lakers, Sixers, Bucks, Hawks and Rockets (with at least one road win over each). I'd say that qualifies as a hot streak.

Playoff run. Surprisingly good considering the talent that season. Jordan went bonkers in the first round (49 in Game 1, 63 in Game 2), but the Celtics still swept the series. They blew a second-round sweep against the frisky Hawks (50 wins, superathletic, led by the runner-up MVP pick), then exacted revenge with one of the all-time closeout ass-whuppings in Game 5. They swept a 57-win Bucks team in the Eastern Finals and convincingly handled a mildly terrifying Rockets team in the Finals. You left that playoffs run thinking, "Wow, those guys couldn't have played any better." That's what we want, right?

Homecourt advantage. Forget about the record-setting 50–1 mark (including playoffs) for a second. Did you know the Celtics nearly went undefeated at home for twelve straight months? After losing to Portland on December 6, 1985, they won *55 straight* home games (including playoffs and the first seven of the next season) before Washington beat them on December 2, 1986. Of those 55 straight wins, only 3 were decided by four or fewer points; 40 of the 55 were by double digits, 11 by more than 20, and five by more than 30. In the '86 playoffs, only Jordan's 63-point game robbed the Celtics of winning all 10 home games by double digits. When I say nobody was touching these guys at home, I mean, *nobody* was touching these guys at home. You have a better chance of seeing another multi-

---

ers bemoaning after the fact that they blew a chance to win 70 by getting bored too often. They also blew four OT games and two more at the buzzer, with Bird clanking FTs in two of them even though he led the league in FT percentage. So it was a slightly fluky 67-win season; they easily could have reached 71 or 72.

permed NBA coaching staff than seeing another NBA team win 55 straight home games in the luxury box era.[62] No way. It will never happen.

Unintentional comedy. The Celts set the standard in three dopey categories: Best Whitewash Ever (Walton, Bird, McHale, Ainge and Wedman, with Sichting, Kite and Carlisle off the bench); Strangest-Looking Championship Team Ever, and Consistently Clumsiest High Fives Ever. Everything culminated in an unforgettable high five/pseudo-hug/half-embrace between Walton and McHale near the end of Game 6 of the '86 Finals. Just an explosion of abnormally long appendages, giant teeth, bad hairdos, hairy armpits and über-Caucasian awkwardness; it's amazing they didn't clunk heads and knock each other unconscious.

Defensive/rebounding prowess. Top of the line in both categories. You were not pounding the '86 Celtics down low or on the boards. Period. Not even the Hakeem/Ralph or Chuck/Moses combos could do it.

Signature playoffs performances. They played three ESPN Classic games—Game 2 vs. Chicago (Jordan's 63), Game 4 vs. Milwaukee (Bird's four threes in the final 4:03 clinched a sweep) and Game 4 at Houston (legitimately exciting)—and three Sistine Chapel games, a list that includes Game 6 of the '86 Finals (the clincher), Game 1 vs. Milwaukee (128–96) and especially Game 5 vs. Atlanta, the greatest evisceration in modern playoffs history: a 36–6 third quarter punctuated by a 24–0 run and the longest standing ovation in NBA history. The *Globe*'s Bob Ryan called it a "scintillating display of interior defense, transition basketball and Globetrotter-like passing which transformed the game into something bordering on legitimate humiliation, but which never degenerated into farce . . . say this for the Hawks: At no point during that surrealistic third

---

62. Assistants Jimmy Rodgers and Chris Ford had ghastly perms this season. Just ghastly. They were right from the Mike Fratello Collection. Ford even threw in a porn mustache and a variety of '80s suits that looked like they came from a Philip Michael Thomas estate sale.

period did they lose dignity. They tried hard at both ends. They simply could not avoid being an accident of basketball history."

Rewatching it on tape, what stands out beyond the crowd (delirious), the passing (exquisite) and the defense (frenetic) was the cumulative effect it had on Atlanta. Mike Fratello called three time-outs trying to stop the bleeding; by the end of the quarter, the Hawks wobbled back to their bench like five guys escaping a violent bar fight. (McHale would say later, "I don't think you'll ever see another quarter of basketball like that again. I mean, the look on the faces of those Atlanta guys leaving the floor after the game, it was like they had just been in a war. It was shell-shock. I think they couldn't wait to get out of there. It was as close to perfection as you are ever going to see.") And it's not like this was a bad Hawks team; they matched up fairly well because Boston had trouble defending Wilkins and Spud Webb.[63] Didn't matter. They got blown out of the building. Ainge told Peter May later, "I call it the Way Basketball Was Supposed to Be Played. That was maybe the most impressive quarter ever played. Atlanta just had no sniff." The tape confirms this. Truly great teams can smell blood and raise it a level; you can see it happening, the fans recognize it, the announcers recognize it, the guys on the bench recognize it, and even the guys playing recognize it. At one point, DJ just starts happily hopping up and down after yet another layup, like even *he* can't believe what's happening. Great moment, transcendant quarter, unforgettable team.

Biggest flaw. The Sichting/Thirdkill spots could have been better. KC Jones inflicted minimal damage other than killing Sam Vincent's confidence. But we're just picking nits. In the fictional round-robin, my biggest concern would be their lack of three-point attempts. Nobody was launching them in the mid-eighties; wouldn't modern defensive teams double McHale and Bird a little more quickly? Then again, Bird and Ainge *became*

---

63. In the regular season, Atlanta went 0–6 against them but every game was close (between three and seven points). There was a memorable game in early January when the Hawks raced out to a 24-point first-half lead, did some trash-talking and got Keyser Söze'd in the second half, with Boston prevailing in OT behind Bird's 41 points, 7 rebounds, 6 assists, 3 steals and 2 blocks. You did *not* talk smack to the '86 Celts.

killer three-point shooters and Wedman certainly had the range, so in a fictional tournament, they could have adjusted. Right? My head hurts.

Dirk Diggler factor. In other words, could they adapt to every conceivable style? The answer is yes. They even had one wrinkle that mortified opponents: a supersized lineup with a front line of Parish, McHale and Walton, then Bird playing guard on offense (which could happen because McHale the Freak could defend almost any two-guard). Every time they played those four guys together at once, you moved to the edge of your seat. They could also handle smallball with Bird-DJ-Ainge-Wedman-McHale, or even Sichting in Wedman's place and DJ playing small forward. You could not throw an opponent at them from any point in history that they wouldn't have handled. Kinda like Dirk Diggler.[64]

Alpha dog. From January to June, Bird peaked as a basketball player. Even said so himself, commenting after Game 6 of the Finals, "That was the only game I thought I was totally prepared for. As far as focus was concerned, none better. Never. I should have quit right there." You think a thirty-three-year-old MJ said that at any point in 1996?

Title defense. The '87 playoffs may have set the standard for "to get rid of us, you're going to have to chop our head off like we're Jason in *Friday the 13th* because that's the only way we're dying" title defenses. See the prologue for the gory details.

Chemistry and swagger. Top of the line. No team loved busting balls more than these guys. They killed Walton for his speech impediment, made fun of McHale's goofy body, rode Ainge like a little brother, teased Wedman about his vegetarian diet . . . there wasn't a single bad apple, or someone who didn't have an exact understanding of his role in the team's hierarchy. Pushing everything over the top were McHale and Ainge (two of the funniest guys who ever played), Bird (the best trash-talker ever) and Walton

---

64. When Wedman broke two ribs during Game 3 of the Bucks series, they played smallball for an extended stretch in Game 4 (Sichting, Ainge, DJ, Bird and McHale), then switched to giantball in crunch time (Ainge, Bird, McHale, Parish and Walton) to pull away. That's ridiculous.

(whose overexuberance defined the season).[65] If anything, they had too much swagger and needed to be challenged at times. Their defining moment: Game 4 of the Milwaukee series, when Bird disdainfully nailed his fourth three in four minutes at the buzzer (the first-ever eff-you three) and jogged off the court like he had just banged everyone's girlfriend in the stands. In the video of that season, Walton runs into the locker room screaming, "Lar-ree Bird! Lar-reeeeee Bird!" We've seen other teams win on that level, but I can't remember any of them getting more of a kick from it.

Trump card. I can't go with passing because Magic's Lakers were just as memorable in that department. So let's go with this: Remember how boxers like Julio Cesar Chavez or Bernard Hopkins would close the ring on opponents over the course of a few rounds, and by the eighth round, suddenly the other guy looked like he was fighting in a phone booth and couldn't move around at all? That's what the Celtics did offensively. They pounded it down low, kept rotating Bird/McHale/Parish/Walton on the low post, kept swinging the ball, kept attacking mismatches, kept getting wide-open 20-footers—only they kept inching closer and closer, and by the second half, suddenly those 20-footers were 15-footers. (Like watching a hockey team pull its goalie and crowd the net with forwards, but in this case the net was the basket.) What's interesting is that had this specific team come along just a few years later, Ainge and Bird would have been gleefully bombing wide-open threes, the spacing would have been better and that boxer/hockey dynamic wouldn't have happened. Would this have made them even more efficient offensively? Probably. But this was memorable. We will never see it again. It's too easy to just jack up threes now.

65. Funniest chemistry story from that season: Bird thought he had clinched the FT title, but Ainge realized before a meaningless Game 82 that if he went 13 for 15, he'd qualify with enough attempts and pass Bird. In the second half, Danny started driving to the basket recklessly, up-faking and trying to draw fouls—totally uncharacteristic—only nobody knew what was going on until the fourth quarter, and KC Jones couldn't remove him because Ainge kept getting to the line. Finally McHale decided he would intentionally commit lane violations to stop Ainge, who was getting heckled by his own bench, but that was averted when there was a whistle and Jones pulled him. And by the way, all of this was for fun and everyone was laughing the whole time.

Biggest luxury. Every time Walton loped off the bench for the first time, the crowd stood and cheered—partly because we liked him, partly because it meant he and Bird would do their "night at the Improv" routine. They experimented that whole season with various no-looks, pick-and-rolls and every other "only we are on this plane and see these angles" offensive play; even on tape two decades later, it's like seeing rare video of Biggie freestyling with Eminem. Their favorite play? Bird dumped the ball in to Walton, then ran by him toward the basket like he was clearing out, only Walton would quickly flip the ball over his head to Bird for an easy layup. When teams caught on, they changed the play a little—now Bird used Walton (holding the ball) to pick his guy, so everything hinged post-pass on whether he ran by Walton's right side or left side (and each time, both defenders had to guess). Nobody could stop it.[66] When teams floated a third defender over to stop them, his guy (usually McHale) just cut to the basket for an easy layup from Walton. And that's how it went. Walton only averaged an 8–7 in 18 minutes a game, but that's reason no. 759 why statistics don't tell the story. Seeing two basketball savants combining their once-in-a-generation passing skills was the pickle for the greatest cheeseburger of a team ever assembled.

Killer instinct. They led by thirty-plus at some point in the fourth quarter or three of four playoff clinchers. The fourth? The one where Bird ripped Milwaukee's heart out with all those threes. And if that's not enough, they defeated their main threat in the West (the Lakers) both times by double digits and their main threats in the East (Atlanta, Milwaukee and Philly) twenty-two of twenty-five times. Well, then.

Iconic relevance (then). Yes.

Iconic relevance (now). Not as much. Yet another reason why we needed a book like this.[67]

---

66. I'm not kidding: when the '86 Celts were feeling it, every time Bird tossed it in to Walton, it was move-up-to-the-edge-of-your-seat exciting. *What are they gonna come up with this time?*

67. One more reason: because I needed an excuse to hit up my boy Hirschy at the NBA for as many '86 Celtics tapes as possible. If I ever get divorced, I guarantee you "He made me watch too many '86 Celtics tapes" will be part of the Sports Gal's irreconcilable differences case.

THIRTEEN

THE WINE CELLAR

FORWARD
LARRY BIRD

26.9
JULIUS ERVING

GUARD
MAGIC JOHNSON

TIME TO PUT the jigsaw pieces together and make a puzzle.

The puzzle revolves around the Martian Premise. Let's say basketball-playing aliens land on earth, blow things up *Independence Day*–style, then challenge us to a seven-game series for control of the universe. And let's say we have access to the time machine from *Lost*, allowing us to travel back Sarah Conner–style and grab any twelve NBA legends from 1946 through 2010, transport them to the present day, then hold practices for eight weeks before the Final Finals. Again, we *have* to prevail or planet Earth as we know it ends. Which twelve players would you pick?

If you learned anything from this book other than "Simmons is incapable of editing himself" and "Rick Barry wore a Burt Reynolds–like wig during the 1975–76 season," I hope and pray that it's this: instead of picking the greatest players, you should pick twelve who complement each other in the best possible way . . . right? (Please nod. Thank you.) You

want a *basketball team*. A group that understands The Secret. A pecking
order of personalities/talents that no rogue player would dare challenge. A
crunch-time unit that includes one vocal leader, one leader by example
and one unquestioned alpha dog. Bench guys who will accept limited
roles and not care about minutes. Roster flexibility with heights, styles
and athleticism. At least four white guys so we can market more jerseys
and posters. (Whoops, I screwed that up—I was thinking of the logic behind the '92 Dream Team. Scratch that one.) In a perfect world, our best
twelve would care only about winning and meshing as a team.

I call it the Wine Cellar Team, and here's why: Whenever someone
makes an all-time team, they casually throw out names without context. *I'll
take Bird, Magic, Jordan, Kareem, LeBron . . .* What does that even mean?
Did you like pre-baseball or post-baseball Jordan? Did you like alpha dog
Magic or unselfish Magic? I need more information. Think like a wine
snob and regard players like vintages of wine and not the brands themselves. Ask any wine connoisseur for their ten favorite Bordeaux of the last
seventy-five years and they wouldn't say, "Mouton-Rothschild, Lafite, Haut
Brion, Latour . . ." They would give you precise vintages. *The '59 Mouton
Rothschild. The '53 Lafite. The '82 Haut-Brion. The '61 Latour.* If you prod-
ded them, they would happily accept the challenge, "I'll give you five dinner menus and you give me the ten best Bordeaux, two per dinner, that
match up with the food." That's part of being a wine connoisseur—not just
knowing the wines but knowing the vintages and how they relate to food.
They would have a grand old time figuring this out.[1]

Doesn't that sound like basketball? It's all about the vintages. I loved
watching Bird, but I *really* loved watching '86 Bird. Why? His teammates
peaked in '86, allowing him to explore parts of his game during his prime
that couldn't be explored otherwise. You could say his career year became
special because of luck and timing. With wines, the determining factors for
career years also hinge on luck and timing—like 1947, an unusually hot
summer in France that created wines of high alcohol and low acidity. That's
how the '47 Cheval Blanc emerged as a famous vintage and the best its vine-

---

1. I never understood the whole wine snob thing. It's so subjective—wines hit everyone
differently and there's no reason to spend hours on end debating which wine is better. Just
drink them and shut up. Nothing's worse than being trapped in a room with someone
who is creating dumb arguments, trying to prove impossible-to-prove things, and hammering you with their insufferable opinions. Unless it's this book. Then it's totally fine.

yard ever produced . . . you know, just like '77 Bill Walton. Not every decision is that easy. Mouton-Rothschild peaked in '53, '59 and '61 . . . you know, like how Magic peaked in different ways in '82, '85 and '87. Wine connoisseurs disagree on the best Mouton-Rothschild vintage, just like we might disagree on the best vintage of Magic. His best scoring season occurred in '87, but I have more than enough firepower on my Wine Cellar Team. If I'm already grabbing a Jordan bottle (either '92 or '96) and a bottle of '86 Bird, and I'm definitely picking a few more scorers, why would I need Magic to assume a bigger scoring load? Why not start '85 Magic (the ultimate for unselfish point guards) or maybe even bring '82 Magic (younger, better defensively, capable of playing four positions, talented enough to average a shade under a triple double) off the bench as my sixth man?

So really, the Wine Cellar Team is a jigsaw puzzle. I made my decisions easier with three ground rules:

1. Only vintage seasons that I remember witnessing live. That makes the ABA-NBA merger our cutoff date and gives us a time frame from 1977 to 2009.[2]
2. Emulate the best basketball team ever (the '86 Celts) as closely as possible, not their talent as much as their unselfishness and we-can-do-anything flexibility.
3. Don't forget that a formula of "unselfishness + character + defense + rebounding + MJ" will run the Martians out of the gym unless they have an eight-foot-three center we didn't know about.[3]

From there, I worked backward and started with the following have-to-have-them guys who received check marks in the following categories: to-

2. Not to get too technical, but we're throwing each pick in the time machine right after his season ends.
3. FYI: We're playing the Final Finals at MSG, selling tickets and everything. I don't want to make the same mistake Rocky made when he fought Drago in Russia on Christmas Day for no money. (Which barely topped these other doozies as the dumbest moment of *Rocky IV*: Apollo dying in the ring for ten solid minutes without medical help and 100 people crowding the ring; Rocky climbing a 20,000-foot Russian mountain in snow boots and a winter coat; and the Soviet crowd turning on Drago and rooting for Rocky.) If the future of the world is at stake, we may as well profit from this thing. By the way, I envision the Final Finals ending like *Rocky IV* did, with the Wine Cellar Team and the Martians forging a mutual respect and Magic Johnson telling the fans, "What you just saw out here was 12 humans and 12 aliens practically killing themselves . . . but I guess it's better than ten billion" and "If the Martians can change, and the humans can change, *everyone can change!*"

tally unselfish, awesome teammate, enjoyed making others better, incredibly high basketball IQ, complete comprehension of The Secret. There were three in all.

'86 Larry Bird

Playoffs: 25.8 PPG, 9.3 RPG, 8.2 APG, 2.1 SPG, 52–93–41 (18 games)

Give him superior teammates and he'd reinvent himself as a complementary player, drain a few threes, post smaller dudes up, rove around on defense like a free safety, make everyone else better and take over if you needed him. Mike Fratello summed up Bird's better-with-great-teammates qualities after coaching an '88 All-Star game in which Bird scored six points and Jordan and 'Nique combined for sixty-nine: "Michael played well, Dominique played well, but the thing which really impressed me was the way Larry Bird subjugated himself. Larry Bird showed me more today than most people could possibly have noticed. From the standpoint of a coach, you've got to love seeing a man do all he did—come up with a couple of key steals, get back on defense continually, and break up about five fast-break opportunities. To me, he was like an overseer of the game. He saw what we needed, and he acted accordingly." Yes. We need an overseer. That will be Bird.

'03 Tim Duncan

Playoffs: 24.7 PPG, 15.4 RPG, 5.3 APG, 3.3 BPG, 53–68 (24 games)

Greatest power forward ever, commander of a double team at all times, the ultimate teammate, and someone capable of playing center when we go small. Fits everything we want to do. A superior version of '86 McHale.

'85 Magic Johnson

Playoffs: 17.5 PPG, 7.1 RPG, 15.2 APG, 51–85 (19 games).

For all the reasons covered in the Mouton-Rothschild paragraph. Like Bird, he would live to make everyone else better.

So that's my three-man foundation along with Jordan. But which Jordan? He peaked athletically and statistically in '91, peaked from a confidence level in '92 and peaked as a competitor and winner in '93 . . . but those three Jordan vintages were a little *too* competitive. Even with the future of the universe at stake, that might not deter him from undermining the confidence of certain teammates (imagine him scrimmaging against Kobe or LeBron) and turning every practice into an all-out war to constantly reaffirm his alpha status. Would we rather have '96 Jordan? You know, the guy who was humbled from his baseball experience, more appreciative of his gifts, a more understanding and supportive teammate, just as competitive and hungry, a little less explosive but more efficient, smarter about his own limitations, someone who treasured The Secret completely? Hmmmmmm. Let's go here.

'92 Michael Jordan

Playoffs: 34.5 PPG, 6.2 RPG, 5.8 APG, 2.8 stocks, 50–86–39 (22 games)[4]

And here's why: prebaseball MJ struggled only to coexist with *shitty* teammates. He's not playing with Brad Sellers and Will Perdue on the Wine Cellar Team. If he didn't cause problems with the Dream Team, he won't cause problems with the greatest team ever assembled. We want our best scorer coming off title number two at the peak of his powers; extending that '86 Celtics framework, imagine switching Jordan with Danny Ainge. Yikes. And since we're running pay-per-viewing scrimmages to raise money for the cities destroyed by the evil Martians, any die-hard hoops fan will pony up to see him battling Young LeBron, Young Wade and/or Young Kobe for eight solid weeks.[5]

For the center spot, I can't hold grudges with the future of the world at

---

4. His most underrated postseason: 7 brutally physical games against the Thugball Knicks, 6 hard-fought games against an excellent Cavs team, and 6 more against a scary Blazers team . . . and he never faded even one iota.

5. Worth noting: I changed my opinion on '92 MJ vs. '96 MJ between 17 and 700 different times. I'm still not sure that I made the right pick. The '92 MJ was athletically superior and had a 90 percent idea of The Secret; the '96 MJ was 90 percent as good but embraced The Secret. So tough. I don't know. Fuck.

stake. I need the surest two points of all time. I need the sky hook. I need Kareem. Any doubts I had about him embracing The Secret were erased in a 1980 *Sports Illustrated* feature, when he explained a decision to play after a debilitating migraine like this: "These guys are my teammates, but they are also my friends. They needed me." Yes! Sounds like something Russell would say. Hence . . .

'77 Kareem Abdul-Jabbar

Playoffs: 34.6 PPG, 17.7 RPG, 4.1 APG, 5.2 stocks, 61–73 (11 games)

That's our starting five: '86 Bird, '03 Duncan, '85 Magic, '92 Jordan and '77 Kareem. You cannot assemble a better five-man unit of modern guys. Our five backups should complement them in every conceivable way (while grasping The Secret, of course).

'86 Kevin McHale

Playoffs: 24.9 PPG, 8.6 RPG, 2.7 APG, 2.4 BPG, 58–79 (18 games)

The most efficient low-post scorer ever. McHale comes in, we post him up, he scores six out of ten times (not counting foul shots). On the other end, he guards players ranging from six-foot-four to seven-foot-four, plays power forward or center and adapts to any style. The Martians *will* have to plan for McHale. In fact, they might look at his body and think he's a fellow alien.

'92 Scottie Pippen

Playoffs: 19.5 PPG, 8.8 RPG, 6.7 APG, 3.0 stocks, 47–76 (22 games)

The best perimeter defender ever, a world-class athlete and someone who can swing between forward and guard and even play point forward. If one of the Martians gets hot, I'm unleashing Jordan or Pippen on him. Also, we need him for our Murderous Press, that's about fifteen paragraphs away from rocking your world.

'77 Bill Walton

Playoffs: 18.2 PPG, 15.2 RPG, 5.5 APG, 3.4 BPG, 51–69 (19 games)

No modern center had a greater effect on his teammates. We want a combination rebounder, shot blocker and passer who would be overjoyed to join forces with the greatest collection of talent ever assembled. And as we learned in '86, the Walton Experience works splendidly in short doses.[6]

'05 Ron Artest

Playoffs: (DNP)

Just kidding. He'd start an intergalactic melee. We need an MJ backup, though. What about . . .

'01 Kobe Bryant

Playoffs: 29.4 PPG, 7.3 RPG, 6.1 APG, 47–82–32 (16 games).

Best-case scenario: Young Kobe performs a reasonable MJ impression as Jordan's caddy. It's conceivable because he hasn't gone Teen Wolf yet and he's young enough to understand his place in the pecking order. If we asked him to play 15 minutes a game, kill himself defensively, push Jordan in practice and serve as his valet during games, Young Kobe probably says yes. Older Kobe would think, "Wait a second, why should I take a backseat to Michael? I'm just as good as he is!" That's why we need Young Kobe.

Worst-case scenario: Young Kobe gets totally caught up in the whole "I need to prove that I'm as good as MJ" thing, jacks up shots in games and keeps challenging Jordan in practice to the point that we can't put them on different teams in scrimmages anymore.

(Actually, why am I even risking it? Couldn't we just go here?)

6. I considered '92 David Robinson here because he averaged a 23–12 with a staggering 6.8 stocks per game (4.5 blocks, 2.3 steals), the highest post-1973 total of all time. And there was no greater teammate or better center candidate for my press. But Robinson had that propensity to choke in the clutch, and if anything happened to Kareem . . .

'09 Dwyane Wade

Regular season: 30.2 PPG, 7.5 APG, 5.2 RPG, 2.2 SPG, 49–77–32 (79 games)

For five reasons: (a) '09 Wade performed the best Jordan imitation yet; (b) it can't be forgotten how he thrived off the bench during the '08 Olympics; (c) I don't have to worry about chemistry; (d) he can handle the ball at point in a pinch; and (e) Lakers fans will be furious that I bumped Kobe. This is a win-win all the way around. Sorry, Kobe. Just remember, I didn't do this . . . *you* did this.[7]

'09 Chris Paul

Regular season: 22.9 PPG, 11.0 APG, 5.5 RPG, 2.8 SPG, 50–87–36 (77 games)

The Evolutionary Isiah and the front of our Murderous Press, as well as the perfect Magic backup (capable of handling any waterbug point guard) and a second ballhandler/cooler for when we're protecting a lead in the last 30 seconds.[P67]

For our last two spots, we're going with luxuries . . .

'10 LeBron James

Regular season: 28.4 PPG, 7.6 RPG, 7.2 APG, 1.69 SPG, 49–78–34 (82 games)

I considered '89 Dennis Rodman before realizing he broke my Only One Head Case (you can get away with one head case, but if you have two, they

---

7. That's an homage to my friend Dave Dameshek, a radio host with a weekly "Jerk List" who starts the segment by telling all of that week's jerks, "Just remember, I didn't do this . . . *you* did this."

P67. Watching Nash live The Secret with the '10 Suns nearly made me switch '07 Nash for '09 Paul on the Wine Cellar team. I changed my mind 20 times. Finally kept Paul, only because we need insurance in case the Martians have a five-foot-eleven waterbug destroying us off the dribble. You never know.

might end up hanging out) and Nobody on My Wine Cellar Team Can
Appear on Celebrity Apprentice at Any Point in Their Lives rules. No
thanks. The '10 LeBron gives us more smallball options, an über-athlete
who can play four positions (à la '82 Magic) and the next to final piece of
our Murderous Press that's now making you giddy.[8] And as we learned with
The Decision, he's more than happy being a supporting piece on a great
team. Even if it means turning the country against him as one hundred Boys
and Girls Club members and Jim Gray are staring him down in disbelief.

'01 Ray Allen

Playoffs: 25.1 PPG, 4.1 RPG, 6.0 APG, 48–92–47 (11 games)

Gets the nod over Reggie Miller as our official thooler (designated three-
point shooter and end-of-the-game cooler).[9] I mean, look at those percentages again! Are you kidding me?

So here's the final Wine Cellar Team: '77 Kareem, '03 Duncan, '86 Bird,
'92 Jordan, '85 Magic (starters); '86 McHale, '92 Pippen, '09 Wade, '77
Walton, '10 LeBron, '09 Paul, '01 Allen (bench). Check out the plethora of
options we have with those twelve guys.

Best crunch-time lineup: Kareem, Bird, Duncan/McHale, Jordan, Magic.
With the following caveats: if McHale is on fire, maybe we play him over
Duncan . . . if Bird/Magic is getting killed defensively, maybe we throw in
Pippen/LeBron and/or Paul/Wade . . . and if we want to downsize, we can
play Duncan/McHale at center and insert LeBron or Wade for Kareem. If
we need a basket, we run something for Jordan or go inside/outside game
with Bird/Kareem. We also have Duncan on the high post if we want to

---

8. When *The Second Book of Basketball* is written LeBron will almost definitely be un-
seating Larry Legend or Duncan from the starting lineup, barring a terrible injury or
someone framing him for a crime. For now, I want an intangibles guy as my backup
small forward and that's Pippen. We'll keep Bron in the garage with a cover on him like
a brand-new Testarossa.
9. You know this book has dragged on too long when I'm coming up with subnicknames
for my nicknames (thooler/cooler). Don't worry, we're almost done. I know you're like
one of those overheated marathon runners on the twenty-sixth mile right now.

run a play through him. And we have Magic ready to run off every miss with Bird, Duncan, and Jordan. Put it this way: we have options, and then some.

Best defensive lineup (bigger): McHale/Duncan/Kareem (two of three), Pippen, Jordan, Wade, Paul. You're not scoring on those guys. Period.

Best defensive lineup (smaller): McHale/Duncan, LeBron, Pippen, Jordan, Wade, Paul. Ditto.[10]

Best fast break lineup: Walton/Duncan, Bird, LeBron/Pippen, Jordan/ Wade, Magic/Paul. Holy schnikes. Lots of options here. We can run with some combination of nearly every guy on our team.

Best smallball lineup: LeBron, Pippen, Jordan, Wade, Paul/Magic. Fascinating because you could get away with this quintet defensively if you pushed the pace and trapped all over the place (it would be like the '07 Warriors on acid). Admit it, you're moving to the edge of your seat when this lineup comes in. You could also insert Magic for Wade or Pippen if you wanted to relive the Magic/Nixon salad days.

Best bigball lineup: Kareem, Walton/Duncan, McHale, LeBron/Pippen, Bird. With LeBron or Pippen at point forward. Yes, you could play them together and it would work—no different from Walton, Parish, McHale, Bird and DJ flourishing in the '86 playoffs. In fact, this might be my favorite look yet.

Best three-point shooting lineup: LeBron, Bird, Jordan, Allen, Paul. My least favorite wrinkle since I only have two deadly bombers and I'd much rather have three. (Note to Steve Nash: You almost made the Wine Cellar

---

10. Conceivably, I could have picked all five members of the '92 or '93 All-Defense First Team: Pippen, Rodman, MJ, Dumars and either Robinson ('92) or Hakeem ('93), then swapped LeBron for MJ and made that my Murderous Press. But that would have involved dumping Walton for Robinson/Hakeem, Wade for Dumars and Ray Allen for Rodman . . . too risky. You wouldn't believe how much time I spent coming up with this team. We are talking dozens and dozens of hours. And every time I thought, "I really need a life," I remembered, "But hey, it's for my book!" and that made it okay.

Team simply as a better version of the '96 Steve Kerr.) On the other hand, I have Larry Bird and Ray Allen. So all isn't lost.

Best free-throw-shooting lineup: Bird, Jordan, Paul, Magic, Allen. Nobody under 85 percent and two over 90 percent. We would not blow a lead in the final 45 seconds.

Most intriguing lineup: Walton, Bird, LeBron, Magic, Jordan. Four superior passers with Jordan. I am giddy.

The murderous press: Duncan, LeBron, Pippen, Wade, Paul. I'm borrowing this idea from Rick Pitino, who told Malcolm Gladwell that if he ever coached in the NBA again, he would pick five of his bench guys to practice exclusively on a full-court press, then play them once a half for four or five minutes at a time. Their sole purpose would be to create havoc, wear opponents down, exploit opposing bench guys and shift momentum. And they would. Would you want to bring the ball up against a press with these five guys prowling around like cheetahs? It would be like throwing against a ten-man secondary, right?[11]

Here's how my playing time would ultimately break down. Keep in mind, we want these guys going all out at all times.

> *First quarter. Jordan, Bird, Magic, Duncan and Kareem start the game. At the 6:00 mark, McHale comes in for Duncan. After the mandatory 3:00 minute time-out, it's time for a Paul-Wade-Pippen-McHale-Walton quintet.*
> *Second quarter. Four minutes of hell with our killer press (Duncan-LeBron-Pippen-Wade-Paul). At the 8:00 mark, Walton, Bird, Magic and Jordan return and play with LeBron at power forward for a little "holy shit, look at this passing" interlude. For the last four minutes, Kareem replaces Walton and McHale replaces LeBron.*
> *Third quarter: Same starters. At 6:00, McHale comes in for Duncan and*

11. Wait a second . . . did I just steal an idea from Rick Pitino, one of the least successful NBA coach/execs in modern basketball history? This book *really* needs to end soon.

Walton replaces Kareem. At 3:00, Paul-Wade-LeBron-McHale-Walton.

Fourth quarter: *Four more minutes of hell with our killer press (and Duncan anchoring it). At the eight-minute mark, Jordan, Kareem, Bird, Magic and McHale return. We bring back Duncan for the final 4:00* unless *McHale is destroying his guy and can't be taken out.*

Minutes breakdown: *Jordan (34), Bird (34), Magic (34), Kareem (27), Duncan (24), McHale (20), LeBron (15), Wade (14), Paul (14), Walton (13), Pippen (11), Allen (0).[12]*

(We are gonna fuck those Martians up! Don't come into our house!)

My toughest omissions: '92 Robinson, '01 Kobe, '89 Rodman, '07 Nash and '96 Kerr (three-point shooting and free-throw shooting), '79 Gervin (instant offense), '84 Bernard (ditto), '04 Garnett (in LeBron's place), '83 Toney (in Wade's spot), '89 Dumars (defense and intangibles), '79 Moses (only for his rebounding), '87 Barkley (in the LeBron spot, although we couldn't press with him), '87 Isiah (over Paul).[13] The toughest cut? I can't believe I'm saying this . . . but it's Rodman. We could have used him on the Murderous Press. Oh, well.

For a head coach, I'm grabbing '07 Gregg Popovich (perfect sense of humor, proven success with veteran teams like this one) over any of the Phil Jackson or Pat Riley vintages, just because we don't need any of their cutesy motivational tricks on a team this good. Pop's assistants: '06 Mike D'Antoni (our offensive guru), '09 Mike Brown (our guru for defending high screens and rotating correctly), '88 Rick Pitino (pulled from college to run our killer press)[14] and '77 Willis Reed (big man coach and protec-

12. Sorry, Ray. You're a luxury. Nobody plays 12 guys; it's nonsensical. If you don't like it, we'll make calls to Nash and Kerr right now. Just say the word. By the way, if LeBron beats out Wade for those backup SG minutes, I'm fine with that. May the best hypothetical man hypothetically win.

13. Poor Isiah even gets cut from the Wine Cellar Team (for a legitimate reason this time: 3-point shooting). But considering MJ hated him enough to keep him off the Dream Team, wouldn't he have said, "Look, I'd rather see Earth blow up over being teammates with that guy?" I feel like the answer is yes.

14. I went with '88 Pitino instead of '96 Pitino because '96 Pitino had too big an ego to be somebody's assistant. This is a guy who once wrote a book called *Lead to Succeed: 10 Traits of Great Leadership in Business and Life* one year *after* he finished ruining the Celtics and the entire team quit on him.

tion just in case an alien starts a bench-clearing brawl). Also, we need 1984 Red Auerbach involved—we're making him the team president, just so we'd have a crusty old guy happily accepting the All-Universe Trophy in the raucous locker room after the game and saying something sarcastic like, "I kept hearing that the aliens were more advanced in every respect." (Holds up the trophy.) "Here's your advancement, I got it right here!"

Speaking of Red, how would a pre-merger team look operating under the same principles? You wouldn't have the same athleticism—hence, no press with the bench guys—and you'd have serious outside shooting issues since nobody consistently drained anything past 20–22 feet back then. So I'd twist this unit around with a different focus. Check it out.

Starters. '74 Kareem (first scoring option); '64 Russell (moves to power forward as my leader, shot blocker, and rebounder); '72 Havlicek (my glue); '66 West (slightly poor man's MJ); '64 Oscar (the maestro). These are my best five guys and the most "modern" of the pre-1977 guys. I want them playing together as much as possible.[15]

Bench. The pre-1977 guys weren't nearly as flexible stylistically and lacked length because the Duncan/KG types just didn't exist. So what do we do? I thought about run-and-gun with '61 Elgin, '59 Cousy, '62 Wilt, '76 Doc and '73 Cowens, but they'd have no outside shooting and might get pancaked defensively. So what if we just unleashed Wilt, revolved the bench around him and re-created the '67 Sixers or '72 Lakers as closely as possible? We tell '67 Wilt going in, "Look, you're not starting. You will never start. You will also never finish a game. Here's all we want from you. For six minutes each half, we want you to score as many points as you possibly can. You will be our number one option for those twelve minutes. We will only care

---

15. If you thought Russell and Wilt should start together, they did so in '61 and '62 and lost by a combined 41 points. Russell mailed in All-Star games (10–12 in 28 MPG) except for after Wilt moved West in '63, when Russell's team won all three years (Russell: 16–19–4; Wilt: 19–18–1). When Wilt returned in '66, the East won two of the next three, as well as in '69 after Wilt went to L.A. (mail-ins from Russell and Wilt). So Russell was 4–0 in All-Stars vs. Wilt and 3–3 as teammates.

about getting you the ball and playing defense. That's it. Otherwise, you're not coming, you'll never see the future and you'll never find out what sex with an alien groupie is like. Do you accept this mission or not?" I think Wilt accepts. Maybe even with a hard-on. Then we build a bench unit around him that resembles the '67 Sixers as closely as possible: '70 Frazier (reasonable Oscar imitation, plus someone to carouse with Wilt after games); '70 DeBusschere (rebounding, defense and long-distance shooting); '75 Barry (passing, long-range shooting, last-minute cooler); '65 Sam Jones (we already know he can score off the bench). Also, I'm going to isolate Barry off the court like a mass murderer so he can't interact with teammates in any way. We'll have to treat him the same way Hannibal Lecter was treated: Keep him on a stretcher with a metal mask covering his face, then wheel him in when we need him for practice and games. This will definitely work.

Deep bench. '75 McAdoo (long-range shooting and added length if we need it); '73 Maravich (three-point specialist, free throw shooting, garbage time fun).

Coach. By himself, '65 Auerbach. Just seven plays and a rolled-up program. We're going old school through and through.

Toughest omissions. The '70 Willis (an enforcer/banger would have been nice); '76 Doc (I don't need more scoring); '59 Cousy (subpar defense and outside shooting); '58 Pettit (Grumpy Old Editor would have killed me); '76 Calvin Murphy (scorer, cooler, strange height matchup for teams); '70 Cunningham (slasher extraordinaire); '73 Cowens (perfect energy guy); '64 Satch Sanders (a Rodman-like defensive stopper); '61 Elgin (just couldn't find a spot for him). The toughest omissions? Doc and Elgin. We already have enough scoring. Sorry, fellas.

What if we had a seven-game series between the pre-1977 and post-1977 guys for the right to play the Martians? I can't imagine the pre-'77's handling Jordan in any conceivable way; he'd definitely annihilate West after Magic kept riling him up that West was the real "Mr. Clutch." The post-'77's could throw four lengthy big guys at Kareem and Wilt and wreak havoc on the Frazier/Jones backcourt with its press.[16] If it came down to the post-'77's protecting a lead, they could toss out a Walton-McHale-Pippen-Jordan-Wade lineup and shackle every pre-'77 guy except '74 Kareem, whom they'd keep doubling by leaving Russell alone from 15 feet (and daring him to shoot). The pre-'77's couldn't take advantage of the three-point line without playing West, Maravich, McAdoo and Barry at the same time . . . and the post-'77's would combat it by unleashing Jordan-Wade-LeBron-Pippen on them and attacking Maravich defensively. If they ran everything through Oscar, the post-'77's would have Pippen, LeBron or Wade hound him everywhere. And again, who's guarding Jordan? Or Wade? Or even LeBron? I can't see the pre-'77's winning a single game.

If you want to combine the two eras, I'm fine with '64 Russell over '77 Walton, '66 West over '09 Wade, and '72 Havlicek over '10 LeBron if we're intent on representing the old guard. But that's it. Do I need to make those switches? Except for Russell, probably not.

So that's the Wine Cellar Team for now. I finished this book in mid-April 2009. When *The Second Book of Basketball: A Quick Influx of Cash* is released in 2016, maybe LeBron replaces Bird as a starter. Maybe Kevin Durant bumps Ray Allen. Maybe Dwight Howard turns into a beast and knocks Walton off. Maybe 2012 LeBron supplants 1992 MJ as the team's alpha dog. I am prepared for anything. I am a basketball fan. I am always ready for the next surprise. You never know when true greatness is lurking around the corner. Just make sure you don't forget the ones who already lurked.

16. Originally, I was worried about '74 Kareem and '77 Kareem hypothetically playing against each other because they couldn't be in two places at the same time. Or so I thought. Because as Season 5 of *Lost* proved, they could be in the same place as long as we didn't disturb the past to make it happen. And that could only happen if it was pre-ordained to happen. So for it to happen, that means even before conceiving of the pre-1977/post-1977 series, I would have already altered Kareem's life back in 1974 and 1977 when Future Bill went back in my time machine and grabbed him at two different points in his life. So even though I didn't think of the idea until last year, '74 and '77 Kareem already will have had the experience of traveling forward in time to hypothetically play each other. Did that make sense? (Waiting.) What? You hate my guts for making your head hurt? How dare you!

Life After The Secret

Bill Walton
CENTER
CLIPPERS

JUNE 30, 2009

WILLIAM THEODORE WALTON III lives in a sprawling house filled with hundreds of books, pictures, mementos, artifacts and everything else that should definitely be in Bill Walton's house. Turn left and you might see a Vietnam book next to a Hunter S. Thompson book. Turn right and you might see a photo of Bill and Bob Dylan hanging next to a picture of Bill and John Wooden. A lifelong resident of the most beautiful city in America, Walton owns a Spanish-style home that makes you think, "I am definitely, undoubtedly in San Diego right now." The house features a basketball half-court and a pool, as well as his lovely wife, Lori, two pooches named Annie and Shasta, and a black cat named Charcoal.

That's right, a black cat.

This blows me away. Bill Walton seems like the last guy who should tempt fate with a black cat. Instead of being mentioned in the same breath with Russell, Wilt and Kareem, he's remembered for bad luck and what could have been. His body continues to pay for an injury-riddled career that ended 22 years ago; only recently could he start moving around after major back surgery left him bedridden for months. His feet betrayed him so egregiously that, within ten minutes of sitting down with him, I glance at his swollen, scarred, almost unrecognizable right foot, become distracted and lose my train of thought. Walton was blessed with a gift and cursed with a body that couldn't handle that gift. The curse trumped the gift. One of the few players who understood The Secret completely and totally, poor Walton never had an extended chance to harvest it.

What would make him want a black cat? Why not hire Spencer Haywood as a butler and stick ladders in front of every doorway? This is one of many questions I plan on asking him. We're chatting fifteen days after the Lakers captured the 2009 title and sent my book into a tailspin. I turned in my manuscript right before the playoffs, then spent the next ten weeks praying nothing would alter The Pyramid or The Secret. You know, like LeBron's team majestically failing and raising legitimate questions about his future in Cleveland. (Damn.) Like Dwight Howard inexplicably leading Orlando to the Finals and creeping up a few Pyramid spots. (Crap.) Like Kobe winning his first title, leapfrogging West and Oscar and reinventing himself as a team player in the minds of many writers and fans. (Shit.) Although the Lakers clearly prevailed as a group, with Pau Gasol (the league's most talented offensive center), Lamar Odom (a gifted all-around forward), Trevor Ariza (a breakout swingman with a little Robert Horry in him) and Derek Fisher (who drained the two biggest shots of the Finals) all shining throughout the playoffs, the media became obsessed that Los Angeles was only winning because "Kobe, really *really* wants this!" and "Kobe *finally* trusts his teammates!" Too bad the relevant per-game numbers didn't back that rhetoric up.[P68]

P68. 2008 Kobe (21 playoff games): 30.1 pts, 5.7 reb, 5.6 ast, 3.3 TO, 22.0 FGA, 9.2 FTA, 47.9 FG%, 81 FT%, 30 3FG%, 41.1 MPG. 2009 Kobe (23 playoff games): 30.2 pts, 5.3 reb, 5.5 ast, 2.6 TO, 23.0 FGA, 8.6 FTA, 45.7 FG%, 88 FT%, 35 3FG%, 40.9 MPG.

If anything, Kobe's circumstances changed. Boston, San Antonio and Houston were crippled by season-ending injuries to Kevin Garnett, Manu Ginobili and Yao Ming. Cleveland made an infuriating and indefensible decision to stand pat at the trade deadline.[1] As all of this was happening, Ariza's maturation pushed the Lakers to another level. This is what I believe. Then again, I am a diehard Boston fan. Do I believe Kobe's "growth" as a teammate was smoke and mirrors because I'm biased, or because it's true? This was why I called Walton. Since his son joined the Lakers in 2003, Luke and Bill probably had every conceivable conversation about Kobe Bryant.[2] Of the living basketball players who understood and executed The Secret—call it The Secret Club—Walton should have the best perspective on him. At least I hope so. Or else I plan on driving my car into oncoming traffic on the way home.

We sit down in Walton's living room and a purring Charcoal nudges against me, jumps on my lap and nestles into my belly. Walton finally shoos her away. You could choke on the irony. We spend the first 30 minutes talking basketball before I explain The Secret to him. I tell him the Isiah/Vegas story and read two excerpts from *The Franchise*. Walton stares ahead and digests everything. Finally . . .

"It's not a secret," he decides, "as much as a choice. Look at the forces fighting against that choice. Look at the forces pushing you to make the other choice, the wrong choice. It's all about you. It's all about material acquisitions, physical gratification, stats and highlights. Everywhere you go, you're bombarded with the opposite message of what really matters. And you wouldn't even know otherwise unless you played with the right player or right coach: the Woodens, the Auerbachs, the Ramseys, the Russells, the Birds. How many people get that lucky? Kobe was blessed to have Phil [Jackson] and eventually realized that. With a truly great coach, it's not about a diagram, it's not about a play, it's not about a practice, it's the

1. The Cavs could have dealt Wally Szezcerbiak's expiring contract for Shaq, Antwan Jamison or Vince Carter and stupidly opted to do nothing. After Orlando shocked them in the Eastern Finals, they traded for Shaq four weeks later. This was like a family buying homeowner's insurance four weeks after robbers cleaned out their house.
2. Thanks to the '09 Finals, Luke and Bill became the third father-son combo to win an NBA title along with the Barrys (Rick and Brent) and Goukases (Matt and Matt). I wanted to make a Nick/Teresa Weatherspoon joke here—badly—but they aren't related.

course of time over history. It's the impact a coach has on the lives around him. That's what Phil has done for Kobe. The history of life is that most people figure it out. Most of the time it's too late. That's the real frustrating part—the squandered opportunities that you can't get back. Kobe figured it out. It took awhile, but he figured it out."

Perfect. Couldn't have scripted a better rebuttal. So what if Walton hijacked my premise and changed it to "The Choice"? (Which, I have to admit, has a nice ring to it.) Jackson definitely wore Kobe down over time—a little like Andy Dufresne believing that his tiny rock hammer scheme would propel him through the walls of Shawshank (remember, pressure over time?)—and that subtle pressure allowed the Lakers to gel. Just enough. It's one more reason why Jackson wears the "greatest NBA coach" title belt: He harnessed the talents of the league's single most difficult superstar other than Wilt. Jackson did this gradually, over the span of a solid decade, even walking away once for effect. You can't credit him for fundamentally changing Kobe, just for nudging him in the right direction and helping him find the balance between dominating and winning. What Kobe did with that understanding, ultimately, was up to him. Remember when I wrote that the vast majority of NBA coaches don't ultimately matter? Jackson matters.

My favorite image of the 2009 Finals was Phil's face after Kobe went one-on-four at the end of Game 2 (ignoring three wide-open teammates) and had a hideous shot blocked. With an overtime period looming, Kobe stormed back to his bench while a sitting Jackson watched from a few seats away, looking slightly amused, slightly disgusted and absolutely unwilling to blow the moment out of proportion.[3] You know what Jackson's reaction reminded me of, actually? Being married. Spend enough time with someone and you accept their strengths and weaknesses for what they are. For instance, I am messy. I leave clothes on the floor. I make coffee in the morning, mistakenly leave grounds on the counter and forget to clean them up. I'm selfishly absentminded like that. My wife stopped complaining about it three years ago. When I do those things now, she makes the Phil Jackson Face. *Crap. I'm stuck with him. It's not even worth*

---

3. In my column the following day, I called it the "Phil Jackson 'Should I point out that MJ would have absolutely passed there? Nahhhhhhh' Face."

getting into it. The plusses outweigh the minuses. Let's move forward. Jackson never made that face with his first wife (MJ); with his second wife (Kobe), he makes it every so often. You could say they're an imperfect match, and if you want to keep the domestic analogy going, they even legally separated in 2004 after a few unhappy years. Now they might go on like this indefinitely. When a coach spends enough time with the same star, they really *do* start to feel like a married couple.[4]

Even Kobe admits that Jackson allowed him to reach his potential. He became more forgiving of teammates and more invested in their individual success. He pushed himself to another level physically, hiring trainer Tim Glover to travel with him full-time, tweaking his game constantly and hoping his work ethic would lift teammates just by proxy. He submitted an unforgettable display of human will from Halloween 2007 through June 2009, leading his team to consecutive Finals, winning an NBA title, and playing in the maximum 164 regular-season games and 44 playoff games without a summer break, thanks to the Olympics. He was the Terminator. He was Schwarzenegger with bullets bouncing off him. For such a polarizing player, I found it fascinating that so many living basketball legends (Walton, Russell, West, Bird and Magic, to name five) professed such profound appreciation of Kobe's talents. The best basketball players are like elite chefs, writers or singers—they know instinctively when someone else has reached their level. When Bird or Walton explains that, yes, Kobe Bryant is truly magnificent, you cannot disagree.[5] Still, I believe that Kobe only became transcendant on *his* terms. He made sacrifices as long as he kept receiving the lion's share of credit and attention. If anything, his teammates and coaches were the ones practicing The Secret—they allowed themselves to be portrayed like backup singers, filled their respective roles, allowed Kobe to thrive, handed over the spotlight and never complained. Like an arrangement of sorts. No different from the Clintons looking at each other once upon a time and probably

4. Russell and Auerbach were the Cleavers. Havlicek and Heinsohn were the Bunkers. Magic and Riley were the Huxtables. Jordan and Jackson were the Simpsons. Duncan and Popovich were the Barones. Phil and Kobe? They were definitely the Sopranos. And I don't need to tell you who was Tony.
5. Bird even blessed Kobe publicly as his favorite active player. I will now peel the skin off my body.

deciding, "Maybe this isn't ideal, but we give each other the best chance to win." Kobe may have bent a little, I tell Walton, but his teammates bent more. Once the Disease of More kicks in, they may not be as willing.[6]

"Kobe only wants to win," Walton counters. "It doesn't matter what your motivation is, or that your game or your style is different, or that it's not perceived to be right or acceptable. We have seen an entire spectrum [of things] from him this decade, and right now he's really really good. Look, you want him to be perfect for *you*. This comes back to your choice—who *your* heroes are. You chose to value a certain type of player over anyone else. He has the right to make his choice, too."

Game, set, match, Walton.

"I guess you're right," I tell him. "Kobe made a choice to play that way, and I made a choice not to totally like it. But I still believe he can get better. I want him to reach the point where I'm watching him and believing that he doesn't care who gets the credit, just who wins. I didn't feel that way after the Finals. Does that make sense?"

"It makes sense." Walton nods. "Your dislike of Kobe's style makes it impossible for you to be happy for the Laker championship. Guys like Bird, Magic and Russell played a style that even opposing fans enjoyed and ultimately liked."

"And you," I add.

"Well . . ."

Walton glances down to the ground. He hates discussing his own career but loves discussing anyone who played with him. Mention Bird to Walton and he starts gushing and rattling off Larry Legend stories. Mention the time Walton dunked on Kareem's head in the '77 playoffs and he reacts like he's awaiting the results of a colonoscopy. That's just the way he is. Thirty-two years later, he still wants people to believe that Maurice

---

6. Not even 36 hours after I visited Walton, the Lakers allowed Ariza to sign with Houston and replaced him with Ron Artest, a loose cannon and attention hog with a penchant for taking bad shots at the wrong times. This won't end well.[P69]

P69. Should have written "This won't end well . . . for the Celtics." Artest ended up locking down Pierce in the 2010 Finals, hitting the biggest three of Game 7, then thanking his psychiatrist and promoting his upcoming record during a hilarious postgame interview with ESPN's Doris Burke. So to recap: this ended well for the Lakers *and* for the state of American comedy.

Lucas was the heart and soul of the '77 Blazers. Even retired, he remains unselfish.[7]

I mention that we may have just figured out the final level of basketball—when a team plays so well together that even opposing fans concede. "I gotta say, even though we got our asses kicked, that was beautiful to watch." Magic's Lakers were like that. Bird's Celtics were like that. The '96 Bulls and '70 Knicks were like that.

"You played on two teams like that," I tell him. "Eighty-six and Seventy-seven."

"I did," he says. "I definitely did."

He changes the subject because that's what Bill Walton does when these things come up. He reveals that he's been watching a lot of international soccer lately, which is interesting because I have been doing the same. A world-class soccer team and a world-class basketball team succeed for the same reason: They control the flow of the proceedings. In soccer, the best players are usually midfielders, like Kaka on Brazil, who can dominate offensively without scoring a goal. Players like Kaka are impossibly skilled.[8] They see angles others can't see. They are always a split-second ahead of their peers. Their unselfishness permeates to everyone else. If you watch closely enough, you will notice Kaka and a teammate occasionally clicking much like Walton and Bird did back in the day. You know, the ESP thing. There isn't enough of it in basketball anymore. How many times can we watch an alpha dog aimlessly dribbling 25 feet from the basket while his teammates stand around watching him? Maybe that's why Bill Walton and I have gravitated toward soccer. Just a little.

"It all starts with the flow," Walton says. "Throw in the performance aspect and that's when you really have something. Larry [Bird] played with passion, persistance, and purpose. There was *meaning* to his performances. Same for Bob Dylan, Neil Young, Jerry Garcia, Jordan, Magic. . . . It was important to them, which made it important to us. The

7. Walton believes basketball's highest level comes down to one question: "Can you make the choice that your happiness can come from someone else's success?" He then added, "My favorite part of the game was starting the fast break." That's the closest he'd come to saying that his way was the best way.
8. You know you've been watching too much soccer when you stop noticing how funny Kaka's name is. At this point, I don't even blink when I hear announcers yell things like "Here comes the great Kaka!"

personality of the lead player brings with it all kinds of responsibilities. Not just a job, it's a way of life. With Larry, people would buy tickets where they couldn't even see the game. Obstructed seats . . . just to be there! People just wanted to be in the arena and feel that golden glow. He was incomparable. He could do things that nobody else could even think of doing and he would do them in the biggest moments on the grandest stages. That's control of the flow. Flow plus meaning equals performance."

"And Kobe controlled the flow in his own way," I add. "Maybe not in the ideal basketball sense for someone like you or me, but still, he's controlling the flow."

"Exactly," Bill Walton says.

We have been talking for two hours now. The '77 Blazers came up earlier when I mentioned an anecdote from *Breaks of the Game* and Walton reacted like he had never heard the story before. And he hadn't. That's how I learned that Bill Walton, one of the most well-read athletes of my lifetime and the focal point of the best sports book ever written, had never actually read the book. *Breaks* was released in 1982. Walton tried to read it when it came out. He couldn't. He tried to read it a few months later. He couldn't. Over the past three decades, Walton estimates that he started *Breaks* fifteen times. He never made it past the first few pages.[9]

"It's too sad," he said wistfully. "Such a special part of my life. So fantastic."

"Wait, wouldn't that make you want to read it?"

"I know how it ended," Walton said grimly.

At the time, I changed topics because he seemed on the verge of breaking down. Two hours later, I come back to it. I have to. The truth is, I don't really care about Kobe. I thought I did . . . but I don't. I didn't drive all the way to San Diego to ask Bill Walton about Kobe Bryant. I had another reason. Even if I didn't want to admit it.

"There are only like fourteen, fifteen guys ever who understood basketball the way you did," I tell him. "You call it a choice, I call it a secret, but either way, it's an exclusive club. You're the only one who didn't really get

9. I brought two '86 Celtics DVDs to watch with Walton: the third quarter of Game 5 vs. Atlanta, and the fourth quarter of Game 4 in Milwaukee. They never came out of my bag. Obviously.

to use that gift. Now we have two generations of people who don't realize that you were one of the best centers who ever lived."

"I'm Luke's dad," Walton jokes.

Only it isn't a joke. Now I'm angry. I glance at his mangled feet. I want to chastise them. I want to scream, "Look at what you did! YOU DID THIS!" Instead, I make an awkward comparison to the late Jerry Garcia— former lead singer of Walton's favorite band—and how Walton lasting for just 517 professional games would be like the Dead's career getting cut short by Garcia's faulty throat.[10] It seems cruel even three decades later. Throw in the undeniable fact that nobody—ever, not in the history of mankind—openly relished and treasured the experience of playing on special teams more than Walton did, and that's when it becomes somewhat tragic. The Secret should never get screwed up like this. Right?

"I can't think about it," Walton explains simply. "It's about what's next. That's what I think about."

And that's how he handles it . . . by not thinking about it. Walton won't watch any tapes from when he played. He won't read an unforgettable book about the pinnacle of his playing career. Something like twenty surgeries later, Bill Walton is still healing. He looks forward and not back. That's why he owns a black cat. He is telling the Gods of Bad Luck, "even after everything that just happened, you cannot break me." I love this about Walton. I love the fact that he has a black cat. I fucking love it.

On the other hand, I am suddenly worried that he won't read my book. I want him to read my book. I tell him this.

"Of course I'll read it," he says. "I read everything you write."

"Yeah, but you're in it, and you said you don't like thinking about—"

"I will absolutely read your book," Bill Walton says again. I wish I could believe him.[P70]

We say our goodbyes a few minutes later. On my way home, I call my

---

10. A better comparison: Springsteen, who openly relished performing with others much like Walton did. Imagine Bruce only appearing on stage for 517 concerts spread over 15 years. Imagine him wistfully remembering those few times he leaned into Little Stevie's microphone and happily spat all over it, wondering why he couldn't have played 5,000 concerts instead of 517. Depressing, right?

P70. One year later, Walton admitted that he never read the book, adding, "I can't read about myself, I just can't." I knew it.

father and recount the entire experience with him, right down to the part where one of Walton's sons (Adam) opened the front door to greet me.

"Wow, remember watching those kids jumping on each other in the Garden?" my father says. "You told them we were right there for those games, right?"

I did.

"What a year that was," my father says. "All our Celtic years blend together for me now, but I can still remember everything about the eighty-six season. You tell him that?"

I did.

Only a few weeks earlier, my father renewed his tickets for the thirty-sixth time. After too many years toiling away in coach, he's back in first class: The Celtics won the 2008 title and should contend for the next few years at least. Funny how life works out. We hang up only because I am entering a highway with my convertible top down. I leave San Diego with my epilogue already written in my head, with Bill Walton's house behind me and the Pacific Ocean to my left, with the sun shining and blue skies above, with my family waiting for me to come home. Picture me rollin'.

ACHNOWLEDGMENTS

This book was a labor of love and could not have been executed correctly without the unyielding support of John Skipper, John Walsh, Gary Hoenig, Gary Belsky and Rob King from ESPN. They believed in this project and afforded me the scheduling flexibility to pull it off. Thanks to all. Special thanks to Hoenig for being the greatest Grumpiest Old Editor ever. His enthusiasm and savvy helped me through some dark times.

Thanks to Malcolm Gladwell for the foreword and for his advice, friendship and feedback. He's one of my top 700 favorite biracial Canadians. Thanks to William Goldman and Chuck Klosterman for making crucial cameos in the book. (I will always remember when Goldman read me a rough draft of what he had written over the phone. One of the true highlights of my career.)

Thanks to Isiah Thomas, Steve Kerr and especially Bill Walton for making this book better.

Thanks a thousand times over to Paul Hirschheimer of NBA Entertainment, a good friend who attached himself to my book from the beginning and made it 9.33 percent better. Thanks as well to David Stern, Adam Silver, Matt Bourne, John Hareas and David Zubrzycki.

Thanks to Hirschy and my buddy Joe House for their early feedback on chapters and Pyramid rankings. House deserves special commendation for twenty-one years of NBA conversations that shaped this book to some degree. Also, thanks to Wally and Gus Ramsey for three decades of friendship, including that fortuitous day when we created the Pyramid while driving to Shea.

Thanks to a remarkable group of friends (a few made cameos in this book) for making me funnier by osmosis. In particular, John O'Connell, Kevin Wildes, Dave Jacoby, Connor Schell, Jamie Horowitz and House had valuable suggestions every time I emailed them footnote-related questions like "Who were the worst celebrity dads ever?" Thanks to my old boss, Jimmy Kimmel, for seven years of friendship and career advice, as well as Shawn Sullivan (the MVP of my wedding) and Rob Strikwerda for their friendship and help with the Celtics/Clippers. Thanks to my friend Russell Sherman for coming up with this book's title. And thanks to every reader who ever took time to email me, especially the ones who appeared in this book.

Thanks to Neil Fine, Kevin Jackson, David Schoenfield, Michael Philbrick, Michael Knisley, Jay Lovinger and Mark Giles for their editing expertise from 2001–2009. And thanks to Gary Sulentic, Bob Holmes and John Wilpers for giving me chances all those years ago.

Thanks to Random House's Mark Tavani for his help and for convincing me that this book wouldn't get screwed up like my first one did. Thanks to everyone else at Random House, as well as Steve Wulf, Sandy DeShong and everyone at ESPN Books. Thanks to my agent, the legendary James "Baby Doll" Dixon, someone who should have become my teammate before 2009. Thanks to Lewis Kay, Dan Klores and Ellie Seifert. Thanks to every writer and teacher who inspired me (too many to list). And thanks to Bill Russell, Larry Bird, Bob Ryan and the late David Halberstam for teaching me Basketball 101 once upon a time.

Thanks to my parents, stepparents and extended family for their unwavering support. You already know how my father affected this book, but my poor mother didn't get enough credit for giving me the writing gene and for being my single biggest fan.

Thanks to my wonderful wife, Kari, for putting up with me these last three years. Her take: "Thank God life is back to normal. If you ever start another seven-hundred-page book, I'm going to murder you in your sleep. Either way, I wish I had married Zack Galifianakis." Good to know.

Thanks to Ben for everything that's about to happen. He's my best-friend-in-training.

Finally, thanks to Zoe. I could have turned into Jack Nicholson in *The Shining* these past three years if not for my beautiful daughter cheering me up, making me laugh and constantly putting a smile on my face. She won't remember this a few years from now, so I wanted to mention it here. I wish I knew her secret.

Bill Simmons
July 4, 2009

BIBLIOGRAPHY

I plowed through nearly one hundred books that helped me write this one. Here's how they broke down by category and influence on my book.

INFLUENTIAL MUST-READS: *Life on the Run* (Bill Bradley) . . . *The Game* (Kenny Dryden) . . . *Wait 'Til Next Year* (William Goldman and Mike Lupica) . . . *The Breaks of the Game; Playing for Keeps* (David Halberstam) . . . *24 Seconds to Shoot* (Leonard Koppett) . . . *Unfinished Business* (Jack MacCallum) . . . *Loose Balls; Tall Tales* (Terry Pluto) . . . *Second Wind* (Bill Russell and Taylor Branch) . . . *The Franchise* (Cameron Stauth)

VERY HELPFUL AND HIGHLY ENJOYABLE: *The City Game* (by Pete Axthelm) . . . *Wilt* (Wilt Chamberlain and David Shaw) . . . *Hang Time* (Bob Greene) . . . *Sacred Hoops* (Phil Jackson) . . . *Wilt, 1962* (Gary Pomerantz) . . . *The Jordan Rules* (Sam Smith) . . . *Foul* (David Wolf)

EXTREMELY USEFUL: *Who's Better, Who's Best in Basketball?* (Elliott Kalb) . . . *Showtime* (Pat Riley) . . . *The Big O* (Oscar Robertson) . . . *The NBA's Top 50* (Ken Shouler) . . . *The Golden Boys* (Cameron Stauth) . . . *The Official 2008–09 NBA Register* . . . *The Official 2008–09 NBA Guide*

ENJOYABLE BOOKS THAT HELPED A LITTLE: *The Fab Five* (Mitch Albom) . . . *Everything They Had* (David Halberstam) . . . *The Best American Sports Writing of the Century* (edited by David Halberstam) . . . *Fathers Playing Catch with Sons* (Donald Hall) . . . *The Last Season* (Phil Jackson with Charley Rosen) . . . *Pistol* (Mark Kriegel) . . . *Best Seat in the House* (Spike Lee and Ralph Wiley) . . . *07 Seconds or Less* (Jack McCallum) . . . *The Franchise* (Michael McCambridge) . . . *A Sense of Where You Are* (John McPhee) . . . *The Short Season* (John Powers) . . . *The Twentieth Century Treasury of Sports* (edited by Al and Brian Silverman) . . . *Classic Wiley* (Ralph Wiley)

HELPFUL, NOT A TOTAL WASTE OF TIME: *Giant Steps* (Kareem Abdul-Jabbar) . . . *Drive* (Larry Bird and Bob Ryan) . . . *Tip Off* (Filip Bondy) . . . *The Perfect Team* (Foreword by Chuck Daly) . . . *The Inside Game* (Waybe Embry with Mary Schmidt Boyer) . . . *Maravich* (Wayne Federman and Marshall Terrell) . . . *Hondo* (John Havlicek with Bob

Ryan) . . . *Give 'Em the Hook* (Tommy Heinsohn and Joe Fitzgerald) . . . *More Than a Game* (Phil Jackson with Charley Rosen) . . . *Sacred Hoops* (Phil Jackson with Hugh Delancy) . . . *My Life* (Magic Johnson and Bill Novak) . . . *Goliath* (Bill Libby) . . . *Only the Strong Survive* (Larry Platt) . . . *Red and Me* (Bill Russell with Alan Steinberg) . . . *48 Minutes* (Bob Ryan and Terry Pluto) . . . *Calling the Shots* (Earl Strom) . . . *The Rivalry* (John Taylor)

NOT PARTICULARLY HELPFUL: *The Long Season* (Rick Adelman and Dwight Jaynes) . . . *Auerbach on Auerbach; On and Off the Court; Red Auerbach* (Red Auerbach with Joe Fitzgerald) . . . *Confessions of a Basketball Gypsy* (Rick Barry and David Wolf) . . . *Out of Bounds* (Jeff Benedict) . . . *The Last Loud Roar* (Bob Cousy) . . . *Covert: My Years Infiltrating the Mob* (Bob Delaney) . . . *The Punch* (John Feinstein) . . . *Champions Remembered* (Ray Fitzgerald) . . . *Rebound* (Bob Greene) . . . *The Jump* (Ian O'Connor) . . . *When Nothing Else Matters* (Michael Leahy) . . . *The Big Three; The Last Banner* (Peter May) . . . *The Drive Within Me* (Bob Pettit with Bob Wolff) . . . *Falling from Grace* (Terry Pluto) . . . *But They Can't Beat Us* (Randy Roberts) . . . *The Pro Game* (Bob Ryan) . . . *Black Planet* (David Shields) . . . *Can I Keep My Jersey?* (Paul Shirley) . . . *Second Coming* (Sam Smith) . . . *Evergreen; Seeing Red* (Dan Shaughnessy) . . . *Basketball My Way* (Jerry West and Bill Libby) . . . *Mr. Clutch* (Jerry West)

Also, I plowed through every relevant NBA feature from 1954 through 2000 in *Sports Illustrated*, as well as countless pieces from *The New York Times* and *The Boston Globe* spanning that same time frame. All can be found online at the *Times/Globe* websites or www.SIVault.com. Old issues of *Inside Sports* from 1980–84 were particularly helpful. Basketball-reference.com, Basketballreference.com and ESPN.com couldn't have been more helpful. For visual references, I burned over three hundred classic games to DVD from NBA TV or ESPN Classic from 2002 to 2007, traded for a few others online and eagerly devoured nearly one hundred rarely seen games that NBA Entertainment was gracious enough to send me. Shows like *Greatest NBA Games* (ESPN 2), *NBA Vault* (ESPN), *SportsCentury* (ESPN Classic) and *Beyond the Glory* (Fox Sports Net) also filled in a few holes. Another unbelievable help: The treasure chest of interviews, highlights and uncut games on YouTube. It would have been nearly impossible to write this particular book as recently as five years ago. So thanks to all.

Last note: Before the release of my book, I am hoping to compile an interactive section of links and YouTube clips that will correspond to the pages and chapters of this book at www.thebookofbasketball.com.

INDEX

PHOTO: STEVEN BARRY

BILL SIMMONS writes the "Sports Guy" column for ESPN
.com's Page 2 and *ESPN: The Magazine.* He is the author of *Now I
Can Die in Peace,* founded the award-winning bostonsportsguy
.com website and was a writer for *Jimmy Kimmel Live.* He com-
mutes between his home in Los Angeles and Fenway Park.